FOURTH
EDITION

COMMUNICATION WORKS

TERI KWAL GAMBLE
College of New Rochelle

MICHAEL GAMBLE
New York Institute of Technology

McGRAW-HILL, INC.

New York   St. Louis   San Francisco   Auckland
Bogotá   Caracas   Lisbon   London   Madrid   Mexico
Milan   Montreal   New Delhi   Paris   San Juan
Singapore   Sydney   Tokyo   Toronto

COMMUNICATION WORKS

2 3 4 5 6 7 8 9 0   VNH   VNH   9 0 9 8 7 6 5 4 3

ISBN 0–07–022793–4

This book was set in Century Old Style by Waldman Graphics, Inc.
The editors were Hilary Jackson and Susan Gamer;
the text was designed by Rafael Hernandez;
the cover was designed by Caliber/Phoenix Color Corp.;
the production supervisor was Friederich W. Schulte.
The photo editor was Barbara Salz.
New drawings were done by Caliber/Phoenix Color Corp.
Von Hoffmann Press, Inc., was printer and binder.

Photos in Contents:

Willie L. Hill/The Image Works (page vii)
Don Klump/The Image Bank (viii)
Randy Matusow/Monkmeyer (x)
Mike Kagan/Monkmeyer (xii)
M. Greco/Stock, Boston (xiv)

Library of Congress Cataloging-in-Publication Data

Gamble, Teri Kwal.
    Communication works / Teri Kwal Gamble, Michael Gamble. — 4th ed.
       p.   cm.
    Includes index.
    ISBN 0-07-022793-4
    1. Oral communication.   I. Gamble, Michael.   II. Title.
P95.G32   1993
302.2'242—dc20   92-25650

ABOUT THE AUTHORS

Teri Kwal Gamble and Michael Gamble both have Ph.D. degrees in communication from New York University. Teri is an Associate Professor of Communication at the College of New Rochelle, and Michael is an Associate Professor of Communication at New York Institute of Technology in Manhattan.

Teri and Michael are award-winning teachers who have conducted seminars and short courses for numerous business and professional organizations across the United States. As the cofounders of Interact Training Systems—a communication consulting firm—they serve as communication trainers, presenting workshops and providing consulting services for many groups, such as real estate companies, manufacturing firms, service organizations, the American Management Association, and even some foreign governments.

The Gambles are also professional writers of educational and training materials. They are coauthors of several textbooks, including *Literature Alive!*, *Introducing Mass Communication*, and *Contacts: Communicating Interpersonally*; and they are currently preparing new texts on public speaking, mass media, and business communication. In addition, they also write for the trade market; among their trade books are *Sales Scripts That Sell*, *The Answer Book*, and *Phone Power*.

Teri and Michael live in New Jersey with their favorite communicators—their son Matthew Jon, age 16; and their daughter Lindsay Michele, age 11.

For Matthew Jon and Lindsay Michele

CONTENTS

LIST OF FEATURED BOXES

Chapter 19

Chapter 20

PREFACE

This fourth edition of *Communication Works* reflects the same intention as the three earlier editions and follows the same approach that contributed to their success. We have designed the text to motivate students to *want to learn* about communication—interpersonal communication, communication in small groups, and public speaking. And we provide materials which encourage students to internalize and practice the key principles of communication.

We have made a special effort to produce a book that students will enjoy reading. How information is presented affects students' level of interest; thus we have once again aimed for clarity of language, participation by our readers, and a lively, colorful format. And we have tested the materials incorporated in the text with students of different ages, cultures, and ethnic groups.

Because we continue to believe that people learn best when they are actively involved, we offer a wide selection of *"Skill Builders"*—learning activities, for use in or outside of class, that have been developed to help students look at communication, assess its effects, and experience the insights and practice they will need to become effective communicators. Instructors have found that these Skill Builders help make the study of communication active, exciting, and rewarding. Of course, we do not expect any instructor to use all the Skill Builders in a single course or semester; each instructor will choose those that fit the needs of his or her own students—and the time available.

In order to meet the needs and reflect the interests of today's increasingly diverse student bodies, and to encourage critical thinking, we have included two new features: *"Culture and Communication"* and *"Ethics and Communication."* These boxes are designed to prompt inquiry on the part of students, to compel students to become involved, and to serve as "starters" for group or class discussions. Now more than ever before, it is essential for students to develop a better understanding of how culture influences communication; it is equally important for them to understand the ethical issues related to communication.

The text also includes many boxed readings chosen specifically because they take the course out of the classroom and into the world, where communication must work. These additional issues and ideas for discussion, which appear in each chapter, are now called *"Points to Ponder."* They highlight an array of thought-provoking topics and, like the other boxes, can be used to encourage critical thinking and analysis in class sessions and independently.

All the boxes—Skill Builders, Culture and Communication, Ethics and Communication, and Points to Ponder—are listed in the front matter (beginning on page xv), so that instructors and students can locate them easily.

We have retained several popular pedagogical features from the previous editions. Each chapter begins with a preview of *behavioral objectives*, specifying what students should be able to do after completing the chapter. These objectives illuminate the material, establish goals, and prepare the readers for the concepts that will be introduced. Within the chapters, students are periodically expected to complete *self-assessment scales* to evaluate their own attitudes and reactions, and to measure their mastery of skills. The chapters also present a broad range of career-oriented examples. Of special interest are the *marginal comments and questions*, which, like the boxes, are there to arouse the students' curiosity—to prompt them to ask and answer questions. At the end of each chapter is a *summary* recapitulating the content and the relevant skills that were emphasized, and a list of *suggestions for further reading* that will broaden students' knowledge and help them with research and writing assignments.

Let's now look at the text part by part and chapter by chapter, noting special features and changes—in addition to the new boxed material—that have been incorporated into the fourth edition.

PART ONE: THE ESSENTIALS OF COMMUNICATION

Part One consists of six chapters offering a unified approach to the study of communication. Models of communication, the self-concept, perception, listening, language, and nonverbal communication are explored with respect to how they affect the ability to relate to others in interpersonal, small-group, and public communication settings. Part One also examines how the media influence our self-images and perceptions, and whether males and females see themselves differently.

Chapter 1: Communication—The Starting Line

- Chapter 1 has been reorganized for greater clarity, smoother flow, and a more natural progression of the material.
- *Communication* has been defined more clearly.
- Some potentially confusing passages have been clarified.
- Skill Builders have been simplified as necessary.

Chapter 2: Communication and the Self-Concept—Who Are You?

- Again, we have simplified the Skill Builders.
- We've added a discussion of cultural issues.
- The coverage of gender differences has been expanded.
- Material has been added on age as a factor in the self-concept.

Chapter 3: Communication and Perception— I Am More Than a Camera

- We've expanded the section on stereotyping.
- We've included additional material on culture.

Chapter 4: Language and Meaning—Helping Minds Meet

- Substantial material has been added on cultural diversity
- The discussion of language and gender has been greatly expanded.
- The "triangle of meaning" has been clarified.

Chapter 5: Nonverbal Communication—Silent Language Speaks

- We've made some additions to the discussion of "eye gaze."
- The discussion of body type and communication has been refined.
- Our discussion of culture and nonverbal behavior has been broadened.

Chapter 6: Listening—A Deliberate Process

- Here, we've substantially increased our discussion of male and female listening behavior and habits.

PART TWO: INTERPERSONAL COMMUNICATION

Part Two has two chapters: one is on understanding relationships; the next provides a unique view of how feelings and emotions affect and are affected by relationships. It includes a special section on "display rules" for males and females, and a thorough discussion of assertiveness. (The chapter on interviewing, which originally appeared in Part Two, has now been moved to Part Five—where it will better help students to consider communication beyond the course and throughout life.)

Chapter 7: Understanding Relationships

- There is a new section on conversation and relationships.
- Our discussion of deception and the development of relationships has been expanded.

Chapter 8: Person to Person— Handling Emotions and Expressing Feelings in Relationships

- Here, we've increased our coverage of the communication of emotions.

PART THREE: COMMUNICATING IN THE SMALL GROUP

Part Three has three chapters focusing on small-group communication and providing ample group experiences for classroom use. It examines, in detail, the steps involved in problem solving; provides a career-oriented discussion of leadership; looks at cooperation, competition, defensiveness, and supportiveness as influences on the climate of a work group; and notes how "groupthink" alters a group's ability to function effectively.

Chapter 9: The Role of the Group in Problem Solving

- We have defined *group* more clearly.
- Some sections of the chapter have been reordered for greater clarity.
- Our discussion of decision-making styles has also been clarified.
- We've added to our coverage of creativity.

Chapter 10: Group Networks, Membership, and Leadership

- We've increased our coverage of male and female roles and leadership.
- We now discuss culture and leadership.

Chapter 11: Handling Group Conflict—
How to Disagree without Becoming Disagreeable

- Instructions for the Skill Builders have been clarified.
- Material has been added on how culture affects conflict and competition.

PART FOUR: COMMUNICATING TO THE PUBLIC

Part Four (which consists of seven chapters) focuses on speechmaking and provides students with a straightforward format—in effect, a "map"—for preparing speeches and similar presentations in class and on the job. Exercises, checklists, and forms for tryouts and evaluation are included.

Chapter 12: The Speaker and the Audience

- Here, we've added material on socioeconomic status.

Chapter 13: The Occasion and the Subject

- Our discussion of a speech's purpose has been expanded.
- We've added brief introductions to several of the "Points to Ponder" boxes.

Chapter 14: Developing Your Speech—Supporting Your Ideas

- There are new sections on computer-aided searches and computer graphics.
- Many new, stimulating examples have been added.

Chapter 15: Designing Your Speech—Organizing Your Ideas

- We've revised our section on conclusions.
- We've added to and refreshed the examples.

Chapter 16: Delivering Your Speech—Presenting Your Ideas

- Here, we've included a new section on "visualization"—imagery used in sports to reduce anxiety.

Chapter 17: Informative Speaking; and Chapter 18: Persuasive Speaking

- Both chapters have new boxes, and some of the material has been clarified.

PART FIVE: CONTINUING COMMUNICATION— TODAY AND TOMORROW

Part Five, consisting of our final two chapters, takes the students beyond the communication course, helping them consider where they will go from here and how to apply course material in their professional and personal lives. As we mentioned above, it now includes our chapter on interviewing; the last chapter considers lifelong development of communication. This is (as far as we know) the only text that includes suggestions and strategies for developing communication skills after the course has ended.

Chapter 19: Interviewing—From Both Sides of the Desk

- We've updated the references.
- Potentially confusing Skill Builders have been clarified.
- We've added more commentary on how culture and ethics might affect the outcome of an interview.
- Our discussion of clothing has been updated.

Chapter 20: Lifelong Development of Communication Skills

- Some passages have been clarified, but this popular section remains essentially the same as the former "Epilogue."

ACKNOWLEDGMENTS

The improvements in this fourth edition of *Communication Works* reflect the experiences of students and the suggestions of colleagues; they are truly the result of a team effort. The contributions of our editors at McGraw-Hill merit special attention. We would like to thank Roth Wilkofsky, our original sponsoring editor; Hilary Jackson, our present editor; Carol Einhorn, our development editor, who coordinated many revisions; Susan Gamer, our editing supervisor, whose sensitivity to changing emphases kept us on track; Rafael Hernandez, our designer, who made sure that the new typography would support the content; and Kathy Bendo, who supervised the photo research.

We would also like to thank our reviewers for their helpful critiques: Allan Broadhurst, Cape Cod Community College; Jerald Carstens, University of Wisconsin–River Falls; Sharon Condon, University of Kansas; Cynthia Cone, San Antonio College; Elizabeth Coughlin, Northern Virginia Community College; Stanley Crane, Hartnell Community College; David Edgecombe, Marian College; Susan Holton, Bridgewater State College; Ann Jaynes, Mattatuck Community College; Kentin Kersting, Labette Community College; Michael L. Lewis, Abilene Christian University; Andre Mickens, North Carolina Agricultural/Technical State University; Don Wallace, Brewton-Parker College; Samuel P. Wallace, University of Dayton; and Paul Westbrooke, Northeastern State University.

Finally, of course, we would again like to thank our children, Matthew and Lindsay, who are growing up with this book and whose communicative instincts continue to make it all worthwhile.

Teri Kwal Gamble
Michael Gamble

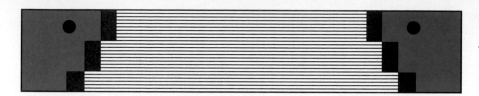

THE ESSENTIALS OF COMMUNICATION

COMMUNICATION: THE STARTING LINE

When you finish this chapter, you should be able to:

Define *communication*

Assess your own effectiveness as a communicator

List and explain the essential elements of communication

Describe representative models of communication

Develop and explain an original model of communication

Describe the characteristics of communication

Identify and provide examples of Watzlawick's axioms of communication

Explain how you can improve your own effectiveness as a communicator

A college student. A corporate vice president. A teenager. An octogenarian. A man and woman in love. A doctor and a patient. A native and a foreigner. Parents. Children. Friends. Enemies. Decision makers. Speakers. You. All these people share at least one thing—a need to communicate.

This book is about *you*, about your need to communicate and how communication can help you relate more effectively to others. It is about how communication can help you establish relationships with strangers you'd like to get to know better. It's about how communication can help you increase your chances of getting a raise. It's about how communication can help you negotiate family disagreements or disagreements among peers. It's about how communication can help you make decisions and solve work-related problems. It's about how communication can help enhance your personal persuasiveness and credibility.

The point is this: Whether or not you possess or develop the ability to communicate effectively with others is essential not only for your own success but also for the success of any organizations you work for, any groups you become part of, and your relationship with any people you come to know. In today's world, job-specific talent, technical expertise, and graduation from a prestigious school do not carry any guarantees for upward mobility or attainment of goals. But one factor shared by people who are able to ascend both the professional and the personal ladders of success is superior communication skills. These people are promoted more rapidly, are happier in their marriages and other relationships, and in general view their lives as being richer and more fulfilling. That is why this book can be of value to you. The topics we cover will help you as you go about your usual business of making friends, informing and persuading others, solving problems, falling in or out of love, and making your personal and professional relationships work.

We all depend on our communication skills to help us meet our needs, find happiness, and attain personal fulfillment. From birth to death, many types of communication are an integral part of your life. Whatever your sex, your occupation, and your goals, communication of one form or another plays a major role. The challenge is to communicate as effectively as possible—to build your communication skills so that communication works for you and not against you.

Whether you are 18 or 80, female or male, married or single, employed or unemployed, it is never too late to learn skills that will enrich and improve the quality of your life. Interpersonal, small-group, and public communication skills are not inborn. You have to develop them, and this development is a process that will continue throughout your life. That is why this book is designed to provide you with a program for lifelong learning. If you want to improve your ability to relate to people in your social life, your job, or your academic life, now is the time to start to make communication work.

We are all one-to-one (interpersonal), one-to-a-few (small-group), and one-to-many (public) communicators.

Top to bottom: Willie L. Hill/The Image Works; Frank Siteman, Stock/Boston; Billy E. Barnes/Stock, Boston

✔ **SKILL BUILDER**

CONTACTS!

Identify five people with whom you recently had a sustained communication contact. (Note: The contact need not have been initiated by you.) For each, indicate the nature of your communication (the subject or message), the context or environment in which it occurred (classroom, office, home, etc.), the type of interaction experienced (interpersonal, small-group, or public), and the outcome (what happened as a result of the interaction). Finally—and this is important—as an assessment of your communication effectiveness, rate each contact on a scale of 1 to 5, with 1 representing "extremely ineffective" and 5 representing "extremely effective," and give your rationale for each rating.

Extremely		Extremely
ineffective	1 2 3 4 5	effective

Now, how would you replay each contact if you were given the opportunity?

WHO IS THE COMMUNICATOR?

Communicators are people who enter into relationships with other people. Without communication, we would be unable to function. During the course of a single day we interact with others to share information and beliefs, exchange ideas and feelings, make plans, and solve problems. Sometimes this is done interpersonally, sometimes in a small group, and sometimes in a public forum. However communication occurs, it is essential in helping us initiate, develop, control, and sustain our contacts with others.

We are all *interpersonal* (one-to-one), *small-group* (one-to-a-few), and *public* (one-to-many) *communicators*. Every time we knowingly or unknowingly send a verbal or nonverbal message to a friend, lover, relative, stranger, audience, acquaintance, supervisor, employee, coworker, or group, communication takes place.[1] In effect, *communication is the deliberate or accidental transfer of meaning*. It occurs whenever someone observes or experiences behavior and attributes meaning to that behavior. It doesn't matter whether the observed or experienced behavior is intentional or accidental, conscious or unconscious. As long as what someone does is interpreted as a message—as long as the behavior of one person affects or influences the behavior of another—communication is occurring. Thus, each facet of our lives from birth to death is dependent on and affected by our communication skills.

Communication is a very significant part of your life. From the day you are born, your ability to communicate is the largest single factor influencing what kinds of relationships you share with others and what happens to you as you make your way in the world.

The examples in the box on the opposite page illustrate the importance of communication.

How might a "hello day" affect your work relationships?

THE IMPORTANCE OF COMMUNICATION

It's a mark of real leadership to take the lead in getting to know people. . . . It's always a big person who walks up to you and offers his/her hand and says hello.

David J. Schwartz, *The Magic of Thinking Big*

"Why didn't you talk to me the first time I approached you?"
"I didn't know what to say."
"You have trouble talking to people?"
"I got out of practice."

Bernard Slade, *Tribute*

"I want him to know how to holler and put up an argument, I want a little guts to show. . . . I want him to know the subtle, sneaky reason why he was born a human being and not a chair."

Herb Gardner, *A Thousand Clowns*

The worst sin towards our fellow creatures is not to hate them, but to be indifferent to them; that's the essence of inhumanity.

Bernard Shaw

"I don't talk to many people—except to say like: give me a beer, or where's the john, or what time does the feature go on, or keep your hands to yourself, buddy. You know—things like that. . . . But every once in a while I like to talk to somebody, really talk; like to get to know somebody, know all about him."

Edward Albee, *The Zoo Story*

I . . . have never been the same person alone that I am with people.

Philip Roth

Communication is the greatest single factor affecting a person's health and relationships to others.

Virginia Satir, *The New Peoplemaking*

NOTICE
STATE OF LOUISIANA
DAVID C. TREEN
GOVERNOR
PROCLAMATION

WHEREAS, November 21 has been declared Worldwide "Hello Day"; and

WHEREAS, we are asking everyone, regardless of what language or nationality, who wants to make it a special day to say "hello" to ten people they have never spoken to before; and

WHEREAS, the purpose is to foster friendship, warmth and good relations among mankind.

NOW, THEREFORE, I, DAVID C. TREEN, Governor of the State of Louisiana, do hereby proclaim November 21 as

"HELLO DAY"

in the State of Louisiana.
(SEAL)
IN WITNESS WHEREOF, I have hereunto set my hand officially and caused to be affixed the Great Seal of the State of Louisiana, at the Capitol, in the City of Baton Rouge, on this the 24th day of February.

DAVID C. TREEN
Governor of Louisiana

ATTEST BY THE GOVERNOR:
Jim Brown
Secretary of State
ST–44–Nov. 18–1

HOW GOOD A COMMUNICATOR ARE YOU?

When has insensitivity caused problems for you or others, on the job or at home?

Being a communicator—simply communicating frequently or having many person-to-person contacts each day—does not mean that you are as *effective* a communicator as you could be. We frequently neglect problems that plague our communicative relationships—although these issues are crucial in our lives and at the heart of much contemporary literature and art.

When we lack sensitivity and fail to consider the feelings of others, our relationships suffer. We can all improve our communication skills. There is no such thing as being *too* effective at establishing, maintaining, and controlling personal and public contacts with others. In the Skill Builder on page 6, you evaluated your own proficiency during a variety of interpersonal, small-group, or public communication experiences. Now let's consider steps that you can take to improve or enhance your ability to relate to others in a variety of communication settings.

First, use the scale of 0 to 100 below to rate your own overall effectiveness as a communicator. Next, using the same scale, rate the communication skills of your best friend, an older relative, a fellow student, a boss or instructor, or a boyfriend, girlfriend, or spouse.

Totally ineffective	0 10 20 30 40 50 60 70 80 90 100	Totally effective

According to the evaluation you have just completed, whose communication skills do you consider better than yours? Why? Whose communication skills do you consider equal to yours? Why? Whose communication skills do you consider inferior to yours? Why?

Now set a goal that indicates the extent to which you would like this course to improve your effectiveness as a communicator. In order to realize this improvement, there are probably a number of skills you should work to maintain, a number of skills you should work to master, and a number of ineffective behaviors you should work to eliminate. To function effectively in interpersonal, small-group, or public communication, you will need to acquire certain skills and perceptions:

1. Ability to understand and communicate with *yourself*
2. Knowledge of how and why you and those with whom you relate see things the way you do
3. Capacity to listen and then process the information you receive
4. Sensitivity to "silent" messages that you and others send
5. Knowledge of how words affect you and those with whom you relate
6. Understanding of how relationships develop
7. Understanding of how feelings and emotions affect relationships
8. Understanding of how to prepare for an interview

9. Ability to handle conflict by learning how to *disagree* without being *disagreeable*
10. Understanding of the behaviors that contribute to successful group decision making
11. Understanding of how beliefs, values, and attitudes affect the formulation and reception of messages and the development of speaker-audience relationships
12. Desire to apply all these skills and perceptions to each communication experience

As we continue exploring and investigating what it means to experience effective interpersonal, small-group, and public communication, you will realize that the objectives just provided describe, in brief, the method and purpose of this book.

WHAT IS COMMUNICATION?

Elements of Communication

All communication encounters have certain common elements that together help define the communication process. The better you understand these elements, the easier it will be for you to develop your own communication abilities. Let's begin by examining the essentials of communication, those components present during every interpersonal, small-group, and public communication contact.

PEOPLE

Obviously, every human communication contact of any kind involves people. Interpersonal, small-group, and public communication encounters take place between and among all types of "senders" and "receivers." *Senders* and *receivers*, respectively, are simply persons who give out and take in messages. Although it is easy to picture an interpersonal, small-group, or public communication experience as beginning with a sender and ending with a receiver, it is important to understand that during communication the role of sender does not belong exclusively to one person and the role of receiver to another. Instead, the processes of sending and receiving are constantly being reversed; thus, when we communicate with one or more people, we simultaneously send and receive.

If we were just senders, we would simply emit signals without ever stopping to consider whom, if anyone, we were affecting. If we were just receivers, we would be no more than receptacles for signals from others, never having an opportunity to let anyone know how we were being affected. Fortunately, this is not how effective communication works. The verbal and nonverbal messages we send are often determined in part by the verbal and nonverbal messages we receive.

In *That's Not What I Meant*, Deborah Tannen writes, "Communication is a continuous stream in which everything is simultaneously a reaction and an instigation, an instigation and a reaction." Why do you think this is so? Provide examples based on situations you have experienced or observed.

RECEIVER-SOURCE-RECEIVER-SOURCE

Choose a partner and role-play one of the following situations: a quarrel between lovers, a conversation between two strangers waiting for a bus during a storm, a controversy between a teacher and a student over a grade, a discussion between friends about the rising cost of tuition. After enacting your scene, explain how what one person did and said influenced what the other person did and said.

MESSAGES

During every interpersonal, small-group, or public communication encounter we all send and receive both verbal and nonverbal messages. What you talk about, the words you use to express your thoughts and feelings, the sounds you make, the way you sit and gesture, your facial expressions, and perhaps even your touch or your smell all communicate information. In effect, a *message* is the content of a communicative act. Some messages we send are private (a kiss accompanied by "I love you"); others are public and may be directed at hundreds or thousands of people. We send some messages purposefully ("I want you to realize . . ."), and others accidentally ("I had no idea you were watching . . ."). Everything a sender or receiver does or says is a potential message as long as someone is there to interpret the behavior. When you smile, frown, shout, whisper, or turn away, you are communicating, and your communication is having some effect.

CHANNELS

Inventory each message you receive during a 2-minute period, and note the channel through which it came.

We send and receive messages with and through all our senses; equally, messages may be sent and received through both verbal and nonverbal modes or *channels*. Thus in effect we are multichannel communicators. We receive sound messages (we hear noises from the street), sight messages (we see how someone looks), taste messages (we savor the flavor of a particular food), smell messages (we smell the cologne a friend is wearing), and touch messages (we feel the roughness of a fabric). Which channel are you most attuned to? Why? To what extent do you rely on one or more channels while excluding or disregarding others? Effective communicators are adept at switching channels. They recognize that communication is a multichannel experience.

NOISE

In the context of communication, *noise* is anything that interferes with or distorts our ability to send or receive messages. Thus, although we are accustomed to thinking of noise as some particular sound or group of sounds, the aware communicator realizes that noise can also be created by, for example, physical discomfort, psychological makeup, intellectual ability, or the environment. Thus noise includes distractions such as a loud siren, a disturbing odor, and a hot room as well as personal factors such as prejudices, daydreaming, and feelings of inadequacy.

✔ SKILL BUILDER

THE "NOISE NOOSE"

In what ways might each of the following elements function as noise and thus choke off effective interpersonal, small-group, or public communication?

1. Black eye
2. Chewing gum
3. Cold, damp room
4. Personal bias
5. Inappropriate choice of words
6. Stomachache
7. Sunglasses
8. Shyness
9. Television
10. A habit of not smiling

✔ SKILL BUILDER

CONTACT IN CONTEXT

Compare and contrast the types of communication that would be most likely to occur in each of the following contexts. Include a description of the nature of each interaction, the probable attire of each interactant, and his or her demeanor.

1. First few minutes of a party
2. Business meeting
3. Your home at mealtime
4. Funeral home
5. College classroom
6. Political rally
7. Football stadium

CONTEXT

Communication always takes place in some *context*, or setting. Sometimes a context is so natural that we hardly notice it. At other times, however, the context makes such an impression on us that it exerts considerable control over our behavior. Consider the extent to which your present environment influences the way you act toward others or determines the nature of the communication encounters you share with them. Consider the extent to which certain environments might cause you to alter or modify your posture, manner of speaking, or attire. Take into account the fact that sometimes conditions of place and time—that is, context—can affect our communications without our consciously realizing it.

FEEDBACK

Whenever we communicate with one or more persons, we also receive information in return. The verbal and nonverbal cues that we perceive in reaction to our communication function as *feedback*. Feedback tells us how we are "coming across." A smile, a frown, a chuckle, a sarcastic remark, a muttered thought,

What positive and negative feedback have you recently given to others? What positive and negative feedback have you received?

or simply silence can cause us to change, modify, continue, or end a transaction. Feedback that encourages us to continue behaving as we are is *positive* feedback, and it enhances whatever behavior is in progress. In contrast, *negative* feedback serves to extinguish a behavior and serves a corrective rather than a reinforcing function. Thus, negative feedback can help to eliminate unwanted, ineffective behaviors. Note that *positive* and *negative* should not be interpreted as "good" and "bad"; these terms simply reflect the way the responses affect behavior.

Both positive and negative feedback can emanate from internal or external sources. Internal feedback is feedback you give yourself as you monitor your own behavior or performance during a transaction. External feedback is feedback from others who are involved in the communication event. To be an effective communicator, you must be sensitive to both types of feedback. You must pay attention to your own reactions and the reactions of others.

EFFECT

As people communicate, they are each changed in some way by the interaction, which in turn influences what follows. In other words, communication can be viewed as an exchange of influences. This means that communication always has some *effect* on you and on the person or people with whom you are interacting. An effect can be emotional, physical, cognitive, or any combination of the three. An interpersonal, small-group, or public communication contact can elicit feelings of joy, anger, or sadness (emotional); communication can cause you to fight, argue, become apathetic, or evade an issue (physical); or it can lead to new insights, increased knowledge, the formulation or reconsideration of opinions, silence, or confusion (cognitive). The result of a communication encounter can also be any combination of the three effects just mentioned. Since effects are not always visible or immediately observable, there is obviously more to a communication reaction than meets the eye, or the ear.

Two Crucial Characteristics of Communication

Besides having specific ingredients, or elements, in common, interpersonal communication, small-group communication, and public communication also share at least two general characteristics.

COMMUNICATION IS DYNAMIC

When we call communication a *dynamic* process, we mean that all its elements constantly interact with and affect each other.[2] Since all people are interconnected, whatever happens to one person determines in part what happens to others.

Like the human interactants who compose them, interpersonal, small-group, and public communication relationships constantly evolve from and affect one another. Nothing about communication is static. Everything is accumulative. We communicate as long as we are alive, and thus every interaction that we engage in is part of connected happenings. In other words, all our present communication experiences may be thought of as points of arrival from past encounters and as points of departure for future ones. (This is well illus-

Can you think of an interpersonal, small-group, or public communication encounter you had that affected a later encounter?

trated by a spiral model of communication developed by Frank Dance and discussed later in this chapter.)

COMMUNICATION IS UNREPEATABLE AND IRREVERSIBLE

Every human contact you experience is unique. It has never happened before, and never again will it happen in just the same way. One interpretation of the old adage "You can never step into the same river twice" is that the experience changes both you and the river forever. Similarly, a communication encounter affects and changes the interactants so that the encounter can never happen in exactly the same way again. Thus communication is both unrepeatable and irreversible. We can neither "take back" something we have said nor "erase" the effects of something we have done. And although we may be greatly influenced by our past, we can never reclaim it. In the words of an old Chinese proverb, "Even the emperor cannot buy back one single day."

FUNCTIONS OF COMMUNICATION: WHAT CAN IT DO FOR YOU?

Every communication experience serves one or more functions. For example, communication can help us discover who we are, help us establish meaningful relationships, or prompt us to examine and try to change either our own attitudes and behaviors or the attitudes and behaviors of others.

Understanding and Insight

One key function of communication is *self-other understanding*: insight into ourselves and others. When you get to know another person, you also get to know yourself; and when you get to know yourself, you learn how others affect you. In other words, we depend on communication to develop self-awareness. The communication theorist Thomas Hora put it this way: "To understand himself man needs to be understood by another. To be understood by another he needs to understand the other."[3]

■ ETHICS AND COMMUNICATION

"I HATE HIM"

How could enhanced self-other understanding help resolve this situation, cited by Gordon Allport in *The Nature of Prejudice?*

> See that man over there?
>   Yes.
> Well, I hate him.
>   But you don't know him.
> That's why I hate him.

Source: Gordon Allport, *The Nature of Prejudice,* Addison-Wesley, Reading, Mass., 1979.

We need feedback from others all the time, and others are constantly in need of feedback from us. Interpersonal, small-group, and public communications offer us numerous opportunities for self-other discovery. Through communication encounters we are able to learn why we are trusting or untrusting, whether we can make our thoughts and feelings clear, under what conditions we have the power to influence others, and whether we can effectively make decisions and resolve conflicts and problems.

Meaningful Relationships

In building relationships, we cannot be overly concerned with ourselves but must consider the needs and wants of others. It is through effective interpersonal, small-group, and public communication contacts that our basic physical and social needs are met.

Psychologists tell us that we need other people just as we need water, food, and shelter. When we are cut off from human contact, we become disoriented and maladjusted, and our life itself may be placed in jeopardy. People who are isolated from others—people who lack satisfying social relationships—are more likely to experience health problems and to die early than people who have an abundance of satisfying relationships.

Communication offers each of us the chance to satisfy what the psychologist William Schutz calls our "needs for inclusion, control, and affection."[4] The *need for inclusion* is our need to be with others, our need for social contact. We like to feel that others accept and value us, and we want to feel like a full partner in a relationship. The *need for control* is our need to feel that we are capable and responsible, that we are able to deal with and manage our environment. We also like to feel that we can influence others. The *need for affection* is our need to express and receive love. Since communication allows each of these needs to be met, we are less likely to feel unwanted, unloved, or incapable if we are able to communicate meaningfully with others. (For a more in-depth discussion of these needs, see Chapter 7.)

Communication also gives us the chance to share our own "reality" with people from our own culture as well as people from different cultures. Whether we live in an east coast urban area, a southern city, a desert community, sunny California, a village in Asia, a plain in Africa, or a town in the middle east, we all engage in similar activities when we communicate. We may use different symbols, rely on different strategies, and desire different outcomes, but the processes we use and the motivations we have are strikingly alike. Equally significant is the fact that insensitivity to another's needs and preferred ways of interacting can hamper our ability to relate effectively.

Influence and Persuasion

During interpersonal, small-group, and public communication, people have ample opportunities to influence each other subtly or overtly. We spend much time trying to persuade one another to think as "we" think, do what "we" do, like what "we" like. Sometimes our efforts meet with success, and sometimes they do not. In any case, our experiences with persuasion afford each of us the chance to influence others so that we may try to realize our own goals.

● CULTURE AND COMMUNICATION

ALIENS

How can communication help alleviate this complaint by the ancient Greek playwright Aeschylus?

"Everyone's quick to blame the alien."

FIVE AXIOMS OF COMMUNICATION

Now that we have looked at elements, characteristics, and functions of communication, it will be useful to turn our attention to five basic axioms of communication (see Figure 1-1). These principles were described in a classic study by Paul Watzlawick, Janet Beavin, and Don Jackson.[5] Each axiom has functional implications and is essential to our understanding of the communication process.

Axiom 1: You Cannot *Not* Communicate

It is not uncommon to assume that we communicate only because we want to communicate and that all communication is purposeful, intentional, and consciously motivated. Obviously, this is often true, but just as often we communicate without any awareness of doing so—and at times even without wanting to!

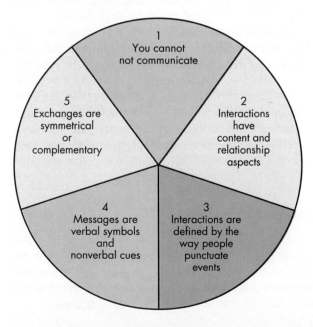

FIGURE 1-1
Five axioms of communication.

✔ SKILL BUILDER

CAN YOU SEND AN UNMESSAGE?

1. Describe a situation in which you tried to avoid communicating with someone. In your description, identify the person you didn't want to communicate with, give your reasons, describe the strategies you used to try to avoid communicating, and describe the results of your efforts.

2. Describe a situation in which someone tried to avoid communicating with you. Again, identify the person involved, give your perception of her or his reasons for not wanting to relate to you, describe the strategies used to try to avoid communicating, and describe the results.

Whenever we are involved in an interaction, we must respond in some way. Even if we do not choose to respond verbally, even if we maintain absolute silence and attempt not to move a muscle, our lack of response *is itself* a response and therefore constitutes a message, influences others, and hence communicates. In other words, we can never voluntarily stop behaving—because behavior has no opposite.

Watzlawick, Beavin, and Jackson identified four basic strategies that we usually employ when trying not to communicate—when we want to avoid making contact with someone. First, we may try to *reject* communication by making it clear to the other person that we are not interested in conversing. By doing this, however, we do not avoid communicating; and we probably create a strained, embarrassing, socially uncomfortable situation. (Furthermore, as a result of this action a relationship now does exist between us and the person we want to avoid.) Second, we may decide to *accept* communication. This strategy involves operating according to the "law of least effort," giving in reluctantly, and agreeing to make conversation in the hope that the person will go away quickly. Third, we may attempt to *disqualify* our communication.[6] That is, we communicate in a way that invalidates our own messages or the messages sent to us by the other person. We contradict ourselves, switch subjects, or utter incomplete sentences or non sequiturs in the hope that the other person will give up. Fourth, we may pretend we would like to talk but that, because we are tired, nervous, sick, drunk, bereaved, deaf, or otherwise incapacitated, we simply cannot communicate at the moment. In other words, we use some *symptom* as a form of communication. To repeat, however, no matter how hard we try, we cannot not communicate, because all behavior is communication and therefore is a message.

Axiom 2: Every Interaction Has a Content Dimension and a Relationship Dimension

The *content* of a communication is its information level, or data level; it describes the behavior expected as a response. In contrast, the *relationship level* of a communication indicates how the exchange is to be interpreted; it signals what one person thinks of the other. For example, "Close the door" is a directive whose content asks the receiver to perform a certain action. However, the communication "Close the door" can be delivered in many ways—as a command, a plea, a request, a come-on, or a turnoff. Each manner of delivery says something about the relationship between the source, or sender, and the receiver. In this way we constantly give others clues about how we see ourselves in relationship to them.

Watzlawick, Beavin, and Jackson identified three types of responses that we use to indicate our reactions to each other. First, we can *confirm* other people's self-definitions, or self-concepts, and thus treat others as they believe they ought to be treated. For example, if your friend Mary believes herself to be competent and smart and if those around her reward her by asking for advice or seeking her help, her self-concept is being confirmed.

Second, we can *reject* the other people's self-definitions by simply refusing to accept their beliefs about themselves. If your friend John imagines himself to be a leader but no one else treats him as if he had the qualities associated with leadership, he may be forced to revise his picture of himself.

Third, we can *disconfirm* other people's self-definitions. Confirmation says, "I accept you as you see yourself. Your self-assessment is correct." Rejection says, "I do not accept you as you see yourself. Your self-assessment is wrong." Disconfirmation, on the other hand, says simply, "You do not exist. You are a nonentity." Disconfirmation implies that we do not care enough to let other people know how we feel, and that we always treat people the same way no matter what they say or do. In other words, we do not offer people *any clues whatever* to indicate that we believe they are or are not performing well. In effect, we totally ignore them. The psychologist William James noted that consistent disconfirmation is perhaps the cruelest psychological punishment that a human being can experience: "No more fiendish punishment could be devised . . . than that we should be turned loose in a society and remain absolutely unnoticed."

✔ SKILL BUILDER

CONFIRM, REJECT, DISCONFIRM

1. Working with a partner, improvise three scenes. In scene A, one person confirms another person's self-image. In scene B, one person rejects the other person's self-image. In scene C, one person disconfirms the other person's self-image. Note the verbal and nonverbal behaviors that aid in confirming, rejecting, or disconfirming the person.

2. Describe communication experiences in which you were (a) confirmed, (b) rejected, and (c) disconfirmed by another person. How did you respond in each case?

3. Describe communication experiences in which you (a) confirmed, (b) rejected, and (c) disconfirmed another person. How did the other person respond in each situation?

Axiom 3: Every Interaction Is Defined by How It Is Punctuated

Think of a recent argument you had that you believe was started by the other person. Describe the situation, and identify that person's stimulus behavior (the apparent starting point). Now, put yourself in the other person's place. How might he or she have answered this same question?

Even though we understand that communication is continuous, we often act as if there were an identifiable starting point or a traceable cause for a particular response. Actually, in many communication interactions it is extremely difficult to determine what is stimulus and what is response. For instance, it is equally possible for a father to believe that he is reading or daydreaming to escape his small daughter's screaming and for the child to believe that she is screaming because her father is reading or daydreaming and won't play with her. The father sees behavior as progressing from screaming to retreating, whereas the child sees it as progressing from retreating to screaming. In other words, what is stimulus for one is response for the other. We all divide up, or punctuate, a particular experience somewhat differently because each of us "sees" it differently. Thus, whenever you suggest that a certain communication began because of a particular stimulus, you are forgetting that communication has no clearly distinguishable starting point or end point. Try to remember that communication is circular—a continuous, ongoing series of events.

Axiom 4: Messages Consist of Verbal Symbols and Nonverbal Cues

When we talk to others, we send out two kinds of messages: (1) discrete, digital, verbal symbols (words) and (2) continuous, analogic, nonverbal cues. According to Watzlawick, Beavin, and Jackson, the content of a message is more likely to be communicated through the digital system, whereas the relationship level of the message is more likely to be carried through the analogic system. Although words are under our control and for the most part are uttered intentionally, many of the nonverbal cues that we send are not. Thus Watzlawick, Beavin, and Jackson write that "it is easy to profess something verbally, but difficult to carry a lie into the realm of the analogic." This means that while you may lie with words, the nonverbal signals you emit are likely to give you away.

Axiom 5: Interactions Are Either Symmetrical or Complementary

The terms *symmetrical* and *complementary* do not refer to "good" (normal) or "bad" (abnormal) communication exchanges but simply represent two basic categories into which all communication interactions can be divided. Each type of interaction serves important functions, and both will be present in a healthy relationship.

During a communication encounter, if the behavior of one person is mirrored by the behavior of the other person, Watzlawick, Beavin, and Jackson would say that a *symmetrical interaction* has occurred. Thus, if you act in a dominating fashion and the person you are relating to acts the same way, or if you act happy and the other person also acts happy, or if you express anger and the other person likewise expresses anger, for the moment the two of you have a symmetrical relationship.

In contrast, if the behavior of one interactant precipitates a different behavior in the other, Watzlawick, Beavin, and Jackson would say that a *complementary interaction* exists. In a complementary relationship you and your partner engage in opposite behaviors, with your behavior serving to elicit the other person's behavior or vice versa. Thus, if you behave in an outgoing manner, your partner might become quiet; if you are aggressive, he or she might become submissive; if you become the "leader," he or she might become the "follower."

Neither a symmetrical nor a complementary relationship is trouble-free. Parties to a symmetrical relationship are apt to experience what is termed *symmetrical escalation*. Since they believe they are "equal," each also believes he or she has a right to assert control. When this happens, the interactants may feel compelled to engage in a battle to show how "equal" they really are. Since it is not uncommon for individuals sharing a symmetrical relationship to find themselves in a status struggle with each other, the main danger of this type of interaction is a runaway sense of competitiveness.

In contrast, the problem that surfaces in many complementary relationships is *rigid complementarity*. This occurs when one party to an interaction begins to feel that control is automatically his or hers and as a result the relationship becomes rigid or fixed. Control no longer alternates between the interactants; thus both persons lose a degree of freedom in choosing how they will behave. For example, a teacher who never pictures himself or herself as a learner, a parent who cannot perceive that his or her child has reached adulthood, and a leader who can never permit himself or herself to act as a follower

"Treat people as equals and the first thing you know they believe they are."

Drawing by Mulligan; © 1982 The New Yorker Magazine, Inc.

How could the attitude expressed here affect the employer-employee relationship?

have all become locked into self-perpetuating, unrealistic, unchanging, and un-healthy patterns of behavior.

In this excerpt from "When Did I Become the Mother and the Mother Become the Child?" Erma Bombeck describes the switch in power that can occur in the parent-child relationship.

> When will the baby catch up with the mother?
> When indeed.
> Does it begin one night when you are asleep and your mother is having a restless night and you go into her room and tuck the blanket around her bare arms?
> Does it appear one afternoon when, in a moment of irritation, you snap, "How can I give you a home permanent if you won't sit still? If you don't care how you look, I do!" (My God, is that an echo?)
> Or did it come the rainy afternoon when you were driving home from the store and you slammed on your brakes and your arms sprang protectively between her and the windshield and your eyes met with a knowing, sad look?
> The transition comes slowly, as it began between her and her mother. The changing of power. The transferring of responsibility. The passing down of duty. Suddenly you are spewing out the familiar phrases learned at the knee of your mother.[7]

Imagine that you have a small daughter. Now imagine how you would feel if some years from now, while you are riding with your daughter in her car, she slams on the brakes and at the same time instinctively places her arm between the windshield and your body? Do you think you would be ready for this shift in power? Or would you say, "My God! So soon"?

The five axioms of communication that we have just explained should provide you with the background knowledge you will need as you prepare to focus on how everything fits together.

MODELS OF COMMUNICATION

Now that we have examined the basic components of communication—people, messages, channels, noise, context, feedback, and effect—some characteristics and functions of communication, and five basic axioms of communication, we are ready to see how our understanding can be reflected in a picture, or model, of the communication process.

Through communication we share meaning with others by sending and receiving messages—sometimes intentional and sometimes unintentional. In other words, communication includes every element that could affect two or more people as they knowingly or unknowingly relate to one another.

At this point we need to remind ourselves that communication occurs whenever one person assigns significance or meaning to the behavior of an-other person. But equally at this point we might ask, "So what? Will knowing this enable me to understand or establish better and more satisfying relation-ships with my friends, my spouse, my employer, my parents?" The answer is yes! If you understand the processes that permit people to contact and influence

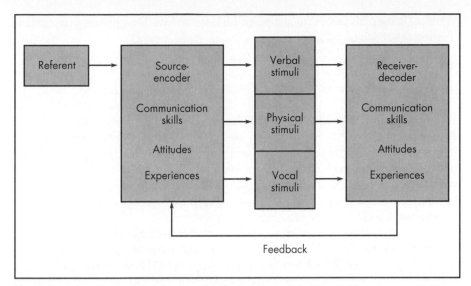

**FIGURE 1-2
Miller's model of
communication.**

Source: Reprinted with the
permission of Macmillan
Publishing Company from
*Speech Communications: A
Behavioral Approach* by
Gerald R. Miller. Copyright
© 1966 by The Bobbs-
Merrill Company.

each other, if you understand the forces that can impede or foster the development of every kind of effective communication, then you stand a better
chance of communicating effectively yourself. Models of communication can
help explain the process by which we initiate and maintain communicative
relationships with others. You will find these models useful tools in discovering
how communication operates and in examining your own communication
encounters.

Figure 1-2 is a model adapted from the work of the communication researcher Gerald R. Miller.[8] It illustrates how a *source-encoder* (a person) sends
out a message to a receiver-decoder (another person) about some *referent* (an
object, act, situation, experience, or idea). The source-encoder's message is
made up of at least three elements: *verbal stimuli* (words), *physical stimuli* (such
as gestures, facial expressions, and movements), and *vocal stimuli* (such as
rate of speaking, loudness and pitch of voice, and emphasis). The receiver-
decoder who receives the message that has been consciously or unconsciously
sent by the source-encoder responds to it in some way (positive or negative
feedback). Both the source's message and the receiver's response are affected
by the context and by each person's communication skills, attitudes, and past
experiences. The message sent differs from the message received because of
noise (remember our earlier definition of *noise*), even though noise is not
shown as an element in this model.

As an illustration of Miller's model, let's analyze the following dialogue
between a husband and wife:

SHE: What's the matter with you? You're late again. We'll never get to the Adamses'
on time.

HE: I tried my best.

SHE: (Sarcastically) Sure, you tried your best. You always try your best, don't you?
(Shaking her finger) I'm not going to put up with this much longer.

HE: (Raising his voice) You don't say! I happen to have been tied up at the office.

SHE: My job is every bit as demanding as yours, you know.

HE: (Lowering his voice) OK. OK. I know you work hard too. I don't question that. Listen, I really did get stuck in a conference. (Puts his hand on her shoulder.) Let's not blow this up. Come on. I'll tell you about it on the way to Bill and Ellen's.

What message is the wife (the initial source-encoder) sending to her husband (the receiver-decoder)? She is letting him know with her words, her voice, and her physical actions that she is upset and angry. Her husband responds in kind, using words, vocal cues, and gestures in an effort to explain his behavior. Both are affected by the nature of the situation (they are late for an appointment), by their attitudes (how they feel about what is occurring), and by their past experiences.

Next, consider a model developed by the communication expert Wilbur Schramm[9] (Figure 1-3). This model shows us more explicitly that human communication is a circle rather than a one-way event. Here each party to the communication process is perceived as both an encoder and a decoder. In addition, each party acts as an interpreter, understanding the messages he or she receives in a somewhat different way. This is because we are each affected by a field of experience or a psychological frame of reference (a form of noise) that we carry with us wherever we go.

Consider this brief dialogue:

WIFE: Hey, kids, don't bother Dad now. He's really tired. I'll play with you.

HUSBAND: Don't isolate me from my own children! You always need to have all their attention.

WIFE: I'm not trying to do that. I just know what it's like to have a really trying day and feel that I have to close my eyes to get back to myself.

HUSBAND: I sure must be wound up.

WIFE: I understand.

Here we see how one's psychological frame of reference can influence the meaning given to a message received. In addition, we come to realize that neither party to the communicative encounter functions solely as a sender or a receiver of messages. Rather, each sends and receives messages simultaneously. The wife receives the message that her husband is exhausted and sends

FIGURE 1-3
Schramm's model of communication.

Source: From *The Process and Effects of Mass Communication* by Wilbur Schramm. Copyright 1954 by the University of Illinois. Used by permission of The University of Illinois Press.

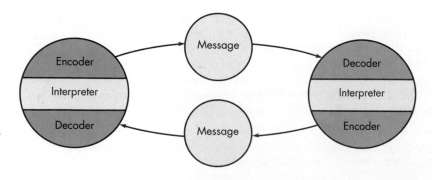

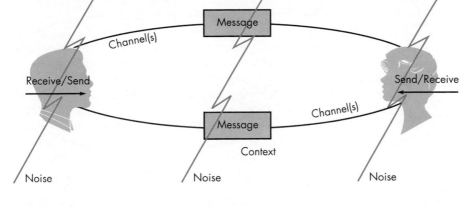

FIGURE 1-4
Gamble and Gamble's
model of
communication.

a message that the kids should let him rest. The husband receives a message that his wife is trying to "alienate" him from the children and sends a message expressing his concern. By listening to her husband's message, the wife is able to determine how he has interpreted *her* message and is thus able to avoid a serious misunderstanding.

A third model, shown in Figure 1-4, combines the strengths of the first two models. Here communication is a circle, and the sending and receiving responsibilities are shared by the communicators. A message or messages may be sent through one or more channels, and the interaction occurs in and is affected by a definite context. Note that noise can enter the interaction at any point and can affect either the sending or the receiving abilities of the interactants. Furthermore, noise can be caused by the context, can be present in the channel, or can pop up in the message itself.

Frank Dance, a noted communication theorist, has created a more abstract model to depict the dynamic nature of the communication process[10] (see Figure 1-5 on page 24). Dance's spiral, or helix, represents the way communication evolves or progresses in a person from birth to the present moment. This model also emphasizes the fact that each person's present behavior is affected by his or her past experience and, likewise, that present behavior will have an impact on his or her future actions. Thus Dance's helix indicates that communication is additive or accumulative; it has no clearly observable beginning and no clearly observable end.

We can picture two communication spirals as meeting in a number of different ways, as shown by Figure 1-6. The point where the spirals touch is the point of contact; each time a contact occurs, messages are sent and received by the interactants. Some helical spirals touch each other only once during a lifetime, whereas others crisscross or intertwine in a pattern that indicates an enduring relationship. Furthermore, the spirals (interactants) may sometimes develop in similar ways (grow together) and sometimes develop in different ways (grow apart) (see Figure 1-7).

The understanding you now have should provide you with some of the background you will need as you work to increase your effectiveness as a communicator. Chapters 2 through 6 provide more background understanding, along with specific steps and guidelines.

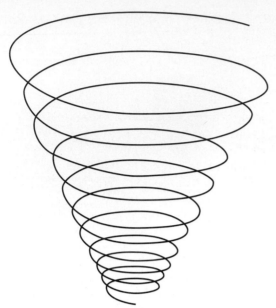

FIGURE 1-5
Dance's communication helix.

Source: From *Human Communication Theory: Original Essays* by Frank E. X. Dance. Holt, Rinehart & Winston. Copyright © 1967 by Frank E. X. Dance. Used by permission of the author.

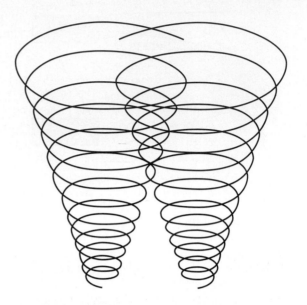

FIGURE 1-6
Meeting of helixes.

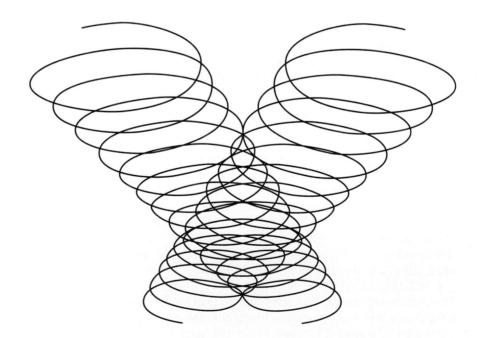

FIGURE 1-7
Model of communication in relationships.

MODELING COMMUNICATION

1. Draw or build something that represents your understanding of communication. You can focus on any or all of the components of the processes we have examined thus far. Your model can be lifelike or abstract. Be ready to present it to the class. Specifically, be sure to do the following.

   a. Describe what your model suggests are the essential elements of the communication process (whether pictured or implied).

   b. Explain what your model says about the communication process.

   c. Develop a saying or epigram that sums up your perception of the state of being in communication.

   d. Explain how your model reflects one or more of the axioms of communication.

   e. Suggest what insights into interpersonal, small-group, and public communication are provided by your model.

2. Identify an important message you want to communicate or must communicate to some person or group within the next few days. Analyze the following:

   a. How you will encode the message

   b. What channel or channels you will use to deliver the message

   c. How the environment or setting might affect the encoding and decoding of your message

   d. How noise could interfere at different points in the process

   e. What feedback you might receive

   f. How one or more of the axioms of communication will come into play during the interaction

   g. What the outcome of the communication transaction will be

IMPROVING YOUR EFFECTIVENESS AS A COMMUNICATOR

The major purpose of this book is to help you gain an understanding of communication and to assist you in developing your skills at interpersonal, small-group, and public communication. To achieve these goals you will need to accomplish the following preliminary tasks.

Understand How This Book Works

Each section of this textbook contains information that clarifies and illuminates the communication experience. Part One (Chapters 1 to 6) defines *communication* and explores how self-concept, perception, listening, language, and nonverbal communication will affect our ability to relate to others in a variety of settings. In Part Two (Chapters 7 and 8) we focus more directly on communicating interpersonally. We examine the nature of relationships and how to handle emotions within relationships. Part Three (Chapters 9 to 11) investigates the role of the group in problem solving; networks, group membership, leadership, and conflict are also examined. In Part Four (Chapters 12 to 18) you will meet the speaker and the audience, and you will have an opportunity to examine how best to prepare for the challenge of speechmaking. Finally, in Part Five we provide materials that will help you carry your communication skills forward, beyond your communication course and beyond this text: Chapter 19 explores a very special type of interpersonal communication, the interview; and Chapter 20 offers guidelines for lifelong learning.

Become Actively Involved in the Study of Communication

The materials in this book will benefit you only if you make a commitment to try out and experience the principles discussed. First, each chapter opening lists targets (behavioral objectives) that specify what you should have learned after completing your study of the chapter. Use these lists to clarify your own communication objectives as you make your way through the book. Next, a plethora of exercises (Skill Builders), self-analyses, and assessment scales are included to help you become aware of what you must know and do to become a more effective communicator. They will give you an opportunity to apply your new knowledge to actual communication experiences. If you use them as directed, you will increase your opportunities to grow because you will be actively testing your own learning and diagnosing your own needs for self-improvement.

Growth takes time, and lasting change does not just happen. Mistakes should be viewed as opportunities for learning, and new learning must be continually practiced. Only in this way can ineffective patterns of behavior be "unfrozen" and new, effective patterns made a part of your communication repertoire.

Believe in Yourself

Above all else, you must believe that you are worth the time and effort needed to develop your communication skills. You must also believe that developing these skills will immeasurably improve the quality of your life. We think you are worth it. And we know that *communication works*! Do you?

SUMMARY

Communication is a deliberate or accidental transfer of meaning. Human communication takes place interpersonally (one to one), in small groups (one to a few), and in public forums (one to many). The essential elements of communication are people, messages, channels, noise, a context, feedback, and some effect or result.

All acts of communication share two general characteristics: (1) Since communication is a dynamic process, each interaction is part of a series of interconnected communication events. (2) Every communication experience is unique, unrepeatable, and irreversible. Communication has a number of essential functions in our lives. It promotes self-other understanding, helps us establish meaningful relationships, and enables us to examine and attempt to change the attitudes and behavior of others.

Watzlawick, Beavin, and Jackson have developed five basic axioms which further clarify the communication process: (1) You cannot not communicate. (2) Every interaction has both a content and a relationship dimension. (3) Every interaction is defined by the way it is punctuated. (4) Messages are digital and analogic (verbal and nonverbal). (5) Communication exchanges are either symmetrical or complementary. Communication theorists have devised a number of models to show how the elements of communication are related and interact.

Developing communication skills is a lifelong process. This book explains the strategies you can use to assess your own communication abilities, improve the effectiveness of your communication relationships, and enhance the quality of your life.

SUGGESTIONS FOR FURTHER READING

Carter, Jay: *Nasty People: How to Stop Being Hurt by Them without Becoming One of Them*, Contemporary Books, New York, 1990. This book describes the tactics people use to bring themselves up by putting others down, and reveals techniques you can use to handle them.

Dance, Frank E. X.: "Toward a Theory of Human Communication," in Frank E. X. Dance (ed.), *Human Communication Theory: Original Essays*, Holt, Rinehart and Winston, New York, 1967. Dance's helical spiral is described in detail.

Gallwey, Timothy W.: *Inner Tennis*, Random House, New York, 1976. This book goes far beyond tennis; it is a guide to self-mastery.

Miller, Gerald R.: *Speech Communication: A Behavioral Approach*, Bobbs-Merrill, Indianapolis, Ind., 1966. Discusses the Miller model of communication.

Schramm, Wilbur: "How Communication Works," in Wilbur Schramm (ed.), *The Process and Effects of Mass Communication*, University of Illinois Press, Urbana, 1954. Describes Schramm's model of the communication process.

Stacks, Don W., Sidney R. Hill, and Mark L. Hickson, III: *Introduction to Communication Theory*, Harcourt Brace Jovanovich, Fort Worth, Tex., 1991. Introduces the student to a multitude of theories explaining human communication. The behavioral implications of each theory are also discussed. An exciting work.

Ting Toomy, Stella, and Felipe Karzenny: *Cross-Cultural Interpersonal Communication*, Sage, Newbury Park, Calif., 1991. Designed to facilitate better understanding of international and intercultural communication processes. Presents a variety of studies that compare communication across cultures.

Watzlawick, Paul H., Janet Beavin, and Don D. Jackson: *Pragmatics of Human Communication: A Study of Interactional Patterns, Pathologies and Paradoxes,* Norton, New York, 1967. This comprehensive work offers an analysis of the systematic nature of communication and the pathologies that can hamper healthy relationships.

NOTES

1. See, for example, E. T. Klemmer and F. W. Snyder, "Measurement of Time Spent Communicating," *Journal of Communication*, vol. 22, 1972, pp. 142–158. These authors reported that people spend 50 to 80 percent of their workdays communicating.

2. See, for example, Alan E. Ivey and James C. Hurse, "Communication as Adaptation," *Journal of Communication*, vol. 21, 1971, pp. 199–207. Ivey and Hurse reaffirm that communication is adaptive, like biological evolution—not an end in itself but a process.

3. Thomas Hora, in Paul H. Watzlawick et al., *Pragmatics of Human Communication: A Study of Interaction Patterns, Pathologies and Paradoxes*, Norton, New York, 1967.

4. William Schutz, *The Interpersonal Underworld*, Science and Behavior Books, Palo Alto, Calif., 1966.

5. Paul H. Watzlawick, Janet Beavin and Don D. Jackson, *Pragmatics of Human Communication: A Study of Interaction Patterns, Pathologies and Paradoxes*, Norton, New York, 1967.

6. For additional information on disqualification, see Janet Beavin Bavelas, "Situations That Lead to Disqualification," *Human Communication Research*, vol. 9, 1983, pp. 130–145.

7. Erma Bombeck, "When Did I Become the Mother and the Mother Become the Child?" in *If Life Is a Bowl of Cherries, What Am I Doing in the Pits?* McGraw-Hill, New York, 1978.

8. Gerald R. Miller, *Speech Communication: A Behavioral Approach*, Indianapolis, Ind., Bobbs-Merrill, 1966, pp. 72–74.

9. Wilbur Schramm, "How Communication Works," in Wilbur Schramm (ed.), *The Process and Effects of Mass Communication*, University of Illinois Press, Urbana, 1954, p. 3–10.

10. Frank E. X. Dance, "Toward a Theory of Human Communication," in Frank E. X. Dance (ed.), *Human Communication Theory: Original Essays*, Holt, Rinehart and Winston, New York, 1967.

COMMUNICATION AND THE SELF-CONCEPT: WHO ARE YOU?

When you finish this chapter, you should be able to:

Define *self-concept*, describe role-taking as a factor in the development of the self-concept, and identify dimensions of yourself that you had not recognized before

Identify how popular culture helps shape your self-concept

Define *self-fulfilling prophecy* and explain how a self-fulfilling prophecy can influence behavior

Identify factors that contribute to the development of a positive or negative self-concept

Compare and contrast the ways male and females, and people from different cultures, see themselves

Describe your own assets and liabilities

Identify the purposes and functions of the Johari window as a model of self-disclosure, and provide examples of information contained in the "open," "blind," "hidden," and "unknown" areas of the self

Describe how you see yourself and how you think others see you

Even the simplest clown manages by gesture and incident to explore the mythology of the self. . . . In him, in his ludicrous contradictions of dignity and embarrassment, of pomp and rags, of assurance and collapse, of sentiment and sadness, of innocence and guile, we learn to see ourselves.

Samuel Howard Miller

The lights in the circus arena are suddenly dimmed. Accompanied by a drumroll and fanfare, an incredibly small car drives into the center ring. A spotlight highlights the red, blue, green, yellow, and orange colors that decorate the tiny automobile. Cymbals crash as the car's door opens and a small clown with a bright, happy face tumbles out. As the elflike figure gets up only to stumble again and again, a larger clown suddenly jumps out of the car. This clown wears a mask of anger and fury and begins to chase the "vulnerable" little clown around the center ring. Suddenly, a third clown timidly and nervously crawls out of the car. Following this clown is a fourth, large, rotund, smiling clown, who rolls about the ring like a Slinky. These antics continue until approximately 15 to 20 clowns have emerged from the single car. Each clown has a distinctive "face," or mask, that depicts a particular attitude or emotion. One looks perpetually happy; another looks perpetually sad; one looks chronically silly; another looks eternally angry; one looks jealous; another appears to be in love; one has eyes that dance; another has a nose that trails on the floor. Finally, the empty clown car backfires a few times and begins to chase the clowns out of the arena as the cheering crowd roars with laughter.

DEFINITIONS: WHAT IS THE SELF-CONCEPT?

How many faces or masks are associated with the word *clown*? One? Two? Ten? An infinite number? Actually, the number of clown faces that can be designed is infinite. Student clowns at the Ringling Brothers Clown College in Florida pride themselves on their ability to create original clown masks. Just as each person who creates such a face is unique, so each mask created is unique. Which face, then, really represents the concept of *clown*? The answer must be that *all* the faces are representations of the word *clown*, for each expresses a different facet, or view, of what a clown is.

Let us consider one other aspect of the clown before we move on. Who are these people who live behind clown masks or faces? What kind of people are they? Presumably a person who performs as a clown takes on that role and behaves in a specified, planned, and rehearsed manner only while the circus performance is in progress. And those of us in the audience assume that a role is being played by each "clown person"—that this is not the real person.[1]

Do you ever wear a special face, or "mask," in your own life? Obviously you do not normally walk around wearing a painted-on clown face any more than the circus performers do, yet you may find that you in fact wear a variety of masks during the course of a single day. For example, does your face look the same when you are happy as it does when you are sad? How do you know? And how does your face look when you are really furious?

What "masks" might people in business wear?

*"Might I point out, sir, that that one goes
particularly well with your tie?"*

Drawing by Gahan Wilson; © 1982 The New Yorker Magazine, Inc.

Actually, we wear many different masks throughout our lives. We wear happy and sad masks, peaceful and angry masks, bored and excited masks, sorry and vengeful masks. Besides the masks we wear to display our innumerable feelings, we also wear those which are associated with the roles we play—student, brother, spouse, sister, boss, or whatever. As the psychologist William James observed: "A man has as many social selves as there are individuals who recognize him and carry an image of him in their mind." We wear so many faces that the question ultimately becomes, "Who am I, really?"

No matter what your age or position, it is important that you spend some time considering who you are and what you intend to do with the rest of your life. It is important that you use each available opportunity to find out about yourself. In this chapter you will be given the chance to explore some aspects of the question, "Who am I?" Your answer will be extremely significant, since who you think you are to a large extent determines what you choose to do, how you choose to act, whom you choose to communicate with, and even whether you choose to communicate at all. Unquestionably, you are the center of your communication system. But who are you, anyway? Jolene Tennis, who has muscular dystrophy, movingly describes her unique sense of self:

> My wheelchair is my life. My wheelchair is my legs, and it gets me wherever I
> want to go. I have climbed Mt. Ranier, and I have gone across swinging foot
> bridges, and I have crossed streams. My wheelchair to me is me. It is part of me.
> I can tell when somebody touches it with two fingers because it is part of my
> skin. I know I live in an able-bodied world, but I don't think of myself as
> disabled. I've never been any other way than the way I am now. I've always been
> in a wheelchair, and that's normal. When David and I decided to get married, I'm

Part of knowing who we are is knowing we are not someone else.
Arthur Miller, *Incident at Vichy*

not even sure David realized people in wheelchairs got married. I showed David that there were a lot of things to do other than physical things, and that you could have fun. Freedom is being able to do what you have to do when you have to do it. I moved away from home when I was two months short of eighteen. I couldn't live at home anymore. I wasn't being allowed to change there, I guess. Being alive is changing. Being able to change. That's what being alive is to me.

I love the sound of water. I can move freely when I am in the water. I can move my body from one place to another and I don't have anything doing it for me. Not anybody or any wheelchair. I don't think about the passage of time anymore. I'm happy now.[2]

If someone were to ask you on 10 different occasions, "Who are you?"— and if each time you had to supply a different answer—what types of responses do you think you would offer? What would you say about yourself? To what extent could your responses be grouped into categories? For example, would you see yourself in reference to your feelings (happy, sad)? Your attitudes (optimistic, insecure)? Your physical attributes (tall, short)? Your intellectual attributes (capable, slow)? Your occupation (student, salesperson)? Your roles and relationships with others (brother, father, sister, mother, son, boss, employee)? Most important, what would your answers tell you about your self-concept?

How do your employer and your friends picture you?

Your *self-concept* is everything that you think and feel about yourself. It is the entire collection of attitudes and beliefs you hold about who and what you are. Even though you are constantly undergoing change, this theory or picture you have of yourself is fairly stable and difficult to alter. For example, have you ever tried to revise your parents' or your friends' opinions about themselves? Did you have much luck? Our opinions about ourselves grow more and more resistant to change as we become older and presumably wiser. The statements we make are more or less accurate "maps" of the "territory" which is ourselves, but some of us map ourselves better than others do—that is, some of us have a more accurate mental picture of our own strengths, weaknesses, and needs than others do.[3]

■ ETHICS AND COMMUNICATION

SELF-CONCERN AND CONCERN FOR OTHERS

According to Virginia Satir in her book *The New Peoplemaking*:

"Every person has a feeling of worth, positive or negative; the question is, Which is it?

Every person communicates; the question is, How, and what happens as a result?

Every person follows rules; the question is, What kind, and how well do they work for her or him?

Every person is linked to society; the question is, In what way, and what are the results?"

How would you answer each of these questions with regard to yourself? Your parents? Your friends? The people you work with? What does each set of answers reveal about self-concern for and concern for others?

Source: Virginia Satir, *The New Peoplemaking*, 2d ed., Science and Behavior Books, Palo Alto, Calif., 1988.

Environment and Experience: Positive and Negative Self-Concepts

How did your self-concept develop? To a large extent it is shaped by your environment and by the people around you, including your parents, relatives, teachers, supervisors, friends, and coworkers. If people who are important to you have "sent you messages" that have made you feel accepted, valued, worthwhile, lovable, and significant, you have probably developed a *positive self-concept*. On the other hand, if those who are important to you have made you feel left out, small, worthless, unloved, or insignificant, you have probably developed a *negative self-concept*. It is not difficult to see how people we value influence the picture we have of ourselves and help determine the ways we behave. The nineteenth-century poet Walt Whitman recognized this:

> There was a child went forth every day,
> And the first object he look'd upon, that object he became,
> And that object became part of him for the day or a certain part of the day,
> Or for many years or stretching cycles of years.

Self-concept, besides being your own theory of who and what you are, is a mental *picture* you have of yourself. This mental image is easily translated into the faces or masks you wear, the roles you play, and the ways you behave. To see this illustrated graphically, examine Figure 2-1. The top panel presents the self-image of a man who thinks of himself as a lowly cockroach. He developed this image because he felt that he was performing a dull job in an impersonal work environment. However, when invited to attend a conference, he alters this perception and as a result changes his demeanor and adopts an "executive appearance." The middle panel shows how our man viewed various colleagues who attended the conference. One is as proud as a peacock, and another is as close-mouthed as a clam; one is ill-tempered like a ram; one is loyal like a dog; one is unforgetful like an elephant; one is a dangerous wolf; and still another is a stubborn mule. Finally, in the bottom panel we see what

---

■ ETHICS AND COMMUNICATION

AGE AND SELF-ESTEEM

Self-esteem may be related to age. According to the researchers Justine Coupland, John F. Nussbaum, and Nikolas Coupland, ". . . elderly people are prone to assimilate society's devalued appraisals of their own social group, and so lower their self-esteem."

What messages do you send older people whom you relate with regarding your estimations of their worth and abilities?

Source: Justine Coupland, John F. Nussbaum, and Nikolas Coupland, "The Reproduction of Aging and Ageism in Intergenerational Talk," in Nikolas Coupland, Howard Giles, and John Wiemann (eds.), *Miscommunication and Problematic Talk*, Sage, Newbury Park, Calif., 1991, p. 85.

FIGURE 2-1
How the self-image can change during a single day.

Source: Adapted from art by Paul Furlinger in *Psychology Today*, August 1972, p. 5. Jules Power Productions.

happens to our man once the meeting is over: He retreats into "roachhood" once more. He reemerges at lunch to play the "knight in shining armor" for his secretary. However, once lunch is finished, he goes back to what he perceives as mindless busywork. To put it politely, he views himself as a donkey. Yet our man has not completely submerged his "better" self. When he is called on to make a decision, he once again changes his self-image and this time pictures himself as a "captain of industry."

We know that if you feel you have little worth, you probably expect to be taken advantage of, stepped on, or otherwise demeaned by others. When you expect the worst, you usually get the worst. Similarly, if you feel you have significant worth, you probably expect to be treated fairly, supported, and otherwise held in esteem by others. When you expect to succeed, you usually find success.

WILL THE REAL SELF-ESTEEM STAND UP?
Anne Taylor Fleming

Los Angeles, Nov. 8—The California Task Force to Promote Self-Esteem and Personal and Social Responsibility: it seemed a parody, an idea born in a hot tub. Even many natives laughed when the task force was created a little over two years ago, though the laughter was checked a little by the realization that they were footing the bill—$735,000—for a three-year exploration into the state of self-esteem of the state's citizenry.

Nonnative Californians were even more amused, most notably the cartoonist Gary Trudeau, who lampooned the new task force in his "Doonesbury" comic strip. But eager applicants were undaunted; more than 300 applied to fill 21 appointive slots on the 25-member commission, the largest number ever to apply to any state task force or commission. The chosen—all unpaid volunteers—include a Christian-school principal from Redding at the top of the state and a turban-wearing Sikh yoga teacher from Del Mar near the bottom. Four more members were named by state officials.

First the members had to agree on a definition of self-esteem. That took more than a year. After considerable discussion, they settled on this: "Appreciating my own worth and importance, and having the character to be accountable for myself and to act responsibly toward others."

Then they had to go about finding out who in the state had self-esteem and why, who didn't and why. Over the past months they have met in daylong forums around the state and listened to everybody: street-gang members and single mothers, counselors and community leaders. They were seeking to find out, as their mandate says, "whether healthy self-esteem relates to the development of personal responsibility and social problems (like crime and alcoholism and violence) and how healthy self-esteem is nurtured, harmed or reduced, and rehabilitated."

So popular has this search become that there are now mini-self-esteem task forces in 42 California counties, including Los Angeles County, which puts out its own chatty little newsletter, The Self-Esteemer. This is clearly an idea whose time has come in California. . . .

Underneath the snickering generated by the task force and the buoyant reach of its own stated goals lies the garrulously tortured soul of its creator: Assemblyman John Vasconcellos of San Jose. There would be no Self-Esteem Task Force without him. It is his baby, born of his own struggle to find self-esteem. . . .

. . . And he is still often in pain, he said, still fighting his own lack of self-esteem, which he defines as "the felt appreciation of my own innate, instinctual being."

That appreciation can be elusive. "I'm not all healed yet," he said in an interview in San Francisco, a rueful smile momentarily lighting up his face. "I wish I were. It started so far back. I'm much more comfortable with my body and my own being, but I'm still a little self-conscious and shy. I came from a very traditional Catholic family. My father was very buttoned down, locked away. I did everything right. I got good grades, ran for class president. I've been running for office since the eighth grade, when I lost by one vote—my own. I just didn't think I should vote for myself."

John Vasconcellos sees the task force as the ultimate self-help program. "I know some people are still frightened by this," he said, "so they deride it as New Age. But after all, 60 to 80 million Americans have already been in some kind of counseling."

The other point of the task force, he emphasized, is to save money: "I've seen the cost of prisons—$17,000 a year to lock somebody up—and dropouts and drugs. We're doing too little too late. We have to get at the root cause; self-esteem informs everything. . . . "

Source: From "Will the Real Self-Esteem Stand Up?" by Ann Taylor Fleming, *The New York Times*, November 9, 1988. Copyright © 1988 by The New York Times Company. Reprinted by permission.

We can conclude that the nature of the self at any given moment is a composite of all the factors that interact in a particular environment. Thus, how you look at yourself is affected by how you look at people, how people actually look at you, and how *you* imagine or perceive that people look at you. In effect, we might say that self-concept is derived from experience and projected into future behavior.

Of course, your self-concept, whether it is positive or negative, may be realistic or unrealistic. Unfortunately, we never really come to know all there is to know about ourselves, and so we keep searching for clues. How accurate is your map of yourself? Some of us have very unrealistic self-concepts. A former baseball star who perceives himself as capable of functioning as a major league manager but turns out to lack the necessary skills will eventually disappoint not only himself but also those who believed in him. On the other hand, if you continually berate yourself with statements like "I'm a failure," you may never discover your actual potential for success; your self-concept prevents you from assuming roles you might be capable of performing.

Role-Taking and Self-Exploration: Categorizing the Self

Throughout each day, we vary the masks we wear and the roles we perform. The language we use, the attitudes we display, and the appearances we present constantly change. In effect, we become different selves as we move from one set of conditions to another. The more we attempt to be ourselves, the more selves we find. It is important to recognize that conditions and circumstances affect the nature of the self. In every situation, how we see ourselves and how we think about ourselves in relation to others direct and modify our behavior.

For example, some of us are optimists when it comes to thinking about the self. If we suffer a defeat, we view it as a temporary setback brought about by circumstances, bad luck, or other people: optimists do not view defeat as their own fault. Some of us are pessimists. In contrast to optimists, pessimists believe that bad events are their own fault, will last a long time, and will undermine whatever they do. For these reasons, pessimists give up more easily.[4] Our self-concept and demeanor are also affected by our perceptions of others and how we think they will respond to us; thus the roles we choose to play are in part a result of the values held by other members of our society.

Clues to self-understanding come to you continually as you interact with others and with your environment. If you are to understand yourself, you need to be open to information that other people give you about yourself. Just as we tend to categorize ourselves and others, so others also tend to categorize themselves and us. For better or worse, the categorization process is a basic part of interpersonal communication. We classify people according to their roles, their status, their material possessions, their personality traits, their physical and vocal qualities, and their skills and accomplishments. Which of these categories are most important to you? Which do you think are most important to the people who are significant in your life? How do others help shape your image of yourself? How do they serve to enhance or belittle your own sense of self?

According to the psychologist Martin P. Seligman, pessimists can learn to be optimists. How do you think optimism would enhance the self-concept?

Are you the person *you* think you are, the person *someone else* thinks you are, or the person you *think* someone else thinks you are? Why?

A DAY IN MY LIFE

1. List the names of all the people with whom you interacted on a single day this week. For each, identify the environment in which you communicated.

2. Next, choose an adjective to describe your image of yourself during each interaction and an adjective to describe your image of the person with whom you spoke.

3. Finally, graph your perceptions on a chart like the one shown here, entering each of your responses

in the appropriate box. (For example, you might see yourself as shy and "person 1" as aggressive.)

4. Answer these questions: What does your chart tell you about the nature of your self-image? To what extent does your view of yourself change as you move from person to person? What factors can you point to in yourself, the individual with whom you were interacting, or the environment that help account for the changes?

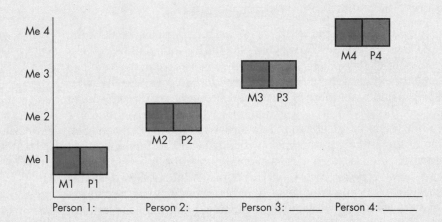

Popular Media: Seeing Ourselves in the Electronic Looking Glass

Thus far we have established that your self-image is made up partly of information and feelings drawn from past experiences and from your interactions with others. There are at least two other important sources that affect your opinion about who you are: television and film. We are all influenced by television and film characters and their lifestyles to a greater extent than we may realize. Subtly but effectively, these two media shape our views of ourselves and our relationship to our world. The poem on the opposite page, although it is based on childhood fantasies, nevertheless reflects a major concern of our culture.

Shel Silverstein

I'll tell you the story of Jimmy Jet—
And you know what I tell you is true.
He loved to watch his TV set
Almost as much as you.

He watched all day, he watched all night
Till he grew pale and lean,
From "The Early Show" to "The Late Late Show"
And all the shows between.

He watched till his eyes were frozen wide,
And his bottom grew into his chair.
And his chin turned into a tuning dial,
And antennae grew out of his hair.

And his brains turned into TV tubes,
And his face to a TV screen.
And two knobs saying "VERT." and "HORIZ."
Grew where his ears had been.

And he grew a plug that looked like a tail
So we plugged in Little Jim.
And now instead of him watching TV
We all sit around and watch him.[5]

Let's consider some actual ways in which the popular media affect the picture you have of yourself. First, through these media we are shown a standard of living few of us can expect to achieve. Thus, our evaluation of ourselves as providers—or even as successful—can be seriously colored by what we see. Second, television and film can affect the ways parents and children perceive themselves and each other. After all, both parents and children are exposed to a steady succession of media counterparts who are either so "perfect" that even their mistakes become the raw material of a closer relationship or so absurd that their foibles can only constitute charming comedy. Third, the visual media can fill our need for a bigger, better, smarter, prettier, stronger personal image. When we were younger, it was easy and fun to "try on" television and film images. For example, we could put on a cape or mask and become Batman, Wonder Woman, Spiderman, Flash Gordon, Superman, or the Bionic Woman. As we mature, however, this process becomes a bit more subtle. As adults, we attempt to become like popular idols or heroes by imitating their fashions, by adopting their speech mannerisms, and by copying their movements and gestures. Thus, we communicate part of the picture we have of ourselves, or the picture we would like to have, through the way we dress, move, speak, and so on. When you put on a certain outfit, comb your hair in a new style, walk or speak in a particular way, or choose to wear a certain artifact, you are telling other people something about who you think you are, whom you would like to resemble, and how you would like to be treated.

Television programs and films can support us or deflate us. They can cause us to feel good, adequate, or inferior.

If you could trade places with any television or film star or character, who would you be? What does this person, real or fictional, "do" for you? Do you have a more positive image of this person than you have of yourself? Why? Would you like to be more like the media image, or would you like the image to be more like you?

SELF-ESTEEM IS SKIN-DEEP
Yvonne Shinhoster Lamb

Why do black children learn to value whiteness more than white children learn to value blackness?
How can communication help eradicate such stereotypes?

Race relations, stripped down to skin color and hair texture, can be a daunting subject to discuss with pre-school children. Particularly if the topic arises, as can occur with children, seemingly out of the blue.

Like the time William, my then 4-year-old son, announced while riding a department store escalator: "I want to be white.

"Whites are good. Being black . . . being an African-American isn't good. That's the reason why," he said as I explored what prompted this revelation.

In response to a question about what is wrong with being a black person, he pointed his finger and pretended to shoot.

Somewhere along the line, my son had received messages that being a black person in America was not something to be proud of. Somewhere in his 4-year-old psyche he had come to the conclusion that to be happy, to achieve success, to reap life's bounty he needed to be white.

My conscious efforts to imbue my son with a positive sense of himself and his race had failed.

Later that night my husband, Greg, spoke with William about being proud of who he is. He reminded him of his uncles, grandfathers, and great-grandfather, who were good, hard-working black men. William listened. They talked about the Rev. Martin Luther King Jr. and other famous blacks, and our son emerged from the conversation saying he was going "to grow up to be a proud black man like Daddy."

Black parents, even those who feel they are instilling in their children racial pride as well as racial tolerance, must not flinch or panic when the time comes to explain the harsh realities of racism and race relations to their young ones.

The sooner those conversations take place, the better, say clinical psychologists Darlene Powell Hopson and Derek Hopson, authors of the book "Different and Wonderful: Raising Black Children in a Race-Conscious Society." Parents should teach their children about race at an early age, they say, because usually around age 3 children begin showing a preference for whites.

The Hopsons and others contend that children are bombarded from infancy with negative messages about being black and positive images about being white from media accounts, commercials, peers, and relatives.

"Black parents who read traditional fairy tales and folklore to their children send them messages very early on that kings, queens, princes, and princesses are white and that the world is controlled and run by white people," psychologist Alvin F. Poussaint, of the Harvard Medical School, said in the foreword to the Hopson book.

"In addition, important cultural symbols and the fantasy heroes who exercise dominant power over children are white, among them Superman, Batman, He-Man, Master of the Universe, and even Captain Midnight."

The Hopsons believe black parents "have an extra responsibility to point out negative racial images, explain their inaccuracies, and teach our children how to separate themselves from them and protect their self-esteem.

"If your child knows and loves the person he is, appreciating his physical appearance, as well as his personal character and his culture, there is little that can undermine him."

In a recent telephone interview, Darlene Powell Hopson pointed out that it's not just students in integrated schools who must sometimes fend off stereotypical and racist comments. Students in predominantly black inner-city schools often confront a kind of black-on-black racism.

"We have those struggles within our own setting," she says, where students and even school officials are "internalizing society's view of what is good and what isn't." Light skin and so-called "good" hair are often considered the desired attributes; dark skin and "nappy" hair are many times targets of ridicule.

Bias Revealed in Doll Play

Parents can learn a lot about their children's self-image and their racial view of the world by watching them play with dolls of various skin hues and hair textures.

It seems not much has changed since psychologist Kenneth Clark performed the famous doll studies nearly 50 years ago in which black children overwhelming selected white dolls and considered them more desirable than their darker counterparts.

Six years ago, clinical psychologists Darlene Powell Hopson and Derek Hopson repeated the Clark study. In their recently released findings, the Hopsons reported that not only did 65 percent of the black children choose white dolls but 76 percent said the black dolls "looked bad."

The results are still relevant today, says Darlene Hopson, adding that they got similar results in June during a filming of preschoolers playing with dolls.

The doll research "is indicative of children picking up on the messages that they are getting in society," Derek Hopson says.

"Sesame Street" research director Valeria Lovelace says the scenario was the same when they organized a group of preschool children to play with dolls as a part of their new programming thrust to gauge how preschoolers view race relations.

Black and white children said they would play with both color dolls, but when given the choice, the children picked the white dolls, Lovelace says.

"Many black children even chose white dolls when asked to pick out the doll that looked more like them," the Hopsons wrote in their book, "Different and Wonderful: Raising Black Children in a Race-Conscious Society." "These results tell us early in their lives, many black children learn that whiteness is more valued than blackness in society."

The Hopsons, in their book, offer suggestions for parents about building their child's self-esteem:

- Use doll play to help children stretch their imagination and express themselves.
- Read the child books and stories that have positive black characters and heroes.
- Expose children to different kinds of people.
- Display pictures of black people you respect or other black art in your home.
- Shield children from negative experiences and avoid using racial stereotypes.

Source: "Self-Esteem Is Skin-Deep" by Yvonne Shinhoster Lamb. © 1992 The Washington Post. Reprinted with permission.

Expectations: The Self-Fulfilling Prophecy and the Pygmalion Effect

Consider this excerpt from *The People Yes*, by the poet Carl Sandburg:

> Drove up a newcomer in a covered wagon. "What kind of folks live around here?" "Well, stranger, what kind of folks was there in the country you come from?" "Well, they was mostly a lowdown, lying, gossiping, backbiting lot of people." "Well, I guess, stranger, that's about the kind of folks you'll find around here." And the dusty grey stranger had just about blended into the dusty grey cottonwoods in a clump on the horizon when another newcomer drove up. "What kind of folks live around here?" "Well, stranger, what kind of folks was there in the country you come from?" "Well, they was mostly a decent, hardworking, law abiding, friendly lot of people." "Well, I guess stranger, that's about the kind of people you'll find around here." And the second wagon moved off and blended with the dusty grey....[6]

The speaker in this passage understands the significance of the self-fulfilling prophecy. A *self-fulfilling prophecy* occurs when expecting some event helps create the very conditions which will permit that event to happen (see Figure 2-2 on page 40). In other words, your predictions can cause you and others to behave in ways that will increase the likelihood of an initially unlikely occur-

> Pessimism is self-fulfilling. Pessimists don't persist in the face of challenges, and therefore fail more frequently—even when success is attainable.
> Martin P. Seligman

39

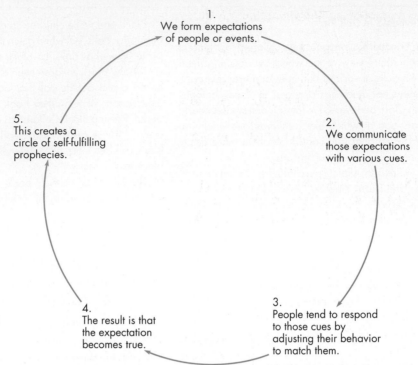

1.
We form expectations
of people or events.

2.
We communicate
those expectations
with various cues.

3.
People tend to respond
to those cues by
adjusting their behavior
to match them.

4.
The result is that
the expectation
becomes true.

5.
This creates a
circle of self-fulfilling
prophecies.

FIGURE 2-2
The self-fulfilling
prophecy in action.

Source: From "Self-Fulfilling
Prophecy: Better
Management by Magic"
by Len Sandler. Reprinted
with permission from the
February 1986 issue of
Training Magazine.
Copyright 1986, Lakewood
Publications Inc.,
Minneapolis, MN, (612)
333-0471. All rights
reserved.

rence. For example, have you ever had to perform a task that others told you would be dull? Was it? Why? If it was dull, did it occur to you that you might have acted in a way that caused the prediction to come true?

Perhaps the most widely known example of the self-fulfilling prophecy is called the *Pygmalion effect*. The term comes to us from a Greek myth in which Pygmalion, a sculptor, falls in love with a beautiful ivory statue of his own creation. The goddess Aphrodite, moved by Pygmalion's obsession with the statue, comes to his rescue and brings it to life. George Bernard Shaw adapted the story to a more modern setting, and Shaw's version in turn served as the basis for the stage and film musical *My Fair Lady*. In this version, Henry Higgins (Pygmalion) transforms a flower girl, Liza Doolittle, into a fine upper-class lady. The play illustrates the principle that we "live up to" labels. We, like Liza Doolittle, act like the sort of person others perceive us to be. In *Pygmalion*, Liza herself understands this when she says:

> "You see, really and truly, apart from the things anyone can pick up [elegant dress, the proper way of speaking, and so on], the difference between a lady and a flower girl is not how she behaves, but how she's treated. I shall always be a flower girl to Professor Higgins because he always treats me as a flower girl, and always will: but I know I can be a lady to you, because you always treat me as a lady, and always will."[7]

A real-life example of the startling effects of self-fulfilling prophecies is a classroom experiment described by psychologist Robert Rosenthal.[8] A number of teachers were notified that certain of their students were expected to "bloom"—that is, do exceptionally well—during the course of the school year.

"I'll make a duchess of this draggle-tailed guttersnipe." The "Pygmalion effect" gets its name from a Greek myth which was adapted in a famous play by George Bernard Shaw that in turn became an equally famous musical, *My Fair Lady*. The Pygmalion effect is an example of the self-fulfilling prophecy—a situation where expecting something to happen actually creates the conditions that allow it to happen.

Archive Photos

What the teachers did not know was that there was no real basis for this determination. The experimenters had simply selected the names of the "bloomers" at random. Do you think the selected students actually bloomed? If you said yes, you are quite right. Those students did perform at a higher level than would otherwise have been expected and did improve their IQ scores. Why? First, the teachers' expectations apparently influenced the way *they* treated these children. The teachers gave these students extra positive verbal and nonverbal reinforcement, waited patiently for them to respond if they hesitated, and did not react negatively when they offered faulty answers. Second, it seems that the way the teachers treated the students had a marked impact on the way the students perceived *themselves* and their own abilities. The "bloomers" responded to the prophecy that had apparently been made about them by fulfilling it.

It should be recognized that the self-fulfilling prophecy has many important implications not only for education but also for our personal life. Have you ever joined a group of people you were convinced would not like you? What happened? Very likely you were proved right. What you probably did was to act in a way that encouraged them to dislike you. Far too frequently we make assumptions about how others will behave and then act as if they had already

Identify people who have functioned as positive or negative "Pygmalions" in your life. Then complete these sentences: "I work best for people who . . ."; "I work *least* for people who . . ."

behaved that way. For example, if you view yourself as a failure in school or in a particular subject, it is likely that you will begin to act the part. Poor study habits, lack of participation in class, and poor grades will reinforce your feelings. In this way a growing negative image can become a vicious, all-consuming spiral.

The Pygmalion effect is also at the root of many business problems.[9] Apparently, some managers treat employees in ways that precipitate superior performance, while many others unconsciously treat workers in ways that precipitate inferior performance. High expectations tend to result in increased productivity, whereas low expectations result in decreased productivity. Thus, subordinates more often than not confirm the expectations of their superiors. For this reason, managers have the potential to function as both *positive* and *negative* "Pygmalions" for those who work under them. In other words, the Pygmalion effect can hinder as well as help.

A variation of the Pygmalion effect is called the *Galatea effect*. The Galatea effect is related to the expectations we have for ourselves rather than the expectations others have for us; in other words, the Galatea effect has to do with self-expectations. Just as we generally live up to—or down to—the expectations others have for us, we also tend to realize the expectations we have for ourselves. That is, we react to the internal messages we continuously send ourselves, not only to the external messages others send us. Our feelings about our own competence and ability can exert an influence on our behavior in much the same way that our performance can be influenced by others' high or low expectations for us. It is important to recognize that we can change and grow each day we exist. Thus how we and others answer the question, "Who are you?" affects how we behave. Remember, however, that at any point in our lives we can begin to acquire higher self-worth.

Biologists have determined that technically speaking, the bumblebee cannot fly. Fortunately, the bumblebee doesn't know this. Remember: people rise no higher than their expectations.

Gender: Do Males and Females See Themselves Differently?

Do you believe you would feel differently about yourself if you were of the opposite sex? Why or why not? If you answered yes, is it because you believe that others would treat you differently? Would they encourage you to exhibit some behaviors or traits while at the same time discouraging you from exhibiting others?

Research tells us that others do treat us differently because of our sex. For

---

✔ **SKILL BUILDER**

GROWING UP MALE; GROWING UP FEMALE

Conduct brief interviews with five males and females from each of these age groups: 5 to 8, 9 to 12, 13 to 16, and 17 to 20 years old. Ask the interviewees what they want to be when they grow up. Compare and contrast their responses. To what extent, if any, do you see a trend emerging? To what extent do the younger or older respondents offer gender-related answers? Explain.

Do men and women see themselves differently? Apparently, they do—and "male characteristics" tend to be valued more than "female characteristics." Today, however, this is beginning to change, as more and more women rise to positions of leadership.

Don Klumpp/The Image Bank

example, we dress male and female babies in different colors and styles, and we even tend to give them different toys to play with. For the most part, our prevalent conceptions of masculinity and femininity are reinforced in the television shows we view, the films we watch, and the books we read.

Unfortunately, studies reveal that women tend to develop a less positive view of themselves than men do. Why? In our society men are expected to exhibit the following personality characteristics to a greater degree than women: aggressiveness, arrogance, assertiveness, an autocratic style, conceit, confidence, cynicism, deliberateness, dominance, an enterprising spirit, forcefulness, foresightedness, frankness, handsomeness, hardheadedness, industriousness, ingeniousness, inventiveness, masculinity, opportunism, outspokenness, sharp-wittedness, shrewdness, sternness, strength, toughness, and vindictiveness. In contrast, women are more likely than men to be perceived as possessing the following traits: appreciativeness, considerateness, contentment, cooperativeness, dependence, emotionality, excitability, fearfulness, femininity, fickleness, a forgiving nature, friendliness, frivolity, helpfulness, joviality, modesty, a tendency to give praise, sensitivity, sentimentality, sincerity, submissiveness, sympathy, talkativeness, timidity, warmth, and a tendency to worry. What is noteworthy for the development of self-worth is that the "male characteristics" are valued more highly overall than the "female characteristics," and that rewards are given out accordingly. Hence, for example, more men than women rise to positions of leadership.

Today, to some extent, this is changing, and education and the media are beginning to contribute to these changes. Whereas women used to be underrepresented in television programming, their numbers are now on the rise; whereas men were typically depicted in professional roles, women are now joining them. In fact, according to the National Commission on Working Women, currently a higher proportion of women on television hold jobs than actual women in the United States. Progress has been made. Not much more than 15 years ago, the researcher Ann Beuf reported a very revealing observation: when asked what he would want to be when he grew up if he were a girl, a young boy said, "Oh, if I were a girl, I'd have to grow up to be nothing."[10] It is unlikely that any boy or girl would give that answer today.

We now know that both men and women can change their self-concepts—and that each of us can function in such a way as to make the change a positive one.

Culture: Do People from Different Cultures See Themselves Differently?

Almost a quarter of a century ago, Marshall McLuhan prophesied that television would create a "global village." If teenagers are representative of the attitudes and concerns shared by society as a whole, McLuhan was on target. Research conducted at the Center for the Study of Adolescence found that psychological maturation appears to be uniform throughout the world. According to the psychiatrist Robert Atkinson, "It consists of increased introspection and self evaluation, leading to the formation of personal identity, ambition, and goals."[11] Young people throughout the world have many attitudes in common (see Figure 2-3). Most are concerned about developing and maintaining social relationships especially with their peers, and most are confident about their ability to assume responsibility for themselves in the future. However, despite this apparent optimism, almost 25 percent of the teenagers in one survey described themselves as frequently sad and lonely, emotionally empty, and overwhelmed by life's problems; these youngsters are burdened with the weight of a poor self-image.

Young people are not the only group describing themselves as lonely today. Loneliness appears to be pervasive. The latest census report found that 23 million Americans live by themselves—over two times the number of single-person households reported in 1970. An editorial in *The New York Times* noted that although solitary living cannot be equated with loneliness, it may certainly involve some loneliness:

> In truth, most of them may not be lonely, those 23 million Americans—a quarter of the nation's households—who the Census Bureau reports live alone. They're more than double the number who lived alone in 1970, and they range from the elderly who've outlived their marital partners to the young who are more eager than ever for their own apartments, and privacy.
>
> That 23 million may love never having to bang on the bathroom door, never having to share the bedroom with a snorer. For them a truly terrific evening may be a date with MacGyver or Murphy Brown, and a truly terrific dining partner, the cat.
>
> If they're elderly, they may take great pleasure in having the wherewithal to live on their own, especially if they remember when the old depended on relatives for meals and a bedroom off the hall. If they're young, they may rejoice that the pressure's off, that marriage is no longer regarded as the ceremony that separates the desirable from the unwanted. On the other hand, they may not. To some of them, a home empty of companions may be synonymous with an empty life.[12]

Percent who agree

Statements	Australia	Bangladesh	Hungary	Israel	Italy	Japan	Taiwan	Turkey	United States	West Germany	International average
A job well done gives me pleasure.	95	95	96	98	96	98	97	96	97	94	96
My parents are ashamed of me.	11	7	4	3	4	15	10	8	7	2	7
I like to help a friend whenever I can.	94	92	92	93	91	90	94	93	94	91	92
Very often I feel that my mother is no good.	11	10	9	9	9	17	15	6	13	6	9
At times I think about what kinds of work I will do in the future.	91	93	87	85	87	91	91	90	94	91	90
My parents will be disappointed in me in the future.	14	10	9	6	7	23	22	13	7	6	11
Being together with other people gives me a good feeling.	93	84	93	88	87	78	76	91	95	94	88
Very often I feel that my father is no good.	19	12	13	6	15	14	18	8	15	9	13
I feel empty emotionally most of the time.	27	39	12	20	29	29	47	42	18	8	27
I often feel that I would rather die than go on living.	30	38	17	19	15	20	14	25	19	19	22
I feel so lonely.	22	43	14	17	20	39	33	32	18	11	25
I find life an endless series of problems—without any solution in sight.	27	39	11	23	13	39	31	37	15	18	25
I frequently feel sad.	27	36	24	28	25	55	26	34	25	17	29

FIGURE 2-3
The universal teenager: common concerns. Teenagers agreed or disagreed with each statement from the Offer Self-Image Questionnaire. Two age groups were surveyed—13 to 15 and 16 to 19—except in Japan, where only the older group responded.

Source: From "The Universal Teenager" by Robert Atkinson, October 1988. Reprinted with permission from Psychology Today Magazine. Copyright © 1988 (Sussex Publishers, Inc.).

In fact, more and more people are reporting that they experience transitory, if not persistent, bouts of loneliness.[13] And people who describe themselves as lonely typically have difficulty making connections with other people. The loneliness they experience seems attributable to a gap between what they want and what they achieve in their social relationships.

Despite many such similarities, however, there are a number of significant differences in the way people from different cultures conceive of the self. For instance, "In North American culture the word 'self' occupies an important place. We speak of self-concept, self-image, self-esteem, self-reliance, self-help, self-awareness, self-actualization, self-determination, and so on. . . . Many cultures do not share our perception of the self as being at the center of the universe. . . . In Japan . . . a person directs his or her loyalty not at the self, but rather at others. . . . The 'I' in the Chinese written language looks very similar to the word for 'selfish.' "[14] In our culture there is a tendency toward development of the self at the expense of the group or others, but some other cultures do not share this tendency.

DEVELOPING SELF-AWARENESS

The Self-Concept versus the Self

The self-concept represents who you *think* you are, not necessarily who you actually are. In general, we are not usually very objective about our self-concepts. Sometimes your image of yourself may be more favorable than the image others have of you. For instance, you might view yourself as an extremely talented writer, but others might consider you a hack. There are many reasons why we are able to maintain a picture of ourselves that others may regard as unrealistic or ridiculous. For one thing, we might be so worried about our presentation of self that we fail to pay attention to feedback from others about how they see us. Or others might send us distorted information about ourselves in an attempt not to hurt our feelings. Or we might be basing our self-view on outdated, obsolete information that allows us to cling to the memories of the past rather than facing the realities of the present.

Just as there are times when we view ourselves more favorably than we should, there are times when we view ourselves more harshly than we should. For example, a woman might be convinced that she is "ugly" despite other people's insistence that she is attractive. Why? This woman might be acting on the basis of *obsolete data*. Perhaps as a child she was gawky or fat, and even though she is now graceful and slender, those past traits are still part of her self-concept. *Distorted feedback* can also perpetuate a negative self-image. People who are strongly influenced by an overly critical parent, friend, teacher, or employer can develop a self-view that is far harsher than the view others hold. Another reason why people often "cheat" themselves of a favorable self-concept is the *social customs of our society*. In the United States, at least, it is far more acceptable for people to downplay, underrate, and criticize themselves than it

▶ **POINTS TO PONDER**

DON'T BE AFRAID TO FAIL

You've failed many times, although you may not remember. You fell down the first time you tried to walk. You almost drowned the first time you tried to swim, didn't you? Did you hit the ball the first time you swung a bat?

Heavy hitters, the ones who hit the most home runs, also strike out a lot. R. H. Macy failed seven times before his store in New York caught on. English novelist John Creasey got 753 rejection slips before he published 564 books.

Babe Ruth struck out 1,330 times but he also hit 714 home runs. Don't worry about failure. Worry about the chances you miss when you don't even try.

Source: United Technologies Corporation 1986.

is for them to praise or boast about themselves or openly display self-appreciation. To put it simply, far too many people are taught "SPS—self-praise stinks."

Walt Whitman, in the poem "Song of Myself," writes, "I celebrate myself and sing myself." To what extent are you able to celebrate yourself? Do you have a predominantly positive or negative self-concept? Take some time now to inventory what you perceive to be your own assets and liabilities. The practice of honestly reviewing your own strong and weak points can help to reshape your image of yourself.

Viewing Ourselves and Others: The Johari Window

We need to realize that self-understanding is the basis of the self-concept. To understand yourself, you must understand your own way of looking at the world. To understand others, you must understand how they look at the world.

Some of your answers to the Skill Builder below may illustrate one of the ideas of the psychiatrist Eric Berne. Berne believes that we sometimes pattern our transactions in such a way that we repeatedly reenact the same script with a different set of players. In other words, it is not uncommon for us to attempt to "stage" dramas with casts of characters drawn from different phases of our lives. This urge toward repetition can become a problem for you if it leads you to fail rather than to succeed. Take some time to examine the extent to which your three sets of responses in the Skill Builder demonstrate flexibility rather than rigidity. Attempt to determine to what degree you have eliminated or extinguished behaviors you did not like. In addition, try to understand what each of your responses says about your past, present, and future needs.

✔ **SKILL BUILDER**

YESTERDAY, TODAY, AND TOMORROW

1. Your instructor will divide the class into small groups.
2. Each group should use the incomplete sentences listed below as "starters" in three rounds of conversations. During the first round you should indicate how you would have responded to each incomplete statement as a young child (between 5 and 8 years old). During the second round you should indicate how you would have responded during later childhood and adolescence. Finally, during the third round you should indicate how you would respond to these statements today.
   a. Other people want me to . . .
   b. The best way to measure personal success is . . .
   c. When I do what I really want to do, I . . .
   d. I get frustrated when . . .
   e. I want to be a . . .
   f. I have fun when . . .
   g. Marriage for me is . . .
   h. People who are "in charge" should be . . .
   i. I miss . . .
   j. What I really like about myself is . . .
   k. When I am with people who do a lot of talking, I . . .
   l. Sometimes I feel like . . .
   m. A decade from now, I . . .
3. What do the responses tell you about yourself and your peers during these three stages of life? Were there discernible consistencies? Were there changes? Why?

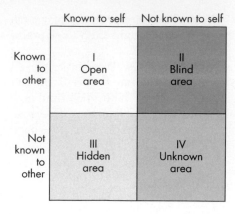

FIGURE 2-4
The Johari window.

Source: From *Group Processes: An Introduction to Group Dynamics* by Joseph Luft by permission of Mayfield Publishing Company. Copyright © 1984, 1970, 1963 by Joseph Luft.

At one time or another we all wish that we knew ourselves or others better. The concept of self-awareness, basic to all functions and forms of communication, may be explored through a psychological testing device known as the *Johari window.* Joseph Luft and Harrington Ingham developed an illustration of a paned window to help us examine both how we view ourselves and how others view us.[15] Before proceeding further, let's look at the window (see Figure 2-4).

The first square, "window pane" I, represents information about yourself that is known to you and to another. At times, for example, your name, age, religious affiliation, and food preferences might all be found in this pane. The size and contents of the quadrant vary from relationship to relationship, depending on the degree of closeness you share with another person. Do you allow some people to know more about you than others? Why?

Pane II, the blind area, contains information about you that others, but not you, are aware of. Some people have a very large blind area and are oblivious to their own faults and virtues. At times, people may feel compelled to seek outside help, such as therapy, to reduce the size of their "blind pane." Do you know something about a friend that he or she does not know? Do you feel free to reveal this information to your friend? Why? What effect do you think your revelation would have on your friend's self-image?

Can you identify some of the things you are hesitant to let others know about yourself? Why are these things easier to hold back than express?

Pane III represents your hidden area. It contains information you know about yourself but do not want others to find out for fear they will reject you. John Powell, author of *Why Am I Afraid to Tell You Who I Am?* expresses the fear of rejection this way: "If I tell you who I am, you may not like who I am, and it is all that I have."[16] Sometimes it takes a great deal of effort to avoid becoming known, but at one time or another each of us feels a need to have people important to us know us well and accept us for what we are. When we move information from quadrant III to quadrant I, we engage in this process of self-disclosure. *Self-disclosure* occurs when we purposefully reveal to another person information about ourselves that he or she would not otherwise know. By self-disclosure we show others that we trust them and care enough about them to reveal to them intimate information we would not willingly share with everyone. Often, our attempts at self-disclosure will be reciprocated, and this

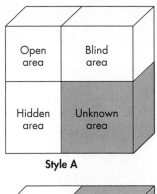

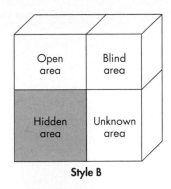

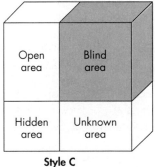

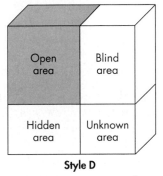

FIGURE 2-5
Interpersonal styles, in
terms of the Johari
window.

sharing of hidden parts is essential if meaningful and lasting relationships are to develop.[17] None of this is to suggest that the hidden area should not be allowed to exist within each of us. It is up to you to decide when it is appropriate for you to share your innermost thoughts, feelings, and intentions with others; it is also up to you to decide when complete openness is not in your best interest.

Pane IV is the unknown area in your makeup. It contains information about which neither you nor others are aware. Eventually education and life experiences may help to bring some of the mysteries contained in this pane to the surface. Only then will its content be available for examination. Have you ever done something that surprised both you and people close to you? Did you and a friend ever exclaim together, "Wow! I didn't know I could do that." "I didn't know you could do that."

People commonly develop a style that is a consistent and preferred way of behaving interpersonally. Figure 2-5 illustrates representative styles. *Style A* is characteristic of people who adopt a fairly impersonal approach to interpersonal relationships. Dominated by their unknown areas, these people usually withdraw from contacts, avoid personal disclosures or involvements, and thus project an image that is rigid, aloof, and uncommunicative. In *style B*, the hidden area, or facade, is the dominant window. Here we find people who desire relationships but also greatly fear exposure and generally mistrust others. Once others become aware of the facade, they are likely to lose trust in these people. *Style C* is dominated by the blind area, and people who are characterized by

Which style appears to be most characteristic of you and the people you interact with?

SYMBOLIZING THE SELF

Bring four objects to class. The first object should reveal something about the way you see yourself, something you believe everyone recognizes about you. In other words, it should represent an aspect of your open area. The second object should reveal something about you that up until this point you believe resided in your hidden area. This second object could symbolize an attitude, feeling, desire, or fear that you had hoped to keep from others but are now willing to move into the open pane. The third object you bring to class should represent how you believe another person sees you. For example, do you believe that a particular friend or relative sees you as you see yourself? How do you think your perceptions are similar? How are they different? Finally, after selecting these three objects, ask someone else to choose an object that represents his or her perception of you. Bring this fourth object to class along with the other three. Be prepared to discuss how your perceptions of yourself and the other person's perception of you conflict or coincide. For example, did the object selected by the other person help you move information from the blind area to the open area? To what extent has each phase of the experience altered the appearance of your Johari window?

this style are overly confident of their own opinions and painfully unaware of how they affect others or are perceived by others. Those who communicate with such people often feel that their own ideas or insights are of little concern, and thus they are apt to develop resentment and hostility. In *style D*, the open area, or area of free activity, is dominant, and relationships involve candor, openness, and sensitivity to the needs and insights of others.

Communication of any depth or significance is difficult if the people involved have little open area in common. In any relationship you hope to sustain, your goal should be to increase the size of the open area while decreasing the size of the hidden, blind, and unknown areas. The open area becomes larger whenever information is moved into it from any of the remaining quadrants, as when you disclose any of your hidden perceptions to others or when others reveal any hidden perceptions they may have about you. We know that as human beings we are constantly thinking about others and what they think about us. The question is whether we are able and willing to share what we are thinking.

IMPROVING SELF-AWARENESS AND AWARENESS OF OTHERS

Throughout this chapter we have stressed that we all carry figurative pictures of ourselves and others with us wherever we go. Together these pictures form a mental "collage." Contained within the collage are past, present, and future images of ourselves—alone or interacting with other people. If you closely examine your various images, you probably will be able to discern that how you look in each is related to when the picture was taken, what environment you were in, and with whom you were communicating. Each picture reveals a somewhat different you, because you change and grow from moment to moment, situation to situation, and year to year.

We sometimes tend to forget that our self-image and our images of others can change. Keeping "self-pictures" updated and current is a challenge. Sharpening a fuzzy image, refocusing an old image, and developing a new image are processes that can help you discard worn-out or inaccurate perceptions of yourself and others. The following guidelines can be used to improve the "picture-taking" skills you have gained while working your way through this chapter.

Take Continual Pictures of Yourself and Others

You can increase your self-awareness by continuing to take the time to examine your self-image and your relationship to others. Developing a clear sense of who you are is one of the most worthwhile goals you can set for yourself. Be willing to watch yourself in action. Periodically examine your own self-perceptions—and your self-*misconceptions*. Consider how you feel about yourself, how you think you look, and to what extent you approve of your values and behaviors. Study the composite picture that emerges from your reflections. How close are you to becoming the person you would like to be? In what ways would you like to alter your various self-portraits? We hope you will take enough time and develop enough courage and open-mindedness to engage in productive and worthwhile self-examination.

Encourage Others To Take Pictures of You

As we have seen, how others perceive you may be very different from how you perceive yourself. Obtaining information from others can help you assess how realistic your self-concept is. Others who come to know you may observe strengths you have overlooked, traits you undervalue, or weaknesses you choose to ignore. However, you do not have to accept all the pictures other people take of you. No one can prevent you from adhering to your own beliefs and rejecting the opinions of others. Looking at other people's pictures of you does mean, however, that you are at least opening yourself to the possibility of change by attempting to see yourself as others see you. Receiving messages from others can help you acquire insight into who others think you are and how they think you are coming across.

Refocus, Refocus, Refocus

Carl Sandburg wrote, "Life is like an onion; you peel off one layer at a time." As you move from yesterday through today and into tomorrow, your self is in constant transition. Try not to let your view of your self today prevent you from adapting to meet the demands of changing circumstances and conditions. Continually formulating new answers to the question "Who am I?" will allow you to discover the vibrant, flexible, and dynamic qualities of your self. Self-discovery is an ongoing, unending way of reacting to life.

SUMMARY

Self-concept is the entire collection of attitudes and beliefs you hold about who and what you are. It is the mental picture you have of yourself. It can be positive or negative, accurate or inaccurate. Your self-concept influences all aspects of your communicative behavior—with whom, where, why, and how you choose to communicate.

You are not born with a self-concept. Rather, your self-concept is shaped by your environment and by those around you, including your parents, your relatives, instructors, supervisors, friends, and coworkers. In addition, television and films, self-expectations and other people's expectations, gender, and culture can shape your opinion of who you are. Particularly, the self-concept can be affected by what is known as the *self-fulfilling prophecy*. A self-fulfilling prophecy occurs when expecting an event helps create the very conditions that permit the event to occur. The media as well as other people help determine which self-fulfilling prophecies we make.

You can change and improve your self-concept by developing greater self-awareness and self-understanding. The Johari window can help you identify the open, blind, hidden, and unknown areas of your self.

Conditions and circumstances affect the nature of the self. Sometimes it seems that we become different "selves" as we move from situation to situation; our demeanor is affected by our perceptions of others and how we imagine they perceive us.

SUGGESTIONS FOR FURTHER READING

Asbell, Bernard: *What They Know about You*, Random House, New York, 1991. A journalist turned college teacher sums up—very readably—research in the field of self-concept and communication.

Branden, Nathaniel: *The Psychology of Self-Esteem*, Bantam, New York, 1969. The author examines our need for self-esteem and discusses the conditions necessary for mental well-being.

Campbell, Colin: "Our Many Versions of the Self: An Interview with Brewster Smith," *Psychology Today*, February 1976, pp. 13–33. Dr. Smith, a psychologist, discusses how the self may be viewed.

Craig, Steve (ed.): *Men, Masculinity, and the Media*, Sage, Newbury Park, Calif., 1992. Explores how the media construct ideals of masculinity and how men respond to media images.

Deetz, Stanley (ed.): *Communication Yearbook/15*, Sage, Newbury Park, Calif., 1992. Contains a plethora of information on the relationship between mass media, the self, and society.

Gergen, Kenneth J.: *The Concept of Self*, Holt, Rinehart and Winston, New York, 1971. In this scholarly work, Gergen examines how the self-concept develops and how it influences behavior.

Goffman, Erving: *The Presentation of Self in Everyday Life*, Doubleday, New York, 1959. A valuable reference in which Goffman explores honest and dishonest ways we reveal who we are to others and ourselves. The concept of "mask" is explained.

Jourard, Sidney M.: *The Transparent Self*, Van Nostrand, New York, 1971. An interesting in-depth look at the self and the nature of the self disclosure process.

Luft, Joseph: *Group Process: An Introduction to Group Dynamics*, 2d ed., Mayfield, Palo Alto, Calif., 1970. Provides a clear, well-written explication of the Johari window and of how it can be used to analyze our relationships.

McWilliams, John-Roger, and Peter McWilliams: *Life 101*, Prelude, Los Angeles, Calif., 1990. The authors take the position that all life is a classroom in communication. This book and their sequel *Do It!* (published in 1991) present a positive outlook on life that would be appreciated by any "Pygmalion."

Powell, John: *Why Am I Afraid to Tell You Who I Am?* Tabor, New York, 1982. A basic introduction to the defenses people construct in an effort to avoid becoming known.

Rosenthal, Robert, and Lenore Jacobson: *Pygmalion in the Classroom*, Holt, Rinehart and Winston, New York, 1968. Reports on the role self-fulfilling prophecies play in education, research, and everyday life.

Schutz, William C.: *The Interpersonal Underworld*, Science and Behavior Books, Palo Alto, Calif., 1966. Contains a discussion of the needs that must be satisfied through human interaction.

Seligman, Martin E. P.: *Learned Optimism*, Knopf, New York, 1991. This study describes theories and techniques relevant to the nurturing of an optimistic attitude. Interesting self-analysis forms are included.

Tuchman, Gaye, Arlene Kaplan Daniels, and James Benet (eds.): *Hearth and Home: Images of Women in the Mass Media*, Oxford University Press, New York, 1978. Contains articles that explore how women are portrayed in the media.

NOTES

1. For an explanation of the differences between role-taking and role-playing, see Robert L. Kelley, W. J. Osborne, and Clyde Hendrick, "Role-Taking and Role-Playing in Human Communication," *Human Communication Research*, vol. 1, 1974, pp. 62–74.
2. From a videotaped speech by Jolene Tennis, aired on a Muscular Dystrophy Telethon, 1984.
3. S. I. Hayakawa and Alan R. Hayakawa, *Language in Thought and Action*, 5th ed., Harcourt Brace Jovanovich, San Diego, Calif., 1990, pp. 217–218.
4. Martin E. P. Seligman, *Learned Optimism*, Knopf, New York, 1991, pp. 4–5.
5. Shel Silverstein, "Jimmy Jet and His TV Set," in *Where the Sidewalk Ends*, Harper and Row, New York, 1974. Copyright © 1974 Evil Eye Music, Inc. Used by permission of HarperCollins Publishers.
6. Carl Sandburg, *The People Yes*, Harcourt Brace Jovanovich, New York, 1936.
7. From *Pygmalion* by Bernard Shaw. Reprinted by permission of The Society of Authors on behalf of the Bernard Shaw Estate.
8. Robert Rosenthal and Lenore Jacobson, *Pygmalion in the Classroom*, Holt, Rinehart and Winston, New York, 1968.
9. J. Sterling Livingston, Sterling Institute, Washington, D.C.; cited in video, *The Self Fulfilling Prophecy*, CRM/McGraw-Hill Films, 1985.
10. Ann Beuf, "Doctor, Lawyer, Household Drudge," *Journal of Communication*, vol. 24, 1974, pp. 142–145.
11. Robert Atkinson, "Respectful, Dutiful Teenagers," *Psychology Today*, October 1988, p. 22.
12. From "In Truth, Most of Them May Not Be Lonely," *The New York Times*, May 9, 1991, p. A24. Copyright © 1991 by The New York Times Company. Reprinted by permission.
13. Robert A. Bell and Michael E. Roloff, "Making a Love Connection: Loneliness and Communication Competence in the Dating Marketplace," *Communication Quarterly*, vol. 39. no. 1, Winter 1991, p. 58.
14. Larry A. Samovar and Richard E. Porter, *Communication between Cultures*, Wadsworth, Belmont, Calif., 1991, pp. 90–91.
15. Joseph Luft, *Group Processes: An Introduction to Group Dynamics*, 2d ed., Mayfield, Palo Alto, Calif., 1970.
16. John Powell, *Why Am I Afraid to Tell You Who I Am?* Tabor, New York, 1982.
17. For example, Morgan Worthy, Albert L. Gay, and Guy M. Kahn found that self-disclosure seems to be reciprocal and regarded as a reward in interpersonal relationships. See their article "Self Disclosure as an Exchange Process," *Journal of Personality and Social Psychology*, vol. 13, 1969, pp. 59–63.

COMMUNICATION AND PERCEPTION: I AM MORE THAN A CAMERA

After you finish this chapter, you should be able to:

Explain why a person is "more than a camera"

Demonstrate how angle of vision, or perspective, affects our perception

Demonstrate how we limit what we perceive

Demonstrate how our sensory capabilities affect perception

Define *perception*

Explain the figure-ground principle

Describe how past experience can influence perception

Discuss how cultural background influences perception

Distinguish between "open" and "closed"

Compare and contrast selective exposure and selective perception

Define *closure*

Explain how first impressions affect perception

Define *stereotyping,* identify some common stereotypes, and explain how the media perpetuate stereotypes

Define and provide examples of "allness"

Explain what is meant by "blindering"

Distinguish between facts and inferences

Identify ways to increase the accuracy of your perceptions

The setting is a football stadium. Larry, Joan, and George are seated next to each other watching the game. Suddenly, a long pass is thrown by the quarterback, caught, and run into the end zone for a touchdown. Larry screams, "Did you see that great pass?" Joan comments, "What do you mean? The receiver saved the day." And George notes, "Forget it. Without that sensational block by 38, there wouldn't have been a play."

Why is it that when we look at the same event, we do not all see the same thing? Do we see things as they are? Do we see things as we want them to be? Or do we see things as *we* are? How do our sensory capabilities affect perception? How do our experiences affect perception? In this chapter we will attempt to answer these questions as we explore how we perceive the world around us and why we are, in effect, "more than a camera."

WHAT IS PERCEPTION?

Perceiving Stimuli: The Eye and the "I"

In many ways, we all live in or inhabit different worlds. Each of us views reality from a different angle, perspective, or vantage point. Our physical location, our interests, our personal desires, our attitudes, our values, our personal experiences, our physical condition, and our psychological states all interact to influence our judgments or perceptions.

Now, how do you absorb information from the world around you? Do you look and listen? Do you touch, taste, and smell your environment and those who interact in it? Certainly. Your senses function as perceptual "antennae" and gather information for you all the time.

However, it is impossible for you to internalize or process all the stimuli or data available to you. Without realizing it, you take steps to limit what you perceive. You will see this for yourself if you try the following test:

1. For the next 60 seconds, attempt to internalize everything that exists in the room you now inhabit. Make an effort to react to each sound, sight, smell, touch, and taste that is present in your environment.
2. Were you able to focus simultaneously on each stimulus or sense experience, or did you find yourself skipping from one stimulus to another and back again?

Most probably, you found yourself switching between stimuli, and thus you are aware that you simply cannot effectively handle, or process, all the sensory experiences that compete for your attention. In many respects, human beings are like television sets: the number of "shows" we can present is limited. Information theorists tell us that the eye can process about 5 million pieces, or

*"Wernock, here, sees your suit as half empty,
but I see it as half full."*

Drawing by Leo Cullum; © 1991 The New Yorker Magazine, Inc.

"bits," of data per second; they also tell us that the brain can utilize only some 500 bits per second. We are therefore forced to identify or *select* those stimuli we will attend to or experience. By doing this, we create a more limited but more coherent and meaningful picture of our world.

Not only are perceptual processes highly selective; they are also personally based. For this reason, different people will experience the same cues in very different ways. The communication expert William Haney emphasized this when he noted that we never really come into direct contact with reality.[1] Instead, everything we experience is "manufactured" by the nervous system. The kind of "sense" we make out of the people and situations in our world depends somewhat on the world outside but more on what kind of perceivers we are. In other words, everything that is seen, heard, tasted, felt, or smelled depends on *who* is seeing, hearing, and so on. Thus your perceptions of a stimulus are shaped by your loves and hatreds, your desires, your physical capabilities, your senses, your organizational processes, and your interpretations and evaluations of past experiences. We could say, then, that your perception of a stimulus and the stimulus itself are not even one and the same thing. The stimulus is "out there," whereas your perception of it is unique, personal, and inside you.

What is perception? As we now realize, perception includes more than just the eye alone, more than just the ear alone, more than just the nose alone, more than just the skin alone, and more than just the tongue alone. Perception is the "I" behind the senses—the I behind the eye. Keeping this in mind, we can define *perception* as the process of selecting, organizing, and interpreting sensory data in a way that enables us to make sense of our world.

Processing Stimuli: The "I" of the Beholder

We have said that perception provides each of us with a unique view of the world—a view sometimes related to, but not necessarily identical with, that held by others. Since we can never actually become one with the world "out there," we are forced to use our senses to help create a personal picture of the people and objects that surround us. How do we make sense out of our world? How do we process the stimuli that compete for our attention?

During the perception process, we are active, not passive. We do not simply relax and absorb stimuli available to us, the way a sponge absorbs liquid. We select, we organize, and we evaluate the multitude of stimuli that bombard us so that what we focus on becomes *figure* and the rest of what we experience becomes the *ground*.[2]

To clarify the concept of figure and ground, look at Figure 3-1 below. What do you see? At first glance, you probably see a vase—or you may see two people facing each other. When stimuli compete for your attention, you can focus on only one, because it is simply impossible to perceive something in two ways at once. Although you may be able to switch your focus rapidly, you will still perceive only one stimulus at any given time. The same holds true for Figure 3-2 on page 58. When you look at Figure 3-2*a*, you may see a duck, a rabbit, or both alternately. In Figure 3-2*b*, you may see the profile of an Indian, the back of an Eskimo walking away, or both alternately.

FIGURE 3-1
Figure and ground.

FIGURE 3-2
Figure-ground
illustrations. (a) Duck or
rabbit? (b) Eskimo or
Indian?

Source: Mitsuko Saito-
Fakunage, "General
Semantics and Intercultural
Communication," *ETC*,
vol. 46, no. 4, Winter
1989, p. 297.

(a)   (b)

In addition, when we are confronted with more input than we can handle, we sometimes need to eliminate or reduce the number of stimuli impinging on our awareness. We cannot "catch" or process each idea or each sensory stimulus in our world or environment. Again, we must select. Thus, each of us sees and evaluates stimuli differently.

Many variables affect us during the perceptual process, interacting to guide us in making our perceptual selections. Some of these constitute "barriers" to perception, as we explain below.

BARRIERS TO PERCEPTION

Perceptual Sets: Is Your Past Following You?

If you took a third-grade boy to one of your college classes, do you think he would perceive the class experience in the same way you do? Of course not. If you asked him to take notes, would his notes be identical to yours? Again, of course not. The child's notes might be scribbled in crayon and supplemented with doodles, and—although doodling is not unknown among adult note-takers—in general they would probably be far inferior to the notes you took. Why? First, you have learned to take notes. Second, you have some familiarity with the material being presented. And third, your intellectual capabilities would almost certainly be superior to the child's. The sum total of all the differences we have been describing can be summed up as *past experience.* Note that age alone does not determine the part played by experience. Even among people of the same age, past experiences differ and hence affect the way stimuli are perceived.

Past experiences often provide us with expectations, or *perceptual sets,* that affect how we process our world.[3] In order to better understand the concept of a perceptual set, quickly read the statements written in the triangles in Figure 3-3. Then examine the words more carefully. During your first reading, did you miss anything that you now perceive? Many people fail to see the second *the* or *a* in the statements at the first reading. Did you? Why? We are so accustomed to seeing words in familiar groups, or clusters, that often we simply

Exchange notes from the same class session with another student. Can you read the other person's notes? Would you be able to study from them? What has this student included that you omitted? What did you include that he or she did not? Why?

Stewart Leeds

"Do you enjoy being a Margarita?"

Drawing by Stewart Leeds; © 1988 The New Yorker Magazine, Inc.

fail to perceive a number of single words when we see them in such phrases. Faster, more accomplished readers make this mistake more readily than slower, less skillful readers. In their attempt to perceive the overall meaning, fast readers simply skip what they perceive as unessential words. How do you think first- and second-graders would respond to Figure 3-3? The authors showed these triangles to a group of children and found that, for the most part, since they were still reading individual words rather than word groups, many noticed the repetition immediately. They were not "set" to perceive the phrases.

Barefoot
in the
the park

Snake
in the
the grass

Busy
as a
a beaver

FIGURE 3-3
Test for perceptual sets.

OPINION: AN ANALYSIS OF MISS MUFFET
Russell Baker

Little Miss Muffet, as everyone knows, sat on a tuffet eating her curds and whey when along came a spider who sat down beside her and frightened Miss Muffet away. While everyone knows it, the significance of the event had never been analyzed until a conference of thinkers recently brought their special insights to bear upon it. Following are excerpts from the transcript of their discussion:

SOCIOLOGIST: Miss Muffet is nutritionally underprivileged, as evidenced by the subminimal diet of curds and whey upon which she is forced to subsist, while the spider's cultural disadvantage is evidenced by such phenomena as legs exceeding standard norms, odd mating habits and so forth.

In this instance, spider expectations lead the culturally disadvantaged to assert demands to share the tuffet with the nutritionally underprivileged. Due to a communications failure, Miss Muffet assumes without evidence that the spider will not be satisfied to share her tuffet, but will also insist on eating her curds and whey. . . .

MILITARIST: Second-strike capability, sir! That's what was lacking. If Miss Muffet had developed a second-strike capability instead of squandering her resources on curds and whey, no spider on earth would have dared launch a first strike capable of carrying him right to the heart of her tuffet. I am confident that Miss Muffet had adequate notice from experts that she could not afford both curds and whey and at the same time support an early-spider-warning system. . . .

BOOK REVIEWER: Written on several levels, this searing, sensitive exploration of the arachnid heart illuminates the agony and splendor of Jewish family life with a candor that is at once breath-taking in its simplicity and soul-shattering in its implied ambiguity. Some will doubtless be shocked to see such subjects as tuffets and whey discussed without flinching, but hereafter writers too timid to call a tuffet a tuffet will no longer . . .

EDITORIALIST: Why has the Government not seen fit to tell the public all it knows about the so-called curds-and-whey affair? It is not enough to suggest that this was merely a random incident involving a lonely spider and a young diner. . . .

PSYCHIATRIST: Little Miss Muffet is, of course, neither little, nor a miss. These are obviously the self she has created in her own fantasies to escape the reality that she is a . . . divorcee whose superego makes it impossible for her to sustain a normal relationship with any man, symbolized by the spider. . . .

FLOWER CHILD: This beautiful kid is on a bad trip. Like . . .

STUDENT: Little Miss Muffet, tuffets, curds, whey and spiders are what's wrong with education today. They're all irrelevant. Tuffets are irrelevant. Curds are irrelevant. Whey is irrelevant.

CHILD: This is about a little girl who gets scared by a spider.

(The child was sent home when the conference broke for lunch. It was agreed that the child was too immature to add anything to the sum of human understanding and should not return until he had grown up.)

Past experiences create perceptual sets in numerous ways. Sometimes *culture* is a factor. In Saudi Arabia, for example, the way women are raised influences how people both within that culture and outside it perceive them. In Saudi Arabia women have few legal rights, are usually not permitted to drive a car, and need a man's permission to obtain a passport; clearly, the Saudis and Americans perceive women very differently.[4]

Motivation is another variable affecting our perceptual sets and thus our perception. Both hunger and poverty, for instance, can alter the way we interpret experience. In one study, researchers showed sailors some ambiguous pictures and asked them to desribe what they saw. Sailors who were hungry "saw with the stomach"—to them, an elongated smudge looked like a fork, and a swirl looked like a fried onion. In a second study, rich and poor children were shown circles of various sizes and were asked which ones were the same size as certain coins. The poor children consistently chose circles that were much too large. Why? A quarter, say, looks bigger to the poor than to the rich.[5]

Obviously, *education* is also an important part of our past experience. How much education and what kind of education we have had will affect the way we process and perceive information. For instance, you may find that your views of television and other media have changed since you were in grade school and that they will change again as you acquire additional education. (Young children, for example, view television commercials as a kind of absolute truth.) At times, education can become a barrier rather than a facilitator or aid to perception. The essay by Russell Baker in the box on the opposite page pokes fun at ridiculously exaggerated perceptions apparently fostered by certain educational backgrounds. Except for the child, each speaker in Baker's essay exhibits a perceptual set, a readiness to process a stimulus in a predetermined or conditioned way. Because of his or her set, each one interprets the nursery rhyme individually—as he or she wanted to.

How might different educational backgrounds create tensions on the job?

As is apparent, perceptual sets are the result of unique experiences. The lessons life has taught you necessarily differ from those life has taught others. As a result, we each perceive the same stimulus differently. This helps explain why a boss and an employee, a teacher and a student, a parent and a child, or two friends can have widely differing opinions and interpretations of a job, a company, an institution, or a situation. For instance, the boss or the person with more power may be situated at the top "looking down," and the employee or the person with less power may be situated at or near the bottom "looking up." One's position in an organization affects how one perceives that organization. Our position or role helps us internalize perceptual sets that in turn cause us to react to people, places, and situations in particular ways.

Selective Exposure: Are You "Open" or "Closed"?

A key factor in how we view our world is the extent to which we open ourselves to experiences. Although numerous sensory stimuli compete for our attention, we tend to select only those experiences which reaffirm existing attitudes, beliefs, and values. We likewise tend to ignore or diminish the significance of those experiences which are incongruent or dissonant with our existing attitudes, beliefs, and values. Just as children sometimes place their hands over their ears to avoid hearing what a parent is saying, so we can select what we will perceive by deciding whether to expose ourselves to a variety of types and sources of information. When driving through poverty-stricken areas, for example, people often roll up their automobile windows. They tell themselves that they are doing this for self-protection, but rolling up the windows is also a means of *self-deception* that helps them avoid contact with some of the depressing sights and sounds of their society.

A 1959 study gave support to the concept of *selective exposure*. The researchers, Wilbur Schramm and Richard Carter, determined that after a massive television campaign by a Republican senatorial candidate, Republicans were twice as likely as Democrats to have seen at least a portion of the campaign.[6] During the 1972 presidential campaign, the researcher Dorothy Bartlett discovered that twice as many Republicans as Democrats failed to open an envelope bearing the return address "Voters for McGovern." Similar results were obtained among Democrats who received a letter with the return address "Voters for Nixon."[7] In each instance voters chose to expose themselves only to information with which they already agreed.

How difficult is it for you to expose yourself to certain ideas, places, or experiences? Why?

Can you cite instances when you chose not to expose yourself to a certain stimulus or idea? Are there some subjects you would prefer not to know about? Are there some people whom you would just as soon avoid?

Selective Perception and Closure: Are You a Distorter?

A concept related to selective exposure is *selective perception*. We see what we want to see and hear what we want to hear. Through the process of selective perception, the same message or stimulus may be interpreted in different ways by different people. Why do we distort stimuli until they conform to what we want or expect?

Each individual's perception of an event is influenced by his or her existing attitudes. Thus, out of the swirling mass of information available to us, we interpret and digest information that confirms our own beliefs, expectations, or convictions, and we reject information that contradicts them. Try viewing the same news broadcast with someone whose political views differ sharply from your own. How similar do you imagine your interpretations of the delivered information will be? Why?

Our selective processes allow us to add information, delete information, or change information so that we can avoid dealing with certain information. Time and time again past experiences, expectations, needs, and wants join forces to determine our present perceptions. Their effect is strengthened by our desire for *closure*—that is, our desire to perceive a complete (and thus secure) world.

Identify each item you see in Figure 3-4. You probably saw a dog rather than a collection of inkblots; and a rectangle, a triangle, and a circle rather than some lines and an arc. We tend to complete familiar figures, mentally. We fill them in on the basis of our previous experiences and our needs. In the same way, we complete stimuli until they make sense to us: we fill in gaps.

What significance does this tendency to fill in missing information have for your everyday perceptions and interpersonal communication? How often do you feel a need to fill in "people gaps"? How often do you make sense out of human actions by "completing" them as you would like to see them?

FIGURE 3-4
Test for closure.

First Impressions: Do You Freeze Your Perceptions of Others?

It is important to realize that your perceptions of a person are a key determinant of the type of relationship you will share with him or her. On what basis do you form first impressions or make initial judgments about the people you meet? What makes you decide if you like or dislike someone? Is it his economic status? Is it the job he or she holds? Perceiving others and the roles they play is an essential part of the communication process. (Can you imagine walking into a bank and not being able to determine to whom you should give your money?) In this section and the next one, we will explore how we form first impressions of other people and why we sometimes stereotype other people. We will attempt to determine why we often feel it necessary to "freeze" people and "squeeze" people until they fit into or conform to our expectations for them.

"You must make a good first impression" is a piece of advice frequently given to people who are starting a new job, preparing for an interview, or getting ready to participate in some other communication encounter. How important is the first impression? Let's find out.

If you analyze the responses you obtain for the Skill Builder on page 64 (adapted from an experiment conducted by Solomon Asch[8]) you'll find that people usually attribute positive qualities to person A, selecting a descriptive word with very positive connotations. In contrast, person B is often perceived as possessing negative qualities, and for this reason the word chosen to de-

WHAT'S ON FIRST?

Person "A." Read the following list of "A"'s character traits to another person, in the order given.

(1) Intelligent   (4) Critical

(2) Industrious   (5) Stubborn

(3) Impulsive   (6) Envious

Ask that person to choose one word to represent his or her impression of "A."

Person "B." Next, read this list of "B"'s character traits to another person, in the order given.

(1) Envious   (4) Impulsive

(2) Stubborn   (5) Industrious

(3) Critical   (6) Intelligent

As before, ask the person to choose one word to represent his or her impression of "B."

scribe B also has negative connotations. Why? The answer seems to be simply that the first list begins with positive traits and the second begins with negative traits; otherwise, each list is precisely the same. Thus first impressions can dramatically affect perception. In addition, a first impression—or *primacy effect,* as it is sometimes called—can even affect the result of communication efforts. Trial lawyers, for example, depend to some degree on the primacy effect when selecting jurors. The first impression that potential jurors make on a lawyer will often determine whether he or she accepts them or uses a peremptory challenge. (Eventually, of course, this decision may have an important impact on the outcome of the case and the future of the defendant.)

Even if our first impressions are wrong, we tend to hold on to them. Doing this can cause a number of different problems. For example, if the opinion we have of someone is erroneous, we can sustain our inaccurate perception by clinging to it and reshaping the conflicting information available to us until it conforms to the image we hold. Thus, we may never come to experience the real person—only our faulty conception of him or her. And it is this faulty conception that will influence the way we respond to that person. Suppose, for instance, you make a new friend, John, at work. You tell an old friend about him. Your old friend tells you: "Yeah. I know that guy. Worked with him two years ago. He's nothing but trouble. Always looking to use people. He'll bleed you of your ideas, pass them off as his own, and leave you far behind as he makes his way to the top. Did it to me. And he'll do it to you. Watch and see." The danger here is that this evaluation may be unfair, biased, or simply wrong. John might have changed during the past two years, or your friend's initial assessment of him might have been all wet. But—sadly—your friend's words will probably influence the way you interact with John, and you will probably find reasons to substantiate your first impression, whether or not such reasons are actually present. You simply may not be able to avoid a basic stumbling block to accurate perception—closing your mind after forming a first impression.

"You're not at all like your answering machine."

Drawing by M. Stevens; © 1991 The New Yorker Magazine, Inc.

In a communication interaction, receivers' psychological states can affect their first impressions of senders. Sometimes a receiver uses cues provided by senders, mixes these cues with his or her own preconceptions, and creates a perception based partly on myth or fiction. When such a perception involves dividing people into groups, it is called *stereotyping*. We explore stereotypes in the next section.

Stereotypes: Do You Squeeze Others into Niches?

A *stereotype* is a generalization about people, places, or events that is held by many members of a society. For example, when we go into a physician's waiting room for the first time, we carry with us a general idea, or stereotype, about what to expect and how to behave in that particular environment. In other words, we have developed an ability to identify and generalize about what we consider appropriate in a physician's office. For example, we would not expect to find flashing colored lights or people dancing to loud music while waiting to be examined. Our stereotype would not allow for this.

It would be difficult for us to operate without stereotypes. If, for example, you had formed no picture of how a salesperson, mechanic, waiter, or politician functions in our society, you would find it somewhat difficult to get along in daily life. Knowing what categories people and things fit into helps us decide how to deal with them. Somehow, knowing whether a stranger is a corporate president, a lawyer, or a teacher helps us decide how to behave in his or her

What are some of the more common stereotypes held by people you know?

■ ETHICS AND COMMUNICATION

PREJUDICE

According to Rod Plotnik and Sandra Mollenauer, "*Prejudice* refers to an unfair, biased or intolerant attitude toward another group of people. An example of prejudice would be the attitude that women should not be in positions of power because they are not as logical or competent as men."

Have you, or has anyone you know, ever made prejudicial statements similar to this example? To what do you attribute the attitude? What can be done to change such attitudes?

Source: Rod Plotnik and Sandra Mollenauer, *Psychology*, Random House, New York 1986.

presence. When we stereotype people, we simply judge them on the basis of what we know about the category to which we feel they belong. We assume that an individual possesses characteristics similar to those we attribute to others in the group, and we simplify our task by overlooking any discrepancies that may exist. By implication, when we stereotype, we say, "Those who belong in the same niche all have the same traits. Those who belong in the same niche are alike."

The media help us to create and maintain stereotypes. Television news programs, for one, help us identify people, places, ideas, and things by providing us with "standard" images of them. In his book, *News from Nowhere*, Edward Jay Epstein explains that television news camera operators and correspondents are told to illustrate their stories with pictures that have universal meaning. "Hence, stories tend to fit into a limited repertoire of images, which explains why so often shabbily dressed children symbolically stand for poverty [and] . . . fire symbolically stands for destruction."[9] If you look closely, you will also notice that producers of television news shows try to select images that illustrate the "human experience." Inflation is portrayed as a housewife shopping in a supermarket; statistics about unemployment are depicted as people on line in an unemployment office. In television news, as in newspapers and magazines, emotionally charged stereotypical images are often chosen to supplement and illustrate factual data that would otherwise seem complicated or uninteresting.

Unfortunately, stereotyping is rarely a positive force in interpersonal relations or in the various institutions that make up our society. Stereotypes are dangerous because even at best they are oversimplifications and overgeneralizations; often, they are gross exaggerations. Stereotypes based on half-truths (or half-lies) and derived from invalid premises pose real problems for us. Ralph Ellison, an African American and the author of *Invisible Man*, noted this:

I am an invisible man. No, I am not a spook like those who haunted Edgar Allan Poe. . . . I am a man of substance, of flesh and bone, fiber and liquid . . . and I might be said to possess a mind. I am invisible, understand, simply because

■ **ETHICS AND COMMUNICATION**

FOR YOUR EYES ONLY

What we see in other people's faces depends on what we know, or think we know, about people. When the researcher Paul Chance showed subjects a set of photographic portraits and asked them to set aside those of Jews, the guesses were not very accurate. He reported that the subjects who were anti-Semitic were not any better at the task than the other subjects, but they set aside more photographs. To their prejudiced eyes, more people looked Jewish.

Why do you think that the prejudiced subjects saw more faces as "Jewish"? How might this affect their ability—for example—to hire people to work for them?

Source: Paul Chance, "Seeing Is Believing," *Psychology Today*, January–February 1989.

people refuse to see me. Like the bodiless heads you see sometimes in circus side shows, it is as though I have been surrounded by mirrors of hard, distorting glass. When they approach me they see only my surroundings, or figments of their imagination—indeed, everything and anything except me.[10]

The practice of stereotyping can be extremely harmful. At one time or another, almost everyone forms fixed impressions of a racial group, an ethnic group, a religious group, an occupational group, or a socioeconomic group.[11] When we stereotype, we project our attitude toward a group of people onto one particular member of that group. If we are not careful, when we are brought together with people about whom we have very little knowledge, we will take the easy way out and stereotype them. It is easy to utter misleading phrases like "All Mexicans are . . . or "She is Catholic; therefore she must . . ." People who stereotype are lazy perceivers and often ineffective communicators.

● **CULTURE AND COMMUNICATION**

FUTURECAST

Interacting with people who appear to be "different" may still often be a novel experience for many of us, but such contacts will probably increase in the years ahead. The Hudson Institute's study for the Department of Labor forecasts that the work force in the United States is changing from one that is white- and male-dominated to one in which women, immigrants, and nonwhite ethnics will be the majority. Could we all benefit by taking the Vulcan greeting of *Star Trek* to heart?

Greetings! I am pleased to see
that we are different.
May we together become greater
than the sum of us both.

Source: William B. Gudykunst, *Bridging Differences*, Sage, Newbury Park, Calif., 1991, p. 1.

What should be emphasized, of course, is that we are *all* individuals. Whenever we interact with another person, we must realize that we are communicating with a person, not with a stereotype. Furthermore, we need to understand that our stereotype of any group is necessarily based on incomplete information and that although stereotypes may be partly true, they are never completely true. In fact, when we stereotype, categorize, or pigeonhole others, we are really stereotyping, categorizing, or pigeonholing ourselves.

Although stereotyping simplifies and gives a sense of order and stability to our lives, it can have very limiting and debilitating effects. Far too frequently we fail to recognize the variations and differences in apparently similar individuals. We overlook differences and emphasize similarities. To some extent, we all enjoy classifying and categorizing, and we tend to find differentiating difficult. Yet to improve our perceptual capabilities, we must make an effort to see differences as well as similarities among people. To paraphrase the communications expert Irving J. Lee, the more we are able to discriminate *among* individuals, the less we will actively discriminate *against* individuals.[12]

In addition to perceptual sets, selective exposure, selective perception and closure, first impressions, and stereotypes, theorists have identified at least three other factors that can function as perceptual blocks. These are "allness," "blindering," and confusing facts with inferences (see Figure 3-5). Let us consider each of these.

"Allness": Do You Assume That's All There Is?

Have you ever noticed how some radio and television commentators speak with great finality? Several have based their careers at least partially on a parent-like image—that is, they seem to have all the answers about everything happening in the world. Is it possible for a commentator—or for any of us, for that matter—to know, much less tell about, all there is to know concerning a topic? Of course not. Knowledge of everything about anything is certainly an impossibility. In his book *Science and Sanity*, Alfred Korzybski coined the term *allness* to refer to the erroneous belief that any one person could possibly know all

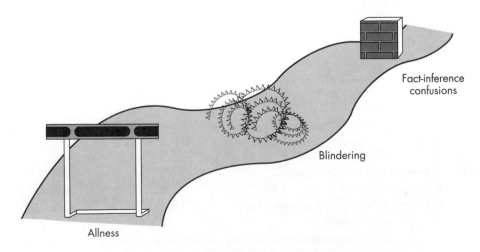

FIGURE 3-5
Barriers to perception.

Fact-inference
confusions

Blindering

Allness

there is to know about everything.[13] Even if we are wise and do not assume that our favorite newscaster (or even our favorite friend) is telling us all there is to know about a topic, we often persist in believing that he or she is telling us all that is *important* about the topic. Did you ever ask someone to "fill you in" on the content of a class session you missed? Did you assume that the person was giving you all the important information? Did a later exam prove you wrong?

The allness fallacy is aptly illustrated in the following poem.

THE BLIND MEN AND THE ELEPHANT
John Godfrey Saxe

It was six men of Indostan
    To learning much inclined
Who went to see the Elephant
    (Though all of them were blind),
That each by observation
    Might satisfy his mind.

The First approached the Elephant,
    And happening to fall
Against his broad and sturdy side,
    At once began to bawl:
"God bless me! but the Elephant
    Is very like a wall."

The Second, feeling of the tusk
    Cried, "Ho! what have we here
So very round and smooth and sharp?
    To me 'tis very clear
This wonder of an Elephant
    Is very like a spear."

The Third approached the animal
    And, happening to take
The squirming trunk within his hands
    Thus boldly up he spake:
"I see," quoth he, "the Elephant
    Is very like a snake!"

The Fourth reached out an eager hand,
    And felt about the knee:
"What most this wondrous beast is like
    Is very plain," quoth he;
" 'Tis clear enough the Elephant
    Is very like a tree!"

The Fifth, who chanced to touch the ear,
    Said: "E'en the blindest man
Can tell what this resembles most;
    Deny the fact who can
This marvel of an Elephant
    Is very like a fan!"

The Sixth no sooner had begun
    About the beast to grope
Than seizing on the swinging tail
    That fell within his scope:
"I see," quoth he, "the Elephant
    Is very like a rope!"

And so these men of Indostan
    Disputed loud and long,
Each in his own opinion
    Exceeding stiff and strong.
Though each was partly in the right,
    They all were in the wrong![14]

Each person in the poem assumed that he knew *all there was to know* about the elephant. Because we sometimes succumb to the allness misevaluation, our perceptions of others and of the world around us can be as limited as those of these six blind men. Remaining open to new ideas and experiences is important for lifelong learning. We fall victims to allness when we close ourselves to new or different information.

How can we avoid allness? We can begin by recognizing that because we can focus on only a portion of a stimulus or an event, we necessarily neglect other aspects of that stimulus or event. Another safeguard is to refrain from thinking of ourselves as the center of the world.

Allness can impede the development of effective relationships. To counteract allness, try to end every assessment you make with the words *et cetera* ("and others"). You can never know everything there is to know about anything, and these words remind you that you should not pretend to "know it all."

"Blindering": Is Your Focus Too Narrow?

The concept of *blindering* as a factor in perception can be illustrated by the following exercise. Attempt to draw four straight lines that will connect each of the dots in Figure 3-6. Do this without lifting your pencil or pen from the page or retracing over a line.

Have you ever considered why the United States almost always appears in the center in our maps of the world? Is there any geographical reason for this? Or could it be an example of "allness" on the part of mapmakers and users?

FIGURE 3-6
Test for blindering.

Did you find the exercise difficult or impossible? Most people do. Why? The problem imposes only one restriction—that you connect the dots with four straight lines without lifting your pen from the page or backtracking over a line. Most of us, however, add another restriction: after examining the dots, we assume that the figure to be formed must be a square. Actually, no such restriction exists, and once you realize this, the solution becomes clear. (The answer appears on page 491.) In effect, the image of a square "blindered" you in your attempts to solve the problem.

Just as we put blinders on a horse to reduce the number of visual stimuli it receives, we can also put blinders on ourselves. Blinders may help a horse, but they can drastically hinder human beings. Because it is a habit that forces us to see only certain things or to see things only in certain ways, blindering can lead to undesirable actions or prevent us from finding solutions. It can also impede or slow down needed actions or decisions.

Inferences: Do You Confuse What You Infer and What You Observe?

Another factor that affects our perception and evaluation of people and events in our world is inability to distinguish what we have *inferred* from what we have *observed*. For example, if you plan to leave your home to drive to a friend's house about a mile away, you probably make some inferences: that when you put the key into the ignition, your automobile will start; that you will not have a flat tire; and that no construction will block your approach to the friend's home. Likewise, when a traffic light turns green, you usually infer that it is safe to cross the street. (The authors found it difficult to walk across many streets in London because the custom there is for the pedestrian to enter the crosswalk and infer that all traffic will stop.)

It is important to distinguish facts from inferences. A *fact* is something that you know to be true, on the basis of observation. You see a woman walking down the street carrying a briefcase. The statement "That woman is carrying a briefcase" is a fact. If the woman with the briefcase has a frown on her face, you may state, "That woman is unhappy." This second statement is an *inference*, since it cannot be verified by observation. In the old crime series *Dragnet*, Jack Webb would often tell witnesses, "All I want is the facts. Just the facts." Facts are not always easy to come by, and sometimes we mistakenly believe we have facts when we actually have inferences. Failing to recognize this distinction can be embarrassing or dangerous.

Sharpen your understanding of facts and inferences by reading the following newspaper story.

> Norwich, N.Y. (AP) They had arrested him for drunken driving, but he insisted he was sober.
>
> Police said his eyes were glassy, his speech thick and his walk unsure.
>
> Roswell Woods was given the usual tests. He was asked to blow up a balloon as a test. He couldn't do it.
>
> He was taken to court. He pleaded not guilty and asked for an attorney.
>
> Before a jury, the 47-year-old veteran heard himself accused. His attorney, Glen F. Carter, asked Woods to stand. He did.

He laughed because he thought that they could not hit him; he didn't imagine that they were practicing how to miss him.

Bertolt Brecht

"Just the facts." In the classic television crime series *Dragnet*, detective Joe Friday would often say this to witnesses. But facts may not be easy to obtain, and often we think we have facts when we really have inferences.

Archive Photos

"It has been testified that your eyes were glassy," the attorney said gently.

The accused pointed to his glass eye, placed there after he had lost an eye in battle.

"It has been testified that your speech was thick," the lawyer continued.

The defendant, speaking with difficulty, said he had partial paralysis of the throat. He said it resulted from one of the 27 injuries received in the line of duty in the South Pacific.

"It is also testified," Carter went on, "that you failed to pick up a coin from off the floor."

He brought out that Woods had been injured in both legs and had undergone an operation in which part of a bone in one leg was used to replace the shattered bone in the other. Woods was unable to stoop, he said.

"And now, the blowing-up of the balloon," the attorney said, "You couldn't blow it up, could you?"

The defendant replied, "I lost one of my lungs in the war. I can't exhale very well."

The jury returned its verdict quickly: "Not guilty."[15]

Acting as if an assumption is a certainty can be risky. When we confuse facts and inferences, we are likely to jump to conclusions. Test your own ability to distinguish facts and inferences by completing the Skill Builder "The Detective." How did you do? (Check your answers against the answer key on page 491.) This test is not designed to discourage you from making inferences. Of necessity, we live our lives on an inferential level. It is designed, however, to discourage you from making inferences without being aware of doing so. It is also designed to help you stop operating as if your inferences were facts.

Are you aware of the inferences you make? As the semanticist S. I. Hayakawa noted, the real question is not whether we make inferences but whether we are cognizant of the inferences we make. One of the key characteristics of a mature relationship is that neither party to it jumps to conclusions or acts on inferences as if they were facts.

The following list summarizes some of the essential differences between facts and inferences:

Facts	Inferences
1. May be made only after observation or experience	1. May be made at any time
2. Are limited to what has been observed	2. Extend beyond observation
3. Can be offered by the observer only	3. Can be offered by anyone
4. May refer to the past or to the present	4. May refer to any time—past, present, or future
5. Approach certainty	5. Represent varying degrees of probability

---

✔ SKILL BUILDER

THE DETECTIVE

Read the story below. Assume that the information contained in it is true and accurate. On a sheet of paper, assess each of the statements that follow the story. Respond to the statements in the order given. Do not go back to change any of your responses. After you read each statement, simply indicate whether you think the statement is definitely true by writing *T*, definitely false by writing *F*, or questionable by writing a question mark. (Note: A question mark indicates that you think the statement could be true or false, but, on the basis of information in the story, you cannot be certain.)

A tired executive had just turned off the lights in the store when an individual approached and demanded money. The owner opened the safe. The contents of the safe were emptied, and the person ran away. The alarm was triggered, notifying the police of the occurrence.

1. An individual appeared after the owner had turned off the store's lights.
2. The robber was a man.
3. The person who appeared did not demand any money.
4. The man who opened the safe was the owner.
5. The owner emptied the safe and ran away.
6. Someone opened the safe.
7. After the individual who demanded the money emptied the safe, he sped away.
8. Although the safe contained money, the story does not reveal how much.
9. The robber opened the safe.
10. The robber did not take the money.
11. In this story, only three persons are referred to.

"*Well, gee, frankly, Mr. Danforth, you being my boss, and asking me to lunch and all, I thought you would pick up the tab.*"

Drawing by Stan Hunt; © 1979 The New Yorker Magazine, Inc.

HOW TO INCREASE THE ACCURACY OF YOUR PERCEPTIONS

Although our effectiveness as communicators is determined in part by our perceptual abilities, we rarely consider ways to increase our perceptual accuracy. Let's examine some suggestions for improving perceptual skills.

Be Aware That Your Perceptual Processes Are Personally Based

As we have mentioned, your perception of a person, thing or event is different from the actual person, thing, or event. The object of your perception is "out there," but your perception is not "out there." Instead, your perception is a composite, or mixture, of what exists "out there" and what exists in you. You are the major actor in the perception process; you are its "star." Thus, what you perceive is determined by physical limitations and by your experiences, needs, fears, desires, and interests. By becoming aware of your role in perception, by recognizing that you have biases, by acknowledging that you do not have a corner on the "truth market," you can increase the probability that your perceptions will provide you with accurate information about the world around you and the people who are a part of it.

Take Your Time

Effective communicators are not in a hurry; they take the time they need to process information fairly and objectively. When we act too quickly, we often make careless decisions that reveal poor judgment. In our haste, we overlook important clues, make inappropriate or unjustified inferences, and jump to conclusions. To combat this, we need to take time to be sure we have assessed a situation correctly. Delaying a response instead of acting impulsively gives us an opportunity to check or verify our perceptions.

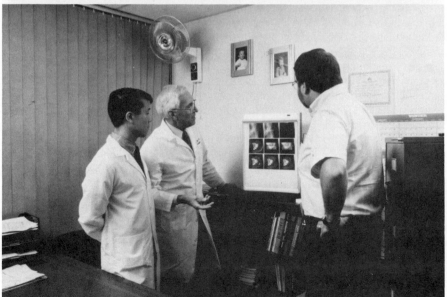

To increase the accuracy of your perceptions, take your time. Lawyers listening to verbal evidence and doctors examining physical evidence have learned that accurate interpretation does not take place instantaneously.

Top, Jay Fries/The Image Bank; *bottom*, Andrée Abecassis/Photo 20-20

Remember that quick, impulsive reactions contribute to faulty perceptions and make us act on inferences as if they were facts. Accurate interpretation of our perceptions does not occur instantaneously.

Try to Be More Open

Frequently, we act like robots or computers that have been programmed to look at the world in a set way. But a person is neither a robot nor a computer. We can take steps to become more observant and broaden our expectations. We need to become willing to expect the unexpected and to expand the size of our perceptual "window." This will happen if we recognize that our reality is subjective, incomplete, and unique. Thus, if we want to cultivate a fuller, more valid perception of our world, we must be willing to review, revise, and update our view of the world.

As we work to internalize the premise of change, we should recognize that if we remove our self-imposed blinders, we will also remove some of the self-imposed restrictions that limit our ability to perceive accurately the people with whom we relate, the situations in which we become involved, and the problems we would like to solve. If we want our perceptions to be valid, we must make a commitment to search out alternatives in an effort to acquire as much information as possible. Furthermore, we cannot expect our perceptions to be accurate or useful if we are unwilling to change them by adding to them, discarding them, or readjusting them as needed. Remember: the more valid your perceptions, the better your chances of communicating effectively with others.

SUMMARY

Perception is the process of selecting, organizing, and interpreting sensory data in a way that enables us to make sense of our world. Perceptions are personally based. They are affected by the perspective we adopt, our sensory capabilities, our past experiences, and our level of motivation. The accuracy of our perceptions is strongly influenced by perceptual sets (readiness to process stimuli in predetermined ways), selective exposure (a tendency to close ourselves to new experiences), and selective perception (an inclination to distort our perceptions of stimuli to make them conform to our need for internal consistency or closure).

How we perceive another person is a key determinant of the kind of relationship we will share with that person. Thus perceiving others and the roles they play is an essential part of the communication process. In this regard, a number of factors can prevent accurate perceptions. We frequently evaluate others on the basis of first impressions, and we tend to stereotype people—to divide them into groups and place them in niches. Stereotyping can be especially harmful by promoting prejudice, since it encourages us to emphasize similarities and ignore differences. Prejudice is an unfair or biased extension of stereotyping, which we must guard against. Other barriers to perceptual accuracy are allness (the habit of thinking we know it all), blindering (the tendency to obscure solutions to problems by adding unnecessary restrictions), and confusion of facts with inferences (inability to distinguish between observations and assumptions).

It is important that you work to increase the validity of your perceptions. As a first step, you need to recognize the role you play in the perceptual process.

SUGGESTIONS FOR FURTHER READING

Allport, Gordon W.: *The Nature of Prejudice*: Doubleday, Garden City, N.Y., 1958. A classic work. A comprehensive treatment of the nature of prejudice and specific stereotypes.

Bartlett, Dorothy L., Pamela B. Drew, Eleanor Fable, and William A. Watts: "Selective Exposure to a Presidential Campaign Appeal," *Public Opinion Quarterly*, vol. 38, 1974, pp. 264–270. Discusses the factors that influence the time of information to which individuals will expose themselves during a campaign.

Berman, Sanford I.: *Why Do We Jump to Conclusions?* International Society for General Semantics, San Francisco, Calif., 1969. A simple but very effective analysis of how we can avoid jumping to conclusions.

Cook, Mark: *Interpersonal Perception*, Penguin, Baltimore, Md., 1971. Discusses the variables that affect perceptual capabilities.

Crouse, Timothy: *The Boys on the Bus*. Ballantine, New York, 1973. A definitive look at the prism through which reporters view events.

Epstein, Edward J.: *News from Nowhere*, Vintage, New York, 1974. A detailed examination of the evening news programs of major networks. Epstein attempts to determine whether television mirrors or creates reality.

Gudykunst, William B.: *Bridging Differences*, Sage, Newbury Park, Calif., 1991. The author, an intercultural consultant and researcher, brings his expertise to bear on this discussion of the importance of perception in intercultural interactions.

Haney, William V.: *Communication and Organizational Behavior*, Irwin, Homewood, Ill., 1973. A comprehensive look at the "misevaluations" we are prone to make and how we can avoid them.

Hastrof, Albert, and Hadley Cantril: "They Saw a Game: A Case Study," *Journal of Abnormal and Social Psychology*, vol. 49, 1954, pp. 129–134. Describes how football fans perceive their home team and the opposition.

Samovar, Larry A., and Richard Porter: *Communication between Cultures*, Belmont, Calif., Wadsworth, 1991. An interesting overview of the role of perception as it relates to communication between cultures.

Schramm, Wilbur, and Richard F. Carter: "Effectiveness of a Political Telethon," *Public Opinion Quarterly*, vol. 23, 1959, pp. 121–126. An analysis and discussion of voter exposure preferences.

Tagiuri, Renato: "Person Perception," in G. Lindzey and E. Aronson (eds.), *The Handbook of Social Psychology*, 2d ed., Addison-Wesley, Reading, Mass., 1969. A classic article, scholarly and thorough.

NOTES

1. William V. Haney, *Communication and Organizational Behavior*, Irwin, Homewood, Ill., 1973, p. 55.
2. E. Rubin, "Figure and Ground," in D. Beardslee and M. Wertheimer (eds.), *Readings in Perception*, Van Nostrand, Princeton, N. J., pp. 194–203.
3. See, for example, Hadley Cantril, "Perception and Interpersonal Relations," *American Journal of Psychiatry*, vol. 114, 1957, pp. 119–126.
4. Larry A. Samovar and Richard E. Porter, *Communication between Cultures*, Wadsworth, Belmont, Calif., 1991, p. 81.
5. Paul Chance, "Seeing Is Believing," *Psychology Today*, January–February 1989, p. 26.
6. Wilbur Schramm and Richard F. Carter, "Effectiveness of a Political Telethon," *Public Opinion Quarterly*, vol. 23, 1959, pp. 121–126.
7. Dorothy L. Bartlett, Pamela B. Drew, Eleanor Fable, and William A. Watts, "Selective Exposure to a Presidential Campaign Appeal," *Public Opinion Quarterly*, vol. 38, 1974, pp. 264–270.
8. Solomon Asch, *Social Psychology*, Oxford University Press, New York, 1987.
9. Edward Jay Epstein, *News from Nowhere*, Vintage, New York, 1974, p. 262.
10. Ralph Ellison, *Invisible Man*, Random House, New York, 1989.
11. See, for example, Gordon W. Allport, *The Nature of Prejudice*, Doubleday, Garden City, N. Y., 1958.
12. Irving J. Lee, *How to Talk with People*, International Society for General Semantics, San Francisco, Calif., 1982.
13. Alfred Korzybski, *Science and Sanity*, 4th ed., Institute of General Semantics, San Francisco, Calif., 1980.
14. Saxe (1816–1887) was a New Englander who edited a weekly newspaper and wrote several volumes of familiar and comic verse.
15. Copyright © Associated Press. Reprinted by permission of Associated Press.

LANGUAGE AND MEANING: HELPING MINDS MEET

After finishing this chaper, you should be able to:

Define *language*

Describe and explain the "triangle of meaning"

Identify a "word barrier"

Discuss the relationship between words and meaning

Explain how time, place, and experience affect meaning

Distinguish between connotative and denotative meaning

Provide examples of bypassing

Distinguish between intensional and extensional orientation

Explain when a sublanguage is appropriate and when it is inappropriate

Provide examples of how word shading can modify meaning

Identify factors that contribute to your own effective or ineffective use of language

Whatever we call a thing, whatever we say it is, it is not.
For whatever we say is words, and words are words and not things.
The words are maps, and the map is not the territory.

Harry L. Weinberg, "Some Limitations of Language"

Have you ever considered what kind of person you would be if you were unable to use words to express yourself? Going even further, have you ever considered what kind of person you would be if you were unable to make a sound? How would it feel to have certain ideas and not be able to communicate them? Like so many other things of importance, the ability to speak is frequently appreciated only when it is threatened or lost. We depend on language to help us communicate meaning to others, and meaning is what communication is all about. If we understand how language works, we will be able to use words to help us share meaning with others.

WHAT LANGUAGE IS

Language is a unified system of symbols that permits a sharing of meaning. A *symbol* stands for, or represents, something else. *Words* are symbols, and thus words represent things. Notice that we have said "represent" and "stand for" rather than "are." This is a very important distinction. Words *stand for or represent* things but are *not* themselves things. Words are spoken sounds or the written representations of sounds that we have agreed will stand for something else. Thus by mutual consent we can make anything stand for anything.

The process of communication involves using words to help create meanings and expectations. However, important as words are in representing and describing objects and ideas, the meaning of a verbal message is not stamped on the face of the words we use. Meanings are in people, not in words. What is important to realize is that you have your meaning and other people have theirs. Even a common word such as *cat* can bring to mind meanings ranging from a fluffy angora to a sleek leopard. Your goal in communicating with another person is to have your meanings overlap so that you can each make sense out of the other's messages and understand each other. Thus, in order to communicate you translate the meaning you want to express into language so that the other person will respond to it by forming a meaning similar to yours. Although language is obviously intended to aid communication, far too often language serves as an obstacle to communication.

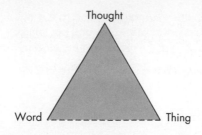

FIGURE 4-1
Triangle of meaning.

HOW LANGUAGE WORKS: WORDS, THINGS, AND THOUGHTS

Language can fulfill its potential only if we use it correctly; to do this, we must understand a number of things. The "triangle of meaning," developed by two communication theorists—C. K. Ogden and I. A. Richards—helps explain how language works.[1] (See Figure 4-1.)

In Ogden and Richards's triangle of meaning, the three points are *thought*, *word*, and *thing*. The broken line connecting *word* (a symbol) and *thing* (a referent, or stimulus) indicates that the word is not the thing and that there is no *direct* relationship or connection between the two. Thus when you use words, you must constantly remind yourself that the only relationships between the words you use and the things they represent are those which exist in people's *thoughts* (including, of course, your own). Frequently, even the existence of an image (a physical object of some type) does not establish meaning. A few years ago, a public service commercial depicting a rat and a child living in a tenement was shown on television. The child was seen beckoning to the rat as she repeated, "Here kitty, kitty! Here kitty, kitty!" Although this example may seem somewhat bizarre, its meaning is really quite clear: it is quite pos-

---

▶ **POINTS TO PONDER**

THE TRIANGLE OF MEANING AT WORK

Situation 1. "Congratulations. You've just given birth to a 3.5-kilogram baby." How do you respond? Your joy is momentarily muted if you don't know what a kilogram is. There is no information in bare facts; information comes from what you do with the facts, and what you bring to them. If you've never stored a mental image of a kilogram, you can't generate a mental image of the baby's weight from the data.

Situation 2. Now imagine that you're at an old Western Union telegraph office. The telegraph opera-

tor hears a message on the wire and bursts into tears. You hear the same dots and dashes, but have no reactions at all. Why not?

If you don't know Morse code, the information means nothing, even if you hear it quite clearly. Meaning is not in the cues reaching our senses, but in the associations we attach to them.

Source: Loretta Breuning, "Networking with Yourself: How the Brain Uses Information (Part 1)," *ETC*, vol. 47, no. 2, Summer 1990, p. 106.

sible for two of us to look at the same object but give it different meanings. No one else will respond to a stimulus (a word or thing) exactly as you do, because the meaning of anything is inside each of us who experiences it.[2] If you are to be a successful communicator, you should understand the relationships that exist between words and people's thoughts and reactions.

■ ETHICS AND COMMUNICATION

LET'S BUST THOSE CHOPS
Rick Reilly

Where do you stand on the issue Reilly takes up here? What changes, if any, would you like to see? Why?

Native Americans have every reason to object to the way they're caricatured by teams. Would you be offended if your dog fetched a morning paper that had this item inside?

> New York—The New York Negroes defeated the Houston Astros 2-1 Friday in front of a stadium full of wild fans waving fried chicken legs and singing gospel songs.

> Chicago—The Chicago Jews defeated the Houston Astros 2-1 Friday in front of a stadium full of wild fans waving yarmulkes and singing *Hava Nagila.*

You would be? Then why shouldn't the two million Native Americans in this country be offended when they read something like this?

> Atlanta—The Atlanta Braves defeated the Houston Astros 2-1 Friday in front of a stadium full of wild fans waving foam rubber tomahawks and chanting war cries.

I know, I know. You've hit your sensitivity ceiling. Your guilt meter is on empty. Your ears will burst if you get scolded one more time about women, blacks, spotted owls, rain forests, landfills, disposable diapers, red meat, whales, or your continued failure to try radicchio.

Now somebody wants you to start worrying about Indian harassment? Take a number.

Not to worry. This one is really nobody's fault. It's simply a lousy little wrong that's been handed down from one year to the next. . . . "It hurts," says Roger Head, a Chippewa who heads the Minnesota Indian Affairs Council. "It's not a true depiction of the Indian people. When we see these folks dressed as Indians and wearing war paint, the stereotypes of Indians come out. They wear headdresses, which are very spiritual in nature, very ceremonial. Would you like it if we went to a game with a lot of Catholics and started giving communion in the stands or hearing confession? It wouldn't show respect."

If we can have the Washington Redskins, why can't we have the Los Angeles Yellowskins? And if we can have the Cleveland Indians—whose grinning injun logo is to American Indians what Stepin Fetchit is to African-Americans—why can't we have the San Diego Chicanos?

If it's a question of respect, listen to this story: An anthropologist was studying Indians in the mid-1800s when he came across an old tribal chief. He asked the chief what America was called before the white man came. The old Indian looked at him and said, "Ours."

WHAT LANGUAGE MEANS

Word Barriers

In talking to others we often assume too quickly that they understand what we mean. There are, however, many reasons why we may not be understood as we want to be and why the words we use can create barriers. In Lewis Carroll's *Alice in Wonderland*, Humpty Dumpty and Alice have the following conversation:

> "I don't know what you mean by 'glory,'" Alice said.
> Humpty Dumpty smiled contemptuously, "Of course you don't—till I tell you. I meant, 'There's a nice knock-down argument for you!'"
> "But 'glory' doesn't mean 'A nice knock-down argument,'" Alice objected.
> "When I use a word," Humpty Dumpty said in a rather scornful tone, "it means just what I choose it to mean—neither more nor less."

We can make words mean whatever we want them to mean. Nothing stops us—except our desire to share meaning with others.

Joseph Jourbert said, "Words, like eyeglasses, blur everything that they do not make more clear." How have words blurred your relationships?

Denotations and Connotations

Sometimes we forget that we may experience a problem in communication if we consider only our own meaning for a word. (*We* know what we mean.) The crucial question is, "What does our word bring to mind for those with whom we are communicating?" When we think about what language means, we must think in terms of both *denotative* (or "dictionary") meaning and *connotative* (or "personal") meaning.

MEANING AND TIME

A definition is not attached to a word forever. Words evolve new meanings from era to era, from generation to generation, and sometimes even from year to year.

For example, *bad* now has a new definition—"good." The word *gay*, now an acceptable term for "homosexual," is losing its former primary meaning of "happy," "bright," or "merry." And in a recent edition of the Random House Webster's College Dictionary, under the entry for the word *girl*, it is noted that "many women today resent being called girls." (To get a good sense of how time affects meaning, try the Skill Builder "A Time Capsule for Words" on the opposite page.)

Time, then, is certainly an important element in determining meaning. Consequently, when we use a word that referred to a particular object at a particular time, we should attempt to determine if it still means the same thing now. "Old" words often acquire vivid new meanings every decade or so. It's often necessary to remember this when speaking with people who are older or younger than you.

A TIME CAPSULE FOR WORDS

1. Briefly define each of the following terms:

radical _____

pot _____

gay _____

high _____

freak _____

trip _____

swing _____

straight _____

rock _____

I'm Elvis _____

crack _____

rap _____

pad _____

grass _____

burning daylight _____

gross _____

hip _____

dust _____

joint _____

stoned _____

dude _____

AIDS _____

2. Show the list, without definitions, to your parents, older relatives, or older friends and ask them to write their definitions for the words.

3. Compare your meaning for each term with the meaning given by others. Why do you suppose their meanings differed from yours?

4. Pretend it is now the year 2020. On a separate sheet of paper, create new meanings for each of the words listed.

Not only do words change meaning over time; they also change meaning from one region of the country to another. For example, what would you envision having if you were to stop for a *soda*? For an *egg cream*? For a *Danish*? For some *pop*? What each word brings to mind probably depends on what region of the country you grew up in. In some parts of the United States a *soda* is a soft drink, but in others it refers to a concoction of ice cream and a soft drink. In some sections of the country an *egg cream* refers to a mixture of seltzer, syrup, and milk, but elsewhere it conjures up the image of an egg mixed with cream. To people in certain parts of the United States a *Danish* is any kind of breakfast pastry; in other regions people expect to be served a particular kind of breakfast pastry. In still other places the waiter or waitress might think that you were ordering a foreign specialty—or even a foreigner! As a further example of the effects of regional differences on communication, consider the piece by William Safire on the opposite page.

MEANING AND CULTURE

Of course, different cultures and subcultures have different languages; hence, usages vary from culture to culture. If a concept is important to a particular culture, there will be a large number of terms to describe it. For example, in our culture, the word *money* is very important and we have many different words to describe it: *wealth, capital, assets, backing, resources,* and *finance* are just a few. Similarly, the Inuit, or Eskimos, have a number of different words for *snow* because they need to be able to make fine distinctions when speaking of it. Thus, for the Inuit, *gana* refers to falling snow, and *akilukah* to fluffy fallen snow. In contrast to the Inuit, Arabs have only one word for "snow"—*talg*—and it refers to either ice or snow. The Arabs are simply not very interested in snow, since it rarely affects them. Similarly, Mandarin (a Chinese language) reflects the interests and concerns of the Chinese people. There are, for example, at least nineteen Chinese words for "silk" and eight for "rice." And since the Chinese care deeply for their families, there are a plethora of words for relations. The Chinese have five words they can use for "uncle," depending on whose brother he is.[3]

As we see, the world we experience helps shape the language we speak, and the language we speak helps sustain our perception of reality and our view of our world. This idea is contained in the Sapir-Whorf hypothesis, which holds that the labels we use help shape the way we think, our world view, and our behavior. In other words, according to the Sapir-Whorf hypothesis, people from different cultures perceive stimuli and communicate differently, at least in part because of their language differences. For this reason you should not assume that the words you use and the words people from other cultures use mean the same thing, nor should you assume that you even see the same reality when viewing the same stimulus. Quite simply, our language and our perception are intertwined.

Japanese culture encourages minimal verbal communication. A Japanese proverb is, "By your mouth you shall perish." What do you think this proverb means?

TRAFFIC TALK
William Safire

What message does this article have for people who visit or relocate in different parts of the United States?

A person whose curiosity causes him to slow traffic is called a *rubbernecker* in Texas, a *gonker* in Detroit and a *lookie-Lou* in L.A. Such obstructive gaping is called *gaper's block* in Denver.

How do traffic-casters refer to stalled cars? By converting adjectives to nouns: A disabled vehicle is called a *disable* in Texas and a *stall* in Baltimore. In Minneapolis, stalls and disables along the icy roadways are called *snowbirds*.

At interchanges, where freeways merge, the traffic-casters have a field day reporting trouble. In Dallas, beware the *Mixmaster*; in Denver, motorists dread *the Mousetrap*; in Detroit, the most jammable interchange is called *the Malfunction Junction*.

Rhyme and alliteration attract the troubadors of traffic trouble. In Detroit on days when roadways are icy, listeners are warned of *bunch and crunch*; after dry spells in Texas, when oil on the road is suddenly mixed with rain, the danger spoken of is *slip and slide*.

MEANING AND GENDER

Sometimes the sex of communicators affects not only the meaning we give to their utterances but also the very structure of those utterances.

Women, for example, use more tentative phrases or qualifiers in their speech than men do. Phrases like *I guess*, *I think*, and *I wonder if* abound in the speech patterns of women but not in those of men. This pattern is also passed on to the very young through their favorite cartoon characters. Just as their real-life counterparts are apt to do, female cartoon characters, more than male characters, use verbs which indicate lack of certainty (*I suppose*) and words judged to be polite.[4] Is art mirroring life, or vice versa? Are cartoons helping to perpetuate stereotypes? Women also tend to turn statements into questions more than men do. Women typically ask something like: "Don't you think it would be better to send them that report first?" Men, in contrast, typically respond with a more definitive "Yes, it would be better to send them that report first." According to Robin Lakoff, a researcher on language and gender, women do not "lay claim to" their statements as frequently as men do. In addition, women use more "tag" questions than men do. A *tag* is midway between an outright statement and a yes-no question. For instance, women often make queries like these: "Joan is here, isn't she?" "It's hot in here, isn't it?" By seeking verbal confirmation for their perceptions, women acquire a reputation for tentativeness. Similarly, women use more disclaimers than men do, prefacing their remarks with statements like "This probably isn't important, but . . ." Such practices weaken the messages women send to others.

Compile a list of differences you believe exist between men's and women's use of language. Why do you think each of these differences has developed?

85

Two factors affecting
what language means
are culture and gender.
For example, in
Mandarin there are at
least nineteen words for
"silk." And according
to one linguist, men and
women speak different
"gender-lects."

Top, Charles Gupton/
Stock, Boston, *bottom,*
J. Barry O'Rourke/The
Stock Market

Interestingly, according to the communications researcher Patricia Hayes Bradley, even if men use tag questions, the perceptual damage done to them by this weaker verbal form is not as great as the damage done to women. Bradley found that when women used tag questions and disclaimers, or failed to support their arguments, they were judged to be less intelligent and knowledgeable—but men were not. Simply talking "like a woman" causes a woman to be judged negatively.[5] Consequently, according to the researchers Nancy Henley and Cheris Kramarae, females face a real disadvantage when interacting with males: "Females are required to develop special sensitivity to interpret males' silence, lack of emotional expression, or brutality, and to help men express themselves. Yet, it is women's communication style that is often labeled as inadequate and maladaptive."[6]

Gender affects how men and women use and process language in a number of other ways as well. According to the linguist Deborah Tannen, men and women speak different "gender-lects." While women speak and hear a language of connection and intimacy, Tannen finds that men speak and hear a language of status and independence.[7] As a result, when conversing with men, women tend to listen attentively rather than interrupt or challenge what the male is saying. Why? Tannen holds that it is because challenging the male could damage the established connection which most women believe must be preserved at all costs.

● CULTURE AND COMMUNICATION

GENDER AND LANGUAGE IN JAPAN

Consider this comment about the Japanese language by Ellen Rudolph:

One of the first verbal hurdles boys and girls have to overcome is the proper way to end sentences. A boy might say "samui yo" to declare "It's cold, I say!" But a girl would say, "samui wa," expressing what is in effect a gentle question: "It's cold, don't you think?" When referring to themselves, boys often use the word "boku," which means "I." Girls can't; they have to say "watashi," a pronoun that can be used by either sex, but that is more polite.

Parents and teachers are vigilant linguistic police, correcting children who use forms of speech reserved for the other sex. Girls in particular are upbraided with "Onnanoko no no ni," which means "You're a girl, don't forget."

What kinds of messages are sent by such semantic practices? To what extent, if any, do Americans send similar messages to young males and females? Do you believe language should be used as a tool to keep males and females in their respective "places"? Why or why not?

Source: "On Language: Women's Talk," *New York Times Magazine*, September 1, 1991, p. 8.

MEANING AND POWER

Both males and females have the potential to influence the way others perceive them by communicating in ways that make them appear more confident, more forceful, and thus more in control of a situation. In other words, the language people use helps us type them as having power or lacking power—as powerful or powerless.[8]

Some people seem to announce their own powerlessness through their language. "Powertalkers," in contrast, make definite statements such as "Let's go out to dinner tonight" rather than weaker "hedges" such as "I think we should go out to dinner tonight." In other words, powertalkers direct the action; they assume control.

Powertalkers also hesitate less in their speech. Instead of making statements filled with "nonfluencies" such as "I wish you wouldn't, uh, keep me waiting so long," powertalkers enhance their sense of self-worth by projecting their opinions with more confidence. They eliminate fillers such as *er, um, you know*, and *like*, and *well* that serve as verbal hiccups and make a speaker appear weak.

Powertalkers use fewer unnecessary intensifiers than more submissive talkers. "I'm not very interested in going" is a less forceful statement than is "I'm not interested in going." Rather than strengthening a position, intensifiers actually can serve to deflate it.

Powerful talk is talk that comes directly to the point. It does not contain disclaimers ("I probably shouldn't mention this, but . . .") or tag questions like those described in the preceding section on language and gender. If you succeed in speaking powertalk, your credibility and your ability to influence others will increase. Changing the power balance may be as simple as changing the words you use.

MEANING AND EXPERIENCE

The meanings we assign to words are based on our past experiences with the words and with the things they represent. Take the word *cancer*, for example. If you were dealing with three different people in a hospital—a surgeon, a patient, and a statistician—how do you imagine each would react to this word? The surgeon might think about operating procedures, diagnostic techniques, or how to tell a patient that he or she has cancer. The patient might think about the odds for recovery and might well be frightened. The statistician might see cancer as an important factor in life-expectancy tables.

Unlike "denotative" ("dictionary") meanings—which are objective, abstract, and general in nature—"connotative" ("personal") meanings are subjective and emotional in nature. Thus, your own experiences influence the meanings you assign to words; that is, your connotative meanings vary according to your own feelings for the object or concept you are considering. (We introduced denotations and connotations briefly at the beginning of this section, on page 82.)

As we mentioned earlier, if we do not make an attempt to analyze how people's backgrounds influence them in assigning meaning, we may have trouble communicating with them. For most of us, words have more than a single meaning. In fact, a commonly used word can frequently have more than 20 different definitions. We know that a "strike" in bowling is different from a "strike" in baseball. We know that "to strike" a match is not the same as "striking up" the band. For this reason, we must pay careful attention to the "context" of a message. Unfortunately, we frequently forget that words are rarely used in one and only one sense, and we assume when we speak to others that our words are being understood in only the way we intend them to be understood. And our receivers may assume that their interpretation of our words is the meaning we intended. Let's explore what happens when this occurs.

BYPASSING: CONFUSING MEANINGS

Sometimes people think they understand each other when in fact they are really missing each other's meaning. This pattern of miscommunication is called *bypassing* because the interactant's meanings simply *pass by* one another.

Think of instances when "bypassing" caused problems for you.

We can identify two main kinds of bypassing.[9] One type occurs when people use different words or phrases to represent the same thing but are unaware that they are both talking about the same thing. For example, two urban politicians once argued vehemently over welfare policies. One held that the city's welfare program should be "overhauled," whereas the other believed that "minor changes" should be made. Far too much time passed before it was realized that the first politician's "overhaul" was actually equivalent to the second politician's "minor changes." How many times have you argued unnecessarily because you were unaware that another person was simply using a different word or words to mean the same thing you were saying?

The second, and more common, type of bypassing occurs when people use the same word or phrase but give it different meanings. In such cases, people appear to be in agreement when they substantially disagree. Sometimes this type of bypass is harmless. Semanticists tell a tall but otherwise useful story about a man who was driving on a parkway when his engine stalled. He managed to flag down another driver, who, after hearing his story, consented to push the stalled car to get it started. "My car has an automatic transmission," the first man explained, "so you'll have to get up to 30 or 35 miles an hour to get me moving." The other driver nodded in understanding, and the stalled motorist then climbed back into his own car and waited for the other car to line up behind him. After much more waiting, he turned around—to see the other driver coming at him at 30 miles per hour!

Developing an awareness that bypassing can occur when you communicate is a first step in preventing it from interfering with or needlessly complicating your relationships. If you believe it is possible for your listener to misunderstand you, then be willing to take the time needed to ensure that your meanings

YOUTHSPEAK
Richard Bernstein

If you think *PC* stands for *personal computer*, what do you think *non-PC* means? Anything that is not a PC? Students these days, while familiar with high technology, are using the term *PC* as an abbreviation for *politically correct*; *non-PC* for its opposite. The term has a leftist connotation and, more likely than not, is used by those who believe the university works hand in glove with the capitalist establishment.

As always, the schools and colleges are producing a lot of slang. Some are invented words; some have been absorbed from street language, rap music, ethnic jargon; others are twists on the special vocabulary of an earlier generation. . . .

Every student generation, of course, wants to make its mark with its own words. In the 1960's, when I was a student, we used to say *cool it* to encourage calmness when all hell breaks loose. The expression has changed slightly; the word is now *chill* (another usage derived from street talk), usually spoken as a command.

Chill also seems to have replaced *to stand somebody up* or *to fail to turn up for a date*. "She chilled on me," the young man said, after waiting disconsolately for several hours. (On the other hand, the word *chillin'*, with origins in rap music, means *first rate, terrific*, as in, "The concert was chillin'.") *Chill* seems a useful and even instructive term. It puts the ice on humiliation, muffles it in the comfort of jargon, helps the sufferer to feign a bit of indifference. Much of the student lexicon has this euphemistic quality, since students, being of a tender age, are a vulnerable lot.

Connie C. Eble, an associate professor of English, at the University of North Carolina at Chapel Hill, who has been collecting student slang for several years—keeping her burgeoning collection on 3 × 5 cards in green file drawers in her office—has a long list of these expressions. Her favorite, she says, is "talking to Ralph on the big white phone."

Ralph, Professor Eble explains, is onomatopoeic, mimicking the sound of regurgitation. *The big white phone* is a metaphor for the toilet bowl, and the expression means to *throw up*; "pray to the porcelain goddess" is a common alternative. . . .

Students have a host of words to refer to other students who study a great deal or who have the sort of seriousness of purpose that, when combined with a pronounced lack of social graces, produces what used to be called "grinds" or "nerds." The new insults are *dweeb, geek, goober* and *wonk*. And *corn dog, goob-a-tron* and *groover*.

A variation on this theme is *granola*, which refers to someone who dresses and acts as students did in the 1960's, perhaps somebody who wears sandals and beads and who says "nerd" instead of "goober." A *buzz crusher* is someone who puts a damper on things, a kill-joy. *Bite moose* is a way of telling somebody to get lost, go to hell. . . .

On the subject of sex, Professor Eble's students have a rich vocabulary describing various forms of behavior that they either indulge in, or wish they did. There is often a defensive quality to this extreme irreverence—a preemptive unwillingness to care too deeply. *To box tonsils*, for example, means *to kiss passionately*, as does *to play tonsil hockey*. The sex act is *parallel parking* or the *horizontal bop*.

Sleep, on the other hand, is not something that students spend a great deal of time doing, and their words for it seem to reflect this. A *rack monster* is a bed; "to get some rack" is "to get some sleep." A *power nap* is a deep sleep induced by extreme exhaustion.

More than any other group, it would seem, students constantly use words in entirely new ways. Take *random*. When something makes no sense and you are resigned to its utter nonsensicalness, "it is random, really random, totally random." "This really random guy" would not be a flattering way of describing a new acquaintance. And *radical* is no longer the make-the-world-over-in-our-own-image word used ad nauseam during the 60's. *Radical*—often shortened to *rad*—means *great, wonderful, remarkable*.

In the old days, we used to say "awesome" to express an approving wonderment, while *radical*, of course, was associated with things revolutionary. *Far out*, for *astonishing* or *wondrous*, was another common term of 20 years ago that seems to have completely disappeared. It just goes to show how much things haven't really changed; the words may be different, but student preoccupations remain the same. . . .

Still, for someone of my generation, it's difficult to think of *radical* as synonymous with *awesome*, just as *far out* is not an allusion to something a great distance away. Perhaps by giving the word *radical* its new twist, students are telling us they aren't so radical anymore. If I objected to this apparent apathy, I would probably be called a *dweeb*, maybe a *granola*. Certainly I would be told to *bite moose*—or should that just be *chill*?

Source: From "On Language: Youthspeak" by Richard Bernstein, *The New York Times Magazine*, December 11, 1988. Copyright © 1988 by The New York Times Company. Reprinted by permission.

for words overlap. Try never to be caught saying, "It never occurred to me that you would think I meant—" or, "I was certain you'd understand." To avoid bypassing, you must be "person-minded" instead of "word-minded." Remind yourself that your words may generate unpredictable or unexpected reactions in others. Trying to anticipate these reactions will help you forestall communication problems.

LABELING: CONFUSING WORDS AND THINGS

Sometimes we forget that it is people, not words, who make meanings. When this happens, we pay far too much attention to labels and far too little attention to reality. We can approach this phase of our study of meaning by considering this problem of labels and how strongly they can influence us.

For example, what type of behavior would you exhibit around vats labeled "Gasoline Drums"? You would probably be careful not to light any matches; and if you smoked, you would be certain not to toss away any cigarette butts. Would you change your behavior if the labels on the containers read "Empty Gasoline Drums"? Chances are, you might relax a bit and give less thought to the possibility of starting a fire—although empty drums are actually more dangerous because they contain explosive vapor.

After studying such situations, the linguistic researcher Benjamin Lee Whorf—who was one of the formulators of the Sapir-Whorf hypothesis—suggested that the way people define or label a situation has a dramatic impact on their behavior. As we discussed earlier in this chapter, according to Whorf, the words we use help mold our perceptions of reality and the world around us.[10] In other words, Whorf believes that our words actually *determine* the reality we are able to perceive. Thus, a person from a tropical country who has rarely if ever experienced snow and who simply calls snow *snow* probably "sees" only one thing (*snow*) when confronted with different kinds of frozen moisture falling from the sky. In contrast, skiers, who depend on snow, seek out snow, and diligently follow snow reports, are able to label and distinguish about six different types of snow.

Each of us has learned to see the world not as it is, but through the distorting glass of our words. It is through words that we are made human, and it is through words that we are dehumanized.
Ashley Montagu, *The Language of Self-Deception*

✔ SKILL BUILDER

"STICKS AND STONES . . ."

Imagine that you are district court judge and are faced with the following case. Simon Maynard Kigler would like to change his name to 1048. That is, Kigler would like to be called One Zero Four Eight, or "One Zero" for short. It is your task to decide whether to grant Kigler this requested name change. Justify your decision with specific reasons.

How important are labels in our culture? The skill builder above may help answer this question. A real-life judge faced with a similar case ruled that the individual could not change his name because a number was totalitarian and an offense to human dignity. What does a number, as opposed to a name, signify? Would *we* change if our names were changed?[11] In *Romeo and Juliet*, Shakespeare offered some thoughts on the significance of names when he had Juliet, of the Capulet family, say these words to Romeo, a Montague:

> 'Tis but thy name that is my enemy;
> Thou art thyself, though not a Montague.
> What's Montague? It is nor hand, nor foot,
> Nor arm, nor face, nor any other part
> Belonging to a man. O! be some other name;
> What's in a name? that which we call a rose
> By any other name would smell as sweet;
> So Romeo would, were he not Romeo call'd.

Are most people blinded by labels? A storekeeper attempted to answer this question by conducting the following test. The storekeeper had just received an order of identical handkerchiefs. He arbitrarily placed half of these handkerchiefs on a table and labeled them "Genuine Irish Linen Handkerchiefs—2 for $3." He placed the other half of the order on another counter and labeled them "Noserags—2 for 25¢." What do you think happened? Right. The storekeeper's customers reacted negatively to the "noserag" label and bought the "Genuine Irish Linen Handkerchiefs" instead. It seems that nobody likes to buy "noserags"—would you?

In examining the effect of labels, the concept of *intensional* versus *extensional orientation* is useful. In his book *Influence*, Robert B. Cialdini provides an example that illustrates *intensional orientation* in action.[12] A friend of his had recently opened an Indian jewelry store in Arizona and wanted to move some turquoise jewelry she had been having trouble selling. She scribbled the following note to her head salesclerk: "Everything in this display case, price × ½." The owner then left for a business trip. When she returned to her jewelry store a few days later, she was not surprised to find that every piece had been sold, but she was surprised to discover that because the employee had read the "½" in her scribbled message as a "2," the entire supply of turquoise jewelry had sold at twice the original price. The customers had displayed intensional orientation. In their mind, "expensive" meant "good," and the higher prices made them believe that the worth of the jewelry must be higher. In other words, a dramatic increase in price led buyers to see the turquoise as more valuable and desirable. But the customers were reacting to a label—the price— and labels don't always tell us all we have to know. The customers had failed to inspect the territory. If you react to a label without examining what the label represents, you are taking an intensional orientation. People who are intensionally oriented are easily fooled by words and labels. In contrast, when you take the time to look beyond a label, when you inspect the thing itself, you are taking an *extensional orientation*. People who are extensionally oriented are disposed to reality rather than to fantasy.

Frequently, our reaction to a person or event is totally changed by words, or by even a single word. We simply confuse words with things. If we are not aware of our responses, we can very easily be manipulated or "conned" by language.

Take some time to analyze the following sets of words to see how your reactions may change as the labels change:

1. coffin — casket — slumber chamber
2. girl — woman — broad
3. backward — developing — underdeveloped
4. the corpse — the deceased — the loved one
5. cheat — evade — find loopholes
6. janitor — custodian — sanitary engineer
7. kill — waste — annihilate
8. war — police action — defensive maneuvers
9. toilet — bathroom — rest room
10. senior citizens — aged — old people
11. air strike — bombing raid — protective reaction
12. broke — poor — disadvantaged
13. bill collector — debt chaser — adjuster
14. love child — illegitimate child — bastard
15. an illegal — an alien — an undocumented resident

Whenever we communicate, we consciously or unconsciously select the level of language we will use. Normally, the words we select depend on the person with whom we are communicating and the situation in which we are communicating. It is important to recognize that different styles of behavior are required in different circumstances.

A Call for Common Sense

It should be apparent that just as particular styles of apparel and behavior are appropriate for certain situations, so certain styles of language are appropriate at certain times and in certain places. Consider slang—a style of language used by special groups but not considered "proper" by society at large. Although we may use slang when conversing with our friends, it would be inappropriate and unwise when speaking to an instructor or when delivering a speech to the town council.

You have the capability to adapt the language you use as you move from one situation to another, but first you need to be aware of the conditions and circumstances that can affect your usages. Jonathan Swift said it long ago when he noted that style is simply "proper words in proper places." Thus it all boils down to deciding what is meant by *proper*. What you think is proper may not always coincide with what someone else thinks is proper.

✔ **SKILL BUILDER**

WHAT'S TABOO TO YOU?

1. Would you feel comfortable using obscenities with any of the following people? Why or why not?

Your grandparent	Your state senator	Your team coach
Your best friend	Your employer	Your instructor
President of your school	Maître d'	Your physician

2. How would your answers to question 1 change if you were in each of the following environments?

Fancy restaurant	Your den	School cafeteria
Truck-stop diner	Classroom	Sports stadium
Your living room	Department store	Auditorium

3. How would your answers change if each person listed in question 1 was a man? How would your answers change if each person was a woman? To what extent, if any, did your responses vary? Why?

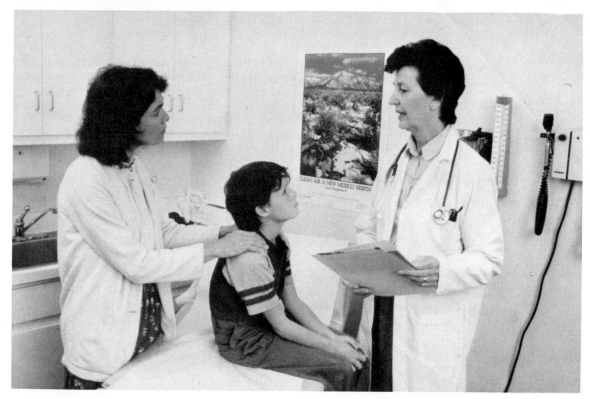

A Call for Clarity

In day-to-day communication, for any one of several reasons, we far too frequently use language that other people cannot easily understand. It doesn't matter how accurately a selected word or phrase expresses *our* ideas if the receivers cannot comprehend it. If you want to be understood, you must make every attempt to select words with meaning for your listeners. If you can accomplish this, you will have taken a giant step toward achieving understanding.

First, as a communicator you want to be sure to use words geared to the *educational level* of your listeners. The following example, adapted from Stewart Chase's *The Power of Words*, aptly illustrates the problems that can arise from failure to consider the receiver's educational background.

A plumber with a limited command of English was aware that hydrochloric acid opened clogged drain pipes quickly and effectively. However, he thought he had better check with the National Bureau of Standards in Washington, D.C., to determine if hydrochloric acid was safe to use in pipes, so he wrote the bureau a letter. A scientist at the bureau wrote back, stating: "The efficacy of hydrochloric acid is indisputable, but the corrosive residue is incompatible with metallic surfaces."

The plumber wrote a second letter, thanking the bureau for the quick reply and for giving him the okay to use hydrochloric acid.

The plumber's second letter bothered the scientist and he showed it to his boss. The boss decided to write another letter to the plumber. The boss's letter read: "We cannot assume responsibility for the production of toxic and noxious residue which hydrochloric acid can produce; we suggest that you use an alternative procedure."

This left the plumber somewhat confused. He dashed off a letter to the bureau telling them that he was glad they agreed with him. "The acid was working just fine."

When this letter arrived, the boss sent it to the "top administrator" at the bureau. The top administrator solved the problem by writing a short note to the plumber: "Don't use hydrochloric acid. It eats the hell out of pipes!"[13]

Another good rule to follow if you hope to achieve clarity is to keep *jargon* to a minimum unless your receiver is schooled in the jargon. In other words, speak the same language as your listener. Most of us who live in the United States share a common language, but many of us also frequently use one or more sublanguages. A *sublanguage* is simply a special language used by members of a particular subculture. We all belong to several subcultures—a national group, an occupational group, an educational group, an ethnic group, and perhaps a religious group. Having a common sublanguage helps members of the group attain a sense of identity. (For example, when some blacks address their acquaintances as "brother" or "sister" in greeting each other in the street, they are affirming their subculture.) However, since all sublanguages are intended to enable communication only within a particular group, a sublanguage is probably not readily understood by outsiders. As an example, consider this brief dialogue between two doctors.

> DOCTOR 1: How's that patient you were telling me about?
>
> DOCTOR 2: Well, she's improving. But now she's suffering from cephalagia complicated by agrypnia.

In analyzing this interchange you would probably not immediately guess that *cephalagia* is the medical term for a headache and that *agrypnia* refers to insomnia. Thus, people schooled in the technical language of a particular group should constantly guard against what may be an innate temptation to impress others rather than to communicate. In short, if we want our receivers to understand us, we must always ask ourselves "Who am I talking to?"

Using readily understandable language need not keep you from aiming for accuracy. Never abandon your efforts to find the exact words that represent the ideas you want to communicate. Remember that a clear message is neither ambiguous nor confusing. Your precise meaning will be shared with other people only if your words tell them precisely what you mean. Thus, select concrete rather than vague words to represent your thoughts. For example, if you were trying to convey how a man sounded when he spoke, you could state: "He said," "He yelled," "He cried," "He purred," "He chuckled," "He growled," "He boomed," or "He sang." Each description would leave your listener with a somewhat different impression and feeling. Your words would shape the meaning you convey to others. As you increase your sensitivity to language, your awareness of the subtle shades of meaning that can be achieved with words will grow.

BUSINESS BABBLE QUIZ
David Olive

Corporate jargon can have its humorous side. Match these ten words with their definitions. David Olive suggests that if you can get them all right, you are ready for the corporate boardroom. (Answers appear on page 491.)

1. ability

2. contract

3. debt

4. dehire

5. historical romance

6. lawyer

7. marketing

8. plausible deniability

9. shark repellent

10. friend

a. the act of keeping the boss informed only of the ends in order that he or she later can deny knowledge of the means

b. the specialist who renders legal what has already been done

c. an enemy with whom you have yet to do business

d. a decision against letting the product speak for itself, recognizing that it may not be the most credible spokesperson

e. a pungent aroma released by the target of a hostile takeover, which, if effective, will encourage the predator to seek its meal elsewhere

f. a handshake that will hold up in court

g. a five year statement of corporate earnings, skillfully adjusted to satisfy investors' expectations of a happy ending

h. the tolerance shown by an employee for coping with superiors whose cognitive endowment would embarrass a tree stump

i. a way of postponing until tomorrow obligations you cannot meet today

j. to terminate with extreme regret and often, little else

Source: Created from *Business Babble* by David Olive. Copyright © 1990, 1991 by David Olive. Reprinted by permission of John Wiley & Sons, Inc.

Guidelines for Developing Language Skills

Throughout this chapter we have stressed that mastery of certain language skills will improve your ability to communicate effectively with others. Use the following guidelines to ensure that your words work for you rather than against you.

IDENTIFY HOW LABELS AFFECT YOUR BEHAVIOR

We can state one of the most fundamental precepts of language simply and directly: *Words are not things*. Always remember that words are nothing more than symbols. No connection *necessarily* exists between a symbol and what people have agreed that symbol represents. In other words, symbols and their representations are independent of each other.

All of us at times respond as if words and things were one and the same, for example, when we make statements like these: "A bathroom is a bathroom. It's certainly not a water closet." "Pigs are called *pigs* because they wallow in mud and grime." Think of how often you buy a product such as Intimate, Brute, Bold, Caress, Secret, or Gleem because of what the label seems to promise. How many times have you turned against a person because he or she is called *liberal*, *conservative*, *feminist*, *chauvinist*, *intellectual*, or *brainless*? Examine your behavior with others. Make certain that you react to *people*, not to the categories in which you or others have placed them.

Too frequently we let words trigger our responses, shape our ideas, affect our attitudes, and direct our behavior, because we assume that words have magical or mystical powers that they do not really have. We foolishly transfer qualities implied by labels to the things those labels represent. Becoming conscious of how labels affect you is the first step in changing your attitudes toward them. Don't permit labels to blind you, mislead you, fool you, or imprison you.

IDENTIFY HOW THE WORDS YOU USE
REFLECT YOUR FEELINGS AND ATTITUDES

It is important to recognize that few of the words you select to describe things are neutral. S. I. Hayakawa, author of *Language in Thought and Action*, noted this:

> We are a little too dignified, perhaps, to growl like dogs, but we do the next best thing and substitute series of words, such as "You dirty double crosser!" "The filthy scum!" Similarly, if we are pleasurably agitated, we may, instead of purring or wagging the tail, say things like "She's the sweetest girl in all the world."[14]

Count the number of times you use "purr words" and "snarl words" each day. What do they reveal about your likes and dislikes? How do your words give you away?

We all use "snarl words" and "purr words." These words do not describe the people or things we are talking about; rather, they describe our personal feelings and attitudes. When we make statements like "He's a great American," "She's a dirty politician," "He's a bore," "She's a radical," "He's a Wall Street slicky," "She's a greedy conservative," "He's a male chauvinist pig," or "She's a crazy feminist," we should not delude ourselves into thinking that we are talking about anything but our own preferences. We are neither making reports nor describing conditions that necessarily exist. Instead, we are expressing our *attitudes* about something. Under such circumstances, if others are to determine what we mean by our descriptions, they are compelled to follow up and ask why.

It is also important to realize that a word which does not function as a snarl word or purr word for you may function that way for someone else, even if you did not intend it to be given such an interpretation. All that matters is the response of the person with whom you are interacting. Therefore, become conscious of how others react to words you use. Listen to people around you and attempt to "read" their responses to your words. Which words that incite them would not incite you? Which words do you find unacceptable or offensive? Why?

We all have our own meanings for words. When engaging in communication, however, we have to be concerned with how others will react to the words we use. We have to consider the possible meanings they may have for our words.

In order to accomplish this, you must make an honest effort to get to know the people with whom you interact. Become familiar with how their background could cause them to respond to certain words or phrases with hostility, anger, approval, or joy. Remember that your ability to communicate effectively with someone else can be affected—either positively or adversely—by the words you use.

IDENTIFY HOW EXPERIENCE CAN AFFECT MEANING

Since we assign meaning on the basis of our experience, and since no two people have had exactly the same set of experiences, it follows that no two people will have exactly the same meanings for the same word. This aspect of language should be neither lauded nor cursed; it should simply be remembered.

Too frequently, we let our words lead us away from where we want to go; we unwittingly antagonize our families, friends, or coworkers. We are infuriated, for example, when an important business deal collapses because our position has not been understood; or we are terrified when the leaders of government miscommunicate and put their countries on a collision course.[15]

In order to avoid or alleviate such problems, we must remember that meanings can change as the people who use words change. You might wear a sport jacket and slacks or a sweater and skirt if you are invited to a "casual" party, but this does not mean that everyone else who is invited to the party would interpret "casual" in the same way. One person might wear jeans and a sport shirt, another shorts and a T shirt. Likewise, you may feel that the word *freak* has only positive connotations, but this does not exclude the possibility that another person might think it has only negative connotations. The meanings people attribute to symbols are affected by their background, age, educational level, and work. Forgetting this can cause misunderstandings and lead to communication difficulties.

Be guided by the fact that the words in themselves have no meaning; remember that meaning resides in the minds of communicators. Try to identify how the life experiences of people with whom you communicate can cause them to respond to words in ways in which you would not respond. Remember that different responses are neither right nor wrong but simply different. Do not take your own language—or anyone else's language—for granted. Do not conclude that everyone thinks as you think or means what you mean. You know what a word means from your own frame of reference, but do you know what it means to someone with a different frame of reference? Take the time and have the patience to find out.

Since intended meanings are not necessarily the same as perceived meanings, you may need to ask people with whom you are speaking such questions as "What do you think about what I've just said?" or "What do my words mean to you?" Their answers can serve two important purposes: they help you determine whether you have been understood, and they permit the other people to become involved in the encounter by expressing their interpretations of your message. If differences in the assignment of meaning surface during this feedback process, you will be immediately able to clarify your meanings by substituting different symbols or by relating your thoughts more closely to the background, state of knowledge, and experiences of your receivers.

Keeping each of these guidelines in mind as you interact with others should help to improve your communication skills. If you recognize that every time you communicate with others you run the risk of being misunderstood, then you will be more likely to become sensitive to the ways in which your words affect those with whom you relate. As John Condon, author of *Semantics and Communication*, advises, "Learning to use language intelligently begins by learning not to be used by language."[16]

SUMMARY

Language is a unified system of symbols that permits a sharing of meaning. Language allows minds to meet, merge, and mesh. When we "make sense" out of people's messages, we learn to understand people.

There is no direct relationship between words and things, as Ogden and Richard's triangle of meaning illustrates. Words don't "mean"; people give meaning to words. A serious barrier to communication is the fact that different people give different meanings to the same words. Words change over time, from place to place, and according to individual experience, and across cultures. Gender also influences the ways men and women process language.

Among the communication problems that result from changes in meaning are bypassing (when people think they understand each other but in fact do not) and mistaking a label for the thing itself (taking an intensional rather than an extensional orientation).

There are two strategies we can use to improve our oral language abilities. First, we can use common sense to recognize that certain styles of language are appropriate at certain times and in certain places. Second, we can seek to make ourselves as clear as possible by selecting words with meaning for our listeners, taking account of their educational level and the sublanguages they understand.

SUGGESTIONS FOR FURTHER READING

Bavelas, Janet Beavin, Alex Black, Nicole Charil, and Jennifer Mullet: *Equivocal Communication*, Sage, Newbury Park, Calif., 1990. Explores the complex nature and diverse consequences of equivocal communication.

Chase, Stuart: *The Power of Words*, Harcourt Brace Jovanovich, New York, 1953. A very readable description of some of the semantic problems that plague us.

Condon, John C.: *Semantics and Communication*, 2d ed., Macmillan, New York, 1975. Contains a good discussion of barriers to verbal interaction.

Haney, William V.: *Communication and Organizational Behavior*, 3d ed., Irwin, Homewood, Ill., 1973. A clear discussion of the misevaluations that impede communication.

Hayakawa, S. I., and Alan R. Hayakawa: *Language, Thought, and Action*, 5th ed., Harcourt Brace Jovanovich, New York, 1990. A comprehensive study of general semantics. The book contains many useful exercises.

Newman, Edwin: *A Civil Tongue*, Bobbs-Merrill, Indianapolis, Ind., 1976. Contains wonderful examples of semantic "atrocities."

Ogden, C. K., and I. A. Richards: *The Meaning of Meaning*, Harcourt Brace Jovanovich, New York, 1930. A classic work. Scholarly discussion of the nature of meaning.

Pearson, Judy Corneila: *Gender and Communication*, Brown, Dubuque, Iowa, 1985. A scholarly compilation about how gender affects communication.

Tannen, Deborah: *You Just Don't Understand*, Ballantine, New York, 1990. A very readable account of the different ways men and women communicate.

Walther, George R.: *Power Talking: Fifty Ways to Say What You Mean and Get What You Want*. Putnam, New York, 1991. Describes the difference between powerless and powerful verbal expression. Filled with anecdotes and examples.

Whorf, Benjamin Lee: "Science and Linguistics," in John B. Carroll (ed.), *Language, Thought and Reality: Selected Writings of Benjamin Lee Whorf*, M. I. T. Press, Cambridge, Mass., 1966. Explores how thinking and language are related.

NOTES

1. C. K. Ogden and I. A. Richards, *The Meaning of Meaning*, Harcourt Brace Jovanovich, New York, 1930.

2. Charles F. Vich and Ray V. Wood, "Similarity of Past Experience and the Communication of Meaning," *Speech Monographs*, vol. 36, pp. 159–162.

3. Nicholas D. Kristof, "Chinese Relations," *The New York Times Magazine*, August 18, 1991, pp. 8–10.

4. A. Mulac, J. Bradac, and S. Mann, "Male/Female Language Differences and Attributional Consequences in Children's Television," *Human Communication Research*, vol. 11, 1985, pp. 481–506.

5. Patricia Hayes Bradley, "The Folk-Linguistics of Women's Speech: An Empirical Examination," *Communication Monographs*, 48, pp. 73–90.

6. Nancy M. Henley and Cheris Kramarae, "Gender, Power and Miscommunication," in Nickolas Coupland, Howard Giles, and John Weimann (eds.), *Miscommunication and Problematic Talk*, Sage, Newbury Park, Calif., 1991, p. 42.

7. Deborah Tannen, *You Just Don't Understand*, Ballantine, New York, 1991, p. 42.

8. Craig Johnson and Larry Vinson, "Placement and Frequency of Powerless Talk and Impression Formation," *Communication Quarterly*, vol. 38, no. 4, Fall 1990, p. 325.

9. See William V. Haney, *Communication and Organizational Behavior*, 3d ed., Irwin, Homewood, Ill., 1973, pp. 247–248.

10. Benjamin Lee Whorf, "Science and Linguistics," in John B. Carroll (ed.), *Language, Thought and Reality: Selected Writings of Benjamin Lee Whorf*, M. I. T. Press, Cambridge, Mass., 1966.

11. For a discussion of names and how they affect us, see Mary Marcus, "The Power of a Name," *Psychology Today*, October 1976, pp. 75–76, 108.

12. For a more complete discussion of this incident, see Robert B. Cialdini, *Influence*, Quill, New York, 1984, pp. 15–27.

13. Stewart Chase, *The Power of Words*, Harcourt Brace Jovanovich, New York, 1953.

14. S. I. Hayakawa and Alan R. Hayakawa, *Language in Thought and Action*, 5th ed., Harcourt Brace Jovanovich, New York, 1990.

15. For more information see *Time*, vol. 136, no. 26, December 17, 1990, p. 114.

16. John Condon, *Semantics and Communication*, 3d ed. Macmillan, New York, 1985.

CHAPTER 5

NONVERBAL COMMUNICATION: SILENT LANGUAGE SPEAKS

After finishing this chapter, you should be able to:

Define *nonverbal communication*

Explain why nonverbal cues can be ambiguous

Define *kinesics*

Explain why the face is an important source of information

Demonstrate how the face is used to send emotionally charged messages

Explain the meaning of *microfacial expressions*

Provide examples of the kinds of messages communicated by postural cues

Explain how clothing can affect communication

Define *paralanguage*; explain how pitch, volume, rate, and pause affect communication

Define *proxemics*

Distinguish between intimate distance, personal distance, social distance, and public distance

Explain why territoriality is an important concept in communication

Describe how color can be used to communicate

Explain the types of messages communicated by touch

Assess your own effectiveness as a nonverbal communicator

Arthur Conan Doyle's most famous character, the detective Sherlock Holmes, frequently used to tell Dr. Watson, "You see, but you do not *observe*." The meaning of this statement is contained in a bit of pithy Holmesian advice: "By a man's finger nails, by his coat-sleeve, by his boots, by his trouser-knees, by the callosites on his forefinger and thumb, by his shirt-cuffs—by each of these things a man's calling is plainly revealed. That all united should fail to enlighten the competent inquirer in any case is almost inconceivable." Sherlock Holmes was of course a fictional creation, able to solve the most perplexing crimes because he noticed minute details that elude most people. His method can be profitably applied to real-life situations and specifically to our study of communication.

COMMUNICATING WITHOUT WORDS

The founder of psychoanalysis, Sigmund Freud, once wrote, "He that has eyes to see and ears to hear may convince himself that no mortal can keep a secret. If his lips are silent, he chatters with his fingertips; betrayal oozes out of him at every pore." Our creative problem-solving abilities are often challenged as we seek to make sense out of communication situations. The following is a mystery that challenged many human minds.

In turn-of-the-century Berlin, a man named Von Osten purchased a horse, which he named Hans. Von Osten trained Hans, not to jump, stand on his hind legs, or even dance, but to count by tapping a front hoof. To his master's astonishment the horse learned to count very quickly, and in a short time Hans also learned to add, multiply, divide, and subtract.

Von Osten exhibited Hans at fairs and carnivals, and the crowds loved it when the horse would correctly count the number of people in the audience, the number of people wearing eyeglasses, or the number of people wearing hats. In addition, Hans thrilled observers by telling time and announcing the date—all by tapping his hoof. Von Osten later decided to teach Hans the alphabet: *A* was one hoof, *B* two taps, and so on. Once he learned this, Hans was able to reply to both oral and written questions, and his proficiency earned him the nickname "Clever Hans."

Naturally, some people who heard about the feats of "Clever Hans" were skeptical and reasoned that no horse could do these things and so there must be some trickery involved. Eventually, a committee was charged with deciding whether there was any deceit involved in Hans's performances. On the committee were professors of psychology and physiology, the head of the Berlin Zoo, a circus director, veterinarians, and cavalry officers. Van Osten was not permitted to be present when the committee tested the horse, but despite the absence of his trainer, Hans was able to answer all the questions put to him. The committee decided that there was no trickery.

Some skeptics, however, were still not satisfied, and so a second investigation was conducted by a new committee. This time, however, the procedures were changed. Von Osten was asked to whisper into Hans's left ear; then another experimenter named Pfungst whispered a number into Hans's right ear. Hans was instructed to add the two numbers—an answer none of the observers, Von Osten, or Pfungst knew. Hans couldn't do it. It seems that Hans could answer a question only if someone in his visual field knew the answer to it.

Why do you suppose Hans had to see someone who knew the answer? Apparently, when the horse was asked a question that all the observers had heard, the observers assumed an *expectant posture* and increased their body tension. When Hans had tapped the correct number of hoofbeats, the observers would relax and move their heads slightly—cues Hans used in order to know when to stop tapping. Thus somehow the horse had the ability to respond to the almost imperceptible movements of people around him. Much as you are able to sense when someone wants you to stop talking or when it is time for you to leave a party, Hans was able to interpret the nonverbal messages of onlookers.

Whether or not we are aware of it, we all communicate nonverbally. The theorists Albert Mehrabian, Mark Knapp, and Ray Birdwhistell agree that in a normal two-person conversation the verbal channel carries less than 35 percent of the social meaning of a message; this means that more than 65 percent of the meaning is communicated nonverbally.[1] (See Figure 5-1.) By analyzing nonverbal cues, we can enhance our understanding of what is really being said when people talk. The nonverbal level can also help us define the nature of each relationship we share with someone else. With practice, we can learn to use the nonverbal mode to provide us with "ways of knowing" that would not otherwise be available to us.[2]

The goal of this chapter is to help you increase your awareness of nonverbal stimuli and expand your ability to use the nonverbal cues you perceive. This increased awareness and ability will help you immeasurably in becoming a more effective communicator.

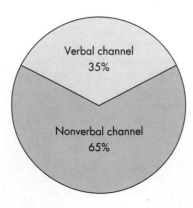

FIGURE 5-1
Communication of social meaning.

CHARACTERISTICS OF NONVERBAL COMMUNICATION:
CUES AND CONTEXTS

105

CHAPTER 5
NONVERBAL
COMMUNICATION:
SILENT LANGUAGE SPEAKS

What is nonverbal communication? How do you recognize it? How can you become a "detective," perceiving and interpreting nonverbal cues? The term *nonverbal communication* designates all the kinds of human responses not expressed in words. This includes a wide range of behaviors. Bernard Gunther, in his book *Sense Relaxation below Your Mind*, has identified some of the factors we should be concerned with when analyzing human communication—our own messages and other people's:

Shaking hands	Your smile
Your posture	How close you stand to others
Facial expressions	How you listen
Your appearance	Your confidence
Voice tone	Your breathing
Hair style	The way you move
Your clothes	The way you stand
The expression in your eyes	How you touch other people

These aspects of you affect your relationship with other people, often without you and them realizing it. . . .

The body talks, its message is how you really are, not how you think you are. . . .

Many in our culture reach forward from the neck because they are anxious to get a-head. Others hold their necks tight; afraid to lose their head. Body language is literal.[3]

Gunther is correct in observing that we communicate with our bodies and appearance. However, nonverbal content is even more extensive than he indicates. We also communicate by sending messages through the environment we create and live in. If, for example, someone entered and walked through your house or apartment at this very moment, what assumptions would they be able to make about you and your family? The spaces we inhabit broadcast information about us to others, even when we are not in them. For instance, are you sloppy or tidy? Do you like roominess, or do you crave the security of cozy places? How you dress your environment and how you dress yourself provide clues about your role, status, age, and goals. Your voice also carries information about you.

Nonverbal communication is perpetual and, frequently, involuntary. We noted in Chapter 1 that, as Paul Watzlawick, author of *Pragmatics of Human Communication*, points out, "no matter how hard one may try, one cannot not communicate." You cannot stop sending nonverbal messages; you cannot stop behaving. As long as one person is observing the actions of another, it is impossible not to communicate. Even if one partner in a conversation suddenly leaves the room, he or she is communicating. If you put a paper bag over your head or sat in class completely encased in a sack, you would still be communicating with those around you. You are communicating nonverbally right now.

For the next 2 minutes, face another person and try not to communicate anything to him or her. What happened? Did you look at each other? Look away? Giggle? Smile? Fidget?

Say "I am really glad to be here," but meanwhile do everything you can to indicate the opposite. What means did you use? Tone of voice? Posture? Facial expressions?

If, at this very moment, someone were to photograph you, what could others surmise by examining the photograph? How are you sitting? Where are you sitting? How are you dressed? What would your facial expression reveal about your reaction to this chapter?

Like verbal communication, nonverbal communication is ambiguous. (Think about the example we just gave—the photograph of yourself reading this chapter. Would different people interpret the photograph in the same way?) Like words, nonverbal messages may not mean what we think they do. Thus, we have to be careful not to misinterpret them. Don't be surprised if you find that the real reason a person glanced at a clock, left a meeting early, or arrived late for class is quite different from what you assumed. It is simply not possible to develop a list of nonverbal behaviors and attach a single meaning to each. All nonverbal communication must be evaluated or interpreted *within the context in which it occurs*. You cannot "read" a person "like a book," nor can others always "read" you. Still, you should realize that those you interact with will attribute meaning to your behavior and make important judgments and decisions on the basis of their observations.

Furthermore, verbal and nonverbal messages can be—and often are—contradictory. When we say one thing but do another, we send a "mixed," or incongruent, message. As you become aware of the nonverbal cues you and others send, you will begin to recognize contradictory messages that impede communication. Wherever you detect an incongruity between *verbal* (word-level) messages, you would probably benefit by paying greater attention to the *nonverbal* messages. Researchers in communication believe that nonverbal cues are more difficult to fake than verbal cues—hence the importance of examining the nonverbal dimension.

If we are going to rely on the nonverbal mode, we must understand it. The following section considers important features of nonverbal communication.

ASPECTS OF NONVERBAL COMMUNICATION

In order to arrive at a better understanding of communication and develop skills that will permit us to both send and receive cues more accurately, we will examine the following areas:

Body language (kinesics)
Clothing
Voice (paralanguage)
Space and distance (proxemic and environmental factors)
Colors
Time
Touch (haptics)

The types of messages that fall within these categories do not occur in isolation; they interact, sometimes supporting and sometimes contradicting one another.

In this section, we will examine these areas separately. In "Assessing Your Effectiveness as a Nonverbal Communicator" later in this chapter (see page 137), we will bring them together so that you can reassemble the nonverbal "puzzle."

Body Language: Kinesics

The study of body communication has received much attention. *Kinesics*—body motion, or *body language*, as it is popularly called—typically includes facial expression (particularly eyebrows, forehead, eyes, and mouth), posture, and gestures. Thus hand movements, a surprised stare, drooping shoulders, a knowing smile, and a tilt of the head are all part of kinesics.

FACIAL EXPRESSIONS

To a large extent, we send messages with our facial muscles. Why is the face so important? First, it is our main channel for communicating our own emotions and for analyzing the feelings and sentiments of others. This is one reason why motion picture and television directors use so many close-ups. Television is often referred to as the "medium of talking heads." It is the face that is relied on to reinforce or contradict what is being communicated through dialogue. Likewise, in your personal relations your face and the faces of those around you broadcast inner feelings and emotions.

Did you know that the 80 muscles in the face can create more than 7,000 expressions?

How well do you read faces? Research has shown that many people are able to decipher facial cues with great accuracy but others lack this ability. It has been proposed that unpopularity, poor grades, and a variety of other problems that plague schoolchildren may be attributed to inability to read the nonverbal messages of teachers and peers. According to the psychologist Stephen Norwicki, "Because they are unaware of the messages they are sending, or misinterpret how other children are feeling, unpopular children may not even realize that they are initiating many of the negative reactions they receive from their peers."[4] Your ability to read someone's face increases when you know the person, understand the context of the interaction, and are able to compare and contrast the person's facial expressions with others you have seen him or her make.

Of all the nonverbal channels, the face is the single most important broadcaster of emotions. You may be able to hide your hands, and you may choose to keep silent, but you cannot hide your face without making people feel you are attempting to deceive them. Since we cannot "put the face away," we take great pains to control the expressions we reveal to others.

How do we do this? To control our facial behavior, we can intensify, deintensify, neutralize, or attempt to mask an emotion. When we *intensify* an emotion, we exaggerate our facial responses to meet what we believe to be the expectations of others who are watching us. Have you ever pretended you loved a gift so as not to disappoint the giver, when in reality you couldn't stand it? When we *deintensify* an emotion, we deemphasize our facial behaviors so that others will judge our reactions to be more appropriate. Were you ever very angry with a professor but compelled to restrain yourself because you feared

To a large extent, we send messages through our facial expressions.

Anthony Edgeworth/The Stock Market

the professor's response if you let your anger show, the way you would with a good friend? When we *neutralize* an emotion, we avoid displaying it at all. Sometimes neutralization is an attempt to display strength, as when we are saddened by the death of a relative but want to appear brave. In our culture men neutralize fear and sadness more frequently than women do. This suppression, or *internalization*, may account for the fact that men have more ulcers than women do. Finally, when we *mask* an emotion, we replace it with another to which we believe others will respond more favorably. Thus, we sometimes conceal feelings of jealousy, disappointment, or rage. George Orwell spoke of the need for masking in his novel *1984:*

Have you ever been guilty of "facecrime"? Were you punished? Should you have been? Why or why not?

> It was terribly dangerous to let your thoughts wander when you were in any public place or within range of a telescreen. The smallest thing could give you away. A nervous tic, an unconscious look of anxiety, a habit of muttering to yourself—anything that carried with it the suggestion of abnormality, of having something to hide. In any case, to wear an improper expression on your face (to look incredulous when a victory was announced, for example), was itself a punishable offense. There was even a word for it in Newspeak: *facecrime,* it was called.[5]

Facially, we may at any time—without realizing it—be communicating multiple emotions rather than one. The researchers Paul Ekman and Wallace Friesen call these facial movements "affect blends."[6] The presence or absence of certain affect blends may help explain why we feel comfortable around some people and uncomfortable around others. It seems that some expressions appear on the face for only a fraction of a second. Thus, what began as a smile may ever so briefly become a grimace and then may be transformed into a smile. These changes may last no more than one-eighth to one-fifth of a second. Researchers call these fleeting emotional displays *microfacial* or *micromomentary expressions*.[7] Microfacial expressions were discovered with slow-motion techniques. What escaped the naked eye at normal speed (24 frames per second) became visible when the film was slowed (to 4 frames per second). Micromomentary expressions are believed to reveal actual emotional states and usually occur when a person is consciously or unconsciously attempting to conceal or disguise an emotion or feeling. Although microexpressions may be little more than a twitch of the mouth or an eyebrow, they can indicate to observers that the message a sender is trying to transmit is not the message the sender is thinking.

By now you are probably beginning to realize the importance of observing facial expressions. But what should you watch for? Read on.

For purposes of analysis, a person's face can be divided into three general areas: (1) the eyebrows and forehead, (2) the eyes, and (3) the mouth. Let us focus on each separately.

How can you use facial cues to determine if others—including your boss, coworkers, and friends—are being honest with you?

When the face assumes an expression of anger, fear, or sadness, the heart rate increases. According to psychologist Robert Levenson, this is because emotions are often associated with a need to behave in a certain way on very short notice. For example, anger and fear are associated with either fighting or fleeing—both of which start the heart pumping.

✔ SKILL BUILDER

FACIAL BROADCAST

1. Choose a partner. Each of you in turn should select at random one of these emotions: happiness, sadness, anger, surprise.

2. Turn away from your partner and formulate a facial expression that you believe portrays the emotion selected. Turn back to your partner, who is to guess the emotion you are portraying. Reverse roles and repeat the exercise. What is it about your partner's face that causes you to identify one feeling rather than another? What did your partner's eyes tell you? Mouth? Nose? Repeat this step a number of times, alternating roles. Your goal during each round is to analyze how various facial features and their positions help broadcast emotions.

3. Now challenge yourselves by adding the following emotions to the list:

Shame	Love
Despair	Sorrow
Humiliation	Rage
Disgust	Astonishment
Coyness	Nervousness

To what extent were the emotions in the second set more difficult for the "performer"? For the "observer"? How accurate were your observations?

Eyebrows and Forehead If you raise your eyebrows, what emotion are you showing? Surprise is probably most common; but fear may also be expressed by raised eyebrows, and when we are experiencing fear, the duration of the movement will probably be longer.

The brows help express other emotions as well. Right now, move your brows into as many different configurations as you can. With each movement analyze your emotional response. What do the brows communicate?

The forehead also helps communicate your physical and emotional state. A furrowed brow suggests tension, worry, or deep thought. A sweating forehead suggests nervousness or great effort.

Eyes The second of the three areas is the eyes. Ralph Waldo Emerson noted, perceptively, "The eyes of men converse at least as much as their tongues."

What do your eyes reveal to others? Various eye movements are associated with emotional expressions: a downward glance suggests modesty; staring suggests coldness; wide eyes suggest wonder, naiveté, honesty, or fright; and excessive blinking suggests nervousness and insecurity. Researchers have also shown that as we begin to take an interest in something, our blinking rate decreases and our pupils dilate.

As an example, consider this:

> Anthropologist Edward T. Hall says PLO leader Yasir Arafat wears dark glasses to take advantage of the pupil response—to keep others from reading his reactions by watching the pupils of his eyes dilate.
>
> Hall is an authority on face-to-face contact between persons of different cultures. In an interview on understanding Arab culture, he says a University of Chicago psychologist discovered the role pupils play as sensitive indicators. Hall says Eckhard Hess found pupils dilate when you are interested in something but tend to contract if something is said that you dislike.
>
> ". . . The Arabs have known about the pupil response for hundreds if not thousands of years," Hall says. "Since people can't control the response of their eyes, which is a dead giveaway, many Arabs, like Arafat, wear dark glasses, even indoors."[8]

Like pupil response, the direction of eye gaze provides interesting insights. For example, have you considered in what direction people look when they are not looking directly at you—and what that might signify? Richard Bandler and John Grinder, two of the founders of neurolinguistic programming, have developed a number of interesting theories. They suggest that people look in one direction when they try to *remember* something and in another direction when they try to *invent* something. To test their hypotheses, try this with a partner: Face each other. One person asks the second the following series of questions; the second person should only *think* of a response to each. When asking the questions, watch for any patterns in the direction your partner looks while thinking of a response.

Questions That Evoke Visually Remembered Images

What color are the carpets in your car?

What color are your mother's eyes?

What color is your instructor's hair?

Questions That Evoke Visually Invented Images

How would you look from my point of view?

How would you look in purple and green hair?

What would your home look like after it had been ravaged by fire?

Questions That Evoke Auditorily Remembered Images

Can you hear your favorite music?

Can you hear music you dislike?

What are the first four notes of Beethoven's Fifth Symphony?

Questions That Evoke Auditorily Invented Images

How would your dog sound singing "Mary Had a Little Lamb"?

What would King Kong sound like tiptoeing through the tulips?

Bandler and Grinder suggest that a right-handed person will look in the directions shown in Figure 5-2. Do your experiences confirm their findings? Could a lawyer or negotiator ask questions and then use these findings to determine whether the person answering had invented the reply? Could a CIA agent use the technique to determine if a paid informant was telling the truth? If the findings are valid, presumably the answer is yes. The agent, for example, could inquire about where hostages were being held: "What does the house look like? Did you see Islamic Jihad members there?" If the informant looked up and to the right, he or she might be creating images rather than actually remembering; in other words, the informant might be lying. Try this experiment yourself.

Whatever your conclusions about the experiment, it is important to maintain eye contact with others to recognize not only when others are not looking at you but also where they are looking, because each cue provides you with potential information about people's unconscious processes and how they internally access data.

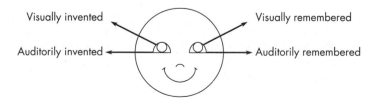

Visually invented   Visually remembered

Auditorily invented   Auditorily remembered

FIGURE 5-2
How direction of gaze varies according to the nature of the item under consideration.

"Perhaps the witness would care to reconsider his answer to the last question?"

Drawing by Stevenson; © 1979 The New Yorker Magazine, Inc.

When we communicate with others—whether in school, on the job, at home, or on a date—"eye accessing" cues are a channel we can use to help make sense of their behavior. Because these cues are not consciously controlled, they will seldom mislead us.

Another eye cue that helps reveal what is on a person's mind is the eye blink. In an article titled "In the Blink of an Eye," Shawna Vogel notes:

> Someone should have told Richard Nixon that his eyelids were giving him away. On August 22, 1973, during his first nationally televised press conference since the Senate's Watergate investigation began six months earlier, the president maintained a calm, controlled tone of voice. But in answering such pointed questions as, "Is there any limitation on the president, short of impeachment, to compel the production of evidence?" Nixon's eyes became a blur. In an average minute he blinked 30 to 40 times. Unimpeachable adults blink only about 10 to 20 times a minute, and even that may be excessive; studies on infants show that the physical need to blink comes just once every two minutes.[9]

How long we look or gaze at a person or thing also communicates a message. In our culture it is deemed acceptable to stare at animals and inanimate objects, such as paintings or sculptures, but rude to stare at people. (Julius Fast, author of the popular book *Body Language*, suggests that we stare at individuals we believe to be "nonpersons."[10]) Instead of staring at others, we are supposed to practice "civil inattention," avoiding sustained eye contact and letting our eyes rest only momentarily on people (in other words, "keeping our eyes to ourselves"). Although it is permissible to look at someone we do not know for 1 or 2 seconds, after that we are expected to "move our eyes along." Notice your own eye behavior the next time you walk down a street. Your eyes will probably wander from face to face. However, if you and a stranger happen to make eye contact while approaching one another from opposite directions, at least one of you will redirect his or her gaze before you actually get too close. If we look at people for a long time, it may make them fidgety and uncomfortable or may seem to imply that we are challenging them. Have you ever innocently rested your eyes on a stranger who then demanded "What are you staring at? You want to start something?"

Despite "civil inattention," in any gathering the first thing most people do is eye one another. Eye contact is important in communication because it gives us certain information. First, it gives us feedback on how we are coming across to others in interpersonal and public situations. Eye contact can indicate that the communication channel is open. It is much easier to avoid talking or listening to people if we have not made eye contact with them. (According to the researchers Michael Argyle and Janet Dean, eye contact almost makes interaction an obligation.[11]) Eye contact between people can also offer clues to the kind of relationship they share. For one thing, it can signal our need for inclusion or affiliation. People who have a high need for affiliation will frequently return the glances of others. There is a high degree of eye contact between people who like each other. We also increase eye contact when communicating with others if the physical distance between us is increased.

What is communicated if eye contact is missing? Lack of eye contact can cause others to think that we are trying to hide something or that we do not like them. It can also suggest that two people are in competition with each other. Others may interpret its absence as signifying either boredom or simply a desire to end an interaction. How do you rate your own eye contact? When are you a looker and when are you a nonlooker?

Of course, we must keep in mind that eye contact is related to culture. Some cultures use eye contact more than we do; other cultures use it less. Arabs, for example, engage in more direct eye contact, and the Japanese in less eye contact, than is typical of Americans. The Japanese, in fact, believe that prolonged eye contact is a sign of disrespect; Japanese children learn at an early age to avoid direct eye contact and to direct their gaze to the area of the Adam's apple instead.[12]

The fact is, the eyes have much to tell us.

Mouth   Like the eyes, the lower facial area has much to communicate. For example, some people smile with just the mouth and lips. For others, like Bette Midler, the smile appears to consume the entire face. As a child, were you ever told to "wipe that smile off your face"? Why? Besides happiness, what can a smile communicate?

How does your face look when you are not smiling—when it is at rest? Some faces have a neutral expression; others have a frown, snarl, or habitual smile—that is, the corners of the mouth seem to normally turn up. (One of

How does eye contact or lack of eye contact affect your interactions with others? You can explore this by using the following experimental "conditions" when talking to others: (1) Keep your eyes on the floor. (2) Glance around continually. (3) Stare at the other person's face. (4) Look at the other person's waist. (5) Maintain comfortable eye contact. Report your findings to the class.

WEDDED FACES
Holly Hall

As is commonly believed, husbands and wives do grow to look alike reports psychologist Robert B. Zajonc.

With several of his graduate students, Zajonc collected facial photographs from husbands and wives in 12 Midwestern couples. Half the photos were taken when the couples first married, half about 25 years later. College undergraduates rated youthful and older pairs of these faces for either their resemblance to one another or for the likelihood that the individuals depicted were married.

With younger faces, students did no better than chance would predict at identifying the husbands and wives. However, "after 25 years the two spouses [were] perceived as more similar in appearance . . . and more likely to be married to each other."

Why should married people look more alike with time? Earlier studies suggest that people in close proximity tend to mimic one another's facial expressions, the researchers say. Daily mimicry among spouses, they write, "would leave wrinkles around the mouth and eyes, alter the bearing of the head, and the overall expression. Eventually [it] would produce . . . changes that make spouses appear more similar than they originally were."

Not only do emotions influence our facial expressions, but in a controversial theory Zajonc has proposed that facial expressions also help produce emotions. Tensing or relaxing facial muscles, he says, can alter the flow of blood to the brain, in turn regulating the release of various neurochemicals that may influence our moods. In this way, mimicked facial expressions may aid spouses in empathizing with one another, since such imitation could lead to shared emotions.

If empathy is gained from facial mimicry, couples who have grown more alike in appearance should have better marriages. In fact the researchers found that the greater the resemblance between spouses, the greater their happiness with their marriage.

The researchers believe that their results may also explain similarities in appearance between other family members. As with married partners, sons and daughters also share a close environment and are vulnerable to the effects of mimicry. Resemblance among family members "may be more than a matter of common genes," the researchers say.

Source: From "Wedded Faces" by Holly Hall, *Psychology Today*, December 1987. Reprinted with permission from Psychology Today Magazine. Copyright © 1987 (Sussex Publishers, Inc.).

your authors had a student who grinned constantly. He could have been told that he had failed the course, and he would still have appeared to grin.)

When you choose to smile, how do people react to your smile? People often find that others will return a smile to those who smile at them but will look away from, or avoid stopping to speak to, a person whose lips are pursed in a frown. To what extent do your experiences confirm this?

Both men and women tend to smile when seeking approval; but in general, women smile more frequently than men do. Women tend to smile even when given negative messages. Why do you think this is so?

Many options are available for expressing emotions through facial expressions. As you watch television actors, comedians, and performers, examine how they use facial expressions. Facial cues communicate a large portion of the messages you send to others. In fact, the researcher Albert Mehrabian has concluded that while verbal and vocal cues are used extensively to help transmit meaning, the face is relied on to an even greater extent than either of these.[13]

Even though women smile more in general than men do, young children think that the smile of a male is friendlier than the smile of a female. Do you agree? Explain.

How many times have you heard the following admonitions?

"Stand up straight!"

"Don't slouch!"

"Why are you slumping?"

"Get your feet off the furniture!"

"Keep your shoulders back!"

"Why are you hunched over that desk?"

When do you stand erect? When do you slouch? What kinds of nonverbal messages does your posture send to others? What conditions cause you to tense up? What conditions allow you to relax? The way we hold ourselves when sitting or standing is a nonverbal broadcast, giving others information that they use to assess our thoughts and feelings.

Describe the posture you consider appropriate for a corporate president.

Although bodily position will not mean precisely the same thing to every observer, research has provided us with enough information to reach some general conclusions about how others are likely to interpret our posture. Nancy Henley, in her book *Body Politics*, suggests that "the *bearing* with which one presents onself proclaims one's position in life."[14] Television and film support this premise by frequently contrasting the upright bearing of a wealthy person with the submissive shuffle of a servant or the slumped demeanor of a "nobody." In line with this, Albert Mehrabian has found that when people are compelled to assume inferior roles, they reflect this by lowering their heads. In contrast, when they are assuming superior roles, people often raise their heads.

Each of us has certain expectations regarding what postures we expect others to display. For instance, a high-ranking military officer would probably adopt an extremely straight and somewhat "official" posture. Henley suggests that "standing tall" in and of itself helps a person achieve dominance. Judith Anderson achieved fame by performing roles of dominant women in Shakespearean and Greek tragedies. Although she was slight in stature, her posture and bearing were such that she seemed to fill the stage.

As a communicator you will want to develop a posture appropriate to and supportive of your goals and aspirations. Stooped shoulders can indicate that you are heavily burdened or submissive; raised shoulders suggest that you are under a great deal of stress. To Americans, square shoulders usually suggest strength. Our emotions or moods and physical bearing are closely related. This relationship is expressed through the verbal idioms that have developed through the years. It is said that we "shoulder a burden," have "no backbone," keep our "chin up," or "shrug off problems." The way we carry ourselves can affect the way we feel and the way others perceive us just as much as the way we feel can affect the way we carry ourselves.

The last aspect of posture we will consider is the way we lean, or orient ourselves, when we communicate. If you were speaking to someone who suddenly turned or leaned away from you, would you consider that a positive sign? Probably not. We usually associate liking and other positive attitudes with lean-

An important aspect of posture is how we lean when communicating. Leaning forward tends to be associated with positive attitudes, such as interest and liking.

Charles Gupton/Stock, Boston

Recall an instance when posture affected your perception of someone else.

"Try on" various postures and see what you feel like in each. To what degree does each posture affect your emotional state?

ing forward, not withdrawing. The next time an interesting bit of gossip is discussed in the cafeteria, notice how most of the listeners, if not all, will lean *forward* to ensure that they do not miss even one detail of the story. When you are communicating with others, a slight forward tilt of your upper body may indicate that you are interested in what they have to say. Mehrabian found that we lean either left or right when communicating with a person of lower status than ourselves. This right or left leaning is a part of our more relaxed demeanor.[15]

Remember that body posture talks. The messages you send by the way you carry yourself vary and reflect whether you are feeling content and confident, angry and belligerent, or worried and discouraged. Your posture helps signal whether you are ready to approach and meet the world or whether you want to avoid and withdraw from it. Equally important, how you hold yourself also helps define the way you feel about others with whom you are communicating.

POSTURE POSES

For this exercise the class is divided into groups of three. Each of you will assume in turn that you are a photographer and that the other two group members are your models. You will pose your models to demonstrate a variety of relationships. The models' arms will remain at their sides, but you may position them to sit or stand; to slump or straighten; and to lean forward, backward, or to either side. Position your models to show one of the relationships listed at the right.

After each "photographer" sets up the models, the remaining class members should attempt to guess which relationship is being displayed. Discuss the cues you used to portray your choices.

Relationships:

Servant and employer

Waiter and customer

Two people who are romantically involved

Two boxers before a fight

Boss and secretary

Instructor and student who is failing

Your choice

GESTURES

The movements of our arms, legs, hands, and feet constitute another important way in which we broadcast nonverbal data. For instance, the way you position your arms transmits information about your attitudes. Cross your arms in front of you. Do you feel closed off from the world? Stand up and put your hands on your hips. How does this stance make you feel? (You may remind yourself of the old stereotype of an army sergeant.) Next, clasp your arms behind your back in a self-assured manner. Then hold your arms stiffly at your sides, as if you were a nervous speaker or a wooden soldier. Finally, dangle your arms at your sides in a relaxed fashion. Become aware of the arm positions that you habitually use. What message does each of these various positions communicate?

Our legs also convey information about us. Try standing as a model would stand. Next, sit down and put your feet up on a desk or table. Then stand with your feet wide apart. Does this last stance make you feel more powerful? Why? Return to a more comfortable position. Shift your weight forward toward the front of your feet. Then rock back so that your weight is on your heels. Watch someone else do this. Does the forward position communicate more energy and enthusiasm? The distribution of body weight and the placement of legs and feet can broadcast stability, femininity, masculinity, anger, happiness, or any number of other qualities. For a communication encounter, choose the stance that most accurately reflects your goals.

It is important to recognize, however, that gestures do not have universal meanings. The meaning one culture gives to a gesture may be very different

Gestures—such as
movements of the arms
and hands—convey a
great deal of nonverbal
information.

Bob Daemmrich/Stock,
Boston

from the meaning another culture gives it. Consider, for example, our "OK" gesture made by forming a circle with the thumb and forefinger. To most Americans, this joining of thumb and forefinger signifies that all is positive; the French and Belgians would interpret the gesture as meaning "you're worth zero."[16]

In summary, it can be said that *gestures* are motions of your limbs or body that you use to express or accentuate your moods and ideas, and that they are culturally related.

Clothing

In addition to body language (facial expressions, posture, and gestures), our style of dress is an important nonverbal cue. Since we adorn our bodies with clothes, decisions about clothing face us every day. "I can't decide what to wear!" "What should I wear?" "What are you wearing?" Some people choose their clothes very carefully; others just seem to "throw on" whatever is at hand.[17] Some of us enjoy shopping for clothes; others have to be dragged to clothing stores. Even careful attention to dress, however, does not guarantee appropriate choices. Have you found yourself extremely overdressed or underdressed for an occasion? How did you feel? Were you able to augment your outfit or take off some part of it to fit in with what everyone else was wearing?

How we dress is extremely important in creating a first impression. What first impressions do people receive from your clothes? What impression would you like to create? It should be apparent that your dress, and your chosen image, should change as your role changes. Automobile mechanics must create the impression that they can repair your car, and corporate presidents must give the impression that they can lead the company through an uncertain fu-

The same dress is indecent 10 years before its time; daring 1 year before its time; chic—that is, characterized by contemporary seductiveness—in its time; dowdy 3 years after its time; hideous 20 years after its time; amusing 30 years after its time; romantic 100 years after its time; and beautiful 150 years after its time.

James Laver

ture. As the caretakers of our health, doctors must inspire confidence. In other words, like it or not, the role we play to some extent dictates the "uniform" we wear. Some organizations, such as fast-food outlets and the armed services, require their employees to wear specific articles of clothing. Most other workers are given some latitude in their choice of dress, although dress codes are followed to a certain extent. John T. Molloy, the author of *Dress for Success* and *The Woman's Dress for Success Book*, gathered data from numerous studies in which people offered their first impressions of the attire of others. Molloy has identified the kinds of clothing he claims should be worn by people who want to become managers or executives. For men, he suggests dark blue pinstripe suits to add a feeling of authority. Dark gray is also accepted as executive attire. Molloy has also created a "uniform" for women in business. The basic outfit is summed up in this statement, which many of the women in Molloy's seminars adopted: "I pledge to wear a highly tailored, dark-colored, traditionally designed, skirted suit whenever possible to the office."[18] What is your reaction to Molloy's advice? Would this kind of attire be appropriate for you in your present position? In the future? Use the exercise in the Skill Builder "Something Different" (page 121) to assess how the clothes you wear affect others.

"Don't say a word! Your eyes, your hair, your T-shirt, your luggage—they say it all."

Drawing by Koren; © 1991 The New Yorker Magazine, Inc.

IS PHYSIQUE A FORM OF NONVERBAL COMMUNICATION?

In general, there are three basic body types: endomorphic (heavy), mesomorphic (muscular), and ectomorphic (thin). Over the years, a number of researchers have tried to establish a relationship between body type and personality. According to the psychologists J. B. Cortes and F. M. Gotti, for example, endomorphs, mesomorphs, and ectomorphs tend to be perceived as having the attributes listed below.

Today, the idea of a link between physique and personality does not find much support among psycholo-

gists, though it still persists in the popular imagination. To what extent do you think your personality and body type reflect the descriptions above? To what extent do you believe your physique influences the way you are treated by others, or other people's expectations about what traits you will exhibit?

In fact, these personality traits are not always associated with the body type under which they are listed; but stereotypes about physique and temperament may affect our perceptions and treatment of others.

Endomorphic	Mesomorphic	Ectomorphic
dependent	dominant	detached
calm	cheerful	tense
relaxed	confident	anxious
complacent	energetic	reticent
sluggish	impetuous	self-conscious
placid	enthusiastic	meticulous
leisurely	competitive	reflective
cooperative	determined	precise
affable	outgoing	thoughtful
tolerant	argumentative	considerate
affected	talkative	shy
warm	active	awkward
forgiving	domineering	cool
sympathetic	courageous	suspicious
soft-hearted	enterprising	introspective
generous	adventurous	serious
affectionate	reckless	cautious
kind	assertive	tactful
sociable	optimistic	sensitive
soft-tempered	hot-tempered	withdrawn

Source: J. B. Cortes and F. M. Gotti, "Physique and Self-Description of Temperament," *Journal of Consulting Psychology*, vol. 29, 1965, pp. 408–414.

✔ SKILL BUILDER

SOMETHING DIFFERENT

Tomorrow, wear something different to class. Your change in dress style should be very noticeable to others. For instance, if you feel that you are usually sloppily dressed, appear as meticulously neat as possible.

The next day, assess the results. How did people respond to you? Did anyone seem surprised? Did anyone ask you questions about your appearance? If so, what kinds of questions were you asked? Compare the reactions you received with the experiences of other people who tried this experiment.

Unquestionably, what you wear causes people to relate to you in particular ways. As a case in point, your authors knew one instructor who wore a black suit and tie to class the first day of each semester just to see how his students would react. His class always believed he was on his way to a funeral. No one spoke a word to him either before or after class. Clothes send forth potent and forceful messages. They are one of the important nonverbal stimuli that influence interpersonal responses.

According to the anthropologist Desmond Morris, "It is impossible to wear clothes without transmitting social signals." What social signals is your clothing transmitting today?

Voice: Paralanguage

In many ways, you either "play" your voice—like a musical instrument—or are a "victim" of your voice. Albert Mehrabian estimates that 38 percent of the meaning of a message delivered during face-to-face conversation is transmitted by voice or vocal cues.[19] Frequently, *how* something is said *is* what is said. How effective are you at playing your voice?

Vocal cues that accompany spoken language are called *paralanguage*. Among the elements of paralanguage are pitch, rate, volume, hesitations, and pauses. Wise communicators realize that the spoken word is never neutral, and they have learned how to use the elements of paralanguage to convey both the emotional and the intellectual meanings of their messages. In other words, adept communicators know how to use vocal nuances to help their listeners appreciate and understand content and "mood." They have made their voices adaptable. Let us examine the elements of paralanguage more closely.

Pitch is the highness or lowness of the voice; it is the counterpart of pitch on a musical scale. We tend to associate higher pitches with female voices and lower pitches with male voices. We also develop vocal stereotypes. We associate low-pitched voices with strength, sexiness, and maturity and high-pitched voices with helplessness, tenseness, and nervousness. Although we all have what is termed a "habitual pitch," we have also learned to vary our pitch to reflect our mood and generate listeners' interest.

Some people tend to overuse one tone to the exclusion of others. These people have monotonous voices that are characterized by too little variety of pitch. Other people speak at or near the upper end of their pitch scale, producing very fragile, unsupported tones. One way to discover a pitch that is not overly high is simply to yawn. Try it now. Permit yourself to experience a good stretch; extend your arms to shoulder level and let out a nice vocalized yawn. Do it again. Now count to 10 out loud. To what extent does the pitch of your voice appear to have changed? Is it more resonant? It should be. If you indulge yourself and yawn once or twice before stressful meetings or occasions, you will be able to pitch your voice at a more pleasing level.

Volume is a second paralinguistic factor that affects perceived meaning. Some people cannot seem to muster enough energy to be heard by others. Others blast through encounters. Have you ever sat in a restaurant and heard more of the conversation at a table several feet away than you could hear at your own table? Volume frequently reflects emotional intensity. Loud people are often perceived as aggressive or overbearing. Soft-spoken people are often perceived as timid or polite.

Volume must be varied if it is to be effective. Knowing how to use volume to control meaning is a useful skill. Try it by participating in this exercise (adapted from Ken Cooper, *Nonverbal Communication for Business Success*[20]): Read the following sentence to yourself: How many animals of *each species* did Moses take aboard the *ark*? (Why is this a riddle? Moses, of course, never had an ark. Noah was the ark builder.) Now tell a friend or acquaintance that you have a riddle. Read the sentence aloud, being careful to increase your volume for each of the italicized words. Keep a tally of the number of people who answer "Two." Try the question again, this time increasing your volume only on the name *Moses*. How did your vocal change affect the reactions of the listeners?

Remember, it is important that the volume you use in communication enhance rather than distort the meaning of your messages. By varying your volume and emphasizing certain words, you can vary and control the meaning attributed to your statements.

The *rate*, or speed, at which we speak is also important. Do you, for example, expect high-pressure salespeople to talk rapidly or slowly? Most often, they speak very quickly. Similarly, "pitch" men and women who are selling gadgets in department stores or on television also speak at a quick clip to retain the audience's interest and involvement. In contrast, more stately or formal occasions require slower speaking rates broken by planned *pauses*. (Politicians at rallies typically punctuate their speeches with pauses that function almost as "Applause" signs.) Goldman-Eisler, a communications researcher, has concluded that two-thirds of spoken language comes to us in chunks of fewer than six words.[21] Therefore, knowing *when* to pause is an essential skill. Pauses serve to slow the rate of speech and give both sender and receiver a chance to gather their thoughts. Unfortunately, many people feel that all pauses must be filled and consciously or unconsciously seek for ways to fill them. Frequently we fill a pause with meaningless sounds or phrases: "Er—Huh—Uh—"; "You know? You know?" "Right! Right!" "OK! OK!" Such "nonfluencies" disrupt the natural flow of speech. Since pauses are a natural part of communication, we should stop trying to eliminate them. Instead, we should give pauses a chance to *function*.

ALPHABET RECITAL

Choose a partner. Each of you will try to convey one of the following emotions, without letting the other know beforehand which it is.

happiness	love
sadness	nervousness
anger	pride
jealousy	satisfaction
fear	sympathy

Now, your partner should close his or her eyes. Your task is to communicate the selected emotion to your partner by reciting the first seven letters of the alphabet (A to G). As you recite the letters, attempt to make your voice reflect the emotion. Your partner's goal is to identify the emotion by listening only to the paralinguistic cues you are sending.

To what extent did the various paralinguistic factors you used (volume, pitch, rate, and pauses) help your partner identify the emotion? If your partner was unable to determine the emotion you were projecting, what could you have done to make the message clearer?

How adept are you at employing the paralinguistic factors we have discussed? Try the Skill Builder "Alphabet Recital." This exercise, a variation of the study conducted by Joel Davitz and Lois Davitz, should prove that you do not always need to see people to tell whether they are happy, sad, angry, fearful, or proud.[22] Many of us can identify someone else's emotional state by voice alone. Of course, some of us encode emotional messages with our voices better than others, and some of us can decode these messages better than others. Accuracy in sending and identifying emotional messages appears to be related to one's own sensitivity and familiarity with the vocal characteristics of emotional expression.

Besides communicating emotional content, the voice also communicates personal characteristics. Listening to a voice can sometimes help you identify the speaker's individual characteristics. For instance, on the telephone we are frequently able to determine a speaker's sex, age, vocation, and place of origin even though we have never met him or her. We also tend to associate particular voice types with particular body or personality types. For example, what type of appearance would you expect in a person who has a breathy, high-pitched voice? How do you think a person who has a throaty, raspy voice would look? Figure 5-3 (page 124) summarizes stereotypes related to vocal cues. As a communicator you should be aware that your voice suggests certain things about you. If receivers are interested in identifying your age, occupation, or status, they are likely to make assumptions based on what your voice says to them. Although the picture or stereotype they form may be far from accurate, your voice can influence their assessment of you as an individual and thus affect the way they interact with you.

How do the voices of 4-year-olds and teenagers differ? The voices of college-age men and retired men? Are there differences in vocal characteristics between, say, a corporation executive and a construction worker?

Vocal cues	Speakers	Stereotypes
Breathiness	Males	Young; artistic
	Females	Feminine; pretty; effervescent; high-strung; shallow
Thinness	Males	Did not alter listener's image of the speaker
	Females	Social, physical, emotional, and mental immaturity; sense of humor and sensitivity
Flatness	Males	Masculine; sluggish; cold; withdrawn
	Females	Masculine; sluggish; cold; withdrawn
Nasality	Males	Wide array of socially undesirable characteristics
	Females	Wide array of socially undesirable characteristics
Tenseness	Males	Old; unyielding; cantankerous
	Females	Young; emotional; feminine; high-strung; less intelligent
Throatiness	Males	Old; realistic; mature; sophisticated; well-adjusted
	Females	Less intelligent; masculine; lazy; boorish; unemotional; ugly; sickly; careless; inartistic; humble; uninteresting; neurotic; apathetic
Orotundity (fullness/richness)	Males	Energetic; healthy; artistic; sophisticated; proud; interesting; enthusiastic
	Females	Lively; gregarious; aesthetically sensitive; proud
Increased rate	Males	Animated and extroverted
	Females	Animated and extroverted
Increased pitch variety	Males	Dynamic; feminine; aesthetic
	Females	Dynamic and extroverted

FIGURE 5-3
Vocal cues and
personality stereotypes.

Source: Adapted from
P. Heinberg, *Voice Training
for Speaking and Reading
Aloud*, 1964.

Space and Distance:
Proxemic and Environmental Factors

How much of the space on our planet do you call your own? How much space do you carry around with you? Are there times when people encroach on your space? In his book *The Hidden Dimension*, Edward Hall uses the term *proxemics* for human beings' "use of space."[23] Thus *proxemics* refers to the space that exists between us as we talk and relate to each other as well as the way we organize the space around us in our homes, offices, and communities.

Hall identified four different distances that we keep between us and other people, depending on the type of encounter and the nature of the relationship:

Intimate distance: 0 to 18 inches

Personal distance: 18 inches to 4 feet

Social distance: 4 to 12 feet

Public distance: 12 feet to limit of sight

Intimate distance ranges from the point of touch to 18 inches from the other person. At this distance, physical contact is natural. We can wrestle, and we can make love. At this distance our senses are in full operation. They are easily stimulated but also easily offended if we find ourselves in an uncomfortable situation. Have you ever had someone come too close to you and wanted that person to "back off"? Did you yourself back away? Sometimes we are forced to endure intimate distance between ourselves and strangers in crowded buses, trains, and elevators. How do you feel and respond in such situations?

Hall's *personal distance* ranges from 18 inches to 4 feet. When communicating at this distance, you can still hold hands or shake hands with another person. This is the most common distance between people talking informally in class, at work, or at parties, and we are apt to conduct most of our conversations within this range. If you reduce personal distance to intimate distance, you are likely to make the other person feel uncomfortable. If you increase it, the other person is likely to begin to feel rejected.

Hall's *social distance* ranges from 4 feet to 12 feet. At the social distance—in contrast to personal distance—we are not likely to share personal concerns. By using social distance, we can keep people at more than an arm's length. Thus, this is a "safer" distance, one at which we would communicate information and feelings that are not particularly private or revealing. Many of our conversations at meals and at business conferences or meetings occur within this space. In business, the primary protector of social space is the desk. Of course, the greater the distance between people, the more formal their encounters. (At a social gathering, you can normally tell how well people know one another by examining how close they stand to each other.)

Public distance (12 feet and further) is commonly reserved for strangers with whom we do not wish to have an interaction. Distances at the farther end of the range are well beyond the area of personal involvement and make interpersonal communication very unlikely. People waiting in an uncrowded lobby for an elevator frequently use public distance. It can be assumed that if a person opts for public distance when he or she could have chosen otherwise, that person does not care to converse.

The concept to remember regarding intimate, personal, social, and public distances is that "space speaks." Becoming aware of how people use space and of how you can use it can improve your communication.

Can you tell how interested people are in you by where they stand in relation to you? Explain. Think of an instance when you unconsciously expressed an interest in someone else by where you stood in relation to him or her.

Edward Hall identified four "distances" between people, illustrated on these pages. At "intimate distances," close physical contact is natural. "Personal distance" is the distance at which we tend to conduct most of our conversations. By using "social distance," we can keep people more than an arm's length away; in business contexts, a desk often serves to establish and maintain this distance. "Public distance" makes any interpersonal communication unlikely.

This page, top, Werner Bokelberg/The Image Bank; *this page, bottom,* Bachmann/The Image Works; *opposite page, top,* Jim Pickerell/The Image Works; *opposite page, bottom,* Ron Sherman/Stock, Boston

SPACES—INFORMAL, SEMIFIXED-FEATURE, AND FIXED-FEATURE

Of course, the nature of our environment affects the amount of distance we are able to maintain between ourselves and others. Researchers in nonverbal communication divide environmental spaces into three classifications: informal, semifixed-feature, and fixed-feature. These categories are based on the perceived permanence of any physical space.

Informal space is a highly mobile, quickly changing space that ranges from intimate to public (from no space between us and others to 25 or more feet). Informal space functions like a personal "bubble" that we can enlarge to keep people at a distance or decrease to permit them to get closer.

"Mr. Smith's office doesn't have a door. You have to batter your way through the wall."
Drawing by Gahan Wilson; © 1991 The New Yorker Magazine, Inc.

In contrast to informal space, *semifixed-feature space* employs objects to create distance. Semifixed features include chairs, benches, sofas, plants, and other movable items. (Today some office walls and partitions can be classified as semifixed features, since they are designed to be relocated as spatial requirements change.) Researchers have found that barriers such as desks can reduce interaction. One study of doctor-patient relationships found that patients were more at ease speaking with a physician seated in a chair across from them than they were when the physician was sitting behind a desk.[24] Why do you think this was so? To what extent do you feel the same way about your instructor? Why do you think police interrogators are sometimes advised to eliminate barriers between themselves and the person they are questioning? In many public places, if interaction is desired, the space will usually contain chairs facing each other. Such arrangements are found in bars, restaurants, and lounges. In contrast, the chairs in waiting rooms at airports or bus terminals are often bolted together in long parallel rows. One manufacturer designed a chair to create an uncomfortable pressure on the spine after the sitter has spent a few moments in it; this chair is meant to be used in spaces where it is con-

Mentally redesign your classroom to promote interaction. Next, redesign it to inhibit interaction. Then consider how you could design an office to promote—or inhibit—interaction.

sidered *un*desirable for people to spend time interacting. How do semifixed features function in homes? Have you ever been in a living room that was created to be "looked at but not lived in"? (Your authors know of a sofa that deteriorated from age rather than from wear because it had been declared "off limits" to an entire household for years.)

Fixed-feature space contains relatively permanent objects that define the environment around us. Fixed features include immovable walls, doors, trees, sidewalks, roads, and highways. Such features help guide and control our actions. For example, most classrooms are rectangular with windows along one side, usually to the students' left. The window location also determines the front of the room. Apartment entrances that open onto a common rotunda increase the opportunity for communication among tenants, as do swimming pools and parks. Fences, on the other hand, can serve to inhibit communication. Shopping malls and department stores rely on fixed features to help route pedestrian traffic in certain directions that will increase sales. The next time you shop in a carefully designed store, examine its fixed features. Can you walk unimpeded to any department, or are you carefully "directed" through the perfumes, lingerie, and knickknacks? Why?

How are the chairs in your classroom arranged? Are they arranged in neat rows? Is the instructor partially hidden by a desk or lectern? Does he or she speak from a raised area or platform?

TERRITORIALITY AND PERSONAL SPACE

Another aspect of proxemics is our need for a defined territory. Some animals mark their territory by urinating around its perimeter and will defend their area against invaders. Human beings also lay out or stake out space, or territory, and territoriality is an important variable in interpersonal communication. What examples of territoriality can you remember encountering? Are you familiar

---

■ ETHICS AND COMMUNICATION

MEN AND SPACE

According to the communication researcher Dale Leathers, "Men use space as a means of asserting their dominance over women." Leathers gives several examples:

1. Men claim more personal space than women.
2. Men more actively defend violations of their territories—which are usually much larger than women's territories.
3. Under conditions of high density, men become more aggressive in their attempts to regain privacy.
4. Men more frequently walk in front of a female partner than vice versa.

In your opinion is it appropriate for one sex to dominate the other as Leathers describes? How should the other sex respond?

Source: Dale Leathers, *Successful Nonverbal Communication: Principles and Applications*, Macmillan, New York, 1986, p. 236.

"Honest, Martha, I don't mean to crowd you."

Drawing by Victoria Roberts; © 1991 The New Yorker Magazine, Inc.

with "Dad's chair"? "Mom's bureau"? How do you feel when someone invades your room—"your territory"? Is it comfortable to look into your rearview mirror and see that you are being tailgated by a tractor-trailer? By a Honda? What happens when someone stands too close to you? How are you treated when you enter another person's territory? For example, did your sister ever "throw you out" of her room? Did she ever ask you to keep your hands off her stereo? Has a friend ever thrown you out of his seat?

To establish territory, we employ markers. At the library, for instance, you may spread your things out, over, and across the table so that others will not find it easy to enter your territory. In large corporations a person's status is often reflected by the size of his or her space. Thus, the president may be accorded a large top-floor territory, while a clerk is given a desk in a second-floor room amid a number of other desks and office machines. Regardless of its size, however, we identify with our location and frequently act as if we owned it.

Colors

Colors seem to have more than a passing effect on us; it has been found that color affects us emotionally and physiologically.

Max Luscher, in his book *The Luscher Color Test*, claims that when people look at pure red for a long time, their blood pressure, respiration rate, and heartbeat all increase.[25] This is because red tends to excite the nervous system. In contrast, when researchers examined the effect of dark blue, they found just the opposite: blood pressure, respiration rate, and heartbeat decreased, and people tended to become calmer. Keeping your own reactions in mind, examine the color schemes used in several public areas, including fast-food chains, stores, and terminals. What colors are used? Do they make you want to move quickly? Do the colors excite you, or are they designed to help you relax?

Color also helps persuade. Law enforcement officials, for example, know that when suspects are questioned under green light, they talk more freely; green helps get people to confess. One study, conducted by the Color Research Institute, was described by Vance Packard.[26] The institute was seeking to determine how the color of a package affected consumers' buying patterns. Women were given three boxes of detergent—one yellow, one blue, and one blue with yellow specks. Although the women thought the boxes contained different detergents, all three contained the same product. After using the products for 3 weeks, the women were asked which detergent they considered most effective for washing delicate clothing. The results of the study were revealing. The women reported that the detergent in the yellow box was too strong and that the one in the blue box was too weak. However, the detergent in the blue box with the splashes of yellow was felt to be just right. How do colors on packages affect you?

Your color preferences may even reflect your personality. In *Color in Your World*, Faber Birren suggests that if you like red, you have a tendency to be outwardly directed, active, impatient, and optimistic.[27] If you dislike red, Birren says, you would probably dislike the qualities exhibited by people who like red. Do you agree?

How do various colors make you feel? If you were a color consultant, what colors would you choose for a fast-food operation? An airline? Your classroom? Why?

Time

Do you have enough time for most of your activities? Are you usually prepared for exams or assignments? Do you arrive for appointments on time, early, or late? Edward Hall says that "time talks."[28] What does your use or misuse of time say about you? To what extent do others communicate with you by their use of time? Would you feel insulted if you were asked out for a date at the last minute by someone you did not know very well? (In the United States, at least, a last-minute invitation is often assumed to indicate that another date fell through or that the inviter is asking only as a last resort.) Some students have a habit of always being 15 minutes late to class—even when their previous class was just down the hall. What cues does such habitual lateness transmit to an instructor? Should the instructor conclude that the student is not interested in the class? That the student does not like the instructor? That the student is unable to organize activities to accomplish even the simplest goal?

Punctuality is one important form of "time communication." Many jobs demand that the worker be on time. Would you wait 30 minutes for a bank teller to arrive? To a military officer, being "on time" really means arriving 15 minutes early. Thus, the armed forces are characterized by the "hurry up

---

● CULTURE AND COMMUNICATION

TWO PROVERBS

What do these proverbs tell you about each culture's orientation toward time?

"He who hesitates is lost."—North American proverb

"Think three times before you act."—Chinese proverb

What kinds of problems might emerge when people from these cultures meet to resolve a controversy?

---

and wait" syndrome familiar to anyone in basic training. (Everyone rushes to arrive, but then everyone stands around for a while with nothing to do.)

Another important factor in "time communication" is the allocation of certain activities to *appropriate times*. It is acceptable to call a friend for a chat at 3 P.M. However, we know of an attorney who goes to work at 5:30 A.M. and by 6:30 A.M. has already made phone calls to a number of people. (How would you react if you were called by a lawyer at 5:30 in the morning?) He does this, he reports, because it gets results: people's "defenses are down" at 5:30 A.M.; consequently they often reveal things they would be prepared to cover up by 9 or 10 o'clock.

We are expected to *structure time* in certain ways to ensure that our activities and tasks are accomplished efficiently. American businesspeople, for instance, seek the greatest return on their "time investment." In other countries, however, time is treated differently in varying degrees. In some cultures, people are accustomed to waiting several hours for a meeting to begin. In others, the meeting begins whenever the second party arrives. The following is an example of how the concept of structuring time is culturally determined:

> A Chinese official matter-of-factly informed an ARCO manager that China would one day be the number one nation in the world. The American said he did not doubt that, considering the size of the country and its population, and the tremendous technological progress that will be made, but he asked, "When do you think that China will be number one?" The Chinese responded, "Oh, in four or five hundred years."[29]

Even within the United States people structure time differently. People from the northeast, for example, usually walk and talk more quickly; provide change more quickly in shops; and are more likely to wear a watch than people from other parts of the country. The authors come from two different regions of the country, and it has taken years of married life for them to adjust to each other's "internal clock." (One of them can start and nearly complete a task before the other manages to be seated.) The phrase *a long time* can mean one thing to one person and something completely different to another.

How long we wait for something or someone is related, first, the value we place on whatever it is we are waiting for; second, to our own status. We are taught to value what we wait for. In fact, if something is too readily available, we may decide we don't want it after all. Status determines who waits. If we are "important," others usually have access to us only by appointment; thus it is easier for us to make others wait—and difficult or impossible for others to make us wait. As the psychologist Robert Levine writes:

> Time is power. With status, then, comes the power to control time, your own and others'. Those who control others' time have power and those who have power control others' time. There is no greater symbol of domination, since time cannot be replaced once it is gone.[30]

How well do you structure your time? In his book *The Time Trap*, Alex MacKenzie lists several barriers to effective use of time:

Attempting too much (taking on too many projects at once)

Estimating time unrealistically (not realizing how long a project will take)

Procrastinating (putting it off, and off, and off . . .)

Allowing too many interruptions (letting yourself be distracted by telephone calls, friends, the media)[31]

Do any of these apply to you? How might you go about improving your use of time?

▶ **POINTS TO PONDER**

POWER WAITING
E. B. White

While waiting in the antechamber of a business firm, where we had gone to seek our fortune, we overheard through a thin partition a brigadier general of industry trying to establish telephone communication with another brigadier general, and they reached, these two men, what seemed to us a most healthy impasse. The phone rang in Mr. Auchincloss's office, and we heard Mr. Auchincloss's secretary take the call. It was Mr. Birstein's secretary, saying that Mr. Birstein would like to speak to Mr. Auchincloss. "All right, put him on," said Mr. Auchincloss's well-drilled secretary, "and I'll give him Mr. Auchincloss." "No," the other girl apparently replied, "you put Mr. Auchincloss on, and I'll give him Mr. Birstein." "Not at all," countered the girl behind the partition. "I wouldn't dream of keeping Mr. Auchincloss waiting."

This battle of the Titans, conducted by their leftenants to determine which Titan's time was the more valuable, raged for five or ten minutes, during which interval the Titans themselves were presumably just sitting around picking their teeth. Finally one of the girls gave in, or was overpowered, but it might easily have ended in a draw. As we sat there ripening in the antechamber, this momentary paralysis of industry seemed rich in promise of a better day to come—a day when true equality enters the business life, and nobody can speak to anybody because all are equally busy.

Source: *The Second Tree from the Corner*, Harper & Row. Originally published in *The New Yorker*.

HUGWORK
Russell Baker

Up till now Americans have never been a people to hug each other indiscriminately, but if a California outfit called the Hug Club has its way that will soon change.

The club of course has something to sell—"Hug Club Membership Paks" at $3 per pak—and its sales pitch is based on the same argument that's making millions for the diet and jogging industries; to wit, hugging will make you healthier. Club literature says, "medical and lay experts" have found that hugging "helped remove depression," "relieved tension and stress," "created a stronger will to live" and "tuned up the body's support systems." In short, hugging is just as healthful as jogging and dieting, and a lot easier.

Club members are supposed to do "hugwork," which consists of "hugging yourself, hugging a pet, hugging a friend and, most difficult, hugging someone you think you don't like."

I've always been cautious about what and whom I hug, so my first instinct was to throw this mailing in the trash. Still—. Well, it couldn't hurt to try. I closed the door so nobody could see me and hugged myself.

While embracing the back of my left shoulder with my right hand, I detected something new. The shoulder seam of my jacket had split. A new jacket too. It was infuriating. The shoddiness of American tailoring, the swindles perpetrated by haberdashers! Was the whole country going down the drain?

So much for hugging's power to help remove depression. Perhaps hugging a pet could have relieved the tension and stress caused by hugging myself, but I don't have a pet. I once kept a tank in which assorted tropical fish died with sad regularity, but even when not on their last fins they were eminently unhuggable.

Hugging somebody else's pet dog was out of the question. Dogs like to bite me for some reason. Maybe it tunes up their bodies' support systems.

I wonder if the Hug Club has thought this thing through. "Hugging someone you think you don't like," for example—that sounds like a great idea. A lot of movies used to reach happy endings by that device. (Movies don't seem to have endings anymore; like modern skyscrapers, they just seem to stop when the workmen get bored with the job.)

In real life, though, hugging someone you think you don't like can produce terrible trauma. One of my most enduring memories of President Nixon is of the night during the Republican Convention of 1972 when Sammy Davis Jr. hugged him on national television. Nixon's broad smile stayed rigidly in place—he was on national television, after all—but his entire body curled in on itself with an instinctive tremor the way a man's body will when it senses that the end is near.

My analysis of that hug is this: Davis thought he didn't like Nixon but, hoping to create a stronger will to live, decided to hug him for theapeutic purposes. Nixon, suspecting that Sammy Davis Jr. didn't like him, thought the life was about to be squeezed out of him when he felt Davis's embrace.

The terrible thing for Nixon was that, being on television, he couldn't scream for help but had to keep smiling. I've always given him high marks in self-control for his refusal to yield to pure terror in that instant.

Most people you think you don't like are fully aware of how you feel about them and likely to panic if you reach for them with both arms. I suppose a hugger with a lot of personality could carry it off without being painfully kicked and pummeled, but I don't advise it for the average person seeking relief from tension and stress.

Hugging friends, of course, is another matter, but even here it is a trickier business than the Hug Club thinks. Hugging is a lot like waltzing. Somebody has to take the lead. In my limited hugging experience, I've always been uncomfortable in any hug that I didn't initiate. A lot of other people really want to be hugged but absolutely cannot get the thing started. They will stand around frustratedly unhugged all their lives rather than step right up and initiate the hugging.

So we are dealing with two distinct classes: huggers and huggees. The trouble arises when two huggers meet. I have a friend who, like me, is a hugger. Our greetings are like the opening steps of a wrestling match. I know he is going to try to hug me, thus reducing me to the status of huggee, which I hate.

If there is any hugging to be done, I want to start it, so I am ready for him when he comes in the door, and for a few seconds we stalk each other as cunningly as two scorpions with a disagreement.

Occasionally I win and humiliate him by reducing him to a huggee. Being a man of great physical strength, he retaliates by clamping me in a bear hug that shuts down the blood flow between my collarbone and hipbone. I prefer hugging female friends, but rarely do it. Very few of those who are huggers by nature have the muscularity to turn you numb when they're reduced to huggees. On the other hand, whether huggers or huggees, female friends tend to be suspicious when subjected to a robust hugging, which complicates friendship.

Babies are the best of all hugging materials. They smell good, can't squeeze the life out of you, never suspect you of lechery and can't do anything but howl if they resent being treated like huggees.

Source: "Sunday Observer: Hugwork" by Russell Baker, *The New York Times*, February 21, 1982. Copyright © 1982 by The New York Times Company. Reprinted by permission.

Touch: Haptics

Our final category of nonverbal communication is touch, also referred to as *haptics*. We have already mentioned touch in relation to space and distance. As we noted, Edward Hall suggests that intimate space begins at the *point of touch* and moves to 18 inches. How important is touch in your own communication encounters? As children we are often admonished not to touch ourselves or things around us: "Don't pick your nose!" "Don't play with yourself!" Yet all humans need to touch and be touched.[32]

Watch a preschool teacher reading a story to 3-year-olds. The children surround the adult, sitting as close as possible to him or her and to one another. In the nineteenth century, some orphaned young children died in hospitals—not because they were ill, but apparently simply because they were seldom or never touched. In hospitals today, children are picked up and held constantly.

How accessible are you to touch? The psychologist Sidney Jourard counted the number of contacts between couples in various cities.[33] He reports the following number of contacts per hour:

San Juan, Puerto Rico	180
Paris, France	110
Gainesville, Florida	2
London, England	0

The evidence seems to indicate that "To touch or not to touch?" is partially a cultural question. Where do you touch your father? Your mother? Your brother? Your sister? A friend of the same sex? A friend of the opposite sex? Men seem to touch their fathers' hands—they shake hands—and women touch their fathers' arms and faces. In general, women seem more accessible to touch. Both men and women will often kiss women in greeting; men who meet usually shake hands. Usually men touch women more than women touch

> You cannot shake hands with a clenched fist.
> Golda Meir

> How do you feel when shaking hands with a friend? A stranger? An employer? Why? What does a pat on the back communicate to you?

135

All humans need to
touch and be touched.
How important is touch
in your own communi-
cations?

Peter Glass/Monkmeyer

men.[34] Physical contact between males is often limited to "contact sports," such as football and soccer.

Touch can also reflect status. The person who initiates touch is usually the one with the higher status. Nancy Henley points out that we are unlikely to go up to our boss and pat her or him on the shoulder.[35] Would you put your arm around the president of your college or university? Why? Would your behavior change if you met the president at a party? Probably not. The president, however, might well put an arm around you or another student. The person who initiates touching usually also controls the interaction.

Touch, of course, functions importantly in sexual communication. If people hold hands, we assume they have a romantic interest in one another. Are we right? The shaving-cream companies have made certain that American men shave every day in order to avoid stubble, which is presumably not "touchable." Most American women shave their legs and underarms and use a variety of lotions to keep their hands soft to the touch. When you were growing up, did your parents touch in your presence? Many adults avoid any contact in front of their children. It is somewhat paradoxical that we spend a great deal of money on creams, razor blades, and other products designed to make us "touchable" and then avoid being touched.

Of course, how we use touch sends many messages about us. It reveals our perceptions of status, our attitudes, and even our needs. For example, in his book *The Broken Heart*, the psychologist James L. Lynch establishes a correlation between many diseases—particularly heart disease—and loneliness.[36] Lynch tells the story of one man, hooked up to heart-monitoring devices, who was in a coma and near death. When a nurse would walk into his room and hold his hand for a few moments, his heartbeat would change from fast and erratic to slow and smooth.

Whom have you
"touched" today? Who
has "touched" you?

Touch communicates. It can make a difference.

ASSESSING YOUR EFFECTIVENESS
AS A NONVERBAL COMMUNICATOR

137

CHAPTER 5
NONVERBAL
COMMUNICATION:
SILENT LANGUAGE SPEAKS

As we have seen, nonverbal communication includes body language, (facial expressions, posture, and gestures), clothing, voice, distances and spaces, colors, time, and touch—all of which can either support or contradict the meaning of the words we speak. Use your knowledge of each of these variables to help you react to interactions you observe and to appropriate pictures in this text. For each, answer the following questions about the interactants and identify the cues that influenced your response:

1. Who is more trustworthy?
2. Who is more dynamic?
3. Who is more credible?
4. Who has more status?
5. Who is older?
6. Who is more intelligent?
7. Who is more powerful?
8. Who is more friendly?
9. What is their relationship to each other?
10. What can you predict about the course of their relationship?

Compare and contrast your responses with those of other students in your class. Discussing your observations will be valuable, since many of our judgments and decisions are based on nonverbal cues.

The following guidelines should prove helpful as you continue to develop your ability to make valid judgments and decisions on the basis of nonverbal communication.

Examine the Environment

For any nonverbal interaction, ask yourself if any environmental stimuli are likely to affect it. Determine if other people present could influence the two communicators. Attempt to determine whether colors and decor will have an impact on the nature and tone of the communication. Analyze the amount of space available to the interactants. Determine whether architectural factors might alter the outcome. Where are chairs, tables, passageways, and desks situated? Why did the interactants situate themselves as they did? What type of behavior would we expect to see in this environment?

Observe the Communicators

Ask yourself if the sex, age, or status of the communicators will exert an influence on their relationship. Assess to what extent, if any, attractiveness, clothing, or physical appearance should affect the interaction. Determine if, in your own mind, the communicators' dress is appropriate to the environment. Decide if the communicators appear to like each other and to have similar goals.

What does each communicator's facial expression reveal? Are his or her facial expressions relatively consistent or fleeting? Do these expressions tend to fluctuate drastically? Assess the extent to which you believe the facial expressions are genuine.

Analyze significant bodily cues. Attempt to decide if hand or foot movements suggest honesty or deception. Decide if either of the interactants moves too much or too little. Ask yourself if both are equally involved in the exchange. Is one more eager to continue the communication than the other? Would one prefer to terminate the communication? How do you know?

Assess the extent to which the interactants mirror each other's posture. Ask yourself how posture supports or contradicts their status relationship. Do the interactants appear to be relaxed or tense? Why? Determine if they have used their bodies to include or exclude others from their conversation. Analyze when and why the communicators alter their postures.

Watch the eye behavior of the participants. Determine if one looks away more than the other. Determine if one stares at the other. To what extent, if any, does excessive blinking occur? When is eye contact most pronounced? How does the eye contact of one participant appear to affect the other?

Listen for Vocal Cues

Assess whether the communicators are using appropriate vocal volumes and rates of speaking, given their situation. Determine if and how the way something that is said verbally supports or contradicts what is being said nonverbally. Analyze how and when silence is used. Be responsive to signals of nervousness and changes in pitch.

Observe Touching

Watch to see if the participants touch each other at all. Determine, if you can, *why* they touched. How did touching or being touched affect the interactants? Was the contact appropriate or inappropriate to the situation? Why?

SUMMARY

Nonverbal communication includes all the human responses that are not expressed in words. Over 65 percent of the social meaning of the messages we send to others is communicated nonverbally. Perceiving and analyzing nonverbal cues can help us understand what is really happening during a conversation.

Nonverbal messages fall into seven main categories: (1) body language or kinesics (facial expressions, posture, eyes and eye contact, and gestures); (2) clothing; (3) voice or paralanguage (including pitch, rate, volume, hesitations or "nonfluencies," and pauses); (4) space and distance or proxemic factors (including both the space that exists between us when we talk to each other and the way we organize space in our homes, offices, and communities); (5) color; (6) time; and (7) touch, or haptics.

You can improve your effectiveness as a nonverbal communicator by observing and analyzing both the physical environment of interactions and the body language, appearance, gestures, vocal cues, eye contact, and touching behavior of the participants.

SUGGESTIONS FOR FURTHER READING

Axtell, Robert E.: *Gestures: The Do's and Taboos of Body Language around the World*, Wiley, New York, 1991. Practical advice on specific nonverbal cues to use and avoid in various cultures.

Bandler, Richard, and John Grinder: *Frogs into Princes: Neuro Linguistic Programming*, Real People Press, Moab, Utah, 1979. A readable and practical work about neurolinguistic programming from the researchers who developed the concept.

Birdwhistell, Ray: *Kinesics and Context*, University of Pennsylvania Press, Philadelphia, 1970. An extensive, scholarly treatment of kinesics and the building blocks of body language.

Birren, Faber: *Color in Your World*, Collier, New York, 1962. An early exploration of the effects of various colors.

Brooks, Michael: *Instant Rapport*, Warner, New York, 1989. A clear, concise book with specific examples of the use of neurolinguistic programming to establish rapport.

Brooks, Michael: *The Power of Business Rapport*, HarperCollins, New York, 1991. Focuses on neurolinguistic programming in business communication. Offers specific techniques for the communicator who wants to improve rapport-building skills.

Burgoon, Judee K., David B. Buller, and W. Gill Woodall: *Nonverbal Communication: The Unspoken Dialogue*, Harper and Row, New York, 1989. A clear, readable book on the principles of nonverbal communication as they apply to our lives.

Cooper, Ken: *Nonverbal Communication for Business Success*, Amacom, New York, 1979. An easy-to-read discussion of how the results of research in nonverbal communication can be directly applied to the world of business.

Cortes, J. B., and F. M. Gatti: "Physique and Self-Description of Temperament," *Journal of Consulting Psychology*, vol. 29, 1965, pp. 408–414.

Decker, Bert: *The Art of Communication*, Crisp, Los Altos, Calif., 1989. Designed with the business communicator in mind, this book presents a system of exercises people can use to help make nonverbal communication work for them.

Ekman, Paul, and Wallace Friesen: *Unmasking the Face*, Prentice-Hall, Englewood Cliffs, N.J., 1975. An immensely understandable work about faces and feelings.

Hall, Edward: *The Silent Language*, Fawcett, Greenwich, Conn., 1959. A popular work on spatial communication from the point of view of an anthropologist.

Hickson, Mark, and Stacks, Don W.: *NVC—Nonverbal Communication: Studies and Applications*, 2d ed., Brown, Dubuque, Iowa, 1989. A discussion of theories and methodologies used to study nonverbal communication. Describes how nonverbal messages reflect cultures and subcultures.

Knapp, Mark L.: *Nonverbal Communication in Human Interaction*, Holt, Rinehart and Winston, New York, 1972. One of the most thorough surveys of nonverbal communication. Contains a wealth of documented information.

Mehrabian, Albert: *Silent Messages*, Wadsworth, Belmont, Calif., 1971. An overview of how we communicate liking, power, and inconsistency with nonverbal cues.

Mehrabian, Albert: *Public Places and Private Spaces*, Basic Books, New York, 1976. Presents theory and research into space and its influence on interaction.

Molloy, John T.: *The Woman's Dress for Success Book*, Warner, New York, 1989. In this volume, Molloy advises women on what to wear to succeed in the business world.

Molloy, John T.: *Dress for Success*, Warner, New York, 1990. An often updated reference for men in business. Discusses what to wear to work and why.

Montagu, Ashley: *Touching: The Human Significance of the Skin*, Harper and Row, New York, 1971. A readable discussion of the value of body touching.

Packard, Vance: *The Hidden Persuaders*, Pocket Books, New York, 1957.

Sommer, R.: *Personal Space*, Prentice-Hall, Englewood Cliffs, N.J., 1969. A description of how we use space to express our feelings and relationships. An analysis of how space controls communication.

1. Ray Birdwhistell, *Kinesics and Context*, University of Pennsylvania Press, Philadelphia, 1970. Mark Knapp, *Essentials of Nonverbal Communication*, Holt, New York, 1980. Albert Mehrabian, *Silent Messages*, 2d ed., Wadsworth, Belmont, Calif., 1981.

2. For some practical advice, see Rowland Cuthill, "How to Read the Other Guy's Silent Signals," *Quest*, May 1977, pp. 46–51.

3. Bernard Gunther, *Sense Relaxation below Your Mind*, Macmillan, New York, 1963.

4. Daniel Goleman, "Sensing Silent Cues Emerges as Key Skill," *The New York Times*, October 10, 1989.

5. George Orwell, *Nineteen Eighty-Four*, New American Library edition, New York, 1983.

6. Paul Ekman and Wallace Friesen, "The Repertoire of Nonverbal Behavior: Categories, Origins, Usage and Coding," *Semiotica*, vol. 1, 1969, pp. 49–98.

7. E. A. Haggard and K. S. Isaacs, "Micromomentary Facial Expressions as Indicators of Ego Mechanisms in Psychotherapy," in L. A. Gottschalk and A. H. Auerback (eds.), *Methods of Research in Psychotherapy*, Appleton-Century-Crofts, New York, 1966.

8. United Press International, 1979.

9. *Discover* magazine, February 1989.

10. Julius Fast, *Body Language*, Evans, New York, 1970.

11. M. Argyle and J. Dean, "Eye Contact, Distance, and Affiliation," *Sociometry*, vol. 28, 1965, pp. 289–394.

12. Helmut Morsbach, "Aspects of Nonverbal Communication in Japan," in Larry Samovar and Richard Porter (eds.), *Intercultural Communication: A Reader*, 3d ed., Wadsworth, Belmont, Calif., 1982, p. 308.

13. Mehrabian, *Silent Messages*.

14. Nancy Henley, *Body Politics: Power, Sex and Nonverbal Communication*, Simon and Schuster, New York, 1986.

15. For a summary of Mehrabian's work in this area, see his article "Significance of Posture and Position in the Communication of Attitude and Status Relationship," *Psychological Bulletin*, vol. 71, 1969, pp. 359–372.

16. Paul Ekman, W. V. Friesen, and J. Baer, "The International Language of Gestures," *Psychology Today*, May 1984, pp. 64–69.

17. For a readable survey of nonverbal communicative aspects of clothing, see Leonard Bickman, "Social Roles and Uniforms: Clothes Make the Person," *Psychology Today*, April 1974, pp. 49–51. For a study of the relationship between dress and personality for both men and women,

see Lawrence B. Rosenfeld and Timothy G. Plax, "Clothing as Communication," *Journal of Communication*, vol. 27, 1977, pp. 24–31.

18. John T. Molloy, *New Dress for Success*, Warner, New York, 1990.

19. Mehrabian, *Silent Messages*.

20. Ken Cooper, *Nonverbal Communication for Business Success*, Amacom, New York, 1980, p. 11.

21. F. Goldman-Eisler, "Continuity of Speech Utterance, Its Determinance and Its Significance," *Language and Speech*, vol. 4, 1961, pp. 220–231.

22. J. R. Davitz and L. Davitz, "The Communication of Feelings by Content-Free Speech," *Journal of Communication*, vol. 9, 1959, pp. 256–257.

23. Edward Hall, *The Hidden Dimension*, Doubleday, New York, 1969.

24. See, for example, A. G. White, "The Patient Sits Down: A Clinical Note," *Psychosomatic Medicine*, vol. 15, 1953, pp. 256–257.

25. Max Luscher, *The Luscher Color Test*, Simon and Schuster, New York, 1980. See also Luscher, *The Four Color Person*, Simon and Schuster, New York, 1980.

26. Vance Packard, *The Hidden Persuaders*, McKay, New York, 1957.

27. Faber Birren, *Color in Your World*, Macmillan, New York, 1985.

28. Hall, op. cit.

29. L. Copland and L. Greggs, *Going International: How to Make Friends and Deal Effectively in the Going Marketplace*, Random House, New York, 1985, p. 10.

30. Robert Levine, "Waiting Is a Power Game," *Psychology Today*, April 1987, p. 30.

31. Alex MacKenzie, *The Time Trap*, McGraw-Hill, New York, 1975.

32. An especially persuasive argument is made by Ashley Montagu in *Touching: The Human Significance of the Skin*, Harper and Row, New York, 1971.

33. Sidney M. Jourard, "An Exploratory Study of Body Accessibility," *British Journal of Social and Clinical Psychology*, vol. 5, 1966, pp. 221–231.

34. Barbara Bales, *Communication and the Sexes*, Harper and Row, New York, 1988, p. 60.

35. Henley, op. cit.

36. James L. Lynch, *The Broken Heart*, Basic Books, New York, 1979. See also Lynch, *The Language of the Heart*, Basic Books, New York, 1986.

LISTENING:
A DELIBERATE PROCESS

After finishing this chapter, you should be able to:

Define *listening*
Explain the nature of serial communication
State how much time you spend listening
Compare and contrast helpful and harmful listening habits
Distinguish between the processes of hearing and listening
Explain the "listening level–energy involvement" scale
Define *feedback*
Describe how feedback affects communication
Use different types of evaluative and nonevaluative feedback
Focus your attention while listening
Set appropriate listening goals
Listen to understand ideas
Listen to retain information
Listen to evaluate and analyze content
Listen empathically

A number of American corporations have run advertising campaigns designed to promote awareness of the importance of listening. Running through their advertisements are slogans such as: "Did you hear that?" "Listening is more than just good philosophy. It's vital to our future." "How can we expect them to learn when we haven't taught them how to listen?"

Do you believe that you listen well? Far too often, listening is something we take for granted. However, listening is a difficult, intricate skill; and, like other skills, it requires training and practice.

LISTENING AND COMMUNICATION

Why Listen?

From the time the alarm clock rings until the late news winds up with the weather, we are inundated with things to listen to. As we proceed through our day, as we move from person to person, from class to lunch, from formal discussions to casual conversations, we are constantly called on to listen. All of us continually engage in "listening activities": we interact face to face with friends and acquaintances, we use the telephone, we attend meetings, we participate in interviews, we take part in arguments, we give or receive instructions, we make decisions based on information received orally, and we generate and receive feedback. Yet we do all this without paying much attention to the role listening plays in these experiences. Consequently, listening problems abound.

At one time, a poll of American teenagers indicated that as many as half of them believed that communication between themselves and their parents was poor—and that a primary cause was poor listening. Parents, too, often feel that communication is failing. As a case in point, one parent was convinced that her daughter must have a severe hearing problem and took her to an audiologist. The audiologist tested both ears and reported back to the distraught parent: "There's nothing wrong with her hearing. She's just tuning you out."

A leading cause of the rising divorce rate (more than half of all marriages end in divorce) is the failure of husbands and wives to interact effectively. They don't listen to each other or respond to each other's messages.

Although we are
constantly called on to
listen, we often give
little consideration to
the role listening plays
in communication.

Richard Pasley/Stock,
Boston

Similarly, political scientists report that a growing number of people believe that their elected and appointed officials are out of touch with the constituents they are supposedly representing. Why? Because they don't believe these officials listen to them. In fact, it seems that sometimes our politicians don't even listen to themselves. Here is a true story: At a national legislative conference held in Albuquerque some years ago, a senator—Joseph Montoya—was handed a copy of a press release by a press aide shortly before he got up to deliver a speech. When he rose to speak, to the horror of his aide and the amusement of his audience, Montoya began reading the press release rather than his speech. He began, "For immediate release. Senator Joseph M. Montoya, Democrat of New Mexico, last night told the National Legislative Conference at Albuquerque . . . ." Montoya read the entire six-page release, concluding with, "Montoya was repeatedly interrupted by applause."

Presidents of major companies also identify listening as one of their major communication problems. One executive asked his secretary for "40 Xeroxes" and sat there with his mouth open a couple of days later when 40 Xerox copiers were wheeled into his office.

It is almost impossible to state a dollar value for the cost of poor listening. But since there are more than 100 million workers in the United States, just one $10 mistake by each of them in a single year would cost $1.6 billion.

Think back over the years you have spent as a student. Did you receive training in writing? Reading? Speaking? The answer to each of these questions is probably yes. In fact, many children now learn to read and write before they start school; and reading and writing skills are taught and emphasized throughout our educational careers. In addition, courses in writing and speed-reading are popular in adult-oriented programs. We often take public-speaking courses, and oral presentations are required in many of our classes. But what about *listening*? How much training have you actually received in listening? It is true that an International Listening Association now exists, and listening is now taught in some schools and colleges. Still, of the four communication skills—

reading, writing, speaking, and listening—listening has received the least attention from educators. Yet listening is the fundamental process through which we initiate and maintain relationships, and it is the primary process through which we take in information. Treat listening as if your very existence depended on it—in many ways, it does.

Studies show that on the average we spend between 42 and 53 percent of our communicative time listening, 16 to 32 percent speaking, 15 to 17 percent reading, and only 9 to 14 percent writing.[1] But we are not born knowing how to listen, or how to listen well. How efficient are your listening skills? Estimate what percentage of information you retain when you listen. This figure represents how good a listener you *think* you are. How good a listener are you really? Let's find out.

Take a moment to review your personal listening situation. Think of interactions you have had that were complicated because you or someone else failed to listen effectively. For example, when was the last time you jumped to a wrong conclusion? Missed an important word? Failed to realize that you were not being understood? Reacted emotionally or let yourself become distracted? Far too often, instead of listening we daydream our way through our daily contacts—we take side trips or otherwise tune out what is said to us. In other words, we adopt destructive "unlistening" behaviors though we are unaware that this is what we are doing. Most people estimate that they listen with 70 to 80 percent accuracy. This means they believe that they can interact with others and accurately retain 70 to 80 percent of what is said. However, Ralph Nichols, a noted researcher, tells us that most of the people he has studied actually listen at only 25 percent efficiency—that is, instead of *retaining* 75 percent of what they hear, they *lose* 75 percent.[2] How effective do you think your writing would be if 75 percent of your work contained errors? What grade would you receive if you misspelled 75 percent of the words you used in an essay or incorrectly punctuated 75 percent of your sentences?

Unfortunately, although most of us have supposedly had many years of practice in listening, errors are extremely common. According to the communication theorist William Haney, we frequently run into problems when we use

List five problems that could result (or have resulted) from "unlistening"—that is, a lack of listening skills. List five benefits that could result from acquiring listening skills.

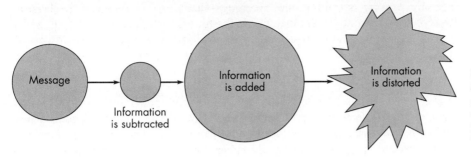

FIGURE 6-1
Message chain.

Source: William Haney,
*Communication and
Organizational Behavior,*
Irwin, Homewood, Ill.,
1973.

serial communication, or chain-of-command transmissions, to relay messages. (See Figure 6-1.) What happens in *serial communication* is that person 1 sends a message to person 2; person 2 then communicates his or her perception of person 1's message (not person 1's message itself) to person 3, who continues the process.

The example in the box on page 146, from an article by Edmond D. Boles, further clarifies the concept of serial communication. Although this example is of course fictional, let's use it to examine what can happen and why. As John R. Freund and Arnold Nelson have noted, whenever one person speaks or delivers a message to a second person, the message occurs in at least four different forms.[3]

1. Message as it exists in the mind of the speaker (his or her thoughts)
2. Message as it is spoken (actually encoded by the speaker)
3. Message as it is interpreted (decoded by the listener)
4. Message as it is ultimately remembered by the listener (affected by the listener's personal selectivity and rejection)

In traveling down this unwieldy "chain of command" from person to person, ideas can become distorted by as much as 80 percent. A number of factors cause this. First, because passing along complex, confusing information poses many problems, we generally like to simplify messages. As a result we unconsciously (and consciously) delete information from the messages we receive before transmitting these messages to others. Second, we like to think the messages we pass along to others make sense. (We feel foolish if we convey a message we ourselves do not understand or deliver a message that appears illogical.) Thus, we try to "*make* sense out of" a message before communicating it to someone else. We do this by adding to, subtracting from, or otherwise altering what we have heard. Unfortunately, as we saw in Figure 6-1, once we "make sense out of" the message, it may no longer correspond to the message originally sent. Such errors occur even though we have had years of practice in listening. The communications expert Gerald Goldhaber estimates that a 20-year-old person has practiced listening for at least 10,000 hours, a 30-year-old at least 15,000 hours, and a typical 40-year-old 20,000 or more hours.[4] These figures are mind-boggling, but have we in reality been practicing listening or "*un*listening"? Research suggests that we have been practicing unlistening.

"Self-talk"—listening to what you say to yourself—can help you make sense of the way you listen to and react to the people in your life.

PERMUTATION PERSONIFIED

Can you cite an experience like this one that has actually occurred in your social, school, or job life?

Despite telemetering advances, improvements in mechanical transmission of data and collating total knowledge, there are occasional breakdowns in communication. We're indebted to a traveler recently returned from Miami for this example.

Operation: Halley's Comet.

COLONEL TO EXECUTIVE OFFICER: Tomorrow evening at approximately 2000 hours Halley's Comet will be visible in this area, an event which occurs only once every 75 years. Have the men fall out in the battalion area in fatigues, and I will explain this rare phenomenon to them. In case of rain, we will not be able to see anything, so assemble the men in the theatre and I will show them films of it.

EXECUTIVE OFFICER TO COMPANY COMMANDER: By order of the colonel, tomorrow at 2000 hours, Halley's Comet will appear above the battalion area. If it rains, fall the men out in fatigues. Then march to the theatre, where the rare phenomenon will take place, something which occurs only once every 75 years.

COMPANY COMMANDER TO LIEUTENANT: By order of the colonel in fatigues at 2000 hours tomorrow evening, the phenomenal Halley's Comet will appear in the theatre. In case of rain in the battalion area, the colonel will give another order, something which occurs once every 75 years.

LIEUTENANT TO SERGEANT: Tomorrow at 2000 hours, the colonel will appear in the theatre with Halley's Comet, something which happens every 75 years. If it rains, the colonel will order the comet into the battalion area.

SERGEANT TO SQUAD: When it rains tomorrow at 2000 hours, the phenomenal 75-year-old General Halley, accompanied by the Colonel, will drive his Comet through the battalion area theatre in fatigues.

Source: "Permutation Personified," *Boles Letter*, 1982, Edmund D. Boles and Associates.

To repeat: listening takes up a very important and very significant portion of your waking day, and since effective listening serves so many purposes, you really do need to listen as if your life depended on it. People who listen effectively demonstrate a sense of caring and concern for those with whom they interact. In contrast, people who do not listen effectively tend to drive people away. By listening accurately, you help avoid communication difficulties and breakdowns.

According to the sociologist Deborah Tannen, "Boys learn to hold center stage by talking; girls learn to listen." Do you agree or disagree? Why?

Who has the primary responsibility for clear and effective communication—the speaker or the listener? An old proverb says, "Nature gave us two ears and one mouth so that we can listen twice as much as we speak." The effective communicator is not afraid to be two parts listener and one part speaker. Actually we believe that since everyone functions as both sender and receiver, everyone must assume "51 percent" of the responsibility for communication. This practice might not be mathematically sound, but it would certainly increase the effectiveness of our interpersonal, small-group, and public communication.

"Because my genetic programming prevents me from stopping to ask directions—that's why!"

Drawing by D. Reilly; © 1991 The New Yorker Magazine, Inc.

■ ETHICS AND COMMUNICATION

ASKING DIRECTIONS

Is it possible that men do not like to put themselves into a listening mode? Could it be that the males' need for independence and control actually makes it harder for them to listen? What are the chances that women, used to seeking help from others, are better than men at listening to advice?

According to Deborah Tannen, author of *You Just Don't Understand: Women and Men in Conversation*, men desire dominance so strongly that they would prefer to drive right past a police officer than to stop and ask for directions. For men, listening to directions implies inferiority. But, according to Tannen, American women are so used to asking for help that they tend to ask strangers for directions even when they are well aware of where they are going.

What do you think? Do men and women listen differently? Should they? Explain.

Source: Deborah Tannen, *You Just Don't Understand: Women and Men in Conversation*, Ballantine, New York, 1990.

Listening versus Hearing

Listening and *hearing* are not one and the same thing. Most people are born with the ability to hear. Thus *hearing* occurs automatically and requires no conscious effort on your part. If the physiological elements within your ears are functioning properly, your brain will process the electrochemical impulses received, and you will hear. However, what you do with the impulses after receiving them belongs to the realm of listening.

What is *listening*? As we will see, it is a deliberate process through which we seek to understand and retain aural (heard) stimuli. Unlike hearing, listening depends on a complex set of skills that we have to acquire. Thus, although hearing simply happens to us and cannot be manipulated, listening requires us to make an active, conscious effort to comprehend and remember what we hear. Furthermore, who we are affects what we listen to. In your environment, from minute to minute, far too many sounds bombard you for you to be able to pay attention to each one. Thus in listening you *process* the external sounds of your environment to select those which are relevant to you, your activities, and your interests. This is not to say that listening is just an external process. It is also an internal process. We listen to the sounds we hear, and we listen to what others say, but we also listen to what we say aloud and what we say to ourselves in response. (Do you ever talk to yourself? Are you your own best listener? Most of us are.)

We have seen that hearing is a natural and passive process. When we hear, we employ little if any conscious effort. Listening, on the other hand, is a deliberate process. How deliberate is it? How much effort must we expend in order to listen effectively? For example, do you work harder when you are listening to an instructor's lecture on important material or when you are listening to a disk jockey announcing your favorite recording on the radio? In many ways listening is similar to reading. Some material we read very carefully and closely; other material we skim quickly to abstract only relevant facts. For still other material we need only check the title and author to know that we do not care to read it. We approach the information that we receive aurally in much the same way. Some information we pass over lightly, and other information we attend to with more care. If the information is important to us, we work harder to retain it.

To help you begin to develop more effective listening skills, we have identified four levels of receiving. An understanding of these levels should help you assess your own effectiveness as a listener. Let's begin by examining the "listening level–energy involvement" scale in Figure 6-2.

As the scale indicates, hearing requires little if any energy expenditure or involvement on your part. In contrast, listening to understand requires a greater expenditure of energy. In listening you need to ensure that you comprehend what is being said. Remembering or retaining a message requires even more effort on your part, and working to analyze and evaluate what is said is still more difficult and thus consumes more energy. Listening to help others (*empathic listening*), requires an even greater degree of involvement and—as we will see—even more energy.

The comedian George Burns once said: "I can't help hearing, but I don't always listen." Describe an occasion when this statement might have been applied to your own behavior. What happened as a result?

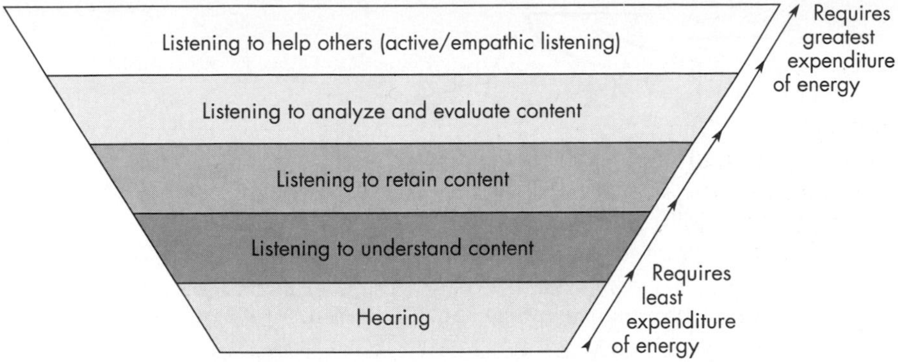
Listening to help others (active/empathic listening)
Listening to analyze and evaluate content
Listening to retain content
Listening to understand content
Hearing
Requires greatest expenditure of energy
Requires least expenditure of energy

FIGURE 6-2
"Listening level–energy involvement" scale.

A common problem of many poor listeners is inability to determine the listening or involvement level appropriate to a situation. For example, in a course with large lecture sections it is not uncommon to find some students "tuning out"—simply hearing when they should be listening to understand, retain, analyze, and evaluate content. All too frequently, these students will later assert adamantly that certain points were "never covered" in class ("I was sitting right there, and I never heard you say that!").

Here is an example of what can happen when people fail to listen effectively at the appropriate level:

> Kevin Daly, founder of Communispond, a company that helps train executives to communicate their ideas more effectively, reports that the president of a steel company in Pittsburgh had aides prepare a news release for him to read at a press conference. The release, as written by his speech writers, was eleven pages. The president did not have time to review the manuscript before arriving at the conference and taking his place on the podium. Nonetheless, he began to read the announcement confidently. As he continued reading the lengthy statement, he realized that page eight had been printed twice. Indeed, he was now reading page eight aloud for the second time. Somewhat flustered, he gazed out at the audience, only to observe that there was "no quiver of recognition" among his listeners. He finished reading the release certain that no one had picked up his error. He was right. The mistake was never reported.[5]

Why didn't the audience members—educated people, all of them—listen more critically to what they were being told? How could they fail to perceive so blatant an error? How could they evaluate what was being said if they were not even aware of the content? Are you a more effective listener than the people in this story? (Are you sure?)

Listening versus Unlistening: How "Unlisteners" Do It

Of course, we do not—probably, we cannot—listen at full capacity all the time. But we should be aware of our "unlistening" behaviors if they prevent us from understanding what could be important to us or to someone else.

"Are you listening to me?"

Drawing by Barsotti; © 1991 The New Yorker Magazine, Inc.

"NODDERS"

"Nodders" pretend that they are listening. They look at the speaker, nod their heads appropriately in agreement or disagreement, and utter remarks such as "mm" or "uh huh" that imply they are paying attention. In actuality, the words are falling on "deaf ears."

"Nodders" adopt the outward appearance of a listener, but they are counterfeiters—pretenders who let no meaning through. Perhaps they unlisten because they are thinking their own private thoughts, are bored with the conversation, or are otherwise occupied. Whatever their motivation, the outcome is similar—no listening has occurred.

"EAR HOGS"

"Ear hogs" want you to listen to them, but they have neither the time nor the desire to listen to you. Intrigued with their own thoughts and ideas, these monopolizers deny your right to be listened to while defending their right to express themselves no matter what the cost.

According to the researcher Alfie Kohn, men have more tendency than women to be "ear hogs." Kohn finds that men interrupt women's statements more frequently than women interrupt men's statements; in fact, in his research 96 percent of the interruptions in male-female interactions were initiated by men.[6]

Using this categorization of "unlisteners," discuss poor listening behaviors you have noticed in yourself or others in daily conversations. To what extent, if any, do the people with whom you are interacting, the nature of the interaction, or the time and place of the interaction influence whether or not these behaviors appear? Explain?

"Gap fillers" never quite get the whole story when they listen. To make up for what they've missed or misinterpreted, they manufacture information to fill in the gaps. While the impression is that they "got it all," nothing could be further from the truth.

"BEES"

"Bees" zero in on only those portions of a speaker's remarks which interest them or have particular importance to them. Everything else the speaker says is considered irrelevant or inconsequential and thus is rejected. "Bees," in their search for just the honey, often miss the flower.

"EAR MUFFS"

"Ear muffs" close their ears to information they would rather not deal with. Sometimes they pretend not to understand what you tell them or act as if they did not hear you at all. Sometimes they simply forget, in short order, what you told them.

"DART THROWERS"

"Dart throwers" wait for you to make a mistake or slip up so that they can attack what you have to say.

To be sure, there are a number of other kinds of deficient listeners. But whatever the individual listening malady, the results are less than desirable. Someone spoke, and someone else failed to listen effectively.

FEEDBACK: A PREREQUISITE FOR EFFECTIVE LISTENING

The feedback process is intimately connected with the listening process. Developing an understanding and appreciation of the way feedback works is essential to improving your listening skills.

What Is Feedback?

The expression *feedback* implies that we are feeding someone by giving something back to him or her. Simply put, *feedback* consists of all the verbal and nonverbal messages that a person consciously or unconsciously sends out in response to another person's communication. As students, you continually provide your instructors with feedback. Many of you, however, are probably not completely honest when you send feedback. At times when you are confused or bored, you may nevertheless put on an "I'm interested" face and nod smilingly, indicating that you understand and agree with everything your instructor is saying. Unfortunately, such behavior tends to encourage the sending of unclear messages. If students admitted their confusion, the instructor might be

✔ SKILL BUILDER

THE EXPECTED VERSUS THE UNEXPECTED

1. Describe a situation in which a feedback message you sent was interpreted as intended. What effect did your feedback have on the nature of the interaction?
2. Describe a situation when a feedback message you sent was misinterpreted. What effect did your feedback have on the nature of that interaction?

more likely to find alternative ways to present the concepts and formulate new, more interesting examples. To cite another instance, some people will respond more actively and talk at greater length when a listener is smiling at them than they will when the listener appears sad or bored.

Whatever the circumstances, we must recognize that the nature of the feedback we give people will affect the communicative interactions we share with them.

Types of Feedback

Imagine someone who writes 50 love letters but receives no answer. Did this person receive feedback?

We constantly provide others with feedback, whether we intend to or not. Everything we do or fail to do in a relationship or interaction with others can be considered feedback. Sometimes we send feedback consciously, intending to evoke a particular response. For example, if you laugh or chuckle at a speaker's joke or story, you may be doing so because you want the speaker to feel that you enjoyed the story and hope he or she will tell more jokes. In contrast, some of the feedback we transmit is sent unconsciously and evokes unintended or unexpected responses. Often, when our words or behaviors prompt a reaction that we never intended, we respond with useless phrases such as "That's not what I meant!" or "I didn't mean it that way!" or "What I meant was . . ."

● CULTURE AND COMMUNICATION

FEEDBACK IN JAPAN

Are you culturally sensitive when giving feedback? For example, most Japanese—unlike most Americans—use an indirect style of communication. Thus, when interacting with someone from Japan, if you give feedback directly (for example, telling someone outright, "You are not working hard enough"), the feedback, instead of being viewed as helpful, might be viewed as a threat. And if it is perceived as a threat, it could well be ineffective.

An American giving feedback to another American, however, can give feedback more directly.

Do you believe we ought to change the way we provide feedback to conform to the preferences of another culture? Explain.

What we intend to convey by feedback, then, may not be what others perceive. Sometimes others intentionally choose not to perceive our messages. At other times, confusion results because feedback that we mean to be *non-evaluative* in tone is interpreted as *evaluative*. Distinguishing between these two categories of feedback will help us use both types effectively and appropriately.

EVALUATIVE FEEDBACK

When we provide another person with an *evaluative response*, we state our opinion about some matter being discussed. For example, "How did you like my speech?" will almost always evoke a response that will be perceived as evaluative. A slight hesitation before the words "I loved it" might be perceived as connoting a negative response. When we give evaluative feedback, we make judgments—either positive or negative—based on our own system of values. As we go about the business of daily life, judgments about the relative worth of ideas, the importance of projects, and the classification of abilities are a necessity. By its very nature, the effect of evaluative feedback is either positive and rewarding or negative and punishing.

Positive Evaluative Feedback *Positive evaluative feedback* tends to keep communication and its resulting behaviors moving in the direction in which they are already heading. If a company places an advertisement and achieves a tremendous growth in sales, the company will tend to place the same or a very similar ad in the same or very similar media in the future. If a person wearing a new hairstyle is complimented, he or she will tend to keep that hairstyle. If you are speaking to an instructor who appears receptive to your ideas and suggestions, you will tend to continue offering ideas and suggestions in the future. Thus, positive evaluative feedback serves to make us continue behaving as we are already behaving and enhances or reinforces existing conditions or actions.

Negative Evaluative Feedback *Negative evaluative feedback* serves a corrective function in that it helps to extinguish undesirable communicative behaviors. When we perceive feedback as negative, we tend to change or modify our performance accordingly. For example, if you were to tell a number of off-color stories that your listeners found in "bad taste," they might send you negative responses. They might turn away, attempt to change the subject, or simply maintain a cold, lengthy silence. Each cue would indicate that your message had overstepped the bounds of propriety, and as a result you would probably discontinue your anecdotes.

Formative Feedback *Formative feedback* is a special kind of negative feedback. Don Tosti, an industrial psychologist, used timed negative feedback with some interesting results[7]. Tosti discovered that in a learning situation it is best to provide positive feedback *immediately after* someone has displayed a desired behavior. Thus, comments such as "You did a good job" and "Keep up the good work" would be offered immediately, because these responses give people a sense of pride and pleasure in themselves and their work. However, Tosti

Feedback consists of all the verbal and nonverbal messages that one person sends in response to another person's communication. Formative feed-back can be especially valuable in learning situations.

Randy Duchaine/The Stock Market

suggests that what he calls "formative negative" feedback should be given only *just before* an undesired behavior (or a similar behavior) is about to be repeated. Tosti believes that withholding negative feedback until the person can use it constructively makes the feedback seem more like coaching than criticism. Comments such as "OK, team, let's eliminate the errors we made last time" and "When you go out there today, try to . . ." reduce the extent to which negative feedback is perceived as harmful rather than helpful. Thus, giving formative feedback just before an activity is to be performed again can help eliminate the feelings of rejection that sometimes accompany negative feedback. (In contrast, it should be remembered that *immediate* positive feedback can do wonders for people's self-image and morale.)

Tosti's findings have many implications for communication. For example, if you handed in a paper to your instructor, following Tosti's guidelines the instructor would hand you a list containing only positive observations. Not until the instructor made the next assignment would you be offered formative or negative feedback in the form of a list containing errors to avoid. Formative feedback can also be used as a memory refresher or as a motivational tool to improve performance. With formative feedback, it is the timing that counts.

Unlike traditional negative feedback, formative feedback does not tend to discourage an individual from attempting to perform an activity again. Nor does it tend to demoralize the person. Test the theory behind formative feedback by using it in our own communication.

Whenever you send evaluative feedback messages, whether positive or negative, preface your statements so as to make it clear that what you are offering is your opinion only. Such phrases as "It seems to me," "In my opinion," and "I think" are usually helpful, because they show your awareness that other interpretations and options are possible. Avoid using phrases like "You must" or "That's stupid." Such comments almost always elicit a certain amount of defensiveness. Expressing either positive or negative feedback in less than adamant terms tends to create a more favorable and receptive climate for the relationship.

NONEVALUATIVE FEEDBACK

In contrast to evaluative feedback, *nonevaluative* (or *nondirective*) *feedback* makes no overt attempt to direct the actions of a communicator. Thus, we use nonevaluative feedback when we want to learn more about a person's feelings or when we want to help another person formulate thoughts about a particular subject. When we offer nonevaluative feedback, we make no reference to our own personal opinions or judgments. Instead, we simply describe, question, or indicate an interest in what the other person is communicating to us.

Despite its nonjudgmental nature, nonevaluative feedback is often construed as being positive. That is, other people's behaviors may be reinforced when we probe, interpret their messages, and offer support as they attempt to work through a problem. Nonevaluative feedback actually reaches beyond positive feedback, however, by providing others with an opportunity to examine their own problems and arrive at their own solutions. For this reason, carefully phrased nonevaluative feedback can be enormously helpful and sustaining to people who are going through a difficult period.

We will consider four kinds of nonevaluative feedback. Three—probing, understanding, and supporting—were identified by David Johnson. The fourth—"I" messages—was identified by Thomas Gordon.[8]

Probing *Probing* is a nonevaluative technique in which we ask people for additional information to draw them out and to demonstrate our willingness to listen to their problems. For example, suppose that a student is concerned about his or her grades in a particular course and says to you, "I'm really upset. All of my friends are doing better in geology than I am." If you use probing, you might ask, "Why does this situation bother you?" or "What is there about not getting good grades that concerns you?" or "What do you suppose caused this to happen?" Responding in this way gives the other person the chance to think through the overall nature of the problem while providing him or her with an opportunity for emotional release. In contrast, comments like "So what? Who cares about that dumb class?" or "Grades don't matter. What are you worrying about?" or "You really were dumb when you stopped studying" would tend to stop the student from thinking through and discussing the problem and instead would probably create defensiveness.

Understanding   A second kind of nonevaluative response is what Johnson calls *understanding*. When we offer *understanding*, we seek to comprehend what the other person is saying to us, and we check ourselves by *paraphrasing* (restating) what we believe we have heard. Paraphrasing shows that we care about other people and the problems they face.

Examine the following paraphrases to develop a feel for the nature of this kind of response:

PERSON 1: I don't think I have the skill to be picked for the team.

PERSON 2: You believe you're not good enough to make the team this year?

PERSON 1: I envy those guys so much.

PERSON 2: You mean you're jealous of the people in that group?

If we use understanding early in a relationship, in effect we communicate that we care enough about the interaction to want to be certain we comprehend what the other person is saying to us. Such a response encourages the relationship because it encourages the other person to describe and detail his or her feelings. By delivering understanding both verbally and nonverbally, we also provide support by showing that we are sensitive to the other person's feelings and are really willing to listen.

Supportive Feedback   A third kind of nonevaluative feedback is what Johnson calls *supportive feedback*. This response indicates that a problem the other person deems important and significant is also viewed by the listener as important and significant.

For example, suppose that a friend comes to you with a problem he or she feels is extremely serious. Perhaps your friend has worked himself or herself into a state of extreme agitation and implies that you cannot possibly understand the situation. In offering supportive feedback you would attempt to calm your friend down by assuring him or her that the world has not ended and that you do understand the problem.

Offering supportive feedback is difficult. We have to be able to reduce the intensity of other people's feelings while letting them know that we consider their problems real and serious. Such comments as "It's stupid to worry about that" or "Is that all that's worrying you?" are certainly not supportive. A better approach might be to say, "I can see you are upset. Let's talk about it. I'm sure you can find a way to solve the problem." A friend who is upset because he or she has just failed an exam needs supportive feedback: "I can see you are worried. I don't blame you for being upset." This is certainly not the time to suggest that there is no valid reason for being upset or that your friend's feelings are inappropriate. It would be foolish to say, "Next time you'll know better. I told you that not studying wouldn't get you anywhere." When we use supportive feedback, we judge the problems to be important, but we do not attempt to solve them ourselves; instead, we encourage people to discover their own solutions.

According to Doris Iarovici, a medical student at Yale, "One of the best things you can do for any patient is to listen and show that you care."[9] This, in a nutshell, is supportive feedback.

"I" Messages   Finally, certain nonevaluative feedback messages are called *"I" messages*, a term coined by Thomas Gordon. When we deliver an *"I"* message, we do not pass judgment on the other person's actions but simply convey our own feelings about the nature of the situation.

According to Gordon, when people interact with us, they are often unaware of how their actions affect us. We have the option of providing these people with either evaluative or nonevaluative feedback. Neither type is inherently good or bad. However, far too often the way we formulate our evaluative feedback adversely affects the nature of our interactions and the growth of our relationships. For example, do any of these statements sound familiar? "You made me angry!" "You're no good!" "You're in my way!" "You're a slob!" What do these statements have in common? As you have probably noticed, each one contains the word *you*. Each also places the blame for something on another person. When relationships experience difficulties, people tend to resort more and more to name-calling and blaming others. Such feedback messages serve to create schisms that are difficult and sometimes even impossible to bridge.

To avoid this, Gordon suggests that we replace "you" messages with "I" messages. If, for example, a parent tells a child, "You're pestering me," the child's interpretation will probably be, "I am bad," and this interpretation will evoke a certain amount of defensivenes or hostility toward the parent ("I am *not* bad!"). But if the parent tells the child, "I'm really very tired and I don't feel like playing right now," the child's reaction is more likely to be, "Mom is tired." Such an approach is more likely to elicit the type of behavior the parent desires than name-calling and blaming ("You are a pest") would be. Keeping this in mind, which of the following messages do you believe would be more likely to elicit a favorable response?

> SUPERVISOR TO WORKERS: You lazy bums! We'll never meet the deadline if you don't work faster!

> SUPERVISOR TO WORKERS: I'm afraid that if we don't work faster, we'll miss the deadline, and the company will lose a lot of money.

Obviously, the second statement would not produce the defensiveness that would be engendered by the first.

"I" messages have one other aspect you should be aware of. It is quite common to say "I am angry" to another person. Anger, however, is a secondary emotion. We are angry *because of* some stimulus or stimuli. In actuality, we *develop* anger. For example, if your child or a child you are watching ran into the street, your first response would probably be fear. Only after the child was safe would you develop anger, and then you would probably share your anger—rather than your fear—with the child. When formulating an angry "I" message, be certain to look beyond or beneath your anger and ask yourself why you are angry. Try to identify the forces that precipitated your anger—these are the feelings that should be expressed. Thus, if someone says something that hurts you, find ways to express the initial *hurt* rather than the resulting *anger*.

Using "I" messages as feedback will not always evoke the behavior you want from the other person, but it will help to prevent the defensive, self-serving behaviors that "you" messages frequently elicit.

At this point, ask yourself which of the types of feedback seem best. Which do you feel are most important? As you probably realize, the categories and types of feedback we have discussed are not necessarily good or bad. Each type can be put to good use. Thus, whether you choose to offer evaluative or nonevaluative responses depends on the person with whom you are interacting and on the nature of the situation in which you find yourself.

Effects of Feedback

How do you think feedback affects interpersonal communication? Suppose, for example, that someone is telling you a funny story. What would happen if you should consciously decide to treat this person politely but neither to smile nor to laugh at the story? Such a reaction—polite but somber—can cause the best of storytellers to stop communicating. Sometimes in the middle of a story, the teller will notice that the listener is not amused. At this point, in an attempt to determine if the receiver heard what was said, the sender will repeat or rephrase key phrases of the story: "Don't you understand? What happened was . . ." or "You see, what this means is . . ." The feedback given by the respondent in any encounter strongly influences the direction and outcome of the interaction.[10] You might want to try the "no laugh" procedure the next time someone begins to relate a humorous incident or tale to you. If you do, note how not laughing affected the sender's ability to formulate a message.

The Skill Builder on the opposite page, adapted from an experiment designed by Harold Leavitt and Ronald Mueller, demonstrates how feedback affects the development of our relationships.[11] Feedback usually increases the accuracy with which information is passed from person to person. However, it also increases the amount of time required to transmit information. Under the "zero feedback" condition (phase 1 of the exercise), the speaker requires less time to transmit the information to the receiver than he or she would under either the "limited feedback" condition (phase 2) or the "free feedback" condition (phase 3). Still, most communicators feel that the added time is more than compensated for by the increased accuracy of the replications. In other words, under "free feedback" condition, time is not wasted.

INCREASING YOUR "EAR POWER": A PROGRAM FOR EFFECTIVE LISTENING

The first step in developing effective listening habits is to become aware of the importance and effects of listening. The second step is to become aware of the importance and effects of feedback. By now, you should have accomplished these two objectives.

NOW YOU HAVE IT, NOW YOU DON'T

Choose a partner. You and your partner should each draw on a card or slip of paper three designs consisting of a random series of straight, interconnecting lines (like the samples shown below). Do not show the diagrams to each other. The purpose of the exercise is to give verbal instructions that will enable your partner to reproduce your diagrams.

Deliver your instructions under three conditions:

1. *"Zero feedback."* When you explain your first design, turn your back to your partner and neither watch nor comment on his or her efforts. Your partner is not allowed to speak to you or look at you during this phase. This situation approximates a zero-feedback (no feedback) condition.

2. *"Limited feedback."* When you describe the second design, you may turn and watch your partner work. You may comment on what he or she is drawing, but your partner may not speak to you or look at you. This approximates a limited-feedback condition.

3. *"Free feedback."* Finally, when you describe your third design to your partner, you may interact openly with each other. You may observe and comment on your partner's efforts, and your partner may interact with you by facing you and asking you questions to check on the accuracy of his or her drawing. This approximates a free-feedback condition.

Next, if time permits, you and your partner should reverse roles and repeat the above three steps.

Which condition produced the fastest replication? Why? Which condition produced the most accurate replication? Why? During which phase of the experience were you most confident? Least confident? Why? How did functioning as sender or receiver alter your feelings during each phase of the experience?

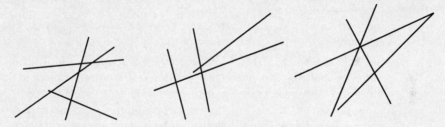

The next step is to sharpen your listening skills by participating in a series of exercises and experiences. If you really want to improve your listening, these exercises should not merely be done once and put aside. Your listening skills will improve only if you return to them—and to similar experiences—repeatedly.

Focusing Your Attention

Let's begin our "effective listening" program by considering the need to be able to focus our attention. It is apparent that if we are to listen effectively, we must be able to pay attention to what is being communicated. However, numerous internal and external stimuli bombard us and compete for our attention.

The difficulties we experience when attempting to focus attention are confirmed by how often, and in how many situations, we are admonished to "Pay

attention!" When was the last time someone said something like "He told us that in class. Weren't you paying attention?" All too frequently the response is, "Well, I thought I was." We will explore several ways you can work to improve your ability to attend consciously to information. Before beginning, we should emphasize that developing this ability will be a lifelong project.

If you are to learn to focus your attention and improve your listening skills, one of your main needs is to handle your *emotions*. Feelings of hate, anger, happiness, and sadness can decrease our listening efficiency. As we become emotionally involved in a conversation, we simply are less able or less willing to focus our attention accurately.

Ralph Nichols in the book *Are You Listening?* notes that certain words often cause us to react emotionally and thus reduce the extent to which we are able to pay attention. He calls these "red-flag words." According to Nichols, red-flag words produce an emotional deafness that sends our listening efficiency down to zero.[12] Among the words known to function as red flags for some listeners are *AIDS, punk, mother-in-law, spastic,* and *income tax.* When some people hear these words, or other red-flag words, they abandon any effort to understand or perceive. Instead, they take "side trips," dwelling on their own feelings and associations. In effect, the emotional eruption they are experiencing causes a listening disruption. It should be noted that, like words and phrases, certain topics can also make us react emotionally and lessen our ability to concentrate. For these reasons it is important to identify words, phrases, or topics that tend to distract you emotionally. Your "distraction words" are personal and unique to you and change as you change. An issue that caused emotional deafness for you in the past may not even distract you momentarily in the future. Thus it is a good practice to keep a record of all your "distractors." If possible, list them on cards, and reexamine them every 3 or 4 months. By keeping and updating your red-flag list, you will be better able to recognize and handle distractions during interpersonal encounters.

Physical factors can also be distractors. For example, the room you are in may be too hot or cold for your comfort, the space may be too small or too large, or the seating arrangement may be inadequate. (Have you ever tried to listen politely and efficiently when the springs in your chair were about to poke through the upholstery and pierce you?)

Compile a list of words and phrases that tend to distract you. Note the reasons for your choices.

"You will like Mr. Woofard. He has an attention-deficit disorder."
Drawing by Booth; © 1991 The New Yorker Magazine, Inc.

In addition to environmental factors, *other people* can also be a distraction. People you are relating to may speak too loudly or too softly. A person may have an accent you find difficult to comprehend or an appearance that interests or perhaps alarms you. (Have you ever been engaged in conversation with someone wearing such an unusual outfit that you found it difficult to focus your attention on what he or she was saying?)

One more factor should also be noted: the *"speech-thought differential."* To put it simply, we can think faster than we can speak. When communicating, we usually speak at a rate of 125 to 150 words a minute. Researchers have found, however, that we can comprehend much higher rates of speech—perhaps even 500 words a minute. What does this mean for you, the listener? It means that when someone speaks at a normal rate, you have free time left over and may therefore tend to take mental excursions and daydream. Then, when

*"I'm sorry, dear, I must have lost consciousness.
What were you saying?"*

Drawing by Chon Day; © 1982 The New Yorker Magazine, Inc.

**Under what conditions
do you "lose
consciousness"?**

you return your attention to the speaker, you may find that he or she is far ahead of you. We must make conscious efforts to use the speech-thought differential effectively. We can do this by internally summarizing and paraphrasing what is being said *as we listen* and by asking ourselves questions that help focus our attention instead of distracting us from the subject at hand. (Several speech-compression devices on the market can speed up the rate of ordinary speech without distorting the speaker's voice.)

Focusing or maintaining your attention is an act you must perform constantly. Smart communicators periodically check to see if their attention has wandered. Make an attention check an integral part of your "effective listening" program. Although the check itself can become an attention distractor, its benefits outweigh this potential deficit.Only after becoming aware that you are not listening can you begin to make the necessary corrections.[13]

Finally, attentive listeners adopt nonverbal behaviors that support listening. Ineffective listeners typically exhibit *passive* listening behaviors—they do not face the person they are interacting with; their posture is defensive and tense; they lean away from the other person; they avoid eye contact. Attentive listeners exhibit *active* listening behaviors—they face the other person directly, adopt an open posture, lean slightly toward the other person, and maintain comfortable eye contact.

We should be aware, however, that culture sometimes interferes with our ability to distinguish between attentive and inattentive listeners. The use of eye contact, for example, differs in traditional black and white cultures. White people typically look away from a conversational partner when speaking and look directly at the partner when listening; black people, in contrast, usually look at the other person when speaking and away when listening. Consequently, whites are apt to perceive blacks who look away while listening to them as not paying attention, when just the opposite is true.

Setting Appropriate Goals

Far too often we find ourselves listening without really knowing what we are listening for, and as a result we become bored and irritated. One way to combat "listening blahs" is to set specific goals when listening. Research indicates that listening effectiveness increases when goals are identified. How can you make this evidence work for you?

Listening goals identify what you personally would like to gain during and after attending to a particular message. When you establish goals, you answer the question, "Why am I listening to this?" Listening goals are closely related to the levels of listening discussed earlier in this chapter. In general, we listen to *understand*, to *retain*, to *analyze and evaluate content*, and to *develop empathic relationships* with others. Thus, one way to set your listening goals is to identify which level of listening is most appropriate in a particular situation. For example, if you are an employee who is expected to internalize a series of direc-

Before beginning an interaction, establish in your own mind one or more listening goals. After the interaction, analyze the extent to which you were able to attain your goal or goals.

"What's wrong with one hundred per cent attention twenty per cent of the time?"

Drawing by Cline; © 1991 The New Yorker Magazine, Inc.

tions for handling highly explosive materials, you will listen to understand and retain instructions. If you are listening to a series of lectures on types of computer operations and your objective is to select a computer for your company, you will listen to understand and retain but also to analyze and evaluate. In contrast, suppose your friend has lost a parent. In this situation your goal will be to listen empathically.

Just as trains switch tracks, so you should be able to switch listening goals. The goals you set are not meant to imprison you; they are meant to help you be flexible, able to adapt to the demands of each situation or experience.

Listening to Understand Ideas

After listening to information from another person, have you ever made a statement like "I'm sure I understand the main point" or "The central idea is crystal-clear"? When we listen to understand, we listen for main ideas or central concepts. Let's examine how this works.

Listening to understand may be compared to a simple tooth extraction. When you visit the dentist to have a tooth pulled, you assume that the dentist will not simply reach into your mouth and pull any tooth at random. Instead, you assume that the dentist will locate the tooth that needs to be extracted, take hold of only that tooth, and remove it. When we listen to understand—a process that underlies all higher levels of listening—we, like the dentist, must locate the central concepts contained in the speaker's message and remove them (in this case for further examination). Since it is almost impossible to remember every word that is said to us, we should work to recall the concepts which are most important—in other words, the ideas which constitute the main points of the message. Thus, when you listen to understand, you seek to identify key words and phrases that will help you accurately summarize the concepts being discussed. But remember that unless the ideas you extract from the messages you receive are accurate representations of what was said, you are only hearing, not listening.

Listening to Retain Information

Robert Montgomery, a training expert who has developed a wealth of material on memory for the American Management Associations, says, "The art of retention is the art of attention."[14] If you are to retain what you hear, you must first learn how to focus your attention and then learn how to make certain that you understand what you have heard. Once you can focus your attention on what another person is saying and can understand what the person has said, you are ready to move up to the next level—listening to retain.

After receiving directions when traveling, did you ever find yourself saying to yourself, "Do I turn right or left here? What was I told?" After having a discussion with a friend and assuming that you understood the friend's point of view, did you ever find yourself wondering what that point of view was? Even worse, after being introduced to someone, do you ever find yourself asking, "What was that person's name?" We will now explore several techniques that you can use to help you retain what you hear. Such aids are commonly referred to as *mnemonic devices*. Use the ones that work best for you.

Your basic tool for retaining the information you hear is *repetition*. The more you repeat a concept or idea, the more likely you are to be able to recall it later. Repetition has two faces: We use repetition when we repeat a statement verbatim (exactly reproduce what was said) and when we paraphrase (restate what was said using other words).

One effective way to remember what others say is to reproduce their words verbatim in writing. The more proficient you are at note-taking, the more information you are likely to be able to retain. Of course, in interpersonal situations, it is neither advisable nor practical to take notes. However, it is a good idea to keep a few index cards or a small notepad handy to record important names, numbers, appointments, and information.

PARAPHRASE

Paraphrasing can also be used to improve your retentiveness. By restating in your own words what a person has said to you, you not only check on your own understanding but also help yourself recall what was said. We will consider the art of paraphrasing in more detail below, when we discuss empathic listening. For now it will suffice to realize that paraphrasing can help alleviate some of the problems created by the "speech-thought differential" we spoke of earlier. If you use some of your extra thinking time to replicate for yourself what has just been said, your mind will be less likely to wander.

VISUALIZATION

Frequently, we are better able to recall information if we picture something about it. For example, many people are able to associate names, places, and numbers with specific visual images. Often, the more outrageous or creative the image, the better it will help them recall a name. For instance, you might picture a person named John Sanderson as standing atop a large sand pile or sand dune, or a person named Susan Grant might be pictured as standing inside Grant's tomb.

Listening to Analyze and Evaluate Content

Being able to analyze and evaluate what you listen to calls for even greater skill than retention. When you learn to analyze and evaluate content effectively, you become adept at spotting fallacies in the arguments and statements you encounter during interpersonal discourse.

Often, we let our prior convictions prevent us from processing and fairly evaluating what we hear. For instance, consider the following conversation:

ALICE: Did you hear? Sandy was arrested by the police for selling drugs.

JIM: Sandy? I don't believe it. The police made a mistake. She isn't that type.

In this interchange Jim is jumping to a conclusion. Instead of analyzing the information he was given, he has reacted on the basis of his prior knowledge. How should Jim have reacted? Should he have agreed that the police were right to arrest Sandy? We don't think so. We think Jim should have asked what evidence the police had to support their claim and what evidence Sandy offered in her own defense. Effective listeners do not let their convictions run away with them but, instead, reserve judgment until the facts are in. In other words, they withhold evaluation until their comprehension of the situation is complete.

Attempts at persuasion often take the form of one person trying to make another believe something because "Everyone else believes it." If we accept such drivel, we may find ourselves swept away on a bandwagon. We might support a candidate simply because we imagine that everyone else does. Or we might join a pyramid scheme because we are convinced that everyone involved will become rich. Effective listeners realize that they have a *choice*. They may join the bandwagon, or they may let it pass them by. Effective listeners do not feel compelled to follow the crowd.

If you become proficient at evaluating and analyzing the information you listen to, you will discover that people frequently argue or talk in circles. For example:

ELLEN: Divorce is wrong.

JOSÉ: Why?

ELLEN: Because my minister told me it is wrong.

JOSÉ: Why did he tell you that?

ELLEN: Because it is wrong!

For 1 week, keep a record of all circular conversations you hear. Point out the fallacy in each instance.

We have a tendency to talk in circles when we are arguing without evidence, particularly if we feel an emotional tie to the topic under discussion or if we believe that our position is closely connected to our value system. When this occurs, we simply insist we are right: "That's all there is to it." We tell ourselves that we do not need reasons. Effective listeners perceive the fallacy inherent in circular reasoning and weigh a speaker's evidence by mentally questioning it. Effective listeners "listen between the lines."

Listening Empathically, Listening Actively

When they are questioning witnesses, attorneys listen for contradictions or irrelevancies: that is, they listen to analyze. In contrast, social workers usually listen to help people work through a personal problem. This, too, is an important level of listening. It is referred to as *empathic*, or *active*, listening, and it is the last type of listening we will consider in our "effective listening" program.

The term *empathic listening* was popularized by the psychotherapist Carl Rogers, who believed that listening could be used to help individuals understand their own situations and problems.[15] When you listen actively, or empathically, you do more than passively absorb the words that are spoken to you. Active listeners also try to internalize the other person's feelings and see life through his or her eyes.

When we listen to help someone else work through a personal problem, we are listening empathically, or actively. A good teacher will use empathic listening when helping a student.

Ron Sherman/Stock, Boston

The following poem by David Ignatow depicts the *non*empathic listener in operation. Are you at all like this?

TWO FRIENDS

I have something to tell you.
I'm listening.
I'm dying.
I'm sorry to hear.
I'm getting old.
It's terrible.
It is, I thought you should know.
Of course, and I'm sorry. Keep in touch.
I will. And you too.
And let me know what's new.
Certainly, though it can't be much.
And stay well.
And you too.
And go slow.
And you, too.[16]

How often do you put on an "I am listening" mask, nod agreement, and utter the appropriate "Ohs" and "I sees," when in reality you are miles away and self-concerned?

We need to be willing to acknowledge the seriousness of other people's problems. We need to take the time required to draw them out so that they can discuss a problem and come to terms with it. We need to show the other person that we understand the problem. We can do this by paraphrasing

▶ **POINTS TO PONDER**

LISTEN HERE: POSSIBLE MOTTO FOR A MAN WHO IS ALL EARS

Mr. Kirk Martin listens, in person and by appointment only. "I will talk, if a person asks me to, or if he looks like he wants me to," Mr. Martin explains. "I can talk eyeball to eyeball to anyone who comes through my front door." Mr. Martin, 48, a professional truck and taxicab driver who sells one-family homes and farms on the side, began his listening enterprise with a newspaper ad: "I will listen to you talk 30 minutes without comment for $5," the ad said. "I get about 10–20 calls a day now, but only a few of those make appointments." He says his clients are from all walks of life. "Many of them are troubled people who need someone to hear them out, just once."

Source: © The Associated Press, 1975.

the person's statements, and also by reinforcing those statements with genuine nonverbal cues—eye contact, physical contact (touching), and facial expressions.

Active, empathic listeners put themselves in the speaker's place in an effort to understand the speaker's feelings. Active, empathic listeners appreciate both the meaning and the feeling behind what another person is saying. Thus, in effect, active, empathic listeners *convey* to the speaker that they are seeing things from the speaker's point of view.

Active, empathic listeners rely heavily on paraphrase:

PERSON 1: I am so mad at my mother.

PERSON 2: If I'm not mistaken, your mother is giving you trouble. Is that right?

PERSON 1: My boss is really trying to fire me.

PERSON 2: If I understand you, you believe your boss is out to replace you. Do I have it straight?

To paraphrase effectively, follow this three-step process:

1. Make a tentative statement that invites correction; e.g., "If I'm not mistaken . . ."
2. Repeat the basic idea or ideas in your own words.
3. Check your paraphrase with the other person; e.g., "Is that correct?"

By paraphrasing a sender's thoughts, listeners accomplish at least two purposes. First, they let the other person know that they care enough to listen. Second, if the speaker's message has not been accurately received, they offer the other person the opportunity to adjust, change, or modify the message so that they can understand it as intended:

PERSON 1: I'm quitting my job soon.

PERSON 2: You're leaving your job tomorrow?

PERSON 1: Well not that soon! But within a few weeks.

In summary, when you listen actively, or empathically, you listen for total meaning, and you listen in order to respond to feelings. When you listen empathically, the following statements will *not* appear in your conversation:

"You must do . . ."

"You should do . . ."

"You're wrong!"

"Let me tell you what to do."

"You sure have a funny way of looking at things."

"You're making a big mistake."

"The best answer is . . ."

"Don't worry about it."

"You think you've got problems! Ha!"

"That reminds me of the time I . . ."

Active, empathic listeners do not judge; they reflect, consider, and often restate in their own words their impressions of the sender's expression. Active listeners also check to determine if their impressions are acceptable to the sender. What kind of a checker are you?

At this point, you should realize why it takes "more than two good ears" to listen.

✔ SKILL BUILDER

WHAT'S THAT YOU SAID?

Choose a partner and select one of the following topics to discuss:

Abortion	Premarital sex
Capital punishment	Socialized medicine
An embarrassing situation	Lying

One person begins the discussion. Before adding ideas, the second person must paraphrase the first speaker's statement. If the paraphrase is accurate, the second person may continue by offering his or her own thought. However, if the paraphrase is inaccurate, the second person must correct any misperceptions. Only when the first speaker agrees that the paraphrase is accurate may the second person continue.

SUMMARY

Listening is a deliberate process through which we seek to understand and retain aural (heard) stimuli. Unlike hearing, which occurs automatically, listening depends on a complex set of acquired skills. The average person listens at only 25 percent efficiency, losing 75 percent of what is heard. A graphic illustration of the results of inefficient listening is distortion of a message in serial communication (when a message is passed from one person to another in a series). A principal reason for poor listening is failure to determine the "involvement level" appropriate in a particular situation. Various behaviors we adopt cause us to *unlisten*—that is, they impede true understanding. Men and women exhibit different listening habits and behaviors.

A prerequisite for effective listening is effective feedback. Feedback consists of all the verbal and nonverbal messages that a person consciously or unconsciously sends out in response to another person's communication. Through feedback we either confirm or correct the impressions others have of us and our attitudes. There are two main types of feedback: (1) Evaluative feedback gives an opinion, positive or negative, and attempts to influence the behavior of others. (2) Nonevaluative feedback gives emotional support. Probing, understanding (or paraphrasing), supportive feedback, and "I" messages are all forms of nonevaluative feedback that help sustain interpersonal relationships. When listening and giving feedback to people from other cultures, it is essential to be extremely sensitive to cultural norms.

You can improve your listening skills by learning to focus your attention while listening and by setting appropriate listening goals. Listening to understand ideas, to retain information, to analyze and evaluate, and to empathize require progressively more effort and attention.

SUGGESTIONS FOR FURTHER READING

Adler, Mortimer J.: *How to Speak, How to Listen,* Macmillan, New York, 1983. Interesting practical advice on listening from a philosopher.

Barker, Larry L.: *Listening Behavior,* Prentice-Hall, Englewood Cliffs, N.J., 1971. A comprehensive, well-documented analysis of listening and feedback.

Bone, Diane: *The Business of Listening,* Crisp, Los Altos, Calif., 1990. A concise program of activities for improving listening. Available with a video program.

Borisoff, Deborah, and Michael Purdy: *Listening in Everyday Life: A Personal and Professional Approach,* University Press of America, Lanham, Md., 1991. Addresses the role listening plays in our personal and professional lives, and gives steps to take to strengthen listening skills.

Floyd, James J.: *Listening: A Practical Approach,* Scott, Foresman, Glenview, Ill., 1985. An easy-to-read, experientially based work.

Friedman, Paul G.: *Listening Processes: Attention, Understanding, Evaluation,* National Education Association, Washington, D.C., 1986. Explores listening and our personal value systems.

Leavitt, H., and R. Mueller: "Some Effects of Feedback on Communication," *Human Relations,* vol. 4, 1951, pp. 401–410. One of the classic studies.

Nichols, Ralph G.: "Do We Know How to Listen?" *The Speech Teacher,* vol. 10, 1961, pp. 118–124. Provides a useful overview of the listening process.

Nichols, Ralph G., and Leonard A. Stevens: *Are You Listening?* McGraw-Hill, New York, 1957. A classic book about listening that helped popularize interest in the field.

Reed, Warren H.: *Positive Listening: Learning to Hear What People Are Really Saying,* Franklin Watts, New York, 1985. A useful guide to effective listening in business.

Rogers, Carl R.: *On Becoming a Person,* Houghton Mifflin, Boston, Mass., 1961. Rogers builds his theory of helping others on sound listening skills.

Steil, Lyman K., Larry L. Barker, and Kittie W. Watson: *Effective Listening: Key to Your Success,* Addison-Wesley, Reading, Mass., 1983. Presents an effective how-to approach to improve listening skills.

Weaver, Carl H.: *Human Listening: Processes and Behavior,* Bobbs-Merrill, Indianapolis, Ind., 1972. Contains useful exercises for improving listening abilities.

Wolf, Florence I., Nadine C. Marsnik, William S. Tracey, and Ralph G. Nichols: *Perceptive Listening,* Holt, Rinehart and Winston, New York, 1983. A comprehensive textbook on listening for college students, including older students.

Wolvin, Andrew, and Carolyn Gwynn Coakley, *Listening,* 3d ed., Brown, Dubuque, Iowa, 1988. Contains a valuable overview of listening theory and activities for practice.

NOTES

1. Paul Tory Rankin, "The Measurement of the Ability to Understand Spoken Language," Ph.D. dissertation, University of Michigan, 1926, p. 43. Larry Barker, R. Edwards, C. Gaines, K. Gladney, and F. Hally, "An Investigation of Proportional Time Spent in Various Communication Activities by College Students," *Journal of Applied Communication Research,* vol. 8, 1980, pp. 101–109.

2. For a detailed discussion, see Ralph G. Nichols and Leonard A. Stevens, *Are You Listening?* New York, McGraw-Hill, New York, 1957.

3. John R. Freund and Arnold Nelson, "Distortion in Communication," in B. Peterson, G. Goldhaber, and R. Pace (eds.), *Communication Probes,* Science Research Associates, Chicago, Ill., 1974, pp. 122–124.

4. Gerald Goldhaber, *Organizational Communication,* 4th ed., Brown, Dubuque, Iowa, 1988.

5. Kevin Daly (president of Communispond, New York City), press release, 1983.

6. Alfie Kohn, "Girl Talk, Guy Talk," *Psychology Today,* February 1988, pp. 65–66.

7. Don Tosti, from a speech, "Operant Conditioning," presented in New York City, fall 1983.

8. David W. Johnson, *Reaching Out: Interpersonal Effectiveness and Self-Actualization,* Prentice-Hall, Englewood Cliffs, N.J., 1972. Thomas Gordon, *Leader Effectiveness Training,* Wyden, New York, 1977.

9. Doris Iarovici, quoted in "Making TLC a Requirement," *Newsweek,* August 12, 1991.

10. For a discussion of the kinds of information conveyed by verbal and nonverbal feedback see Dale G. Leathers, "The Informational Potential of the Nonverbal and Verbal Components of Feedback Responses," *Southern Speech Communication Journal,* vol. 44, 1979, pp. 331–354.

11. H. Leavitt and R. Mueller, "Some Effects of Feedback on Communication," *Human Relations.* vol. 4, 1951, pp. 401–410.

12. Ralph Nichols and Leonard A. Stevens, *Are You Listening?* McGraw-Hill, New York, 1957.

13. Ralph G. Nichols, "Listening Is a Ten-Part Skill," *Nation's Business,* vol. 45, 1957, p. 4.

14. Robert Montgomery, *Memory Made Easy,* Amacom, New York, 1990.

15. See Carl Rogers, *Becoming Partners,* 1973: Dell, New York, and *On Becoming a Person,* Houghton Mifflin, Boston, Mass., 1972.

16. David Ignatow, "Two Friends," *Figures of the Human.* Copyright 1963 by David Ignatow. Wesleyan University Press by permission of University Press of New England.

INTERPERSONAL
COMMUNICATION

UNDERSTANDING RELATIONSHIPS

After finishing this chapter, you should be able to:

Explain the reasons behind our need for person-to-person contacts

Define *inclusion, control,* and *affection*

Discuss what can happen when our need for inclusion, control, or affection is not met

Describe relationships in terms of breadth and depth

Explain the theory of social penetration

Discuss and distinguish between 10 stages of relationships

Explain cost-benefit theory

Identify ways to enhance your satisfaction with your relationships

People meet and separate. But funny things happen in between.

Mark L. Knapp

In *Peoplemaking*, Virginia Satir notes: "Once a human being has arrived on this earth, communication is the largest single factor determining what kinds of relationships he makes with others and what happens to him in the world about him. How he manages his survival, how he develops intimacy, how productive he is, how he makes sense . . . are largely dependent on his communication skills."[1] This chapter explores the nature of the relationships we share with others, our satisfaction or dissatisfaction with them, and how we can improve them. One thing all our relationships have in common is communication. Through communication we not only establish and maintain but also withdraw from and end relationships. Through communication we define what we think of ourselves in relationship to others. Through communication we express ourselves and our needs to others. Some relationships we share with others are rich and intense; some are superficial and almost meaningless. The communication that characterizes these relationships will also be rich or superficial. Whatever the nature of the experience, what causes us to come together in a relationship is communication, and what happens to the relationship over time is a result of communication. Communication can function as either the lifeblood or the death blow of a relationship. Let us examine how and why.

THE ROLE OF RELATIONSHIPS

As society becomes increasingly technological, we cannot help feeling that the environment in which we live is becoming less personal. It is only natural that we seem impelled to seek warm, personal relationships to compensate; consequently, a major theme of our time has become our desire for closer, more personal ties. As John Naisbitt writes in *Megatrends*, the future may be high-tech, but it must also become "high-touch" if we are to live comfortably in it.[2] We shall now explore why we need such person-to-person contacts.

Functions of Relationships: Three Basic Needs

A vast body of research consistently attests that we attempt to meet our needs for inclusion, control, and affection through our relationships.[3]

Inclusion has to do with the varying degrees to which we all need to establish and maintain a feeling of mutual interest with other people—a sense that we can take an interest in others and that others can take an interest in us. We want others to pay attention to us, to take the time to understand us. Wanting to be included is normal. We all remember how it feels to be left out— to be the last person asked to join a team, not to be invited to an important party, or to be ignored during a mealtime conversation. When our need for

Our relationships help us to meet our needs for inclusion, control, and affection. Inclusion *(top)* has to do with taking an interest in other people and feeling that others are interested in us. Control *(middle)* has to do with our need for a satisfactory level of influence and power. Affection *(bottom),* of course, has to do with our need for emotional closeness.

Top to bottom: Jim Raycroft/The Stock Market; Jon Feingersh 1990/The Stock Market; Elyse Lewin/ Image Bank

● CULTURE AND COMMUNICATION

WOMEN, INTIMACY, AND ISOLATION

According to the sociologist Deborah Tannen, for women life is a struggle to preserve intimacy and avoid isolation. Do you believe this is true only of American women? What about women from other cultures? What about men?

Source: Deborah Tannen, *You Just Don't Understand: Women and Men in Conversation*, Ballantine, New York, 1991.

inclusion is met, we tend to feel worthwhile and fulfilled. If it goes unmet, we tend to feel lonely, and our health may even suffer.

To be sure, loneliness is an all too common affliction of our age. But what exactly is it? A consensus has emerged that loneliness begins with a recognition that the interpersonal relationships we have are not the kinds we would like to have.[4] Thus, loneliness can be considered a result of a perceived discrepancy between desired and achieved social relationships.[5] Lonely people find it difficult to make connections with others. When our person-to-person contacts are deficient, we feel alone, and we seek substitutes for these contacts—sometimes, for example, opting for the company of professional "contact people" such as physicians or even radio talk show hosts. Inclusion is so interconnected with our well-being that in the early 1980s the California State Department of Mental Health mounted an advertising campaign designed to convince people that social relationships could enhance their physical and mental health and increase their life span.

Control has to do with our need to establish and maintain satisfactory levels of influence and power in our relationships. To varying degrees, we need to feel that we can take charge of a situation, whereas at other times we need to feel comfortable assuming a more submissive role. When our control need goes unmet, we may conclude that others do not respect or value our abilities and that we are viewed as incapable of making a sound decision or of directing others' or our own future.

Finally, *affection* has to do with our need to give and receive love and to experience emotionally close relationships. If our need for affection goes unfulfilled, we are likely to conclude that we are unlovable and that therefore people will remain emotionally detached from us (that is, they will try to avoid establishing close ties with us). In contrast, if our experiences with affection have been more pleasant, we are probably comfortable handling both close and distant relationships, and most likely we recognize that not everyone we come into contact with will necessarily care for us in the same way.

Do you think males and females differ in their need for inclusion, control, or affection? Do they differ in the way they express their needs? Why or why not?

These three basic needs differ from each other in a significant way. Inclusion comes first; that is, it is our need for inclusion that impels us to establish a relationship in the first place. By comparison, our needs for control and affection are met through the relationships we have already established. Thus, as the psychologist William Schutz notes, "Generally speaking, inclusion is cornered with the problem of *in* or *out*, control is concerned with *top* or *bottom*, and affection with *close* or *far*."[6]

The extent to which needs are felt and met differs from person to person. We can therefore categorize people according to "need levels." If people do not attempt to satisfy a need, we say that their need level is deficient. In contrast, if people try constantly to satisfy a need, we say that their "need level" is excessive. A person who has a deficient need for inclusion, control, or affection might be described as, respectively, "undersocial," an "abdicrat," or "underpersonal"; and a person whose needs in these areas were excessive could be called, respectively, "oversocial," an "autocrat," or "overpersonal." Undersocial people tend to avoid interacting with others, insisting instead that they value privacy. Oversocial people seek to be with others at all times. The fears experienced by these two types are similar—both fear being ignored or being left out—but the overt behaviors they use to compensate for their fears are different. Similarly, the "abdicrat" typically assumes a submissive or subordinate role, whereas the "autocrat" wants to dominate at all times. Again, however, both types fear being viewed as incapable or irresponsible; they just compensate in different ways. "Underpersonal" people attempt to keep all their relationships superficial, and "overpersonal" people try to become very close to others. Both are motivated by the same strong need for affection, and both fear rejection; but they express their needs through opposite behaviors.

We are not suggesting that people who are satisfied with their relationships are rare; many of us have what we consider ideal—or at least adequate—relationships that satisfy our needs. We are "social" (comfortable with people or alone), "democratic" (content to give or take orders depending on the situation), and "personal" (able to share close or distant relationships).

As we try to understand our own interpersonal needs and try to make sense out of our relationships, we should remember these classifications and how we express needs through our behavior.

Relationships and Conversation

According to Robert E. Nofsinger, author of *Everyday Conversation*, "Almost everything we do that concerns other people involves us in conversation."[7]

Some of our conversations help us accomplish our "relationship goals"; others end up impeding our ability to attain these goals. Sometimes we embarrass ourselves when conversing; sometimes we embarrass the people we are with. Sometimes we find ourselves unable to "get a word in edgewise"; sometimes we find that we seem to be talking mainly to ourselves—no one else is paying attention. Sometimes we say what we know we shouldn't say; sometimes we listen when others wish we wouldn't. It is through conversation that we establish and strengthen—or weaken and terminate—every one of our relationships. As Nofsinger reminds us, "Our family life is created and enacted each day through conversation. And, in large part, we find employment (or fail to) through our everyday talk."

Our conversations have outcomes. They produce results. Through our "moves," through "taking turns" or refusing to take turns, we influence the direction of our relationships. Thus, some of our relationships go nowhere, while others are particularly effective—usually because we worked to make them that way.

DIMENSIONS OF RELATIONSHIPS: BREADTH AND DEPTH

Every relationship—with a friend, a family member, or a coworker—can be described in terms of two concepts: *breadth* and *depth*. *Breadth* has to do with how many topics you discuss with the other person. *Depth* has to do with how central the topics are to your self-concept and how much you reveal.

According to the social psychologists Irwin Altman and Dalmas Taylor can be schematized as shown in Figure 7-1.[8] Central to their theory of "social penetration" is the idea that relationships begin with relatively narrow breadth (few topics are spoken about) and shallow depth (the inner circles are not penetrated) and progress over time in intensity and intimacy as both breadth and depth increase. Thus our relationships may develop incrementally as we move from discussing few to many topics, and from superficial topics (the periphery of the circle) to intensely personal topics (the center of the circle). Figure 7-2 is an exercise using these concepts.

The breadth of topics we discuss may be wide for casual as well as for intimate relationships, but the depth of penetration usually increases as a relationship becomes more intimate. Consequently, a highly intimate relationship

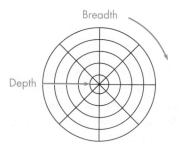

FIGURE 7-1
Breadth and depth in relationships.

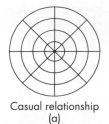

Casual relationship
(a)

Intimate relationship
(b)

FIGURE 7-2
Use arrows with the segmented concentric circles to show the contrast between one of your casual relationships and one of your more intimate relationships.

will probably have both considerable breadth and considerable depth as the people involved extend the range of topics they discuss and reveal more about how they feel about these topics.

The social-penetration model is useful for a number of reasons. First, it can help us visualize the nature of the relationships we share by indicating the range of topics we communicate about and the extent to which we reveal ourselves through our discussions. Second, the model can help explain why certain relationships seem stronger than others. For example, is there one person to whom you reveal more about a particular topic than you would reveal to anyone else? Is there someone with whom you would not even consider discussing a particular topic? Do you reveal more of yourself to some people at work than to others? Is the same true for members of your family? What about your friends? Although we may behave in ways that limit some people's access to certain portions of our "relationship circle," others may have access to its entire scope; although we may keep some from straying too far from the periphery, we may let others venture close to the center. When your communication with another person lacks breadth, depth, or both, it should not surprise you that you feel little if any bond to each other; to enhance the strength of your relationship, you would have to alter the nature and extent of your interactions.

Sometimes, in an effort to get to know another person quickly, we may discuss topics at a depth that would normally be reserved for those with whom we are more intimate. When such disclosures occur too rapidly or prematurely in the development of a relationship, they may create a feeling that "something is wrong," a signal that one participant was not ready for the relationship to progress that quickly or to be that intense. For example, employees in one company complained when a supervisor discussed personal aspects of his marriage with them during the business day; noting that hearing such intimate disclosures made them feel uncomfortable, they requested that he limit the depth and scope of his communications with them.

When interactants are ready to deepen a relationship, they see increases in breadth and depth as a natural and comfortable development.

How do you feel when someone reveals more to you than you are ready for? Have you ever made anyone feel uncomfortable by revealing too much too quickly? What prompted you to do it? How did the other person react?

DEVELOPMENT OF RELATIONSHIPS

Stages of Relationships: From Beginning to Ending to Beginning . . .

All relationships we share are complex (each of us is a unique bundle of experiences, thoughts, fears, and needs) and ever-changing (as we change, our relationships change—they grow stronger or weaker over time). Relationships pass through a number of stages as they strengthen or dissolve.[9]

"Initiating" and "experimenting"—at social gatherings, for example—are the first stages of a relationship.

Comstock

STAGE 1: INITIATING

Stage 1 involves the things that happen when we first make contact with each other. At this time, we look for signals that either impel us to initiate a conversation or tell us that we have nothing to gain by interacting. If we decide to make contact, we search for an appropriate conversation opener, for example, "Nice to meet you" or "What's happening?"

What happens when we can't find an appropriate opener? The following passage from *Conventionally Speaking* by Alan Garner describes one such possibility:

> I decided to marry her. Courtship would be a mere formality. But what to say to begin the courtship? "Would you like some of my gum?" sounded too low-class. "Hello," was too trite a greeting for my future bride. "I love you! I am hot with passion!" was too forward. "I want to make you the mother of my children," seemed a bit premature.
>
> Nothing. That's right, I said nothing. And after a while, the bus reached her stop, she got off, and I never saw her again.
>
> End of story.[10]

STAGE 2: EXPERIMENTING

Once we have initiated contact, we try to find out more about the other person; we begin to probe the unknown. This is the stage of experimenting. Often we exchange small talk—for example, we tell the other where we're from and who we know in an effort to get acquainted. Although many of us may hate small talk or "cocktail party chatter," according to Mark Knapp it serves several useful functions.

1. It provides a process for uncovering integrating topics and openings for more penetrating conversations.

2. It can serve as an audition for a future friendship or a way to increase the scope of a current friendship.

3. It provides a safe procedure for indicating who we are and how the other person can come to know us better (reduction of uncertainty).

4. It allows us to maintain a sense of community with our fellow human beings.[11]

In an article on small talk, Michael Korda notes, "The aim of small talk is to make people comfortable—to put them at their ease—not to teach, preach, or impress. It's a game, like tennis, in which the object is to keep the ball in the air for as long as possible."[12]

At this stage our relationships lack "depth": they are quite casual and superficial. The vast majority of them never progress beyond this point.

STAGE 3: INTENSIFYING

When a relationship does progress beyond experimenting, it enters the third stage, intensifying. During this stage people become "good friends"—they begin to share things in common, disclose more, become better at predicting each other's behavior, and may even adopt nicknames for each other or exhibit similar postural or clothing cues. In a sense, they are beginning to be transformed from an "I" and an "I" into a "we."

Have you had some relationships which did not pass beyond the experimentation phase but which you now wish had gone further? What kept them from intensifying?

STAGE 4: INTEGRATING

The fusion of "I" and "I" really takes place in stage 4. Two individuals are now identified as a pair, a couple, or "a package." Interpersonal synchrony is heightened; the two people may dress, act, and speak more and more alike or share a song ("our song"), a bankbook, or a project.

STAGE 5: BONDING

In stage 5, the interactants announce that their commitment to each other has been formally contracted. Their relationship is now institutionalized, formally recognized. This recognition can be a wedding license or a business contract, for example. The relationship takes on a new character: it is no longer informal. It is now guided by specified rules and regulations. Sometimes this alteration causes initial discomfort or rebellion as the interactants attempt to adjust to the change.

STAGE 6: DIFFERENTIATING

In stage 6, instead of continuing to emphasize "we," the interactants attempt to reestablish an "I" orientation, to regain a unique identity. They ask, "How are we different?" "How can I distinguish me from you?" During this phase, previously designated joint possessions take on a more individualized charac-

In the "integrating" stage of a relationship, a fusion of two individuals takes place, so that they are identified as a pair. "Bonding" is the stage at which such a relationship is formalized.

Joel Gordon

ter; "our friends" become "my friends," "our bedroom" becomes "my bedroom," "our child" becomes "your son" (especially when he misbehaves). Although an urge to differentiate the self from the other is not uncommon (we need to be individuals as well as members of a relationship), if it persists, it can signal that the relationship is in trouble or that the process of uncoupling has begun.

STAGE 7: CIRCUMSCRIBING

In stage 7, both the quality and the quantity of communication between the interactants decrease. Sometimes a careful effort is made to limit areas open for discussion to those considered "safe." Other times there is no actual decrease in breadth of topics, but the topics are no longer discussed with any real depth. In other words, fewer and less intimate disclosures are made, signaling that mental or physical withdrawal from the relationship is desired.[13] Dynamic communication has all but ceased; the relationship is characterized by lack of energy, shrinking interest, and a general feeling of exhaustion.

STAGE 8: STAGNATING

When circumscribing continues, the relationship stagnates. In stage 8, the participants feel that they no longer need to relate to each other because they know how the interaction will proceed; thus, they conclude that it is "better to say nothing." Communication is at a standstill. Only the shadow of a relationship remains: the participants mark time by going through the motions while feeling nothing. In reality, they are like strangers inhabiting the hollow shell of what once was a thriving relationship. They still live in the same environment, but they share little else.

STAGE 9: AVOIDING

During the stage of avoiding, the participants actually go out of their way to be apart; they avoid contact with each other. Relating face to face or voice to voice has simply become so unpleasant that one or both can no longer continue the "act." Although communicated more directly at some times than at others (sometimes the "symptom" is used as a form of communication; at other times an effort is made to disconfirm the other person), the dominant message is "I don't want to see you anymore; I don't want to continue this relationship." At this point, the end of the relationship is in sight.

STAGE 10: TERMINATION

At stage 10, the bonds that used to hold the relationship together are severed; the relationship ends. Depending on how the participants feel (whether or not they agree on termination), this stage can be short or drawn out over time, can end cordially (in person, over the telephone, with a letter or legal document) or bitterly. All relationships eventually terminate (by the death of one participant if not before), but this doesn't mean that "saying good-bye" is easy or pleasant.[14]

It is noteworthy that a relationship may stabilize at any one of these stages. For example, as we have noted, many relationships never proceed beyond the experimenting stage; others stabilize at the intensifying stage, the bonding stage, etc. When the participants disagree about the point of stabilization, difficulties can arise. We should also recognize that movement through the stages may be forward or backward. For instance, we may advance and then retreat, deciding that a more superficial relationship is what we really desire. Additionally, we proceed through the stages at our own pace. Some relationships, especially those in which time is perceived to be limited, develop more quickly than others; the rate at which the participants grow together or apart, however, usually depends on their individual needs.

Identify relationships in your own life that have stabilized at one or more of Knapp's "coming together" stages: initiating, experimenting, intensifying, integrating, bonding.

Cost-Benefit Theory and Development of Relationships

Although the stages described above can serve as a guide, relationships are not always predictable. No relationship is foreordained in heaven or hell for success or failure. Rather, our relationships develop as a consequence of the energy we are willing to commit to them and as a result of what we are willing to do with and for one another.

Unless the people who share a relationship are able to continue to grow together and adapt to their continually changing environment, the relationship may begin to deteriorate at any point. According to *cost-benefit theory*, we will work to maintain a relationship only as long as the benefits we perceive for

---

✔ **SKILL BUILDER**

COSTS AND BENEFITS OF RELATIONSHIPS

Make a cost-benefit analysis of a relationship you are now experiencing by identifying both the benefits you receive and the costs you expend as a result of the relationship. On the basis of your analysis, what is your prognosis for the future of this relationship?

---

ourselves outweigh the costs.[15] These benefits include feeling better about the self, personal growth, a greater sense of security, additional resources for accomplishing tasks, and an increased ability to cope with problems. In comparison, costs include the time spent trying to make the relationship work, psychological and physical stress, and a damaged self-image.

The greater our rewards and the lower our costs, the more satisfying a relationship will be. When costs begin to outweigh benefits, we are more and more likely to decide to terminate the relationship. In contrast, when benefits outweigh costs, the relationship will probably continue to develop.

Deception and Development of Relationships

Why are you lying to me who are my friend?
Moroccan proverb

How do you define the word *lie*? To whom would you lie? What kinds of situations call for a lie? How many times in the past month have you lied to someone with whom you share a relationship? How many times were you caught? What happened as a result? It is noteworthy that distortion and concealment of sensitive information appear to be relatively common in everyday interactions: deceptive messages are frequently delivered.

When we lie to someone, we do not merely deliver wrong information; we also intentionally seek to deceive him or her. Sissela Bok, the author of *Lying*, says that when we lie, it is both our hope and our expectation that we will succeed in making the target of our efforts believe something we do not believe.[16] This description is supported by the communication theorists Steven A. McCornack and Timothy R. Levine, who note: "Deception is the deliberate falsification or omission of information by a communicator, with the intent being to mislead the conversational partner."[17]

It is rare to tell someone only one lie. To sustain our original lie, we usually need to tell more lies. As Bok writes, "The liar always has more mending to do." And the liar has to expend a great deal of energy remembering who he or she told what and why.

In Tennessee Williams's play *A Streetcar Named Desire*, one of the characters—Blanche DuBois—says, "I don't tell the truth. I tell what ought to be truth." Does this practice help or hinder the development of relationships? Why?

Why do people lie? Of course, the reasons are as numerous as the situations that precipitate a need to lie in the first place. However, two main reasons appear to dominate: most people lie to gain a reward or to avoid punishment. What kinds of reward are we after in our relationships, and what kinds of punishment are we avoiding?

According to the researchers Carl Camden, Michael Motley, and Ann Wilson, we lie to continue to satisfy the basic needs fulfilled by our relationships,

Needs	Benefit self	Benefit other	Benefit third party
Basic needs	68	1	1
A. Acquire resources	29	0	0
B. Protect resources	39	1	1
Affiliation	128	1	6
A. Positive	65	0	0
1. Initiate interaction	8	0	0
2. Continue interaction	6	0	0
3. Avoid conflict	48	0	0
4. Obligatory acceptance	3	0	0
B. Negative	43	1	3
1. Avoid interaction	34	1	3
2. Leave-taking	9	0	0
C. Conversational control	20	0	3
1. Redirect conversation	3	0	0
2. Avoid self-disclosure	17	0	3
Self-esteem	35	63	1
A. Competence	8	26	0
B. Taste	0	18	1
C. Social desirability	27	19	0
Other	13	5	0
A. Dissonance reduction	3	5	0
B. Practical joke	2	0	0
C. Exaggeration	8	0	0

FIGURE 7-3
Types of white lies and their frequency.

Source: From "White Lies in Interpersonal Communication: A Taxonomy and Preliminary Investigation of Social Motivations" by C. Camden, M. T. Motley, and A. Wilson, *Western Journal of Speech Communication*, vol. 48 (1984), p. 315.

to increase or decrease desired and undesired affiliations, to protect our self-esteem, and to achieve personal satisfaction.[18] Most often, when we lie we benefit ourselves, though a percentage of our lies are designed to protect the person or persons we are lying to, and an even smaller percentage benefit a third party (see Figure 7-3).

Why is lying a strategy we use? We may use lying as a strategy because lies help us manage what we perceive to be difficult situations, situations that make us more vulnerable than we would like to be.

How does a lie affect our relationships once it is uncovered? Imagine sharing a relationship, no matter how ideal in other aspects, in which you could never rely on the words or gestures of the other person. Information exchanged in that relationship would be virtually worthless, and the feelings expressed would be practically meaningless. No one likes to be duped. No one likes to appear gullible. No one likes to play the fool. When someone does deceive us, we become suspicious and resentful; we are disappointed both in the other person and in ourselves.

As Sissela Bok observed, people who discover that they have been lied to "are resentful, disappointed and suspicious. They feel wronged; they are wary of new overtures." Further, Bok notes, people "look back on their past beliefs and actions in the new light of the discovered lies." While "bending the truth" to sustain a relationship may be a common practice, unless trust and truthfulness are present, it is only a matter of time before the relationship will die.

How is a liar like a counterfeiter?

✔ **SKILL BUILDER**

LIES, LIES, LIES

1. Report on an experience of being lied to. Indicate who lied to you, the nature of the lie, and your reactions when you found out you had been lied to. How did the lie affect your relationship with the liar?

2. Report on an experience when you lied to someone else. Indicate whom you lied to, the nature of the lie, your reason for lying, and the other person's reaction when he or she found out that you had lied. How did your lie affect the relationship you shared?

Quite simply, lies are fundamentally destructive and often kill a relationship. Few factors have more influence on a relationship than trust. In fact, the reason most commonly cited for terminating a relationship is a loss of trust in one's partner. And nearly all breakups due to deception are reported to be initiated by the recipient of the lie.

Trust and Development of Relationships

Trust gives us the ability to rise above our doubts.
John K. Rempel, John G. Holmes

Of course, there is a potential for trouble in any relationship. As we have just seen, one cause of trouble is lying. Another, equally important cause is misreading the other person's desires with regard to the depth of the relationship—that is, how much he or she trusts you at a particular point in time. The degree of trust you place in another person to accept information you disclose to him or her without hurting you or the relationship is your "tolerance of vulnerability." Your tolerance of vulnerability varies from person to person, topic to topic, and situation to situation.

The researcher William Rawlins designed a matrix, shown in Figure 7-4, that we can use to analyze the amount of trust we place in different people at different times in a relationship's development. We can also use this matrix to determine which of our relationships have more stability or staying power than others. A relationship in which the partners have difficulty trusting one another is a troubled relationship.

**FIGURE 7-4
Rawlins's "trust matrix."**

Source: Matrix created by William K. Rawlins from "Openness as Problematic in Ongoing Friendships: Two Conversational Dilemmas" by W. K. Rawlins, *Communication Monographs*, vol. 50 (March 1983), p. 11. Copyright by the Speech Communication Association; reprinted by permission of the publisher and author.

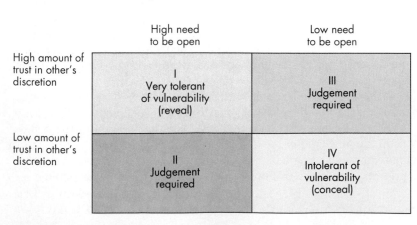

BUILDING A TRUSTING RELATIONSHIP

What, in your opinion, is appropriate behavior, given the following paradox?

Some of us are more trusting than others, primarily because of the way we have been treated. British psychologist John Bowlby, for instance, suggests that adult concerns about trust may be related to unresponsive parenting in infancy. Erik Erikson contends that attitudes toward trust continue to develop during early explorations of intimacy. And throughout our adult lives, important relationships can either reinforce our confidence or consolidate our fears about the risks of emotional commitment. But even if our past relationships have sown the seeds of doubt, it may be possible to find ways of building trust.

Clearly, based on past behavior, some people merit our trust and others do not. But the behavior on which we base our judgments cannot always be described in black and white. We have to interpret what the behavior means to us and our relationship. We may not be able to bring about an immediate change in a partner's behavior, but we can change how we interpret his or her actions and begin to build trust.

One thing to guard against is overinterpreting negative behavior, which is most likely to happen when we are reminded of sensitive issues from the past. In a recent study we asked couples to think about times in their relationship when they felt disappointed by their partner. This simple intrusion of negative thoughts had a profound effect on the way they interpreted a subsequent situation. In short, they saw what they expected to see. They became insensitive to their partner's present actions and relied on the past to judge the interaction.

Because our past relationships can so powerfully color our perceptions of the present, we should be especially vigilant for issues that trigger our emotional insecurities. To combat this we can focus on concrete behavior rather than jumping to harsh conclusions about our partner's motives and character. We can also become more sensitive to and appreciative of positive behavior. In essence, we allow ourselves to trust by giving our partner some credit and providing him or her with the necessary room to make mistakes.

These are risky suggestions, and they may not be appropriate for everyone. To believe in someone, especially when there is good reason for uncertainty, means leaving yourself open to hurt and disappointment. Yet the paradox remains: To be able to trust, you must be willing to take the risk of trusting. Indeed, if we try to see new evidence of caring in a partner we risk being wrong, but if we do not try we can never be right.

Source: From "How Do I Trust Thee?" John K. Rempel and John G. Holmes, *Psychology Today*, February 1986. Reprinted with permission from Psychology Today Magazine. Copyright © 1986 (Sussex Publishers, Inc.).

IMPROVING YOUR "RELATIONSHIP SATISFACTION"

Our relationships can contribute to feelings of happiness or unhappiness, elation or depression. They can enrich and stimulate us, or they can limit and harm us. To enhance your ability to develop relationships that satisfy, follow these guidelines.

Actively Seek Information from Others and Reinforce Others for Attempting to Seek Information from You

People who fail to initiate contacts or fail to reinforce the conversational attempts of others are less likely to build stable foundations for effective relationships. Passive, restrained communicators are simply more likely to remain chronically lonely. Although we all experience short-term loneliness from time to time, sustained chronic loneliness leads to social apathy, which in turn increases loneliness.

Recognize the Characteristics of Friendship

People who share effective friendships report that the following qualities are present: enjoyment (they enjoy each other's company most of the time), acceptance (they accept each other as they are), trust (both assume that one will act in the other's best interest), respect (each assumes that the other will exercise good judgment in making life choices), mutual assistance (they are willing to assist and support each other), confidences (they share experiences and feelings with each other), understanding (they have a sense of what the other thinks is important and why the other behaves as he or she does), and spontaneity (they feel free to be themselves).[19]

Recognize That Relationships Evolve

Ours is a mobile society in which each change we experience has the potential to bring us different relationships. Be prepared for changes in relationships; recognize that in our lives we are likely to experience a certain amount of turnover and change. As we grow and develop, so will our relationships.

Know When to Sever a Relationship

Not all relationships or connections are meant to continue. When a relationship is draining our energies and our confidence, we need to extricate ourselves from it before it destroys us.

Recognize That Communication Is the Lifeblood of a Relationship

Without communication, relationships shrivel and die. Any relationship that is worth your time and energy depends on effective communication to sustain and nourish it. Your desire and motivation to communicate are key ingredients in the establishment and growth of a relationship.

SUMMARY

Communication is one variable common to all relationships. As a result of communication, we establish and nurture or withdraw from and end our relationships.

Relationships play many roles in our lives. They fulfill our needs for inclusion, control, and affection. We each need to feel that others take an interest in us, that they view us as capable of exerting control over our lives, and that we are lovable. It is through conversation that we establish, maintain, and end our relationships.

Every relationship we share is unique and varies in breadth (how many topics we discuss with the other person) and depth (how much we are willing to reveal to the other person about our feelings). Most relationships develop according to a social-penetration model, beginning with narrow breadth and shallow depth; over time, some relationships increase in breadth and depth, becoming wider, more intimate, or both.

Researchers have identified a number of stages our relationships may pass through: initiating, experimenting, intensifying, integrating, bonding, differentiating, circumscribing, stagnating, avoiding, and terminating. Note that a relationship may stabilize at any stage. When the participants disagree about the point of stabilization, problems are likely to arise.

It is important to recognize that how we communicate plays a key part in determining whether our relationships are as effective and rewarding for us as they could be. Relationships are also affected by lies or deception, and by vulnerability and trust.

SUGGESTIONS FOR FURTHER READING

Borisoff, Deborah, and Lisa Merrill: *The Power to Communicate*, Waveland, Prospect Heights, Ill., 1985. Explores the impact of stereotyped gender differences on males' and females' development, communication, and professional contexts.

Gamble, Teri, and Michael Gamble: *Contacts: Communicating Interpersonally*, Random House, New York, 1982. An introduction to the nature of interpersonal communication and an exploration of the roles we play in developing effective relationships.

Garner, Alan: *Conversationally Speaking*, McGraw-Hill, New York, 1989. A readable approach to conversation by a consultant to business and industry. An interesting handbook for people interested in improving conversational skills quickly.

Gibb, Jack: *Trust*, Newcastle, North Hollywood, Calif., 1991. Explores the nature of trust. Interesting discussion of fear and the barriers it can create between people.

Knapp, Mark L.: *Interpersonal Communication and Human Relationships*, Allyn and Bacon, Boston, Mass., 1984. An examination of how people communicate in developing and deteriorating relationships.

Laing, R. D.: *Knots*, Random House, New York, 1970. Each chapter, composed of dialogue scenarios or poems, describes a different kind of relationship. A highly thought-provoking work.

Nofsinger, Robert E.: *Everyday Conversation*, Sage, Newbury Park, Calif., 1991. A comprehensive discussion of both research and practical conversational techniques.

Satir, Virginia: *Peoplemaking*, Science and Behavior Books, Palo Alto, Calif., 1972. A clear and inclusive treatment of family communication and person-to-person interaction.

NOTES

1. Virginia Satir, *Peoplemaking*, Science and Behavior Books, Palo Alto, Calif., 1972, p. 30.
2. John Naisbitt, *Megatrends*, Warner, New York, 1984, pp. 35–52.
3. William C. Schutz, *The Interpersonal Underworld*, Science and Behavior Books, Palo Alto, Calif., 1966, pp. 18–20.
4. See Robert A. Bell, *The Interpersonal Underworld*, Science and Behavior Books, Palo Alto, Calif., 1966, pp. 18–20.
5. Robert A. Bell and Michael Roloff, "Making a Love Connection: Loneliness and Communication Competence in the Dating Marketplace," *Communication Quarterly*, vol. 39, no. 1, Winter 1991, pp. 58–74.
6. Schutz, op. cit., p. 24.
7. Robert E. Nofsinger, *Everyday Conversation*, Sage, Newbury Park, Calif., 1991, p. 1.
8. T. Altman and D. A. Taylor, *Social Penetration: The Development of Interpersonal Relationships*, Holt, Rinehart and Winston, New York, 1973.
9. Mark L. Knapp, *Interpersonal Communication and Human Relationships*, Allyn and Bacon, Boston, 1984, pp. 35–44.
10. Alan Garner, *Conversationally Speaking*, McGraw-Hill, New York, 1981, p. 69.
11. Knapp, op. cit.
12. Michael Korda, "Small Talk," *Signature*, 1986, p. 78.
13. See Lawrence B. Rosenfield and Daniella Bordaray-Sciolino, "Self Disclosure as a Communication Strategy during Relationship Termination," presented at the national meeting of the Speech Communication Association, Denver, Colorado, November 1985.
14. Ibid.
15. J. W. Thibaut and H. H. Kelly, *The Social Psychology of Groups*, Wiley, New York, 1959.
16. Sissela Bok, *Lying*, Pantheon, New York, 1978. See also Bok, *Secrets*, Random House, New York, 1989.
17. Steven A. McCornack and Timothy R. Levine, "When Lies Are Uncovered: Emotional and Relational Outcomes of Discovered Deception," *Communication Monographs*, vol. 57, June 1990, p. 119.
18. C. Camden, M. T. Motley, and A. Wilson, "White Lies in Interpersonal Communication: A Taxonomy and Preliminary Investigation of Social Motivations," *Western Journal of Speech Communication*, vol. 48, 1984, pp. 309–325.
19. Keith E. Davis, "Near and Dear: Friendship and Love Compared," *Psychology Today*, February 1985, pp. 22–30.

CHAPTER 8

PERSON TO PERSON: HANDLING EMOTIONS AND EXPRESSING FEELINGS IN RELATIONSHIPS

After finishing this chapter, you should be able to:

Determine how well you "read" and express feelings

Define the terms *emotion state* and *emotion trait*

Identify the physical sensations and facial expressions that accompany particular emotions

Explain how attraction, proximity, reinforcement, similarity, and complementarity function as determiners of relationships

Explain how suppression and disclosure of feelings can affect the development of a relationship

Compare and contrast rules for men and women regarding emotional display

Explain how feelings can be handled effectively during conflicts

Explain how assertiveness, nonassertiveness, and aggressiveness differ

Identify behaviors that foster and impede the development of a relationship based on assertiveness

Draw and explain a "relationship window"

Create and explain a "DESC script"

Explain how you can protect your emotional rights in the relationships you share

This chapter is about feelings—your feelings and the feelings of people with whom you share relationships. Although everyone knows that feelings exist, and although everyone uses terms to identify and label feelings—*anger, sadness, fear,* and *happiness,* for example—few of us really understand how we and others experience these emotions, and even fewer of us realize how these emotions affect our *intrapersonal and interpersonal* lives.

Let us begin to examine the communication of emotion. By exploring what feelings "feel" like, "look" like, and "sound" like and by attempting to analyze how people handle their feelings, we will increase our ability to establish and sustain meaningful relationships with others. Since feelings can either enhance or disrupt our interpersonal lives, only when we are able to respond appropriately to our own feelings and to those of others will we be able to communicate effectively.

YOU AND YOUR EMOTIONS

What is it really like to be angry? What does your body feel like when you get angry? What happens to your face? Can you identify the types of situations that make you angry? Can you recall that you ever enjoyed being angry? Can you tell when a friend, family member, or coworker becomes angry? How well do you read or express feelings?

An Emotions Survey

Consider these emotions:

Anger
Happiness
Surprise
Fear
Sadness

Which of these feelings do you experience most frequently? Least frequently? Which of these feelings do you least enjoy expressing? Which do you least enjoy observing in others?

Now, for each emotion, answer the following questions:

1. Identify an occasion when you felt this emotion.
2. On a scale ranging from 1 (mild) to 5 (intense), indicate the strength of the emotion.
3. Describe what you felt like and what you imagine you looked like when you experienced the emotion.
4. Describe how you attempted to handle the emotion.
5. Describe how others around you reacted to you.
6. Identify when you perceived an occasion that someone you were with was experiencing this emotion.
7. Describe your perceptions of how this person felt and looked.
8. Describe how he or she attempted to handle the emotion.
9. Describe your reactions to his or her behavior.

You can use the information you have just gathered in at least three ways: (1) to help you clarify how you feel about emotions, (2) to help you understand other people's emotions, and (3) to help other people understand your emotions.

Emotional States and Traits

Whether you realize it or not, at any given time you are experiencing some emotion to some degree. In any particular context with any particular people, you will almost certainly have certain thoughts or attitudes about the situation. These thoughts or attitudes will give rise to a particular emotion state. According to the theorist Carroll E. Izard, an *emotion state* is a particular emotional process of limited duration, lasting from seconds to hours and varying from mild to intense. An example would be a state of sadness. Izard notes that "chronically intense emotions, or frequent episodes of intense emotion, may indicate psychopathology."[1] Thus a person who *always* feels an emotion intensely—who is always in an extreme state of joy, depression, or anger—is unusual.

In addition to emotion states (such as sadness), people may also exhibit *emotion traits.* For instance, if you were described as exhibiting a "sadness trait," this would indicate that you had a tendency to experience sadness frequently in your daily interactions.[2]

What emotion traits have you experienced or observed in others in the past 24 hours? Does any particular emotion trait punctuate either your own interpersonal behavior or the behavior of those with whom you habitually relate?

Every emotion you experience is accompanied by physiological changes in your body and physical changes in your appearance. Are you "fine-tuned" to the physiological and visual signals the body and face send as a person experiences an emotion? Let's find out.

What Do Feelings Feel Like?

195

CHAPTER 8
PERSON TO PERSON:
HANDLING EMOTIONS AND
EXPRESSING FEELINGS
IN RELATIONSHIPS

Feelings can be accompanied by a wide range of physical sensations and changes. Sometimes, as with anger, blood rushes to your face, so that your face reddens; your heartbeat and pulse quicken; and you may experience an urge to wave your arms and legs, raise your voice, and use strong words to express what you are feeling. Likewise, when you are exposed to a threat or become anxious or frightened, your body will respond by releasing certain hormones into your bloodstream. According to David Viscott, in times of stress the blood supply to the muscles is increased while the supply to the abdomen and skin is decreased.[3] Thus, cold feet and pallor are two physical symptoms of the feeling of anxiety. In these and similar ways, your feelings let you know how people, ideas, and the environment affect you. In other words they reveal to you what is important to you.

Becoming aware of our feelings can help us understand our reactions to ourselves and to those with whom we interact. Understanding bodily reactions to emotion can help us understand how we try to cope with emotion. Not everyone experiences feelings in the same way. Your ability to accept the reactions of other people indicates an awareness that they can experience unique physical sensations—responses quite separate and distinct from your own. Emotions affect us in many different ways. As we have seen, they may cause changes to occur in the circulatory or respiratory system. Increases or decreases in blood pressure and breathing rate can in turn affect our perceptions, outlook, and actions. As Carroll Izard observes, "The joyful person is more apt to see the world through 'rose colored glasses,' the distressed or sad individual is more apt to construe the remarks of others as critical, and the fearful person is inclined only to see the frightening object (tunnel vision)."[4] Feelings are our reaction to what we perceive; they define and color our image of the world.

What Do Feelings Look Like?

Your face is the prime revealer of your emotions (see the boxes "Anatomy of a Smile" and "Faces of Emotion"). In fact, although rules for displaying emotions vary from culture to culture, the facial expressions associated with certain emotions (specifically, fear, happiness, surprise, anger, and sadness) appear to be nearly universal and thus are recognizable anywhere in the world. As early as 1872, Charles Darwin, in *The Expression of the Emotions in Man and Animals,* observed that people the world over express basic feelings in similar ways. Without understanding a person's language, you can frequently determine whether he or she is angry, frightened, or amused. Moreover, it appears that these basic facial expressions are innate. Paul Ekman, a prominent researcher in the area of nonverbal emotion, has gone so far as to assert that the face will eventually become the most important source of information on human emotion: "The face is the one social fact that accurately reflects our subjective experience. It's the only reflection of man's inner emotional life that is visible to the world."[5] Of course, although facial representations of emotions may be remarkably consistent from culture to culture, social rules for displaying emotion do vary; the Japanese, for example, are much more likely than Americans to refrain from expressing negative emotions in public. (We discuss "display rules" later in this chapter.)

Describe some of the ways in which "face reading" might affect the atmosphere of a workplace and the workers' productivity.

The facial expressions associated with certain emotions seem to be nearly universal; these emotions are *(clockwise from top of this page)* anger, fear, happiness, surprise, and sadness.

This page: Roy Morsch/The Stock Market. *Opposite page:* Bill Horsman/Stock, Boston *(top)*; Harrit Gans/The Image Works *(bottom left)*; Dave Schaefer/The Picture Cube *(bottom right)*

197

CHAPTER 8
PERSON TO PERSON:
HANDLING EMOTIONS AND
EXPRESSING FEELINGS
IN RELATIONSHIPS

FALSE OR GENUINE? ANATOMY OF A SMILE

Not all smiles are the same. Psychologist Paul Ekman describes 18 different types, including the miserable smile, the false "cocktail party" smile and the smile of relief, each marked by different movements of the facial muscles. Most striking is the disparity between the "social" smile and the smile of true enjoyment, called the "Duchenne smile" after French anatomist Duchenne de Boulogne, who first described it in 1862. Smiles of real joy draw in the *Orbicularis oculi* muscle around the eyes, as well as the *Zygomaticus major* cheek muscle (see below). But when people put on a phony expression of pleasure, they smile only with their cheeks, not their eyes. Ten-month-old infants, experts find, are more apt to display a Duchenne smile when their mother approaches, while the approach of strangers often elicits "false" smiles.

Source: Copyright *U.S. News & World Report*, June 24, 1991, p. 56.

Both Ekman and Izard have identified facial patterns (changes involving the facial muscles) that are apparently specific to basic emotions. According to these researchers, *surprise* is a transient state and the briefest of all emotions, moving onto and off the face quickly. Surprise is typically expressed by lifted eyebrows that create horizontal wrinkles across the forehead, slightly raised upper eyelids, and (usually) an open, oval-shaped mouth. Surprise can turn to happiness if the event that precipitated it promises something favorable, but it can turn to fear or anger if the event poses a threat or foretells aggression.

Anger results most typically from interference with the pursuit of our goals. Being either physically or psychologically restrained from doing what you would like to do can produce anger. So can being personally insulted or rejected. Thus an action that shows someone's disregard for our feelings and needs may anger us. When a person is angry, the eyebrows are usually lowered and drawn together, creating a frown. The eyes appear to stare at the object of anger, and the lips are tightly compressed or are drawn back in a squarish shape, revealing clenched teeth. Often the face reddens, and veins on the neck and head become more clearly visible. (It can be noted, with regard to anger and a closely related emotion, hostility, that these are potentially damaging states. For some time, a general personality type characterized by competitiveness, impatience, and aggression was believed to be strongly predictive of heart disease. More recently, the focus has shifted to hostility. According to Redford Williams, a professor of psychiatry, there is strong evidence that hostility alone damages the heart: "It isn't the impatience, the ambition or the work drive. It's the anger. It sends your blood pressure skyrocketing. It provokes your body to create unhealthy chemicals. For hostile people, anger is poison."[6] Some people have "free-floating hostility," meaning that they are usually angry, often without real cause. These people are most at risk.)

Happiness is the easiest emotion for observers to recognize when expressed on the face. Happiness is the feeling that pulls the lips back and curves them gently upward. The raised cheek and lip corners create wrinkles, or dimples, that run down from the nose outward beyond the lips and from the eyes outward around the cheeks.

Angry, cynical people are five times as likely to die before 50 as people who are calm and trusting.
Dr. Redford B. Williams

199

CHAPTER 8
PERSON TO PERSON:
HANDLING EMOTIONS AND
EXPRESSING FEELINGS
IN RELATIONSHIPS

With *sadness*, the opposite of happiness, there is often a loss of facial muscle tone. Typically, the inner corners of the eyebrows are arched upward and may be drawn together. The lower eyelid may appear to be raised, the corners of the mouth are drawn down, and the lips may begin to tremble.

When a person is experiencing *fear*, the eyebrows appear to be slightly raised and drawn together. The eyes are opened more widely than usual, and the lower eyelid is tensed. The lips may be stretched tightly back, and wrinkles appear in the center of, rather than across, the entire forehead.

Interestingly, according to research reported by Daniel Goleman, putting on a sad, happy, or frightened face can actually produce the feeling that the expression represents. In other words, facial expressions in and of themselves elicit or cause feelings; they are not simply the visible sign of an emotion.[7] Thus, while our emotions may influence our facial expressions, our facial expressions may also influence our emotions.

When feelings reveal themselves on your face, do other people observe, listen to, and react to them? When they reveal themselves on the faces of persons with whom you interact, do you observe, listen, and react to them? We cannot communicate effectively if we fail to respond to the feelings of others or if others fail to respond to our feelings. This is why it is important to be highly attuned to facial expressions. We cannot afford to let emotions pass by unattended or unnoticed.

Think of an instance when you read and responded to someone else's feelings. Think of an instance when you failed to do so. How was the relationship you shared affected in each case?

■ ETHICS AND COMMUNICATION

HAPPY OR SAD, A MOOD CAN PROVE CONTAGIOUS
Daniel Goleman

Should a person who is experiencing a bout of "sadness," or a similar depressive emotion, be kept isolated from others so as not to "infect" them with the same feeling? In other words, would we be better off if we were exposed only to people who were in a good mood? Why or why not?

"Emotions are contagious," wrote the Swiss psycho-analyst Carl Jung. His observation is now being borne out and given precision by scientific studies of the subtle interplay of moods as they are passed from person to person.

The new data depict moods as akin to social viruses, with some people having a natural ability to transmit them while others are more susceptible to contagion. And moods seem to perpetuate themselves by leading a person to do things that reinforce the feeling, no matter how unpleasant it may be.

The transmission of moods seems to occur instantaneously and unconsciously as one person mimics, for example, the physical movement of another's facial expressions. It also appears that a feeling of harmonious interaction between two people is achieved when they synchronize their moods, and this can be done by a series of precisely timed nods and other nonverbal cues.

"Emotional contagion happens within milliseconds, so quick you can't control it, and so subtly that you're not really aware it's going on," said Dr. Elaine Hatfield, a psychologist at the University of Hawaii who presented her findings at a meeting of the American Psychological Society in Washington last June.

The new understanding of who is more likely to pass along emotional contagion and who is more susceptible to picking up someone else's mood comes from psychophysiological studies of how people express their emotions. The data distinguished people by the degree to which their moods were freely expressed in their faces and gestures or in responses of the autonomic nervous system, which controls involuntary activities of the organs, like sweating or a jump in heart rate.

(Continued)

The moods studied are relatively mild, like cheerfulness, melancholy or irritability, because the vast majority of emotional life, researchers have found, is in this range. For example, in a study of more than 5,000 days of people's moods, subjects reported being intensely happy on fewer than 3 days in 100.

Women report being in negative moods about twice as often as men, according to Dr. Ed Diener, a psychologist at the University of Illinois, even though women also say they are, over all, as happy as men. "One reason seems to be that women's moods tend to be more intense than men's," Dr. Diener said. "While they may have unhappy moods more often, they also report more intense joy than men, so it averages out about the same."

The more emotionally expressive people are, the more apt they are to transmit their moods to someone they talk with, said Dr. John Cacciopo, a psychologist at Ohio State University. People who are easily affected by the moods of others, on the other hand, have especially forceful autonomic reactions when they unconsciously mimic someone who is highly expressive, he said.

Such people are far more likely to feel sad after a chat with someone who is depressed, or to feel buoyed by seeing an upbeat commercial, Dr. Cacciopo said. While the spread of strong emotions between people is obvious, the transmission of moods can be almost insidious in its subtlety. For example, in one study, two volunteers simply sat quietly facing each other, waiting for an experimenter to return to the room. The volunteers had been paired because one was highly expressive of emotions, the other more deadpan.

Two minutes later, when the experimenter came back and had them fill out a mood checklist, the mood of the more expressive of the pair had taken over the other person, presumably through body language. The study, reported in the April issue of The Personality and Social Psychology Bulletin, was done by Dr. Ellen Sullins, a psychologist at Northern Arizona University.

The transmission seems to be instantaneous as well as unconscious. "Just seeing someone express an emotion can evoke that mood in you," Dr. Cacciopo said. "This dance of moods goes on between people all the time."

One mechanism at work in this transmission is the tendency for people to imitate the expressions of faces they look at. For example, Swedish researchers reported in 1986 that when people viewed pictures of smiling or angry faces, their facial muscles changed slightly to mimic those faces.

While the changes were fleeting and not visible to eye, they were detected using electrodes that measured electrical activity in the muscles. Dr. Cacciopo repeated the study and found that seeing the faces evoked the moods.

Dr. Cacciopo and Dr. Hatfield theorize in an article to appear later this year in The Review of Personality and Social Psychology that it is through such unconscious mimicry of another person's facial expression, gestures and movements, tone of voice and the like that people create in themselves the mood of the person they are imitating.

Synchronization Is Crucial

This approach has long been used by actors who evoke emotions by recalling times when they felt a particular way and purposely repeat expressions and gestures from that moment.

An ability to synchronize moods with another person appears to be crucial to smooth interaction. "It determines if your interactions are effective or not," said Dr. Cacciopo. "If you're poor at both sending and receiving moods, you'll be likely to have problems in your relationships."

Just how awkward or comfortable people feel together depends to a large extent on how tightly orchestrated their physical movements are as they talk, according to studies by Dr. Frank Bernieri, a psychologist at Oregon State University. His work focuses on the nonverbal markers that punctuate an interaction, like whether one person nods on cue at the precise moment the other makes a conversational point, or whether people shift in their chairs simultaneously or rock at the same rhythm.

"The degree to which people's movements seem orchestrated determines how much emotional rapport they will feel," Dr. Bernieri said. "When people are in sync, it's like watching a long series of volleys in tennis, with one person's movements precisely linked in timing to the other's."

In one study, pairs of volunteers spent 10 minutes trying to teach the other a set of made-up words and their definitions. Analysis of videotapes of their interaction found that those pairs whose movements were in greatest synchrony also felt the most emotional rapport with each other.

"Even if the final mood was something negative, like being bored, if both partners felt the same way, there was greater synchrony in their movements," said Dr. Bernieri.

Such physical synchrony seems to pave the way for the transmission of moods. In another study, Dr. Bernieri had women who scored high on a test of depression come to the lab with their romantic partners and discuss a problem in their relationship.

"The most highly synchronous couples felt lousy after the talk," said Dr. Bernieri. "The men in those couples left feeling as frustrated and depressed as their partners."

People who are feeling an intense emotion like depression seem to choose activities that perpetuate their moods, other researchers have found. While it is no surprise that people in a joyous mood stoke the feeling by, for instance, rehashing a victory, psychologists find that people do the same with unpleasant moods.

Seeking a Confirming View

The effect is most striking for sadness. For example, William Swann, a psychologist at the University of Texas, had volunteers who scored either very high or very low on a test of depression read what were supposed to be sketches of their personality. Each student saw three sketches, one portraying him or her in a positive light, one neutral and one highly critical.

The volunteers were then told they could meet one of the psychology interns who had purportedly done the sketch. Those volunteers who were least depressed tended to choose the intern who wrote the flattering profile. But those who were most depressed tended to choose the person who had done the critical profile.

"People seek to confirm whatever view they hold of themselves, even if for the moment, it is a negative one," said Dr. Gordon Bower, a psychologist at Stanford University who is a leader in the research on moods. "In general, you seek out people who are in the same mood you are in."

Much of the research showing how moods perpetuate themselves comes from experiments in which good or bad moods are induced in volunteers, and their actions once in that mood are carefully studied. For example, in research by Dr. Bower's graduate students, volunteers first immersed themselves in recalling an event in their past that made them very happy or very sad. Then they were asked to view an array of slides, half depicting happy moments, half upsetting ones.

"On average, the sad people looked about a second longer at the unpleasant slides, while happy people looked longer at the happy ones," said Dr. Bower.

In a similar study by Dr. Mark Snyder at the University of Minnesota, volunteers who were put into a good or bad mood through hypnosis were then asked to judge snippets of music. Those who were happy preferred light-hearted tunes; those who were sad preferred dirges.

It is perhaps no surprise that people's moods affect how they see their future. But psychologists point out that people are largely unaware that a good or bad mood is creating an optimistic or pessimistic outlook: it simply seems that the facts support one or another view.

Research by Dr. Bower and others shows that moods influence people's judgments by making either positive or negative memories more readily available. Thus a rational weighing of the evidence is swayed in one direction or the other by the bias that moods introduce in what can be brought to mind.

For example, an Australian study found that people who had just seen the comedy "Back to the Future" made positive judgments of such things as how their marriages and careers were working out, while those who had just seen "The Killing Fields" tended to make more negative evaluations.

Source: "Happy or Sad, a Mood Can Prove Contagious," Daniel Goleman, *The New York Times*, October 15, 1991. Copyright © 1991 by The New York Times Company. Reprinted by permission.

It is our feelings that make us human. It is our feelings that color our relationships by adding warmth, vitality, and spirit. It is our feelings that cause us to move or be moved. In fact, feelings are at the heart of our relationships. In order to create liking, build trust, engage in self-disclosure, resolve conflicts, and influence others, it is necessary to communicate feelings.

Factors in Attraction

The first step in the study of how feelings affect our relationships is to recognize what causes us to seek out some people and not others. What is *interpersonal attraction*? Why are we attracted to one person and not to another? Why do we develop a positive attitude toward one person and a negative attitude toward another? A number of researchers have identified variables that influence how attracted people feel toward one another.[8] Attractiveness (not surprisingly), proximity, similarity, reinforcement, and complementarity are consistently named as determiners of attraction.

The first kind of information we process when we interact with someone is that person's *outward attractiveness*. For the most part, we tend to like physically attractive people more than physically unattractive people, and we tend to like people who exhibit pleasant personalities more than those who exhibit unpleasant personalities. Of course, judgments of what is "physically attractive" and what constitutes a "pleasant personality" are subjective. However, whatever we perceive as pleasing functions as an important element in creating and sustaining interpersonal attraction.

A second factor influencing attraction is *proximity*. When we consider the people with whom we enjoy interacting, we usually find that for the most part they are people with whom we work or people who live close to us. Apparently physical nearness affects the amount of attraction we feel. Living physically close to another person or working near another person gives us ample opportunity to interact, talk, share similar activities, and thus form an attachment. Research indicates that, for these reasons, the closer two people of the opposite sex are geographically, the more likely it is that they will be attracted to each other and marry. In all fairness, however, we should examine an opposite effect of proximity. According to Ellen Berscheid and Elaine Walster, authors of *Interpersonal Attraction*, the closer people are located, the more likely it is that they can come to dislike each other. Berscheid and Walster note, "While propinquity may be a necessary condition for attraction, it probably is also a necessary condition for hatred."[9] What do you think?

Reinforcement is a third factor appearing in practically all theories of interpersonal attraction. Simply put, we will feel positive about people who reward us or who are associated with our experiences of being rewarded, and we will feel animosity or dislike for people who punish us or are associated with our experiences of punishment. Thus, for the most part, we like people who praise us more than people who criticize us, we like people who like us more than those who dislike us, and we like people who cooperate with us more than

Explore relationships you shared with a person who was critical of you, one who praised you, one who cooperated with you, and one who competed with you. Which relationship caused the most problems? Which was the most satisfying? Which was the most productive?

203

CHAPTER 8
PERSON TO PERSON:
HANDLING EMOTIONS AND
EXPRESSING FEELINGS
IN RELATIONSHIPS

Factors in attraction include *(top)* proximity and *(bottom)* similarity. Physical nearness apparently tends to increase attraction; we also tend to be attracted to people who are like us.

Top, Grant Leduc/Monkmeyer; *bottom,* G & M De Lossy/The Image Bank

© Mell Lazarus. By permission of Lemm Lazarus and Creators Syndicate.

those who oppose us or compete with us. Of course, reinforcement can back-fire: if people become overzealous in their praise and fawn over us too much, we will question their sincerity and motivation. But in general, as the social psychologist Eliot Aronson notes, "We like people whose behavior provides us with a maximum reward at minimum cost."[10]

Similarity also affects our attraction to others. We are attracted to people whose attitudes and interests are similar to our own and who like and dislike the things we like and dislike. Thus, we usually like people who agree with us more than we like those who disagree with us, especially when we are discussing issues we consider salient or significant. In effect, similarity helps provide us with "social validation": it gives us the evidence we need to evaluate the "correctness" of our opinions or beliefs. We also expect people who hold attitudes similar to our own to like us more than people who hold attitudes that are dissimilar to ours. Perhaps if we believed that everyone we met could not help liking us, we would more readily associate with unfamiliar people who held attitudes different from our own. By seeking the company of "similars," we play it safe.

Not all the evidence suggests that we seek to relate only to "carbon copies" of ourselves, however. In fact, *complementarity*—the last of these factors influencing interpersonal attraction—suggests just the opposite. Instead of being attracted to people who are similar to us, we frequently find ourselves attracted to people who are dissimilar in one or more ways. Both the psychologist Theodore Reik and the sociologist Robert Winch note that we often tend to fall in love with people who possess characteristics that we admire but do not ourselves possess. Thus, a dominant woman might seek a submissive man, and a socially awkward man might seek a socially poised woman.

✔ **SKILL BUILDER**

LIKES AND DISLIKES

1. Identify five people to whom you are strongly attracted. How might each of the factors discussed in the text—attractiveness, proximity, reinforcement, similarity, and complementarity—help to explain the attraction?

2. Identify five people to whom you are not attracted. Using the same factors, attempt to explain why you do not find these people attractive.

Our relationships with most of the people we contact in the course of a lifetime will be transitory and will not amount to much. At times, however, for one reason or another we find that our interchanges continue, and then it becomes quite important to be able to determine what the person with whom we are communicating is feeling. At that point, it is just as necessary for us to understand the world of the other person as it is for us to understand ourselves. We need to realize that other people are as easily able to experience happiness, sadness, anger, fear, or surprise as we are, and indeed, that the feelings we express toward another person are likely to be reciprocated.

By themselves or inherently, feelings are neither good nor bad. Feelings as such do not disrupt relationships, "build walls," or add problems to your life. Rather, it is *what you think and how you act* when experiencing feelings that can affect a relationship for better or worse. For example, anger and fear are not necessarily harmful. As Izard notes, "Anger is sometimes positively correlated with survival, and more often with the defense and maintenance of personal integrity and the correction of social injustice."[11] Fear may also be associated with survival and at times serves to help us regulate destructive aggressive urges. Thus, it is not any emotion itself that is an issue but how you deal with the emotion and the effect it has on you and on those who are important to you.

According to John Powell—the author of *Why Am I Afraid to Tell You Who I Am?*—our feelings tell us about our needs and about the state of our relationships.[12] People who share healthy relationships are able to pay direct attention to the emotional reactions that occur during their interactions with others. They take time to become aware of these emotions by periodically asking themselves, "What am I feeling?" Once the feeling has been identified, their next step is to estimate its strength: "How strong is this feeling?" Next, they ask: "How did I get to feel this way?" "Where did the feeling come from?" "How did I contribute?" In healthy relationships, an emotion is reported as experienced; for instance, "I'm getting angry, and I'm beginning to say things I really don't mean."

It must be understood that healthy relationships do not consist totally of positive feelings. Other feelings are also important. Unfortunately, many of us lack the commitment, courage, and skill needed to express our own feelings—particularly when these feelings are not positive—or to allow other people to express their feelings to us. Many people are reluctant to work their feelings through; instead, they ignore or deny a feeling until it eventually becomes unmanageable.

Thus, we often keep our feelings too much in check or, when we do express them, we express them ineptly and incompletely. Did you know that the majority of people who are fired from their jobs are asked to leave not because of incompetence but because of "personality conflicts"? It may well be that many of the problems we have with friends, parents, or employers are due to inability to express or accept messages about feelings. Efforts to sacrifice or disregard feelings inevitably lead to problems with relationships or failures of relationships. In the next section, we will examine how this happens.

Suppression and Disclosure of Feelings

Sometimes the way we handle feelings impedes our relationships with others. For example, we may bury our real feelings, hesitate to express them, or unleash them uncontrollably.

CENSORING YOUR FEELINGS

Feelings are not the enemy of healthy human relationships. However, for some reason we are taught to act as if they were. As a result, many of us grow up afraid of feelings.

Have important people in your life ever expressed sentiments similar to the following to you?

> "You shouldn't feel depressed about what happened."
>
> "Don't ever let me hear you say you hate your boss."
>
> "If you can't tell me you're pleased with the way it looks, then don't say anything."
>
> "Don't you scream at me! You have no right to get angry with me!"
>
> "If you were strong, you would turn the other cheek and smile."
>
> "There's nothing to be afraid of! Why are you such a baby?"

Compile a list of feelings you try, or have tried, to avoid exhibiting. Explain why you feel it necessary to conceal them.

As these examples clearly imply, feelings and emotions are frequently perceived as dangerous, harmful, and shameful. When this is the case, we in effect censor our feelings and become overly hesitant to express our feelings to others or to let others express their feelings to us. We allow ourselves to exhibit only socially approved feelings for fear of being considered irrational or emotionally volatile. This leads to communication that is shallow, contrived, and frequently inappropriate.

Often, so as not to "make waves" or alienate others, both males and females act the part of "nice guy." At times people desperately want others to like them and so are willing to pretend to feel, or not feel, a particular emotion. People may also become what Theodore Isaac Rubin calls "emotional isolationists."[13] That is, they may try to protect themselves from any exchange of feelings by minding their own business and avoiding entanglements or involvements. Or they may overintellectualize every experience in an attempt to render their emotions impotent. Each of these techniques is counterproductive and can ultimately cause problems with relationships.

"DISPLAY RULES"

Various types of unwritten laws guide us in deciding when or when not to show our emotions. For instance, when we are young, we may be told not to cry at school, not to yell in front of strangers, or not to kiss in public. As adults we may be advised not to flirt at office parties, not to display anger when disciplined, or not to be too outspoken during a meeting.

207

CHAPTER 8
PERSON TO PERSON:
HANDLING EMOTIONS AND
EXPRESSING FEELINGS
IN RELATIONSHIPS

Are these people "breaking" display rules? Is crying "unmanly"? Is a strong display of anger "unwomanly"?

Left, David Woo/Stock, Boston; *below*, Lee Snider/The Image Works

"Do you know how masculine it is to risk crying?"
Drawing by Koren. © 1981 The New Yorker Magazine, Inc.

One determinant of "display rules" is gender. Although feelings do not discriminate between the sexes, and although members of both sexes obviously are equally capable of emotions of all kinds, our society for some reason deems it appropriate for men and women to behave differently with regard to their emotions. For example, Theodore Isaac Rubin, author of *The Angry Book*, gives the following examples of confused ideas about anger:

Big anger displays are not feminine.
Big anger displays are only feminine and are not masculine.
Gentlemen simply don't show anger.
Ladies must not get angry at gentlemen.
Gentlemen must not get angry at ladies.
Very loud anger displays are evidence of homosexuality.[14]

As Rubin observes, "members of both sexes get equally angry" and "are equally expressive"; nevertheless, different rules and taboos regarding the expression of anger, and other emotions, have been internalized by males and females. According to Sidney Jourard, males in our society are compelled to play a dangerous role—they are taught not to disclose. Because of this, Jourard believes, their tension accumulates and they tend to die early.[15] Marc Feigen-Fasteau, author of *The Male Machine*, echoes this. With regard to the emotional restraints placed on males, he puts it this way: "If others know how you really feel, you can be hurt, and that in itself is incompatible with manhood."[16] Do you agree with this statement? Why?

209

CHAPTER 8
PERSON TO PERSON:
HANDLING EMOTIONS AND
EXPRESSING FEELINGS
IN RELATIONSHIPS

In our society, men are generally viewed as more rational, objective, and independent than women. Women are perceived to be more emotional, subjective, and dependent than men. Women are also supposed to do more disclosing than men. When asked, people typically indicate that the "male" traits are more desirable than the "female" traits. But Kay Deaux notes in *The Behavior of Women and Men* that the supposedly female characteristics are not seen as all bad:

> There is a cluster of positively valued traits that people see as more typical of women than men; these traits generally reflect warmth and expressiveness. Women are described as tactful, gentle, aware of the feelings of others, and able to express tender feelings easily. Men in contrast are viewed as blunt, rough, unaware of the feelings of others, and unable to express their own feelings.[17]

For example, for the most part women are perceived as warm and men as competent. Which do you feel is the more desirable trait?

A second important determinant of "display rules" is culture. For example, in some African societies, people will assume that you are friendly until you prove to them that you are not. When they smile, it means that they like you; if they don't smile, it means that they distrust or even hate you. The Japanese, on the other hand, often laugh and smile to mask anger, sorrow, or disgust. People from Mediterranean countries often intensify emotions such as grief, sadness, and happiness, whereas the British deintensify, or understate, these emotions.

A third determinant of "display rules" is *personal values*. That is, we each tend to formulate *personal* "display rules." In effect, we decide for ourselves under what conditions and with whom we will freely share or inhibit our emotional expressions. You might, for instance, feel it inappropriate to show anger before a parent, but you might readily reveal it to a boyfriend, girlfriend, or spouse. You might be hesitant to express your innermost fears to an instructor or employer, but you might readily disclose them to a close friend.

To whom do you feel free to say, "I'm frightened of that," or "What you just did disappointed me," or, "I really care about you"?

Our personal "display rules" might also cause us to develop a characteristic style of emotional expression. We might become "withholders" and try never to show how we feel, or we might become "revealers" and try always to show how we feel. Or we might become what Paul Ekman and Wallace V. Friesen call "unwitting expressors," "blanked expressors," or "substitute expressors."[18] "Unwitting expressors" reveal their feelings without being aware that they have done so. (They then wonder how someone could "read their emotions.") "Blanked expressors" are certain that they are communicating feelings to others but in fact are not. (They are then confused or upset when people fail to "pick up on" their cues.) "Substitute expressors" substitute the appearance of one emotion for another emotion without realizing that they have done so. (They then cannot understand why people react in unexpected ways.) Thus, personal "display rules" sometimes work to impede interpersonal relationships.

SEX ROLES REIGN POWERFUL AS EVER IN THE EMOTIONS
Daniel Goleman

How might the different messages sent by males and females about emotions and appropriate emotional responses affect their ability to communicate honestly and effectively with each other?

Despite two decades of assaults on sexual stereotypes, new research shows that when it comes to emotional life, men and women seem as bound as ever by traditional sex roles.

The differences are starkest in the suppression of feeling. Psychologists are finding that men generally are still more reticent when it comes to emotions like sympathy, sadness and distress, while women are more inhibited when it comes to anger and sexuality.

Yet studies are finding that men and women differ little, if at all, in the actual physiology of these feelings; the differences appear only when it comes to their expression.

Beyond the expression of feeling, men and women also differ in how they explain an emotional outburst—especially intense feelings like anger and sadness—and what the appropriate response might be.

And these differences seem destined to last. Recent studies show that parents still treat boys and girls differently in regard to their emotional life.

"The stereotypes of emotionality for men and women are as strong as ever, in spite of two decades of efforts to break them down," said Dr. Virginia O'Leary, a psychologist at Radcliffe College. Dr. O'Leary was one of several psychologists presenting findings on sex differences in emotions at a meeting of the American Psychological Association last week.

Some of the most compelling laboratory research shows, for instance, that when provoked, men and women had equivalent reactions in terms of heart rate and other physiological responses. But when questioned, the men usually said they were angry while the women usually said they were hurt or sad.

In a study, men and women viewed scenes of accidents and their victims. The men's faces showed no expression, while the women expressed sympathy. Physiological measures, meanwhile, showed that both men and women were equally affected by the scenes.

"Although women don't admit to feeling angry as much as do men, they may feel just as angry inside," said Leslie Brody, a psychologist at Boston University. "It's their early training that tells women not to be as open about their anger. And the same is true for men with emotions like sympathy."

Dr. Brody has reviewed much of the research on sex differences in emotion in "Gender and Personality," published by Duke University Press. In Dr. Brody's own research, men and women are presented with situations intended to elicit various emotions. In those that elicit anger—for instance, descriptions of betrayal or criticism—men simply react with anger. Women, on the other hand, were as likely to say that they would be sad, hurt or disappointed.

"Men are about four times more likely to commit acts of violence than are women, while women are about twice as likely to become depressed as men," Dr. Brody said. "When men are in conflict, they turn their anger against the other person, while women tend to turn it against themselves by taking the blame."

The inhibitions in expressing emotion seem strongest in social situations, and weakest in situations where a person is most at ease. For instance, in a study where people were asked to reveal an emotionally upsetting secret, men did so as readily as women when they could tell the secret by talking into a tape recorder or by writing in a private journal.

But in face-to-face situations, differences emerge between men and women, said James Pennebaker, a psychologist at Southern Methodist University, who did the research on confessions. "It's more threatening for men to express emotion that shows they are troubled," he said.

In the emotional politics of life, the relative ease with which men express their anger may lead to unsuspected difficulties. In a survey of women who work as secretaries, the single most disliked characteristic of male bosses was anger, Dr. O'Leary said.

(Continued)

Sexuality is another arena where there is a marked difference between the sexes in inhibition. One study found that as many as 42 percent of women said they were not sexually aroused, even as readings of vaginal temperature showed that they were responding physiologically. The women in the study were listening to a tape of an erotic story while the measurements were made. In the same study, not a single man was unaware of his sexual arousal.

More recent studies have had similar findings, said Dr. Patricia Morokoff of the University of Rhode Island. Dr. Morokoff has found that, particularly among women with less sexual experience, there tended to be a disparity between physiological arousal and the arousal they reported, measured during both erotic films and sex fantasies.

"Girls are taught to restrict knowledge of their genitals and genital responses," while boys are freer to explore their genitals, Dr. Morokoff said.

"Society presents an ambivalent message to women about sex: It is desirable to be sexually responsive with one's partner, but it is not desirable to be interested in sex for gratification of one's own sexual needs," she added. "One way out of this double-bind is physiological response without awareness of arousal."

For men, the greatest suppression is for a range of emotions that, in terms of gender stereotypes, are seen as "unmanly," said Dr. O'Leary of Radcliffe.

In research with Devorah Smith, a psychologist at Boston University, Dr. O'Leary found that men and women differ in the causes they attribute for emotions like anger, fear or sadness in themselves or others.

"Men are more likely to explain a strong emotion in terms of some impersonal event, something that happened in the situation, while women are more likely to see the cause as something in a personal relationship or the person's mood," Dr. O'Leary said.

This difference between men and women has greatest implications for arguments between the sexes, she said.

"If a couple fight, the man is likely to make an instrumental response—to look for something in the situation to change and make things better," Dr. O'Leary said. "But the woman is likely to read the argument as an index of trouble in the relationship itself, and become critical of their relationship."

The difference between the sexes in the causes they use to explain life's difficulties may be one reason women tend to be more susceptible to depression than men, said Ellen McGrath, a psychologist in New York City who addressed the psychology meeting on women and depression.

"If men fail at something, they tend to attribute it to some external cause, like the challenge being impossible, or not enough support from their boss," Dr. McGrath said. "For women, though, the tendency is to see a failure as due to something about themselves, as the result of some personal inadequacy."

The influence of sex roles on depression was reported in another study at the psychology meeting by Rosalind Cartwright, a psychologist at Rush-Presbyterian-St. Luke's Medical Center in Chicago. The research, which is continuing, involves 157 men and women who are going through separation or divorce. So far, half of the men and women in the study have become severely depressed.

While the usual sex ratio for those being treated for depression shows a rate of twice as many women as men, the Chicago study found that the rates were identical for men and women.

But when the volunteers were asked questions to assess how they conform to the traditional sex roles, the 2-to-1 ratio emerged. Among the most traditional men and women, there were twice as many depressed women as men. Among the least traditional, the ratio was reversed.

The emotional differences seem destined to remain, researchers say, since the ways parents treat boys and girls appear to be as distinctive as ever. Studies at Pennsylvania State University have shown that parents ask their 18-month-old girls how they are feeling more often than they ask boys of the same age. Mothers were also found to talk to their 2-year-old daughters about feelings more than they do to their 2-year-old sons.

The patterns of emotional inhibition among adult men and women seem in large part attributable to how parents treat their children. Parents insist more that boys control their emotions, for instance, but with girls emphasize emotional closeness, studies have found. And research shows, too, that when parents tell stories to children, they tend to use more emotional words with girls, with one exception: they refer more to anger in stories they tell to boys.

As Jerry Gillies, the author of *Friendship*, writes, "You are not making contact if you are not putting out what you really are."[19] The interpersonal communication theorist Sydney Jourard noted that dissembling, concealing, and being hesitant to reveal feelings are "lethal" habits for males.[20] Jourard believed that men, because they are not as apt to express their feelings as women, encounter stresses that actually cause them to have a shorter life span than women. Now that women are assuming what were traditionally male roles, will they too feel more compelled to keep their feelings to themselves? Whatever the answer, it is acknowledged that *all* people are likely to experience personal and interpersonal difficulties when they try to repress or disguise their feelings.

According to the communication expert David Johnson, many people mistakenly assume that all we need to ensure the development of effective interpersonal relationships is rationality, logic, and objectivity. "To the contrary," writes Johnson, "a person's interpersonal effectiveness increases as all the relevant information (including feelings) becomes conscious, discussable, and controllable."[21] Thus, he holds, suppression of feelings results in ineffective interpersonal behavior. The psychologist Thomas Gordon notes that besides reducing your interpersonal effectiveness, continually "bottling up" your feelings can cause you to develop ulcers, headaches, heartburn, high blood pressure, a spastic colon, and various psychosomatic problems.[22] There is also evidence linking emotion, disease, and the immune system. Researchers have found that strong emotional responses may bolster the immune system. For example, cancer patients who openly showed that they were upset and showed a fighting spirit seemed able to marshall stronger immune defenses than patients who suppressed their feelings.[23] David Viscott, a medical doctor, states, "When we lose touch with our feelings, we lose touch with our most human qualities. To paraphrase Descartes, 'I feel, therefore, I am.' "[24]

How might suppressing your feelings affect your ability to perform effectively in school? On the job?

If either interactant in a relationship attempts to suppress his or her feelings, one or more of the following consequences may result. First, it may become increasingly difficult to solve interpersonal problems. Research reveals that in a relationship the quality of problem solving improves when the participants feel free to express both positive and negative feelings. When the participants feel inhibited, the quality of communication is diminished. Second, unresolved feelings foster a climate in which misinterpretation, distortion, and nonobjective judgments and actions can thrive. Unresolved feelings create or enlarge blind spots in our interpretation of people and events. Third, repression of emotions can lead to serious conflicts and blowups. Intense feelings that are not dealt with fester beneath the surface until they erupt as a result of mounting internal (self) and external (other) pressures. (Holding in such feelings can make it impossible for you to think clearly.) Fourth, maintaining an effective relationship means that participants are honest with each other. To penalize or reject a person for expressing emotions honestly is to tell him or her that you deny the right to reveal an authentic self. You also deny yourself the ability to know the person. Finally, continued repression of feelings can in time cause you to obliterate your capacity to feel anything.

213

CHAPTER 8
PERSON TO PERSON:
HANDLING EMOTIONS AND
EXPRESSING FEELINGS
IN RELATIONSHIPS

When you can take the risk of revealing your feelings to another person, your relationship is likely to be strengthened.

R. Michael Stuckey/Comstock

EFFECTS OF DISCLOSED FEELINGS ON RELATIONSHIPS

Certainly, there are people to whom you may not choose to reveal your feelings, and there are also situations in which you decide that disclosure of your feelings would be inappropriate. However, consider this. When you do take the risk of revealing your feelings to others, your relationship is likely to reap definite benefits.

First, by honestly revealing your feelings, you make it less threatening for the other person to reveal his or her feelings. You demonstrate that you care enough to share your feelings, and thus risk taking becomes a reciprocal process. Second, you acknowledge that emotions are acceptable. You do not censor the feelings the other person experiences, nor do you decide which feelings he or she may and may not feel. You express an interest in the whole person, and instead of using emotions as weapons, you show that you are willing to use them as tools. Third, by describing your feelings and by sharing your perceptions with others, you become more aware of what it is *you* are actually feeling. Fourth, you give yourself the opportunity to resolve difficulties and conflicts in a productive way. Fifth, by revealing your feelings you can indicate to others how you want to be treated. In contrast, by keeping quiet—by saying nothing—you encourage others to continue behavior of which you may disapprove. Feelings, when respected, are friendly, not dangerous.

CONFLICTS AND RELATIONSHIPS

Managing Conflict: Handling Feelings during Conflicts

One of our objectives in this chapter is to investigate conflict to see how we can learn to handle it effectively. This makes sense when you consider that you have been, and will be, faced with conflicts all your life. Observing your own conflicts and giving more thought to them can be a positive experience.

Conflict develops for a multitude of reasons and takes a multitude of forms. It can arise from people's different needs, attitudes, or beliefs. We can say that conflict tests each relationship we share with another person and in so doing helps us assess the health or effectiveness of the relationship. Handled well, conflict can help each participant develop a clearer picture of the other, and thus it can strengthen and cement a relationship. Handled poorly, conflict can create schisms, inflict psychological scars, inflame hostilities, and cause lasting resentments. Thus, conflicts can produce highly constructive or highly destructive consequences.

We need to realize that every relationship worth maintaining, every relationship worth working at, is certain to experience moments of conflict. As David Johnson notes, "A conflict-free relationship is a sign that you really have no relationship at all, not that you have a good relationship."[25] Thus, to say there should be no conflict amounts to saying that we should have no relationships. If a relationship is healthy, conflicts will occur regularly. If a relationship is healthy, conflicts will also be handled effectively. A survey by *Redbook* magazine suggests that how people express themselves in conflict situations is fre-

What conflicts have you been involved in recently—in class, at work, or at home? Why did you define each situation as a conflict?

"Since there are no women or children on board, Mr. Aaron here has suggested that we go in alphabetical order."

215

CHAPTER 8
PERSON TO PERSON:
HANDLING EMOTIONS AND
EXPRESSING FEELINGS
IN RELATIONSHIPS

Ralph and Alice
Kramden, played by
Jackie Gleason and
Audrey Meadows in the
famous television series
The Honeymooners,
have almost come to
symbolize marital
conflict. It might be
interesting to analyze
some episodes in light
of the conflict strategies
discussed in this
chapter.

Viacom

quently more important than what they disagree about.[26] *Redbook* asked female readers how they were most likely to behave when displeased with their husbands and how their husbands were most likely to behave when displeased with them. Readers were asked whether they were most apt to "say nothing, brood about it, hint they were unhappy, express their feelings, or start an argument." They were also asked how they handled themselves when they did argue with their spouses. For instance, were they most likely to "leave the room, sulk, sit in silence, swear, shout, hit out, cry, or break things"? The results indicated that the most happily married women were those who said that both they and their husbands were able to reveal displeasure, discuss it, and try to resolve the problem calmly and rationally. They also noted that they rarely if ever felt compelled to resort to active aggressive fighting (swearing, shouting, hitting out, crying, or breaking things) or to passive aggressive fighting (leaving the room, sulking, or keeping silent). Thus it appears that avoiding conflicts, trying to settle them prematurely, or prohibiting the discussion of differences can lead to serious problems.

At this point, reexamine your personal "conflict inventory" to identify your style of managing conflict. Do you or people you know use any ineffective or "pseudo" methods of dealing with conflicts? Do you feel a need to deny that a conflict exists, withdraw, surrender, placate, or distract by introducing irrelevancies? Do you intellectualize, blame, find fault, or force the other person to accept your ideas by physically or emotionally overpowering him or her? Why? What elements of your relationship elicit irrational responses instead of a rational discussion of the disputed issues?

✔ SKILL BUILDER

THE CONFLICT INFERNO

1. Pretend that you and the other members of your class are trapped by fire on the top floor of a skyscraper. An explosion could occur at any time. Only one very narrow stairway remains open to lead the group to safety. You decide to form a line, single file, to go down this stairway. Of course, those nearest the front of the line will have the greatest chance of survival. Your task is to determine the order in which people will take their places in the line. You must give reasons why you yourself should head the line.

2. How successful were you in handling the conflicts that arose? What communication strategies did you use? What effects did they have?

My idea of an agreeable person is a person who agrees with me.
Benjamin Disraeli

Can you think of situations in your own life that illustrate the four functions of conflict discussed here?

Of the strategies available, only discussion, or "leveling," can break impasses and solve difficulties. Thus, the fate of any conflict is related to the communication strategies employed. Conflict forces people to select response patterns that will forge an effective network of communication. We can choose either disruptive or constructive responses. Try using constructive strategies as you participate in the Skill Builder above ("The Conflict Inferno").

We see that in any situation problems can develop if we fail to deal with conflict appropriately. We can also see that there are certain definite benefits to be derived from handling conflict effectively. Alan Filley, in the book *Interpersonal Conflict Resolution*, identifies four major values arising from conflict. First, many conflict situations can function to reduce or even eliminate the probability of more serious conflict in the future. Second, conflict can foster innovation by helping us acquire new ways of looking at things, new ways of thinking, and new behaviors. Third, conflict can develop our sense of cohesiveness and "togetherness" by increasing closeness and trust. Fourth, it can provide us with an invaluable opportunity to measure the strength or viability of our relationships.[27] Conflict, after all, is a natural result of diversity.

How Conflict Arises: Categorizing Conflicts

We have examined what conflict is and how we feel about it. Now let us explore how and why it arises. We can begin by saying that conflict is likely to occur wherever human differences meet. As we have seen, conflict is a clash of opposing beliefs, opinions, values, needs, assumptions, and goals. It can result from honest differences, from misunderstandings, from anger, or from expecting either too much or too little from people and situations. Note that conflict does not always require two or more people; you can sometimes be in conflict with yourself. Self-conflict occurs when we find ourselves having to choose between two or more mutually exclusive options—two cars, two classes, two potential spouses, two activities; the internal struggle in such a situation is called *intrapersonal conflict*. In contrast, *interpersonal conflict* refers to the same type of struggle between two or more people. Interpersonal conflict

217

CHAPTER 8
PERSON TO PERSON:
HANDLING EMOTIONS AND
EXPRESSING FEELINGS
IN RELATIONSHIPS

can be prompted by differences in perceptions and interests; by a scarcity of resources or rewards such as money, time, and position; or by rivalry—situations in which we find ourselves competing with someone else. Those involved in an intrapersonal or interpersonal conflict usually feel "pulled" in different directions at the same time.

Consider the Skill Builder below ("Tied in Knots"). How did this experience feel? Of course, when engaged in conflict you do not have real ropes tugging at you, but we are certain that you sometimes feel as if you did. When you are able to handle a conflict, the "ropes" do not get in the way. At other times, however, a conflict escalates out of control. Before you know it, you are "tied up in knots" and unable to extricate yourself. In any case, the exercise probably demonstrated that those who see themselves in conflict with each other are interdependent and have the power to reward or punish one another. Thus whenever two or more people get together, conflicts serious enough to damage their relationship may develop.

We can categorize conflict in different ways. First, we can classify the *goal* or *objective* about which a conflict revolves. Goals or objectives can be nonshareable (for example, two teams cannot win the same basketball game) or shareable (your team can win some games and the other team can win some). Or they can be fully claimed and possessed by each party to the conflict. (You can each win everything—members of the rival Teamsters and Independent Truckers unions both get a raise.)

Second, conflicts can be categorized according to their *level of intensity*. In low-intensity conflicts, the interactants do not want to destroy each other; they devise an acceptable procedure to help control their communications and permit them to discover a solution that is beneficial to each. In medium-intensity conflicts each interactant feels committed to win, but winning is seen as sufficient. No one feels that the opposition must be destroyed. In high-intensity conflicts, one interactant intends to destroy or at least seriously hurt the other. In high-intensity conflicts, winning as such is not necessarily sufficient; to mean anything, victory must be total.

Describe and give examples (real or hypothetical) of low-, medium-, and high-intensity conflicts. At which "temperature" do you prefer to keep your conflict thermometer? Why?

✔ SKILL BUILDER

"TIED IN KNOTS"

This exercise was suggested by an experience included in Virginia Satir's book *Peoplemaking*.

1. Think of some idea, belief, value, need, or goal that has involved you in a conflict situation.

2. Identify the relevant aspects of yourself or the other person or persons involved. Briefly summarize each position.

3. Choose class members to play the parts of those you perceived yourself to be in conflict with.

4. Cut heavy twine or rope into 10-foot lengths, one for each player. Also cut a number of 3-foot lengths to tie around each player's waist, including your own. Next, tie your 10-foot "lead" rope to the rope around your waist. Then, hand your rope to the person with whom you perceive yourself to be in conflict, who will also hand his or her rope to you.

5. While tied to each other, begin to talk about the issue that is the cause of conflict.

Source: Virginia Satir, *Peoplemaking*, Science and Behavior Books, Palo Alto, Calif., 1988.

A conflict can also be classified as a *pseudo conflict*, a *content conflict*, a *value conflict*, or an *ego conflict*.

A *pseudo conflict* (as the term implies) is not really a conflict but gives the appearance of a conflict. It occurs when a person mistakenly believes that two or more goals cannot be simultaneously achieved. Pseudo conflicts frequently revolve around false either-or judgments ("Either I win or you win") or around simple misunderstandings (failing to realize that you really agree with the other person). A pseudo conflict is resolved when the people realize that no conflict actually exists.

A *content conflict* occurs when people disagree over matters of fact: the accuracy or implications of information; the definition of a term; the solution to a problem. If the interactants realize that facts can be verified, inferences tested, definitions checked, and solutions evaluated against criteria, they can be shown that a content conflict can be settled rationally.

A *value conflict* arises when people hold different views on some issue of a particular nature. As an example, take the American welfare system. A person who values individual independence and self-assertiveness will have very different opinions about public welfare from someone who believes that we are ultimately responsible for the well-being of others. The realistic outcome of such a conflict would be that the interactants would disagree without becoming disagreeable—that is, they would discuss the issue and learn something from one another, even though they might continue to disagree. In effect, they would agree that it is acceptable to disagree.

Ego conflicts have the greatest potential to destroy a relationship. An *ego conflict* occurs when the interactants believe that "winning" or "losing" is a reflection of their own self-worth, prestige, or competence. When this happens, the issue itself is no longer important because each person perceives himself or herself to be on the line. Thus it becomes almost impossible to deal with the situation rationally.

At this point, you should understand that conflict can develop for a number of different reasons; and you should be aware of the types of disagreements and problems that can arise during intrapersonal and interpersonal conflict. We now need to realize that particular conflict-generating behaviors affect each of us differently. We can see this in the excerpt from Neil Simon's play *The Odd Couple* in the box on pages 219–220. Felix and Oscar function almost as a symbol of the roommate relationship. Through them, the human contrasts that precipitate conflict are exposed. Are you a Felix or an Oscar? Are you both of them? Are you neither of them?

What types of problems would Felix and Oscar experience if they were coworkers?

Some of us perceive ourselves to be involved in a conflict if we are deprived of a need; others do not. Some of us perceive ourselves to be involved in a conflict if someone impinges on our territory or disagrees with us about the way we define a role; others do not. Take some time to discover your own personal sources of conflict. Making such observations will help you understand the types of issues that draw you into disharmony with yourself and others. It will also let you see how you tend to respond when faced with a conflict situation. We will now examine constructive and destructive ways of handling conflict in greater detail.

THE ODD COUPLE
Neil Simon

(FELIX *comes out of the kitchen carrying a tray with steaming dish of spaghetti. As he crosses behind* OSCAR *to the table, he smells it "deliciously" and passes it close to* OSCAR *to make sure* OSCAR *smells the fantastic dish he's missing. As* FELIX *sits and begins to eat,* OSCAR *takes can of aerosol spray from the bar, and circling the table sprays all about* FELIX, *puts can down next to him and goes back to his newspaper.*)

FELIX. *(Pushing spaghetti away.)* All right, how much longer is this gonna go on?

OSCAR. *(Reading his paper.)* Are you talking to me?

FELIX. That's right, I'm talking to you.

OSCAR. What do you want to know?

FELIX. I want to know if you're going to spend the rest of your life not talking to me. Because if you are, I'm going to buy a radio. *(No reply.)* Well? *(No reply.)* I see. You're not going to talk to me. *(No reply.)* All right. Two can play at this game. *(Pause)* If you're not going to talk to me, I'm not going to talk to you. *(No reply.)* I can act childish too, you know. *(No reply.)* I can go on without talking just as long as you can.

OSCAR. Then why the hell don't you shut up?

FELIX. Are you talking to me?

OSCAR. You had your chance to talk last night. I begged you to come upstairs with me. From now on I never want to hear a word from that shampooed head as long as you live. That's a warning, Felix.

FELIX. *(Stares at him.)* I stand warned. . . . Over and out!

OSCAR. *(Gets up taking key out of his pocket and slams it on the table.)* There's a key to the back door. If you stick to the hallway and your room, you won't get hurt. *(Sits back down on couch.)*

FELIX. I don't think I gather the entire meaning of that remark.

OSCAR. Then I'll explain it to you. Stay out of my way.

FELIX. *(Picks up key and moves to couch.)* I think you're serious. I think you're really serious. . . . Are you serious?

OSCAR. This is my apartment. Everything in my apartment is mine. The only thing here that's yours is you. Just stay in your room and speak softly.

FELIX. Yeah, you're serious. . . . Well, let me remind you that I pay half the rent and I'll go into any room I want. *(He gets up angrily and starts toward hallway.)*

OSCAR. Where are you going?

FELIX. I'm going to walk around your bedroom.

OSCAR. *(Slams down newspaper.)* You stay out of there.

FELIX. *(Steaming.)* Don't tell me where I go. I pay a hundred and twenty dollars a month.

OSCAR. That was off-season. Starting tomorrow the rates are twelve dollars a day.

FELIX. All right. *(He takes some bills out of his pocket and slams them down on table.)* There you are. I'm paid up for today. Now I'm going to walk in your bedroom. *(He starts to storm off.)*

OSCAR. Stay out of there! Stay out of my room! *(He chases after him.* FELIX *dodges around the table as* OSCAR *blocks the hallway.)*

FELIX. *(Backing away, keeping table between them.)* Watch yourself! Just watch yourself, Oscar!

OSCAR. *(With a pointing finger.)* I'm warning you. You want to live here, I don't want to see you, I don't want to hear you and I don't want to smell your cooking. Now get this spaghetti off my poker table.

FELIX. Ha! Haha!

OSCAR. What the hell's so funny?

(Continued)

FELIX. It's not spaghetti. It's linguini! *(OSCAR picks up the plate of linguini, crosses to the doorway, and hurls it into the kitchen.)*

OSCAR. Now it's garbage! *(Paces around the couch.)*

FELIX. *(Looks at OSCAR unbelievingly.)* What an insane thing to do. You are crazy! . . . I'm a neurotic nut but you *are crazy!*

OSCAR. I'm crazy, heh? That's really funny coming from a fruitcake like you.

FELIX. *(Goes to kitchen door and looks in at the mess. Turns back to OSCAR.)* I'm not cleaning that up.

OSCAR. Is that a promise?

FELIX. Did you hear what I said? I'm not cleaning it up. It's your mess. *(Looking into kitchen again.)* Look at it. Hanging all over the walls.

OSCAR. *(Crosses up on landing and looks at kitchen door.)* I like it. *(Closes door and paces right.)*

FELIX. *(Fumes.)* You'd just let it lie there, wouldn't you? Until it turns hard and brown and . . . yich. . . . It's disgusting. . . . I'm cleaning it up. *(He goes into the kitchen. OSCAR chases after him. There is the sound of a struggle and falling pots.)*

OSCAR. *(Off.)* Leave it alone! . . . You touch one strand of that linguini—and I'm gonna punch you right in your sinuses.

FELIX. *(Dashes out of kitchen with OSCAR in pursuit. Stops and tries to calm OSCAR down.)* Oscar. . . . I'd like you to take a couple of phenobarbital.

OSCAR. *(Points.)* Go to your room! . . . Did you hear what I said? *Go to your room!*

Source: From *The Odd Couple* by Neil Simon. Copyright © 1966 by Neil Simon. Reprinted by permission of Random House, Inc. This play or any portion thereof cannot be performed, recited, recorded, or broadcast in any media without a license from the author, and requests should be addressed to Samuel French, Inc., 45 West 25th Street, New York, NY 10010.

Resolving Conflict: Styles of Expression

As we have seen, your emotions and how you handle them can "make or break" the relationships you enter into. In other words, you can make your feelings work for or against you. There are three basic ways of handling emotionally charged or conflict-producing situations: nonassertively, aggressively, and assertively. Let's examine the characteristics of each approach.

NONASSERTIVENESS

Have there been moments in your life when you believed you had to suppress your feelings to avoid rejection or conflict or when you felt unable to state your feelings clearly? Are you ever afraid to let others know how you feel? If you have ever felt hesitant to express your feelings to others, intimidated by another person, or reluctant to speak up when you believed you were being treated unfairly, then you know what it is to be *nonassertive*. When you behave nonassertively, you force yourself to keep your real feelings inside. Frequently, you function like a weather vane or "change colors like a chameleon" in order to fit the situation in which you find yourself. In other words, you become an echo of the feelings around you. Unfortunately, nonassertive people rarely take the steps needed to improve a relationship that is causing problems, and as a result they frequently end up with something they don't really want. With so much at stake, why do people refrain from asserting themselves?

Experience shows that we hesitate to assert ourselves in our relationships for a number of reasons. Sometimes inertia or laziness is a factor: the easiest response is simply no response at all. (After all, assertion can be hard work.) At other times apathy or lack of interest leads us to be nonassertive; we simply do not care enough to become actively involved. Frequently, fear can lead to nonassertiveness. In particular, we may fear that rejection might result from active self-assertion. (We become convinced that speaking up may make someone angry.) Or we may simply feel we lack the interpersonal skills needed for assertiveness.

Why might you hesitate to protect your rights—that is, why would you be reluctant to assert yourself? Under what circumstances would nonassertiveness be most likely to occur?

Another important cause of nonassertiveness is shyness. Each of us feels inadequate from time to time. We may feel exploited, stifled, or imposed upon. These feelings manifest themselves in a variety of ways—as depression, as weakness, as loneliness—but most of all, according to the psychologist Philip G. Zimbardo, as shyness. In a survey reported in *Psychology Today*, more than 80 percent of the American high school and college students interviewed said that they had been disturbingly shy for a great portion of their lives.[28] What effect does this have? Zimbardo sums it up in his work *Shyness*, where he states: "The shy person shrinks from self-assertion."[29]

Which situations and people in your life make you feel shy? What are the consequences of your shyness?

According to Zimbardo and Shirley L. Radl, coauthors of *The Shyness Workbook*, few shy people consider their shyness a positive trait; they see it as evidence that something is wrong with them. Actually, Zimbardo and Radl note, "shyness is not a permanent trait but rather is a response to other people evoked by certain situations. The unpleasant feelings of shyness come from having low self-esteem and worrying about what other people will think of you."[30]

According to Lynn Z. Bloom, Karen Coburn, and Joan Pearlman, authors of *The New Assertive Woman*, in our society shyness or nonassertiveness is often considered an asset for women but a liability for men.[31] To what extent do your experiences support this? Do you think women gain more from being nonassertive than men lose? Why?

There are many degrees of shyness. For example, shyness can take the form of mild bashfulness, or it can simply cause you to increase the distance you like to keep between yourself and others. Unfortunately, extreme shyness can make you fear all social relationships and can prevent you from expressing or even acknowledging your emotions.

The polar opposite of the shy, nonassertive person is the aggressor, whom we examine next.

AGGRESSIVENESS

Unlike nonassertive people, who often permit others to victimize them and are reluctant to express their feelings, aggressive people insist on standing up for their own rights to the point where they ignore and violate the rights of others. Aggressive people manage to have more of their needs met than nonassertive people do; but they generally accomplish this at someone else's expense. The aggressor always aims to dominate and "win" in a relationship; breaking even is not enough. The message of the aggressive person is selfish: "This is the way I feel. You're stupid if you feel differently. This is what I want. What you want doesn't count and is of no consequence to me." In contrast to the nonassertive person, who ventures forth in communication hesitantly, the aggressive person begins by attacking, thereby precipitating conflict. It is therefore not surprising that a conversation with an aggressive person will often escalate out of control: the target of the aggressor frequently feels a need to retaliate. In such situations no one really wins, and the end result is a stalemated relationship.

People feel a need to act aggressively for a number of different reasons. First, according to two "assertiveness counselors," Arthur J. Lange and Patricia Jakubowski, we tend to lash out when we feel ourselves becoming vulnerable; we attempt to protect ourselves from the perceived threat of powerlessness.[32] Second, emotionally volatile experiences that remain unresolved may cause us to overreact when faced with a difficulty in a relationship. Third, we may firmly believe that aggression is the only way to get our ideas and feelings across to the other person. For some reason, we may think that people will neither listen to nor react to what we say if we take a mild-mannered approach. Fourth, we may simply never have learned to channel or handle our aggressive impulses. (In other words, we may not have mastered a number of necessary interpersonal skills.) Fifth, aggression may be related to a pattern of repeated nonassertion in the past; the hurt, disappointment, bewilderment, and sense of personal violation that resulted from nonassertion may have mounted to the boiling point. No longer able to keep these feelings inside, we abruptly vent them as aggressiveness.

Needless to say, damaged or destroyed relationships are a frequent result of aggression. In fact, neither the nonassertive nor the aggressive person has many meaningful relationships. For this reason we need to find a middle ground or "golden mean" between the extremes of nonassertion and aggression.

ASSERTIVENESS

The intent of nonassertive behavior is to avoid conflict of any kind; the intent of aggressive behavior is to dominate. By contrast, the intent of assertive behavior is to communicate honestly, clearly, and directly and to support your beliefs and ideas without either harming others or allowing yourself to be harmed. If we can assume that both nonassertion and aggression are due at least partly to having learned inappropriate ways of reacting in interpersonal encounters we should be able to improve our interpersonal relationships if we work to develop appropriate ways of reacting. Understanding the nature of assertiveness will help us accomplish this.

When you assert yourself, you protect yourself from being victimized; you meet more of your interpersonal needs, make more decisions about your own life, think and say what you believe, and establish closer interpersonal relationships without infringing on the rights of others. To be assertive is to recognize that all people have the same fundamental rights and that neither titles nor roles alter this fact. We all have a right to influence the way others behave toward us; we all have a right to protect ourselves from mistreatment. Furthermore, we all have the right to accomplish these objectives without guilt.

Describe an interpersonal situation in which someone took advantage of you and you permitted it. What do you believe motivated the other person? What motivated you? Describe a situation in which you took advantage of someone else. Why do you believe the other person allowed you to victimize him or her?

Assertive people have learned how to stop themselves from sending inappropriate nonassertive or aggressive messages. Thus assertive people announce what they think and feel without apologizing but without dominating. This involves learning to say "No," "Yes," "I like," and "I think." In this way neither oneself nor the other person is demeaned; both are respected.

The focus of assertiveness is *negotiation*. Assertive people try to balance social power in order to equalize the relationships they share. Whereas aggressive people often hurt others and nonassertive people often hurt themselves, assertive people protect themselves as well as those with whom they interact. This means attending to feelings and using specific verbal and nonverbal skills to help solve interpersonal problems.

Remember that being assertive does not mean being insensitive, selfish, stubborn, or pushy. It does mean being willing to defend your rights and communicate your needs, and it does mean being willing to attempt to find mutually satisfactory solutions to interpersonal problems and conflicts. It is up to you to decide whether you would like to redefine some of the ways you relate to others. It is up to you to determine whether you need to shake off any inappropriate and unproductive ways of behaving in favor of assertiveness.

You may, of course, encounter difficulties as you attempt, through assertiveness, to promote more successful and open communication with others. Sherwin B. Cotler and Julio J. Guerra point out that most "assertion situations" fall into at least one of four categories: (1) an interaction with a stranger where you are requesting something, (2) an interaction with a friend or intimate where you are requesting something, (3) an interaction with a stranger where you are refusing something, (4) an interaction with a friend or intimate where you are refusing something.[33] These situations may be represented as a "relationship window" (see Figure 8-1).

Most people will experience the majority of their difficulties with assertiveness in one or more of the quadrants shown in Figure 8-1. For example, some people may find it easy to refuse a stranger's request but difficult to deny that of a friend. For others, refusing close friends or strangers alike may pose few problems; instead, they may experience great anxiety when making requests of others. Where do you experience the most difficulty?

223

CHAPTER 8
PERSON TO PERSON:
HANDLING EMOTIONS AND
EXPRESSING FEELINGS
IN RELATIONSHIPS

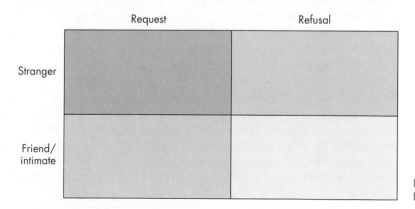

FIGURE 8-1
Relationship window.

✔ SKILL BUILDER

THE RELATIONSHIP THERMOMETER

The "emotional response index" of nonassertive people is usually too low or "below normal" (they do not permit themselves to react). The emotional response index of aggressive people is usually too high or "above normal" (they overreact). The emotional response index of assertive people is "normal." Examine your own "relationship temperature" by trying to send the following messages (a) nonassertively, (b) aggressively, and (c) assertively.

1. You would like a stranger seated near you to stop smoking.
2. You do not wish to drive a friend to the airport.
3. You do not want to move your seat on an airplane so that two friends whom you do not know can sit together.
4. You would like a friend to help you plan a club function.

At which "temperature setting"—nonassertiveness, aggressiveness, or assertiveness—did you find it easiest to operate? Why? Which style was hardest for you to adopt? Why?

It is important to realize that at one time or another we will all have some difficulty in at least one of the quadrants. Once you have identified your own problem areas, however, you can begin to examine your behavior more closely. You can begin to recognize when you feel a need to fight, when you feel a need to flee, and when you feel a need to assert yourself. Fighting or fleeing makes sense for animals and is therefore characteristic of their behavior. These alternatives do not necessarily make sense for human beings in dealing with one another; still, you and I do sometimes flee from each other, and we do sometimes fight with each other. Sometimes we display these behaviors because we want to, sometimes because we feel we must, and sometimes because we don't know what else to do or may think we lack the social skills to do anything else. What we can do, however, is use our problem-solving ability to develop assertive ways to handle interpersonal difficulties. We can learn to be *socially adept.*

In order for any relationship to grow, the participants need to demonstrate at least a minimal level of assertiveness in their communication with each other. The important thing is to try to let your actions be dictated by the circumstances and the people. There is no single "right" way to act in every interpersonal encounter, and the choice of how you act should be your own. In general, however, we can all increase our feelings of self-worth by learning to be more assertive.

As we have seen, many of us have trouble expressing our feelings. Either we behave nonassertively and keep our emotions too much in check, or we behave aggressively and become excessively demanding or belligerent. The result is that our emotions impede the development of healthy relationships and foster the development of unhealthy relationships.

It is sad that we are rarely if ever taught to reveal our emotions in ways that will help our relationships. The key to using our feelings to promote effective relationships is learning to express them effectively. The following guidelines should help you communicate feelings in positive ways and thereby enrich the quality of your interpersonal encounters and relationships.

Work On Feelings You Have Difficulty Expressing or Handling

By now you should have a good idea of what feelings you have trouble expressing or responding to. Now concentrate on expressing or responding to these feelings when they arise. A first step is to let others know what feelings cause problems for you.

Stand Up for Your Emotional Rights

When we sacrifice our rights, we teach others to take advantage of us. When we demand rights that are not ours, we take advantage of others. Not revealing your feelings and thoughts to others can be just as damaging as disregarding the feelings and thoughts of others. Here is what we consider a "bill of rights" for every person:

1. The right to be treated with respect
2. The right to make your own choices or decisions
3. The right to make mistakes and to change your mind
4. The right to have needs and have your needs considered as important as the needs of others
5. The right to express your feelings and opinions
6. The right to judge your own behavior
7. The right to set your own priorities
8. The right to say no without feeling guilty
9. The right not to make choices for others
10. The right not to assert yourself

These rights provide a structure on which you can build effective relationships. Internalizing them will enable you to learn new habits and formulate new expectations. Accepting your personal rights and the personal rights of others is an important first step.

Check Your Perceptions

So far we've spoken about your feelings, but what about the other person's feelings? Sometimes our interpretations of another person's feelings are determined by our own. "Checking your perceptions" requires that you *express* your assessment of the other's feelings in a tentative fashion. You want to communicate to other people that you would like to understand their feelings and that you would like to refrain from acting on the basis of false assumptions which you might later regret. Sample "perception checks" include the following:

"Were you surprised at what Jim said to you?"

"Am I right in thinking that you feel angry because no one paid attention to your ideas?"

"I get the feeling that what I said annoyed you. Am I right?"

"I'm not certain if your behavior means you're confused or embarrassed."

Show Respect for Feelings

Don't try to persuade yourself or others to deny honest feelings. Comments like "Don't feel that way," "Calm down," and "Don't cry over spilt milk" communicate that you believe the other person has no right to feel that way. (You should avoid advising yourself or others to repress or ignore feelings.) Feelings are potentially constructive and should not be treated as destructive.

Use a "Script" to Handle Feelings Assertively

In their book *Asserting Your Self,* Sharon Bower and Gordon Bower present a technique you can use to handle interpersonal dilemmas effectively.[34] This approach utilizes what is called a "DESC script" (*DESC* stands for describe, express, specify, consequences). A script contains characters (you and the person with whom you are relating), a plot (an event or situation that has left you dissatisfied), a setting (the time and place the interaction occurred), and a message (the words and nonverbal cues of the actors).

You begin the script by *describing,* as specifically and objectively as possible, the behavior of another person that troubles you and makes you feel inadequate. By describing the bothersome occurrence, you give yourself a chance to examine the situation and define your personal needs and goals. Once you have identified what it is about the other person's behavior that you find undesirable, you are in a better position to handle it. Use simple, concrete, specific, and unbiased terms to describe the other's actions. For example, instead of saying, "You're always overcharging me, you dirty cheat!" try, "You told me the repairs would cost $50, and now you're charging me $110." Instead of saying, "You're ignoring me; you don't care about me," say, "You never look at me when we speak." Instead of guessing at motives and saying, "You resent me and want Lisa," use, "The last two times we've gone out to eat with Jack and Lisa, you've criticized me in front of them."

227

CHAPTER 8
PERSON TO PERSON:
HANDLING EMOTIONS AND
EXPRESSING FEELINGS
IN RELATIONSHIPS

After you have written a direct description of a behavior that bothers you (identifying the characters, the plot, and the setting) you next add a few sentences expressing how you feel and what you think about the behavior. To do this, get in touch with your emotions and use personal statements. Using personal statements makes it clear that you are referring to what *you* are feeling and what *you* are thinking. The distinguishing feature of a personal statement is a pronoun such as *I, me,* or *my*; for example, "I feel," "I believe," "My feelings," "It appears to me." Thus, when hurt by the behavior of an unthinking friend, you might say, "I feel humiliated and demeaned when you make fun of me." Realize that there are a number of ways in which feelings can be expressed. You can name a feeling: "I feel disappointed. I feel angry." You can use comparisons: "I feel like mashed potatoes without salt" or "I feel like a rose whose petals have been ripped off one by one." Or you can indicate the type of action your feelings are prompting you to exhibit: "I feel like leaving the room" or "I feel like putting cotton in my ears." By disclosing such feelings tactfully, you can make your position known without alienating the other person.

Once you have described the bothersome behavior and expressed your feelings or thoughts about it, your next step is to write down your request for a specific different behavior. That is, you *specify* the behavior you would like substituted. In effect, you are asking the other person to stop doing one thing and start doing something else. As before, make your request concrete and particular. It would be more effective to say, "Please stop playing the drums after 11 P.M." than to yell, "Stop being so damn noisy!"

Finally, you note possible *consequences*—positive and negative—in terms of your own and the other person's behavior and feelings. Then review your script and rehearse it until you feel that your verbal and nonverbal cues support your goal.

Practice Four Basic Assertive Behaviors

Practice the following assertive behaviors:

1. Stop automatically asking permission to speak, think, or behave. Instead of saying, "Do you mind if I ask to have this point clarified?" say, "I'd like to know if . . ." In other words, substitute *declarative statements* for requests for permission.

2. Establish eye contact with people with whom you interact. Instead of looking down or to the side (cues that imply uncertainty or insecurity), look into the eyes of the person you are speaking to. This lets people know you have the confidence to relate to them honestly and directly.

3. Eliminate hesitations and fillers ("uh," *"you know,"* "hmms") from your speech. It's better to talk more slowly and deliberately than to broadcast the impression that you are unprepared or lack self-assurance.

4. Say no calmly, firmly, and quietly; say yes sincerely and honestly; say "I want" without fear or guilt.

SUMMARY

Our emotions have an impact on our inner life and our interpersonal life. They can enhance or disrupt our relationships. They can increase our understanding of other people, or they can prevent us from relating to other people effectively. We are experiencing some emotion to some degree at any given time. A temporary emotional reaction to a situation is an *emotion state*; a tendency to experience one particular emotion repeatedly is an *emotion trait*.

Feelings can be accompanied by a wide range of physical sensations. A number of basic feelings (including surprise, anger, happiness, sadness, and fear) are also reflected by characteristic facial expressions that are similar around the world. We can improve our communication abilities by learning to read the facial expressions of others to discover their feelings and by letting our own expressions convey our emotions to others. It is believed that emotions are contagious—others frequently pick up an emotion displayed by one person during an interaction.

Feelings are at the heart of our important interpersonal relationships. Among the factors that can cause us to establish relationships with some people but not others are attractiveness, proximity, reinforcement, similarity, and complementarity. How we deal with our emotions often influences the course of our relationships. When we censor or fail to disclose our feelings, we are likely to engage in interactions that are shallow or contrived rather than fulfilling and real. Sometimes we are simply obeying unwritten "display rules"—often based on gender or culture—when we decide which feelings we will reveal or conceal. Not expressing our feelings honestly can lead to misunderstandings and even breakdowns in our relationships.

There are three ways of expressing feelings in emotionally charged or conflict-producing interpersonal situations: nonassertively, aggressively, and assertively. Only the assertive style enables us to express our beliefs and ideas without harming others or being victimized ourselves. We can use a "relationship window" to identify the kinds of interactions in which we find it most difficult to be assertive. We can then analyze and learn to handle a typical situation by using a DESC script.

SUGGESTIONS FOR FURTHER READING

Aronson, Eliot: *The Social Animal*, 6th ed., Freeman, San Francisco, Calif., 1992. Contains an excellent chapter on attraction; explores why people like each other.

Bach, George R., and Ronald M. Deutsch: *Stop! You're Driving Me Crazy*, Putnam, New York, 1979. This readable work explains how to recognize the "crazy making" behavior of those closest to you as well as how to put an end to it.

Berscheid, Ellen, and Elaine Hatfield Walster: *Interpersonal Attraction*, 2d ed., Addison-Wesley, Reading, Mass., 1978. A scholarly examination of theories of interpersonal attraction.

Bower, Sharon Anthony, and Gordon H. Bower: *Asserting Yourself*, Addison-Wesley, Reading, Mass., 1976. An easy-to-follow assertiveness training program; explains DESC scripts.

Coupland, Nikolas, Howard Giles, and John M. Wiemann (eds.): *Miscommunication and Problematic Talk*, Sage, Newbury Park, Calif., 1991. Offers new insights into communication behavior in a variety of relationships and social contexts. Explores such issues as misunderstanding, inequality, and conflict.

Deaux, Kay: *The Behavior of Women and Men*, Brooks/Cole, Belmont, Calif., 1976. Brings together a considerable amount of information about the behavioral styles of women and men. Topics include emotional stereotypes, aggression, and attraction.

Dyer, Wayne: *Pulling Your Own Strings*, Avon, New York, 1978. Identifies effective ways of dealing with people. Dyer offers strategies for eliminating self-defeating behaviors.

Egan, Gerard: *You and Me: The Skills of Communicating and Relating to Others*, Brooks/Cole, Monterey, Calif., 1977. Contains a readable chapter on expressing feelings and emotions. Good exercises are suggested.

Gaylin, Willard: *Feelings*, Ballantine, New York, 1979. Establishes the thesis that feelings are not barriers to a happy life but an integral part of it.

Gillies, Jerry: *Friends: The Power and Potential of the Company You Keep*, Coward-McCann, New York, 1976. Explores what friends mean to you and what roles they play in your life.

Goleman, Daniel: "The 7000 Faces of Dr. Ekman," *Psychology Today*, February 1981, pp. 42–49. Updates Ekman's work on nonverbal expression.

Izard, Carroll E.: *Human Emotions*, Plenum, New York, 1977. A scholarly, thoughtful look at human emotions and their management.

Lange, Arthur J., and Patricia Jakubowski: *Responsible Assertive Behavior*, Research Press, Champaign, Ill., 1976. A guide for trainers. Contains useful, structured exercises.

Powell, John. *Why Am I Afraid to Tell You Who I Am?* Argus, Niles, Ill., 1969. Contains a composite of suggestions for dealing with our emotions.

Vincent, Jean-Didion: *The Biology of Emotions*, Basil Blackwell, Cambridge, Mass., 1990. Discussion of research that explores the links between our physical selves and our emotional selves. Considers the relationship between emotions and thought.

Viscott, David: *The Language of Feelings*, Pocket Books, New York, 1976. An in-depth examination of the feelings that guide our lives.

Zimbardo, Philip G.: *Shyness*, Jove, New York, 1977. A highly readable work. Discusses what we can do about the "social disease" that is reaching epidemic proportions.

Zimbardo, Philip G., and Shirley L. Radl: *The Shyness Workbook*, A&W Visual Library, New York, 1979. Contains worksheets for analyzing the role shyness plays in your life.

NOTES

1. Carroll E. Izard, *Human Emotions*, Plenum, New York, 1977, p. 5.
2. Ibid.
3. David Viscott, *The Language of Feelings*, Pocket Books, New York, 1976, p. 54.
4. Izard, op. cit., p. 10.
5. Paul Ekman, *Darwin and Facial Expression*, Academic, New York, 1973. See also Paul Ekman, *Why Kids Lie*, Scribner, New York, 1989.
6. Earl Ubell, "The Deadly Emotions," *Parade Magazine*, February 11, 1990, pp. 3–5.
7. See Daniel Goleman, "A Feel-Good Theory: A Smile Affects Mood," *The New York Times*, Tuesday, July 18, 1989, pp. C1 and C9.
8. For example, Ellen Berscheid and Elaine Hatfield Walster, *Interpersonal Attraction*, 2d ed., Addison-Wesley, Reading, Mass., 1978.
9. Berscheid and Walsher, op. cit.
10. Eliot Aronson, *The Social Animal*, 3d ed., Freeman, San Francisco, Calif., 1980, p. 239.
11. Izard, op. cit.
12. John Powell, *Why Am I Afraid to Tell You Who I Am?* Argus, Niles, Ill., 1969.
13. Theodore Isaac Rubin, *The Angry Book*, Macmillan, New York, 1970; and *Emotional Common Sense*, Harper and Row, New York, 1986.
14. Rubin, *The Angry Book*.
15. Sidney Jourard, *The Transparent Self*, Van Nostrand, New York, 1971. See also Sidney Jourard and Ted Landsman, *Healthy Personality*, Macmillan, New York, 1980.
16. Mark Feigen-Fasteau, *The Male Machine*, McGraw-Hill, New York, 1974.
17. Kay Deaux, *The Behavior of Women and Men*, Brooks/Cole, Belmont, Calif., 1976.
18. Paul Ekman and Wallace Friesen, *Unmasking the Face*, Consulting Psychology, Los Angeles, Calif., 1984.
19. Jerry Gillies, *Friends: The Power and Potential of the Company You Keep*, Coward-McCann, New York, 1976.
20. Jourard, op. cit.; Jourard and Landsman, op. cit.
21. David Johnson, *Reaching Out: Interpersonal Effectiveness and Self Actualization*, Prentice-Hall, Englewood Cliffs, N.J., 1972.
22. Thomas Gordon, *Parent Effectiveness Training*, Plume, New York, 1988.
23. Daniel Goleman, "Strong Emotional Response to Disease May Bolster Patients' Immune System," *The New York Times*, October 22, 1985. pp. C1, C3.
24. Viscott, op. cit.
25. Johnson, op. cit.
26. *Redbook*, June 1976.
27. Alan C. Filley, *Interpersonal Conflict Resolution*, Scott, Foresman, Glenview, Ill., 1975.
28. *Psychology Today*, May 1975.
29. Philip Zimbardo, *Shyness*, 2d ed., Jove, New York, 1987.
30. Philip Zimbardo and Shirley L. Radl, *The Shyness Workbook*, A&W Visual Library, New York, 1979.
31. Lynn Z. Bloom, Karen Coburn, and Joan Pearlman, *The New Assertive Woman*, Dell, New York, 1975.
32. Arthur J. Lange and Patricia Jakubowski, *Responsible Assertive Behavior*, Research Press, Champaign, Ill., 1976.
33. Sherwin B. Cotler and Julio J. Guerra, *Assertive Training*, Research Press, Champaign, Ill., 1976, pp. 15–22.
34. Sharon Bower and Gordon Bower, *Asserting Yourself*, Addison-Wesley, Reading, Mass., 1977.

COMMUNICATING IN THE SMALL GROUP

THE ROLE OF
THE GROUP IN
PROBLEM SOLVING

After finishing this chapter, you should be able to:

Define *group*

Explain the role groups play in your life

Identify occasions when it is appropriate to have a group, rather than an individual, attempt to solve a problem

Enumerate advantages and disadvantages of group problem solving

Provide examples of how a group's climate affects its operations

Compare and contrast various decision-making methods

Use a decision-making grid

Apply the reflective-thinking framework to increase your effectiveness at problem solving

Describe and use brainstorming

Talented administrators know that they do not know all there is to know.

Anonymous

A group is a collection of people who communicate with each other, usually face to face, over time in order to reach decisions and accomplish objectives. If you think about it, you'll probably realize that you spend a great deal of time interacting in groups. A large part of your socialization—your adaptation to society—occurred in your family group. Much of your leisure time is spent in the company of groups of friends. If you attend a religious service, you become part of a group. If you participate in student government you are part of a group. As a class member, you belong to a group. Even at work you are probably expected to function as part of a team of some sort. Thus, from your earliest days to the present and into the future, you have been and will continue to be a member of a variety of groups. In fact, in the United States there are more groups than people. Most of us belong to a number of different groups. Are you a member of two groups? Ten groups? Twenty groups? Take a moment to assess the nature of your group membership.

GROUPS AND YOU

Compile a list of groups to which you belong, groups to which you aspire to belong, and groups to which you would refuse to belong. Give your reasons for accepting, seeking, or refusing membership.

As you probably realize, groups are everywhere. You belong to some groups for fun and to some for profit. You join some to increase your prestige, and you join others simply because you have to. Some help you fulfill personal or professional objectives, and others meet your moral and ethical needs and give you a sense of well-being. Groups help you define who you are. The groups to which you belong or aspire to belong tell you about your own preferences and goals. The groups you refuse to join tell you about your dislikes, fears, and values. The simple fact is that groups have a great impact on your daily life, and you need to belong to a number of them to survive in today's world.

Some of your most important communication will take place in one group or another. It is estimated that over 11 million meetings are held each day and that at least 40 percent of your work life will be spent attending group meetings and conferences. A recent survey showed that the typical executive spends about 700 hours per year interacting in groups. That is the equivalent of two out of every five days on the job. Thus, knowing how to relate to others in a group setting is not only vital if you are to attain personal success but also critical if you are to attain professional success.[1] For this reason, although we realize that social groups are important, in these chapters we will focus on the work-related problem-solving or task group.

By the time you conclude your study of small-group communication, you will have internalized the information you need to understand the forces that shape and modify group behavior. We hope you will also have gained the skills you need to improve the quality of interactions in task groups. The knowledge and abilities you gain will be transferable to other areas of your life. Let's begin by inquiring into the nature of small-group communication.

Groups are everywhere
in our lives. We often
join groups as part of
our work, for instance.

Randy Matusow/
Monkmeyer

CHARACTERISTICS AND COMPONENTS OF GROUPS

Is it easy to explain what the word *group* means? Try your hand at it now.
Generate five different ways of completing each of the following:

1. A group *is* . . .
2. A group is *not* . . .

Defining a group is tricky business.[2] A *group* is a collection of people. But it is
not just a random assemblage of independent individuals; rather, it is composed
of individuals who interact verbally and nonverbally, occupy certain roles with
respect to one another, and cooperate to accomplish a definite goal. The members of a group recognize the other individuals who are part of the activity,
have certain kinds of attitudes toward these people, and obtain some degree
of satisfaction from belonging to or participating in the group. The interactants
acknowledge the do's and don'ts of group life, the norms that specify and regulate the behavior expected of members. Furthermore, communication within
a group involves more than the casual banter that occurs between strangers at
bus stops or in department stores.

The fact that a number of people are present in a particular space at the
same time does not mean that a group exists. For example, under ordinary
conditions passengers in a train or an elevator are not a group. (However,
should the train or elevator break down or experience some other difficulty,
they might become a group in order to meet the demands of the new situation.)
Rather, the members of a group consistently influence each other and are
influenced by each other; that is, interaction in the form of mutual influence
occurs. The individual members affect the character of the group and are also
affected by it.

What *is* a group? What is *not* a group? People standing on line do not ordinarily constitute a group; members of a jury, on the other hand, do become a group.

Top, Crandall/The Image Works; *bottom*, Comstock

Researchers have found that for most tasks, groups of five to seven people work best. This size enables members to communicate directly with each other as they work on a common task or goal, such as solving problems, exchanging information, or improving interpersonal relationships.

Every group establishes its own goals, its own structure and patterns of communication, its own norms, and its own "climate." Every participant in the group usually has a stake in the outcome, will develop relationships with the other members of the group, and will assume roles and relationships that relate to group tasks and either foster or impede the group's effectiveness. Thus the members' styles of interaction will have an impact on the kind of atmosphere or climate that develops in the group. Conversely, the climate will affect what members say to each other and how they say it. For example, have you ever belonged to a group that had too "hot" a climate—one in which members were intolerant of each other and tempers flared? Have you ever belonged to a group that had too "cold" a climate—one in which members were aloof, sarcastic, unconcerned about hurting one another's feelings, or too self-centered to notice that the needs of others were not being adequately met?

A group's climate tends to persist. If the group climate is cold, closed, mistrustful, or uncooperative, individual members will frequently react in ways that perpetuate those characteristics. In contrast, if the group climate is warm, open, trusting, and cooperative, members will usually react in ways that reinforce *those* characteristics. In the book *Communication within the Organization*, Charles Redding has suggested that an effective climate is characterized by (1) supportiveness, (2) participative decision making, (3) trust among group members, (4) openness and candor, and (5) high performance goals.[3] The healthier the group climate, the more cohesive the group.

Group climate affects group norms—the explicit and implicit rules that members internalize concerning their behavior. In some groups we would exhibit certain behaviors that we would not dare exhibit in others. For example, in which groups that you belong to would you feel free to ask a question that might be considered "dumb," interrupt someone who is talking, express disagreement with another member, openly express support for an unpopular position, point out that someone isn't making sense, offer a comment unrelated to the topic, or simply not attend a meeting? In some groups interaction is formal and stuffy; in others it is informal and relaxed. Groups invariably create standards that they expect members to live up to. In this way a group is able to foster a certain degree of uniformity.

In Chapters 10 and 11, we'll take a closer look at the communication patterns, roles, leadership behaviors, and problems that develop in groups. For now, let us recognize that certain attributes can facilitate the group process whereas others work against it. Douglas McGregor, an expert in organizational communication, summarizes the characteristics of an effective and well-functioning group as follows:

1. The atmosphere tends to be informal, comfortable, and relaxed.

2. There is a lot of discussion in which virtually everyone participates, but it remains pertinent to the task.

3. The task or objective is well understood and accepted by the members. There will have been free discussion of the objective at some point, until it was formulated in such a way that the group members could commit themselves to it.

4. The members listen to each other. Every idea is given a hearing. People do not appear to be afraid of being foolish; they will offer a creative thought even if it seems fairly extreme.

> Select two groups you have belonged to that represent what you consider effective and ineffective climates. For each group, identify the types of behavior exhibited by members. How did each climate affect your own participation in the group? How did each climate affect your relationship with other group members?

5. There is disagreement. Disagreements are not suppressed or overriden by premature action. The reasons are carefully examined, and the group seeks to resolve disagreements rather than dominate dissenters.

6. Most decisions are reached by a kind of consensus in which it is clear that everyone is in general agreement and willing to go along. Formal voting is at a minimum; the group does not accept a simple majority as a proper basis for action.

7. Criticism is frequent, frank, and relatively comfortable. There is little evidence of personal attack, either overt or hidden.

8. People are free to express their feelings and their ideas about the problem and the group's operation.

9. When action is taken, clear assignments are made and accepted.

10. The chairperson of the group does not dominate it, nor does the group defer unduly to him or her. In fact, the leadership shifts from time to time, depending on the circumstances. There is little evidence of a struggle for power as the group operates. The issue is not who controls but how to get the job done.

11. The group is self-conscious of its own operation.[4]

USING GROUPS TO SOLVE PROBLEMS

We form small groups to share information that will permit us to solve common problems and make decisions about achieving certain identified common goals. But why use a small group instead of a single person?

Groups as Problem Solvers: Pros and Cons

ADVANTAGES OF THE SMALL GROUP

In many ways, using a group to solve a complex problem is more logical than relying on one individual. Group problem solving offers a number of important advantages.

First, it permits a variety of people with different information and different points of view to contribute to the problem-solving, decision-making process. That is, a small group facilitates the pooling of resources. The broader the array of knowledge that is brought to bear on any problem, the more likely an effective solution becomes. Second, participating in a group apparently increases individual motivation. Group efforts often lead to greater commitment to finding a solution and then to greater commitment to the solution that has been arrived at. Third, group functioning makes it easier to identify other people's mistakes and filter out errors before they can become costly or damaging. Groups are frequently better equipped than individuals to foresee difficulties, detect weaknesses, visualize consequences, and explore possibilities. As a result they tend to produce superior decisions and solutions. Fourth, the decisions or solutions of a group tend to be better received than those of an individual. As the old adage says, "There is strength in numbers." The person or people to whom a group solution is reported will tend to respect the fact that

You know ... everybody is ignorant, only of different subjects.
Will Rogers

THE GROUP VERSUS THE INDIVIDUAL

The purpose of this exercise is to explore the differences between individual and group decisions.

1. Complete each of the following tasks—first working alone and then as a member of a problem-solving group.
2. When the tasks have been completed in both ways, answer these questions: How did the group's response differ from you own? Which were you more satisfied with? Why?

Task A: States

Arrange the following 20 states geographically, from easternmost (number 1) to westernmost (number 20). Disregard north and south. Do not use maps. (See page 492 for answers.)

Alabama	Maine	Ohio
Arkansas	Minnesota	Oklahoma
Colorado	Mississippi	Utah
Delaware	New Jersey	Washington
Georgia	New Mexico	Wisconsin
Idaho	New York	Wyoming
Illinois	North Dakota	

Task B: A Foundation

You are a foundation, empowered to grant $1 million to one and only one of the following applicants. The money may not be divided among the candidates. The person to whom the grant is awarded may not put it to personal use. The following profiles are the only information you have about the candidates. Rank the candidates 1 (most deserving) to 10 (least deserving).

Angela is a 52-year-old nun who teaches in a depressed area. She says she will use the money to clothe, feed, house, and educate the poor.

Billy is a 7-year-old boy who has had bone cancer for 4 years. He will die unless new and expensive lifesaving procedures are used. In addition, his family would like to use the money for some of the joys of childhood he has missed—including a trip to Disneyland. They say they will donate the remaining money to the Cancer Research Fund.

Charles is the 45-year-old director of the School for Human Resources, an organization that educates youngsters with muscular disorders. He needs the money to improve the school's facilities, increase its educational offerings, and hire a full-time psychologist for the students.

Douglas is a 60-year-old union president and founder of the Needy Children's Scholarship Fund. He says he would use the money to send disadvantaged minority young people to college.

Evelyn is a 40-year-old, prosperous real estate developer. She says that she will use the money to become a partner in real estate deals that will return 10 times the initial investment in 5 years. With part of the profit she expects to build a modern housing project for the elderly.

Felipe is a 37-year-old paraplegic who received his injuries during the Vietnamese war. Although he is eligible for disability benefits, he refuses to accept them. Felipe would use the money to help other disabled veterans lead a more normal life.

Greg is an orphaned college student majoring in physics. He supports himself and his two younger sisters by taking odd jobs. Greg hopes to become a nuclear physicist. He would use the money to take care of his family and pay for his education.

Hannah is 24 years old and a promising medical student. She was adopted as a newborn. Although she loves her adoptive parents, Hannah would like to find her natural parents. She needs the money to fund her search and help with her medical school expenses.

(Continued)

Inez is a 20-year-old struggling artist who refuses to use her family's money to further her career. She says she would use the award to lease or build space and purchase the materials that would give her and a group of other aspiring artists the security they need to develop and show their work.

Jenny is a mildly retarded 6-month-old whose parents were killed in an automobile accident. She has been adopted by an aunt and uncle. The money would be placed in a trust and given to her when she reaches her twenty-first birthday.

a number of people working together came to one conclusion. Fifth, group efforts are generally more pleasant and fulfilling than working alone. The group provides companionship, a chance to affirm ideas and feelings, and an opportunity for self-confirmation. It is rewarding to know that others respect us enough to listen and react to what we have to say. It is even more rewarding to have our thoughts and concerns accepted by others. (These advantages are summarized in Figure 9-1 below.)

DISADVANTAGES OF THE SMALL GROUP

This is not to suggest that using a group does not have potential drawbacks. Several disadvantages of group problem solving have been identified.

> "random thoughts by archy"
> i have noticed that
> when chickens quit
> quarrelling over
> their food they
> often find that
> there is enough
> for all of them
> i wonder if it might not
> be the same way with
> the human race
>
> Don Marquis, *Archys Life of Mehitabel*

First, when we are working with a number of other people, it sometimes becomes very tempting to "lie back" and let someone else handle your duties and responsibilities. A lazy group member can maintain a low profile and simply coast along on the efforts of others. Second, personal goals sometimes conflict with group goals. As a result, people may try to use the group to achieve self-oriented objectives that might interfere with or even sabotage group objectives. Third, the decision-making, problem-solving process may be dominated by a few forceful, persistent members who do not take the time to ensure that all members have a chance to speak and be heard. Actual or perceived status plays a part here. Group members may be hesitant to criticize the comments of high-status people, and low-status people may be reluctant to participate at all. Consequently, position and power can affect whether ideas are offered, listened to, or incorporated into group decisions. Fourth, certain people who are set on having their ideas and only their ideas accepted may be unwilling to compromise. When this happens, the group decision-making "machinery"

Advantages	Disadvantages
Facilitates pooling of resources	Encourages laziness
Increases motivation	Conflicting personal and group goals
Makes identification of errors easier	Domination by a few
Decisions are better received	Stubbornness leads to deadlock
Provides rewards of working with others	Riskier decisions are made
	Takes longer to reach decision

FIGURE 9-1
Why use teamwork?

240

● **CULTURE AND COMMUNICATION**

MEN, WOMEN, AND GROUPS

Do men talk more than women during group meetings? Two communication researchers, Barbara Eakins and Gene Eakins, studied university faculty meetings and found that almost without exception, men spoke more frequently and for longer periods of time than women. In fact, even the longest "speaking turns" of women were shorter than the shortest "turns" of men.

If this is true, where does the stereotype that "women talk too much" come from?

What do you think? Do you talk more in single-sex or mixed-sex groups?

Source: Barbara Eakins and Gene Eakins, *Sex Differences in Communication*, Houghton Mifflin, Boston, Mass., 1978.

■ **ETHICS AND COMMUNICATION**

AVOIDING PROBLEMS

What consequences might a group face if instead of handling a problem, the members opted to run away from the problem, rationalize it, or otherwise avoid confronting it directly?

In your opinion, is running away from a problem a viable alternative to solving the problem?

PEANUTS reprinted by permission of UFS, Inc.

breaks down, and frequently no solution can be agreed on. In other words, the group becomes deadlocked. Fifth, the decisions reached and the actions taken after a group discussion are often riskier than the decisions individuals would have made or the actions individuals would have taken. This phenomenon has been called the *risky shift*. Sixth, it often takes longer to reach a group solution than an individual decision. In business and industry, where time is frequently equated with money, the group can be a costly tool. (See Figure 9-1 for a summary of these drawbacks.)

In view of these pros and cons, we may now ask: When does it make sense to use a group? At what point do the advantages outweigh the possible disadvantages?

Experience suggests that a group rather than an individual should be used to solve a problem if the answer to most of the following questions is *yes*:

1. Is the problem complex rather than simple?
2. Does the problem have many parts or facets?
3. Would any one person be unlikely to possess all the information needed to solve the problem?
4. Would it be advisable to divide the responsibility for problem solving?
5. Are many potential solutions desired, rather than just one?
6. Would an examination of diverse attitudes be helpful?
7. Are group members more likely to engage in "tasklike" than "nontasklike" behavior?

As a new employee, what problems might you experience when interacting with others in a problem-solving group?

In these complex times, it often makes sense for individuals of varied expertise to join together and pool their knowledge and insight to solve problems. Note that we said "pool their *knowledge* and *insight*." Group effort is futile if the members pool only ignorance and obstinacy. As we shall see, the kind of interaction that yields an array of relevant data is an essential ingredient in successful group work. The more information the members can gather and share, the more likely they are to rid themselves of bias, and in turn the more objective their work becomes.

Decision Making in Groups: Reaching Goals

Thus far, we have established what a group is and when and why it makes sense to use a group. We have also noted that every group has a goal—a reason for existing. We turn now to examining how groups reach their goals.

In our society, critical decisions are usually relegated to groups; depending on the group, a wide variety of decision-making strategies or approaches may be used. In this section we investigate the diverse methods members can adopt to arrive at a decision as well as the advantages and disadvantages of each approach. Let's start by considering these questions: How do the groups to which you belong make decisions? Do different groups use different strategies? Why? Does the method any one group uses change from time to time? Why? Are you happy with each group's approach?

STRATEGIES: METHODS OF DECISION MAKING

Before we examine the different methods that groups use in making decisions, consider the following list to decide which decision-making strategy or strategies a group you belong to would employ most often if you had your way. Do this by ranking the possibilities from 1 (your first choice) to 8 (your last choice).

_____ Ask an expert to decide.

_____ Flip a coin.

_____ Let the majority rule.

_____ Let the group leader decide.

_____ Stall until a decision no longer needs to be made.

_____ Let the minority rule, because that's sometimes fair.

_____ Determine the "average" position, since this will be least offensive to anyone.

_____ Reach a decision by consensus, that is, be certain all have had input into the discussion, understood the decision, can rephrase it, and will publicly support it.

Then, consider the implications of your ranking.

As the preceding list suggests, the methods employed by groups to make decisions include (1) decision by an expert, (2) decision by chance, (3) decision by the majority, (4) decision by the leader, (5) total deferral of decision, (6) decision by the minority, (7) decision by averaging individual decisions, and (8) decision by consensus. Each method has certain advantages and is more appropriate and workable than others under certain conditions. An effective group bases its decision-making strategy on a number of variables, including (1) the nature of the problem, (2) the time available to solve the problem, and (3) the kind of climate in which the group is operating or would prefer to operate. Try the exercise in the Skill Builder "Lost on the Moon" to see how effective each strategy is for your group.

✔ SKILL BUILDER

"LOST ON THE MOON"

You are a member of a space crew originally scheduled to rendezvous with another ship on the bright side of the moon. Mechanical difficulties, however, have forced your ship to crash-land some 200 miles from the rendezvous point. The landing has damaged much of your equipment. Your survival depends on reaching the other ship, and the most critical items available must be chosen for the 200-mile trip. Below are listed the only items left intact after landing. There are fifteen of them. Your task is to rank them in order of importance to you and your crew as you attempt to reach the rendezvous point. Choice 1 should be the most important item, choice 2 the next most important, and so on, down to choice 15, the least important item.

One box of matches

Food concentrate

Nylon rope (50 feet)

Parachute silk

(Continued)

✔ **SKILL BUILDER (Continued)**

Two .45-caliber pistols

One case of dehydrated milk

Two 100-pound tanks of oxygen

Map of constellations as seen from the moon

Life raft

Magnetic compass

Five gallons of water

Signal flares

First-aid kit with injection needles

Solar-powered FM receiver-transmitter

Portable heating unit

For this exercise, proceed as follows:

1. The class is divided into groups. Each group designates one of its members as "leader" and another (presumably one with the most knowledge on the topic) as "expert."

2. Next, working individually and without discussion, rank the listed items in terms of their importance in reaching your destination.

3. Make a copy of your individual ranking. (Leaders should write "Leader" on their copies, and experts should write "Expert." Submit your sheets to your instructor, who will then compute "leader", "expert", "average", "majority", and "minority" rankings for the class as a whole.

4. Next, each group should attempt to reach a group ranking of the items by employing the strategy of consensus.

5. At the end of the work period, your instructor will provide the correct rankings.
   a. Determine the numerical difference between your group's score and the correct answers.
   b. Add all differences together to determine the overall rating of your group. The lower the score, the more accurate the ranking.

6. Finally, compare and contrast the effectiveness of the various decision-making methods.

Notes
A problem can develop when you have a group meeting and the boss acts as if he or she is sitting on a perfect score of "15" when actually it is an imperfect "89." What can be done to prevent this from damaging the group's effectiveness? Remember, at issue is how well the group handles all its resources. (Answers can be found on page 492.)

Source: Adapted from a release of the National Aeronautic and Space Administration (NASA).

Groups use various
methods of decision
making; "decision by
the majority" is
typically arrived at
by voting.

Spratt/The Image Works

Experience has shown that the various methods of group decision making vary considerably in their effectiveness. *Majority vote* is the method used most frequently. Most elections are decided and many laws are passed using this approach, and a large number of other decisions are made on the basis of the vote of at least 51 percent of a group's members. Lest we overlook the importance of the *minority*, however, we should note that it too can carry weight. Think of how often committees subdivide responsibilities with the result that subgroups actually end up making the key recommendations and thus the key decisions.

Another popular decision-making strategy is *averaging*, by which the most popular decision becomes the group's decision. (In "Lost on the Moon," on pages 243–244, the average response of each group could have been obtained by summing all individual answers and then dividing by the number of members in the group.)

Letting the *expert* member decide what the group should do is also fairly common. In this case, the group simply defers its decision-making power to its most knowledgeable member.

In many groups the *leader* retains all the decision-making power. Sometimes this is done after consultation with group members; at other times it is done without consultation.

Although each of these methods has been used successfully by a variety of groups, the most effective decision-making strategy is *decision by consensus*. When a group achieves consensus, all members agree on the decision. Even more important, all of them help formulate the decision by voicing their feelings and airing their differences of opinion. Thus they all understand the decision and will support it.

Identify the methods of decision making that are used most often in your class, at home, and at work. Are you satisfied with them? Why?

Research shows that the greater the *involvement* of members in the decision-making process, the more effective the decision will be. Of course, decisions by a leader, by an expert, or by a majority or minority vote all take less time than consensus; however, it should be remembered that after all, it is the group that will usually be responsible for implementing the decision. If members disagree with a decision or do not understand it, they may not work very hard to make it succeed. A leader may make routine decisions or may be called on to make decisions when little time is available for a real discussion of the issues; but under most circumstances, one person cannot be the best resource for all decisions. A drawback of the decision-by-expert method is that it is sometimes difficult to determine who the expert is. Also, decision by an expert—like decision by a leader—fails to involve other group members. Decision by averaging, on the whole, is superior to either decision by a leader or decision by an expert. With averaging, all members can be consulted and individual errors will cancel each other out, and an "average" position will usually not dissatisfy anyone too much. On the other hand, an "average" position usually doesn't satisfy anyone very much; thus commitment to the decision tends to be rather low.

How do you influence a group? What behaviors let some people exert more influence than others?

Thus, under most circumstances the quality of decision making and the satisfaction of the participants are higher when consensus is used. Consensus puts the resources of the entire group to effective use, permits discussion of all issues and alternatives, and ensures the commitment of all members. From this we can see that it is not the decision alone which is important in group interaction; we must also be concerned with the reactions and feelings of group members.

PERSONAL STYLES: A DECISION-MAKING GRID

How do you behave when you are engaged in collective problem solving? The following list will provide you with a general indication of your own behavior in a problem-solving group. From the possibilities given, choose the approach that best characterizes your personal decision-making style. Rank your behavior from 1 (most characteristic) to 5 (least characteristic).

When my group is engaged in decision making I:

Sit back and let others make the decision for me.

Am concerned that a decision work, not whether others like it.

Am concerned that members are satisfied with the decision, not whether it will work.

Sacrifice my own feelings in order to reach a decision that can be implemented.

Work so that everyone will discuss, understand, agree to, and be satisfied with a decision.

The decision-making grid in Figure 9-2, adapted from the work of Jay Hall, Vincent O'Leary, and Martha Williams, can help you understand your responses. It shows the relationship between concern that a decision work ("concern for adequacy") and concern for commitment of others to the decision

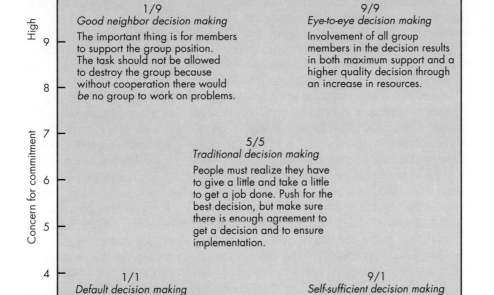

FIGURE 9-2
Decision-making grid.

Source: © 1964 by the
Regents of the University of
California. Reprinted from
*California Management
Review*, vol. 7, no. 2, by
permission of the Regents.

("concern for commitment").[6] If you characteristically sit back and let others do the decision making, you exemplify the "default" style (you are a 1/1 with low concern for adequacy and low concern for commitment). If you insist that the quality of a decision is more important than the "happiness" of group members, you represent the "self-sufficient" style. The exact opposite of this type is the person who is more concerned about group support for a decision than about its quality or workability—the "good neighbor" style. The middle position, the "traditional" style, is typical of a "sacrificer-compromiser," who is willing to give in in order to get a job done. Finally, if you characteristically employ an "eye-to-eye" style, you believe that consensus is possible if all group resources are used, if members feel free to express their opinions and ideas, and if consideration is given to the task itself and to the "maintenance dimension" of the decision-making process—that is, to social and emotional aspects and to members' satisfaction.

QUESTIONS FOR DECISION MAKERS: FACTS, VALUES, AND POLICIES

The actual content of decision making is based on three key kinds of questions: questions of fact, questions of value, and questions of policy.

Questions of fact are concerned with the truth or falsity of a statement. Existing information may be inconsistent or contradictory, and group members are required to ferret out the truth. For example, a group might be asked to determine whether evidence proved beyond a doubt that Bruno Hauptmann kidnapped and murdered Charles and Anne Lindbergh's child or that Sam Shepherd murdered his wife. Questions of fact might be phrased like this: "What evidence supports the guilt or innocence of _____?" Similarly, a group might wrestle with questions like these: "What is the likelihood that a nuclear winter will follow a nuclear war?" "What are the effects of depletion of the ozone layer of the atmosphere?" As you can see, answering questions like these requires that a group examine and interpret the available data carefully.

In contrast, *questions of value* are not factual; they involve subjective judgments. "Who was the best president to serve in the last 100 years?" is a question of value. So are the following: "To what extent is a college education valuable to all Americans?" "How desirable are physical fitness programs?" "To what extent, if any, is the use of laboratory animals for scientific research justified?"

Questions of policy are designed to help us determine what future actions, if any, should be taken. In fact, the key word in a question of policy is the word *should*: "What should colleges do to prevent student suicides?" "What should the United States do to discourage terrorism?" "What should federal policy be regarding the sale of semiautomatic military-style weapons to members of the general public?"

A FRAMEWORK FOR DECISION MAKING: REFLECTIVE THINKING

> Groups can bring out the worst as well as the best in human decision making.
>
> Irving Janis

The quality of a group's decisions depends at least partly on the nature of its decision-making system. There is a generally agreed upon structure, consisting of several stages, which, if used properly, can increase the problem-solving effectiveness of most groups. This is called the *reflective-thinking framework*, and it was first proposed by John Dewey in 1910. It is probably still the sequence most commonly used by problem-solving groups.[7]

The reflective-thinking framework has six basic components:

1. *What is the problem?* Is it clearly defined? Do we understand the general situation in which it is occurring? Is it stated so as not to arouse defensiveness? Is it phrased so as not to permit a simple yes or no answer? (For example, "What should the college's policy be toward final exams for seniors?" instead of "Should the college stop wasting the time of its seniors and eliminate final exams?" or "What should the government's policy be toward gun control?" instead of "Should the government restrain trigger-happy hunters?")

2. *What are the facts of the situation?* What are its causes? What is its history? Why is it important? Whom does it affect, and how?

3. *What criteria must an acceptable solution meet?* By which and whose standards must a solution be evaluated? What are the principal requirements of the solution? How important is each criterion?

4. *What are the possible solutions?* How would each remedy the problem? How well does each satisfy the criteria? What are the advantages and disadvantages of each?

5. *Which is the best solution?* How would you rank the solutions? Which offers the greatest number of advantages and the smallest number of disadvantages? Would some combination of solutions be beneficial?

6. *How can the solution be implemented?* What steps need to be taken to put the solution into effect?

To make this framework function, it is necessary for every member of the group to suspend judgment. This means that the interactants must be open to all available ideas, facts, and opinions. They must guard against "early concurrence," which could force them to conclude the discussion prematurely. All data and alternative courses of action must be appraised thoroughly. Instead of insisting on your own position and closing yourself to new information, you will need to explore all the major variables that contributed to the problem and investigate all the major issues that may be involved in producing a workable solution.

As you make your way through the framework, ask yourself if (1) the resources of all the group members are being well used, (2) the group is using its time to advantage, (3) the group is emphasizing fact finding and inquiry, (4) members are listening to and respecting one another's opinions and feelings, (5) pressure to conform is being kept to a minimum while an honest search for diverse ideas is made, and (6) the atmosphere is supportive (noncritical), trusting (nonthreatening), and cooperative (noncompetitive). Remember, if group members are afraid to speak up, close-minded, reluctant to search for information, or unmotivated, they will not perform effectively.

THE SEARCH FOR BETTER IDEAS: BRAINSTORMING

According to Jay Cocks, a business theorist and writer, "In an era of global competition, fresh ideas have become the most precious raw materials."[8] Where do fresh ideas come from? Betty Edwards, author of *Drawing on the Right Side of the Brain*, believes that fresh ideas come from developing creative problem-solving skills, as well as from encouraging creativity in the workplace.[9] To prepare students like yourselves to meet the demands of the 1990s and beyond, colleges and universities across the country are offering entire courses on creativity. According to the instructional technologist Jeff DeGroff, "The lesson of the twentieth century is that people must change patterns of thinking."[10] Thus, if you can come up with creative solutions, you may find yourself of great value to the companies and corporations of today and tomorrow. Brainstorming is one key technique used to "thaw" frozen patterns of thinking and encourage creativity. What is brainstorming?

A number of researchers have suggested that the best way to have a *good* idea is to have *lots* of ideas. Frequently, however, instead of suspending judgment and permitting ideas to develop freely, problem solvers tend to grasp at the first solution that comes to mind. Recognizing that this practice inhibits the search for new avenues of thought, Alex Osborn devised a technique called *brainstorming*.[11] This method is used primarily to promote a free flow of ideas and can be incorporated into the problem-solving process. For instance, although brainstorming is used most frequently when group members are attempting to identify a solution, it can also be used to help identify the factors

Brainstorming is a key technique for generating ideas, and thus can be a useful part of the problem-solving process.

Seth Resnick/Stock, Boston

that caused a problem, the criteria that a solution should meet, and the ways the solution could be implemented.

To ensure that brainstorming sessions are successful, group members need to adhere to certain guidelines:

1. Temporarily suspend judgment. That is, do *not* evaluate or criticize ideas. Instead, adopt a "try anything" attitude. This will encourage rather than stifle the flow of ideas.

2. Encourage freewheeling. The wilder the ideas that are offered, the better. It is easier to tame a wild idea later than it is to replace or invigorate an inert idea. At this point, the practicality of an idea is not of primary importance.

3. Think of as many ideas as you can. At this stage, it is the quantity—not the quality—of ideas that is important. The greater the number of ideas, the better the chance of finding a good one. Thus, in a brainstorming session no self-censorship or group censorship is permitted. All ideas should be expressed.

4. Build on and improve or modify the ideas of others. Work to mix ideas until they form interesting combinations. Remember, brainstorming is a group effort.

5. Record all ideas. This ensures that the group will have available all the ideas that have been generated during the session.

6. Only after the brainstorming session is finished should group members evaluate the ideas for usefulness and applicability.

Brainstorming is effective because it lessens the inhibitions of members and makes it easier for them to get their ideas heard; promotes a warmer, more playful, enthusiastic, and cooperative atmosphere; and encourages each individual's potential for creativity. But the unique aspect of brainstorming—and perhaps its most important benefit—is suspended judgment.

Too often, one or two group members stifle the creative thinking effort of a brainstorming group. Despite the lip service they may pay to suspending judgment, they have come to the problem-solving experience with an "evaluative set." According to Sidney Parnes, who studies creative thinking, this attitude surfaces in the form of "killer phrases," words that stop the flow of ideas.[12] This practice strikes at the heart and nature of brainstorming. It replaces the "green light" of brainstorming not so much with a "yellow light" of criticism or thoughtful evaluation as with a "red light" of frozen judgment. We should note that "killer phrases" are often accompanied (or replaced) by "killer looks"—looks that discourage or inhibit the generation of ideas. (How often do killer phrases or looks intrude upon your group experiences?) By gaining insight into types of "killers," and their effects, you can increase your ability to analyze your own behavior and change it if necessary.

> I had an immense advantage over many others dealing with the problem inasmuch as I had no fixed ideas derived from long-established practice to control and bias my mind, and did not suffer from the general belief that whatever is, is right.
>
> Henry Bessemer (discoverer of a new way of making steel)

✔ **SKILL BUILDER**

BRAIN POWER

Case A: "A Stitch in Time . . ."

A woman was surprised to discover that her somewhat eccentric uncle had left her over 1 million empty spools of thread in his will. Since she was an enterprising person, she decided to turn her inheritance into a business. Working with four to six other students, use the next few minutes to generate as many uses as you can for empty spools of thread.

Case B: Warning Signs

How can we warn people who will be alive 10,000 years from now that they should stay away from the sites where we dumped nuclear wastes? Working with your group, your task is to generate as many ways as you can to warn people.

After completing these activities, answer the following questions:

1. How satisfied were you with the group effort? Why?

   Case A: Satisfied 1 2 3 4 5 Dissatisfied
   Case B: Satisfied 1 2 3 4 5 Dissatisfied

2. Which brainstorming guidelines were adhered to? How do you know?

3. Which brainstorming guidelines were ignored or violated? Why?

ORIGINAL SPIN
Leslie Dorman and Peter Edidin

Pamela Webb Moore, director of naming services (she helps companies figure out good names for their products at Synectics, a creativity consulting firm) uses a number of techniques to encourage creativity.

One technique she uses to limber up the minds of tightly focused corporate managers is "sleight of head." While working on a particular problem, she'll ask clients to pretend to work on something else. In one real-life example, a Synectics-trained facilitator took a group of product development and marketing managers from the Etonic shoe corporation on an "excursion," a conscious walk away from the problem—in this case, to come up with a new kind of tennis shoe.

The facilitator asked the Etonic people to imagine they were at their favorite vacation spot. "One guy," Moore says, "was on a tropical island, walking on the beach in his bare feet. He described how wonderful the water and sand felt on his feet, and he said, 'I wish I could play tennis barefoot.' The whole thing would have stopped right there if somebody had complained

that while his colleague was wandering around barefoot, they were supposed to come up with a shoe. Instead, one of the marketing people there was intrigued, and the whole group decided to go off to play tennis barefoot on a rented court at 10 at night."

While the Etonic people played tennis, the facilitator listed everything they said about how it felt. The next morning, the group looked at her assembled list of comments, and they realized that what they liked about playing barefoot was the lightness of being without shoes, and the ability to pivot easily on both the ball of the foot and the heel. Nine months later, the company produced an extremely light shoe called the Catalyst, which featured an innovative two-piece sole that made it easier for players to pivot.

Source: From "Original Spin" by Leslie Dorman and Peter Edidin, *Psychology Today*, July 8, 1989. Reprinted with permission from Psychology Today Magazine. Copyright © 1989 (Sussex Publishers, Inc.).

It is interesting to consider how brainstorming is related to what the researcher Rosabeth Moss Kanter calls "kaleidoscope thinking." According to Kanter:

A kaleidoscope takes a set of fragments and forms them into a pattern. But when the kaleidoscope is twisted or approached from a new angle, the same fragments form a different pattern. Kaleidoscope thinking, then, involves taking existing data and twisting it or looking at it from another angle in order to see and analyze the new patterns that appear.[13]

For a problem-solving group to be effective, certain characteristics need to be present, and concerned members must work to develop these qualities. By becoming aware of the difference between optimal or ideal problem-solving behaviors and the actual behaviors of you and your fellow group members, you can begin to improve your group's method and style of operation.

An effective group exhibits these characteristics:

1. Group goals are clearly understood and cooperatively formulated by the members. Goals are not merely imposed. If group members are confused about the nature of a problem, they will not be able to solve it. (As the theorists Bobby R. Patton and Kim Giffin stress, "If we aim at nothing, we are pretty apt to hit it.")[14]

2. All members of the group are encouraged to communicate their ideas and feelings freely. Ideas and feelings are valued; they are neither ignored nor suppressed. "Keynote" phrases are *I think*, *I see*, and *I feel*. These phrases reveal a personal point of view and indicate that you recognize that someone else may feel, think, or see differently from you.

3. Group members seek to reach a consensus when the decision is important. Input from all members is sought. Each member's involvement is considered critical. Thus, the decision is not left to an "authority" to make on the basis of little or no discussion.

4. Consideration is given to both the "task" dimensions and the "maintenance" dimensions of the problem-solving effort. Both the quality of the decision and the well-being of the group members are considered important.

5. Group members do not set about problem solving haphazardly. A problem-solving framework is used, and an outline is followed that aids the group in its search for relevant information.

6. Motivation is high. Group members are anxious to search for information, speak up, listen to others, and engage in an active and honest search for a "better" solution. They neither jump impetuously at the first solution that presents itself nor prematurely evaluate and criticize ideas.

7. An effort is made to assess the group's problem-solving style to identify and alleviate factors that impede its effectiveness as well as to identify and foster factors that enhance its effectiveness.

Do you see a problem as a game or as work? According to Mary Ann Glyn, who teaches organization behavior at Yale University, people who see problems as games come up with more creative solutions than those who consider the same problems work.

SUMMARY

In communication theory, a *group* is defined as a collection of people who interact verbally and nonverbally, occupy certain roles with respect to one another, and cooperate with each other to accomplish a definite goal. Some of our most important communication experiences take place in small groups. Small groups are used to solve common problems and make decisions by sharing information.

The advantages of using a group instead of an individual are that resources can be pooled, motivation is increased, errors are more likely to be detected, decisions are more readily accepted by those outside the group, and the group members can enjoy the companionship and rewards of working with others. There are, however, potential disadvantages to group problem solving: it may encourage laziness among some members; conflict may arise between personal and group goals; the group may be dominated by a few; one or two stubborn members may create a deadlock; the group may make an excessively risky decision; and the decision itself usually takes longer to reach.

To operate effectively, group members need to be supportive; exercise participative decision making; show trust, openness, and candor; and set high performance goals. The healthier the group climate, the more cohesive the group. Keep in mind that in group meetings, men tend to speak more often, and longer, than women. Thus women should make an effort to take the initiative, and men should give women the opportunity to air their views.

There are a number of different methods groups use to make decisions—decision by an expert, by chance, by majority, by the leader, by the minority, by averaging individual decisions, and by consensus—or the group can defer a decision entirely. Making decisions by consensus is considered the most effective strategy. When a group achieves consensus, all members have helped formulate the decision, all have agreed on it, and all will support it.

The behavior of group members can be plotted and analyzed on a decision-making grid, which provides a picture of the relationship between concern that a decision will actually work and concern that group members will be committed to the decision. Most groups can improve their problem-solving effectiveness by using the reflective-thinking framework, a systematic six-step approach to decision making. Another technique that is useful in some situations is brainstorming, which encourages each member's potential for creativity. Brainstorming can help you change your patterns of thinking and find new solutions.

SUGGESTIONS FOR FURTHER READING

Bormann, Ernest G.: *Small Group Communication: Theory and Practice*, Harper and Row, New York, 1990. A thorough examination of small groups.

Fritz, Robert: *Creating*, Fawcett, New York, 1991. Discusses the basics of creativity. Suggests techniques that can be applied to any field.

Johnson, David W., and Frank P. Johnson: *Joining Together: Group Theory and Group Skills*, Prentice-Hall, Englewood Cliffs, N.J., 1991. Provides both theory and practice opportunities. Readable examination of the dynamics of small-group communication.

Kayser, Thomas: *Mining Group Gold*, Serif, El Segundo, Calif., 1990. Gives specific tools to help teams work effectively. Stresses building consensus through preparation and planning.

McGregor, Douglas: "The Human Side of Enterprise," in K. Davis and W. Scott (eds.), *Human Relations and Organizational Behavior*, McGraw-Hill, New York, 1969. Clearly compares and contrasts "theory X" with "theory Y."

Napier, Robert, and M. Gershenfeld: *Groups: Theory and Experiences*, Houghton Mifflin, Boston, 1989. Combines group theory with practice.

Phillips, Gerald M., Douglas J. Pedersen, and Julia T. Wood: *Group Discussion: A Practical Guide to Participation and Leadership*, Houghton Mifflin, Boston, 1979. A practical resource for problem solvers.

Redding, Charles: *Communication within the Organization*, Industrial Communication Council, New York, 1972. Very readable and comprehensive, but hard to find.

Rothwell, J. Dan: *In Mixed Company: Small Group Communication*, Harcourt Brace Jovanovich, Fort Worth, Texas, 1992. A comprehensive, innovative, and user-friendly work.

Van Oech, Robert: *A Whack on the Side of the Head*, Warner, New York, 1990. One of a series of books by this author, focusing on practical approaches to creativity. Offers specific techniques, puzzles, and exercises designed to spur creativity.

1. Vincent DiSalvo, "A Summary of Current Research Identifying Communication Skills in Various Organizational Contexts," *Communication Education*, vol. 29, 1980, pp. 281–290.

2. There are numerous definitions of the word *group*. For a sampling, see Robert S. Cathcart and Larry A. Samovar (eds.), *Small Group Communication: A Reader*, 3d ed., Brown, Dubuque, Iowa, 1979: David W. Johnson and Frank P. Johnson, *Joining Together: Group Theory and Group Skills*, Prentice-Hall, Englewood Cliffs, N.J., 1975; and Marvin E. Shaw, *Group Dynamics: The Psychology of Small Group Behavior*, 3d ed., McGraw-Hill, New York, 1981.

3. Charles Redding, *Communication within the Organization*, Industrial Communication Council, New York, 1972.

4. Douglas McGregor, *The Human Side of Enterprise*, McGraw-Hill, New York, 1960.

5. For a discussion of the issue of individual versus group decision making see G. Walson and D. W. Johnson, *Social Psychology: Issues and Insights*, 2d ed., Lippincott, Philadelphia, 1972.

6. J. Hall, V. O'Leary, and M. Williams, "The Decision-Making Grid: A Model of Decision-Making Styles," *California Management Review*, Winter 1964, pp. 45–46.

7. John Dewey, *How We Think*, Heath, Boston, 1910.

8. Jay Cocks, "Let's Get Crazy!" *Newsweek*, July 19, 1991.

9. Betty Edwards, *Drawing on the Right Side of the Brain*, St. Martin's, New York, 1979.

10. Jeff DeGroff, in "Grab Your Textbook and Your Poker Cards," Maryanne George, *The Record*, Knight Ridder News Service, January 28, 1991.

11. A. F. Osborne, *Applied Imagination*, Scribner, New York, 1957.

12. Sidney Parnes, *A Source Book for Creative Thinking*, Scribner, New York, 1962.

13. Rosabeth Moss Kanter, "How to Be an Entrepreneur without Leaving Your Company," *Working Woman*, November 1988, p. 44. See also Kanter, *When Giants Learn to Dance*, Touchstone, New York, 1990.

14. Bobby R. Patton and Kim Giffin, *Decision Making: Group Interaction*, Harper and Row, New York, 1978.

GROUP NETWORKS, MEMBERSHIP, AND LEADERSHIP

After finishing this chapter, you should be able to:

Explain how networks affect group interaction

Define *group role*

Compare and contrast task, maintenance, and self-serving roles

Define *leadership*

Distinguish among various leadership styles: type X, type Y, autocratic, democratic, laissez-faire

Describe how trait theory, situation theory, and functional theory contribute to our understanding of leadership

Explain how cooperation and competition manifest themselves in group interactions

Identify behaviors that contribute to defensive or supportive group climate

Demonstrate an ability to improve communication among members of a group

In this chapter we will explore the various dimensions of group membership and the meaning of leadership; we will also elaborate on the characteristics of effective group communication. By gaining insights into the various roles performed by members and leaders, by familiarizing ourselves with the communication styles open to us, and by seeing how role expectations, leadership, and networks (communication patterns) affect group performance, we will be better equipped to analyze our own behavior in problem-solving groups.

NETWORKS: PATTERNS OF COMMUNICATION

Any group's ability to accomplish its task is related to the interactions among its members. It is all but impossible for a small group to communicate well unless the members are comfortable in speaking with one another, feel free to express their ideas and feelings to each other, and have an opportunity to receive feedback about how they are coming across.

If you are able and willing to communicate with most, if not all, the members of your group, you can be said to occupy a *central position* in the group. In contrast, if you relate to only one or at the most a few people in your group, you occupy a *peripheral position*. It is the group's networks that determine the communication paths open to members and the effectiveness of their interactions. Figure 10-1 on page 258 shows representative types of networks.

The first studies of group networks were conducted by the sociological researchers Bavelas and Leavitt.[1] Bavelas studied four communication patterns: circle, line (or chain), star (or wheel), and "Y." For each pattern, he measured the time it took group members to solve a simple problem and the satisfaction of group members with the operation of the group. Bavelas discovered that the Y pattern was the most efficient; that is, it enabled the members to solve the problem presented to them in the shortest time. However, he found that the circle pattern was associated with the highest morale. Bavelas also found that members who occupied central positions in group networks were more satisfied with the group's operation than members who occupied peripheral positions.

Very few ideas and very few projects of any significance are implemented by one person alone.
Rosabeth Moss Kanter

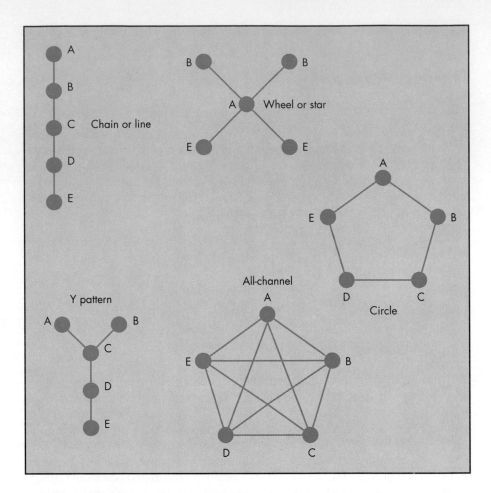

FIGURE 10-1
Communication
networks.

Leavitt studied the same four patterns of communication. In Leavitt's experiments, members of a "circle" group, a "chain" group, a "Y" group, and a "wheel" group had to discover a common symbol included on cards provided to them. He found that the network with the greatest degree of shared centrality—the circle—produced the highest morale among group members; the network with the lowest degree of shared centrality—the wheel—required the shortest time to come up with an accurate solution. In most of the groups Leavitt studied, the person who occupied the most central position was identified as the leader. The circle was described as having shared leadership; each of the other groups had one clearly emergent leader.

We can see that the particular type of communication network a group develops will determine which communication channels are open and which channels are closed, and thus the network will affect who talks to whom. The network also affects morale. When people are cut off from relating to each other, individual satisfaction decreases.

CENTRAL OR PERIPHERAL?

The purpose of this exercise is to increase your awareness of the effect of networks on satisfaction and efficiency in problem-solving groups. Your instructor will divide the class into groups of five or six members. Each group will be required to use one of the networks shown in Figure 10-1. You may communicate with only the members to whom you are directly linked. Thus, in the wheel pattern, for example, only if you are A can you communicate with all the members of the group; if you are B, C, D, or E, you may communicate with other members only through A. (Note that only in the all-channel network are the lines of communication completely free and open to each member.) Complete the following tasks:

Task A

Using only written messages sent directly to the person or people with whom you are permitted to communicate, your task is to reach unanimous agreement on the number of squares contained in the following diagram. Your group will be considered to have completed the task when each person in the group has reported the group's decision to your instructor.

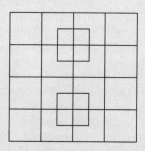

Task B

Maintaining the same network pattern as in task 1, rank the following list of attributes of a communicator in a small group from 1 (most important) to 10 (least important). Your group will be considered to have completed the task when each member has reported the group's decision to your instructor.

Has high self-esteem

Is able to express himself or herself fluently

Gets along well with others

Is goal-oriented

Is highly intelligent

Is a prolific generator of ideas

Has strong problem-solving ability

Has strong leadership qualities

Does not automatically agree with superiors

Is self-disciplined

When tasks A and B have been completed, answer these questions.

1. Network my group used: _____

2. Time we required to complete the task: _____

3. How did the time your group used compare with the time consumed by other groups?

4. Rank the extent to which you enjoyed being a member of your group:

   Very much   1 2 3 4 5   Not at all

5. What was your group's average "level of enjoyment"? (To compute this, add the individual scores from item 4 together and divide by the number of people in your group.)

6. How did your group's "enjoyment level" compare with the "enjoyment levels" of the other groups?

7. Do you think your group had a leader? If so, who?

8. To what extent do you think your group's network helped or hindered your own performance? Explain.

Thus it makes sense that overall group morale increases when a decentralized network (a network with *shared centrality*) is used. And as we have seen, the network can also affect efficiency. In addition to Bevalas's and Leavitt's findings about efficiency, other studies have shown that although centralized networks (networks with many isolated, or peripheral, members) produce faster solutions to a simple problem, decentralized networks are more efficient if the problem is more complex. (It seems that if a problem is complex and the group network is centralized, the member in the central position begins to suffer from "information overload.")

From studies like these, we see that if we can trace the types of communication patterns groups use for problem solving, we will more readily understand why some members feel frustrated while others feel content, why some feel they are able to exert power while others feel powerless, and why some enjoy the group experience while others abhor it. Having an opportunity to interact with others, give others information, gain information directly from others, and exert some control over the operation of the group is essential if members are to believe they can contribute to the group, be satisfied with the group process, and be motivated to continue their participation in the group. For a group to be effective, the members need to realize that it is up to them to elicit contributions from one another and to encourage effective communication among all members. Thus, a completely connected pattern of group communication is usually the most desirable.

GROUP MEMBERS: ROLES AND RESPONSIBILITIES

What type of group member do you consider yourself? To be an effective member, you need to consider the assets and liabilities you bring to the group experience, the roles you perform in your group, and how your behavior either contributes to or detracts from your group's effectiveness.

Defining Group Roles

At this point it will be useful for us to examine a number of different group roles in order to determine how each contributes to or detracts from a group's performance. First, however, let us clarify the term *group role*. A group role is a type of behavior: a particular kind of communicative act exhibited by a group member. Naturally, a group will perform more effectively when group members assume positive roles (functions that help accomplish the group's purpose) and avoid negative roles (behaviors that distract or frustrate the group). We may perform a number of different roles in a group, or we may prefer to perform a single role. We may also perform certain roles in one group and completely different roles in another. For example, sometimes we may contribute in ways that promote the accomplishment of the group task, at other times we may function in ways that help maintain relationships among group members, and at still other times we may deemphasize group objectives by exhibiting self-serving behaviors and actively seeking to meet only personal needs or goals.

List three positive and three negative qualities you bring to groups. What could others do to make you a more effective group member? How could they make you an ineffective member?

Studies indicate that if men and women talk equally in a group, people think that the women have talked more. How would you account for this?

MORE ON MEN, WOMEN, AND GROUPS

According to the researcher Elizabeth Aries, a professor of psychology at Amherst College, women and men perform different group roles when interacting in mixed-sex groups. Whereas men tend to set the agenda by offering opinions, suggestions and information, women tend to react by agreeing or disagreeing. Also, Aries notes that men tend to sit more relaxed, with legs outstretched, while women tend to sit more close-bodied.

What in your opinion accounts for these disparities in contribution and demeanor? Do these differences pose a problem for either sex? Can women be perceived as equally helpful to the progress of the discussion if it is the men who typically provide the bulk of information and opinions while women typically provide support?

Should members of both sexes become more adept at exchanging roles and functions in a group? Why or why not?

Source: Elizabeth Aries, "Gender and Communication," in Phillip Shaver and Clyde Hendrick (eds.), *Sex and Gender*, Sage, Newbury Park, Calif., 1987, p. 127.

Classifying Roles

Even though their role-classification model was formulated more than 40 years ago, the system proposed by Kenneth Benne and Paul Sheats is still commonly used today. It describes the functions participants should seek to assume—and the functions they should avoid—during the life of a group.[2] Benne and Sheats considered *goal achievement* (completing the task) and *group maintenance* (building relationships) the two basic objectives of any group. They further reasoned that eliminating nonfunctional behaviors is a requirement or condition that must be met if the preceding goals are to be realized. Guided by these assumptions, Benne and Sheats identified three categories of roles:

1. Task-oriented roles
2. Maintenance-oriented roles
3. Self-serving roles

Task-oriented roles include these:

Initiating. The member defines a problem; suggests methods, goals, and procedures; and starts the group moving along new paths or in different directions by offering a plan.

Information seeking. The member asks for facts and opinions and seeks relevant information about the problem.

Opinion seeking. The member solicits expressions of feeling and value in order to discover the values underlying the group effort.

Information giving. The member provides ideas and suggestions and supplies personal experiences as well as factual data.

Opinion giving. The member supplies opinions, values, and beliefs and reveals his or her feelings about what is being discussed.

Clarifying. The member elaborates on the ideas of others, supplies paraphrases, offers examples or illustrations, and tries to eliminate confusion and increase clarity.

Coordinating. The member summarizes ideas and tries to draw various contributions together constructively.

Evaluating. The member evaluates the group's decisions or proposed solutions and helps establish standards for judgment.

Consensus testing. The member checks on the state of group agreement to see if the group is nearing a decision.

Maintenance-oriented roles include these:

Encouraging. The member is warm, receptive, and responsive to others and praises others and their ideas.

Gatekeeping. The member attempts to keep communication channels open; he or she helps reticent members contribute to the group and works to keep the discussion from being dominated by one or two members.

Harmonizing. The member mediates differences between participants and attempts to reconcile misunderstandings or disagreements; he or she also tries to reduce tension by using humor or other forms of relief at appropriate junctures.

Compromising. The member is willing to compromise his or her position to maintain group cohesion; he or she is willing to admit error and modify beliefs to achieve group growth.

Standard setting. The member assesses whether group members are satisfied with the procedures being used and indicates that criteria have been set for evaluating group functioning.

Self-serving roles include these:

Blocking. The member is disagreeable and digresses in an effort to ensure that nothing is accomplished.

Aggression. The member criticizes or blames others and works to deflate the egos of other group members in an effort to enhance his or her own status.

Recognition seeking. The member attempts to become the focus of attention by boasting about his or her own accomplishments rather than dealing with the group task; he or she may speak loudly and exhibit behavior that is unusual.

Withdrawing. The member appears indifferent, daydreams, is lost in thought, or sulks.

Dominating. The member insists on getting his or her own way, interrupts others, and gives directions in an effort to "run" or control the group.

Joking. The member appears cynical or engages in horseplay or other inappropriate or irrelevant behaviors.

Self-confessing. The member uses other group members as an audience and reveals personal "feelings" or "insights" that are not oriented toward group concerns.

Help seeking. The member tries to elicit sympathy or pity from other members.

Which roles in each of these categories do you find yourself performing most frequently? What conditions in the group, or what personal needs, do you think precipitate such behavior on your part?

✔ SKILL BUILDER

ROLE CALL

Form groups of five to seven members. Designate two members of each group as group-process observers who will chart the roles members perform during the life of the group.

Each group is to complete both of the following tasks:

Task A

Use materials like cotton, pipe-cleaners, construction paper, tape, glue, scissors, and string to build a container that will support and catch an uncooked egg dropped from a height of 5 feet without damaging the shell.

Task B

Choose a group name and design a group symbol to affix to your egg container.

With the aid of your process observers, answer these questions:

1. How did the group organize for work?
2. To what extent was the members' participation evenly distributed?
3. Which task or maintenance functions did various members perform?
4. Which task or maintenance functions were lacking or not sufficiently present, inhibiting the group's performance?
5. Which self-serving roles were present? How did they affect the group's operation?
6. Summarize what the group needs to do to enhance its ability to function in the future.

As we have seen, every group member affects the operation of his or her group; sometimes the members exhibit behaviors that improve task performance in specific ways, and sometimes they exhibit behaviors that reflect their general concern for human needs and feelings. Sometimes they exhibit helpful behaviors, and sometimes they exhibit behaviors that seem to announce a minimal regard for the group experience. Developing an understanding of membership roles and behavior is essential if we are to meaningfully evaluate the effectiveness of the groups to which we belong. Developing an understanding of group leadership is also essential; after all, membership and leadership go hand in hand. Let's turn now to leadership.

APPROACHES TO LEADERSHIP: THE LEADER IN YOU

What is leadership? Are you a leader or a potential leader? What qualities does a good leader possess? Are effective leaders born or made?

What Is Leadership?

Explore what leadership means to you by completing these sentences:
A leader is a person who . . .
I like a leader who . . .
I am a leader when . . .
It is essential for a leader to . . .
I possess the following leadership skills: . . .
I lack the following leadership skills: . . .

Leadership is the ability to influence others. Thus, every person who influences others can be said to exert leadership.[3] Leadership can be either a positive or a negative force. When its influence is positive, leadership facilitates task accomplishment by a group. But if its influence is negative, task accomplishment is inhibited. Every group member is a potential leader. Whether this potential is used wisely or abused—or whether it is used effectively or ineffectively—depends on individual skills, on personal objectives, and on commitment to the group.

Groups, especially problem-solving groups, need effective leadership in order to achieve their goals. Effective leadership can be demonstrated by one or more of the members. We should point out here that there is a difference between being appointed a leader—that is, serving as a designated leader—and exhibiting leadership behaviors. When you function as a designated leader, you have been "dubbed" the leader; this means that an outside force has given you the authority to exert your influence within the group. When you simply engage in effective leadership behavior without being appointed or directed to do so, you achieve leadership, that is, you are automatically performing roles that help a group attain task or maintenance objectives.

Effective leaders perform combinations of the task and maintenance roles we described above. They demonstrate *role versatility*. Such leaders help establish a group climate that encourages and stimulates interaction; they make certain that an agenda is planned for a meeting; they take responsibility for ensuring that group communication proceeds smoothly. When group members get off the track, it is this type of leader who asks relevant questions, offers internal summaries, and keeps the discussion going. This is also the kind of leader who encourages continual evaluation and improvement by group members.

The successful organization has one major attribute that sets it apart from unsuccessful organizations: dynamic and effective leadership.
P. Hersey and K. Blanchard

Giving information is one of the "task-oriented" roles a group member may assume.

D. MacTavish/Comstock

Among the "maintenance-oriented" roles group members may play is keeping harmony—
by reconciling disagreements or clearing up misunderstandings.

Jon Feingersh/The Stock Market

Leadership Styles

TAKING RISKS: "X" AND "Y" LEADERS

The assumptions we make about how people work together will influence the type of leadership style we adopt. Here are eight assumptions that a leader might make about how and why people work. Choose the four you are most comfortable with.

1. The average group member will avoid working if he or she can.
2. The average group member views work as a natural activity.
3. The typical group member must be forced to work and must be closely supervised.
4. The typical group member is self-directed when it comes to meeting performance standards and realizing group objectives.
5. A group member should be threatened with punishment to get him or her to put forth an adequate effort.
6. A group member's commitment to objectives is related not to punishment but to rewards.
7. The average person prefers to avoid responsibility and would rather be led.
8. The average person not only can learn to accept responsibility but actually seeks responsibility.

If you picked mostly odd-numbered items in the list above, you represent what the management theorist Douglas McGregor calls a type X leader. In contrast, if you checked mostly even-numbered items, you represent what McGregor calls a *type Y* leader.[4] The type Y leader is more of a risk taker than the type X leader. Y leaders are willing to let each group member grow and develop in order to realize his or her individual potential. X leaders, however, do not readily delegate responsibility; unlike Y leaders, X leaders are not concerned with group members' personal sense of achievement. (Are you satisfied with the set of assumptions you chose? What consequences could they have?)

AUTOCRATIC, LAISSEZ-FAIRE, AND DEMOCRATIC LEADERS

In most discussions of leadership styles, three categories in addition to type X and type Y usually come up: the *autocratic* leader (the "boss"), the *democratic* leader (the "participator"), and the *laissez-faire* leader (the "do-your-own-thing" leader).[5] Let's examine each briefly.

Autocratic or *authoritarian leaders* are dominators who view their task as directive. In a group with an autocratic leader, it is the leader who determines all policies and gives orders to the other group members. In other words, one boss typically assumes almost all leadership roles; thus in effect this person becomes the sole decision maker. Although such an approach may be effective and efficient during a crisis, the usual outcome of this behavior is low group satisfaction.

Divide into groups. Create a problem-solving situation and explain how an authoritarian, a laissez-faire, and a democratic leader might handle it. For example, imagine that a corporation needs to purchase data-processing equipment. What behaviors might each type of leader exhibit in a group discussion on this topic? In turn, each group will role-play each example of leadership style.

Three commonly identified leadership styles are autocratic, laissez-faire, and democratic. A drill sergeant would be a good example of an autocratic leader; the leader of an informal folksinging group could appropriately adopt a laissez-faire style; the editor of a college newspaper would probably adopt a democratic style.

Top, Larry Kolvoord/The Image Works: *middle,* J. Muir Hamilton/Stock, Boston; *bottom,* Richard Pasley/Stock, Boston

The opposite of the authoritarian leader is the *laissez-faire leader*. This type of leader adopts a "leave them alone" attitude. In other words, this person diminishes the leadership function to the point where it is almost nonexistent. The result is that group members are free to develop and progress on their own; they are indeed free to "do their own thing." Unfortunately, the members of a laissez-faire group may often be distracted from the task at hand and lose their sense of direction, with the result that the quality of their work suffers.

The middle leadership position—and the one that has proved most effective—is *democratic leadership*. In groups with democratic leadership, members are directly involved in the problem-solving process; the power to make decisions is neither usurped by a "boss" nor abandoned by a laissez-faire leader. Instead, the leader's behavior represents a reasonable compromise between these two extremes. Democratic leaders do not dominate the group with one point of view, but they do attempt to provide direction to ensure that both task and maintenance functions are carried out. The group is free to identify its own goals, follow its own procedures, and reach its own conclusions. Most people prefer democratic groups. Morale, motivation, group-mindedness, and the desire to communicate all increase under the guidance of a democratic leader.

It should be emphasized that although democratic leadership is traditionally preferred, all three leadership styles can be effective under the appropriate conditions. Thus, when an urgent decision is required, the autocratic style may be in the group's best interest. When a minimum of interference is needed for members to work together effectively, the laissez-faire style may be more effective. When commitment to the group decision is of greatest importance, the democratic style should be practiced.

Theories of Leadership

Where does leadership ability come from? Why do some people exert more leadership than others? Why are some people more effective leaders than others? Are some people born to be leaders? Or does every situation "find" its own leader? Or is leadership a matter of learned abilities and skills? Over the years, theorists have given various answers to these questions.

TRAIT THEORY

Describe a person who you believe was born to be a leader. What attributes do you believe destined this person to lead?

The earliest view of leadership was *trait theory*. According to trait theory, leaders are people who are born to lead.[6] (Do you know any men or women who seem to have been "born to lead"?) Trait theorists also believed that there are special, built-in, identifiable leadership traits. Accordingly, attempts were made to design a test that could predict whether any person would become a leader.

After many years of research, proof of trait theory is still lacking. Simply put, personality traits are not surefire predictors of leadership. For one thing, no one set of characteristics is common to all leaders, and leaders and followers share many of the same characteristics. Also, the situation appears at least in part to determine who will come forward to exert leadership. This is not to suggest, however, that trait research did not yield valuable findings. In fact, while the statement "Leaders *must* possess the following personality traits . . ." is not valid, the research does enable us to note that certain traits are indeed *more likely* to be found in leaders than in nonleaders.

(WO)MEN AT WORK: LEADERSHIP STYLE IS COMING OF AGE
Bettijane Levine

Social power, like leadership, concerns the ability to influence others, or to control the outcomes of others. Currently, in the United States, more men than women occupy power positions. However, as is noted in this article by Bettijane Levine, the leadership styles men and women use may cause this imbalance to change in the years ahead.

Women, take heart. Men, take note. A new ground-breaking study shows that the two sexes differ dramatically when it comes to leadership—and that the feminine approach may be the wave of the future.

Male executives tend to lead the traditional way; by command and control, according to the study, conducted by Judith B. Rosener at the University of California, Irvine. Men give an order, explain the reward for a job that's well-done, and pretty much keep their power and knowledge to themselves.

Female executives, on the other hand, tend to lead in non-traditional ways: by sharing information and power. They inspire good work by interacting with the staff, by encouraging employee participation, and by showing how employees' personal goals can be reached as they meet organizational ones.

The findings were based on the response of 355 women and 101 men, matched for their position and for the type and size of organization.

The "female" style of leadership may be especially appropriate for the corporate climate of the Nineties and may be one reason that more women will quickly achieve positions of great power in the next few years, explains Rosener, a professor in UC Irvine's graduate school of management. The International Women's Forum commissioned the study.

"The male leadership model of command and control is not necessarily better or worse than the female model," Rosener says. "If there is a fire, for example, you need a command-control-type leader to order everyone out, with no questions asked."

In fact, for years the traditional male leadership style has been the *only* style at top corporations. No other style was thought to exist. Rosener says it's still in place "at most Fortune 500-type" companies, where strict hierarchical structure means that all orders flow from the top, with everyone below following them.

But the hierarchical structure is starting to look anachronistic in a world where corporations have international headquarters and where decision-making is required at lower levels, Rosener says.

It does not function as well in a global economy of multinational companies, service industries, and fast-changing technology businesses, where it's impractical to have only a few top people from whom all planning and orders flow.

The structure could actually be harmful to corporations in which far-flung, lower-level employees need to make quick, accurate decisions, backed by knowledge and power to make the decisions.

The female tendency to share knowledge, power, and responsibility may be what's needed next, Rosener says. The trouble is, most executives at top companies would still consider these to be non-managerial skills, not qualifications for the top job.

Why? Until now, there has been little research and no proof to document the existence and efficacy of leadership techniques.

Indeed, says Rosener, studies had found that there was little or no difference between leadership styles of men and women who make it to the top.

"That's because researchers always looked at Fortune 500-type companies, where there are no women," Rosener says. "And any woman who made it in a firm like that would have to do so by emulating the male management style."

She says that other studies focus on mid-level management, giving no clue about how women really function once at the top.

Rosener says her study, which will be featured in the November-December issue of the Harvard Business Review, also found that women "are enthusiastic about work" and "think it is 'fun,' " whereas "men describe work as work."

(Continued)

Other significant findings:

• Top executive women earn about the same as men. The mean income for women studied is $140,000 per year; the mean for men is $136,000. This contradicts most other studies saying that women are paid less than men.

• Sixty-eight percent of the women studied were married. This is inconsistent with previous findings, which indicate that top executive women sacrifice their personal lives in pursuit of success.

Rosener says the good news from this study is that high-achieving women can have it all. They can marry, earn as much as men, use a leadership style that comes naturally, and still ascend to the top spot.

But to do all that, they'll have to find a company that appreciates the female leadership style—or start a company of their own.

Source: From "(Wo)Men at Work" Bettijane Levine, *Los Angeles Times*, October 29, 1990. Copyright 1990, Los Angeles Times. Reprinted by permission.

Use the scale in Figure 10-2 to measure the extent to which you possess leadership attributes. Calculate your "leadership score" by adding up the numbers you have chosen. Next, use the scale to rate a person you definitely perceive as a leader. Finally, use the scale to rate a person you definitely perceive as *not* a leader. To what extent did you see yourself as having leadership traits? The highest possible score is 55. Such a score probably indicates strong leadership potential and means that a person perceives himself or herself as a leader or is so perceived by others. How does your total score compare with that of the person you considered a leader? With that of the person you considered a nonleader? If you are interested, you can compute an average score for men and women. Which sex do you think would score higher? Why do you think each set of results turned out as it did?

According to the researcher Marvin Shaw, the characteristics identified in Figure 10-2 indicate leadership potential. Shaw notes that a person who does not exhibit these traits is unlikely to be a leader.[7] Of course, having "leadership potential" doesn't guarantee that you will actually emerge a leader. A number of group members may have the qualities of leadership, but the final assertion of leadership will depend on more than "potential."

Trait	Low				High
Dependability	1	2	3	4	5
Cooperativeness	1	2	3	4	5
Desire to win	1	2	3	4	5
Enthusiasm	1	2	3	4	5
Drive	1	2	3	4	5
Persistence	1	2	3	4	5
Responsibility	1	2	3	4	5
Intelligence	1	2	3	4	5
Foresight	1	2	3	4	5
Communication ability	1	2	3	4	5
Popularity	1	2	3	4	5

FIGURE 10-2
Evaluating your
leadership traits.

✔ SKILL BUILDER

HOW ARE YOU SITUATED?

1. What conditions are necessary for you to feel comfortable exerting leadership? Explain.

2. What conditions could inhibit you from making an attempt to become a leader? Explain.

3. Describe an instance when either you or someone you knew tried to lead a group but failed. What factors can you point to as contributing to the failure?

4. Describe an instance when either you or someone you knew emerged as the leader of a group. What factors can you point to as contributing to this development of leadership?

SITUATIONAL THEORY

The second theory of leadership is *situational theory.* According to this theory, whether an individual displays leadership skills and behaviors and exercises actual leadership depends on the situation.[8] The development and emergence of leadership can be affected by such factors as the nature of the problem, the social climate, the personalities of the group members, the size of the group, and the time available to accomplish the task. As the organizational behavior theorist Keith Davis notes in *Human Relations at Work*, leader and group "interact not in a vacuum, but at a particular time and within a specific set of circumstances."[9] A leader is not necessarily a person "for all seasons."

FUNCTIONAL THEORY

The third theory of leadership is *functional theory.* In contrast to trait theory and situational theory, which emphasize the emergence of one person as a leader, functional theory suggests that several group members should be ready to lead because various actions are needed to achieve group goals.

Functional theorists believe that any of the task or maintenance activities can be considered leadership functions. In other words, when you perform any needed task or maintenance function, you are exercising leadership. Thus, according to functional theory, leadership shifts from person to person and is shared. Of course, sometimes one or two group members perform more leadership functions than others do. Consequently, one member might become the main "task leader," whereas another might become the main "socioemotional leader." However, the point is that we can enhance our leadership potential by learning to perform needed group functions more effectively.

From the functional viewpoint, then, leadership is not necessarily a birthright; nor is it simply a matter of being in the right situation at a critical juncture. Instead, we are all capable of leadership, and what is required is that we have enough self-assertion and sensitivity to perform the functions that are needed *as* they are needed. In effect, this is asserting that good membership is good leadership. And the converse is also true: good leadership is good membership.

■ ETHICS AND COMMUNICATION

KEEPING DOWN WITH THE COMPETITION

What problems are encountered when a group aspires, not to produce the best work it possibly can, but rather to produce work that is only as good as what competing groups produce?

"That's settled, then. We'll lower our standards to meet the competition."

Drawing by Weber; © 1989 The New Yorker Magazine, Inc.

In your opinion, is a group as good as its strongest member? As bad as its weakest member? More than the sum of its parts? Explain.

GROUP RELATIONSHIPS AND GROUP INTERACTION

273

CHAPTER 10
GROUP NETWORKS,
MEMBERSHIP, AND
LEADERSHIP

A number of other variables affect the quality of group interaction. Most important, the nature of the relationships shared by members of a group is highly significant in determining whether the group will operate effectively. For this reason, the following questions deserve our attention: To what extent do members of a group cooperate or compete with one another? To what extent do the members foster a defensive or a supportive environment?

Cooperation versus Competition

Obviously, the personal goals of each member have an impact on the operation of a group. If individual members view their goals as congruent or coinciding, an atmosphere of cooperation can be fostered. However, if individual members see their goals as mutually contradictory, a competitive atmosphere will develop. Too frequently, group members attempt to compete with one another when cooperating would be more beneficial to the group. The psychologists Linden L. Nelson and Spencer Kagen believe that it is irrational and self-defeating to compete if cooperating would make better sense.[10] When a group experience develops into a "dog-eat-dog" situation, all the members may go "hungry."

Few factors do more to damage a group's ability to maintain itself and complete a task than competition among members. Yet highly competitive individuals do belong to groups and do in fact affect the group's communication climate and emergent goal structure. The term *goal structure* describes the way members relate to each other. Under a *cooperative goal structure*, the members of a group work together to achieve their objectives, and the goals of each person are perceived as compatible with or complementary to those of the others. Group members readily pool resources and coordinate their efforts to obtain what they consider common aims. In contrast, when a group develops a *competitive goal structure*, members do not share resources, efforts are not coordinated, and, consciously or unconsciously, individuals work to hinder one another's efforts to obtain the goal. According to the psychologist Morton Deutsch, group members who have a competitive orientation believe that they can achieve their goals only if other members fail to do so.[11]

In order for the members of a group to cooperate with each other, certain requirements need to be met. First, the members need to agree that each has an equal right to satisfy needs. Second, conditions must be such that each person in the group is able to get what he or she wants at least some of the time. Third, plays for power that rely on techniques such as threatening, yelling, or demanding are viewed with disdain and are avoided. Finally, members do not attempt to manipulate each other by withholding information or dissembling. Consequently, when you cooperate as a group member, you do not aim to "win" or to "beat" or "outsmart" others. Unlike competition, cooperation does not require "gaining an edge" over the other members of your group; for this reason, unlike competition, cooperation does not promote defensiveness.

How do you act in group situations you define as cooperative? In situations you define as competitive? To what extent does the sex of the other group members appear to make a difference?

Supportiveness versus Defensiveness

For our purposes, *defensive behavior* can be said to occur when a group member perceives or anticipates a threat.

When you feel yourself becoming defensive, you may experience one or more of the following symptoms: a change in voice tone (as you become nervous, your throat and vocal mechanism grow tense and your vocal pitch tends to rise), a tightening of your muscles and some degree of rigidity throughout your body, and a rush of adrenaline accompanied by an urge to fight or flee. Now let us examine the behaviors that can precipitate such reactions.

In general, we tend to become defensive when we perceive others as attacking our self-concept. In fact, when we behave defensively, we devote a great amount of energy to defending the *self*. We becomed preoccupied with thinking about how the self appears to others, and we become obsessed with discovering ways to make others see us more favorably. When a member of a group becomes overly concerned with self-protection, he or she may compensate either by withdrawing or by attacking the other members. When this happens, the conditions necessary for the maintenance of the group begin to deteriorate. In short, defensive behavior on your part gives rise to "defensive listening" in others. The postural, facial, and vocal cues that accompany words can also raise the "defense level." Once the defensiveness of a group member has been aroused, that person no longer feels free to concentrate on the actual meaning of messages others are trying to send. Instead, the defensive member feels compelled to distort messages. Thus as group members become more and more defensive, they become less and less able to process each other's emotions, values, and intentions accurately. For this reason the consequences of defensiveness include destroyed or badly damaged individual relationships, continuing conflicts and increased personal anxiety within the group, wounded egos, and hurt feelings.

Before we can work to eliminate or even reduce defensiveness in our group relationships, we must understand the stimuli that can cause us to become defensive in the first place. The sociological researcher Jack R. Gibb identified six behaviors that cause defensiveness and six contrasting behaviors that allay or reduce the perceived level of threat.[12] (See Figure 10-3.) Let us examine these.

Defensive climate	Supportive climate
1. Evaluation	1. Description
2. Control	2. Problem orientation
3. Strategy	3. Spontaneity
4. Neutrality	4. Empathy
5. Superiority	5. Equality
6. Certainty	6. Provisionalism

FIGURE 10-3
Behaviors characteristic of defensive and supportive climates.

✔ SKILL BUILDER

ON THE DEFENSIVE

Think of several group experiences during which you found yourself becoming defensive. Use a three-column format to record your reactions.

- In column 1, identify the nature of the group experience.
- In column 2, describe specific events and specific actions of group members that you believe led to your feeling threatened, anxious, or frightened.
- In column 3, describe the feelings you experienced and the behaviors you adopted during the incident.

Gibb's first pair of contrasting behaviors is *evaluation* versus *description*. Group relationships can run into trouble if a member makes judgmental or *evaluative statements*. As Gibb notes in an article, "Defensive Communication," "If by expression, manner of speech, tone of voice, or verbal content the sender seems to be evaluating or judging the listener, then the receiver goes on guard." Far too often, we are apt to offhandedly label the actions of others "stupid," "ridiculous," "absurd," "wonderful," or "extraordinary" because we simply are predisposed to use judgmental terms. Although it is true that some people do not mind having their actions praised, it is also true that most of us do mind having our actions condemned; moreover, whether judgment is positive or negative, the *anticipation* of judgment can hinder the creation of an open communication climate. In contrast to evaluative statements, *descriptive* statements recount particular observable actions without labeling those behaviors as good or bad, right or wrong. When you are descriptive, you do not advise changes in behavior. Instead, you simply report or question what you saw, heard, or felt.

Gibb's second pair is *control* versus *problem orientation*. Communication that group members see as seeking to *control* them can arouse defensiveness. In other words, if your intent is to control other group members, to get them to do something or change their beliefs, you are likely to evoke resistance. How much resistance you meet will depend partly on how openly you approach these people and on whether your behavior causes them to question or doubt your motives. When we conclude that someone is trying to control us, we also tend to conclude that he or she considers us ignorant or unable to make our own decisions. A *problem orientation*, however, promotes the opposite response. When senders communicate that they have not already formulated solutions and will not attempt to force their opinions on us, we feel free to cooperate in solving the problems at hand.

Gibb's third pair is *strategy* versus *spontaneity*. Our defensiveness will increase if we feel that another group member is using a *strategy* or is trying to "put something over on us." No one likes to be "conned," and no one likes to be the victim of a hidden plan. We are suspicious of strategies that are concealed or tricky. We do not want others to make decisions for us then try to persuade us that we made the decisions ourselves. Thus when we perceive ourselves as being manipulated, we become defensive and self-protective. In contrast, *spontaneous* behavior that is honest and free of deception reduces defensiveness. Under such conditions the receiver does not feel a need to question the motivations of the sender, and trust is engendered.

Gibb's fourth pair is *neutrality* versus *empathy*. *Neutrality* is another behavior that can increase defensiveness in group members. For the most part, we need to feel that others empathize with us, that we are liked and are seen as worthwhile and valued. We need to feel that others care about us and will take the time to establish a meaningful relationship with us. If, instead of communicating empathy, warmth, and concern, a group member communicates neutrality or indifference, we may well see this as worse than rejection. We feel that he or she is not interested in us; we may even conclude that he or she perceives us as a "nonperson."

Gibb's fifth pair is *superiority* versus *equality*. Our defensiveness will be aroused if another group member communicates feelings of *superiority* about social position, power, wealth, intelligence, appearance, or other characteristics. When we receive such a message, we tend to react by attempting to compete with the sender, by feeling frustrated or jealous, or by disregarding or forgetting the sender's message altogether. On the other hand, a sender who communicates equality can decrease our defensive behavior. We perceive him or her as willing to develop a shared problem-solving relationship with us, as willing to trust us, and as feeling that any differences between us are unimportant.

Gibb's sixth and last pair is *certainty* versus *provisionalism*. The expression of absolute *certainty* or dogmatism on the part of a group member will probably succeed in making us defensive. We are suspicious of those who believe they have all the answers, view themselves as our guides rather than as our fellow travelers, and reject all information that we attempt to offer. In contrast, an attitude of *provisionalism* or open-mindedness encourages the development of trust. People who communicate a spirit of provisionalism—instead of attempting to win arguments, to be right, and to defend their ideas to the bitter end—are perceived as flexible and open rather than rigid and closed.

Gibb described behaviors associated with a defensive or supportive climate; Linda Heun and Richard Heun, in *Developing Skills for Human Interaction*, and Anita Taylor, in *Communicating*, identified nonverbal cues that usually accompany such behaviors. Figure 10-4 on the opposite page is adapted from their work.

Take some time to examine the ways in which you feel you elicit defensiveness or support in the groups to which you belong.

Defensive behaviors	Supportive behaviors
1. **Evaluation** Maintaining extended eye contact Pointing at the other person Placing hands on hips Shaking your head Shaking your index finger	1. **Description** Maintaining comfortable eye contact Leaning forward

2. **Control**
Sitting in the focal position
 	
Placing hands on hips
 	
Shaking your head
Maintaining extended eye contact
Invading the personal space of the
    other person
	2. **Problem orientation**
	Maintaining comfortable personal
	    distance
	Crossing your legs in the direction of
	    the other person
	Leaning forward
	Maintaining comfortable eye contact

3. **Strategy** Maintaining extended eye contact Shaking your head Using forced gestures	3. **Spontaneity** Maintaining comfortable eye contact Crossing your legs in the direction of the other person Using animated natural gestures Leaning forward

4. **Neutrality**
Crossing your legs away from the
    other person
Using a monotone voice
Staring elsewhere
 	
Leaning back
Maintaining a large body distance
    (4½–5 feet)
	4. **Empathy**
	Maintaining a close personal distance
	    (20–36 inches)
	Maintaining comfortable eye contact
	Crossing your legs in the direction of
	    the other person
	Nodding your head
	Leaning toward the other person

5. **Superiority**
Maintaining extended eye contact
Placing hands on hips
Situating oneself at a higher elevation
Invading the other person's personal
    space
	5. **Equality**
	Maintaining comfortable eye contact
	Leaning forward
	Situating oneself at the same elevation
	Maintaining a comfortable personal
	    distance

6. **Certainty** Maintaining extended eye contact Crossing your arms Placing hands on hips Using a dogmatic tone of voice	6. **Provisionalism** Maintaining comfortable eye contact Nodding your head Tilting your head to one side

FIGURE 10-4
Nonverbal cues
contributing to the
development of a
defensive or a
supportive climate.

Sources: Adapted from
Linda Heun and Richard
Heun, *Developing Skills for
Human Interaction*, 2d ed.,
Merrill, Columbus, Ohio,
1978; and Anita Taylor,
Teresa Rosengrant, Arthur
Meyer, and Thomas B.
Samples, *Communicating*,
Prentice-Hall, Englewood
Cliffs, N.J., 1977.

A good group is supportive.

J. Pickerell/The Image Works

HOW TO IMPROVE COMMUNICATION AMONG GROUP MEMBERS

Here are four things you can do to help ensure that the members of your group communicate and function effectively.

1. *Encourage an open, supportive environment.* Group members must feel free to contribute ideas and feelings. They must also believe that their ideas and feelings will be listened to. Unless members feel free to exchange information and feelings, they are unlikely to achieve their objectives. It is only through the transmission and accurate reception of task- and maintenance-related content that groups progress toward their goals. Thus, experienced group members realize how essential it is to elicit contributions from all members and to encourage communication among all members.

2. *Establish a cooperative climate.* As we have seen, a competitive goal structure can impede effective group interaction. Members of a cooperative group deal honestly with each other, but members of a competitive group sometimes begin to dissemble and deliberately mislead each other. In or-

der to guard against destructive competition and foster a cooperative orientation, members need to work to demonstrate mutual trust and respect. Thus, participative planning is essential. The key is coordination, not manipulation.

3. *Be ready to perform needed leadership and membership roles.* Members can help the group accomplish its tasks if they contribute to rather than detract from effective group functioning. To the extent that (1) task roles are "present and accounted for," (2) maintenance roles are effectively carried out, and (3) negative, individual, or self-centered roles are deemphasized, members' satisfaction with the group experience will increase and the group will prosper.

4. *Encourage continual improvement.* Since there is no such thing as being *too* effective at communicating with others in a group setting, we should continually make every effort to improve our communication ability. Become a "communication-process" observer within your group. Pay careful attention to how your behavior affects others and how theirs affects you. Only in this way can you develop the insights needed to facilitate more effective group interaction.

SUMMARY

A group's ability to complete a task depends on how its members interact. The five most common kinds of communication networks in groups are the chain (or line), star (or wheel), circle, Y, and decentralized networks. The decentralized network is usually the most effective and satisfying, since each group member communicates directly with all the others and no one occupies a peripheral position.

Every group member performs specific group roles. We contribute to the group's objective when we assume a task-oriented role (behaving in a way that promotes the accomplishment of the task) or a maintenance-oriented role (helping to maintain the relationships among group members). However, we can undercut the group's effectiveness by playing a self-serving role—seeking to satisfy only our own needs or goals.

In order to achieve their objectives, groups need effective leadership. Leadership is simply the ability to influence others, and there are many different leadership styles. For example, the autocratic leader dominates and directs all the other members of the group,

but the laissez-faire leader lets them "do their own thing." In most situations the democratic leader, who encourages all the members to be involved constructively in decision making and problem solving, is preferred.

There are three principal explanations of how people become leaders. Trait theory holds that some men and women are simply born to lead; situational theory holds that the situation itself—the nature of the problem and the characteristics of the group—determines who assumes leadership; functional theory holds that a number of group members can and should share the various leadership functions that need to be performed if the group is to achieve its goals. Interestingly, some research suggests that women tend to share power and information, while men tend to keep power and information for themselves.

In addition to effective leadership, a group needs cooperation among its members and a supportive group climate to be able to work toward achieving its objectives. In effect, a group creates its own culture in which to function.

Appelbaum, Ronald L., Edward M. Bodaken, Kenneth K. Sereno, and Karl W. E. Anatol: *The Process of Group Communication*, Science Research Associates, Chicago, Ill., 1979. Successfully integrates theory and application.

Bavelas, A.: "Communication Patterns in Task-Oriented Groups," *Journal of the Acoustical Society of America*, vol. 22, 1950, pp. 725–730. Describes early network studies.

Benne, Kenneth, and Paul Sheats: "Functional Roles of Group Members," *Journal of Social Issues*, vol. 4, 1948, pp. 41–49. Classic explanation of role functions.

Bethel, Sheila Murray: *Making a Difference: Twelve Qualities That Make You a Leader*, Putnam, New York, 1990. Presents communication that can help people move up the corporate ladder.

Clampett, Philip G.: *Communicating for Managerial Effectiveness*, Sage, Newbury Park, Calif., 1991. Provides a very thorough picture of effective managerial communication. Contains very interesting pragmatic insights.

Cohen, William A.: *The Art of the Leader*, Prentice Hall, Englewood Cliffs, N.J., 1990. A guide for strengthening leadership abilities. Offers a clear discussion of qualities leaders must cultivate to be effective.

Fiedler, Fred: *A Theory of Leadership Effectiveness*, McGraw-Hill, New York, 1967. Gives the reader a chance to understand this psychologist's situational theory of leadership.

Gardner, John: *On Leadership*. New York: The Free Press/Macmillan, 1990. Former Secretary of Health, Education and Welfare discusses the importance of leadership in business and government. Provides specific steps for effective leadership.

Gibb, Jack R.: "Defensive Communication," *Journal of Communication*, vol. 2, 1961, pp. 141–148. Identifies behaviors that elicit defensive or supportive reactions.

Goldhaber, Gerald: *Organizational Communication*, Brown, Dubuque, Iowa, 1990. Includes an effective unit on the roles of group membership and leadership within an organization.

Helgesen, Sally: *The Female Advantage: Women's Ways in Leadership*, Doubleday, New York, 1990. Looks at leadership and management techniques employed by women. Important reading for both men and women preparing to enter the work force.

Heun, Linda R., and Richard E. Heun: *Developing Skills for Human Interaction*, 2d ed., Merrill, Columbus, Ohio, 1978. Offers a clear discussion of nonverbal cues that contribute to a defensive or supportive climate.

Koestenbaum, Peter: *Leadership*, Jossey-Bass, San Francisco, Calif., 1991. A unique view of what constitutes exceptional leadership. Stresses the importance of commitment to excellence.

Leavitt, H. J.: "Some Effects of Certain Communication Patterns on Group Performance," *Journal of Abnormal Social Psychology*, vol. 46, 1951, pp. 38–50. Provides clear examples of how networks affect interaction.

National Institute of Business Management, *Mastering Meetings*, Berkley, New York, 1990. A very readable guide for conducting effective meetings. An easy-to-use reference manual.

Nelson, Linden L., and Spencer Kagen: "Competition: The Star-Spangled Scramble," *Psychology Today*, September 1972, pp. 53–56, 90–91. A readable study of how culture influences the development of the competitive spirit.

Patton, Bobby R., and Kim Giffin: *Decision-Making Group Interaction*, 2d ed. Harper and Row, New York, 1978. A comprehensive overview of relevant research and theory.

Shaw, Marvin E.: *Group Dynamics: The Psychology of Small Group Behavior*, 3d ed., McGraw-Hill, New York, 1981. A comprehensive guide to small-group research.

NOTES

1. See A. Bavelas, "Communication Patterns in Task-Oriented Groups," *Journal of the Acoustical Society of America*, vol. 22, 1950, pp. 725–730; and H. J. Leavitt, "Some Effects of Certain Communication Patterns on Group Performance," *Journal of Abnormal Social Psychology*, vol. 46, 1951, pp. 38–50.

2. Kenneth Benne and Paul Sheats, "Functional Roles of Group Members," *Journal of Social Issues*, vol. 4, 1948, pp. 41–49.

3. For a summary and critique of 114 studies on small groups, focusing on leadership, discussion, and pedagogy, see John F. Cragan and David W. Wright, "Small Group Communication Research of the 1970s: A Synthesis and Critique," *Central States Speech Journal*, vol. 31, 1980, pp. 197–213.

4. Douglas McGregor, *The Human Side of Enterprise*, McGraw-Hill, New York, 1960.

5. For a classic study on leadership style, see K. Lewin, R. Lippit, and R. K. White, "Patterns of Aggressive Behavior in Experimentally Created Social Climates," *Journal of Social Psychology*, vol. 10, 1939, pp. 271–299.

6. For an early study on trait theory, see Frederick Thrasher, *The Gang: A Study of 1313 Gangs in Chicago*, University of Chicago Press, Chicago, Ill., 1927.

7. Marvin Shaw, *Group Dynamics: The Psychology of Small Group Behavior*, 3d ed., McGraw-Hill, New York, 1981.

8. See Fred Fiedler, *A Theory of Leadership Effectiveness*, McGraw-Hill, New York, 1967.

9. Keith Davis, *Human Relations at Work*, McGraw-Hill, New York, 1967.

10. Linden L. Nelson and Spencer Kagen, "Competition: The Star-Spangled Scramble," *Psychology Today*, September 1972, pp. 53–56, 90–91.

11. Morton Deutsch, "A Theory of Cooperation and Competition," *Human Relations*, vol. 2, 1949, pp. 129–152.

12. Jack R. Gibb, "Defensive Communication," *Journal of Communication*, vol. 2, 1961, pp. 141–148.

CHAPTER 1

HANDLING GROUP CONFLICT: HOW TO DISAGREE WITHOUT BECOMING DISAGREEABLE

After finishing this chapter, you should be able to:

Define *conflict*

Explain how you feel when involved in a group conflict

Define *groupthink* and explain its consequences

Identify the benefits that can be derived from effective handling of group conflict

Provide examples of what can happen if group conflicts are handled poorly

Distinguish between healthy and unhealthy conflict management styles or strategies

Demonstrate an ability to use constructive strategies to resolve conflicts

Discuss how conflicts can be categorized

Explain the difference between a competitive and a cooperative conflict orientation

Identify behaviors that can be used to resolve conflicts effectively

> Man is the only animal that can remain on friendly terms with the victims he intends to eat until he eats them.
>
> Samuel Butler
>
> You can't eat your friends and have them too.
>
> Budd Schulberg

Conflict is an inevitable part of the life of any group, and sooner or later it touches all group members. A conflict can be started by anyone and can occur at any point in a group's existence. Opposed or contradictory forces within us can create inner conflicts, or we can find ourselves experiencing tension as external forces build and create interpersonal conflicts. Thus, a conflict can originate within a single group member or between two or more group members.

A group experiences *conflict* whenever a member's thoughts or acts limit, prevent, or interfere with his or her own thoughts or acts or with those of any other member. If you think about your recent group experiences, you will probably discover that you have been involved in conflicts. Some involved only you; some involved you and another. Probably, some were mild and subtle; others were intense and hostile. In any case, probably all of them were interesting.

Our goal in this chapter is to explore what conflict is, how it arises, how it affects us as group members, and how we can handle it productively. In doing so, we will develop skills to help us deal more effectively with group problem solving and decision making.

WHAT DOES CONFLICT MEAN TO YOU?

The word *conflict* means different things to different people. What does it mean to you? The following test will help you find out.

1. State your personal definition of *conflict* and indicate how you feel when involved in a conflict.
2. Next, use the scale in Figure 11-1 (page 284) to measure the extent to which you consider conflict in a small group positive or negative.
   a. Add your circled numbers together. If your score is 10–14, you believe that conflict is definitely positive. If your score is 15–20, you believe that conflict can be helpful. If your score is 21–30, you do not like to think about conflict; you have very ambivalent feelings. If your score is 31–40, you believe that conflict is something to try to avoid. If your score is 41–50, you believe that conflict is definitely negative.
   b. Determine the average scores for men and for women in the class. How do they compare? If they differ, what do you believe caused the difference? How does your score compare with the average for your sex?
   c. Compute the average score for your class as a whole. How does your score compare with the class average?

Good	1	2	3	4	5	Bad
Rewarding	1	2	3	4	5	Threatening
Normal	1	2	3	4	5	Abnormal
Constructive	1	2	3	4	5	Destructive
Necessary	1	2	3	4	5	Unnecessary
Challenging	1	2	3	4	5	Overwhelming
Desirable	1	2	3	4	5	Undesirable
Inevitable	1	2	3	4	5	Avoidable
Healthy	1	2	3	4	5	Unhealthy
Clean	1	2	3	4	5	Dirty

FIGURE 11-1
Conflict: positive or negative? For each item, circle the number that best reflects your attitude.

3. Complete these sentences:
   a. The time I felt worst about dealing with conflict in a group was when . . .
   b. The time I felt best about dealing with conflict in a group was when . . .
   c. I think the most important outcome of group conflict is . . .
   d. When I am in conflict with a group member I really care about, I . . .
   e. When I am in conflict with a group member I am not close to, I . . .
   f. When a group member attempts to avoid entering into a conflict with me, I . . .
   g. My greatest difficulty in handling group conflict is . . .
   h. My greatest strength in handling group conflict is . . .

How would being given the silent treatment affect your ability to function on the job?

The dictionary defines *conflict* as "disagreement . . . war, battle, and collision. . . ." These definitions suggest that conflict is a negative force that of necessity leads to undesirable consequences. To what extent does your score suggest that you support this premise? To what extent do you believe that conflict is undesirable and should be avoided at all times and at all costs? Do you feel that conflict is taboo? Why? Unfortunately, many of us have been led to believe that conflict is "evil"—one of the prime causes of divorce, disorder, or violence—and that to disagree, argue, or fight with another person will either dissolve whatever relationship exists or prevent any relationship from forming. Somehow many of us grow up thinking that nice people do not fight, do not make waves. They believe that if they do not smile and act cheerful, people will not like them and they will not be accepted or valued as group members.

AVOIDING CONFLICT: GROUPTHINK

What is *groupthink*? How does it come about? According to Irving Janis, author of *Victims of Groupthink*, it occurs when groups let the desire for consensus override careful analysis and reasoned decision making.[1] In effect, then, groupthink is an extreme way of avoiding conflict. While cohesiveness is normally a desirable group characteristic, when carried to an extreme it can become dysfunctional or even destructive.

285

CHAPTER 11
HANDLING GROUP
CONFLICT: HOW TO
DISAGREE WITHOUT
BECOMING DISAGREEABLE

What is conflict? We often think of conflict in negative terms like "war" and "battle" (above); but conflict can be positive—constructive and productive—if a group handles it effectively, as in the town meeting shown here (below).

Top, Baldelli/Contrasto/Saba; *bottom*, Peter Byron/Monkmeyer

The fatal explosion of the space shuttle *Challenger* in 1986 was widely attributed (at least in part) to "groupthink": team members were said to have ignored or stifled the "mavericks" who protested that something was wrong. Do some research to see if you agree that groupthink was a factor.

NASA

In groups characterized by groupthink, members try to maintain harmony by forgoing critical decision making. Did you or anyone you know ever feel a need for self-censorship at a meeting because it seemed dangerous to challenge the leader or boss? Did you ever feel it necessary to twist facts around to please a boss or leader or agree with whatever he or she said? If so, how did this influence the course of the meeting? If not, why not?

Are you a groupthinker? To find out, answer yes or no to each of the following questions, and explain your answers.

1. Have you ever felt so secure about a group decision that you ignored all warning signs that the decision was wrong? Why?

2. Have you ever been party to a rationalization justifying a group decision? Why?

3. Have you ever defended a group decision by pointing to your group's inherent sense of morality?

4. Have you ever participated in feeding a "we versus they" feeling—that is, in depicting those opposed to you in simplistic, stereotyped ways?

5. Have you ever censored your own comments because you feared destroying the sense of unanimity in your group?

6. Have you ever applied direct pressure to dissenting members in an effort to get them to agree with the will of the group?

7. Have you ever served as a "mind guard"—that is, have you ever attempted to preserve your group's cohesiveness by preventing disturbing outside ideas or opinions from becoming known to other group members?

8. Have you ever assumed that the silence of other group members implied agreement?

287

CHAPTER 11
HANDLING GROUP
CONFLICT: HOW TO
DISAGREE WITHOUT
BECOMING DISAGREEABLE

Each time you answered yes to one of these questions, you indicated that you have contributed to an illusion of group unanimity. In effect, you let a tendency to agree interfere with your ability to think critically. In so doing, you became a groupthinker. We contend that groupthink impedes effective group functioning; we believe that when all group members try to think alike, no one thinks very much.

In our opinion, conflict as such is neither a positive nor a negative phenomenon. For this reason, we will not show you how to avoid it. We do believe, however, that how you view conflict and how you handle it in any group to which you belong will determine the nature of the group's experience and your satisfaction with it. Conflict can be productive if you meet its challenge, but it can be counterproductive if you deal with it improperly. In other words, whether a group conflict is helpful or harmful, destructive or facilitative, depends on how constructively you cope with it.

RESOLVING CONFLICTS

Cooperative versus Competitive Conflict: Win-Win or Win-Lose?

A lion used to prowl about a field in which four oxen used to dwell. Many a time he tried to attack them; but, whenever he came near, they turned their tails to one another, so that whichever way he approached them he was met by the horns of one of them. At last, however, they fell a-quarreling among themselves, and each went off to the pasture alone in a separate corner of the field. Then the lion attacked them one-by-one and soon made an end to all four.

Like it or not, you are a negotiator. Negotiation is a fact of life. . . . Everyone negotiates something everyday.
Roger Fisher and William Ury, *Getting to Yes*

How does this story from *Aesop's Fables* apply to our study of conflict? Let's find out by trying the Skill Builder "Brown Paper."

 SKILL BUILDER

BROWN PAPER

1. Divide into groups of three to five.
2. A 3- by 5-foot length of brown wrapping paper will be given to each group.
3. At a signal, each individual in the group will take hold of a section of the brown paper.
4. On receiving a second signal, each individual will pull the brown paper toward himself or herself and away from the other members of the group. Each member's personal goal is to get as much brown paper as possible.

What happens in "Brown Paper"? The "goal" is probably ripped to shreds because like the oxen, instead of cooperating, you all pull in separate directions. Unlike the oxen, however, you can learn to handle your conflicts constructively and can learn to disagree without becoming disagreeable. To do this, you need to put conflict into a mutual, noncompetitive framework. Unfortunately, sometimes this is more easily said than done. In many conflict situations we are too quick to view our own position as "correct" or "true" while condemning and misperceiving the other person's position. Also, besides causing us to be too hasty in defending our own position and condemning someone else's, conflict in and of itself can make us compete when we should cooperate. When a conflict first develops, one of the key variables affecting the outcome is whether the participants' attitude is *cooperative* or *competitive*. Will one person achieve victory by destroying the positions of others? Will the participants argue to a draw? Or will they share the goal?

In general, we can say that people come to a conflict situation with one of two orientations or perspectives: competition or cooperation. People who have a competitive set perceive a conflict situation in all-or-nothing terms and believe that to attain victory they must defeat the other participants. They do not believe that their own interests and those of others are compatible. By contrast, people with a cooperative set believe that a way to share the rewards of the situation can be discovered.

If people bring a competitive orientation to a conflict, each of them will tend to be ego-involved and will see winning as a test of personal worth and competence. In contrast, if people bring a cooperative orientation to a conflict, each of them will tend to look for a mutually beneficial way to resolve the disagreement.

For a conflict to be defined as *cooperative*, each participant must demonstrate a willingness to resolve it in a mutually satisfactory way. In other words, each person must avoid behaving in any way that would escalate the conflict. If the people involved in a conflict are treated with respect by all the others involved, if they are neither demeaned nor provoked, and if communication is free and open instead of underhanded and closed, the disagreement may be settled amicably.

With whom have you had to negotiate recently: friend, spouse, coworker, boss, etc.? Over what: money, goods, services, information, rules, prestige, etc.? What was the outcome?

Interview a manager. Ask about the nature of a conflict he or she had to resolve, and strategies he or she used to handle it.

■ ETHICS AND COMMUNICATION

"LET US SIT DOWN AND TAKE COUNSEL"

Woodrow Wilson once said, "If you come at me with your fists doubled, I think I can promise you that mine will double as fast as yours; but if you come to me and say, 'Let us sit down and take counsel together, and if we differ from one another, decide just what points are at issue,' we will presently find that we are not so far apart after all, the points on which we differ are few, and the points on which we agree are many, and if we only have the patience and the candor and the desire to get together, we will get together."

Where do you stand? Are patience, candor, and desire all that is necessary for resolution of conflicts?

"GOLD RUSH"

When do we "rush to compete"? When do we "rush to cooperate"? To find out, divide the class into groups of six to eight. Designate one person in each group as "auctioneer." The auctioneer has an unlimited supply of "gold bars"—represented by rectangular pieces of yellow poster board—to "auction off" to the group members.

The group members sit in a row. As the auctioneer puts a gold bar up for sale, each person in turn offers a bid or "passes." Bidding is done in pennies, and each group member has a "bank" of 100. A gold bar is considered "sold" when all group members but one have passed on it in turn.

Whenever a new gold bar is placed on the auction block, the first chance to bid is passed down the line of group members. Keep a record of how much each member ends up paying for each bar. Members may meet to discuss their strategy after each round of play—that is, after each person has had a turn to bid or pass. At the end of play, those who have purchased the most gold bars are the winners. (Note: A group can have no winners or any number of winners.)

When 10 complete rounds have been played or 20 minutes has elapsed, the group should discuss what has just occurred. Members should attempt to answer these questions:

1. Who behaved cooperatively? How do you know?

2. Who behaved competitively? How do you know?

3. What factors affected the way your group defined the situation?

4. What dangers are inherent in "rushing to compete"?

If a conflict is defined as *competitive*, the participants become "combatants"—they believe that to attain victory they must defeat the other side. Unfortunately, competing with or defeating another person with whom we are interacting is characteristic of encounters in our society. Many phrases we use reflect this orientation: we speak of "outsmarting" others, of putting people "in their place," of getting ourselves "one up" and someone else "one down."

The Skill Builder "Gold Rush" explores how situations come to be defined as cooperative or competitive. The auction is "competitive" if at any time the group members bid against one another or raise the bidding level. It is "cooperative" if the group members permit each bidder to buy an equal number of gold blocks at the minimum price of one penny each.

To put all this another way, we can define a conflict as a win-lose situation, or we can define it as a win-win situation. If we define it as *win-lose*, we will tend to pursue our own goals, misrepresent our needs, attempt to avoid empathizing with or understanding the feelings of others, and use threats or promises to get others to go along with us. If we define a conflict as *win-win*, we will tend to view it as a common problem, try to pursue common goals, honestly reveal our needs to others, work to understand their position and frame of reference, and make every effort to reduce rather than increase defensiveness.

To transform a conflict from competitive to cooperative, you must use effective communication techniques.[2] One of our goals is to help you discover workable strategies and give you an opportunity to practice them until you can use them for yourself. You should aim to become a "conflict processor" and develop the ability to view a conflict from the standpoint of other people.

CONFLICT CORNER: CAN YOU SEE IT MY WAY?

Choose a current issue that is significant and controversial (for example, abortion, the war on drugs, capital punishment, nuclear energy). You will be assigned to defend or oppose it. Defenders and opposers will have a chance to meet and prepare their cases. Each defender (A) will be paired with an opposer (B). Person A will have 5 minutes to present the defense's position to person B. Person B then has 5 minutes to present the opposition's position to person A.

Players will then switch roles, so that B presents A's case and A presents B's case.

1. To what extent did reversing roles help you understand and appreciate another point of view?

2. How could such a procedure help a person change from a win-lose orientation to a win-win orientation?

Role reversal can help people involved in a conflict to understand each other, find creative ways to integrate their interests and concerns, and work toward a common goal. Reversing roles helps you avoid judging others by enabling you to see things from their perspective. Once you can replace a statement like "You're wrong" or "You're stupid" with one like "What you believe is not what I believe," you will be on your way to developing a cooperative orientation.

● CULTURE AND COMMUNICATION

A new teacher—let's call her Mary—arrived at a Navaho Indian reservation. Each day in her classroom, something like this would occur. Mary would ask five of her young Navaho students to go to the chalkboard and complete a simple mathematics problem from their homework. All five students would go to the chalkboard, but not one of them would work the problem as requested. Instead, they would all stand silent and motionless.

Mary, of course, wondered what was going on. She repeatedly asked herself if she might possibly be calling on students who could not do the assigned problems. "No, it couldn't be that," she reasoned. Finally, Mary asked her students what the problem was. Their answer displayed an understanding not many people attain in a lifetime.

Evidently, the students realized that not everyone in the class would be able to complete the problems correctly. But they respected each other's uniqueness, and they understood, even at their young age, the dangers of a "win-lose" approach. In their opinion, no one would "win" if anyone was embarrassed or humiliated at the chalkboard, and so they refused to compete publicly with each other. Yes, the Navaho students wanted to learn—but not at the expense of their peers.

Where do you stand? In your opinion would typical American schoolchildren behave similarly? Why or why not? Should they behave like the Navahos?

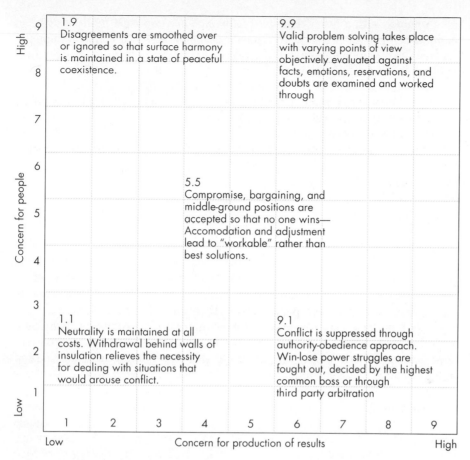

FIGURE 11-2
Blake and Mouton's conflict grid.

Source: Reprinted with permission of NTL, "Conflict Grid," "The Fifth Achievement" by Robert Blake and Jane Srygley Mouton, pp. 418, vol. 6, no. 4, *Journal of Applied Behavioral Science*, Copyright 1970.

The figure contains the following labelled cells on the grid (vertical axis "Concern for people" from Low to High, horizontal axis "Concern for production of results" from Low to High):

1,9 Disagreements are smoothed over or ignored so that surface harmony is maintained in a state of peaceful coexistence.

9,9 Valid problem solving takes place with varying points of view objectively evaluated against facts, emotions, reservations, and doubts are examined and worked through

5,5 Compromise, bargaining, and middle-ground positions are accepted so that no one wins— Accomodation and adjustment lead to "workable" rather than best solutions.

1,1 Neutrality is maintained at all costs. Withdrawal behind walls of insulation relieves the necessity for dealing with situations that would arouse conflict.

9,1 Conflict is suppressed through authority-obedience approach. Win-lose power struggles are fought out, decided by the highest common boss or through third party arbitration

Goals and Styles: A Conflict Grid

A number of different paradigms, or models, have been proposed to represent the ways we try to resolve conflicts. Among them is Blake and Mouton's "conflict grid"[3] (see Figure 11-2). This grid has two sides. The horizontal scale represents the extent to which a person wants to attain personal goals. The vertical scale represents the extent to which the person is concerned for others. The interface between the two scales indicates how strongly the person feels about these concerns—that is, how his or her concern is apportioned.

Both scales range from 1 (low) to 9 (high), representing increasing importance of personal goals ("concern for production of results") and of other people ("concern for people"). On the basis of this measure, Blake and Mouton identified five main "conflict styles." As you consider their grid and the following descriptions of their five styles, try to identify your own conflict style.

A person with a 1/1 conflict style can be described as an *"avoider"*; the avoider's attitude can be summed up as "lose and walk away." If you have a 1/1 style, your goal is to maintain neutrality at all costs. You probably view conflict as a useless and punishing experience, one that you would prefer to do without. Rather than tolerate the frustrations that can accompany conflict, you physically or mentally remove yourself from the conflict situation.

A person with a 1/9 style is an *"accommodator"* whose attitude is "give in and lose." If you are a 1/9, your behavior demonstrates that you overvalue the maintenance of relationships and undervalue the achievement of your own goals. Your main concern is to ensure that others accept you, like you, and "coexist in peace" with you. You are afraid to make others angry, and you will do anything to avoid being perceived as a troublemaker. Although conflicts may exist in your world, you refuse to deal with them. You feel a need to maintain the appearance of harmony at all costs. This discrepancy leads to an uneasy, tense state characterized by a great deal of smiling and nervous laughter.

A person with a 5/5 style is a *"compromiser"* whose attitude is "find a middle ground." If you are a 5/5, your guiding principle is compromise. Thus, you work to find a way to permit each participant in a conflict to gain something. Compromise is of course a valid strategy in some cases. But it can be a problem if you always settle for a workable solution because you are afraid the conflict may escalate if you try to find the *best* solution. It is undeniable that "half a loaf is better than none," and this conflict style will leave participants half-satisfied; but it can also be said to leave them half-*dis*satisfied. Thus compromise is sometimes referred to as the "lose-lose" approach.

Why would people who are competitors (9/1) enjoy being surrounded by "yes people" (1/9)? What dangers could such a mix pose?

A person with a 9/1 style is a *"competing forcer"* who takes a "win-lose" attitude. If you are a 9/1, attaining your personal goals is far more important to you than concern for people. You have an overwhelming need to win and dominate others; you will defend your position and battle with others, whatever the cost or harm to them.

A person with a 9/9 style is a *"problem-solving collaborator"* who takes a "win-win" attitude. If you are a 9/9, you actively seek to satisfy your own goals (you are result-oriented) as well as those of others (you are also person-oriented). This, of course, is the optimum style when you are seeking to reduce conflict. As a problem solver, you realize that conflicts are normal and can be helpful; you also realize that each person in a conflict holds legitimate opinions that deserve to be aired and considered. You are able to discuss differences without making personal attacks.

Which conflict-resolving strategies do you use? Why?

According to Alan Filley, effective conflict resolvers rely to a large extent on problem solving (9/9) and smoothing (1/9), whereas ineffective conflict resolvers rely extensively on forcing (9/1) and withdrawal (1/1).[4]

Outcomes:
Productive versus Destructive Results

If we are to develop and sustain meaningful group relationships, we need to learn to handle conflicts constructively. According to the psychologist Morton Deutsch, a conflict has been productive if all the participants are satisfied with the outcomes and believe they have gained something.[5] In other words, no one loses; everyone wins. In contrast, a conflict has been destructive if all the participants are dissatisfied with the outcomes and believe that they have lost something. Perhaps one of the most important questions facing each of us is whether we can turn our conflicts into productive rather than destructive interactions.

293

CHAPTER 11
HANDLING GROUP
CONFLICT: HOW TO
DISAGREE WITHOUT
BECOMING DISAGREEABLE

When can the outcome of a conflict be considered productive? Morton Deutsch defines a conflict as productive if all the participants are satisfied with the outcome and feel they have gained something. Another way of putting this is to say that a productive conflict is a win-win conflict: everyone wins; no one loses.

Skjold/The Image Works

When individuals or groups fail to achieve important goals, they may feel a need to strike out. Consider this:

DREAM DEFERRED

Langston Hughes

What happens to a dream deferred?
  Does it dry up
  like a raisin in the sun?
  Or fester like a sore—
  And then run?
  Does it stink like rotten meat?
  Or crust and sugar over—
  like a syrupy sweet?

Maybe it just sags
like a heavy load.

Or does it explode?[6]

We will be most likely to create constructive rather than destructive inter-actions if our conflicts are characterized by cooperative problem-solving meth-ods, attempts to reach mutual understanding, accurate and complete commu-nication, and a demonstrated willingness to trust each other. We will be most likely to fail if our conflicts become win-lose encounters characterized by mis-conceptions and misperceptions; inaccurate, sketchy, and disruptive communi-cation; and a demonstrated hesitancy to trust each other. It is apparent that in a conflict situation the best approach to a constructive resolution is cooperation.

MANAGING CONFLICT SUCCESSFULLY: SKILLS AND STRATEGIES

Conflict can be resolved productively by applying principles of effective communication. When you use effective communication techniques, you reduce the likelihood that your comments will escalate a conflict by eliciting angry, defensive, or belligerent reactions. Learning to handle conflict successfully is an attainable goal that can lead to increased self-confidence, improved relationships, and a greater ability to handle stressful situations. All that is required is a commitment to practice and apply the necessary skills. Anyone who is willing can learn creative and effective ways of managing conflict—ways that will increase the likelihood of future harmony and cooperation.

Let us now examine the behaviors that can turn conflict situations into problem-solving situations. The following suggestions are a basic guide to conflict resolution.

Recognize That Conflicts Can Be Settled Rationally

A conflict stands a better chance of being settled rationally if you avoid certain unproductive behaviors:

Don't pretend that the conflict simply does not exist (that is, don't be an ostrich).

Don't withdraw from discussing it (don't be a turtle).

Don't placate or surrender to the people with whom you are in conflict (don't be a sheep).

Don't try to create distractions so that the conflict will not be dealt with (don't be a cuckoo).

Don't overintellectualize the conflict or rationalize the conflict (don't be an owl).

Don't blame or find fault with the other people (don't sound like a screeching parrot).

Don't attempt to force the others to accept your way of seeing things (don't be a gorilla).

Recognizing unproductive behaviors is a first step in learning to handle conflicts more effectively. Being willing to express your feelings openly, directly, and constructively without resorting to irrational techniques that destroy trust and respect is a prerequisite for becoming a productive conflict manager. Thus, instead of insulting or attacking others or withdrawing from a conflict, be willing to describe whatever action; behavior, or situation you find upsetting. Do this without negatively evaluating other people or causing them to become defensive. Focus on *issues*, not *personalities*. Be willing to listen to and react to what the other person is saying.

Conflicts can be settled rationally if you act like a capable, competent problem solver and adopt a person-to-person orientation.

TO BE RATIONAL OR IRRATIONAL? "THAT IS THE QUESTION"

Identify two group conflict situations that you attempted to settle through nonrational means, rational means, or both. Use the questions and charts below to help you identify your own behaviors and those of the other people involved. For example, did you begin the interaction by acting like a "screeching parrot" or an overly intellectual "owl"? Did you switch strategies during the interaction? Why? What was your behavior like at the conclusion of the interaction? If possible, ask the other people to fill out similar charts. Then compare and contrast your perceptions.

Then, for each situation, answer the following questions:

1. Which ineffective behaviors did you find yourself using during the course of the interaction?

2. What consequences did these behaviors of yours have?

3. Which factors or occurrences do you believe kept you from functioning in a human-to-human or person-to-person manner?

Conflict interaction 1

Issue: _____

| | Myself | | Others | |
	Start	End	Start	End
Human				
Gorilla				
Parrot				
Owl				
Cuckoo				
Sheep				
Turtle				
Ostrich				

Conflict interaction 2

Issue: _____

| | Myself | | Others | |
	Start	End	Start	End
Human				
Gorilla				
Parrot				
Owl				
Cuckoo				
Sheep				
Turtle				
Ostrich				

Define the Conflict

Once you have recognized that conflicts can be handled rationally, you are ready to ask, "Why are we in conflict? What is the nature of the conflict? Which of us feels more strongly about the issue? What can we do about it?" Here again, it is crucial to send "I" messages ("I think it is unfair for me to do all the work around here"; "I don't like going to the library for everyone else") and to avoid sending "blame" messages ("You do everything wrong"; "You are a spoiled brat"; "You will make us fail"). Be very clear that you would like to join with the other group members in discovering a solution that will be acceptable and beneficial for all of you—a solution where none of you will lose and each will win.

FEIFFER

Check Your Perceptions

A situation is a conflict when it is perceived as a conflict. In "conflict-ripe" situations we often distort the behavior, position, or motivations of the other person involved. We prefer to "see" one set of motivations rather than another because it meets our own needs to interpret the situation that way. When we do this, we deny the legitimacy of any other position. Thus, it is not uncommon for each person in a conflict to believe, mistakenly, that the other person is committing underhanded and even vicious acts. It is not extraordinary for each person to make erroneous assumptions about the other's feelings, nor is it unusual for people to think they disagree with each other simply because they have been unable to communicate their agreement. For these reasons, it is important for each person to take some time to explain his or her assumptions and frame of reference to the others. It is also important for all the people involved to feel that their contributions are listened to and taken seriously.

After each of you has identified how you feel, it is time to determine whether you understand one another. This calls for active, empathic listening. Each of you should be able to paraphrase what the other has said in a way the other finds satisfactory. Doing this before you respond to the feelings expressed can help avert escalation of the conflict. Along with active listening, role reversal can also help people in conflict understand one another. Like active listening, role reversal permits us to see things as others in the group see them. If we are willing to listen to and experience another person's point of view, that person will be more likely to listen to and experience ours.

Suggest Possible Solutions

The goal during the "possible solutions" phase is for the group members to put your heads together and come up with a variety of solutions. Most important, neither you nor anyone else in the group should evaluate, condemn, or make fun of any of the suggestions. You must suspend judgment and honestly believe that, potentially, the conflict can be resolved in a variety of ways.

Assess Alternative Solutions and Choose the One That Seems Best

297

CHAPTER 11
HANDLING GROUP
CONFLICT: HOW TO
DISAGREE WITHOUT
BECOMING DISAGREEABLE

After possible solutions have been generated, it is time to see which solution each person considers best. It is legitimate to try to determine which solutions will let one side "win" at the other's expense, which will make everyone "lose," and which will let everyone "win." Your objective is to discover which solutions are totally *unacceptable* to each side and which are *mutually acceptable.* (It is crucially important to be honest during this stage.) Once all the solutions have been assessed, you are in a position to determine if one of the mutually acceptable solutions is clearly superior to all the others—that is, if it has the most advantages and the fewest disadvantages. Also, be sure to explore whether it is the most constructive solution.

Try Out Your Solution and Evaluate It

During the "tryout" stage we see how well the chosen solution is working. We try to ascertain who is doing what, when, where, and under what conditions, and we ask how all this is affecting each person in the group. We want to know if the people involved were able to carry out the job as planned, whether the solution we adopted has solved the problem, and whether the outcome has been rewarding to everyone. If not, we know it is time to begin the conflict resolution process again.

Remember that conflict situations can be learning experiences. If handled properly, they can help us discover ways of improving our ability to relate to others. Thus, your goal should be not necessarily to have fewer conflicts, but rather to make the conflicts you do have *constructive.* Instead of eliminating conflicts from our group relationships, we simply need to learn how to use them.

SUMMARY

Conflict is an inevitable part of the life of any group. A group experiences conflict whenever a member's thoughts or acts limit, prevent, or interfere with his or her own thoughts or acts or with those of another member. However, conflict is not always a negative force. In fact, the absence or avoidance of conflict can result in groupthink, a problem which occurs when a group allows the desire for consensus to override careful analysis and reasoned decision making.

Whether a conflict helps or hinders a group's operation depends on how the members react to it. If they resort to strategies such as blaming, withdrawing, intellectualizing, distracting, and forcing, their effectiveness will be impaired. However, if they discuss the issues calmly, they can break impasses and solve difficulties. Various styles of handling conflict can be plotted on Blake and Mouton's "conflict grid." The most effective style is that of the "problem-solving" collaborator, who takes a "win-win" approach and has high concern both for results and for the feelings of other people. It is essential to take into account the various cultures that people may reflect in their approaches to conflict and conflict resolution.

A number of communication techniques can help us resolve conflicts. The first step is simply to recognize that conflicts can be settled rationally—by focusing on the issues, not on personalities. Next we should define the conflict and check the accuracy of our perceptions, using "I" messages, empathic listening, and role reversal, as appropriate. Then we should suggest and assess a variety of solutions to the conflict, choose the best one that is mutually acceptable, and try it out.

SUGGESTIONS FOR FURTHER READING

Blake, Robert, and Jane Mouton: "The Fifth Achievement," *Journal of Applied Behavioral Science*, vol. 6, 1970, pp. 413–426. Contains an explanation of the "conflict grid."

Borisoff, Deborah: *Conflict Management: A Communication Skills Approach*, Prentice-Hall, Englewood Cliffs, N.J., 1989. A practical treatment of conflict management techniques.

Cline, Rebecca J. Welch: "Detecting Groupthink: Methods for Observing the Illusion of Unanimity," *Communication Quarterly*, vol. 38, no. 2, Spring 1990, pp. 112–126. Contains some fresh insights about groupthink.

Deutsch, Morton: "Conflicts: Productive and Destructive," *Journal of Social Issues*, vol. 25, 1969, pp. 7–43. Compares and contrasts constructive and destructive conflicts.

Janis, Irving: "Groupthink," *Psychology Today*, vol. 5, 1971, pp. 43–46, 74–76. A readable and useful overview of this dangerous phenomenon.

Janis, Irving: *Groupthink: Psychological Studies of Policy Decisions and Fiascos*, Houghton Mifflin, Boston, Mass., 1983. Offers a more detailed treatment and careful analysis of groupthink.

Johnson, David, and Frank Johnson: *Cooperation and Competition*, Erlbaum, Hillsdale, N.J., 1987. Demonstrates that conflict is necessary in healthy relationships.

Kindler, Herbert S.: *Managing Disagreement Constructively*, Crisp, Los Altos, Calif., 1988. Very readable; offers guidelines that are easy to put into practice.

Olsen, Harry A.: *The New Way to Compete*, Lexington, Lexington, Mass., 1990. A practical and innovative discussion of competition, cooperation, and conflict resolution.

Ruben, Harvey L.: *Competing*, Lippincott and Crowell, New York, 1980. A popular, insightful account of the role competition plays in our lives.

Thompson, Leigh: "An Examination of Naive and Experienced Negotiators," *Journal of Personality and Social Psychology*, vol. 59, no. 1, 1990, pp. 82–90. Compares and contrasts negotiation approaches.

Woolf, Bob: *Friendly Persuasion*, Berkley, New York, 1991. A consultant offers tactics for effective negotiation in business contexts. Stresses the need for maintaining a relationship during negotiation.

NOTES

1. Irving Janis, *Victims of Groupthink: A Psychological Study of Foreign Policy Decisions and Fiascos*, Houghton Mifflin, Boston, Mass., 1972.

2. For a description of how to promote a win-win approach to conflict, see Deborah Weider-Hatfield, "A Unit in Conflict Management Communication Skills," *Communication Education*, vol. 30, 1981, pp. 265–273.

3. Robert Blake and Jane Mouton, "The Fifth Achievement," *Journal of Applied Behavioral Science*, vol. 6, 1970, pp. 413–426.

4. Allan Filley, *Interpersonal Conflict Resolution*, Scott, Foresman, Glenview, Ill., 1975.

5. Morton Deutsch, "Conflicts: Productive and Destructive," *Journal of Social Issues*, vol. 25, 1969, pp. 7–43.

6. "Dream Deferred" from *The Panther and the Lash* by Langston Hughes. Copyright 1951 by Langston Hughes. Reprinted by permission of Alfred A. Knopf, Inc.

COMMUNICATING TO THE PUBLIC

THE SPEAKER
AND THE AUDIENCE

After finishing this chapter, you should be able to:

Identify the characteristics of effective public speakers

Enumerate steps to be taken in approaching public speaking systematically

Explain why self-analysis is a prerequisite to effective speechmaking

Conduct a thorough audience analysis

Explain how the attitudes of audience members can affect their reception of a presentation.

> In the United States there are more than twenty thousand different ways of earning a living, and effective speech is essential to every one.
>
> Andrew Weaver

Public speaking: two seemingly harmless words: *Public speaking*: the act of preparing, staging, and delivering a presentation to an audience. We speak every day. Under ordinary circumstances, we rarely give speaking, or our skills in speaking, a second thought—that is, until we're asked to deliver a speech or simply to speak in public. Once we know that this is what we're going to have to do, if we're like most Americans, we fear it more than we fear bee stings, accidents, heights, or our own death.[1] When we are told that we will have to speak in public, terrifying thoughts and feelings consume us.

But just as we can learn to handle ourselves more effectively in our interpersonal and group relation-relationships if we take the time that is needed to analyze and practice successful behaviors, we can also learn to handle ourselves more effectively as public speakers. With practice, we can develop the understanding and master the skills that will make us articulate speakers who are organized, confident, and competent and can communicate ideas in such a way that others will be interested in them and persuaded by them.

Unfortunately, far too few of us ever bother to analyze our effectiveness in speaking until after we have stepped into the spotlight. We believe that it is time to correct this error. With that end in mind, the chapters in Part Four have been designed to help you gain the understanding and master the skills you need to speak like a pro and to feel like a winner after addressing an audience. We believe that developing understanding and skills and putting them to work for you can set you a step above the crowd.

Consider this: your ability to communicate will probably play the greatest role in determining whether you are as successful in your chosen career as you could be. A typical person speaks over 34,000 words each day; that adds up to more than 238,000 words per week, or 12 million words per year. Some percentage of those words will be delivered in the form of public speaking. If we do not want to waste our words, and if we do not want our words to be ignored or misunderstood, we must learn to use tools that will help people understand us, help them believe us, and help them respond to us. We must prepare to meet the challenge of speechmaking.

● CULTURE AND COMMUNICATION

"REPORT TALK" AND "RAPPORT TALK"

According to the researcher Deborah Tannen, men are more comfortable speaking in public than women are, while women are more comfortable speaking in private than men are. Tannen finds that men excel at "report talk" while women excel at "rapport talk."

Do your experiences confirm or contradict this? If this disparity exists, what, if anything, do you think should be done to change it?

Source: Deborah Tannen, *You Just Don't Understand: Women and Men in Conversation*, Ballantine, New York, 1991, pp. 74–75.

APPROACHING PUBLIC SPEAKING SYSTEMATICALLY

People respond to the challenge of public speaking in a variety of ways. Some believe that speechmaking is an inborn skill: "I talk a lot, so this public speaking business poses no difficulty for me." Others view it as torture: "I'm scared stiff! This will be traumatic!" These attitudes represent two extremes, and both can cause problems. Overconfident people can run a risk of being inadequate speakers because they conduct little research and thus are ill prepared. People who are overly anxious or fearful may find it terribly trying and nerve-racking to stand before an audience and deliver a talk. The most effective speakers are those who display a healthy respect for the challenges involved in speaking before others and who work systematically to create, prepare, and deliver an admirable presentation.

How can you become an effective speaker? Of course you must work at it. To help you, we will put the entire speechmaking process into a logical format that you can examine and follow in detail. The process we will describe should serve you as a "road map"—one you can use to prepare every public presentation you will ever make. We will also help you learn to control your nervous energy to make it work for and not against you as you deliver a speech. In short, we will provide you with procedures for speechmaking. Then, it will be up to you to supply the material, and the creative energy, that will help you develop your material into an effective presentation. Let's begin.

It is important to realize that public speaking is a creative undertaking—not something that just happens when you stand up to speak. The process actually begins when you first consider addressing a group of people, and it is not finished until you have completed a postpresentation analysis of your work. We believe this creative process can be approached systematically, as shown in Figure 12-1. This chart divides speechmaking into four main stages: topic selection, topic development, presentation, and postpresentation analysis.

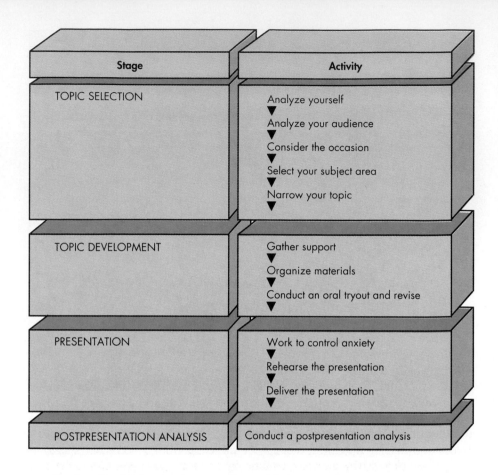

FIGURE 12-1
Systematic speaking
process.

During the *topic selection stage*, your job is to analyze yourself, your audience, and the nature of the occasion; choose a general subject area; focus on the subject; and narrow its scope until you hit on a particular aspect of the topic that you can handle in the time allotted. This then becomes your purpose or reason for speaking. During the *development stage*, you gather your evidence, organize the evidence according to your purpose, prepare visuals, and rehearse. During the *presentation stage*, your main task is to control your anxiety so that you will be able to deliver your ideas clearly and effectively. During the *postpresentation analysis stage*, you determine (with the aid of others—such as your instructor or fellow class members—or on your own) the strengths and weaknesses of your presentation in order to be better prepared to meet the challenge when the next occasion arises.

It is important to realize that not every phase of this sequence consumes the same amount of time; in fact, the time you will need for each stage will vary from speech to speech. Sometimes you will need to spend a great deal of time analyzing your audience and identifying the needs of your listeners. At other times you will know your audience well and will need to spend relatively little time determining whether your speech is appropriate. Sometimes the subject of your talk will be provided for you. At other times, you will be required to come up with your own topic. Sometimes you will be asked to fill a brief time period; other times you will be allotted as much time as you need to share your ideas effectively with others. For example, as a manager you may be required to deliver a detailed report on work that your unit has been doing and instructed to "take as much time as you need to inform us of your progress." On the other hand, you may find yourself asked to "say just a few words" or to "give a brief progress report." For some speeches you may find that you need to spend a great deal of time researching and gathering material. For others, the primary problem will lie not in gathering materials but in organizing them so the speech will flow smoothly and accomplish its objectives.

Because circumstances and occasions vary so widely, we suggest that you consider each step of the systematic speaking process for every speech you prepare. Skipping over any phase without at least being certain that you have adequately considered it can lead to embarassing and uncomfortable moments for you and your audience.

Let's begin now to work our way through the speechmaking process.

CONSIDERING THE SPEAKER

Criteria: Expectations for Speechmakers

When you listen to a speaker—either in person or through the media—how do you expect him or her to behave? What do you want the speaker to do for you? We believe it is helpful to view the process of speechmaking from the standpoint of the listeners. After all, without listeners, we would be speaking to ourselves—and that is not what public speaking is all about. Good speakers have certain characteristics that you may want to keep in mind as you prepare your own presentations.

First, *good speakers have insight.* They know their own strengths and limitations. They understand and have considered the reservoir of experience on which they may draw. Second, *good speakers know their audiences.* They work to understand the nature and concerns of the people they have been called on to address. They are able to feel the pulse of this "public," to stand in the shoes of the audience members, and to view the event or occasion through the audience's eyes so that they are able to share something that will be of value.

✔ SKILL BUILDER

FROM THE LISTENER'S POINT OF VIEW

1. Describe the behaviors exhibited by the most effective speaker you have had the good fortune to hear.
2. Contrast that description with a description of the most ineffective speaker you ever had the misfortune to hear.

As people living during a "media explosion," we have become accustomed to highly professional speakers. On television, Carole Simpson, Ted Koppel, and Carl Sagan *(counterclockwise from top)* are examples of this trend.

Top, Steve Fenn/ABC, Inc.; *bottom left*, M. Katz/ Outline Press; *bottom right*, Bill Bernstein/Outline Press

Third, *good speakers believe that what they are doing is important;* they know why they are speaking, and they know what they hope to accomplish by speaking. They are clear about their purpose and about the main ideas they want to communicate. In addition, they are adept at formulating and delivering a message that is organized to support their purpose. Fourth, *good speakers always practice.* They conduct dry runs of the presentation, adapting it to potential changes in the audience and the audience members' needs. They also prepare well for questions audience members may ask. Fifth, *good speakers think of the speech as if it were a performance.* They know that they will need to work hard to keep the audience interested in what they have to say; they understand the essential fickleness of audiences, and so they make it easy and pleasurable for listeners to "stay tuned" to their ideas. Finally, *good speakers make a critique or postpresentation analysis of the speech.* They know that there is much to learn from each experience, much that they may be able to apply the next time they are in the spotlight.

It is noteworthy that because of the media explosion, our society has grown accustomed to high-quality speeches. Talk shows, television news programs, and entertainers bring professional speechmaking into our homes every day. Newscasters, for example, have had years of training and practice in speaking. Public relations practitioners are often carefully schooled in public speaking to ensure that they know how to communicate a positive image to an audience. Many corporate executives employ speech writers and speech coaches to help them communicate with diverse audiences. All this presents a difficult, though not impossible, task for the student who is about to step into the spotlight. The communication environment you find yourself in is challenging. You will need to add the skills of sharing information and persuading audiences to your credentials, for only then will you have the expertise to communicate effectively in our multifaceted environment. From the classroom to the corporation, from the boardroom to the television studio, from the steps of city hall to the podium in a local auditorium, your challenge is to develop the skills and confidence you need to deliver—clearly and persuasively—the messages that are important to you and important to the people you represent.

Self-Analysis: You and Your Topic

Thorough self-analysis is a prerequisite for effective speechmaking. Although at times subjects or topics may be assigned, under many circumstances the choice will be left to you, the speaker. Even when a topic is specified, it is recommended that you conduct a self-analysis to help you uncover aspects that you may find particularly interesting or appealing. Such an analysis could also become the basis for personal stories or anecdotes that can eventually be integrated into your presentation.

There are more topics and subject areas for speeches than you could possibly exhaust in a lifetime.[2] Still, "I just don't know what to say" is an all-too-familiar lament.

But where was I to start? The world is so vast, I shall start with the country I know best, my own. But my country is so very large. I had better start with my town. But my town, too, is large, I had best start with my street. No: my home. No: my family. Never mind, I shall start with myself.[3]

We suggest that at the outset of your preparation, you take some time for what corporate trainers call a *front-end analysis*—a preliminary examination of possibilities. Following are three useful forms that a front-end analysis can take. First, you can begin by *reviewing your life* in terms of potential topics:

1. Divide your life (thus far) into thirds: early, middle, more recent. Compose one sentence to sum up what your life consisted of during each segment. (For example, "I lived in ——— with my two brothers and mother and went to elementary school.")
2. Under each summary statement, identify your main interests and concerns at that time of your life.
3. Examine the interests and concerns you listed. Which of them keep recurring? Which have you left behind? Which have you developed only recently?

A second approach is to *consider this very moment* as a source of potential topics:

1. On the left side of a sheet of paper, list sensory experiences; that is, list everything you are able to see, hear, taste, smell, or touch from your present vantage point.
2. When you have listed 10 to 15 items, go back over the list and note subjects or topics that might be suggested by each observation or experience. Arrange these in a corresponding list on the right side of the paper. For example, if you listed a "passing train" in the left column, you might enter "mass transportation" in the right column. Note: If you are not satisfied with the topics you have identified, move to another location and begin the process again.

A third approach is to *work with a newspaper* to find potential topics:

1. Take today's newspaper and, beginning with the front page, read a story and compile a list of topics suggested by it.
2. Do not prejudge your ideas. Simply work your way through the paper looking for possibilities.

Your "autobiography," your "this moment" observations, and today's news should provide you with an ample number of potential subjects. You may want to go over the list, ranking the ideas in order of interest (A for the "most promising," B for "also promising," C for "less promising," and so on). These approaches should be considered tentative, but they will provide you with raw data that you'll need as you move ahead.

GENERATING TOPICS THROUGH BRAINSTORMING

You can generate literally hundreds of topics for speeches by taking simple everyday objects and listing all the topics these objects bring to mind. For example, list topics that come to mind for these objects:

Safety pin

Watch

Diamond

Paper clip

You should find that you're generating 25 or more topics for each object. If you're not generating that many, you need to allow your mind to wander and flow more freely. You may want to work with a partner and share your lists.

Once your lists are complete, identify the five most interesting topics which might be developed into speeches for your class.

CONSIDERING THE AUDIENCE

Having conducted a search of yourself, it is now time to determine where your audience fits in.

Unfortunately, a pitfall for many speakers is speaking to please themselves—approaching speechmaking with only their own interests and their own point of view in mind, and neglecting the needs and interests of their audience. These speakers will often choose an inappropriate topic, dress improperly, or deliver a presentation that is either too simple or too technical for the audience. We have all heard medical experts address general audiences using such complex language that their listeners were baffled and bored. We have also heard speakers address highly educated groups in such simple language and about such mundane topics that everyone was not only bored but insulted.

Your focus during the initial stages of speech preparation should, therefore, not be solely on yourself. Be prepared to consider a potential topic from the point of view of your audience. Just as you bring your own background and experiences to a presentation, the audience members will bring theirs. Thus, it is important to consider what your listeners are thinking about, what their needs and hopes are. You may start by considering where you are, but you must not be so self-centered as to stop there. Successful communicators, in a sense, enlarge the area of the spotlight to include the audience.

To pay proper attention to your audience, you must know something about it. For example, how familiar are the audience members with what you are going to talk about? What is their attitude toward your topic? What are they anxious about? What would they like to know? What are their expectations? If you don't find out the answers to questions like these, you run the risk of having your words fall on deaf ears. Unfortunately, of all the steps in the process of public speaking, audience analysis is most often overlooked. "Speaking to hear yourself speak" is a trap you will want to take steps to avoid every time you must speak before others.

During the early stages of preparing a speech, it's important to consider a potential topic from the audience's point of view—to consider your listeners' concerns, their needs, and their hopes.

Spencer Grant/Photo Researchers

Speech . . . preserves contact—it is silence which isolates.

Thomas Mann

In other words, when preparing any speech, you must be audience-centered. Without an audience, you would be in trouble. You could of course speak in a room alone—to yourself—but this would be of little value if your goal is to change the attitudes, values, beliefs, or behavior of others. No one would be enlightened by your ideas; no one would chuckle at your humor; no one would give you a pat on the back for a job well done. Making a speech without considering the audience is in effect like talking to yourself. Or, to put it another way, if you make a speech without considering the audience, you are like a chef who cooks a banquet and then eats it all alone, or an artist who stores a painting of great beauty in a garage. It is from behind the eyes of your audience that you must approach speechmaking. Let's see how this works.

■ ETHICS AND COMMUNICATION

THE "MAGIC BULLET" OF SPEECHMAKING

Roger Ailes, chairman of Ailes Communication, Inc., and a communications consultant to many corporations and their chief executive officers, says that being likable is the "magic bullet" of communication. Ailes writes: "With it, your audience will forgive just about everything else you do wrong. Without it, you can hit every bull's-eye in the room, and no one will be impressed."

What do you think? What makes you dislike a speaker? In your opinion, is being likable more important for a speaker's success than having something significant to say? Should it be? How do you react when you dislike a speaker?

Source: Roger Ailes, *You Are the Message: Getting What You Want by Being Who You Are*, Doubleday, New York, 1989, p. 110.

THE MAKEUP OF YOUR AUDIENCE

How can you know, or how can you try to determine, precisely who will attend your presentation? For example, can you expect certain interested groups or individuals to come? Will others whom you do not expect surprise you by showing up?

Finding information about the people you will be speaking to can often seem difficult or even impossible. But it is important to make educated guesses about the makeup of your intended audience—and actually, this is a simple task. What you are doing at this stage of the process is creating a mental picture of the people to whom you are going to speak.[4] Once you have created such an image or "snapshot" for yourself, you will be better able to continue planning your presentation.

Fortunately for most speakers, audiences seldom just "happen." Unless people are in a park or a shopping mall or walking down a street when someone—such as a politician—begins to speak out about some issue, they tend to gather to hear a speaker for specific reasons. People meet to listen to speakers in a number of different settings, including lecture halls, auditoriums, parties, and houses of worship, as well as in front of radio and television sets. And they meet for a number of different purposes: to gain information, to evaluate ideas and proposals, to praise or pay homage to others, to assess attitudes and beliefs, to be entertained, to be spiritually uplifted, and to be comforted in sorrow. Our primary emphasis in this book is on the first two of these purposes—that is, speechmaking for audiences who have gathered to listen to an *informative* or *persuasive address.*

Just as an economist might gather data, synthesize them, and use them to predict the future value of the dollar in the world market, so you must gather, synthesize, and use data to predict the makeup of your audience and its reaction to your presentation. Of course, we cannot be right 100 percent of the time. As any stockbroker will tell you when you have lost money on a recommended investment, "No one can foretell the future." Nonetheless, it would be foolhardy not to at least attempt to make reasonable predictions. To stay in business, a stockbroker or an economist must make forecasts, and these forecasts must be right more often than they are wrong. Equally, you must try to predict your audience and its reactions, and your aim must be to make accurate predictions more often than inaccurate ones. Otherwise, in the future you may find a grade, a promotion, or even your career in jeopardy.

SOURCES OF INFORMATION

Information about your audience should come from two key sources:

1. Your personal experience with the group
2. Original research

Let's consider each of these.

Personal Experience   The best source of information about your audience is your personal experience with the group—either as a speaker or as an audience member. If you have attended several functions or are a member of the class or organization you are expected to address, you have personal knowledge of the audience members. Thus you will probably be able to formulate reasonably accurate predictions about the appropriateness of your material for that particular group.

Research   What if you have had no previous contact with the group you are to address? If this is the case, you might ask the program planner to provide you with relevant information. For instance, if you have been asked to speak at a professional convention, you would be concerned with specific information about the makeup of the audience: How many will attend the lecture? Will there be students present? Government officials? All these factors would have to be taken into account in preparing and customizing the presentation.

Another way to gather information about a group is to obtain copies of public relations material. Recent news releases highlighting the organization may help put you on the same "track" as your audience. Corporate newsletters can also be valuable, as can a trip to the local library for information describing the organization.

Original research often takes the form of discussions with members of the potential audience. Robert Orben, a speech consultant and writer for former president Gerald Ford, tells this story.[5] A presidential address had been planned for a college campus in Minnesota. The speechwriters knew that many of the students were not supporters of the president. They therefore spent a great deal of time on the telephone with students and school officials in an effort to obtain specific bits of information that could be included in the speech to help create a bond between the president and his audience. Finally, a somewhat disgruntled student provided the writers with the "gem" they felt they needed. They completed the speech confident that they had done their job well—and they had. Ford began his address by saying, "Washington may have the new subway, Montreal may have the monorail, but this campus has the Quickie!" The students in the audience laughed and applauded warmly. Why? The drinking age was 21 in Minnesota but 18 in a neighboring state. And the 15-mile trip students often took to get to the first bar across the state line was known as "the Quickie." In this instance, talking at length to potential members of the audience provided information that helped establish an atmosphere in which the listeners, although not necessarily in agreement with the speaker, were at least rendered friendly enough to listen to his views.

Demographics of Audiences: What Are They Like?

Since the background and composition of your audience are important factors to consider in planning a speech, every effort must be made to determine audience *demographics*: age, sex, marital status, religion, cultural background, occupations, socioeconomic status, education, and membership in special organizations. Despite the fact that no one audience will be entirely uniform in all these categories, you should consider each one during your initial planning sessions.

Would you give precisely the same presentation to a group of children that you would give to your class? Almost certainly not. How might your presentations differ? Could you even deal with the same subject? The adult students would bring many more years of experience to your presentation than the children would. Adults may have been through economic hassles and even a war, for instance—experiences that children have probably not yet faced. Of course, the maturity of the two audiences would also differ. These contrasts may seem obvious, but age is a factor often overlooked in planning speeches. You might choose to speak on draft registration or birth control to a college audience, but you might fail to realize the same material would probably have less intrinsic appeal to an audience of senior citizens.

It's also wise to consider how your own age will affect your presentation. How close are you to the mean, or average, age of your anticipated listeners? If you are about the same age as the audience members, your job may be a little easier. If you are much older or much younger than the audience members, you will need to attempt to see your topic through their eyes and adjust it accordingly.

The average age of your audience might also lead you to make certain adaptations in your manner of presentation. A study by Donald Kausler and Charles Lair indicated that age can affect information-processing abilities. According to these researchers, younger people can process oral information at a somewhat faster rate than older people. Thus older audiences might prefer a slower, more evenly paced step-by-step delivery than would appeal to younger people.[6]

Choose a topic of current interest. How would you approach the topic for a presentation to people of your own age? How would you change your approach to appeal to an older or younger audience?

SEX

Sex can also influence an audience's reaction to your speech. There are, admittedly, some myths and misconceptions about effects of sex. (For example, in the past researchers believed that women could be more easily persuaded than men.[7] Do you think this is a valid statement today?) Still, you need to consider sex differences, especially if you speak to an audience composed entirely or mainly of one sex. Be sure to study your potential audience before drawing any conclusions. Although the same topics may appeal to both men and women, gender may affect the ways in which male and female audience members respond. For example, a discussion of rape or abortion may elicit a stronger emotional reaction from the women in your class, whereas a discussion of vasectomy or animal castration may elicit a stronger response from the men. (Veterinarians, in fact, report that men, but not women, tend to overfeed castrated male dogs, presumably to overcome the owners' sense of guilt.) Be aware, though, that the so-called traditional roles of men and women are changing, and that stereotypes once attributed to both groups are beginning to crumble.

MARITAL STATUS

Are most of the members of your audience single? Married? Divorced? Widowed? These factors might also influence their reactions to your presentation. The concerns of one group are not necessarily the concerns of another.

RELIGION

If you are speaking to a religious group with whom you have little familiarity, make a point of discussing your topic in advance with some group members. Some groups have formulated very clear guidelines regarding issues such as divorce, birth control, and abortion. It is important for you to understand the audience and its feelings if you are to be able to relate effectively to its members.

CULTURAL BACKGROUND

Use your knowledge of an audience's culture and mind set to create a bond with your listeners. During the Iranian hostage crisis of 1980–1981, for example, one Iranian student at an American university handled the cultural difference problem in a particularly effective manner. From his perspective, his American audience was composed of foreigners who had been provoked to the point where they resented his presence; in fact, anti-Iranian graffiti had become a common sight on his campus. He began his speech—called "Stereotypes"— by noting, "I am an Iranian student. I am not holding anyone hostage. I have not demonstrated against the United States. I am simply trying to better myself by receiving a college education, just as you are." In this way, he established an understanding with his audience. He reached beyond nationality to the human factor—a strategy that helps unite speaker and audience.

OCCUPATIONS

People are interested in issues that relate to their own work and the work of those important to them. Consequently, if possible, relate your subject to the occupational concerns of your audience. Also, if you are speaking before an audience whose members belong to a particular occupational group, you must attempt to find or create examples and illustrations that reflect their concerns.

SOCIOECONOMIC STATUS

Researchers have found that there are psychological as well as economic differences between upper-class, middle-class, and lower-class people. Having or lacking discretionary income, power, and prestige evidently influences our attitudes and beliefs. Since our society is socially mobile, with a "move up" philosophy, as a speaker you can usually assume that your audience members want to get ahead and improve their position in life, and you can adjust your presentation to appeal to that desire.

EDUCATION

Although it is important to determine your listeners' educational level, you cannot let your findings trap you into making unwarranted assumptions— either positive or negative—regarding their intellectual ability. Still, in general you will probably find that the higher people's level of education, the more general their knowledge and the more insightful their questions. In addition, the more knowledgeable members of your audience may have specific data to dispute your stand on controversial issues. An educated and sophisticated audience may be far more aware of the impact of various political and social programs than, say, a group of high school dropouts. A less educated audience may need background information that a more educated audience may consider superfluous.

Whatever the education level of your listeners, here are three precepts to keep in mind:

1. Don't underestimate the intelligence of your listeners; don't speak down to them.
2. Don't overestimate their need for information; don't try to do too much in the time that is available to you.
3. Don't use jargon if there's a chance that your listeners are unfamiliar with it; listeners will quickly "tune out" what they don't understand.

ADDITIONAL FACTORS

You may find that you need to consider several additional variables as you prepare your presentation. For example, if your audience is your class, do class members belong to a particular campus organization? Do members of the class involve themselves in any particular types of projects? Do the interests of the class relate in any way to your speech? Do class members have any identifiable goals, fears, frustrations, loves, or hates that could be tied in? How has their environment influenced their perception of key issues?

If used wisely, your knowledge of audience demographics can help you achieve your purpose as a speechmaker. It can permit you to draw inferences about the predispositions of audience members and their probable responses to your presentation. Thus, when planning your next presentation, fill out a chart like the one in Figure 12-2.

Average age of audience members:
Sexual makeup:
Marital status:
Religious preferences:
Cultural background:
Education:
Occupation:
Additional relevant factors:

Your topic:
Examples of ways you will use the demographic information:

FIGURE 12-2
Audience
demographics.

*"I am here tonight, gentlemen, to speak to you not
of guns but of, God help me, butter."*

Drawing by Ziegler; © 1981 The New Yorker Magazine, Inc.

**Do you think it would
be possible for the
speaker in the cartoon
to obtain a fair hearing
from such an audience?
How?**

Attitudes of Audiences: What Do They Care About?

Once you have considered audience demographics, your next step is to try to predict the attitudes your listeners will have toward you and toward your presentation. For example, you should consider whether or not the audience members are required to attend, whether the audience is homogeneous or heterogeneous, and whether the audience members favor your stand or are actively opposed to it.[8]

MOTIVATION: IS ATTENDANCE OPTIONAL OR REQUIRED?

People may attend or "tune in on" a presentation because they want to (that is, they do so willingly), because they have to (they are required to do so), or simply because they are curious. You might attend a town council meeting because a proposed increase in property taxes is being considered; you might attend a parents' meeting at school out of a sense of duty or because your spouse insisted that you go; you might attend a lecture on the fur industry because you are curious about what might be discussed.

Try to rate your audience on the following scale with respect to audience members' overall motivation:

Required to attend   1   2   3   4   5   Strongly desire to attend

Since the audience's willingness to attend can affect how your presentation is received, it is important to make an educated guess regarding its probable level of enthusiasm. (Of course, it's also important to remember that just because audience members want to attend your talk, they will not necessarily agree with what you have to say.)

Audiences can be heterogeneous (mixed) or homogeneous (similar) in terms of various characteristics. For example, the audience shown at top is homogeneous in terms of sex, and the audience shown at bottom is homogeneous in terms of race.

Top, Ken Kaminsky/The Picture Cube; *bottom,* D. Wells/The Image Works

VALUES: IS THE AUDIENCE HOMOGENEOUS OR HETEROGENEOUS?

A second factor for consideration is the degree of *homogeneity,* that is, the extent to which everyone in the audience has similar values and attitudes. Of course, it is easier to address a homogeneous audience than a heterogeneous one. In addressing heterogeneous groups, speakers need to vary their appeals to ensure that all segments of the audience "spectrum" are considered.

Use the following scale to measure the extent to which the members of your audience share similar characteristics and values:

Homogeneous   1   2   3   4   5   Heterogeneous

LEVEL OF AGREEMENT:
DOES THE AUDIENCE AGREE WITH YOUR POSITION?

Whatever your topic, you must attempt to predict your audience's reaction to the stance you take. For example, they may oppose you, they may support you, or they may be neutral or uninterested. The accuracy of your prediction will to some extent determine how your presentation is received.

Use the following scale to help you assess your audience's position in terms of its similarity or dissimilarity to your own.

Agrees with me   1   2   3   4   5   Disagrees with me

Your objective when speaking to an audience that *agrees* with your position is to maintain its support. Your objective when speaking to a *neutral* audience is to gain your listeners' attention and show them how your presentation can be of value to them. When facing an audience that *disagrees* with you, you need to be especially careful and diplomatic in your approach. In this case, your objective is to change your listeners' minds—to move the audience closer to the "agree with me" side of the continuum. This task becomes easier if you establish a common ground with audience members, that is, if you first stress values and interests that you share. Keep in mind that your goal is to increase the likelihood that a voluntary audience will attend to your message and that a "captive" audience will give you a fair hearing.

LEVEL OF COMMITMENT:
HOW MUCH DO THEY CARE?

Finally you need to consider how much the audience cares about your topic. Is it very important to them? Do they feel strongly enough to be moved to action? Or are your concerns irrelevant to your listeners?

Use the following scale to represent your audience's commitment.

Passive   1   2   3   4   5   Active

Together, the three attitudinal scales will indicate how much background and motivational material you need to include in your presentation.

ATTITUDE CHECK

1. For practice, select three to five current, controversial topics.
2. Each member of the class should fill out the following scales for each topic.
   a. If a speech was being given on this topic, would you:

   Attend only if   1   2   3   4   5   Have a great
   required to   desire to attend

   b. Do you feel that your attitudes and values are similar or dissimilar to those of other members of your group?

   Similar   1   2   3   4   5   Dissimilar
   (homogeneous)   (heterogeneous)

   c. Do you support this issue?

   Favor   1   2   3   4   5   Disapprove

   d. Is your involvement in or commitment to your position active or passive?

   Passive   1   2   3   4   5   Active
   involvement   involvement

3. Using your knowledge about the class members, estimate where on each scale the average response will fall. Then, add up the scores for each issue and divide by the number of class members participating to determine the actual class average for each issue. How accurate were your predictions? Would you have been off base if you had spoken to the class on one or more of the identified topics? Why? How can the information you gathered help you become a more effective speaker?

Predicting the Audience's Reaction

Once you have completed your audience research, you will be in a position to predict your listeners' reception of any topic you select. Consider the following questions:

1. What do the audience members now know about my topic?
2. To what extent are they interested in my topic?
3. What are their current attitudes toward this topic?

Thus, as you develop your presentation, you must keep in mind the audience's knowledge of, interest in, and attitude toward the subject matter. These important factors will help you select and shape material specifically for the audience members.

SUMMARY

Public communication, unlike interpersonal communication, occurs in a somewhat formal setting and requires the communicator to be well prepared. Effective speakers understand the challenges involved in speaking before others and work in a systematic manner to create, prepare, and deliver their presentations.

The public speaking process begins when you first consider addressing a group of people. Four main stages of speechmaking follow: topic selection, topic development, the presentation itself, and the postpresentation analysis.

A thorough analysis of yourself and a thorough analysis of your audience are the essential preliminary steps in topic selection. Information about your audience should come from your personal experience with the group, from original research (e.g., news releases and interviews), or both. First, you need to determine audience demographics, including such factors as age, sex, marital status, religion, cultural background, occupation, economic status, education, and membership in organizations. Then you should try to predict the attitudes the listeners will have toward you and your presentation. It will help you to know whether audience members are required to attend, are homogeneous or heterogeneous in their attitudes, are favorably or unfavorably disposed toward your position, or are uninterested in your topic altogether.

SUGGESTIONS FOR FURTHER READING

Boylan, Bob: *What's Your Point?* Warner, New York, 1990. A consultant describes some innovative presentation techniques that have worked for his corporate audiences.

Eisenberg, Abne, and Teri Kwal Gamble: *Painless Public Speaking*, University Press of America, Lanham, Md., 1991. A workbook approach; guides the speechmaker easily through the audience-analysis process.

Frank, Milo: *How to Get Your Point Across in 30 Seconds or Less*, Pocket Books, New York, 1990. A concise book, directed at business speakers, written by a former media specialist and film producer.

Lucas, Stephen: *The Art of Public Speaking*, 4th ed., McGraw-Hill, New York, 1992. Contains valuable information about both the speaker and the audience.

Tarshis, Barry: *The "Average American" Book*, Atheneum, New York, 1979. Highly readable; contains a wealth of information related to audience analysis.

Van Ekeren, Glenn: *The Speaker's Source Book*, Prentice Hall, Englewood Cliffs, N.J., 1988. A refreshing compilation of stories, anecdotes, and quotations about many topics. They can be adapted to fit many subjects.

NOTES

1. David Wallechinsky, Irving Wallace, and Amy Wallace, *The Book of Lists*, Morrow, New York, 1977, p. 469.
2. For an overview of the speech selection process, see Martin P. Andersen, E. Ray Nichols, Jr., and Herbert W. Booth, *The Speaker and His Audience*, 2d ed., Harper and Row, (New York, 1974, chap. 10, "Determining the Subject and Thesis Statement"; and John F. Wilson and Carroll C. Arnold, *Dimensions of Public Communication*, Allyn & Bacon, Boston, Mass., 1976, chap. 2, "First Considerations."
3. Elie Wiesel, *Souls on Fire*, Summit, New York, 1982.
4. The following sources expand on our discussion of audience analysis: Douglas Ehninger, Alan H. Monroe, and Bruce E. Gronbeck, *Principles and Types of Speech Communication*, 8th ed., Scott, Foresman, Glenview, Ill., 1978; and Steven W. King, *Communication and Social Influence*, Addison-Wesley, Reading, Mass., 1975.
5. Robert Orben, "Speech Writing for Presidents," presentation delivered in Washington, D.C., 1983.
6. Donald H. Kausler and Charles V. Lair, "Information, Feedback Conditions and Verbal Discrimination Learning in Elderly Subjects," *Psychonomic Science*, 1968, pp. 193–194.
7. Thomas M. Scheidel, "Sex and Persuasability," *Speech Monographs*, vol. 30, 1963, pp. 353–368.
8. See Lawrence R. Wheeless, "The Effects of Attitude Credibility and Homophily on Selective Exposure to Information," *Speech Monographs*, vol. 41, 1974, pp. 329–338.

THE OCCASION AND THE SUBJECT

After finishing this chapter, you should be able to:

Explain how the nature of the occasion influences a speech

Narrow your topic appropriately

Evaluate a topic according to its worth, appropriateness, and interest, and in terms of availability of research material

Formulate clear and precise purpose statements for yourself and behavioral objectives for your audience

Whenever you give a speech, you should have a clear idea of the nature of the occasion and how your topic relates to it. Clearly, both the occasion and your subject will affect the way you develop your presentation, stage it, and deliver it.

CONSIDERING THE OCCASION

If asked to speak before a group—including your own class—your first response might well be, "Why? What's the occasion?" Identifying the occasion and your role in it are essential steps in the process of preparing a speech. Fortunately much, if not all, of what you need to know about the occasion is relatively easy to determine. Essentially, only the following need to be specified:

Date and time of the presentation
Length of presentation
Location of the presentation
Nature of the occasion
Size of the audience

Date and Time: When and How Long?

Date and time are the most obvious—and among the most important—bits of information you need to acquire. We have seen student speakers and professional speakers arrive an hour early, an hour late, and even a day early or a day late. (Of course, it's far better to be early than late, but being a day early is surely excessive.)

Timing can influence a speaker's effectiveness. For example, one well-known speaker arrived late at a New York college and found a hostile audience that had waited nearly an hour. Some professional speakers schedule their engagements so close together—two or three a day—that they must rush out the door rudely, almost before they have completed their talks. In a situation like this, the audience may react angrily.

What's the occasion? An essential step in preparing a speech is considering the occasion and your role in it.

Hugh Rogers/Monkmeyer

The length of the presentation can also influence its effectiveness. For instance, one student speaker was supposed to deliver a 10-minute informative speech, "The History of the Corvette." Although it was suggested that he limit his consideration of the topic to two or three major model changes, he attempted to discuss every minute body and grill alteration in the Chevrolet Corvette from 1954 to the present. The instructor made several attempts to stop him, but 40 minutes into the speech he was still going strong. At this point the instructor announced a class break. The student responded, "That's fine. I'll just continue." And he did—although the majority of his audience had departed.

Sometimes we are not actually given as much speaking time as we have been led to expect. For example, lunch or after-dinner speakers are often told that they will have 45 minutes to fill, but after introductions and comments by preliminary speakers they suddenly find themselves left with 30 minutes or less. In his book *Public Speaking for Private People*, Art Linkletter notes that he tells groups he will speak the full allotted time, no more and no less. If he is originally asked to speak for 45 minutes and only 5 minutes remains when he is introduced, he will nevertheless speak for 45 minutes.[1] Most speakers are not in a position to make such a demand. Are you able to plan a presentation to ensure that you will not run over or under your time limit?

MR. KENNEDY, YOU REMEMBER MRS. . . . UH . . .

For at least one of the participants, a trip down memory lane yesterday proved just a bit too far back.

Barbara B. Kennelly, daughter of the late John M. Bailey, the Democratic leader in Connecticut, is a candidate to fill the unexpired term of a deceased United States Representative, and she invited Senator Edward M. Kennedy, an old family friend, to a campaign rally in Hartford.

Mrs. Kennelly said she remembered vividly how the two had met in 1958, when her father was a valued supporter of John F. Kennedy's Presidential aspirations.

But Senator Kennedy's memory proved not quite so keen as his old friend's.

At one point he called her "Mrs. Connelly."

At another, he referred to her as "this outstanding candidate, Barbara McNelly."

While Irish eyes are smiling or crying over the bloopers, Mrs. Kennelly corrected her old friend each time.

Then Mr. Kennedy referred to her as "Barbara Kanally" and someone in the crowd shouted, "It's Kennelly."

"South Boston," said the Senator, sheepishly referring to his home town to explain the gaffes.

But by the end of his speech endorsing Mrs. Kennelly, Mr. Kennedy had adapted a safe means of referring to the woman he called "my old friend."

"Elect Barbara your Congresswoman," he said.

Source: From "Mr. Kennedy, You Remember Mrs. . . . Uh, . . . " *The New York Times*, January 6, 1982. Copyright © 1982 by The New York Times Company. Reprinted by permission.

Location and Participants: Where?

Reminding yourself of the location of your presentation and of the people directly connected with it is an important aspect of preparing a speech. This may seem obvious, but it is sometimes neglected, with absurd and embarrassing results. We recall being present at a speech by a world-famous psychologist whose audience consisted of members of the host college and the surrounding community. Early in his speech, the eminent Dr. M——— mumbled what seemed to be the name of another college, though most of his listeners failed to notice. The second time, however, he clearly announced how happy he was to be here at X———, mentioning the wrong college again. (Doubly unfortunate was the fact that X was a rival of the host college.) By then, some members of the audience appeared embarrassed for the speaker, and others appeared hostile. The third time, the psychologist mentioned not only the wrong school but the wrong town as well. At this point, there was sufficient commotion in the audience for him to realize his error, and in evident confusion he turned to the college president to ask where he was.

Here is another example: During a state visit to South America, former president Ronald Reagan delivered a few words at the airport: "It was so nice to be here in Bolivia." Unfortunately, he was in Brazil. Realizing his mistake, he noted, "Bolivia is my next stop." Unfortunately, Bolivia wasn't on his itinerary.

How can you avoid such problems? The minister who officiated at our marriage had a possible solution. During the wedding rehearsal, we noticed that a page in his Bible was marked with a paper clip that held a slip of paper, and later we asked him about it. The minister showed us that it had our names clearly written on it. He explained that because he was somewhat nervous when conducting a wedding, he frequently tended to forget the names of the bride and groom, even if they (in our case the bride) had belonged to the congregation for years. The slip of paper provided an unobtrusive reminder. Taking our cue from this experience, we now each attach a slip of paper to the first page of our notes whenever we address a group. The slip bears the name of the organization, its location, the name of the person introducing us, the names of the officers, and other important information. Thus we have at our disposal the data we need, to be integrated as appropriate. You may also want to adopt this simple procedure to avoid unnecessary embarrassment or loss of credibility.

Of course, there are other aspects to "location" besides merely the site where you are and the people who are present. Also of concern is the nature of the physical space you are to speak in. Is the space nicely or shabbily decorated? Hot, cold, or comfortable? Quiet or noisy? If appropriate, you might refer to the environment in your talk, as did one student who was speaking on the effects of AIDS (acquired immune deficiency syndrome):

> Take a look around you. What do you see? Desks, chairs, fluorescent lights, a chalkboard, your friends? Sights you take for granted every day. Eight-year-old Jane Doe doesn't take these sights for granted, though. Not any more. Jane has AIDS, and has been barred by a court order from attending a public school. No more will she sit at a desk as you are sitting, glance at the board as you do, share the fun of learning with friends. AIDS is changing her life.

Type of Occasion: Why and How Many?

Why have you been asked to speak? Although every occasion is unique to some extent, you can ask some general questions to clarify the situation in your own mind. For example, is it a class session? Right now it probably is, but in the future it could well be a sales meeting, a management planning session, a convention, or a funeral. Is your presentation part of the observance of a special event? For example, is the occasion in honor of a retirement? A promotion? Is it some other type of recognition? Who else, if anyone, will be sharing the program with you? Factors like these can affect the nature of your presentation. An appropriate topic for a retirement party, for instance, might be considered inappropriate for a more formal occasion.

Determining how many people will show up to listen to any particular presentation is difficult. In a classroom situation, for example, on one day the room may be filled, but on another day a speaker may arrive and find that a number of students are out sick or off on a special project for another course. The same problem confronts the professional speaker. In our work we always multiply and divide the sponsor's estimate by two. Thus we are prepared to

A STIRRING BREEZE SPARKS FEELINGS, THEN WORDS FOR A PRESIDENT'S VISION
Maureen Dowd

Washington, Jan. 20—Peggy Noonan was sitting on a couch in a West Wing office at the White House two weeks ago, her black fake-crocodile notebook in her lap. She was tired and drained. She had just finished working on Ronald Reagan's farewell speech, and now she was beginning to scribble notes for George Bush's Inaugural Address.

With an unorthodox time-sharing scheme, both men had chosen the 38-year-old speech writer to help them express themselves, one with his partisan musings as he left the Oval Office and the other with his bipartisan dreams as he entered it.

Ms. Noonan began daydreaming about her privileged perch. "I thought this must be the most special place in history, 40 feet down from the retiring President and 20 feet from the incoming President," she recalled at lunch Thursday. "And here I am, sitting on this couch between this President and that one."

Down the hall in the direction of the Oval Office, there was stillness that day two weeks ago. Down the other way, toward Mr. Bush's Vice-Presidential office, there was noise and laughter and aides and secretaries and Secret Service agents bustling about.

"It felt like a new breeze," she recalled. "There was a literal movement of air. A new history beginning today."

And so President Bush's inaugural message was born. "A new breeze is blowing, and a nation refreshed by freedom stands ready to push on," he told America today.

Ms. Noonan was one of a handful of people, watching from the reviewing stand as Mr. Bush took the oath of office, who were pivotal in helping the new President win the prize he had sought so long and so hard.

It was an odd pairing in some ways, the passionate and eloquent writer from an Irish working-class family in New Jersey interpreting the proper and less-than-articulate politician from an upper-crust, Anglo-Saxon clan.

But, from "warts and all" and "read my lips" to "a quiet man" and "kinder, gentler," the partnership worked so well that many of the phrases Ms. Noonan coined for Mr. Bush became so famous so fast that they are now clichés.

Ms. Noonan began her career in Newark as a premium adjuster at the Aetna Insurance Company and wrote radio commentaries for Dan Rather at CBS News before moving to the Reagan White House staff.

She provided some of Mr. Reagan's most moving moments, including his speech in Normandy in 1984 to mark the 40th anniversary of the D-Day invasion and his remarks in 1986 after the explosion of the space shuttle Challenger. So moving were her words that she was dubbed "La Pasionaria" after Dolores Ibarruri, whose fiery speeches in the Spanish Civil War rallied Communists against Franco.

Ms. Noonan had left the White House and was at home nursing her infant, Will, and working on a book about Washington politics and mores when she heard Mr. Bush on the radio campaigning in New Hampshire. He was "recycling" Bob Dole's I-am-one-of-you slogan, she recalled.

She asked her husband, Richard Rahn, and her mother if they could take care of the baby for a week. Then she flew north.

She found Mr. Bush impatient. Tapping his fingers on his chest, he told her, "They gotta get to know me out there." She traveled with him and ate with him and watched him with his children and grandchildren. She got a pad and pen and interviewed him like a reporter, asking him how he imagined his Presidency and what events had shaped his ideas on social issues.

Accustomed to the response from the public that President Reagan received, she was struck by the different way people reacted to Mr. Bush. Waitresses kissed him and locals stopped by the table to shake hands and say, "Hang in there, George."

"When you traveled with Reagan, it was like traveling with a God," she said. "People were struck by his radiance and looked at him with slack jaws. With Bush, it was cuter."

Ms. Noonan, who detests "faux Kennedy speeches rendered in gummy hands," dissected Mr. Bush and gave him a simpler, self-deprecating style—not high drama and trumpets, as he said today.

"He doesn't have the rolling roundness of Reagan," Ms. Noonan said. "He's more of a brisk bounder."

Ms. Noonan, who says she always tries "to hit a home run," said she was "the most scared I ever was" as she watched Mr. Bush give his speech at the Republican National Convention. The speech was widely hailed as the best of his career and the one that helped change the tide for his lagging campaign.

"Before he had even finished, a lady in the Delaware delegation held up a placard saying 'Read my lips,' " she recalled, "and I said to myself, 'O.K., we have a hit, ladies and gentlemen.' "

One Bush aide had asked her to take the word "gentle" out of the speech. "Don't you think this will start up the wimp thing again?" he complained. Ms. Noonan explained, with barely restrained anger, that "only a man utterly confident of his own strength can talk like this."

For those who had watched Mr. Bush talk with his own words and then talk with Ms. Noonan's, the effect was eerie. Pre-Noonan, if Mr. Bush wanted to talk about drugs, he would talk about "narced-up terrorist kind of guys," not, as he did today under Ms. Noonan's influence, "deadly scourge."

Pre-Noonan, Mr. Bush could answer only, "Challenges, rewards," when asked why he was in politics. Today he could talk about being the man who could help a country "celebrate the quieter, deeper successes that are made not of gold and silk."

Other Bush aides may refer to his speeches as "rah, rah," but Ms. Noonan, who is returning full time to her book and baby after today, has a more lofty view of a great political speech: "It makes people less lonely. It connects strangers with simple truths."

Source: From "The 41st President, Speed Writer, A Stirring Breeze Sparks Feelings, Then Words for a President's Vision" by Maureen Dowd, *The New York Times*, January 21, 1989. Copyright 1989 by The New York Times Company. Reprinted by permission.

speak to a small group—that is, possibly 20—if 40 were expected; or to a large group—possibly 100—if 50 was the estimate. We make it a policy to be prepared with large visuals and ample handouts, although we are also psychologically ready to decrease the formality of the presentation if a smaller audience actually arrives.

If you are speaking in a situation where chairs must be set up, we recommend putting a small number of chairs in place and stacking additional chairs nearby. If a small group arrives, it will appear that the audience was just as anticipated; if a larger crowd shows up, people come away with the impression that you were prepared for an overflow.

The articles by Maureen Dowd (these pages) and Jerry Bruno (page 328) describe how professional planners and speechwriters consider the nature of the occasion and the audience when preparing a speech. Which parts of their advice can you apply to your own speechmaking situations?

Since you are not likely to have an "advance" person at your disposal when preparing to deliver your presentation—at least not yet—you must do all the advance thinking for yourself. Make it a habit to complete an analysis of both your audience and the occasion before completing work on any presentation. The predictions you make will serve you well as you continue preparing your speech.

THE ADVANCE MAN
Jerry Bruno

There's nothing really rewarding about being de-nounced in front of five thousand people by a con-gressman. . . . It's just one of those things—or two or five of those things—that I ran into in politics. It just seemed that, working for Robert Kennedy, I happened to run into them all the time. . . .

The particular denunciation was the result of a fight with Congresswoman Edith Green of Oregon. . . . Edith Green is a very tough politician—one of the toughest anywhere—and as a lot of badly scarred peo-ple in Washington will tell you, when she wants some-thing, she knows how to fight for it. She's also some-body Robert Kennedy felt a debt to, because of her help to John Kennedy in 1960.

Now my business is crowds: how to get them in, how to get them out, even how to count them. . . . Edith Green had her ideas about what Bob Kennedy should do—namely, speak at this new auditorium in Portland that seated 14,000. Remember the first rule of crowds: 25,000 people in a 50,000-seat stadium is a half-empty turnout. But 4,000 people in a hall that seats 3,000 is an overflow crowd. And it works that way on a crowd. People want the sense of being somewhere special, somewhere a lot of people are trying to get to. It depresses people to see empty seats all around them, makes them feel they've been conned into turning out for an event that wasn't all that special.

In this case I took a look around and realized that you couldn't fill those 14,000 seats if Raquel Welch and Paul Newman put on a stag show as a warm-up.

So I called the Washington office.

"Joe," I said to Dolan, "you just can't fill this hall Edith wants us to go to. It'll be just terrible."

"Well," Dolan said, "don't do it."

So I looked around and found a Labor Temple that was perfect. It held maybe four thousand people and I knew we could get an overflow crowd out to that au-ditorium. It was just right. At least, that's what I thought until I spoke to Edith Green.

"That Temple can't hold the crowd that's going to turn out for Kennedy," she said.

"How many do you think will come out?" I asked.

"Maybe six thousand people," she said.

"Yeah, but that won't even half fill the new hall," I said. "It'll be terrible."

"Why can't we hang a curtain over the empty seats?" she said.

This is a common trick in political advance, and it really works great in places like the old Madison Square Garden where you can barely see the balcony from the floor. The press never notices those things. But when we went out to look at this new hall, it was one of those well-lit modern places, with no posts and no hidden corners. There was just no way to hide eight thousand empty seats, not from newsmen, and God knows not from Robert Kennedy.

The argument showed no signs of settlement, so I settled it myself. I had thousands of flyers printed up announcing that Robert Kennedy and Edith Green would appear at the Labor Temple. Edith Green just about hit the ceiling and threatened to cancel the whole affair.

"I don't think you can do that," I said. "You've got fifty thousand flyers saying you and Kennedy will be there. That could mean a lot of disappointed voters."

So Bob Kennedy came to Portland, and at the Labor Temple they were hanging from the rafters, and I mean literally up there in the rafters. There were two thousand people or so outside, the hall was packed, the press was impressed by the turnout, and it was the kind of evening Kennedy loved. And then Edith Green stood up to introduce Kennedy.

"I want all you people to know," she said, turning in my direction, "that had I had my way, we would all have been comfortable and able to hear Bob Kennedy. But because of that man there"—and she points to me—"we're in this crowded, sweaty room. And I want you to know, Senator Kennedy, that it was that man who caused this problem."

There I am—my first public recognition in all my years in politics! And there's Bob Kennedy, his head down as though in deep thought, trying to keep from bursting out laughing on the stage. . . .

Source: *The Advance Man* by Jerry Bruno and Jeff Greenfield. Re-printed by permission of Sterling Lord Literistic, Inc. Copyright © 1970 by Jerry Bruno and Jeff Greenfield.

■ ETHICS AND COMMUNICATION

SPEECHMAKING AND THE GOLDEN RULE

Charles Osgood, anchor at *CBS Sunday Night News* and writer and anchor of *The Osgood File* on CBS radio, notes:

Speakers sometimes overlook the Golden Rule, I fear,

They go ahead and give a speech that they would hate to hear.

Where do you stand? In your opinion, is it more important for a speaker to deliver a speech containing ideas that audience members *need* to hear, or one containing ideas that they would *like* to hear? Explain.

Source: Charles Osgood, *Osgood on Speaking: How to Think on Your Feet without Falling on Your Face,* Morrow, New York, 1988.

CONSIDERING THE SUBJECT

Selecting a Topic: Criteria

Now let's move on to the next phase of preparing a speech: selecting your subject. To continue preparing your speech without having selected a subject—on the basis of self-analysis, audience analysis, and occasion analysis—would be like trying to buy an airline ticket without knowing your destination.

You must carefully examine the list of possible topics you generated during the self-analysis and audience-analysis phases of your preparation. During this examination, you evaluate your ideas according to specific criteria. These criteria include (1) apparent worth, (2) appropriateness, (3) interest, and (4) availability of material. When you keep these criteria in mind, selecting a topic will be easier—if only because few of your choices will meet each of the criteria equally well with regard to the needs of particular audiences.[2]

 SKILL BUILDER

TOPIC EVALUATION TIME

1. Working individually or in groups, develop a list of criteria by which you believe a topic for a class speech should be assessed.

2. Share your criteria with others. Which criteria seem to be most important in the selection process? Which appear to be least important? Why?

3. Compare the criteria you developed with those we have identified. How are they similar or different?

✔ **SKILL BUILDER**

WHAT IS THIS TOPIC WORTH?

1. Working individually or with a group, draw up a list of 10 topics that you believe are worthy of your time and attention.
2. Next, compile a list of 10 seemingly worthless or trivial topics.
3. Compare your list with lists made by others.

IS THE TOPIC WORTHWHILE?

At this point, you need to determine if the topic is important to you and to the people who will listen to you. Many speakers—including college students and business people—often fall into the trap of choosing topics that are of little value to the audience. One of the authors recalls a time in a military training institute when he heard one colonel tell another, "After 25 years as an officer, I'm expected to waste my time hearing how to inspect a fork!" To that audience of high-ranking officers, the topic "Fork Inspection Techniques" was clearly trivial. You may also find that some topics chosen by others are trivial from your perspective. They may be so commonplace—how to set a table, for example—that they don't merit the time and energy you must expend in listening to them. Many subjects that are acceptable for interpersonal discourse may be inconsequential when presented in a public setting where the speaker's purpose is to inform or persuade. Which topics do you judge to be worth your time? Which, in your opinion, are unworthy of consideration?

IS THE TOPIC APPROPRIATE?

We have already discussed how important it is to determine if a topic is appropriate to you and your personal interests. Two additional facets of this criterion must also be considered: (1) Is the topic appropriate to the audience? (2) Is it appropriate to the occasion? Let's examine each in turn.

● **CULTURE AND COMMUNICATION**

AUDIENCES—MELTING POTS OR MULTICULTURAL?

None of us is culture-free. Everyone is subject to cultural influences. In your opinion, should public communication help bring about a mingling and melding of human cultures, or should it help create an audience of multiculturalists—people who recognize, accept, and appreciate the basic differences that distinguish people of diverse cultures? Explain.

By this time, you should have developed a profile of your audience. That is, you have either determined precisely or made educated guesses about the age, sex, and educational level of the majority of the people who are going to hear your speech. It then becomes imperative for you to ask which of your possible topics is most appropriate for such a mix of people. Sometimes this determination is easy. For instance, you would not ordinarily give a talk about the evils of television to a group of network representatives. Nor, ordinarily, would you opt to speak on the advantages of a women's college to an audience already attending a women's college. You might not choose to speak on baseball trivia to an audience of highly educated professional women. Or would you? Is there a way to make seemingly inappropriate topics appropriate? Every subject area must be seen through the eyes of its intended audience. Just as an automobile is customized for a particular owner, so a subject area must be customized to reflect the needs of a particular group of listeners. Just as the automobile is painted, pinstriped, and upholstered with an owner or type of owner in mind, so you as a speaker must "outfit" your topic to appeal to the audience members you hope to reach. This takes work, but it can be done.

The appropriateness of the topic to the occasion must also be considered. For example, you can probably think of any number of occasions on which a humorous topic would be ill conceived. Can you think of occasions where a humorous topic would be an asset? To choose two obvious examples, a humorous topic would be inappropriate for an event commemorating servicemen and -women who have given their lives for their country, whereas it would be welcomed at a "roast."

> Make a list of 10 subjects you believe would be *inappropriate* for delivery to your class. Discuss how each topic might be approached to make it appropriate.

IS THE TOPIC INTERESTING?

Speechmakers often make the mistake of selecting topics they think they *should* speak about rather than topics they *want* to speak about. Student speakers, for instance, will sometimes turn to a newspaper or news magazine and, without further thought, select a story at random as the basis for a speech. We know one student who insisted on talking about labor-management relations. Why? He thought it sounded like an important subject. Unfortunately, he had spent little time in the labor force and no time in management. And because he did not care enough to do much—if any—research, the entire subject remained foreign to him. Not surprisingly, the speech he delivered was dull, "tired," and disjointed. A lazy, unenthusiastic speaker can make almost any topic uninteresting—even a potentially fascinating or exciting one.

It cannot be overemphasized that if others are to believe that what you are speaking about is important, you yourself must first believe that it is important. John Silverstein, a spokesman for General Dynamics, put it this way, "You need to believe in your idea. This is very important. What a listener often gauges is how convinced the speaker is. If he has lived it, breathed it, and is himself really sold on it, it generally is enough to sell the argument."[3] Of course, selecting a topic that is appealing to you is a personal matter and can be relatively simple, but determining what will interest your audience can be somewhat more challenging.

> We like to hear what makes us feel comfortable and self-assured. Yet this is exactly what we have no need of hearing; only those who disturb us can improve us.
> Sydney J. Harris

✔ **SKILL BUILDER**

WHAT'S IN IT FOR THEM?

Why might each of the following topics interest the identified audiences?

1. Topic: "Gun Control"
   Audience: Senior citizens
   Audience: Your class

2. Topic: "Teenage Suicide"
   Audience: Members of a parent-teacher association
   Audience: Your class

3. Topic: "The Art of Chinese Cooking"
   Audience: Weight-control self-help group
   Audience: Your class

Here, students have an advantage. As a student, you know your fellow students, and you should be able to identify topics that will interest them. When addressing less familiar audiences, however, you should feel free to return to your audience analysis and make some educated guesses. Determining an audience's interests is a never-ending challenge—one that some unadventurous speechmakers prefer not to tackle. One corporate executive, for example, once delivered a speech that was gratifyingly well received. Unfortunately, he then delivered essentially the same speech for the next 5 years, although times and needs kept changing. Needless to say, his current audiences are not interested in his topic. As times change, people's interests change, and so should the topics selected by speakers. Topics must be updated to match the moods, needs, and concerns of listeners; only by updating can you ensure that your topic treats an issue of interest to your audience.

Advertising executives discovered long ago that people are interested primarily in themselves and in how products relate to them. Speechmakers are in an analogous position. Keep this in mind when considering the interests of your audience members. Ask yourself how your subject relates to them. Ask yourself what they stand to gain from listening to you. Create an "inventory" for each of your possible subjects. If you are unable to identify significant ways in which your audience will benefit from hearing about a topic, there is good reason for you *not* to speak on that topic.

IS SUFFICIENT RESEARCH MATERIAL AVAILABLE?

Before choosing a topic, you must be certain that material on the subject exists and that you can find it readily—in a library or somewhere else. Many a speaker falls into the trap of writing for material that is unavailable in a school or local library, only to have it arrive too late or turn out to be unpromising. Such an experience can cause last-minute panic, and the result is an inadequately prepared speechmaker and an inadequate presentation. Avoid this pitfall by giving careful attention to your library and other nearby sources during the selection phase of your preparation.

Is sufficient research material available? When choosing a topic for a speech, it's essential to make sure that you can find the information you need—in the library or somewhere else.

George Disario/The Stock Market

Narrowing the Topic

It is essential to consider how much time is available for your speech. We know an army chaplain who more than once demonstrated how adept he was at handling time constraints. The chaplain's job was to address groups of recruits during basic training, and on each occasion he was given only 3 minutes to get his message across. One day his objective was to persuade soldiers not to use foul language. (It was his belief that such a practice degraded both individuals and the service.) Realizing that he could accomplish only so much in the time permitted, he chose to focus on a single word—the particular word that he found most offensive. During his 3-minute talk, he suggested that the troops avoid using just that one term. By doing this, the chaplain demonstrated that he understood how important it is to narrow a topic to manageable proportions and, incidentally, succeeded in realizing his objective. (After his speech, the abused word was heard much less frequently around the base.)

Far too many speakers attempt to give audiences "the world" in 5 minutes. (Even Mel Brooks, in his satiric film *History of the World*, limited himself to *Part One*.) It is essential to narrow your topic to fit the constraints imposed by the situation. Don't try to take on too much. Five minutes is not sufficient to discuss the history of Russia, the industrial revolution, or even pedigreed dogs.

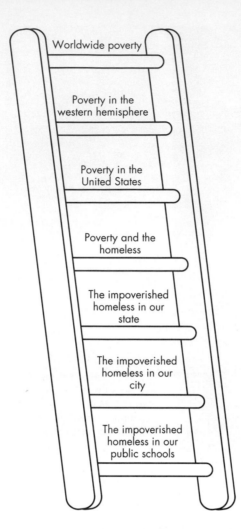

FIGURE 13-1
Technique for narrowing a topic.

Let us share with you a strategy you can use to avoid "biting off more than you can chew"—or talk about. Select a topic and place it at the top of a "ladder." Then subdivide the topic into constituent parts; that is, break it down into smaller and smaller units, as shown in Figure 13-1. The smallest unit should appear on the lowest step of the ladder. This process is like whittling or carving a stick of wood. The more you shave off, the narrower the topic becomes. Like the carver, you decide what shape to give your topic and when to stop shaving. For example, assume that you want to speak on the welfare system. One way to narrow your topic would be to focus on how the welfare system helps women. Your topic could be focused even further. You might explore how the welfare system helps women in California or, more specifically, women in Los Angeles. To take another possibility, if you want to talk on the computer revolution, you might focus on how the computer has revolutionized education or, more specifically, on how computers are used to teach writing skills.

You can use the "manageability" chart in the "Skill Builder" on page 335 for overall assessment of each speaking assignment you undertake.

✔ **SKILL BUILDER**

MANAGEABILITY SCALE

Answer each of the following questions about your subject by awarding yourself a score from 1 to 10, where 1 represents "poor" and 10 represents "excellent." The highest possible score is 100.

1. Is your subject *worthwhile?*
   From your perspective?   _____
   From your audience's perspective?   _____

2. Is your subject *appropriate?*
   From your perspective?   _____
   From your audience's perspective?   _____

3. Is your subject *interesting?*
   From your perspective?   _____
   From your audience's perspective?   _____

4. Is *sufficient material* available?
   Material exists.   _____
   Material can be obtained in time.   _____

5. Have you *narrowed your topic* to fit the situation?   _____

6. What are your *overall feelings* at this stage?   _____

                                              Score   _____

Formulating a Purpose Statement and Behavioral Objectives

Once you have identified a topic and narrowed its scope, reexamine exactly *why* you are speaking. What is your purpose? What do you hope to accomplish?[4] What kind of response would you like from your audience? What do you want your listeners to think or do as a result of your presentation? What, in other words, is your ultimate objective?

Most speakers have one of two general objectives when they prepare to deliver a speech: they aim either to *inform* listeners (to share new information or insights with the audience) or to *persuade* listeners (to convince audience members to believe in or do something). However, in actual speaking situations, the purpose is not always so clear. Persuasive speeches usually contain informative material, and informative speeches may sometimes include elements of persuasion. (Informative and persuasive speaking are discussed in more detail in Chapters 17 and 18.)

If your purpose is to inform, your primary responsibility is to relay information to your audience in an interesting, well-organized, and professional manner. Informative speakers may explain something, demonstrate how something functions, or describe how something is structured. When speaking informatively, you hope to provide a learning experience for your listeners, sharing information they did not possess before your talk. In other words, if your main goal is to inform an audience, you must be certain that the data you provide will enhance your listeners' understanding, and you must find ways to help the audience remember what you say.

To ensure that your purpose is clear—initially to yourself and ultimately to your listeners—it helps to develop a *purpose statement*. What this means is that you commit to writing a summary of what you want to accomplish; you describe what you hope to do with your speech. The purpose statement of an informative speech often contains such words as *show, explain, report, instruct, describe*, and (not surprisingly) *inform*.

The following are examples of purpose statements for various kinds of informative speeches:

> To *explain* how selected Chinese character letters evolved
>
> To *describe* how a recession affects college students
>
> To *inform* class members about current Internal Revenue Service (IRS) regulations that affect them
>
> To *instruct* class members in how to give an insulin injection
>
> To *report* on the Rastafarian cult of Jamaica

Notice that each example takes the form of an infinitive verb phrase; thus it begins with *To*. Notice also that each statement contains one and only one idea and that it is written from the speaker's perspective.

Sometimes, in addition to developing a purpose statement, we also find it helpful to view the speech from the perspective of its listeners. To facilitate this process, you can formulate *behavioral objectives*. Objectives identify what you want the audience to take away after hearing your presentation; that is, they describe the behavior or response you want the audience to exhibit as a result of listening to your speech. For instance, you may want your listeners to be able to *list, explain, summarize, state,* or *apply* certain information. The following are examples of behavioral objectives:

> After listening to this presentation, the audience will be able to *explain* the process of photographic development.
>
> After listening to this speech, the audience will be able to *name* three kinds of questions that are unlawful in employment interviews.
>
> After listening to this presentation, the audience will be able to *discuss* the three main reasons why college students fail to graduate.

✔ SKILL BUILDER

PRACTICE IN PURPOSE STATEMENTS

1. Working individually or with a group, compile a list of five potential topics for informative speeches to be delivered in class. (Approximate speaking time is 7 minutes.)

2. Formulate a purpose statement for each topic and evaluate it according to these criteria: Is it clearly stated? Does it contain a single idea? Can the material be covered in the time available?

3. Develop an appropriate behavioral objective for each purpose statement.

THE PERSUASIVE SPEECH

The same principles used for informative speeches may be applied in formulating purpose statements and behavioral objectives for a persuasive speech. During a persuasive speech your main goal is to reinforce or change an audience's beliefs, or to make the audience behave in a certain way. The words *convince, persuade, motivate,* and *act* commonly turn up in purpose statements for persuasive speeches. Here are some examples:

To *persuade* audience members to buy investment real estate.

To *motivate* listeners to contribute money to the American Cancer Society.

To *persuade* class members to become actively involved in the anti-nuclear-weapons movement.

To *convince* class members to ask their dentists to apply a newly developed plastic coating to their teeth to prevent tooth decay.

With regard to behavioral objectives, you might want your audience to support a plan or take some overt action. Here are examples of behavioral objectives:

After listening to my presentation, audience members will purchase savings bonds.

After listening to my presentation, students will sign up to will their eyes to an eye bank.

After listening to my speech, students will boycott stores that sell products made of ivory.

To sum up, formulating precise purpose statements and behavioral objectives makes good sense. Both can help you focus your efforts and clarify your goals.

In recent years, public-speaking theorists have begun to look more closely at guidelines for writing. As a result, speakers are now often encouraged to develop theses for their speeches, just as writers do for papers. A *thesis* simply divides a topic into its major components. For example:

> *Thesis:* A recession affects college students by increasing tuition costs, reducing availability of courses, and limiting career opportunities after graduation.
>
> *Thesis:* Investment real estate can provide you with income, security, increasing equity, and some tax benefits.

As you can see from these examples, the thesis brings you a step closer to the structure of the speech itself.

USING ANALYSIS EFFECTIVELY

Effective speechmakers do not approach their task haphazardly. As we have seen, careful thought precedes the actual speech. Every speaker, from novice to professional, can benefit from following these suggestions:

1. Focus your attention on the characteristics of people you consider to be good speakers. Assess the extent to which you measure up to the standards they represent. Begin to identify ways of improving your speaking skills.

2. Conduct a systematic self-analysis as a preparation for speechmaking. Take the time you need to survey your own likes, dislikes, and concerns. Effective speakers know themselves well. They know what they care about, and they know what ideas they would like to share with others.

3. Analyze your audience. Effective speakers adapt their ideas to reflect the needs and interests of their listeners. Speeches are not meant to be delivered in an echo chamber or a vacuum. Rather, they are delivered with the specific purpose of informing or persuading others—of affecting others in certain specific ways. The degree to which you will succeed is directly related to how well you know your listeners and how accurately you are able to predict their reactions.

4. Analyze the occasion. It is essential that you learn why, when, where, and for how long you are expected to speak. Without this information, your preparation will be incomplete and insufficient.

5. Determine if your topic is supported by your own interests, your audience's interests, and the demands of the occasion. Be certain to evaluate your subject according to these criteria: Is the topic worthwhile? Is the topic appropriate? Is the topic interesting? Is sufficient research material available? Have I sufficiently narrowed my focus?

SUMMARY

Identifying the occasion and your role in it is an essential step in the process of preparing a speech. Once you have determined the date, time limit, and location of the speech as well as the nature of the occasion and the audience, you can start thinking about a suitable topic. Choosing a topic usually involves two steps: selecting a general subject and narrowing it down to a manageable topic. You can evaluate your topic by answering these questions: Is the topic worthwhile? Is it appropriate for the intended audience? Is it interesting? Is sufficient research material available? Will there be enough time to cover the topic adequately?

After you have chosen your topic, you need to reexamine your purpose for speaking. Most speakers have one of two general objectives when they prepare to deliver a speech: to inform listeners (to share new information or insights) or to persuade listeners (to convince the audience to believe or do something). To ensure that your purpose is clear, you should formulate a purpose statement—a summary of what you want to accomplish, expressed as an infinitive phrase. For example, you may want to inform your audience about something, to describe something, or to explain how something is done. You can also list behavioral objectives—abilities you want the audience to have internalized after listening to your presentation.

SUGGESTIONS FOR FURTHER READING

DeVito, Joseph A.: *The Elements of Public Speaking*, HarperCollins, New York, 1991. Helpful for speakers who find it difficult to select a topic.

Ehninger, Douglas, Bruce Gronbeck, Ray McKerrow, and Alan Monroe: *Principles and Types of Speech Communication*, HarperCollins, New York, 1992. Includes useful material on subjects for speeches and occasions for public speaking.

Fletcher, Leon: *How to Design and Deliver a Speech*, 4th ed., HarperCollins, New York, 1990. Offers step-by-step procedures for making a topic manageable.

Ilardo, Joseph: *Speaking Persuasively*, Macmillan, New York, 1981. Provides a detailed theory of topic selection.

Osborn, Michael, and Suzanne Osborn: *Public Speaking*, 2d ed., Houghton Mifflin, Boston, Mass., 1991. Provides helpful strategies for determining the purpose of a speech.

NOTES

1. Art Linkletter, *Public Speaking for Private People*, Bobbs-Merrill, Indianapolis, Ind., 1980, pp. 106–107.
2. For a study of the topics treated in public speeches by the leaders of the largest corporations in the United States, see Robert J. Myers and Martha Stout Kessler, "Business Speaks: A Study of the Themes in Speeches by America's Corporate Leaders," *Journal of Business Communication*, 17: vol. 3, pp. 5–17.
3. Thomas Leech, *How to Prepare, Stage, and Deliver Winning Presentations*, Amacom, New York, 1982, p. 11.
4. For a step-by-step explanation of how to establish your purpose, see Leon Fletcher, *How to Design and Deliver a Speech*, 2d ed., Harper and Row, New York, 1979, chap. 6.

DEVELOPING YOUR SPEECH: SUPPORTING YOUR IDEAS

After finishing this chapter, you should be able to:

Identify and use the various research resources available to you

Provide examples of how personal observations can be integrated into a presentation

Conduct an informal survey

Conduct a personal interview

Identify various types of supporting material, including definitions, statistics, examples, illustrations, and testimonials

Use comparison and contrast, repetition and restatement

Explain how visual and audio aids can enhance a presentation

Research is the process of going up alleys to see if they are blind.

Marston Bates

The world is already full of speakers who are too busy to prepare their speeches properly; the world would be better off if they were also too busy to give them.

William Norwood Brigance

Basic research is what I am doing when I don't know what I am doing.

Wernher von Braun

Your first step in the topic development stage of speech preparation is to gather material, such as illustrations, statistical evidence, expert opinions, and quotations, to integrate into your speech.

CONDUCTING RESEARCH: FINDING SUPPORTING MATERIAL

During the process of preparing a speech, one of your chief tasks is gathering information. Potential sources available to you include published works, other people, and, of course, yourself. Most of the time, you will have some personal knowledge of your topic. If you are discussing some aspect of sports medicine, for instance, you may have been injured in football, baseball, track, tennis, or swimming. If your topic is related to music or music education, you may have played the piano as a child. If your topic has to do with business or technology, you may work in an industry which relates directly to it. Far too often, speakers fail to realize that their personal experiences can be used to establish credibility and add interesting and pertinent examples.

Library Research

Libraries contain information storage and retrieval systems—resources that are invaluable for every type of research. Whatever your topic, the odds are that some library has relevant information. The library is one of the few real bargains left in our society. A huge array of material is available free; other materials and services (those available through a variety of photographic and electronic systems) are yours for only a minimal cost. In addition, every academic and public library has on its staff knowledgeable people who have been trained to aid you with your investigatory work.

When you begin library research, you will need to consult several reference sources—sources you may have already encountered during your educational career. Your goal during this phase of research is to compile a preliminary bibliography. Thus, your first stop may well be the library's card catalog.

The library is one of the few real bargains in today's world. Much of a library's material is available free, and its other materials and services cost very little to use.

D. Ogust/The Image Works

Next, you will move on to a variety of newspaper, magazine, and journal indexes. Depending on your subject, you may also consult bibliographical sources, encyclopedias, and almanacs. And you will almost certainly encounter forms of computer-assisted searches.

CARD CATALOGS

Card catalogs are traditionally organized according to the Dewey decimal system, which was developed during the nineteenth century; the more recently developed Library of Congress system; or a combination of both.

The *Dewey decimal system* classifies knowledge into nine areas, with a separate category for encyclopedias and works of general information. Here are its major categories:

000	General works		500	Pure science
100	Philosophy		600	Technology
200	Religion		620	Engineering
300	Social sciences		640	Home economics
	310	Statistics	650	Business
	330	Economics	670	Manufactures
	340	Law	680	Other manufactures
	350	Public administration	700	The arts
	380	Public services and utilities	800	Literature
400	Language		900	History

Each major class is divided into sections; shown here are the subsections for the social sciences and technology. Although the Dewey decimal system is found in libraries all over the country, its method of division is too restricted to accommodate the collections of large libraries.

Larger libraries use the *Library of Congress (LC) system,* which combines the Dewey numbering system with an alphabetical system. This permits a much larger number of categories. There are 20 major sections in the Library of Congress system:

A	General works	M	Music
B	Philosophy-religion	N	Fine arts
C	History-auxiliary sciences	P	Language and literature
D	History and topography (except America)	Q	Science
		R	Medicine
E–F	America	S	Agriculture
G	Geography-anthropology	T	Technology
H	Social sciences	U	Military science
J	Political science	V	Naval science
K	Law	Z	Bibliography and library science
L	Education		

Whatever the system, when consulting a card catalog, your task is to use its author, title, and subject cards to locate relevant books. Figure 14-1 is a sample title card.

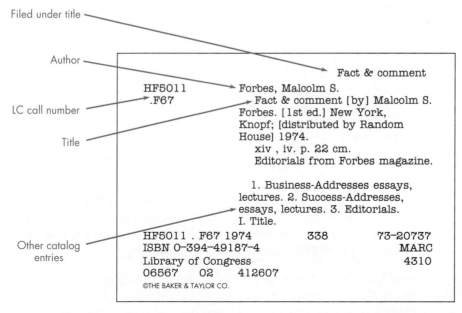

FIGURE 14-1
Title card.

In addition, if your library has an "open stack" policy, browse through other titles near those you've identified, because they too may contain information you can use.

REFERENCE WORKS

Since magazines, newspapers, and scholarly periodicals may contain information valuable to you, indexes are critical resources. One of the first indexes you will consult will probably be *The Reader's Guide to Periodical Literature*. It can lead you to a variety of popular and mass-distribution magazines, including *Time*, *Newsweek*, and *U.S. News & World Report*, all of which may contain information relevant to your subject. *The New York Times Index* and *The Wall Street Journal Index* are also high on the list of indexes you should consider. If your topic warrants it, you may also need to explore issues of *Education Index*, *Psychological Abstracts*, and *Sociological Abstracts*. These sources will offer you leads to articles that have appeared in a number of scholarly journals.

The *World Almanac*, *Statistical Abstract of the United States*, and *Information Please Almanac* are only three of many such reference works that can provide the speechmaker with interesting factual and statistical evidence. Multivolume encyclopedias, such as the *Britannica* and the *Americana*, and one-volume versions, such as the *Random House Encyclopedia* and the *Columbia Encyclopedia*, may also be consulted. Specialized encyclopedias such as the *McGraw-Hill Encyclopedia of Science and Technology* may be useful for technologically oriented topics.

Biographical materials can be located in the *Dictionary of National Biography*, the *Dictionary of American Biography*, and even *The New York Times Obituary Index*. Similarly, *Current Biography* can help you research the lives of contemporary public figures.

COMPUTER-AIDED SEARCHES

Computers and laser disks can facilitate your research. Many college libraries now have computerized card catalog systems that make the research process faster and more efficient. When you are looking for magazine articles, you can access *Reader's Guide to Periodical Literature*, *Magazine Index*, *Business Index*, and other bibliographic sources simply by pushing a button. *The New York Times* and the *Wall Street Journal* are just two of the newspapers covered by the electronic *National Newspaper Index*. If you are interested in computers, you may already be familiar with Compuserve, Prodigy, and other such services which provide researchers and consumers with valuable information.

More complex computer-assisted searches are routinely conducted by college reference librarians. Information is accessed through a large number of data bases available to librarians. Since these searches often require the payment of a fee and may take some time, you will want to be certain of your topic and of the specific information you need before using them.

If you have not visited your college library recently, now is the time to do so. You might ask your instructor to arrange to have the library staff give you a tour, or you may simply explore the library on your own or with other class members.

A CRIMINAL INVESTIGATION

1. Working individually within groups, choose a well-known crime to investigate. Possibilities for investigation include the Sam Shepherd case, the Jean Harris-Herman Tarnower ("diet doctor") case, the Sacco-Vanzetti case, the Charles Manson case, the Lee Harvey Oswald case, and the Bruno Hauptmann case.

2. Using the resources available in your library, compile a bibliography of relevant materials.

3. Rank the entries in your bibliography from 1 ("most promising") for what seems to be the most useful source, to 2 for the next most promising source, and so on down.

4. Compare your list with the lists developed by the other members of your group. Discuss the number of sources cited by each individual in your group, the most unusual material located, and the decisions you made in ranking your references.

Generating Your Own Information

You may also want to generate information to support or "flesh out" your presentation. Three primary techniques for generating your own information are (1) personal observation, (2) the survey, and (3) the interview.

PERSONAL OBSERVATION AND EXPERIENCE

One of the best ways to research a topic is to examine what you yourself know about it. Search your own background and experiences for materials you might want to integrate into your presentation.

If your topic is one for which direct observation of an event, person, or stimulus would be appropriate, then by all means go out and observe. An observational excursion might take you to a biology laboratory, an airport, a supermarket, or a construction site, for example. Direct observation can provide you with a better understanding of your topic and enable you to incorporate new personal experiences into your presentation in the form of examples, illustrations, or quotations. When conducting a direct observation, be sure to take careful notes. If possible, arrive at the location with tape recorder or video recorder in hand. Sit down immediately after the experience and record your thoughts and feelings. All your firsthand notes should be filed with the materials gathered during your library research.

INFORMAL SURVEYS

Developing a reliable scientific survey instrument is complicated. However, informal surveys can be used to provide the speechmaker with useful and often entertaining information. For example, if you are investigating the possibility of adding cable television courses to the curriculum, a survey at your school may produce data you can use. (For instance, you might be able to discover the percentage of students interested in enrolling for such courses.)

Ways of generating your own information include personal observation *(top)* **and surveys** *(bottom).*

Top, Geoffrey Nilsen/Photo Researchers; *bottom,* Rhoda Sidney/Monkmeyer

A SURVEY

1. Divide into groups. Each group should select a controversial topic.

2. Working together, develop a list of 5 to 10 questions about your chosen topic.

3. Each member of the group should proceed to a particular campus location where he or she will seek the cooperation of 5 to 10 people, asking each of them to answer the questionnaire that was devised in step 2.

4. Group members then come together and pool the information they have collected. Work out percentage responses for questions, if possible. (For example: "Thirty percent of those surveyed noted that they would not attend a televised course if given the choice.")

5. Present your results to the class.

6. How useful is this type of research? Of what value can it be to a speaker?

Informal surveys normally consist of no more than 5 to 10 questions. To conduct an informal survey with a prospect, you need to identify yourself first and state the purpose of your survey: "Hello, I'm ——. I'm investigating the feasibility of incorporating cable televised courses into the regular curriculum of the college." The survey can be conducted either orally or in writing. A sample of 25 to 50 people and some simple mathematical calculations should provide adequate statistical information to integrate into your presentation. When you conduct an informal survey, you may gain more than expected. While running the survey or examining the results, you may find interesting off-the-cuff remarks to incorporate in your speech.

INTERVIEWS

An interview is similar to a survey except that it is usually more detailed and assumes that the person being interviewed is in some way an expert on the topic under consideration. On your campus or in your community you will probably find knowledgeable people to interview about current issues and many other topics. Political, business, and religious leaders, for instance, can often be persuaded to talk to student speakers. And of course the faculty members of a college are often eager to cooperate.

Be advised that to obtain useful information, you must carefully analyze beforehand what it is you want to know. You must then ask your respondents specific questions that will provide the information you need to develop your speech. However, remember to allow your interviewees to talk freely when answering a question. Many responses are interesting in themselves or give rise to new, possibly exciting lines of questioning.

Be sure to record accurately the information gathered during an interview. Take careful notes and repeat or verify any direct quotations you intend to use in your presentation. Also be certain during the speech to credit the interviewee as your source, unless he or she has asked not to be mentioned by name.

Interviews conducted by professionals on radio or television can also provide you with useful expert information. Remember to check local listings for potentially interesting programs.

A Note on Recording Information

It is important to organize the information you collect so that it is easily retrievable and usable. We suggest that you buy a pack of 5-by-7-inch note cards to record the information you gather. For example, you might note the source of your data at the top of the card and write below that a direct quotation or summary of the information gathered. This procedure can be used for material derived from print, nonprint, survey, and interview sources. Also, since it's impossible to "make appointments" with ideas, you should plan to record any of your own thoughts in the same way. For instance, an idea about a possible format for your speech may occur to you. If so, write it down. Don't rely on your memory. Ideas that are not committed to paper are easily lost and often not easily found. During the process of gathering information and developing ideas, your stack of reference cards should continue to grow.

INTEGRATING YOUR RESEARCH: TYPES OF SUPPORTING MATERIAL

Taken together, your research and your experiences should yield a wealth of information to integrate into your presentation. But making your research and experiences "live" for an audience is not an easy task; in fact, it is a key challenge facing the speechmaker. Following are some major ways to make research and experience understandable and believable for an audience.[1]

Definitions

Choose a word for which people have different associations— for example, an abstract concept like *honesty, jealousy, freedom, justice,* or *love.* Write your own definition and share it with the class.

Definitions can be used to help explain what a stimulus is or what a word or concept means. It is especially important to use definitions when your listeners are unfamiliar with terms you are using or when their associations for words or concepts might differ from yours. Only if you explain *how you are defining a term* can you hope to share your meanings with your listeners. Thus, the purpose of a definition is to increase the audience's understanding.

For example, in a famous speech, "On Woman's Right to Suffrage," Susan B. Anthony took pains to define what she believed was meant by "we, the people": "It was we, the people, not we, the white male citizens; nor yet we, the male citizens; but we, the whole people who formed the union."

Statistics

Statistics are simply facts expressed in numerical form. They may be cited to explain relationships or to indicate trends. To be effective as support, statistics must be honest and credible. If used appropriately, they can make the ideas you are presenting memorable and significant.

For example, on a WNEW-TV program "Teenage Suicide: Don't Try It!" a speaker noted:

> The reason that we're talking about adolescent suicide is that it has grown 250 percent in the last 5 years in our country. It's a very, very serious problem. Today when we're together in the next hour, 57 of your peers will attempt to take their own life—will attempt to kill themselves. Fifty-seven in an hour. That's a lot. Eighteen of those kids your age will make it today. They'll die, and they'll die at their own hand.[2]

Statistics also added impact to a speech by Janeen Rohovit of Arizona State University:

> Each of us in this room stands a one-in-two chance of being killed or seriously injured in an automobile accident in our lifetime. According to the National Safety Council's publication *Accident Facts*, American teenage drivers manage to kill themselves and each other at a rate of nearly 10,000 every year. Indeed, automobile accidents are the number one cause of death for teenagers age 16 to 19 years old. And since we all share the roads, these young drivers manage to kill and injure their share of the rest of us as well.[3]

In the excerpt below, Russell Baker explains his view of how statistics are used in Washington.

▶ **POINTS TO PONDER**

POOR RUSSELL'S ALMANAC
Russell Baker

Numbers in Washington are much easier to understand than in most places because there are only five. There are (1) the million, (2) the hundred million, (3) the billion, (4) the trillion and (5) the megaton.

In counting, strangers are often confused by the Washington system of modifying numbers with the phrases "give or take," "estimated at" and "on the order of magnitude of." Each of these phrases significantly alters the number's value.

For example, "twenty billion give or take a billion" means that the final cost of, say a new excavation will probably not exceed the contractor's quoted price by more than three or four billion dollars.

By contrast, the expression "on the order of magnitude of twenty billion dollars" means that the excavation will cost approximately thirty billion dollars, while "estimated at twenty billion dollars" means the hole will probably cost between forty and fifty billion dollars.

In general, "on the order of magnitude of" increases the value of the number by 50 percent, and "estimated at" increases it on the order of magnitude of 100 percent.

Source: Russell Baker, from *Poor Russell's Almanac*, Congdon, New York, 1981.

■ ETHICS AND COMMUNICATION

HYPOTHETICAL EXAMPLES

Speakers use both factual and hypothetical examples and illustrations to involve audience members in a presentation. Examples and illustrations help make a speaker's material specific, personal, and compelling.

In your opinion, must speakers let audience members know when they are using hypothetical examples or illustrations? Do speakers have an obligation to let listeners know when material is not factual but merely possible? As an audience member, would you feel betrayed if a speaker used an example to add human interest and you discovered later that the example was not real?

Examples and Illustrations

Examples are representative cases; as such, they serve to specify particular instances.[4] *Illustrations*, on the other hand, tell stories and thus create more detailed narrative pictures. (See page 435 for effective use of an illustration.) Both examples and illustrations may be factual or hypothetical.

Jacqueline D. St. John, in a speech entitled "Reflections and Perspectives on the Women's Movement," used brief examples effectively to show that history—or the people who write history—had ignored women:

> How could such women as these be left out of revolutionary history? Margaret Cochran Corbin, "Captain Molly," who was buried with military honors at West Point; Deborah Sampson Gannet, who fought under the assumed name of Robert Shurtleff and served with the Fourth Massachusetts Regiment fighting against British, Tories, and Indians; and Mary Hays, "Molly Pitcher," who fired artillery cannons against Hessian and British troops.[5]

Kelly McInerney of Regis College in Colorado used an extended example to add impact to a speech on the horrors of ivory poaching:

> As the sun rises in Kenya, an elephant crosses the savanna to the edge of a water hole, its trunk raised to catch the first scent of danger. Satisfied that the way is clear, it signals and is joined by a companion. In greeting, the two twist their trunks together, flap their ears and hit tusk against tusk, sending a sharp cracking sound across the hills. That same crack of ivory can be heard 10,000 miles away in Hong Kong and Tokyo, where ivory traders stack tusk upon tusk—more than 800 tons laundered free of illegality.[6]

Testimonials

Whenever you cite someone else's opinions or conclusions, you are using *testimony* or a *testimonial*. Testimony gives you an opportunity to connect the ideas in your speech with the thoughts and attitudes of respected and competent people. The testimony you include in a presentation need not be derived exclusively from present-day sources; words of people from the past may also be used to tie today and yesterday together. When using testimonials, be sure to consider whether the people you cite as authorities are credible sources, whether their ideas are understandable, and whether their comments are relevant to your purpose.

In a speech on book censorship in the United States, one student explained her stand eloquently by quoting the Nobel Prize–winning author Aleksandr Solzhenitsyn:

> Woe to that nation whose literature is disturbed by the intervention of power. Because that is not just a violation against "freedom of print," it is the closing down of the heart of the nation, a slashing to pieces of its memory.

In a speech delivered before the House Judiciary Committee, Representative Barbara Jordan explained her stand on the impeachment of Richard Nixon by quoting James Madison: "If the President be connected in any suspicious manner with any person and there be grounds to believe that he will shelter him, he may be impeached."

As we see, testimony reinforces a speaker's claims. It may be quoted directly, as in the preceding examples; or it may be paraphrased, as in the following example. Gregory Solomon, a student at Northern Illinois University, used testimony in a speech called "The Maturing of the American Motorist" to support his position that we must be able to spot warning signs of declining skills among elderly drivers.[7] Referring to a recent research study, Solomon said:

> According to a 1988 study conducted by the National Research Board, when a driver reaches the age of 75, he or she is twice as likely as the average driver to be involved in an automobile accident, based upon miles driven. And once that driver reaches 80 the chances double again.

● CULTURE AND COMMUNICATION

EXPERTS AND CULTURAL GROUPS

If the testimony of others influences us in making decisions and assessing situations, then an audience's judgments about a public speaker—and about his or her speech—ought to be influenced by people the speaker quotes or refers to, who presumably have special knowledge or experience relevant to the topic.

In your opinion, does it matter whether a speaker uses experts from the same cultural group as the audience, or would experts from other cultural groups serve just as well in adding strength and impact to the speaker's ideas?

Explain your position.

Solomon added more support to his ideas by noting:

> According to Dr. Harvey Sterns, Director of the Institute for Life Span
> Development and Gerontology at Northeastern Ohio College of Medicine, after
> the age of 70 an individual's reflexes, vision and attention span—skills vitally
> important to driving—may all start to gradually diminish, or in some cases these
> skills may be lost abruptly.

Use direct quotations when you believe that the language and the length
of an expert's remarks are appropriate for your audience. Use a paraphrase
when you need to summarize an expert's opinion in fewer words, or when you
need to simplify its language.

Comparisons and Contrasts

Comparisons stress similarities between two entities; *contrasts* stress differences. Both are employed by speakers to help audiences understand something that is unknown, unfamiliar, or unclear.

William L. Laurence combined comparison and contrast when he described the atomic bombing of Nagasaki:

> As the first mushroom floated off into the blue, it changed its shape into a
> flower-like form, its grand petals curving downward, creamy white outside,
> rose-colored inside. . . . Much living substance had gone into those rainbows.
> The quivering top of the pillar was protruding to a great height through the
> white clouds, giving the appearance of a monstrous prehistoric creature with a
> ruff around its neck, a fleecy ruff extending in all directions, as far as the eye
> could see.[8]

Similarly, a spokesperson for Rockwell International used an analogy to explain
the amount of energy needed to launch a rocket into space:

> If you ran all the rivers and streams of America through steam turbines at the
> same time—you'd get only half of the 160 million horse-power that all five of the
> Saturn's F-1 engines generate.[9]

Gregory Solomon used similarities and differences to clarify his position on
closer scrutiny of elderly drivers:

> The Transportation Research Board of the National Research Council found that
> drivers over the age of 65 rank second, behind teenagers, in percentage of
> accidents per mile driven. So why aren't we concentrating on teens behind the
> wheel? There's one difference: teenagers will improve with experience and
> maturity, while the elderly's skills will only continue to diminish.[10]

President Ronald Reagan used comparison and contrast to eulogize the crew
of the ill-fated space shuttle *Challenger* in a speech to the nation on January 28,
1986:

There's a coincidence today. On this day 390 years ago, the great explorer Sir Francis Drake died aboard ship off the coast of Panama. In his lifetime the great frontiers were the oceans, and a historian later said, "He lived by the sea, died on it and was buried in it." Well, today we can say of the *Challenger* crew: Their dedication was, like Drake's, complete. The crew of the space shuttle *Challenger* honored us by the manner in which they lived their lives. We will never forget them nor the last time we saw them this morning as they prepared for their journey and waved goodbye and "slipped the surly bonds of earth to touch the face of God."

Repetition and Restatement

When a speaker uses *repetition*, the same words are repeated verbatim. When a speaker uses *restatement*, an idea is presented again, in different words. If used sparingly, these devices can add impact to a speechmaker's remarks and thereby increase memorability.[11]

One of the most famous examples of successful use of repetition is the speech delivered by Martin Luther King, Jr., in 1963 at the Lincoln Memorial:

I say to you today, my friends, so even though we face the difficulties of today and tomorrow, I still have a dream. It is a dream deeply rooted in the American dream. I have a dream that one day this nation will rise up . . . live out the true meaning of its creed—we hold these truths to be self-evident, that all men are created equal. . . .

I have a dream that my four little children will one day live in a nation where they will not be judged by the color of their skin but by the content of their character. I have a dream today. . . .

I have a dream that one day every valley shall be exalted, and every hill and mountain shall be made low, the rough places shall be made plain, and the crooked places shall be made straight and the glory of the Lord will be revealed and all flesh shall see it together.

 SKILL BUILDER

TYPES OF SUPPORT

Identify specific ways in which each of the following types of support could be integrated into one or more forthcoming class presentations.

1. Definition
2. Statistics
3. Examples and illustrations
4. Testimonials
5. Comparison and contrast
6. Repetition and restatement

Carolyn Lockwood, a student at Geneva College in Pennsylvania, used restatement and repetition to emphasize a call for involvement in helping those less fortunate than ourselves:

> The first three words of our United States Constitution are "We the People." We the people compose our government, one person at a time; and one person at a time, we can effect change. You might not think this penny is worth much, but I ask you: What is this dollar? Nothing more than one hundred pennies. This dollar would not be a dollar without this one penny; it would only be 99 cents. And just as this one penny is so crucial for this dollar being a dollar, so one person can make a difference.
>
> And you cannot tell me that one person cannot make a difference, for by just giving this speech, I have forced you to think of this issue for at least ten minutes.
>
> And you cannot tell me that one person cannot make a difference, when Florence Nightingale, a young girl, innovated the nursing profession by providing medical treatment for British soldiers during the Crimean War.
>
> When Dr. Ardell Thomas, a small-town doctor, had a vision of a low-cost boarding home for the elderly and founded the Lucy Austin Shared Home in Wellsboro, Pennsylvania.
>
> And when Lech Walesa, an electrician, fights for the cause of human rights in Poland. One person can definitely make a difference.[12]

H. Norman Schwarzkopf, former commander-in-chief of the United States Central Command, also knew the value of repetition. When he delivered his "Operation Desert Storm" speech before a joint session of Congress on May 8, 1991, he intoned:

> So, for every soldier: thank you, America. For every sailor: thank you, America. For every marine: thank you, America. For every airman: thank you, America. For every coast guardsman: thank you, America. From all of us who proudly served in the middle east in your armed forces, thank you to the great people of the United States of America.

ILLUSTRATING YOUR RESEARCH: PRESENTATION AIDS

The first question to ask yourself about audio and visual aids is, "Do I need them?" Many speakers make the mistake of not using such aids when the content really demands them. Other speakers use too many audio and visual aids; they clutter the content so much that the presentation becomes confusing and loses momentum. In this section we consider (1) how you can determine whether your presentation would be improved by audio and visual aids and (2) how you can select and prepare such aids when they are needed.

Why Use Presentation Aids?

Presentation aids have several functions. Ideally, they make it easier for the audience to follow, understand, respond to, and remember your speech. Thus when deciding whether to use an audio or visual aid, begin by asking yourself if it will serve at least one of these purposes.

MEDIA AIDS

Watch a 30-minute newscast, alone or with a group. As you watch the program, complete a chart like this one:

Date: _____

Newscast: _____

Time: _____

Audio and visual aids:

Aid	Purpose	Effect

You might determine, for example, that a film clip of a woman shopping in a supermarket was used to aid the viewer's understanding of inflation ("Purpose"). If you felt that this image was overused and trite, you would indicate this in the "Effect" column. On the other hand, you might determine that a graph showing a sharp increase in urban crime in the past 5 years added impact to the discussion; this too would be entered under "Effect."

Compare your observations with those of others in your class or group. Which aids used on television would have been equally effective if integrated into a speech? Were some audio or visual aids more appropriate for television than they would be for a live presentation? Why?

For example, if your presentation contains highly technical information, the use of an appropriate aid may help reduce your listeners' confusion. If the presentation needs additional impact, an audio or visual aid can help increase listeners' motivation. If you want to highlight an important point, an audio or visual can add emphasis. A three-dimensional model of the molecular structure of a virus might, for instance, evoke more interest than would words alone. The damage smoking does to a human lung can be depicted with visuals to capture the attention of smokers and nonsmokers alike. Audio and visual aids can also help an audience remember what you have said. A chart can dramatize statistical data, indicating, for instance, the number of infants who fall prey to sudden-death syndrome each year or symbolizing a decline in real income. By providing your audience with an additional "channel," audio and visual aids give needed reinforcement to key points and ideas.[13]

Selecting and creating materials to help accomplish your speechmaking goals is not easy.[14] Once you decide to use audio or visual aids, there are a number of serious decisions to be made. Initially, you will need to identify precise points in your presentation when aids will be effective. One way to prepare yourself to make such a judgment is to examine how producers of newscasts select audio and visual aids to complement the work of on-camera reporters. After all, in many ways you are the "producer" of your speech.

Another strategy is "material brainstorming." Examine the information you have and repeatedly ask yourself the following question: Which specific pieces of information could be improved with audio or visual aids?

Keep a record of each idea that comes to mind, being sure to indicate how the audio or visual support would actually be used.

Once you have analyzed your needs for audio and visual reinforcement, it is time to reconsider the possibilities you've identified.

TYPES OF VISUAL AIDS

Let's now examine a sampling of the types of visual aids at your disposal.

Objects and Models   In your brainstorming session, you may have decided that you would like to use an object to illustrate a certain concept. The object you choose can be the "real thing," for example, a set of earphones, a food processor, or a computer.

However, using an actual object is often impractical: objects like automobiles are obviously too large, and objects like microelectronic chips may be too small. In such cases it may be necessary to use a model instead. A model can be made of clay, papier-mâché, wood scraps, or other materials. If used creatively, inexpensive materials can serve your purpose very well. Your aim is simply to make a reasonable facsimile of the object—something that will enable you to share information more meaningfully.

In the following example, a speaker used objects—two oranges—to help explain the chemical properties of shrink-wrapping:

> In front of me are two oranges. One is wrapped in shrink-wrap. One is not. After this presentation I will take both oranges and put them on a windowsill in our classroom. I guarantee you that 2 months from now, the one that is not wrapped will have shrivelled up. It will be about the size of my thumb. The one that is shrink-wrapped will be the same size that it is today. Two months from now, I will cut both oranges open and I will take a bite out of the one that was shrink-wrapped. I am confident it will still taste as good as any orange I could purchase fresh in a supermarket.

Objects and models make it easier for you to pull your audience into your speech. Since they are tangible, they can make your points more realistic, and they can add drama to your presentation.

Graphs   You can use graphs to make an effective presentation even more successful. The most commonly used graphs are circle or pie graphs, bar graphs, line graphs, and pictographs.

A *pie graph* is simply a circle with the various percentages of the whole indicated by "wedges." By focusing on relationships, pie graphs show how items compare with each other and with the whole. Since the entire circle represents 100 percent, the pie graph is an effective way to show percentage relationships or proportions. In a speech on local systems of taxation, for example, one student used a pie graph to stress the large percentage of the municipal budget allocated to schools (see Figure 14-2).

If your goal is to show the performance of one variable over time, a *bar graph* might be appropriate (see Figure 14-3). Bar graphs can also be used to contrast various events at one point in time. In Figure 14-4, for example, a student compared rates of sexual harassment charges filed in four states and the District of Columbia. The bar graph clearly shows a wide discrepancy—from a rate of 7.25 per 100,000 population to a rate of 3.92.

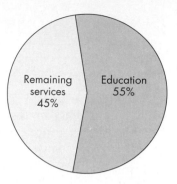

FIGURE 14-2
Pie graph.

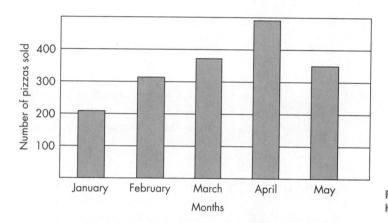

FIGURE 14-3
Hypothetical bar graph.

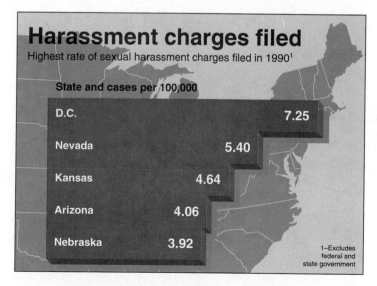

FIGURE 14-4
An actual bar graph.

Source: EEOC, Bureau of
the Census; from *USA
Today.*

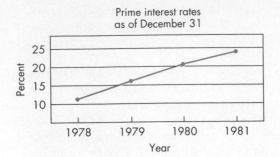

FIGURE 14-5
Line graph.

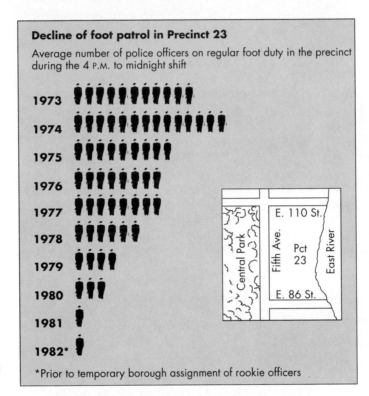

FIGURE 14-6
Pictograph.

Source: From "Decline of Foot Patrol Officers in Precinct 23." Copyright © 1982 by The New York Times Company. Reprinted by permission.

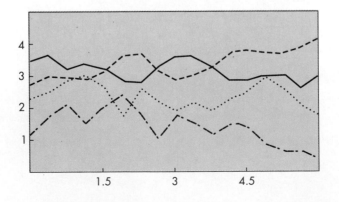

FIGURE 14-7
Poorly designed line graph.

Like bar graphs, line graphs can illustrate trends, relationships, or comparisons over time (see Figure 14-5). A line graph can show whether or not a perceptible trend is visible. The line graph is one of the easiest types for audiences to follow.

Pictographs utilize sketches of figures to represent a concept (see Figure 14-6). During your research, you may discover sketches or pictures that could be integrated into a pictograph to help vitalize your content.

The general rule to follow in making and using graphs is that a single graph should be used to communicate only one concept or idea. Consider the graph in Figure 14-7. Such a graph is far too "busy" or cluttered for an audience to read easily and quickly. Your goal in devising a graph is to eliminate extraneous information and to focus, rather than diffuse, the audience's attention. Emphasize the essentials.

Photographs and Drawings Finally, you may find photographs or drawings that can add interest or impact to your presentation and provide greater reality. For example, one student juxtaposed a photograph of the deceased singer Karen Carpenter (taken from the cover of a national weekly magazine) with one of her own sister to illustrate that anorexia nervosa is a disease afflicting both famous and ordinary people.

Drawings, like photographs, can help generate a mood, clarify, or identify. In explaining a sequence of plays that led to a success for his football team, one speaker used a sketch like the drawing in Figure 14-8. Would you recommend simplifying this sketch?

If possible, use a variety of dark, rich colors like red, black, blue, and green to add contrast to a drawing. But remember, unless a drawing is large enough to be seen, it will not increase your audience's attention or strengthen your presentation.

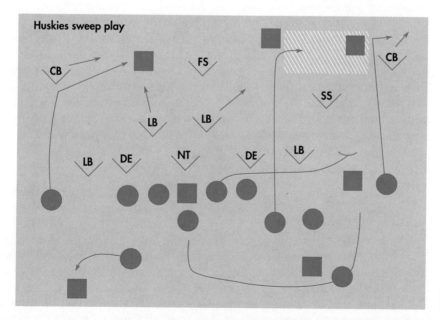

FIGURE 14-8
Drawing.

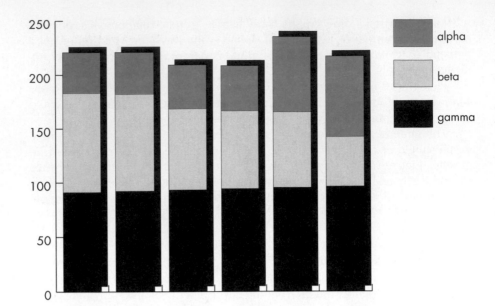

FIGURE 14-9
Computer-generated
graph.

Computer Graphics   Recent advances in computer technology make it possible for speechmakers to use computer-generated visual aids. Most college speakers have traditionally used poster board and marking pens to enlarge charts and graphs so that they can be easily seen, but now computer graphics hardware and software are making it easier and easier for students to develop professional-looking charts and graphs.

For IBM systems with at least 512K of memory, Harvard Graphics is one of the more sophisticated programs available. The program provides model charts and graphs; you input your own data and then make a printout. You can print on a transparency and use the graphic with an overhead projector. The leading program available for Macintosh users is *Persuasion*. It works much like *Harvard Graphics* and also produces high-quality graphics. Figure 14-9 shows samples of graphics generated by *Persuasion* and *Harvard Graphics*. Either system takes some "up front" time to learn. If you are "computer-literate" and learn quickly, you can probably experiment with graphics programs that your school has available. But be sure to have a backup plan for poster board and markers in case the computer turns out to be too time-intensive.

GUIDELINES FOR USING VISUAL AIDS

Criteria   When evaluating visuals, remember that they must be appropriate to the audience, the occasion, the location, and the content of your speech—and to you yourself.

In developing visual materials, keep these three criteria in mind: (1) simplicity, (2) clarity, (3) visibility. By *simplicity* we mean that the visuals should be as transportable as possible (so that you can easily bring them with you to the presentation) and as easy as possible to use. Give careful consideration to the size and weight of large items. Ask yourself if a visual can be displayed without disrupting the environment. Ask yourself if it can be set up and taken down in a minimum amount of time. With regard to *clarity*, remember that the purpose of a visual aid is to enhance understanding, not to cause confusion. Ideally each visual should depict only one idea or concept, or at least should be displayed so that only the relevant portions are visible at the appropriate point in your speech. *Visibility* is the third criterion. Since a visual aid obviously serves no purpose if it cannot be seen and read, you must determine if your audience will be able to see and read it. Make sure that lettering is tall enough (¾ inch high or larger) and that photographs or pictures are large enough.

Methods and Equipment   The most popular way to present "flat" visuals is to display them on a chartboard or on oaktag. Given a number of variously colored felt markers, a yardstick, and a little time, you should be able to create appealing and functional visuals. If you are willing to invest a bit more time, energy, and money, the "press-on" letters that are widely available in stationery stores can give your work a professional look. You may also use more sophisticated equipment to present visuals—overhead projectors, film, videotape, and 35-mm slides. Overhead projectors are often used by training professionals and salespeople. Transparencies can be created from almost any 8½- by 11-inch original of a photograph, illustration, or graph. Then the image can be projected onto a screen or a light-colored wall (if no screen is available). The room need not be completely darkened to use an overhead projector, but be sure to rehearse with transparencies, to be sure they are clearly visible. (Setup time is about 10 minutes.)

Film clips can also be used to add life and motion to a presentation. For film, you need a screen or light-colored wall in a room that can be darkened. It will take about 15 minutes to prepare the room and equipment. Without adequate setup time, a film clip can become more of a hindrance than a help.

Slides are easier to use than film. However, we suggest that unless you have been trained in multimedia or multi-image production, the number of slides you use should be kept to a minimum. (Also, be prepared to deal with jammed slide trays and burned-out bulbs.)

Videotape recorders have improved greatly in recent years and make it much easier for speakers to use videos and film clips. Video stores have many tapes that can be used to arouse audiences' interest. One speaker used a clip of Abbott and Costello's "Who's on First?" routine to introduce the topic of language. A speaker on real estate used examples from a local real estate program on cable television. A company president regularly uses clips from the various *Rocky* films to motivate the sales force. The channel C-Span makes it convenient to incorporate current events into speeches. If your topic is current, check the C-Span listings—if they are available in your area—to determine if and when the topic will be covered. Then, in addition to quoting a public official, you can actually have him or her as a "video guest" to briefly illustrate a point.

When using videotape, carefully edit the segment to 30 seconds or less and cue up the tape before you begin the speech. Far too many speakers press the "play" button only to find that they have no picture or sound on the monitor. One speaker we heard recently had scarcely begun his presentation before he had to call a coffee break while repairs were done on the video equipment. Audiences today are simply not willing to sit while you and others tinker with electronic gadgetry. Prepare it carefully in advance, and rehearse.

Audio Aids

Audiotape is readily available and easy to use as an accompaniment to a speech. Cassette players come in a variety of forms and sizes, many of which are easily portable. Since speechmakers often find it advantageous to integrate a brief excerpt from a song or a segment from an interview or newscast into their presentations, audiotape has become a popular support medium. One student, for example, reinforced an informative presentation entitled "The Speech Capabilities of Dolphins" with a few moments of dolphin sounds that she had recorded during a visit to an aquarium. Another added impact to a speech called "Teenage Runaways" by using a segment of the Beatles' song "She's Leaving Home."

If you decide to use audiotape, cue the tape to the precise point at which you want to begin. Do this before you arrive at the front of the room, so that "finding the right spot" on the tape will not bring your presentation to an untimely halt.

To conclude: once you have decided on your topic and conducted your research, it's time to begin to think actively about integrating presentation aids into your speech. There is little doubt that a well-chosen, well-designed visual or audio aid can add interest and impact to your message.

IMPROVING YOUR ABILITY TO SUPPORT YOUR IDEAS

A speech devoid of support is like a skeleton; the structure is there, but the flesh is missing. By developing an understanding of the way support functions to "flesh out" ideas, you increase your chances of becoming a proficient speaker. Speakers who are adept at finding and using support realize the following:

1. Support rarely if ever surfaces on its own. You need to search for it by examining yourself, other people, and published materials.
2. In order for ideas to affect listeners, the audience's imagination must be stirred. Supportive devices can serve this function. Definitions, statistics, examples and illustrations, testimonials, comparison and contrast, and repetition and restatement can all be used to make spoken words more understandable and more believable, and to give them greater impact.
3. Audio and visual aids can also be used to enhance the effectiveness of a presentation. If appropriately designed and integrated, they will increase listeners' comprehension, retention, and motivation.

SUMMARY

The first step in the topic development stage of preparing a speech is to gather a variety of effective research materials to integrate into your presentation. You may consult published works, including books, journals, magazines, and newspapers available in the library. You may be able to draw on your own personal observations and experiences. You can also interview other people or conduct a survey.

Depending on the nature of your topic, you can make your research interesting and understandable to your audience by using various kinds of verbal support: definitions, statistics, examples and illustrations, testi-

monials (quotations), and comparisons and contrasts. You can often increase the impact and memorability of your speech by using repetition and restatement. You can use either factual or hypothetical examples when developing ideas.

Many speeches can be enhanced with visual and audio support. Objects, models, graphs, photographs, drawings, slides, videotapes, and audiotapes can be incorporated into the presentation to reinforce, clarify, and dramatize concepts. Computer graphics programs are now making professional-looking graphics available even to student speakers.

SUGGESTIONS FOR FURTHER READING

Brandt, Richard C.: *Flip Charts: How to Draw Them and How to Use Them*, University Associates, San Diego, Calif., 1986. Excellent techniques for designing, using, and storing flip-chart visuals for business presentations.

Ehninger, Douglas, Bruce Gronbeck, Ray McKerrow, and Alan Monroe: *Principles and Types of Speech Communication*, HarperCollins, New York, 1992. An excellent overview of the speech support process.

Nelson, Robert B., and Jennifer Wallich: *Making Effective Presentations*, Scott, Foresman, Glenview, Ill.,

1991. A concise look at the process of designing speeches for the business environment.

Todd, Alden: *Finding Facts Fast*, Ten Speed Press, Berkeley, Calif., 1979. A readable and usable tool; guaranteed to save you time.

Wilder, Claudyne: *The Presentation Kit*, Wiley, New York, 1990. Offers many suggestions for increasing the effectiveness of presentations.

Zelazny, Gene: *Say It with Charts*, Irwin, Homewood, Ill., 1991. Guidelines for improving presentations. Contains an abundance of charts to use as models for your own work.

NOTES

1. For a more comprehensive treatment of supporting materials, see Douglas Ehninger, Alan Monroe, and Bruce Gronbeck, *Principles and Types of Speech Communication*, 8th ed., Scott, Foresman, Glenview, Ill., 1978, chap. 7.
2. "Teenage Suicide: Don't Try It!" WNEW Television, New York, December 10, 1981.
3. Janeen Rohovit, "One in Two," in *Winning Orations*, Interstate Oratorical Association, Mankato, Minn., 1990, p. 8.
4. For a discussion of the power of examples in public speaking, see Scott Consigny, "The Rhetorical Example," *Southern Speech Communication Journal*, vol. 41, 1976, pp. 121–134.
5. Jacqueline D. St. John, "Reflections and Perspectives on the Women's Movement," speech presented in Washington, D.C., 1976.
6. Kelly McInerney, "Ivory Tusks: White Gold," in *Winning Orations*, p. 15.

7. Gregory Solomon, "The Maturing of the American Motorist," in *Winning Orations*, p. 26.
8. William Laurence (student, New York Institute of Technology), speech 1023, presented 1983.
9. Provided by Rockwell International, 1988.
10. Solomon, op. cit.
11. The power of restatement is explained in a study by R. Ehrensberger, "An Experimental Study of the Relative Effects of Certain Forms of Emphasis in Public Speaking," *Speech Monographs*, vol. 12, 1945, pp. 94–111.
12. Carolyn Lockwood, "The Buck Stops Here," in *Winning Orations*, 1990, p. 98.
13. For a discussion of research that reveals how visual aids increase recall, see W. Linkugel and D. Berg, *A Time to Speak*, Wadsworth, Belmont, Calif., 1970.
14. For a work on how to prepare and use visual aids, see James W. Brown, Richard B. Lewis, and Fred F. Harcleroad, *AV Instruction: Techniques, Media and Methods*, McGraw-Hill, New York, 1973.

DESIGNING YOUR SPEECH: ORGANIZING YOUR IDEAS

After finishing this chapter, you should be able to:

Explain how the principle of redundancy affects communication
Describe the basic framework for any speech
Identify main and subordinate ideas
Create a complete sentence outline
Identify five methods of ordering ideas
Use internal summaries and transitions effectively
Develop an effective introduction
Develop an effective conclusion
Use a tryout to refine a speech

Every speech ought to be put together like a living creature, with a body of its own, so as to be neither without head nor without feet, but to have both a middle and extremities, described proportionately to each other and to the whole.

Plato

You can have the best ideas in the world and the most impressive and eye-opening support, but if you are unable to organize your ideas and integrate your support so that the audience can follow what you're trying to communicate, you might as well not speak at all. Organization is one of the main challenges you will have to face as a speechmaker. It is the second step in the topic development stage of preparing a speech.

What is your goal when you are organizing ideas? Primarily, you want to order your materials in such a way that communication between you and your audience will be facilitated. How can you accomplish this? You must plan. Just as an architect develops a plan for a building, so you must develop a plan for your speech. Your plan shows the structure you will adhere to—the developmental sequence you think will work best. Of course, just as an architect considers numerous designs before selecting one, you should test potential patterns to determine which one will best clarify and amplify your ideas. Fortunately, you do not have to grope your way through a thicket of possibilities. Communication theorists have developed guidelines to help you with this phase.

BUILDING THE FRAMEWORK: A BASIC FORMAT

Because of the nature of a speech, it is usually impossible for an audience to go back over the material and reexamine it. Your listeners need to be able to comprehend your message the first time they hear it, because they will probably never hear it again. There is no "rewind" button for audiences to push if they become distracted or confused. Speakers must therefore structure their messages so that confusion is kept to a minimum.[1]

As we saw in Chapter 6, not everyone is a skillful listener. For this reason, we advise you to base your organization on the *principle of redundancy*. In other words, to ensure comprehension, you will need to build a certain amount of repetition into your speech. Only if this is done will listeners be able to follow your ideas easily. This basic developmental principle is often expressed as follows: *Tell them what you are going to tell them, then tell them, and finally, tell them what you have told them.*

One of the best ways to organize a speech is the *introduction-body-conclusion format* (see Figure 15-1, page 366). We refer to this format as a *speech framework*, because it provides a frame or skeleton on which any speech or formal presentation can be built.

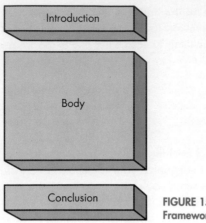

FIGURE 15-1
Framework for a speech.

Any speech you develop should be organized according to this framework. Your introductory remarks and your concluding statements should each take up approximately 10 to 15 percent of the total presentation. This leaves 70 to 80 percent of your time for developing the ideas contained in the body of your speech. Since the body will be the main portion of your presentation, it is often advisable to begin by preparing this part of the speech; once the body is set, you can move on to develop the introduction and the conclusion. Let's consider the three key parts of a speech in that order: body, introduction, conclusion.

THE BODY OF YOUR PRESENTATION

Outlining: Identifying Main and Subordinate Ideas

As you begin to organize the body of your speech, you must think in terms of a logical structure for your ideas. Your audience will be unlikely to recall a long, wandering, unstructured collection of data. In examining the evidence you have gathered, you will need to distinguish between your main ideas and your subordinate ideas. By *subordinate*, we mean those ideas which function as amplification for more important ones. In many ways, subordinate ideas can be viewed as the base or the foundation on which larger ideas are constructed (see Figure 15-2). Consequently, you should begin the organizational process

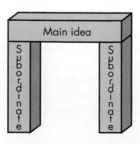

FIGURE 15-2
Construction of an idea.

by arranging your materials into "clusters" of main and subordinate ideas. As you do this, you will be able to determine which evidence supports the main ideas and which supports the subordinate ideas.

Your main ideas will be, say, two to five major points that you want the audience to remember. If, for example, you want listeners to recall three significant outcomes of World War II, those outcomes should be the three major points in your speech. One way to begin to structure your research material is to state your specific purpose and your thesis and put the main ideas in numbered boxes just below them.

Specific purpose: _____

Thesis: _____

I	II	III

For example, if you are developing a speech on computer viruses, you might begin as follows:

Purpose: To inform the audience about computer viruses.

Thesis: The audience will understand what a computer virus is, how it is spread, and how it can be prevented.

I	II	III
Definition of computer virus	Spread of computer viruses	Preventive measures

You are now off to a good start. Next, you need to develop these major points into complete sentences, using parallel structure.

   I. Computer viruses can be defined in two ways.
  II. Computer viruses are spread by people and machines.
III. Computer viruses can be prevented in three ways.

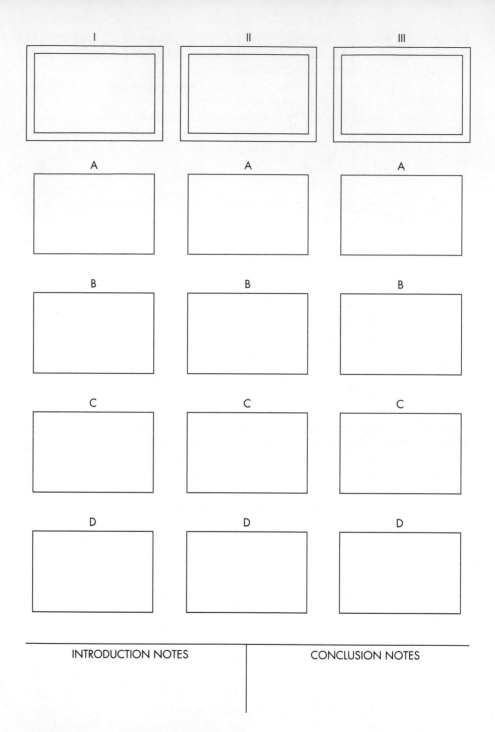

INTRODUCTION NOTES   CONCLUSION NOTES

FIGURE 15-3
Presentation planning
worksheet.

Many people find it helpful to develop material using a system like the one shown in Figure 15-3 above. Here we see the entire process with places to "plug in" information contained in the main idea and the supporting ideas. Once you have completed such a structure, you are ready to develop a more traditional outline.

As you continue pulling clusters together, arrange them like this:

I. Main idea
  A. Subordinate idea
    1. Sub-subordinate idea
    2. Sub-subordinate idea
  B. Subordinate idea
    1. Sub-subordinate idea
    2. Sub-subordinate idea

If you have taken notes on cards, you can "lay out" or "pattern" the body of your speech in the following way:

Purpose statement

I. Main idea
  A. (Supports I)
    1. (Supports A)
    2. (Supports A)
    3. (Supports A)
  B. (Supports I)
    1. (Supports B)
    2. (Supports B)

II. Main idea
  A. (Supports II)
  B. (Supports II)

Notice that the outline you develop indicates the relative importance of each item included in it. The main points—roman numerals I, II, III, and so on—are the most important items you want your audience to remember. Your subpoints—capital letters A, B, C, etc.—are supportive of but less important than the main points. Likewise, sub-subpoints—Arabic numbers 1, 2, 3, etc.—are supportive of but less important than subpoints.

A final outline, using symbols and indentations, would look like this:

Purpose: To inform audience members about myths and realities concerning acquired immune deficiency syndrome (AIDS).

I. Several myths about the disease AIDS are prevalent in society today.
  A. Many people believe that they can contract AIDS by touching objects an infected person has recently touched.
    1. They use handkerchiefs to open doorknobs.
    2. They wear gloves to handle money.
    3. They will not sit on toilet seats.
  B. Others are afraid to touch people they suspect could have the disease.
    1. They avoid shaking hands.
    2. Kissing is out of the question.
    3. They avoid coming into contact with someone who is crying.

II. Much is known about how AIDS is actually spread.
  A. When the virus is dry, it is dead.
  B. It doesn't live long when exposed to air.
  C. The disease is transmitted by exposure to the semen or blood of an infected person through a break in the skin.

LAY IT ALL OUT

1. For practice, record each of the following items on a 3- by 5-inch card.

   Barry W. Keenan and Joseph Amsler kidnapped Frank Sinatra, Jr., from his hotel room in Lake Tahoe on December 8, 1963.

   C. Burke Elbrick, U.S. ambassador to Brazil, was kidnapped by revolutionaries on September 4, 1969.

   Children of wealthy people are easy prey for kidnappers.

   Lt. Colonel Donald J. Crowley, United States air attaché in the Dominican Republic, was kidnapped by terrorists.

   J. Paul Getty, 3d, grandson of an American oil mogul, was kidnapped by people who demanded $2.8 million in exchange for his life.

   Kidnapping victimizes the rich.

   Kidnapping victimizes the famous.

   Patricia Hearst was kidnapped by members of the Symbionese Liberation Army, who demanded that her father, Randolph Hearst, donate $2 million in food to the poor.

   Daniel A. Mitrione, an American diplomat to Uruguay, was abducted by terrorists who demanded the release of political prisoners.

   An Exxon executive living in Campana, Argentina, was kidnapped by Marxist guerrillas.

   Terrorist organizations have used kidnapping to publicize their varied causes.

   Kidnappers prey on the rich, the famous, and those they perceive to be in a position to help further their political ends.

   Charles A. Lindbergh, Jr., son of the famous aviator, was abducted and eventually killed by kidnappers who demanded a $50,000 ransom.

2. Lay the cards out on a large table or some other open surface. After examining various options, develop a purpose statement. Then arrange the items into a main idea and subordinate ideas. Note: You need not use all the cards. Select only those which support your purpose statement and main idea.

3. Compare your layout with other students' arrangements.

4. Last, you should put the information into the standard outline form given in the text.

Ordering Your Ideas: Finding the Right Approach

Obviously, the ideas in your speech should be ordered in a way that will make sense to your audience. There are five generally accepted approaches to ordering material: (1) chronological, or time, order, (2) spatial order, (3) cause-effect order, (4) problem-solution order, and (5) topical order. We will examine each in turn.

CHRONOLOGICAL ORDER

Chronological, or time, order involves developing an idea or a problem in the order in which it occurs or occurred in time.

For example, one student used chronological order to describe the events that resulted in the elephant's becoming an endangered species.

Purpose statement: To explain why the elephant is becoming an endangered species.

I. Until the early 1900s, elephants had little reason to fear people.
II. During the 1920s, elephants were slaughtered as the demand for ivory products increased in the United States and Europe.
III. Within the past 20 years, products made from ivory have also come to be prized in the far east.

As you can see, this student has considered the steps leading up to the present situation in the order in which they occurred. Another student used chronological order for a speech on the insanity defense.

Purpose statement: To examine the history of the insanity defense in criminal jurisprudence.

I. In the seventeenth and eighteenth centuries, belief in witchcraft influenced popular legal conceptions of mental disorder.
II. The nineteenth-century showcase for the insanity defense was the trial of Daniel M'Naghten, a political assassin.
III. Not until 1954 did the courts begin to acknowledge that a wide variety of diseases or defects may impair the mind.
IV. In 1982, the John Hinckley case and the public's reactions to it again raised questions regarding our attitude toward crime, punishment, and personal responsibility.

Any event that has occurred in time can be examined chronologically. With a time-ordered presentation, it is up to you to decide where to begin and end your chronology and what events to include. As you might expect, time order is most often used in informative speeches.

SPATIAL ORDER

Spatial order describes an object, a person, or a phenomenon as it exists in space. An object, for example, might be described from

Top to bottom
Bottom to top
Left to right
Right to left
Inside to outside
Outside to inside

The point is that you must select one orientation and carry it through.

Think of three topics you could develop using chronological order. Why do they lend themselves to that arrangement?

How could you use spatial order to describe yourself? (For practice, try it.)

Ideas in a speech can be ordered in any of several ways, depending on what will make most sense to the audience. Spatial order describes an object as it exists in space; how might this speaker describe the object spatially?

Cary Wolinsky/Stock, Boston

One student used spatial order to explain the appearance and functioning of a beehive:

I. Outside the hive
II. Inside the hive

Another student used spatial order to describe the interior design of the White House:

I. The entrance is a study in perspective.
II. The first floor is a study in contrasts.
III. The second floor, containing the living quarters, is a study in the personality of the occupant.

Like chronological order, spatial order is used most frequently in informative speeches.

 SKILL BUILDER

SPEAKER'S CHOICE

1. Find a rock, a shell, a piece of driftwood, or some other natural object.
2. Describe the object to a partner, a group of students, or the entire class, using spatial order.
3. Explain why your spatial ordering took the form it did.
4. Would approaching the object from a different angle have altered your audience's understanding and appreciation? How?

Visuals can be used effectively to reinforce information contained in a spatially ordered presentation—whether you intend to discuss the components of a computer, the terrain of a national park, the design of a new car, or the floor plan of a house or apartment. Using spatial order involves organizing your ideas according to an "area concept," which should be reflected in the main points of the outline.

CAUSE-AND-EFFECT ORDER

Cause-and-effect order requires you to categorize your material into things related to the causes of a problem and things related to its effects. It is then up to you to decide which aspect you will explore first. Thus, in a speech on drunk driving, you might begin by discussing the percentage of drivers during a certain period who were drunk when involved in car accidents (cause). You might then discuss the number of deaths each year that are attributed directly to drunk driving (effect).

One student used cause-effect order in a speech on obesity, first discussing the physiological and psychological causes of obesity and then considering the health-related effects of being overweight:

I. Obesity appears to have several causes, some physical and some psychological.
II. Obesity can have adverse effects on health.

You can vary this approach by discussing the effect before the cause. In the following example, a student used effect-cause order to reveal the causes of excessive stress among students:

I. The number of students suffering from stress-related ailments is increasing at an alarming rate.
II. Experts on such ailments have identified four major explanations for this increase.

As you can see, cause-effect order and effect-cause order are quite versatile. They are used in both informative and persuasive speeches.

How could you use cause-and-effect order to explain a recent disagreement you had with an instructor, an employer, a friend, or a family member?

PROBLEM-AND-SOLUTION ORDER

Problem-and-solution order requires you to (1) determine what problems are inherent in a situation and (2) present a solution to remedy them. Thus you might discuss the problems that develop when many students entering college are deficient in writing skills. The second portion of your speech could then suggest a number of ways in which the identified problem could be alleviated (perhaps, for example, by expanding tutoring programs or offering noncredit remedial courses). If you wanted to speak about increased crime in your community using problem-and-solution order, your first task might be to establish in the minds of your listeners that a problem does indeed exist. From there you could proceed to suggest various solutions.

■ ETHICS AND COMMUNICATION

SOUND BITES

"Hey, do you want to be on the news tonight or not? This is a sound bite, not the Gettysburg Address. Just say what you have to say, Senator, and get the hell off."

Drawing by Ziegler; © 1989 The New Yorker Magazine, Inc.

In your opinion, are "sound bites"—public presentations of positions that usually last no more than 90 seconds—an effective way of informing the electorate? Why or why not?

How organized must a speaker be to present ideas or urge action in this manner? What organizational format do you believe lends itself best to this type of presentation? Is 90 seconds or less enough time to deliver a message designed not just to inform, but to influence? Explain your position.

One student used problem-and-solution order to argue that her state should raise the legal drinking age to 21:

I. The problems caused by intoxicated teenagers are increasing.
II. Raising the legal drinking age to 21 will do much to alleviate the situation.

Problem-and-solution order is most frequently employed in persuasive speeches.

TOPICAL ORDER

At times, a speech may not fit neatly into any of the patterns described above. When this happens, you may choose to develop or cluster your material by dividing it into a series of appropriate topics. This is topical order. Examples of topical order include the following categorical arrangements: advantages and disadvantages of a proposal; social, political, and economic factors that contribute to a problem; perceptions of upper-class, middle-class, and lower-class people on an issue. When you use topical order, you may find that you can integrate or intermingle cause-and-effect, time, problem-and-solution, or spatial order with it.

One student used topical order to explain various factors that shape attitudes toward abortion:

I. The family is a prime influence on attitudes.
II. Religious groups play a role.
III. Economic pressures also have an effect.

Another student used topical order to argue in favor of shield laws (laws that protect journalists from having to reveal their sources):

I. Shield laws protect the public's right to know.
II. Shield laws protect the reporter from having to serve as an informer.

Because of its wide applicability, topical order is used very frequently.

Selecting an appropriate order is an important factor in whether your speech will be successful. Just as fashion designers must create an exciting pattern or design, you must select an appealing pattern for your presentation.

Connecting Your Ideas: Internal Summaries and Transitions

In order to transmit your ideas to an audience with clarity and fluidity, it will be necessary for you to discover ways to move from one idea to the next. To do this, you must become acquainted with internal summaries and transitions.

The body of the speech should contain brief, internal summaries; these are designed to help listeners remember the content. Examples: "Thus far we have examined two key housing problems. Let us now consider a third." "The four characteristics we have discussed thus far are . . . ." Besides helping the audience recall the material, transitional words or phrases serve to facilitate the speaker's movement from one idea to another; in effect, they bridge gaps between ideas, so that there are no abrupt switches.[2]

To indicate that additional information is forthcoming, you might use transitional words and phrases such as *equally important, next, second, furthermore, in addition*, and *finally*. To signal that you will be discussing a cause-effect relationship, you could use expressions like *as a result* and *consequently*. To indicate that there is a contrasting view to the one being elaborated, you would use phrases such as *after all, in spite of, on the other hand*, and *and yet*. To indicate that you are summing up or recapitulating briefly, you can say *in short*. Expressions such as *likewise* and *similarly* signal that a comparison will be made. Phrases like *for example* and *for instance* let the listeners know that a point will be illustrated.

BEGINNINGS AND ENDINGS

Once you've outlined the body of your speech and considered the need for transitional devices, you are ready to "tell them what you are going to tell them" and "tell them what you have told them." In other words, it's time to develop your introduction and conclusion.[3]

The Introduction

FUNCTIONS OF THE INTRODUCTION

Use brainstorming to devise a number of ways you could introduce yourself to a group of people you don't know.

The function of your introduction is to gain the attention of the audience members, make them want to listen to your speech, and provide them with an overview of the subject you will be discussing. The art of designing introductions is much like any other art; that is, it requires creative thinking. You will need to examine your purpose, the speech itself as you have developed it, your analysis of the audience, and your own abilities.

All too frequently, the introduction is overlooked or neglected because speakers are in too much of a hurry to get to the "heart of the matter." However, in public speaking, just as in interpersonal communication, first impressions count. The opening moments of contact, with one person or with a multitude, can affect the developing relationship either positively or negatively. Unquestionably the first few moments of your speech—the introduction—will affect your audience's willingness to process the remainder. It is at this point that people will decide whether what you have to say is interesting and important or dull and inconsequential. If your introduction is poorly designed, your audience may "tune you out" for the remainder of your speech. On the other hand, a well-designed introduction can help you develop a solid rapport with the audience and thus will make it easier for you to share your thoughts.

The material you include in your introduction must be selected with care. Since in all likelihood your listeners have not been waiting in line for several days to hear you speak, you will need to work to spark their interest; you will need to motivate them to listen to you. Student speakers sometimes go overboard in trying to accomplish this objective. Some have been known to yell or

● CULTURE AND COMMUNICATION

IS PAYING ATTENTION CULTURAL?

Edward T. Hall suggests that "Culture . . . designates what we pay attention to and what we ignore." If this is so, how can speakers ensure that audience members who belong to other cultural groups will pay attention to the right things? In other words, how can speakers "target" crucial ideas and emphasized points? How can a speaker be sure that listeners are not paying attention to the wrong thing and screening out what they should be concentrating on?

Source: Edward T. Hall, *The Hidden Dimension*, Doubleday, New York, 1966.

throw books across the room; in one recent case, a student fired a blank from a starter pistol. Such devices are certainly attention-getters; but startling an audience can turn your listeners against you. (After all, it is difficult to listen to ideas or evaluate content if you fear for your own safety.) Other speakers look for a joke—*any* joke—to use as an attention-getter. Unfortunately, a joke chosen at random is seldom related to the topic and thus can confuse or even alienate listeners rather than interest and involve them. (A well-chosen anecdote, however, can be very effective.) Some speakers insist on beginning with statements like "My purpose here today is . . ." or "Today, I hope to convince you . . ." Such openings suggest mainly that the speechmaker has forgotten to consider motivation and attention.

Consider this. Years ago, television shows began simply by flashing the title of the program onto the screen. Today, however, it is common to use a "teaser" to open a show. The teaser usually reveals segments of the show designed to arouse the interest of potential viewers—to encourage them to "stay tuned." Without this device, many viewers would probably switch channels. Your listeners, of course, cannot "switch" speakers, but they can decide not to listen *actively* to what you have to say. Therefore, you too must design a teaser to include in your introduction—material that will interest and appeal to your audience.

TYPES OF INTRODUCTIONS

Effective speechmakers begin in a number of different ways. They may relate an unusual fact, make a surprising statement, or cite shocking statistics. Or they might ask a question, compliment the audience, or refer to the occasion. Sometimes they will use a humorous story or illustration as a lead-in. Sometimes they rely on a suspenseful story or a human interest story to capture their listeners' attention. Audiences respond to stories about people. For this reason, the plight of a family left homeless by a fire might be used effectively to open a speech on fire prevention, and a description of people severely injured in an automobile accident might introduce a speech supporting the use of air bags. If you have selected a topic because you have a personal interest in it, you can use a personal anecdote to begin your presentation. Let us examine a few examples of these various approaches.

Some of the most effective introductions use *humor*, as in the following examples—the first from a speech by former president Ronald Reagan; and the second from a speech by a commissioner, Barbara Franklin:

> The story is that there was an agent overseas who happened to be in Ireland and there was an emergency and it was necessary to contact him immediately. So they called in another agent and they said, "Now, you'll go there. His name is Murphy and your recognition will be to say, " 'Tis a fair day but it'll be lovelier this evening.' "
>
> So he went to Ireland and—a little town in Ireland, into the pub, elbowed himself up to the bar, ordered a drink and then said to the bartender, "How would I get in touch with Murphy?"
>
> And the bartender says, "Well, if it's Murphy the farmer you want, it's two miles down the road and it's the farm on the left." He said, "If it's Murphy the bootmaker, he's on the second floor of the building across the street. And," he says, "my name is Murphy."
>
> So he picked up the drink and he said, "Well, 'tis a fair day, but it'll be lovelier this evening."
>
> "Oh," he said, "it's Murphy the spy you want."[4]

> As a federal regulator, I accept speaking engagements these days with more and more trepidation. The trepidation turns to outright fear as the day of the speech arrives and the experience of Winston Churchill comes to mind.
>
> On one of his trans-Atlantic tours, a student asked, "Mr. Churchill, doesn't it thrill you to know that every time you make a speech the hall is packed to overflowing?"
>
> Churchill pondered the question for a moment. Then he replied, "Of course, it is flattering. But always remember that if I were being hanged, the crowd would be twice as big."
>
> Churchill's point is not lost today. In view of predictions that government regulation is an idea whose time is passing, the prospect of a public lynching is very intimidating—especially to a potential "lynchee."
>
> I'll take my chances this evening. In fact, I welcome this opportunity to discuss the issue of regulation with those of you who ultimately will decide where it goes—consumers, the business community, and government officials.[5]

Another kind of effective introduction is an *illustration*—which can also add drama to a presentation, as it does in the following remarks by William Stanmeyer:

> On July 2, 1972, four-year-old Joyce Ann Huff, a beautiful little girl to judge by the newspaper photo, happily went out to play in the yard of her home in Los Angeles County. She played awhile, her mother occasionally glancing at her from a kitchen a few feet away. . . .
>
> Neither Joyce Ann nor her mother noticed a yellow 1966 Chevrolet carrying three men roll up the street and pause while a man in the back seat took aim with a shotgun at the little girl. But they heard a thunderous explosion as the shotgun drove forty-two pellets into Joyce Ann's body and drove her soul forever from the face of the earth. Splattered with blood, Joyce Ann died within five minutes in the arms of her sobbing mother. . . .
>
> What, if anything, under our present system of criminal justice, will happen to the murderers?[6]

Here is an example of a third kind of effective introduction. Representative Paul Findley combined a rhetorical *question* and a *surprising statement* to make his point:

Have you ever considered this question: What was America's greatest invention? Was it Alexander Graham Bell's telephone? . . .

Was it the Wright brothers' airplane, which gave men wings, for good or ill? . . .

Was it atomic energy, which ushered in an age that is only now beginning to unfold?

Each has a claim to greatness. Each is uniquely American. Each has contributed immensely to progress. Which would you choose?

My choice may surprise you. It is none of these. My choice is nothing more tangible than a manuscript, and yet it has become the most vital force for freedom and progress history has known. It is uniquely an American invention. It is the federal union plan for government as embodied in the United States Constitution.[7]

One student began a speech in a similar way—asking a rhetorical question:

Do you know who you voted for in the last presidential election? I bet you don't. I bet you think you voted for the Democratic, Republican, or Independent candidate. But you didn't. You voted to elect members of the electoral college. In the course of my speech, I will explain why this practice is undemocratic, un-American, and unacceptable.

Another student used *frightening facts* to jolt her audience:

In the time it takes me to complete this sentence, a child in America will drop out of school. In the time it takes me to complete this sentence, a child in this country will run away from home. Before I finish this presentation, another teenage girl will have a baby.

We have a country which is gripped by a lost generation. This is an invisible group of kids lost and alone on the streets. On their own, they are hungry, sick, and scared. They are victims of our society. They are victims who desperately need help.

In this presentation I will show you how we can all help these kids.

Finally, many speakers use *startling statistics* to capture the audience's interest. Here are two examples:

Why exercise? There are some 50 million adult Americans who do not engage in physical activity for the purpose of exercise. That's equivalent to the entire population of France—and it was once said that 50 million Frenchmen can't be wrong. Can 50 million Americans be wrong? We think they are, and that's why we are here.[8]

According to figures published by the U.S. Department of Justice, 192,000 women will be raped this year. The majority of these women will be young—in fact most will be between the ages of 16 and 34. Will you, your sister, your wife or your girlfriend be one of them? Research shows many of these attacks can be avoided. I'd like to tell you how.[9]

The Preview

After you have used your introduction to spark interest and motivate your audience to continue listening, it is necessary for you to *preview* your speech. That is, you need to let your audience know what you will be discussing.

Consider these examples of previews by student speakers:

> There are three "weight classes" of people in our society: the overweight, the underweight, and those who are the right weight. Unfortunately, many people fail to understand the role weight plays in their lives. Your weight affects how your body functions. Let's explore how.

> People have traditionally relied on oil or gas to heat their homes. Today, solar energy is gaining favor as an alternative. However, I believe there are four good reasons why it is inappropriate to consider installing a solar energy system in your home at this time.

Your preview should correspond to your purpose statement. As such, it should let your audience know what to listen for. Additionally, by presenting it after you have gotten your listeners' attention and motivated them to continue paying attention, you ensure that your purpose statement will get a fair hearing.

The Conclusion

FUNCTIONS OF THE CONCLUSION

The conclusion summarizes the presentation and leaves your listeners thinking about what they have just heard. The conclusion provides a sense of completion. The conclusion's summary function may be considered a "preview in reverse." During your preview, you looked ahead, revealing to your listeners the subject of your efforts. During the summary, you will review for them the material you have covered.

For example, a summary might begin, "We have examined three benefits you will derive from a new town library." During the remainder of this summation, the three benefits might be restated, to "cement" them in the minds of the listeners.

Inexperienced speechmakers sometimes say that the summary appears to be superfluous. ("After all, I've just said all of that not more than two minutes ago.") However, it is important to remember that you are speaking for your listeners, not for yourself. The summary provides some of the redundancy mentioned earlier; it enables audience members to leave with your ideas freshly impressed on their minds. In addition to refreshing your listeners' memory, the conclusion can help clarify the issues or ideas you have just discussed.

Besides serving as a summary, your conclusion should be used to heighten the impact of the presentation. You can do this in a number of different ways. One popular technique is to refer back to your introductory remarks; this gives your speech a sense of "closure." If, for example, you are speaking about child abuse and you begin your presentation by showing pictures of abused children, you might paraphrase your opening remarks and show the pictures again, to arouse sympathy and support. Quotations and illustrations also make effective conclusions. For example, if you are speaking about the problems faced by veterans of the Vietnamese war, you could provide a moving conclusion by quoting some veterans or retelling some of the challenges they face. Of course, you are also free to draw on your own experiences when designing a conclusion. Keep in mind that, as with introductions, audiences respond to conclusions that include personal references, surprising statements, startling statistics, or relevant humor.

TYPES OF CONCLUSIONS

Let's examine how some of these conclusion techniques work in practice. One student, for example, used *illustration* to end a speech called "The Nature of AIDS":

> I take their hand and talk to them. I tell them I was happy I could make things easier. Then I say, "Thank you for letting me work for you." But every night before Jerry Cirasulolo goes to sleep, he also recites a little prayer: "Please God, give me the strength to keep on caring. And please don't let me get AIDS."

Tara Trainor, a student at Essex Community College, ended a speech on mistreatment and abuse of dolphins by using an example that personified the dolphin:

> Yes, he was kind and loving. He always took care of his family and other families too. He travels in wide social circles. In fact, maybe you have met him in his confused, cramped position. He has offered us a tidal wave of love, and we have offered him a whirlpool of death. It is time, now, to put the dolphin in our hearts, not in our fishermen's nets.[10]

In the speech on physical fitness quoted earlier, Theodore Klumpp concluded with a *surprising statement* to keep his audience thinking about his remarks:

> Unfortunately, nature does not appear to favor mind over matter, and the full utilization of only our mental capacities does not appear to be enough. I believe that we must do everything we can, as we grow older, to resist the inclination to slow down the tempo of our living. I am convinced that if you will just sit and wait for death to come along, you will not have to wait long.[11]

Recognizing the effectiveness of *statistics and rhetorical questions*, Brian Swenson—a student at Dakota Wesleyan in South Dakota—ended a speech on guns and children with these words:

> Today we have looked at a few cases of child shootings, some facts and statistics about child shootings, and what you should do if you own a gun to prevent this from happening to your children or other children. Now, maybe you still think that you don't need to lock up your gun and that this won't happen to you; but I have one more figure for you. One child is killed every day with a handgun, and for every child killed ten others are injured. Now, I have a question for you. Is your child going to be one of the ten that are injured, or is it going to be the one that is killed? The choice is yours.[12]

Robert Kennedy
understood how to
conclude a speech
effectively. One of his
techniques was the use
of quotations.

Bettmann

Quotations can increase the impact of a conclusion. Robert Kennedy often ended his speeches with these words by the poet Robert Browning:

> Some men see things as they are, and ask, "Why?" I dare to dream of things that never were, and ask—"Why not?"

Humor, when used appropriately, can help keep people on your side. One student concluded a speech on healthy living by saying:

> Medical experts tell us that even laughter is healthy. In fact, it is bad to suppress laughter. It goes back down and spreads your hips!

Another student ended a speech directed at new, first-year students with the following "letter":

> Dear Mom and Dad:
> Just thought I'd drop you a note to clue you in on my plans.
> I've fallen in love with a guy named Buck. He quit high school between his sophomore and junior years to travel with his motorcycle gang. He was married at 18 and has two sons. About a year ago he got a divorce.
> We plan to get married in the fall. He thinks he will be able to get a job by then. I've decided to move into his apartment. At any rate, I dropped out of school last week. Maybe I will finish college sometime in the future.
> Mom and Dad, I just want you to know that everything in this letter so far is false. NONE OF IT IS TRUE.
> But it is true that I got a C in French and a D in math. And I am in need of money for tuition and miscellaneous.
>
> Love, _____

In a speech on automobile insurance, one speaker included these quotations from accident reports in his conclusion:

> Coming home, I drove into the wrong house and collided with a tree I don't have.
>
> The other car collided with mine without giving warning of its intention.
>
> I thought my window was down, but found it was up when I put my head through it.
>
> I pulled away from the side of the road, glanced at my mother-in-law, and headed over the embankment.
>
> I had been driving for 40 years when I fell asleep at the wheel and had an accident.
>
> I had been shopping for plants and was on my way home. As I reached an intersection, a hedge sprang up, obscuring my vision.

In Summary: Using Introductions and Conclusions Effectively

To increase the effectiveness of your introductions and conclusions, then, use some of these techniques:

Humor, when appropriate

Interesting illustrations or quotations

Rhetorical questions

Surprising statements or unusual facts

Startling statistics

ANALYZING YOUR PRESENTATION: THE TRYOUT

In the theater, playwrights, producers, directors, and performers would never "open" an important show without first conducting a series of tryouts, or preview performances. These performances, often staged before invited guests or audiences who pay reduced prices, give the cast and backers an opportunity to experience audiences' reaction and, if necessary, make needed alterations. As a speechmaker, you would be wise to give yourself the same advantage.

Once you've researched your topic, identified your supporting materials, and outlined your presentation, it's time to become your own audience—to explore the "sound" and "feel" of your speech. Two essential ingredients in your first tryout are your speech notes and a clock or wristwatch. If possible, use a tape recorder so that you can review the exact words you use to express your ideas. Before starting, check the time and turn on the recorder. You can then begin speaking. In effect, what you are doing is preparing an oral rough draft of your presentation.

What are you trying to determine? First, you want to know if your presentation consumes too much or too little time. If a run-through takes 25 minutes and your time limit is 5 minutes, you have serious revision work ahead of you. If, on the other hand, you have designed a "60-second wonder," you may find that you need to go back to the library for more material. Second, as you actually listen to your speech, you should be alert for ideas that are not expressed as clearly as you would like. Third, you may find that the same thoughts are reiterated again and again and again—more than is necessary for "redundancy." Fourth, you may realize that the structure is confusing because of missing or inappropriate transitions. Fifth, you may have failed to develop an effective attention-getter. Sixth, the information in the body of your presentation may be too detailed or too technical for your audience. Seventh, your conclusion may not satisfy the psychological requirements you've established for it.

You can use the items on the following checklist to analyze the first tryout of your speech:

Topic
Date
Specific purpose
Length of presentation
Introduction
    Attention-getter
    Preview
    Most effective components
    Changes needed
Body
    Main points
    Support
    Most effective components
    Changes needed
Conclusion
    Summation function
    Psychological appeal
    Most effective components
    Changes needed

An oral run-through of a speech often shows where revision is needed. The speech may be too long or too short, or the ideas may need clearer expression.

When it's time to make revisions, we suggest a "modular" approach. Electronic equipment is often designed with modules that can be removed for repairs or replacement; similarly, you can extract selected modules from your outline in order to revise them, replace them, or delete them. For example, if you find that your main attention-getter is not as effective as it could be— improve it. If the supporting material under, say, the second main point in the body of your speech is confusing, rewrite it. If an illustration is too long and drawn out, shorten it. In other words, your goal during the tryout is to refine your speech until it is as close as possible to the one you will actually present. Once you reach that point, it is time to think about your delivery; we'll consider delivery next, in Chapter 16.

SUMMARY

Organization is one of the main challenges facing the speechmaker. One of the best ways to organize your speech is the introduction-body-conclusion format. Since the body of the speech is the main part of your presentation, it should be prepared first. There are five generally accepted ways to order the ideas in a speech: (1) *chronological order*, (2) *spatial order*, (3) *causes and effects*, (4) *problem and solution*, (5) *topical order*. The body of your presentation must also have internal summaries and transitions to help listeners recall the content. (Professional speakers today must be prepared to give very short synopses—"sound bites"—to the media if they want to appear on the air.)

After the body of the speech has been completed, you are ready to prepare the introduction and conclusion. The introduction should gain the attention of the audience members, make them want to listen to your speech, and provide them with an overview of the subject to be discussed. Devices used to enhance introductions include humor, illustrations, questions, surprising statements, and statistics.

The purpose of the conclusion is to summarize the material covered, heighten the impact of the presentation, and enable the audience to leave the occasion with your ideas freshly impressed on their minds. Devices used to increase the effectiveness of conclusions include surprising statements, rhetorical questions, quotations, and humor.

When you have completed the outline for the entire speech, you should become your own audience: try it out and analyze the results. Be sure to take into account any cultural barriers that might affect your presentation; be sure that your presentation is clear to all members of your audience.

SUGGESTIONS FOR FURTHER READING

Beebe, Steven A., and Susan J. Beebe: *Public Speaking: An Audience-Centered Approach*, Prentice-Hall, Englewood Cliffs, N.J., 1991. A "tell and show" approach to public speaking. Contains a multitude of examples that you can use as models for your own presentation.

Berg, Karen, and Andrew Gilman: *Get to the Point: How to Say What You Mean and Get What You Want*, Bantam, New York, 1990. This is a quick reference guide by two public speaking consultants. The publisher offers an audio program from the book that is especially helpful for business speakers.

McKenzie, E.C.: *14,000 Quips and Quotes*, Baker Book House, Grand Rapids, Mich., 1991. Offers quick reference to a wealth of useful, brief, and to-the-point material covering over 500 topics.

Osborne, John W.: *Talking Your Way to the Top*, Avant, San Marcos, Calif., 1990. An overview of the career skills needed by today's executive, including organizational skills.

Perret, Gene, and Linda Perret: *Funny Business*, Prentice-Hall, Englewood Cliffs, N.J., 1991. Extensive source of humor for the public speaker in business. Examples can be edited to suit many different topics and speaking situations.

Van Ekeren, Glenn: *The Speaker's Sourcebook*, Prentice-Hall, Englewood Cliffs, N.J., 1988. A fine source of humorous stories for many topics.

NOTES

1. A number of studies reveal how organization affects reception. For example, see Christopher Spicer and Ronald E. Bassett, "The Effect of Organization on Learning from an Informative Message," *Southern States Communication Journal*, vol. 41, 1976, pp. 290–299; and John E. Baird, Jr., "The Effects of Speech Summaries upon Audience Comprehension of Expository Speeches of Varying Quality and Complexity," *Central States Speech Journal*, vol. 25, 1974, pp. 119–127.

2. D. L. Thistlethwaite, H. deHaan, and J. Kamenetsky suggest that a message is more easily understood and accepted if transitions are used. See "The Effect of 'Directive' and 'Non-Directive' Communication Procedures on Attitudes," *Journal of Abnormal and Social Psychology*, vol. 51, 1955, pp. 107–118. Also of value on this aspect of speech organization is E. Thompson, "Some Effects of Message Structure on Listeners' Comprehension," *Speech Monographs*, vol. 34, 1967, pp. 51–57.

3. For a more comprehensive treatment of introductions and conclusions, see Loren Reid, *Speaking Well*, McGraw-Hill, New York, 1977, chap. 11.
4. From a speech by President Reagan at a bill-signing ceremony at the Central Intelligence Agency, Langley, Va. White House transcript, June 23, 1982. © 1982 by The New York Times Company. Reprinted by permission.
5. From a speech by Barbara Hackman Franklin, commissioner of Consumer Product Safety Commission, delivered at a conference, "The Conspicuous Consumer," Boston College, Boston, Mass., November 29, 1978.
6. From a speech by Dr. William Stanmeyer, reprinted in *Vital Speeches of the Day*, January 1973, pp. 182–186.
7. From a speech by Congressman Paul Findley, reprinted in *Vital Speeches of the Day*, October 15, 1962, p. 26.
8. From a speech by Theodore G. Klumpp, consultant to President's Council on Physical Fitness and Sports. Reprinted in *Vital Speeches of the Day*, December 15, 1974, pp. 135–138.
9. Student group presentation, New York Institute of Technology, 1991.
10. Tara Trainor, "A Loyal Friend," in *Winning Orations*, Interstate Oratorical Association, Mankato, Minn., 1990, p. 51.
11. Klumpp, op. cit.
12. Brian Swenson, "Gun Safety and Children," in *Winning Orations*, 1990, p. 101.

DELIVERING YOUR SPEECH: PRESENTING YOUR IDEAS

After finishing this chapter, you should be able to:

Assess your "speech anxiety"

Use deep-muscle relaxation, thought-stopping, visualization, and other techniques to reduce speech anxiety

Discuss four types of delivery: manuscript, memorized, impromptu, and extemporaneous speeches

Demonstrate how appropriate nonverbal behaviors can enhance effectiveness

Develop an effective rehearsal schedule

Analyze a speechmaker's performance (including your own) in terms of content, organization, language, and delivery

> The human brain is a wonderful thing. It operates from the moment you're born until the first time you get up to make a speech.
>
> Howard Goshorn

Your research is finished. Your speech is prepared. The date for your presentation is set. What happens next? If you're like most speakers, your mind turns to delivery. You wonder if you will really gather the courage to stand and speak before an audience. The answer is "Of course!" You've come this far, and it's now time to complete the journey. Actually, there are only two more hurdles: overcoming your own anxiety and finding a way to rehearse effectively.

DEALING WITH ANXIETY AND "SPEECH FRIGHT"

Fear, or anxiety, is something that affects *all* public speakers.[1] Thus if you experience a certain amount of apprehension before, during, or after presenting a speech, rest assured that you are not alone. Students sometimes allow their fears to get the better of them. Instead of using anxiety as a positive force, they let it overwhelm them. To combat this, we'll suggest ways to make "speech fright" actually work *for* you.

Understanding Your Fears

SELF-ANALYSIS: HOW ANXIOUS ARE YOU?

How anxious are you about delivering your speech? Use the inventory on the opposite page to find out.

Although this inventory is not a scientific instrument, it should give you some indication of your level of fear. Note that you must display *some* level of anxiety to be categorized as "normal." If you had no anxiety about speaking in public, you would not be considered "normal"; what's more, you would probably not be a very effective speechmaker.

For each statement, circle the number that best represents your response.

1. I am afraid I will forget what I have to say.

   Not afraid   1 2 3 4 5   Extremely afraid

2. I am afraid my ideas will sound confused and jumbled.

   Not afraid   1 2 3 4 5   Extremely afraid

3. I am afraid my appearance will be inappropriate.

   Not afraid   1 2 3 4 5   Extremely afraid

4. I am afraid the audience will find my speech boring.

   Not afraid   1 2 3 4 5   Extremely afraid

5. I am afraid people in the audience will laugh at me.

   Not afraid   1 2 3 4 5   Extremely afraid

6. I am afraid I will not know what to do with my hands.

   Not afraid   1 2 3 4 5   Extremely afraid

7. I am afraid my instructor will embarrass me.

   Not afraid   1 2 3 4 5   Extremely afraid

8. I am afraid audience members will think my ideas are simplistic.

   Not afraid   1 2 3 4 5   Extremely afraid

9. I am afraid I will make grammatical mistakes.

   Not afraid   1 2 3 4 5   Extremely afraid

10. I am afraid everyone will stare at me.

   Not afraid   1 2 3 4 5   Extremely afraid

Next, add the numbers you chose and score yourself as follows:

41–50	Very apprehensive	11–20	Overconfident
31–40	Apprehensive	10	Are you alive?
21–30	Normally concerned		

■ ETHICS AND COMMUNICATION

IS COMPULSORY SPEECHMAKING FAIR?

Studies show that many students fear public speaking more than they fear death. Is it fair to demand that all students face up to their fear and take a course that requires them to deliver at least one speech? Are there other options that could provide the same skills without actually involving standing in front of an audience? Explain your opinion.

CAUSES OF "SPEECH FRIGHT"

We are largely the playthings of our fears.
Horace Walpole

Before we can cope with our fears, we need to develop a clearer understanding of what causes them. Following are some of the more common causes of speech fright.

Fear of Inadequacy If adequacy is a state of feeling confident and capable, *inadequacy* is just the opposite—that is, feeling inferior and incapable. Feeling inadequate may cause us to assume that we will be unable to cope with writing or speaking. Do you fear to take risks because you imagine your performance will not be good enough or will be judged inadequate or not up to par? When you disagree with something you have read or heard, do you feel more comfortable swallowing hard and sitting quietly than you do speaking up for or writing about what you think is right? Is it easier for you to go along with a group than to write or speak your objections to other people's actions or words? If you feel inadequate, you probably prefer to play it safe; you do not want to put yourself in a position where you might feel even more inadequate.

Fear of the Unknown A new job may cause us to feel fearful because our coworkers, the situation, and our responsibilities are unfamiliar, unknown, or still unclear. We may fear writing a paper or delivering a speech for the same reasons. Each new event has a threatening, unknown quality—a quality that many people prefer not to deal with. When such an event involves writing or speaking, we may be afraid because we do not know how people will react to what we write or say. We simply are more comfortable with what is familiar— with the tried and true. Although we have a cognitive understanding of what is and is not likely to happen before an audience or in the mind of a reader, we let our feelings take charge, causing us to react emotionally and behave irrationally.

Fear of Being Judged How sensitive are you to the judgment of others? Are you concerned about a friend's opinion of or judgment about you? An instructor's? Do you believe that what an audience, a reader, or an instructor concludes about you is necessarily true? Sometimes we become so sensitive to the judgments of others that we try to avoid judgment altogether. Public speaking is one situation in which such an attitude is common.

Fear of Consequences   Basically, one of two things can result from giving a speech: the audience may like it or dislike it. That is, it may be a success or a failure. This basic result may then have further consequences. In the classroom, for example, an unsatisfactory speech may result in a failing grade. In a business situation, it can result in the loss of an important account. Whatever the consequences, the speaker must be prepared to deal with them.

Learning to Cope with Your Fears: Controlling Anxiety

One of the best ways to cope with the fear of speechmaking is to design and rehearse your presentation carefully. The systematic approach that we suggest, for example, covers both design and rehearsal and should—at least in theory—decrease your anxiety by increasing your self-confidence. However, theory and reality do sometimes diverge, and preparation notwithstanding, you may still find that you experience some anxiety about your speech. Let us now see how such anxiety can be controlled.

SYMPTOMS OF ANXIETY

The first thing you need to do is recognize the actual bodily sensations and thoughts that accompany and support your feelings of nervousness. Try the Skill Builder "What Does Anxiety Mean to You?"

Examine the symptoms that you and others in your class identified in this "Skill Builder." Did your lists include any of these physical symptoms?

Rapid or irregular heartbeat

Stomach "knots"

Shaking hands, arms, or legs

Dry mouth

Stiff neck

Lump in the throat

Nausea

Diarrhea

Dizziness

 SKILL BUILDER

WHAT DOES ANXIETY MEAN TO YOU?

1. Describe the bodily sensations you experience when you are nervous, anxious, or afraid.
2. Compile a list of thoughts that pass through your mind when you are nervous, anxious, or afraid.

When people are asked about fear-related thoughts, they often make state-ments like the following. Were any of these included on your lists?

"I just can't cope."

"I'm irritable."

"I'm under such pressure."

"This is a nightmare."

"I know something terrible is going to happen."

"Why does the world have to crumble around me?"

Once you have identified the physical and mental sensations that accom-pany fear, your next step is to learn how to control these reactions.[2] The next sections describe behavior-modification techniques that can help you.

"DEEP-MUSCLE RELAXATION": OVERCOMING PHYSICAL SYMPTOMS

It is well established that muscle tension commonly accompanies fear and anxi-ety. However, we also know that a muscle will relax after being tensed. Deep-muscle relaxation is based on this fact.

Try this: Tense one arm. Count to 10. Now relax your arm. What feelings did you experience? Did your arm seem to become heavier? Did it then seem to become warmer? Next, try tensing and relaxing one or both of your legs. When you examine what happens, you'll see why it is reasonable to expect that you can calm yourself by systematically tensing and relaxing various parts of your body in turn.

✔ SKILL BUILDER

TENSE AND RELAX

1. Imagine that your body is divided into four basic sections:
   a. Hands and arms
   b. Face and neck
   c. Torso
   d. Legs and feet

2. Sit comfortably. In turn, practice tensing and relax-ing each of these four sections of your body.
   a. *Hands and arms.* Clench your fists. Tense each arm from shoulder to fingertips. Notice the warm feeling that develops in your hands, forearm, and upper arms. Count to 10. Relax.
   b. *Face and neck.* Wrinkle your face as tightly as you can. Press your head back as far as it will go. Count to 10. Relax. Roll your head slowly to the front, side, back, and side in a circular move-ment. Relax.
   c. *Torso.* Shrug your shoulders. Count to 10 in this position. Relax. Tighten your stomach. Hold it. Relax.
   d. *Legs and feet.* Tighten your hips and thighs. Re-lax. Tense your calves and feet. Relax.

> ✔ SKILL BUILDER
>
> **"CALM"**
>
> 1. Work through the procedure described in the text for releasing tension.
> 2. As soon as you experience the "warm feeling" throughout your body, say to yourself: "Calm." Try this several times, each time working to associate the "detensed" feeling with the word *calm*.
> 3. The next time you find yourself in a stress-producing situation, say "Calm" to yourself and attempt to achieve the "detensed" state.

You will want to try using the Skill Builder "Tense and Relax" several times before you actually present a speech. Many students report that "butterflies" or tensions tend to settle in particular bodily sections. Thus, it can be helpful to check the bodily sensations you listed in "What Does Anxiety Mean to You?" and personalize "Tense and Relax" to deal with your individual symptoms.

"THOUGHT STOPPING": OVERCOMING MENTAL SYMPTOMS

Anxiety is not simply a physical phenomenon; it also manifests itself cognitively—that is, in thoughts. Thus it is important to work to eliminate the thoughts associated with anxiety and fear, as well as the bodily symptoms.

Many people use the word *relax* to calm themselves. Unfortunately, *relax* doesn't sound very relaxing to some people. We advise you to substitute the word *calm*. Try the Skill Builder "Calm."

A variation on the "calm technique" is to precede the word *calm* with the word *stop*. When you begin to think upsetting thoughts, say to yourself, "Stop!" Then follow that command with, "Calm." For example:

> "I just can't get up in front of all those people. Look at their cold stares and mean smirks."
> "Stop!"
> "Calm."

You may find that you can adapt this thought-stopping technique to help you handle symptoms of anxiety in interpersonal situations.

"VISUALIZATION": A POSITIVE APPROACH

Sports psychologists use a technique called *visualization* to help athletes compete more effectively. The athletes are guided in visualizing the successful completion of a play or a game. They are asked to imagine how they will feel when they win. Eventually, when they go out on the field to compete, it is almost as if they have been there before—and have already won.

You may want to try this technique to boost your confidence as a speaker. Sit in a quiet place. Picture yourself approaching the podium. See yourself delivering your presentation. Then hear your audience applaud appreciatively. After you have actually delivered the speech, answer these questions: Did the experience help you control your anxiety? Did it help you succeed?

OTHER TECHNIQUES

Speakers report that other techniques can also help reduce "speech fright." Some try to include a bit of humor early in the speech to get a favorable response from the audience right away. They say that such a reaction helps them calm their nerves for the remainder of the presentation. Others look for a friendly face and talk to that person for a moment or two early in the speech. Others use charts, graphs, and other visuals to help them organize the material. In this technique, the visual shows the next major point to be covered, eliminating the necessity for the speaker to remember it or refer to notes. Still others report that they rehearse a speech aloud, standing in front of an imaginary audience and "talking through" the material again and again and again. What other techniques have you and your classmates found helpful?

Remember, no matter how you choose to deal with it, fear is a natural response to public speaking and can probably never be eliminated completely. But you do need to learn to *cope* with fear; only in this way will you be able to deliver a successful, well-received presentation.

Think you can or think you can't, either way you will be right.
Henry Ford

REHEARSING YOUR PRESENTATION

All speakers need to rehearse their presentations. It is common knowledge that presidents practice by videotaping and reviewing their performance before delivering an address. Corporate leaders often spend hours rehearsing and refining the presentations they will deliver at sales meetings, stockholders' meetings, and so on. Actors, obviously, rehearse before a new play or production opens. It stands to reason that only the most foolhardy and unconcerned souls would undertake to deliver a speech that they have not adequately rehearsed.

By now you have tried out your presentation orally at least once. During the tryout stage your purpose was to analyze your speech in order to identify any changes that needed to be made. This done, you are now ready to begin rehearsing the speech *as you will deliver it.*

Options for Delivery

There are four general types of delivery available to you as a speechmaker: (1) manuscript, (2) memorization, (3) impromptu, and (4) extemporaneous. Although we recommend the extemporaneous style of delivery, we will briefly examine all four options.

A *manuscript speech* is written out word for word and then read aloud by the speechmaker. Manuscript speeches are most common in situations where it is imperative that precise language be used. For example, since presidential addresses are likely to be under close scrutiny not only in this country but throughout the world, they will often be read from a typed page or a teleprompter. When corporate speakers are discussing matters with sensitive legal and commercial aspects, they may choose to deliver a manuscript speech.

Unfortunately, use of a manuscript tends to reduce eye contact between speaker and audience. Furthermore, speakers reading aloud often sound as if they are reading to, rather than talking to, the audience, and thus it is difficult if not impossible to establish the much-needed conversational tone.

MEMORIZED SPEECHES

A *memorized speech* is a manuscript speech that the speaker has committed to memory. This delivery style often takes on a "canned" tone—often glaringly. Also, speakers who have memorized their lines are less able to respond to audience feedback, or "vibes," than they would be if they were working from notes. Additionally, of course, there is a problem of retention. Speechmakers who insist on memorizing their presentations word for word often find themselves plagued by memory lapses, leading to long, awkward silences during which they valiantly attempt to recall forgotten material. You may, naturally, want to memorize certain key words, phrases, or segments of your speech, but at this point in your career there is little reason for you to commit the entire presentation to memory.

IMPROMPTU SPEECHES

An *impromptu* speech is in many ways the antithesis of a memorized speech. Memorization requires extensive preparation, but someone who must deliver an impromptu speech often has no more than a few seconds or minutes to gather his or her thoughts. An impromptu speaking situation may arise, for example, when a boss unexpectedly asks an employee to discuss the status of a project that is still in its developmental stages. If you are faced with such a request, you will need to rely on what you have learned about patterning your ideas; using the introduction-body-conclusion format will facilitate your task.

EXTEMPORANEOUS SPEECHES

An *extemporaneous speech* is researched, outlined, and then delivered after careful rehearsal. Extemporaneous speaking is more audience-centered than any of the preceding options. Since it is prepared in advance and rehearsed, the speaker is free to establish eye contact with the members of the audience and is also free to respond to feedback. In addition, because extemporaneous speakers may use notes, they are not constrained by a need to commit the entire presentation to memory. Nor are they handicapped by a manuscript that must be read word for word, inhibiting their adaptability.

Unfortunately, many speakers confuse manuscript, memorized, and impromptu speeches with extemporaneous speeches. Although asked to give an extemporaneous speech, they may insist on writing it out word for word and then either memorizing or reading it. Or they may spend too little time preparing the speech and deliver what is essentially a poorly developed impromptu presentation. This sort of misconception defeats their purpose and decreases their effectiveness as speechmakers. Since the extemporaneous speech has been found most effective for most public speakers, we suggest that you use it. Above all, don't turn extemporaneous speaking into what it is not.

Visual Considerations

When we speak in public, we have three basic kinds of tools at our disposal: (1) verbal, (2) visual, and (3) vocal. By this time, you have exerted considerable effort to develop the verbal aspects of your presentation. We now need to devote some time and attention to the visual and vocal dimensions. This section takes up visual considerations; the next section will discuss vocal considerations.

In addition to your ideas, what aspects of yourself do you want to communicate to an audience? If you're like most speakers, you want your audience to accept you as a credible source. As we will see in Chapter 18, this means that you want your listeners to consider you:

Competent

Trustworthy

Dynamic

How is credibility communicated? Obviously, it is conveyed verbally, through the content and structure of language. However, far too frequently speakers forget that credibility is also conveyed through visual and vocal cues. As we noted in Chapter 5, the nonverbal components of a message account for at least 65 percent of the total meaning transmitted to listeners. Thus the visual and vocal dimensions of your speech merit careful attention.

Let's first consider visual cues. How do you think a speechmaker should *look* standing before an audience? Close your eyes and picture his or her clothing, posture, gestures, facial expressions, movements, and use of eye contact.

 SKILL BUILDER

A PICTURE OF SUCCESS

1. Bring to class a picture of someone you think looks like a credible speaker.
2. Describe the attributes that contribute to this person's apparent credibility.

The topic, the audience, and the occasion are all factors you should consider in deciding what to wear when you deliver your speech. Sometimes speakers make thoughtless errors in dress. For example, one student delivered a very serious tribute to a well-known leader while wearing a shirt emblazoned with a huge Mickey Mouse emblem. (When asked why, he responded, "I didn't think anyone would notice.") One woman addressing a group of executives on the need for conservatism in office attire chose to wear a bright red suit, polka-dot silver blouse, and floppy red and silver hat. (Audience members later commented on the dichotomy between her topic and her own clothing.)

Be aware that it's up to you to choose what you will wear. Your clothing does not choose you.

POSTURE

As a public speaker you will almost always be expected to stand up when addressing your audience. Thus, unless you are physically disabled—in which case your audience will of course understand—you should expect to be on your feet. Although this may seem obvious, the problem is that standing is something many of us do not do very well. Your posture communicates; it sends potent messages to the audience. Speakers often seem to forget this, assuming a stance or position that works against them rather than for them. For example, some speakers lean on the lectern or actually drape themselves over it as if unable to stand without its assistance. Some perch on one foot like a pigeon. Some prop themselves against the wall behind them, giving the impression that they want to disappear into it.

To prepare yourself to stand properly in public, we suggest that you assume your natural posture and ask others to evaluate it. Are you too stiff? Do you slouch? Do you appear too relaxed? Feedback can help you "put your best posture forward" when you rise to speak.

GESTURES

As we noted in Chapter 5, *gestures* are movements of a speaker's hands and arms. The gestures you use when speaking in public may be purposeful, helping to reinforce the content of your speech, or purposeless, detracting from your message. A problem most of us encounter is that we have certain favorite gestures which are so habitual that we are no longer conscious of them. Thus we are often unaware of it when we do things like scratch our neck, put our hands into and out of our pockets, jingle our keys or jewelry, or smooth our hair. Such mannerisms often become intensified when we find ourselves faced with a stressful situation such as speaking in public. In fact, when people are nervous, it is not unusual for them to add new gestures to their repertoire of annoying mannerisms. Speakers will sometimes tap a pencil or ring on the lectern or even crack their knuckles—things they would never do in normal circumstances.

Stand up before the class and recite the alphabet. As you do so, make as many annoying gestures as you can. Then recite the alphabet a second time. During this second recitation, make gestures that are as appropriate as possible.

Gestures can, however, serve a number of useful purposes. They can help you emphasize important points, enumerate your ideas, or suggest shapes or sizes. Thus your job with regard to gestures is really twofold. First, you need to work to *eliminate annoying* gestures; second, you need to *incorporate appropriate* gestures that can be used to enhance the ideas contained in your speech.

MOVEMENTS AND FACIAL EXPRESSIONS

It's important to understand that your presentation really begins as soon as you are introduced or called on to speak—that is, before you have uttered your first syllable. The way you rise and approach the speaker's stand communicates a first impression to your listeners. Similarly, your facial expressions as you complete your speech and your walk as you return to your seat also send important signals to your audience. Far too many speechmakers approach the lectern in inappropriate ways. For example, they may walk in a way that "broadcasts" a lack of preparation. Some even verbalize this by mumbling something like "I'm really not ready. This will be terrible." Others apologize for a poor showing all the way back to their seats.

Consider carefully your way of moving to and from the speaker's stand. The way you move communicates whether or not you are in control. You may have noticed that confident people walk with head erect, follow a straight rather than a circuitous path, proceed at an assured rather than a hesitant or frenetic pace, and use open rather than closed arm movements.

✔ SKILL BUILDER

MOVING TO AND FROM THE PODIUM

1. Your instructor will introduce you to the class as if it were actually your turn to speak. When called on, rise and approach the podium while displaying one of the following:
   a. Extreme fear
   b. Anger at having to make a speech
   c. Fatigue and exhaustion
   d. A hangover
   e. Frantic last-minute attempts to organize your ideas
   f. Total lack of preparation
   g. Anything else of your own choice
   h. Confidence

2. Next, begin at the podium and return to your seat while displaying one of the following:
   a. Disappointment
   b. Buffoonery
   c. A "lost" feeling
   d. Nervous shuffling of papers
   e. Timidity
   f. Exhilaration
   g. Confidence

Establishing eye contact with your listeners shows that you consider them important and want to share your message with them.

Sepp Seitz/Woodfin Camp & Associates

EYE CONTACT

Eye contact also communicates. Unfortunately, some speakers "talk" to walls, chalkboards, windows, trees, or the floor rather than to their listeners. Some speakers seem embarrassed to look at any audience members; others seek the attention of one person and avoid looking at anyone else. Some student speakers avoid meeting the eyes of the instructor during a speech; others focus on him or her exclusively.

Be sure that your gaze includes all the members of the audience. Look at each individual as you deliver your speech. Such contact will draw even the most reluctant listeners into your presentation.

Vocal Considerations

Obviously, the voice is one of our main tools in speechmaking. Your voice is to your speech as the artist's brush is to a painting. The brush carries colors to the canvas just as your voice transmits ideas to your listeners. In Chapter 5 we considered four basic vocal dimensions: volume, rate, pitch, and quality. We suggest that you review this material during your rehearsals, keeping in mind that your goal is to use your voice to reinforce the content of your speech.

In order to respond to your ideas your audience must of course first hear them. Maintaining your voice at an appropriate *volume* is your responsibility. If you are to address a group in a large auditorium, a public address system

THE TOP TEN ERRORS

Your instructor will write the following "top 10" presentation errors on the chalkboard:

1. Inappropriate dresser
2. Slumper
3. Hyperactive speaker
4. "Hare"
5. "Tortoise"
6. Pacer
7. Blaster
8. Eye avoider
9. Mad gesturer
10. "Scaredy cat"

In turn, each student is to select one error. Reading from the front page of the newspaper or from a telephone directory, the students' task is to "act out" the errors they have chosen. (For "inappropriate dresser," of course, some props or advance preparation may be needed.)

Observers are to identify the error being exhibited in each case.

The *class* as a whole should then discuss the various factors that cause speakers to commit each of the "top ten" errors.

MULTICULTURAL COMMUNICATION CLASSES

If Dean Barnlund, author of *Communication in a Global Village,* is right, few communication classes today are composed of students who are "cultural replicas" of each other. A number of students in your class may speak in different native tongues (English is their second language); they may also move at different paces, gesture in different ways, and respond to or seek different values.

What kinds of challenges do situations like these pose for speakers and for listeners? Explain.

Should we require that foreign students in the United States speak and act as Americans do? Why or why not?

Source: Dean Barnlund, "Communication in a Global Village" in *Public and Private Self in Japan and the United States,* Simul, Tokyo, 1975, pp. 3–24.

will probably be provided. The system should be of good quality and have sufficient power for the space. If you are addressing a group in a smaller room, you will probably be expected to speak without amplification. By observing the people in the rear, you should be able to determine if you are speaking loudly enough for them to hear you easily. If you notice that any of the audience members look confused or upset, speak up. On the other hand, if your voice is normally loud and you notice that those seated nearest to you are cringing, "turn down" your volume a bit.

With regard to *pitch,* try not to fall into the "monotone trap." If you maintain one predominant tone throughout your presentation, you will create a sense of boredom in the audience. Use pitch to reflect the emotional content of your material; use it to create interest.

Like volume and pitch, *rate* also communicates. Speaking too quickly or to slowly can impede understanding. Thus, respond to feedback from your audience and speed up or slow down your pace as appropriate.

Nonfluencies are a problem every public speaker needs to consider. "Uhs" or "ums" are normal in communication encounters, but they are not expected in speechmaking. During person-to-person conversations, we realize that people are thinking about or planning what they are going to say next. In contrast, we expect public speakers to have prepared their remarks carefully, and thus we are less tolerant of their nonfluencies.

We suggest that you attempt to eliminate nonfluencies from your delivery as far as possible.

Synthesize your understanding of the visual and vocal dimensions of public communication by trying the Skill Builder "The Top Ten Errors" on the opposite page. Awareness of common errors should help you avoid them. So, of course, will adequate rehearsal of your presentation. We'll discuss rehearsal procedures next.

Rehearsal Procedures: Communicating Confidence

Rehearsal—careful practice of your presentation—can help you acquire the confidence you need to deliver an effective speech. At this point you have prepared an outline and appropriate visuals. Your task is to synthesize these ingredients into a polished presentation. Although rehearsal is a highly individualized matter, we can provide you with some basic guidelines.

First, begin the rehearsal process by reading through your outline several times, developing a list of key words and main points to be covered. These may become the basis of your delivery notes.

Second, *learn* your first and last sentences. Many speakers find it helpful to commit the first and last sentences of an address to memory. If you do not memorize your opening and closing sentences, you should at least become very familiar with them. (As one student put it, "That way I know that I'll be able to start and stop the speech.")

Keep a log of your progress during rehearsals. Each time you rehearse, note the location of the rehearsal, the problems you encountered, the changes you made, and any progress you observed.

Rehearsal helps you put all the ingredients of speechmaking together as a polished presentation.

Mike Kagan/Monkmeyer

Third, conduct a preliminary auditory rehearsal. Stand up and face an imaginary audience. Present the entire speech. Time yourself. This will give you an idea of how the final address will sound.

Fourth, conduct additional rehearsals. Rehearse for several days, sometimes alone, at other times before a small group of friends or relatives. If you want, use an audio or videocassette recorder.

When rehearsing, be sure to incorporate all your audio and visual aids into the presentation. Also, practice delivering the speech in several different locations; this will help you to get used to the "foreign" feel of the room where the speech will actually be presented. Your goal is to develop a flexible delivery—one that will enable you to meet the unique demands of the "live" audience.

GIVING THE SPEECH: SOME FINAL TIPS

If you follow the developmental plan we have outlined, you should find yourself ready and eager to deliver your speech. Not only will you have carefully prepared and rehearsed your address; you will also have at your disposal tested techniques to help you control your nerves. At this juncture, we need to offer only a few additional pointers.

1. Arrive at your speaking location with ample time to spare. Be sure that you have prepared equipment to hold your notes and presentation aids.

2. If you are going to use a public address system or other electronic equipment, test it so that you will not have to adjust the volume or replace bulbs or batteries unnecessarily during your presentation.

3. Give ample consideration to your clothing and appearance. Your confidence and believability will increase if you "look the part." (But don't distract yourself with worries about your appearance *while* you are speaking.)

4. Let your audience know you are prepared by the way you rise when introduced and by walking confidently to the podium.

5. While speaking, work to transmit a sense of enthusiasm and commitment to your listeners. Some speechmakers actually find it useful to write the word *enthusiasm, commitment* or *confidence* on a 3- by 5-inch card that they take with them to the speaker's stand. The card helps them remember to communicate these qualities.

6. Complete your speech before returning to your seat. You've worked hard to communicate your credibility to audience members; don't blow it in the last few seconds. Last impressions, like first impressions, count.

At this point there is little more we can advise, except to say, "Have fun!" Public speaking should be a rewarding and enjoyable experience, not just for your audience but for you as well.

AFTER THE SPEECH: EVALUATING YOUR EFFECTIVENESS

As soon as you have completed your presentation, the first question you will ask yourself is, "How did I do?" No doubt you will also want to know what your peers and your instructor thought of your performance.[3] You and your listeners can evaluate your speech by analyzing how effectively you were able to handle each of the following: content, organization, language, and delivery.

Content

Was the subject of your speech appropriate? Was it worthwhile? Was your purpose communicated clearly? Did you research the topic carefully? Were your audiovisual aids helpful? Did you use a variety of supports? Were your main points adequately developed? Were your main divisions of speech effectively bridged by transitional words and phrases?

Organization

How effective was your organizational approach? Did you begin with material that gained the attention of the audience? Did you preview each of the main points? Were your main points arranged in a logical sequence? Was the number of main points appropriate for the time allotted? Was your organizational design easily discernible? Did your conclusion provide a sense of closure? Did it motivate listeners to continue thinking about your presentation?

Language

Was the language you used to explain your ideas clear? Was it vivid? Did your speech sound as if it should be listened to rather than read? Could any of the words or phrases you used have been considered offensive to any audience members?

Delivery

Did you maintain effective eye contact with the members of the audience? Did you approach the speaking situation confidently? Were you able to use an extemporaneous style of delivery? Could you be heard easily? Was your speaking rate appropriate? Did you articulate clearly? Were you able to convey a sense of enthusiasm as you spoke? Did your gestures help reinforce your content?

A Performance Inventory

The Skill Builder "Debriefing Yourself" can help you conduct a personal performance inventory.

When it is time for the audience to comment on your presentation, we suggest that they, like you, consider the positive dimensions of your performance before making recommendations for improvement. Speaker and audience alike should remember that analysis is designed to be constructive, not destructive. It should help build confidence. It should not destroy the speaker's desire to try again.

Your instructor will probably provide you with a more formal analysis of your work, using an evaluation form similar to the one shown in Figure 16-1 on the opposite page. Whether or not your instructor uses Figure 16-1, you will find it helpful as a personal guide.

 SKILL BUILDER

DEBRIEFING YOURSELF

Before joining in a discussion of your effectiveness as a speechmaker, make two lists:

1. What I believe I did well
2. What areas need improvement

Name: _____ Speech: _____

Specific purpose: _____

1. **Content**
____ Based on accurate analysis of speaking situation
____ Specific goal of speech was apparent
____ Subject appropriate, relevant, and interesting to intended audience
____ All material clearly contributed to purpose
____ Had specific facts and opinions to support and explain statements
____ Support was logical
____ Handled material ethically
____ Used audiovisual aids when appropriate
____ Included a variety of data—statistics, quotations, etc.
____ Moved from point to point with smooth transitions

2. **Organization**
____ Began with effective attention-getter
____ Main points were clear statements that proved or explained specific goals
____ Points were arranged in logical order
____ Each point was adequately supported
____ Concluded with memorable statement that tied speech together

3. **Language**
____ Ideas were clear
____ Ideas were presented vividly
____ Ideas were presented emphatically
____ Language was appropriate for intended audience

4. **Delivery**
____ Got set before speaking
____ Stepped up to speak with confidence
____ Maintained contact with audience
____ Sounded extemporaneous, not read or memorized
____ Referred to notes only occasionally
____ Sounded enthusiastic
____ Maintained good posture
____ Used vocal variety, pitch, emphasis, and rate effectively
____ Gestured effectively
____ Used face to add interest
____ Articulation was satisfactory
____ On finishing, moved out with confidence
____ Fit time allotted

Additional comments:

FIGURE 16-1
Evaluation form.

THE LECTURE LIFE
Charles Osgood

One Friday afternoon right after lunch, I got a phone call from Bob Keedick. The Keedick family has been in the lecture business for a long time. Bob's father used to book Lowell Thomas's famous talks on "Lawrence in Arabia" before there was such a thing as radio. Anyway, Bob had a problem. Rex Reed, the movie columnist, was supposed to be speaking at a dinner in Phoenix that very night and had come down with such a bad case of laryngitis he couldn't talk at all. Could I hop on the next flight to Phoenix and fill in? I'd been up since four o'clock in the morning New York time, but aside from that, I couldn't think of a good reason not to go and the price was right, so off I went.

It was the annual dinner of a Phoenix business group, and everybody seemed quite relieved when I showed up. However disappointed that Rex Reed couldn't make it they might have been, they showed me nothing but courtesy and hospitality. There was a little cocktail reception for the headtable guests before the dinner, and then we all filed into the main dining room. Turned out to be a big dinner, several hundred people, all the movers and shakers of the Phoenix business world, it seemed to me.

The president of the organization explained to me that most of the people in the room would have no way of knowing that Rex Reed hadn't made it. There was a very nice picture of Rex Reed on the banquet program. I could see people at the tables looking at the picture of Rex Reed on the program and then looking up at me. I could imagine what they were whispering to each other: "Reed doesn't look anything like his picture, does he?"

After a full meal, dessert, coffee, some announcements, introduction of officers, acknowledgment of committees, handing out of awards, acceptances, preliminary remarks, etc., it was my turn. The introduction was most gracious. Rex Reed had this terrible case of laryngitis, but they were most fortunate indeed that CBS News correspondent Charles Osgood could be there and so on.

I started out by apologizing that I was unable to talk about movie stars since I didn't know any movie stars. In fact, I admitted, I didn't even know Rex Reed. But I spoke about news broadcasting for twenty minutes or so, explaining the sort of assignments I'd been getting, talking about Walter Cronkite, Dan Rather, people like that. The audience was attentive. They laughed at the right places and frowned at the right places, and when I finished, they applauded as if they meant it. I was right pleased with myself. Then it was time for questions. The first question was this:

"Mr. Reed, why do they have to use all those dirty words in the movies these days?"

Source: Reprinted by permission of The Putnam Publishing Group from *The Osgood Files* by Charles Osgood. Copyright © 1991 by Charles Osgood.

SUMMARY

Anxiety or fear affects all speechmakers. One of the best ways to cope with "speech fright" is to design and rehearse your presentation carefully. In addition, you should learn to recognize the causes of fear and the physical and mental sensations that accompany it, so that you can learn to control them with appropriate behavior-modification techniques such as "thought stopping" and visualization.

There are four general options for delivery. (1) A manuscript speech is written out word for word and then read aloud. (2) A memorized speech is a manuscript speech committed to memory. (3) An impromptu speech is delivered on the spur of the moment. (4) An extemporaneous speech is researched, outlined, and delivered after careful rehearsal.

In delivering the speech, you have three basic kinds of tools at your disposal: verbal, visual, and vocal. Far too often, the verbal component is overemphasized while the nonverbal aspects are underemphasized. Effective speechmaking requires that you pay attention to the visual aspects of your delivery, such as your clothing, posture, gestures, movements, and use of eye contact; and that your vocal cues reinforce—rather than sabotage—the content.

Careful rehearsal of your presentation can help you develop the confidence and competence required to deliver an outstanding speech. To ensure continued improvement, you should conduct postpresentation analyses, which will enable you to profit from each speaking experience. (If English is your second language, feedback can help you make certain that your audience understood you.)

SUGGESTIONS FOR FURTHER READING

Eisenberg, Abne, and Teri Kwal Gamble: *Painless Public Speaking,* University Press of America, Lanham, Md., 1991. Includes a concise chapter on the voice and its relationship to public speaking.

Hegstrom, Timothy G.: "Message Impact: What Percentage Is Nonverbal?" *Western Journal of Speech Communication,* vol. 43, 1979, pp. 134–142. Discusses how nonverbal messages affect a speaker's performance.

Kaplan, Burton: *The Manager's Complete Guide to Speech Writing,* Macmillan, New York, 1988. A unique approach to speech preparation and delivery, based on the author's experience as a professional speechwriter.

Kuschner, Malcolm: *The Light Touch,* Simon and Schuster, New York, 1990. A consultant who specializes in humor offers suggestions for sharing your sense of humor with your audience.

Mandel, Steve: *Effective Presentation Skills,* Crisp, Los Altos, Calif., 1987. A concise source of techniques for confident and enthusiastic presentation.

Martel, Myles: *Mastering the Art of Q and A,* Irwin, Homewood, Ill., 1989. A readable guide to delivering nearly every type of presentation, including media appearances.

Sarnoff, Dorothy: *Speech Can Change Your Life,* Doubleday, New York, 1970. This popular book offers a variety of presentation tips.

Wilder, Claudyne: *The Presentation Kit,* Wiley, New York, 1990. Offers a host of suggestions for presenting a speech in an effective and professional manner.

NOTES

1. See James C. McCroskey, "Oral Communication Apprehension: A Summary of Recent Theory and Research," *Human Communication Research*, vol. 4, Fall 1977, pp. 78–96. Also note that *Communication Education*, vol. 29, no. 3, 1980, is devoted exclusively to communication apprehension, theory and practice.

2. For a more detailed guide to "fear control training," see Herbert Fensterheim and Jean Baer, *Stop Running Scared!* Dell, New York, 1977.

3. For a listing of behavioral objectives for representative grade A, B, and C speeches, see Valgene Littlefield, "Behavioral Criteria for Evaluating Performance in Public Speaking," *The Speech Teacher (Communication Education)*, vol. 24, 1975, pp. 143–145.

INFORMATIVE SPEAKING

After finishing this chapter, you should be able to:

Define *informative speaking*

Explain why it is important to develop an ability to send and receive informative messages

Distinguish between three types of informative discourse

Explain how to create "information hunger" and increase listeners' comprehension

Develop and present an informative speech

There are things that are known and things that are unknown; in between are doors.

Anonymous

In Chapter 13 we introduced you to two categories of speechmaking—informative and persuasive—and gave you an opportunity to formulate sample purpose statements for each type. At this point we want to increase your ability to prepare and deliver effective informative speeches by showing you how you can apply your general knowledge and skills to this particular situation.

SPEAKING INFORMATIVELY

"What's happening?" "How does it work?" "What's going on?" "What is it?" "What does it mean?" These are the kinds of questions that an informative speech attempts to answer. Whenever you prepare an informative speech, your goal is to offer your audience more information than they already have about the topic. Your objective is to update and add to their knowledge, refine their understanding, or provide background.[1]

How does the informative speech relate to your life? What informative messages have you received recently? Have you listened to a televised news report? A radio commentary? Have you received instructions or directions from a friend, employer, coworker, or instructor? Our world is filled with informative messages that we depend on. Many of these messages are informal, but others have been carefully planned, structured, and rehearsed to achieve maximum impact. The simple fact is that in today's world it has become increasingly important to develop the ability to share information with other people. Unless you are adept at sending and receiving informative messages, you will be unable to establish common understanding.

We once worked with a corporate vice president who—although he had a fine mind and excellent analytical abilities—considered the process of passing information on to people above and below him in the organizational hierarchy a "deadly bore." He saw little need to inform others of his activities or his

How many people do you know whose job requires them to deliver speeches? What percentage of their time is devoted to preparing and delivering speeches?

■ ETHICS AND COMMUNICATION

ASSESSING INFORMATIVE SPEAKING SKILLS

A majority of people surveyed report that they rely on informative speaking almost constantly when on the job; and the need to inform others and be informed by others is experienced daily throughout life. Should we, therefore, assess who has and who has not mastered the skills needed to deliver and process informative discourse?

If not, why not? If so, how?

accomplishments. Not surprisingly, he no longer holds his former position of power and influence. When his company merged with another organization, he lost his job—primarily because he was unable to explain his responsibilities and achievements to the new administration. Knowing how to design and deliver effective informative messages has important implications for our careers and our lives.[2]

TYPES OF INFORMATIVE PRESENTATIONS

Let's now consider three types of informative speeches: (1) messages of explanation, (2) messages of description, and (3) messages of definition.

Explanations of Processes

What processes are you equipped to speak about?

If your purpose is to explain how to do something (for example, how to motivate employees), how something is made (for example, how to make glass), or how something works (for example, how a slot machine works), then you are preparing to deliver an *explanation of a process*. Your primary goal is to share your understanding of the process or procedure with your listeners and, in some instances, to give them the skills they need to replicate it.

"*Your instructions were perfect.*"

Drawing by Koren; © 1982 The New Yorker Magazine, Inc.

One type of informative speech is explaining a process—for example, this lecture by a chef.

Patrick Ward/Stock, Boston

When organizing a process speech, you must be especially careful to avoid overcondensing the data. It is not uncommon for an inexperienced speaker to recite a long list of facts that merely enumerate the steps involved in a particular process. This kind of perfunctory outline is hard for an audience to follow. You would be wise, instead, to use *meaningful information groups*. For example, grouping information under such headings as "Gathering Ingredients," "Blending Ingredients," and "Adding the Garnish" would be considerably more effective than simply relaying, say, 15 steps involved in preparing a chocolate mousse. Besides facilitating understanding, this "grouping" system also helps the audience retain the material.

It is also important to consider the length of time it will actually take to accomplish your objectives in a process speech. Take a tip from televised cooking shows. Notice how an "on-the-air" chef always demonstrates some parts of the process "live" but has other parts of the dish already prepared in advance to save time. This technique can be of great value to you too.

 SKILL BUILDER

A DEMONSTRATION

Design and present a 3- to 5-minute speech in which it is your purpose to demonstrate how to do something or to explain how something works. An outline is required.

SKILL BUILDER

PROCESS PROBERS

1. Accompanied by two to three students, go to a location of your choice. Once there, observe the environment and compile individual lists of possible topics for a process speech, suggested by the stimuli around you.

2. Compare your own list with the lists made by others in your group. (Feel free to brainstorm additional possibilities for topics.)

3. To determine whether the topics generated will be suitable for delivery, consider these questions:
   a. Is the process of interest to me?
   b. Do I know or want to learn about it?
   c. Can I accomplish my objectives in the time allotted?
   d. Will my presentation provide the audience with new, useful information?

4. Develop a 5- to 6-minute presentation demonstrating how to do or make something or explaining how something works. Prepare an outline and use accompanying visuals.

Descriptions

One of your responsibilities as a speaker is to be able to *describe* a person, place, or thing, for your listeners. For instance, if you were a "site-location specialist" for a fast-food chain, you would have to describe potential store locations to the management. If you were a spokesperson for a nuclear plant that had experienced a radiation leak, you would have to describe the location and extent of the mishap to the media. Whatever the nature of a descriptive message, your aim is to help your listeners form mental "close-ups" of places, people, or things. To do this you will need to find ways to describe condition, size, shape, color, age, and so on, to make your subject "live" for your audience.

✔ **SKILL BUILDER**

A DESCRIPTION

Design and present a 3- to 5-minute speech in which you describe an object, a place, a structure, or a person. Use spatial order, as discussed in Chapter 15, to organize the speech. An outline is required.

One of your responsibilities as a speaker is describing something for your listeners; to do this effectively, you need to find ways to make the subject "come alive."

Jürgen Vogt 1988/The Image Works

Of course, visual aids of the type discussed in Chapters 14 and 17 will be particularly relevant to a descriptive presentation. For example, photographs, maps, and drawings can make it easier for you to describe a significant archeological dig, the pathos of a homeless person, the appearance of the "Elephant Man," or the blight of an inner-city slum. In a descriptive speech, you "paint" with words.

Whatever your topic, you will want to ensure that the words and phrases you select will evoke the appropriate sensory responses in your listeners. To do this you will need to communicate how your subject looks, tastes, smells, feels, and sounds.

✔ SKILL BUILDER

IMAGERY

1. Find a natural object—such as a piece of driftwood, a large shell—or a photograph of a bird or animal. Put it at the front of the classroom.

2. Divide into pairs of partners. Each pair is to use as many sensory images as possible to describe the object or photo.

3. Compare the images.

4. Repeat the experience, substituting a new object or photo.

SKILL BUILDER

WHAT DOES IT MEAN?

1. Working individually or in groups, list topics for a speech of definition.
2. Select five of the topics and develop purpose statements (see Chapter 15) for them.
3. Design and present a 3- to 5-minute speech in which you define a concept or idea. Organize it carefully and submit an outline.

Definitions

"What do you mean?" is a common question. In most cases, it is used when the questioner is seeking clarification or elaboration of ideas from a speaker. Sometimes a satisfactory answer can be supplied in a sentence or two. At other times, however, it takes a speech, or even a book, to define a concept adequately. For example, books with titles like *Theory Z, Leader Effectiveness Training, The Preppy Handbook*, and *Happiness Is . . .* are actually extended definitions: the authors are discussing their meaning for a particular concept or idea. An informative speech of *definition* likewise serves to provide an audience with an explanation of a term. "Dancercise," "Aerobics," "ESP," and "Muscular Dystrophy" are among the topics for which a definitional presentation would be appropriate. Can you think of others? Many students find that topics such as "The Meaning of Obscenity," "Prejudice," "Friendship," or "Shyness" give them the freedom they need to develop effective speeches of definition.

Since many of the concepts you may choose to define will have connotative or subjective meanings not traditionally found in dictionaries, not all members of your audience will agree with the definition you present. On one television talk show, for example, two experts on shyness were unable to agree on what it means to be shy. It is therefore necessary to organize a definitional speech in a way that will be clear and persuasive. For example, how would you define *shyness*? To explain your meaning for the term, you might offer examples of what it feels like to be shy, describe how a shy person behaves, and then go on to discuss the consequences of shyness. Perhaps you would explain shyness by comparing and contrasting a shy person with an extrovert. Or you might choose to discuss the causes of shyness and then focus on different types or categories of shyness. No matter how you choose to order your ideas, your organization should be suggested by the topic and grow out of it.

 SKILL BUILDER

YOUR CHOICE—DEFINE OR DESCRIBE

1. Prepare a 5-minute speech of definition or description. Be sure to use whatever speaking aids you believe will help bring your presentation to life for the audience.
2. Prepare an outline. Prepare a bibliography of sources you consulted.

To develop an effective informative speech, you need to accomplish several tasks: (1) make your listeners want to learn more about the topic; (2) communicate the information clearly by avoiding "overload" and stressing key points; (3) find ways to involve audience members in your presentation; (4) provide the information in ways that will make it memorable, by using novelty, creativity, and audiovisuals. Let's look at each of these tasks.

Create "Information Hunger"

Your primary goal in an informative speech is to deliver a message of explanation, description, or definition, but it is equally important to make your presentation interesting and relevant (that is, significant) for your listeners. In other words, you need to work to increase each listener's "hunger" to receive your message.

Which speakers succeeded in increasing your hunger for knowledge about a topic? What did they do to accomplish this?

You will be more adept at creating "information hunger" if you have analyzed your audience carefully (see Chapter 12). Then, by using appropriate "vehicles," you will be able to generate the interest that will motivate them to listen to the information you want to share. Remember to use the attention-getting devices we discussed in Chapter 15. For example, you can relate your own experiences or the experiences of others; you can ask rhetorical questions; you can draw analogies for your listeners to consider. You can also arouse the audience's curiosity; and you can incorporate humor or use eye-catching visual aids.

Obviously, your effectiveness as a speaker will increase to the extent that you are successful in creating a desire and a need to know among audience members.

Avoid "Information Overload"

Listeners will become informed as a result of your speech only if they are capable of processing the information you deliver. A common danger in informative speaking is that your audience will experience "information overload."

Information overload is created in two ways: (1) The speechmaker delivers far more data about the topic than the audience needs or wants. This confuses the listeners and causes them to "tune out" or "turn off" what is being communicated. (2) The speechmaker "dresses" ideas in words the listeners do not understand. Instead of using clear language and speaking at a level the audience can comprehend, the speaker creates frustration among audience members by using unfamiliar jargon or words that soar beyond the reach of the listeners' vocabulary. Forgetting that an informative speech will fail if its ideas are superfluous or unclear, some speakers end up talking to themselves rather than to the audience.

Remember, your speech does not have to be encyclopedic in length or sound impressively complicated to merit the audience's attention. But it must by all means be understandable.

Avoid "Information Underload"

A speaker who tries to avoid information overload will often overcompensate and create a situation of "information underload." Such a speaker underestimates the sophistication or intelligence of the audience members and tells them little that they do not already know. As a speechmaker you need to strike a balance, providing neither too little information nor too much. As a rule, effective speechmakers neither underestimate nor overestimate the capabilities of the audience. Instead, they motivate their listeners to want to fill in any "information gaps." To motivate your listeners, do not "overkill" your subject by saturating the listeners with so much material that they lose interest; instead, choose supporting materials carefully to achieve your objectives, using an appropriate mix of new information and more familiar support. Once one point is made, be ready to move on to the next one.

Emphasize Key Points

As we have seen in Chapter 14, emphasis can be created through repetition (saying the same thing over again) and restatement (saying the same thing in another way). As long as you do not become *overly* repetitious and redundant, these devices will help your listeners process and retain the main points of your speech.

The organization of your speech can also reinforce your main ideas. Remember that you can use your introduction to preview ideas, and you can use your conclusion to help make those ideas memorable. Transitions and internal summaries also help create a sense of cohesiveness.

Involve Your Listeners

People learn more if they become involved with the material that is being presented to them. Effective speechmakers do not view the audience as a passive receptacle; rather, they work to find ways to let the audience take an active

---

● CULTURE AND COMMUNICATION

CONVEYING INFORMATION ACROSS CULTURES

Through informative presentations, speakers attempt to describe something, demonstrate how something works, or explain some concept. Their goal is to convey knowledge and understanding. For this goal to be realized, the information they want to share must be communicated clearly.

But people who seem to "speak the same language" may in reality come from very divergent backgrounds. How can such speakers hope to communicate clearly with each other? How can an appreciation of the communicative behavior of people from cultures different from your own facilitate this effort?

Effective speakers find
ways to involve their
listeners—to let the
audience take an active
part in the presentation.

Richard Hutchings/Photo
Researchers

part in the presentation. For example, the audience may be called on to perform
some activity during the presentation. If you were giving a speech on how to
reduce stress, say, you might have your listeners actually try one or two stress-
reducing exercises. Or if your speech was "How to Read an EKG," you might
pass out sample EKGs for audience members to decipher.

Provide Information Memorably

Remember that people want to understand and remember information that they
perceive as *relevant* to their own lives. Few of us would have much interest in
a speech on the development of bees. If, however, we found that the bees we
are hearing about are a new species of "killer" bee which is extremely resistant
to common insecticides, and that droves of these bees are on the way to our
community and will arrive within the next 2 weeks, we would develop an intense interest very quickly.

Audiences also want to listen to "*new*" information. In this case the term
new means "new to them." A historical blunder may be new in this sense, and
it may be relevant to a college or business audience today. The cable television
industry has found that weather is worthy of its own channel; the weather
forecast is constantly being updated and is therefore considered "new."

Audiences also respond well to information that is *emphasized.* You can use
your organization of main ideas to emphasize material you want people to
retain.

Repetition can help as well; audiences respond to information that is *repeated.* Martin Luther King understood the value of repetition in his "I Have a
Dream" speech. Jesse Jackson uses repetition to foster his audiences' retention
as well as their emotional involvement. As you prepare your informative speech,
look for ways to let repetition augment your message.

Martin Luther King used repetition memorably in his "I Have A Dream" speech.

UPI/Bettmann

Take your mind out every now and then and dance on it. It is getting all caked up.

Mark Twain

NOVELTY AND CREATIVITY

An effective speaker looks constantly for ways to approach information from an unusual direction. If you are the fifth speaker that your audience will hear on the homeless, you must find a different slant or approach to the topic, or the audience may be bored from the outset. You might try taking a different point of view—through the eyes of a child, for example. Look for analogies that bring topics home to an audience. "The number of people entering teaching today is diminishing. It is like _____ (a stream drying up?)" Try other ways to complete this analogy. As you prepare your presentation, remember that you are looking for creative ways of bringing your topic to life for the audience.

AUDIOVISUAL AIDS

You will want to include visual aids in an informative presentation. Remember first, though, that you are your primary visual aid. The way you stand, walk, talk, and gesture is extremely important to the effectiveness of your presentation. Avoid hiding behind the lectern; avoid reading your notes. Move to the

---

 SKILL BUILDER

BRAIN GAME

1. How many uses can you find for a block of wood?

2. How many uses can you find for an old tire?

3. How might you approach a speech entitled "Pins and Needles"?

side. Use gestures to show the size and shape of objects. If some article of clothing is important to your topic, you may want to wear it. Foreign students, for example, sometimes wear clothing from their homeland when they give informative speeches about their culture.

Bring objects, or make simple models if you cannot bring the objects themselves. Use charts and graphs when appropriate. If you have access to a computer and can manipulate spreadsheet software, you can create computer-generated bar, line, and pie graphs. You can then have a graph converted to a transparency at a local copy shop so that it can be used with an overhead projector.

You can also consider using video and audio clips to create interest. Camcorders can be used to conduct interviews or show processes at work. For example, one student interviewed other students about campus parking problems. Another showed a brief tape of a chemical reaction which could not have been demonstrated safely in the classroom.

The more visuals you use, the more planning you will need. As we mentioned in Chapter 16, audiences today are not willing to wait while you activate and cue up a VCR or audiotape recorder. Make sure that the equipment is in place and ready before you begin the speech.

Visual aids can increase the clarity of your presentation and arouse your audience's interest—but they call for careful planning.

Matthew Borkoski/Stock, Boston

An Outline: "The Unthinkable"[3]

Purpose: To inform the audience about the potential results of a nuclear war.

Introduction

The purpose statement guides the speaker in developing the outline.

   I. Are you familiar with these lyrics by the satirist Tom Lehrer?

A rhetorical question gets the audience involved.

> We will all go together when we go,
> All suffused with an incandescent glow.
> No one will have the endurance
> To collect on his insurance
> Lloyd's of London will be loaded when we go![4]

Lines from a protest song set the ironic tone of the speech.

  II. Today I would like to explain what the results of a nuclear war would be.

Tells the audience the purpose of the speech.

Body

   I. Nuclear war has been proposed as a way to solve a number of the world's problems.
     A. Some feel it will solve the population problem.
     B. It has also been discussed by officials as a way to solve the oil problems in the middle east.

The body is organized into three main points, each with a number of subpoints. Note that every entry is a complete sentence and contains only a single idea.

  II. Our government has taken steps to ensure that we will survive as a nation.
     A. The U.S. Postal Service plans to distribute special change-of-address cards to survivors of a nuclear blast.
     B. The Federal Preparedness Agency has stockpiled 71,000 pounds of opium near Washington, D.C.
     C. The Department of Housing and Urban Development has made plans to rent the homes of owners who cannot be located.
     D. The Constitution, Bill of Rights, and Declaration of Independence will be safe.
       1. When war breaks out, a National Archives Guard will push a button causing these documents to descend into a 50-ton vault.
       2. They will remain there until the war is over.
     E. A command post for top-echelon leaders has been built at Mount Weather, 80 miles west of Washington, D.C.
     F. The president will be safe.
       1. He or she will be aboard a $250 million 747.
       2. The plane is designed to fly far above the nuclear fallout.

Gives dramatic examples of the government's hopelessly inadequate plans in case of a nuclear attack.

  III. To discover what would happen to the general population if the "unthinkable" occurred, we need only look at the results of the bomb that leveled Hiroshima.
     A. Parents and children were separated.
       1. When found, some children looked like boiled octopuses.
       2. Others were never seen again.

The third main point stands in contrast to the second main point, showing what a nuclear bombing is really like.

Vivid descriptions and startling statistics convey the horrors of a nuclear attack.

B. People suffered greatly.
   1. Some ran screaming back into the fire that was consuming the city.
   2. Others developed an abnormal thirst and spent their last agonizing hours screaming for water.
C. In Hiroshima, destruction ruled.
   1. The death toll was 130,000.
   2. Sixty-eight percent of all buildings were destroyed.
   3. Thousands who survived the initial blast eventually succumbed to radiation sickness and cancer.
D. The bomb that leveled Hiroshima in 1945 was only one-millionth as powerful as today's nuclear weapons.

A surprising statement makes Hiroshima relevant to the present time.

Conclusion

I. Nuclear war is truly the "unthinkable" force on earth today.
II. "We will all go together when we go, All suffused with an incandescent glow...."

States the conclusion. Repeating the first two lines of the protest song provides a sense of unity.

Sources

Glasstone, Samuel, and Philip Dolan, eds.: *The Effects of Nuclear Weapons*, Department of Defense and Energy Research and Development Administration, 1977.
National Academy of Sciences: *Long Term World Wide Effects of Multiple Nuclear Weapons Detonations*, National Academy of Sciences, 1975.
O'Brien, Ellen: "Memoirs of Preparing for a Nuclear War," *The Record*, March 5, 1982.
Schell, Jonathan: "Reflections: The Fate of the Earth," *The New Yorker*, February 1, 1982.
Zuckerman, Ed: "How Would the U.S. Survive a Nuclear War?" *Esquire*, March 1982.

Lists the sources used in preparing the speech.

A Speech: "Computer Viruses—A Growing Menace"[5]

As human beings, we all suffer from a variety of illnesses ranging from the common cold to more serious maladies such as pneumonia. Perhaps the most annoying illness for most of us is one caused by a virus. A virus leaves us with many unanswered questions, such as, Where did it come from? How do I get rid of it? What if I cannot get over it?

The speaker gains attention by establishing common ground with the listeners.

Computers are susceptible to viruses as well. These viruses, like their human counterparts, are contagious and leave many unanswered questions. The idea of a computer having a virus may sound like something out of science fiction, but it is very real and can be extremely frightening. I would like to take the next few minutes to explore computer viruses—what they are, where they have occurred, and what we are doing to eliminate them.

The use of personal pronouns involves the audience.

The speaker personifies computers. An effective analogy is used.

The speaker forecasts the speech's development.

A virus, whether biological or electronic, is basically an information disorder. Biological viruses are tiny scraps of genetic code—DNA or RNA—that can take over the machinery of a living cell and trick it into making thousands of flawless replicas of the original virus. Like its biological counterpart, a computer virus carries in its instructional code the recipe for making copies of itself. When it invades a host computer, the typical virus takes temporary control of the disk operating system. Then, whenever the infected computer comes into

The speaker begins to consider the first main point of the speech.

A definition is used to clarify the subject under discussion.

Comparison and
contrast are used.

An analogy is carried
through the discussion.

A question is used to
raise the second main
point of the speech.

Statistics enhance the
credibility of the data.

Evidence is used to
summarize known
information.

Specific instances add
support.

Questions are raised for
us to ponder together
with the speaker.

The speaker continues
with more examples as
support.

The virus is personified.

Again, evidence and
highly credible people
are used to increase the
importance of the
information provided.

The speaker gives us
the facts, using parallel
structure for emphasis.

A question introduces
the third main point of
the speech.

Once more, an analogy
is used. A definition
also adds clarity.

contact with an uninfected piece of software, a fresh copy of the virus passes into the new program. Thus, the infection can be spread from computer to computer by unsuspecting users who swap disks or send programs to one another over telephone lines. A single strategically placed computer with an infected memory—say, an electronic bulletin board—can rapidly infect thousands of other systems.

Where have these viruses hit? The most serious outbreaks so far have occurred in personal computers. But security experts say that the greatest risk would come from infected large mainframe computers, such as those used by the IRS and air traffic controllers. Forty years after the dawn of the computer era, when we are dependent on high-speed information processing, the computer world is being threatened by an enemy from within. Some 250,000 computers may have been hit with viruses in the very recent past.

Computer experts began warning of the possibility of viruses as early as 1984, but the viruses did not begin to surface until 1988, when IBM, Hewlett-Packard, and Apple all began to report incidents of viruses. The University of Delaware and Lehigh University both reported that faculty and student personal computers were infected. How did this happen? In one case, Drew Davidson, a 23-year-old programmer, caused a message called "Universal Message of Peace" to flash across thousands of Macintosh screens (though it did no harm, since it erased its own instructions and thus disappeared without a trace). How did Davidson accomplish this task? Apparently he inserted the virus into some game software that was distributed to a Macintosh users group. The game was subsequently published with the virus in it.

In a more serious incident, a Christmas greeting appeared mysteriously on terminals connected to a worldwide network owned by IBM. Users who followed the instructions inadvertently triggered a viruslike self-replicating mechanism, sending an identical copy of the original program to every name on their electronic mailing lists. In a matter of days, the virus clogged the 350,000-terminal network.

Some viruses have been playful. In one instance the screen featured the likeness of the Cookie Monster from *Sesame Street*. It would not disappear until the user typed in the letters "COOKIE." Many viruses are not playful, however, One example was called GOTCHA. It displayed a likeness of Madonna and then proceeded to erase all the files on the user's disk.

Most states have laws which prohibit computer tampering, and a federal law spells out harsh penalties for tampering with government computer data. Texas is just one of 48 states that have passed laws against computer mischief, and during his presidency Ronald Reagan signed a law that established penalties for unauthorized tampering with government computers. Recently, the Software Development Council, led by Michael Odawa, launched a movement to plug any loopholes in that law. Said Odawa, "I say, release a virus, go to jail!"

So far, real disaster has been avoided. No insurance company rolls have been wiped out. No air traffic systems have been jammed. No military data have been erased. But the possibility of tragedy still is real.

What are we doing to eliminate viruses? Many "vaccinations" have been and are being created to protect our computer software from these viruses. Like a biological vaccination, a vaccine program is a preventive measure—an attempt to protect an uninfected disk from invasion by an uninvited program.

Vaccines surround memory locations in computers and sound alarms when tampering occurs. However, there are many strains of viruses. Thus, vaccines are often ineffective.

As an individual computer operator, you can practice safe computing. Remember, if you get a floppy disk from someone, it may have been in everybody else's computer, too. So don't share disks. Don't copy software. Don't let anyone touch your machine. Just say *no*! A computer virus is truly a menace to be avoided by individuals, corporations, and governments alike. Hopefully, a disaster can be avoided.

The audience is involved as an argument parallel to the one used in the war on drugs is offered. This adds impact to the conclusion.

Sources

"A Virus Carries Fatal Complications," *The New York Times*, June 26, 1988.
"Computer Systems under Siege," *The New York Times*, January 31, 1988.
"Invasion of the Data Snatchers," *Time*, September 26, 1988.
Interview with Robert Hoffer, programmer and manager of The Computer Center, Montvale, N.J., January 18, 1989.

SUMMARY

An informative speech gives an audience more information about something than they already have. It can update and add to their knowledge, refine their understanding, or provide background material. There are three basic types of informative presentations: speeches that *explain* a process; speeches that *describe* a person, place, or thing; and speeches that *define* a term.

In order to be effective, an informational speaker needs to accomplish several tasks: (1) make the listeners want to learn more about the topic; (2) communicate the material clearly by avoiding "information overload" and stressing the key points; (3) find ways to involve the members of the audience in the presentation; (4) provide the information in ways that will make it memorable.

SUGGESTIONS FOR FURTHER READING

Arredondo, Lani: *How to Present Like a Pro*, McGraw-Hill, New York, 1991. Well-written material on preparing to present an informative speech in an organizational setting.

Berg, Karen, and Andrew Gilman: *Get to the Point: How to Say What You Mean and Get What You Want*, Bantam, New York, 1990. A reference guide with many suggestions for informative speakers.

DeVito, Joseph: *Elements of Public Speaking*, HarperCollins, New York, 1990. Useful examples of informative speeches and helpful treatment of research.

Goss, Blaine: *Processing Communication*, Wadsworth, Belmont, Calif., 1982. A readable treatment of information processing as it relates to public speaking.

Lucas, Stephen: *The Art of Public Speaking*, 4th ed., McGraw-Hill, New York, 1992. Includes a fine unit on specifics of informative speaking, and excellent examples.

Timm, Paul R.: *Functional Business Presentations*, Prentice-Hall, Englewood Cliffs, N.J., 1981. Discusses the informative speech in the organizational setting.

Wilcox, Paul: *Oral Reporting in Business and Industry*, Prentice-Hall, Englewood Cliffs, N.J., 1967. Focuses on informative speaking in the business setting.

NOTES

1. Although compiled years ago, a valuable source to consult is Charles Petrie, "Informative Speaking: A Summary and Bibliography of Related Research," *Speech Monographs*, vol. 30, 1963, pp. 79–91.

2. For a fine chapter on the informative speech, see Douglas Ehninger, Alan H. Monroe, and Bruce E. Gronbeck, *Principles and Types of Speech Communication*, 8th ed., Scott, Foresman, Glenview, Ill., 1978, chap. 7.

3. Developed as part of a class exercise by students in the course "Basic Speech Communication" at New York Institute of Technology.

4. Tom Lehrer, *Tom Lehrer's Song Book*, Crown, New York, 1968.

5. Developed by students as part of a class project at the College of New Rochelle.

PERSUASIVE SPEAKING

After finishing this chapter, you should be able to:

Define *persuasive speaking*

Identify how your perception of your goal and your audience influences your effectiveness as a persuader

Define and distinguish between *attitudes* and *beliefs*

Explain the concept of *credibility*

Develop and present a persuasive speech

Our aim in this chapter is to increase your ability to prepare and present persuasive speeches by showing you how to apply your general knowledge and skills to this special type of discourse.

SPEAKING PERSUASIVELY

When you deliver a *persuasive speech*, your goal is to modify the thoughts, feelings, or actions of your audience. You hope that your listeners will change attitudes or behaviors you do not approve of and adopt attitudes and behaviors which are compatible with your interests and the way you see the world. Persuasive discourse is becoming increasingly important; more than ever, in fact, we are concerned with being able to influence others.[1]

Today's business environment demands effective persuasion skills. If you are negotiating a piece of property for your new corporate headquarters, trying to persuade a town planning board to change zoning laws, speaking to a jury to persuade them to decide in favor of your client, attempting to convince a company to use your services, running for public office, or working in any of thousands of other situations, you will have opportunities to practice and refine the presentation skills you are learning in this class.

PURPOSES OF PERSUASION: THOUGHT AND ACTION

Many theorists contend that to persuade audience members to act differently you must first persuade them to think differently. Do you agree?

We can analyze the goals of persuasive speakers by examining what they want their speeches to accomplish. For example, a speaker may believe that flying saucers exist even though most of the audience may not. A speaker may oppose bilingual education while others support it. A speaker may want audience members to become organ donors, and the audience members may feel some real reluctance about committing themselves. The objective of the speaker, sometimes referred to as the *proposition* of the speech, indicates what type of change the speaker would like to create in audience members. Typically, speakers want one or both of two general outcomes: they want to convince listeners that

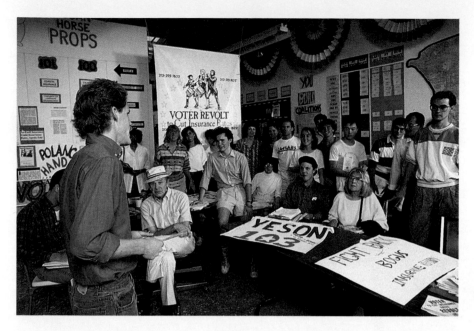

The goal of a persuasive speech is change: you want to modify your listeners' thoughts, feelings, or behavior.

M. Greco/Stock, Boston

something is so (that is, to change the way audience members *think*), or they want to cause audience members to take some action (that is, to change the way they *behave*). Whatever the general nature of the proposition, it most likely will reflect at least one of the following goals: adoption, discontinuance, deterrence, or continuance.[2]

When your goal is *adoption*, you hope to persuade the audience to accept a new idea, attitude, or belief (for example, that saccharin is hazardous to health), with the hope that in time that belief will also be supported by action (your listeners will eliminate saccharin from their diet). When your goal is *discontinuance*, you hope to persuade audience members to stop doing something they are now doing (drinking while pregnant, for example). When your goal is *deterrence*, you want to persuade the audience to avoid some activity or way of thinking (for example, "If you don't smoke now, don't begin." "If you believe that every woman has the right to exercise control over her own body, don't vote for candidates who would make abortions illegal"). Finally, if your goal is *continuance* of a way of believing or acting, you want to encourage people to continue to think or behave as they now do (for instance, "Keep purchasing products made in the United States").

Adoption and discontinuance goals involve asking listeners to alter their way of thinking or behaving, whereas deterrence and continuance goals involve asking them *not* to alter the way they think or behave but rather to reinforce or sustain it. In general, persuaders find it easier to accomplish deterrence and continuance objectives. That doesn't mean, however, that accomplishing adoption or discontinuance goals is impossible. They may be more difficult to achieve, but if the speaker uses a variety of appeals and a sound organizational scheme and has credibility, these goals can also be realized.

To what extent do you think job effectiveness is related to the ability to influence others? Explain your answer.

"I found the old format much more exciting."

Drawing by Levin; © 1982 The New Yorker Magazine, Inc.

PERSUADING EFFECTIVELY

Whenever we try to cause others to change their beliefs, attitudes, or behaviors, or whenever others try to influence us, we are participating in the *persuasive process*.[3] Let's examine some procedures you can use to increase your persuasiveness as a speaker.

Identify Your Goal

To be a successful persuader, you must have a clearly defined purpose. You must, in fact, be able to answer these questions:

What response do I want from audience members?

Would I like them to think differently, act differently, or both?

Which of their attitudes or beliefs am I trying to alter? Why?

Unless you know what you want your listeners to think, feel, or do, you will not be able to realize your objective.

Acting on a good idea
is better than just
having a good idea.
Robert Half

The nature of your task is partly related to the extent and type of change you hope to bring about in people. The task will be simplified if you have some idea of how the audience members feel about whatever change you are proposing. For example, to what extent do they favor the change? How important is it to them? What is at stake? The more "ego-involved" the members of your audience are, the more committed they will be to their current position and hence the harder it will be for you to affect them.[4]

Understand Factors Affecting Your Listeners' Attitudes

In order to be able to influence others, you need to understand the favorable and unfavorable mental sets or predispositions that audience members bring to a speech; that is, you need to understand *attitudes*—how they are formed, how they are sustained, and how they may be changed by you. The following forces or factors are among the most important influences on our attitudes.

FAMILY

Few of us escape the strong influence exerted by our families. Many of our parents' attitudes are communicated to us and are eventually acquired by us. As the communication theorists Scott Cutlip and Alan Center write, "It is the family that bends the tender twig in the direction it is likely to grow."[5]

RELIGION

Not only believers but also nonbelievers are affected by religion. In fact, the impact of religion is becoming ever more widespread as churches strive to generate and guide attitudes on such social issues as abortion, civil rights, the death penalty, child abuse, and divorce.

EDUCATION

More people than ever are attending school; they start young (sometimes before the age of 5), and many attend until they are in or beyond their twenties. Moreover, the traditional role of the school has expanded since large numbers of adults are now returning to complete their education. The courses taught, the instructors who teach them, the books assigned, and the films shown all help shape attitudes.

 SKILL BUILDER

CONTROVERSIAL ISSUES

Prepare a 3- to 4-minute presentation explaining your attitude on a controversial issue such as busing, abortion, or gun control. Discuss the forces and factors that led you to form your attitude, and explain what would have to happen for you to change your attitude.

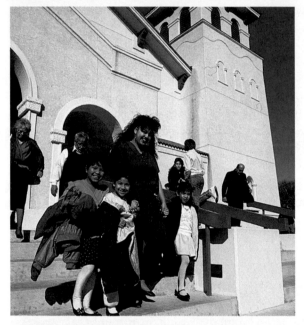

Factors that shape our attitudes include *(top to bottom)* the family, religion, and education.

Top to bottom, Arlene Collins/Monkmeyer; Bob Daemmrich/The Image Works; Alon Reininger/Contact Press Images/Woodfin Camp & Associates

Economic status and social status also shape our attitudes. Our economic status helps determine the social arena we frequent. Our view of the world is likewise affected by the company we keep and the amount of money we have.

CULTURE

As the seventeenth-century poet John Donne wrote, "No man is an island, entire of itself. . . ." From the crib to the coffin we are influenced by others—in person and through the media. The groups we belong to, our friends, and the fabric of the society in which we find ourselves all help form and mold us. Our social environment contains ingredients that help determine our mental sets and in turn our attitudes. We shape our social institutions and are reciprocally shaped by them.

In *The Female Eunuch*, Germaine Greer describes how society has traditionally defined and shaped what a woman is—and she rejects the stereotype:

> I'm sick of pretending eternal youth. I'm sick of belying my own intelligence, my own will, my own sex. I'm sick of peering at the world through false eyelashes, so everything I see is mixed with a shadow of bought hairs; I'm sick of weighting my head with a dead mane, unable to move my neck freely, terrified of rain, of wind, of dancing too vigorously in case I sweat into my lacquered curls. I'm sick of the Powder Room. I'm sick of pretending that some male's self-important pronouncements are the objects of my undivided attention. I'm sick of going to films and plays when someone else wants to, and sick of having no opinions of my own about either. I'm sick of being a transvestite. I refuse to be a female impersonator. I am a woman. . . .[6]

Understand Your Listeners' Beliefs

Your persuasive efforts will be facilitated if you understand not only your listeners' attitudes but also their beliefs—and if you understand how audiences might respond when their important beliefs are challenged.[7]

Attitudes and *beliefs* are, of course, related—in fact, the two terms are sometimes used interchangeably—but they are not really the same thing. We might say that attitudes and beliefs are related to each other as buildings are related to bricks, beams, boards, and so on. That is, in a sense beliefs are the "building blocks" of attitudes. Whereas attitudes are measured on a "favorable-unfavorable" scale, beliefs are measured on a "probable-improbable" scale. Thus, if you say that you think something is true, you are really saying that you believe it. According to the psychologist Milton Rokeach, your "belief system" is made up of everything you agree is true. This includes all the information and biases you have accumulated from birth. Your "disbelief system," which is composed of all the things you do *not* think are true, develops along with your belief system. Together, the two significantly affect the way you process information.[8]

It is necessary to recognize that, to your listener, some beliefs will be more important than others. The more central or important a belief is, the harder audience members will work to defend it, the less willing they will be to change it, and the more resistant they will be to your persuasive efforts.

How do you react when someone questions your position on what you consider a critical issue? Why?

BELIEF AND DISBELIEF

1. Think of 10 different ways to complete the sentence "*I believe . . .*"

2. Next, think of 10 different ways to complete the sentence "*I do not believe . . .*"

3. Attempt to identify how what you *believe* and what you *do not believe* influence you by describing how each belief and nonbelief listed above affected what you did or said in a particular situation.

4. Finally, attempt to describe how your behavior would change if you *did not believe* what you said you believed and if you *believed* what you said you did not believe.

Use Two Principles of Influence: Consistency and Social Proof

When you are speaking persuasively, you should be aware of two significant principles.

First, we all have a desire to be consistent with what we have already done. In other words, once we take a stand, our tendency is to behave consistently with that commitment.[9] Therefore, it is important to determine how your speech can engage this tendency toward *consistency*. If you can find a way to get audience members to make a commitment (to take a stand or go on record), you will have "set the stage" for them to behave in ways consistent with that stand.

Second, we all respond to *social proof*. That is, one method we use to determine what is right is to find out what other people think is right.[10] You can use the actions of others to convince your listeners that what you're advocating is right. As the motivation consultant Cavett Robert notes: "Since 95 percent of the people are imitators and only 5 percent initiators, people are persuaded more by the action of others than by any proof we can offer."[11]

Reason Logically

You will be more apt to achieve the goal of a persuasive speech if you can give your listeners logical *reasons* why they should support what you advocate. The most common forms of logical reasoning are deduction, induction, reasoning from causes and effects, and reasoning from analogy.

DEDUCTION

When we reason deductively, we move from the general to the specific. In other words, we offer general evidence that leads to a specific conclusion. The following example moves from the general to the specific.

Major premise: People who study regularly instead of cramming usually get better grades.

Minor premise: You want to get better grades.

Conclusion: Therefore, you should study regularly instead of cramming.

You can evaluate deductive reasoning by asking

1. Are the major premise and the minor premise (or minor premises) true?
2. Does the conclusion follow logically from the premises?

Be sure to give the necessary evidence to buttress your major and minor premises.

INDUCTION

When we reason inductively, we move from specific evidence to a general conclusion. The following example moves from the specific to the general—from a series of facts to a conclusion.

> After growing up on a diet of television violence, Ronnie Zamora committed a murder.
>
> After watching a television show, *Born Innocent*, a group of teenagers imitated the rape scene shown on the program.
>
> After the movie the *Deerhunter* was televised, 28 people died imitating its Russian roulette scene.
>
> Violence depicted on television is copied in real life.

Whenever speakers use what is true in particular cases to draw a general conclusion, they are reasoning by induction. For instance, we are reasoning inductively if we conclude that sexualized violence against women shown on MTV videos leads to acts of sexualized violence against women in real life because in a number of cases men have enacted in real life the situations they saw on the videos.

You can evaluate inductive reasoning by asking the following two questions:

1. Is the sample of specific instances large enough to justify the conclusion drawn from them?
2. Are the instances cited representative or typical ones?

CAUSAL REASONING

When we reason from causes and effects, we either cite observed causes and hypothesize effects or cite observed effects and hypothesize causes. We use causal reasoning every day. Something happens, and we ask ourselves, "Why?" Similarly, we speculate about the consequences of certain acts; that is, we wonder about what effects they have. The following statements illustrate causal reasoning:

> Smoking cigarettes causes cancer.
>
> Smoking cigarettes causes heart disease.
>
> Smoking cigarettes can cause problems during pregnancy.
>
> Cigarette smoking is hazardous to your health and should be eliminated.

To evaluate the soundness of causal reasoning, ask these questions:

1. Is the presumed cause real or false?
2. Is the presumed cause an oversimplification?

REASONING FROM ANALOGY

When we reason from analogy, we compare like things and conclude that since they are alike in a number of respects, they are also alike in some respect that until this point has not been examined. For example, if you wanted to argue that the methods used to decrease the high school dropout rate in a nearby city would also work in your city, you would first have to establish that your city is similar to the other city in a number of important ways—number of young people, number of schools, skilled personnel, financial resources, etc. If you said that the two cities were alike except for the fact that your city had not instituted such a program and that its dropout rate was therefore significantly higher, you would be arguing by analogy.

To check the validity of analogical reasoning, ask these questions:

1. Are the two things being compared alike in essential respects? That is, do the points of similarity outweigh the points of difference?
2. Do the differences that do exist matter?

✔ **SKILL BUILDER**

REASONS

Individually or with a partner, select one topic for a persuasive speech. Write three to five basic reasons why people should believe what you believe about this topic, or why they should take whatever action you are proposing.

Topic: _____
Reason 1: _____
_____
Reason 2: _____
_____
Reason 3: _____
_____
Reason 4: _____
_____
Reason 5: _____
_____

What seem to be the best reasons? Are you incorporating logical as well as emotional appeals or reasons in your plan? Share your ideas with the class members.

Before you can persuade or convince other people, you must first get their attention. In his book *The Art of Persuasion*, Wayne Minnick relates how a 9-year-old girl succeeded in getting the undivided attention of a male guest at her party. It seems that all the boys had gathered at one end of the room, talking to each other and ignoring the girls. "But I got one of them to pay attention to me, all right," the little girl assured her mother. "How?" inquired the mother. "I knocked him down!" was the undaunted reply.[12]

We are not suggesting that you knock your listeners down to get their attention, but you will need to find other ways to encourage them to listen to you. It is your responsibility to put them into a receptive frame of mind. You can do this in several different ways. You can compliment your listeners. You can question them. You can relate your message directly to their interests, or you can surprise them by relating to them in an unexpected way. Once you have the attention of your listeners, you must continue to work to hold it.

To what extent must friends, coworkers, politicians, and advertisers compete to get your attention? Which strategies are the most effective? Why?

Make Your Listeners Feel as Well as Think

Following is an excerpt from a student's speech. Why is it effective?

> My father had lung cancer and cancer of the spinal column. He was ill for only 5 weeks. The last weeks of his life were spent in a hospital. He was operated on, given radiation treatments, and placed in a medical contraption that was supposed to increase his limited mobility. It didn't. The bill for his 5-week stay in the hospital amounted to $20,000. My father was by no means a wealthy man. However, neither was he eligible for Medicaid. Thus, his illness consumed my parents' entire savings. There is something terribly wrong with a health care system that is permitted to inflict such a terrible blow on patients and their families. National health care has become a necessity.

Many changes in human behavior have resulted from messages that combined emotional appeals with rational reasons. Since few people will change their attitudes or take action if they are unmoved or bored, effective speakers develop emotional appeals that are designed to make listeners feel.[13] Whether the feeling evoked is sadness, anger, fear, sympathy, happiness, greed, nostalgia, jealousy, pride, or guilt depends on the speaker's topic and the response desired.

Here is how Edward R. Murrow, a renowned radio broadcaster, used emotional appeal to heighten one of his reports during World War II:

> April 15, 1945
> . . . Permit me to tell you what you would have seen, and heard, had you been with me on Thursday. It will not be pleasant listening. If you are at lunch, or if you have no appetite to hear what Germans have done, now is a good time to switch off the radio, for I propose to tell you of Buchenwald. It is on a small hill about four miles outside Weimar, and it was one of the largest concentration camps in Germany, and it was built to last. As we approached it, we saw about a hundred men in civilian clothes with rifles advancing in open order across the fields. There were a few shops; we stopped to inquire. We were told that some of

In his radio broadcasts during World War II, Ed Murrow used emotional appeals to heighten his reporting.

The Bettmann Archive

the prisoners had a couple of SS men cornered in there. We drove on, reached the main gate. The prisoners crowded up behind the wire. We entered.

And now, let me tell this in the first person, for I was the least important person there, as you shall hear. There surged around me an evil-smelling horde. Men and boys reached out to touch me; they were in rags and the remnants of uniform. Death had already marked many of them, but they were smiling with their eyes. I looked out over that mass of men to the green fields beyond where well-fed Germans were ploughing.

A German, Fritz Kersheimer, came up and said, "May I show you round the camp? I've been here ten years." An Englishman stood to attention, saying, "May I introduce myself, delighted to see you, and can you tell me when some of our blokes will be along?" I told him soon and asked to see one of the barracks. It happened to be occupied by Czechoslovakians. When I entered, men crowded around, tried to lift me to their shoulders. They were too weak. Many of them could not get out of bed. I was told that this building had once stabled eighty horses. There were twelve hundred men in it, five to a bunk. The stink was beyond all description.

When I reached the center of the barracks, a man came up and said, "You remember me. I'm Peter Zenkl, one-time mayor of Prague." I remembered him, but did not recognize him. . . .

As I walked down to the end of the barracks, there was applause from the men too weak to get out of bed. It sounded like the hand clapping of babies; they were so weak. The doctor's name was Paul Heller. He had been there since 1938.

As we walked out into the courtyard, a man fell dead. Two others—they must have been over sixty—were crawling toward the latrine. I saw it but will not describe it.

In another part of the camp they showed me the children, hundreds of them. Some were only six. One rolled up his sleeve, showed me his number. It was tattooed on his arm. D-6030, it was. The others showed me their numbers; they will carry them till they die.

An elderly man standing beside me said, "The children, enemies of the state." I could see their ribs through their thin shirts. The old man said, "I am Professor Charles Richer of the Sorbonne." The children clung to my hands and stared. We crossed to the courtyard. Men kept coming up to speak to me and touch me, professors from Poland, doctors from Vienna, men from all Europe. Men from the countries that made America.

We went to the hospital; it was full. The doctor told me that two hundred had died the day before. . . . Dr. Heller pulled back the blankets from a man's feet to show me how swollen they were. The man was dead. Most of the patients could not move. . . .

I asked to see the kitchen; it was clean. The German in charge had been a communist, had been at Buchenwald for nine years, had a picture of his daughter in Hamburg. He hadn't seen her for almost twelve years, and if I got to Hamburg, would I look her up? He showed me the daily ration—one piece of brown bread about as thick as your thumb, on top of it a piece of margarine as big as three sticks of chewing gum. That, and a little stew, was what they received every twenty-four hours. . . .

Dr. Heller, the Czech, asked if I would care to see the crematorium. He said it wouldn't be very interesting because the Germans had run out of coke some days ago and had taken to dumping the bodies into a great hole nearby. Professor Richer said perhaps I would care to see the small courtyard. I said yes. . . . The wall was about eight feet high; it adjoined what had been a stable or garage. We entered. It was floored with concrete. There were two rows of bodies stacked up like cordwood. They were thin and very white. Some of the bodies were terribly bruised, though there seemed to be little flesh to bruise. . . . I tried to count them as best I could and arrived at the conclusion that all that was mortal of more than five hundred men and boys lay there in two neat piles.

There was a German trailer which must have contained another fifty, but it wasn't possible to count them. . . . It appeared that most of the men and boys had died of starvation. . . . But the manner of death seemed unimportant. Murder had been done at Buchenwald. God alone knows how many men and boys have died there during the last twelve years. . . .

As I left that camp, a Frenchman who used to work for Havas in Paris came up to me and said, "You will write something about this, perhaps?" And he added, "To write about this you must have been here at least two years, and after that—you don't want to write any more."

I pray you to believe what I have said about Buchenwald; I have reported what I saw and heard, but only part of it. For most of it I have no words. . . .[14]

The people who listened to Murrow's broadcasts did not soon forget them.

Ronald Reagan also understood the need for emotion. He chose a poem to close his presidential tribute to the astronauts lost in the *Challenger* disaster.

> Let us close with these lines written by a 19-year-old World War II fighter pilot, John Gillespie Magee, Jr., shortly before his own death in the air:

HIGH FLIGHT

> Oh, I have slipped the surly bonds of Earth.
> And danced the skies on laughter-silvered wings:
> Sunward I've climbed and joined the tumbling mirth
> Of sun-split cloud—and done a hundred things
> You have not dreamed of—wheeled and soared and swung
> High in the sunlit silence. Hov'ring there.
> I've chased the shouting wind along and flung
> My eager craft through footless halls of air.
> Up, up, the long delirious burning blue
> I've topped the wind-swept heights' easy grace
> Where never lark or even eagle flew—
> And, while with silent lifting wing I've trod
> The high untrespassed sanctity of space.
> Put out my hand and touched the face of God.[15]

Your goal should be to compel your listeners to remember your ideas and proposals, and to do this you will need to arouse their feelings. As a speaker, you must appeal not just to your listeners' heads but also to their hearts. Thus, although your speech should be grounded in a firm foundation of logic and fact, it should also be built on feelings.

Evoke Relevant Needs and Issues

Balance is a state of psychological health or comfort in which our actions, feelings, and beliefs are related to each other as we would like them to be. When we are in a balanced state, we are content or satisfied. Thus we engage in a continual struggle to keep ourselves "in balance." What does this imply for you as a persuasive speaker? If you want to convince your listeners to change their attitudes or beliefs, you must first demonstrate to them that some current situation or state of affairs has created an *imbalance* in their lives and that you can help restore their balance.

Remember that human behavior depends on motivation. If you are to convince people to believe and do what you would like them to do, you must make your message appeal to their needs and goals.

One popular device used to analyze human motivation is a schematic framework devised by the famous psychologist Abraham Maslow.[16] In Maslow's "hierarchy of needs," motivation is seen as a pyramid with our most basic needs at its base and our most sophisticated needs at its apex (see Figure 18-1). Maslow defined *survival needs* as the basic necessities of life: shelter, food, water, and procreation. *Safety needs* include the need for security and the need to know that our survival requirements will be satisfied. At the third level

FIGURE 18-1
Maslow's hierarchy of needs.

Source: From Abraham Maslow: *Toward a Psychology of Being*, with permission of the publisher, Van Nostrand Reinhold N.Y.

are *love* and *belonging needs*. Once these are met, our *esteem* needs can be addressed. Esteem needs include self-respect and the respect of others. Our efforts to succeed are often attempts to satisfy our esteem needs, because success tends to attract respect and attention. At the peak of Maslow's hierarchy is the need for *self-actualization*. When we satisfy this, we have realized our potential; that is, we have become everything we are capable of becoming.

How does Maslow's hierarchy relate to you as a persuasive speaker? Find out by trying the Skill Builder below. Remember that salient needs make salient motives. Your goal is to make your receivers identify your proposal with their needs. Whenever you attempt to do this, you will probably have to involve personal feelings.

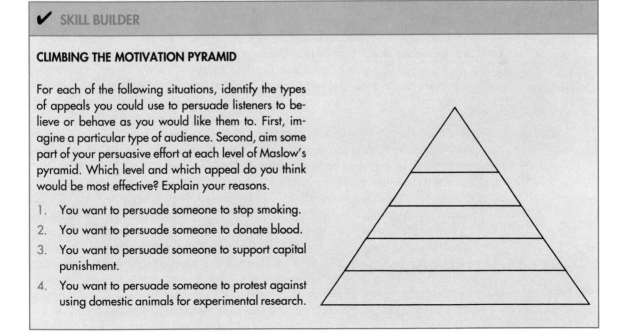

✔ **SKILL BUILDER**

CLIMBING THE MOTIVATION PYRAMID

For each of the following situations, identify the types of appeals you could use to persuade listeners to believe or behave as you would like them to. First, imagine a particular type of audience. Second, aim some part of your persuasive effort at each level of Maslow's pyramid. Which level and which appeal do you think would be most effective? Explain your reasons.

1. You want to persuade someone to stop smoking.

2. You want to persuade someone to donate blood.

3. You want to persuade someone to support capital punishment.

4. You want to persuade someone to protest against using domestic animals for experimental research.

● **CULTURE AND COMMUNICATION**

PERSUASION AND "ASSUMED SIMILARITY"

LaRay M. Barna, an intercultural communication theorist, points out that we are all influenced by our cultural upbringing, and while we tend to assume that other people's needs, desires, and basic assumptions are the same as our own, often they are not. How can "assumed similarity"—the belief that we all have similar thoughts, feelings, attitudes, and nonverbal codes—cause problems for persuasive speakers?

Do you think that it would be more beneficial for a persuasive speaker to "assume differences" rather than similarity? Explain.

Promise a Reward

When you are speaking persuasively, demonstrate how your listeners' personal needs can be satisfied by your proposal. You should stress how your ideas can benefit the people you are trying to persuade. Make them believe that your proposal will supply a reward.

Remember, however, that different audiences value different types of rewards. For practice, think of three different types of audience and identify the most important needs of each. Imagine that you are a salesperson trying to persuade each of these audiences to buy one of the following items: (1) guitar, (2) plant, (3) dog, (4) hat, (5) attaché case. Describe the strategies you would use with each group. What adaptations would you make? To what extent would you display your awareness of individual differences?

What are your own most important needs? How might someone use this information to persuade you to buy one of the items listed here?

It is important to remember that people are usually preoccupied with how something will benefit them personally. Your listeners, whoever they are, will want something in return for behaving as you would like them to behave.

BECOMING A MORE CREDIBLE PERSUADER

Consider the interview with Gerry Spence in the box on the opposite page. As Spence realizes, your success as a persuader will be determined in part by what your "targets" think of you—in other words, by your credibility.[17]

When we use the term *credibility,* we are talking not about what you are "really" like but about how an audience *perceives* you. If your listeners accept you as credible, they probably believe that you are a person of *good character* (trustworthy and fair), *knowledgeable* (trained, competent to discuss your topic, and a reliable source of information), and *personable* (dynamic, charismatic, active, and energetic). As a result, your ideas are more likely to get a fair hearing. However, if your listeners believe that you are a liar (untrustworthy), incompetent (not sufficiently knowledgeable about your topic), and passive (lacking in dynamism), they are less likely to respond as you desire.

"THE BEST IN THE WEST"

ED BRADLEY: In the Old West, when a man wanted to settle a score, he went out and found himself a hired gun. Today, when he wants to settle a score, he goes out and finds himself a lawyer. And if he's lucky, he finds Gerry Spence, who dresses more like a hired gun than a hired lawyer. Spence sees himself as a Marshall Dillon, a good guy fighting the bad guys for causes he believes in and for causes he feels are just and significant. . . . You're on the stand; you're under oath. How good are you as a lawyer?

GERRY SPENCE: I'm the best lawyer I ever knew. . . .

ED BRADLEY: Gerry Spence isn't modest, but he probably isn't wrong. He just may be the best trial lawyer in America. He hasn't lost a trial since 1969.

GERRY SPENCE: . . . Gerry Spence walks up to a jury, and he gives that jury everything that he is. He gives—he says, "Here I am. Here is all of me. Here is my heart and my guts and my soul, and the truth, and my belief, and everything that I am. Here it is, and I—and I—and I ask you to take it."

It is entirely possible—even probable—that your listeners may consider you more credible about some topics than others. For example, here are two pairs of imaginary statements. Which statement in each pair would you be more inclined to accept?

> The United States must never negotiate with terrorists. Strength is the only language they will understand.—George Bush
>
> The United States must never negotiate with terrorists. Strength is the only language they will understand.—Madonna

> The world of contemporary music has room in it for everyone. The message music sends is tolerance.—Michael Jackson
>
> The world of contemporary music has room in it for everyone. The message music sends is tolerance.—Bill Bradley

If you're like most people, you found the first statement in each pair more credible. The source cited for the first statement seems obviously more knowledgeable about the subject. Another way of saying this is that you may be judged more credible by certain types of audiences than by others.

Regardless of the circumstances, however, it will be up to you to build your credibility by giving your listeners reasons to consider you competent, trustworthy, and dynamic.[18] To help listeners see you as competent, you can describe your own experiences with the subject and suggest why you feel you've earned the right to share your ideas. You can help your listeners see you as trustworthy by demonstrating respect for different points of view and communicating a sense of sincerity. To help listeners see you as dynamic, speak with energy, use assured and forceful gestures, and create vocal variety.[19]

FACING QUESTIONS OF PRIVATE LIFE, KENNEDY APOLOGIZES TO THE VOTERS
Alessandra Stanley

Where do you stand? In your opinion, how do speeches containing apologies and revelations about the private lives of public figures enhance or detract from a speaker's credibility? Explain.

Cambridge, Mass., Oct. 25—Senator Edward M. Kennedy went to the John F. Kennedy School of Government at Harvard University today to discuss his future in politics, and to do so he stepped back and tried to address the hurdle of his past. He apologized to his constituents in Massachusetts without specifying what he had done wrong in his private life, but he suggested that in the future he would mend his ways.

"I am painfully aware that the criticism directed at me in recent months involves far more than honest disagreements with my positions, or the usual criticism from the far right," he said steadily, looking up from his prepared text, over the heads of 800 members of the audience and straight into a bank of television cameras. "It also involves the disappointment of friends and many others who rely on me to fight the good fight.

"To them I say: I recognize my own shortcomings—the faults in the conduct of my private life. I realize that I alone am responsible for them, and I am the one who must confront them." He added, "I believe that each of us as individuals must not only struggle to make a better world, but to make ourselves better, too."

It was the Senator's first and only allusion to the damage his reputation had sustained in the aftermath of the Palm Beach scandal involving an accusation of rape against his nephew—whose trial begins next week—a reputation still troubled by a 1969 car accident at Chappaquiddick Island in Massachusetts in which a young woman died. And it was his only reference to the way that reputation had blunted his performance in the Judiciary Committee hearings on Prof. Anita F. Hill's assertions of sexual harassment against the Supreme Court nominee Judge Clarence Thomas.

Senator Kennedy had been widely criticized and mocked by Republican adversaries and even fellow liberals. His closest friend across the aisle, Senator Orrin G. Hatch of Utah, made a crack on the Senate floor about the Chappaquiddick accident, although he later apologized for it.

Senator Kennedy received a 22 percent approval rating in a national Gallup Poll after the hearings adjourned—the lowest rating of any Senator on the committee. Mr. Kennedy will be up for re-election in 1994.

"He knew people had concerns and he felt it was important to address these concerns," said Paul Donovan, a spokesman for the Senator. "He felt he owed it to the people of Massachusetts."

Mr. Donovan said the Senator's office began preparing the speech after the hearings concluded, but he said it was not in direct response to unfavorable polls.

Senator Kennedy's admission of "shortcomings" was tersely worded and unemotionally expressed, and it had an entirely different ring than the pained, personal and uncertain speech he gave immediately after the accident at Chappaquiddick in 1969, when he asked Massachusetts voters to help him decide whether he should remain in office. He later pleaded guilty to leaving the scene of an accident.

Mr. Kennedy chose the sympathetic setting of a university he once attended, among mainly liberal academics and students, in what was his first attempt to fight back, to repair the damage and restore, if not his personal reputation, then his political standing as the voice of American liberalism. Unlike most guests who speak at the Kennedy School, the Senator left without taking questions from the audience.

Some who waited in line for as long as an hour to hear the speech, did so because they had heard rumors that Mr. Kennedy would announce either his resignation or his intention not to run again. "People were buzzing all day that he might resign or choose not to run," said Marina McCarthy, a teacher at the Harvard University Extension School. A Kennedy supporter, Ms. McCarthy said she thought the speech was "done tactfully and gracefully," adding, "I think he can push on."

Far from leaving public office, Senator Kennedy vowed, "I will continue to fight the good fight."

"Some of the anger of recent days," he said, referring to the public reaction to the Thomas hearings, "reflects the pain of a new idea still being born—the idea of a society where sex discrimination is ended and sexual harassment is unacceptable—the idea of an America where the majority who are women are truly and finally equal citizens."

Mr. Kennedy, who wore an earnest expression and an earnest navy blue business suit, spoke for half an hour in a hot, crowded room in the Institute of Politics at the Kennedy School, which is celebrating its 25th anniversary. He vividly denounced Republican policies as "the negative politics" of the right. He included a sharp dig at Louisiana State Representative David Duke, a former Ku Klux Klan member now running for Governor of that state, describing him as "racism in a business suit."

He called civil rights the "unfinished business of America," and he hailed the accord reached between Congress and the White House on a civil rights bill as "a well-deserved defeat for those who would misuse race as a political weapon."

He referred to many of his causes, including education, national health insurance and gun control. He also referred to his family. "I know something of the feelings of pain shared by legions of families across this land who have been victimized by the instant, tragic, terrible violence of gunshots," he said before reminding the audience, "I fought for the Gun Control Act of 1968 and I intend to continue the fight for gun control in the 90's.

"Unlike my brothers, I have been given length of years and time, and as I approach my 60th birthday, I am determined to give all that I have to advance the causes for which I have stood for almost a quarter of a century."

Ronald H. Brown, chairman of the Democratic National Committee, attended the forum and lavishly praised Mr. Kennedy after the speech.

Some students in the audience were more blasé. "I didn't think he said anything different in terms of policy," said Steve Cohen, a Harvard graduate student, "but on the personal stuff, I respected him more as an individual because he confronted issues of his past."

Note that the audience's assessment of your credibility can change during your presentation or as a result of it. Thus, we can identify three types of credibility:

Initial credibility—your credibility before you actually start to speak

Derived credibility—your credibility during your speech

Terminal credibility—your credibility at the end of your speech.

Of course, if your initial credibility is high, your task should be easier. But keep in mind that your speech can lower your initial credibility—and that it can also raise your initial credibility. What you say and how you say it are important determiners of credibility. For instance, in the box on page 444, do you consider Art Buchwald's character Randolph Habermeyer, chief lobbyist for the American Hot and Cold Steel Company, a credible source?

As Ralph Waldo Emerson wrote:

The reason why anyone refuses his assent to your opinion, or his aid to your benevolent design, is in you. He refuses to accept you as a bringer of truth, because, though you think you have it, he feels that you have it not. You have not given him the authentic sign.

THE LOBBYIST AGAINST IMPORTS
Art Buchwald

Randolph Habermeyer, chief lobbyist for the American Hot and Cold Steel Company, was awakened by his Swiss-made Computer Alarm Clock. He got up and turned on his Sony television set to hear the news.

Then he showered and shaved with the new electric razor his wife had bought which said Made in Germany.

He then started dressing. Since he was going to testify in front of a congressional committee he selected his suit carefully, deciding on an imported Pierre Cardin pin stripe. He also chose a conservative silk tie that came from Thailand. Finally he put on his Italian-made Gucci shoes. He filled his Paris-made Hermes briefcase with all the papers he would need for his testimony.

It was raining out so he grabbed his trench coat. It was his favorite coat, and he was amazed that the Spanish, of all people, could manufacture trench coats at a third the price of the American ones.

Habermeyer kissed his wife good-bye and got into his Mercedes-Benz to drive from Potomac to the Capitol. In the Mercedes he had a phone, which had been made in Taiwan, and he called his office to dictate several messages to his secretary on a German-made Grundig machine.

He also had a pocket-size Dutch-made Philips recorder in the car to remind him of things he wanted to do the next day.

Suddenly he looked at his gas gauge and realized he was short of gas.

He stopped at a BP (British Petroleum) station and filled up the tank.

Habermeyer was listening to his radio as he drove along. They were advertising a new "Star Wars" rocket ship from Hong Kong. He made a note to buy one for his son for Christmas.

The next commercial had to do with a French Cuisinart blender. Habermeyer decided to get one for his wife because she had said they were still the best on the market.

As he was driving along he realized he had time to buy some cigars. Since Cuban ones were still not on the market, he favored the ones made in the Canary Islands.

The clerk was pushing a new cigar that had been manufactured in the Philippines, but Habermeyer said he'd stick with his Flamencos.

He also bought a throwaway lighter made in South Korea.

Then he got back into his Mercedes and drove up to the Hill.

Before going to the committee room to testify, he dropped off to see a congressman friend and gave him a box of Swiss chocolates that one of the people from the company had brought back on a recent trip. The lobbyist knew the congressman had a sweet tooth, and he couldn't think of a better gift to give him.

Finally Habermeyer went to the committee room to testify. He was the second witness. He sat at the table, took out his prepared statement and began to read.

"On behalf of the American Hot and Cold Steel Company, as well as all American steel companies, I am raising my voice in angry protest over the flagrant dumping of foreign steel in this country. Mr. Chairman, this committee must decide whether we will permit the importation of foreign steel at the price of sacrificing American jobs and doing mortal damage to the American economy.

"The time has come for us to say, 'Enough is enough.' We cannot survive when we have to compete with the labor costs of other nations. It is your patriotic duty to see that the United States is protected from the flooding of foreign imports which I, as an American citizen, find despicable . . ."

Habermeyer took 30 minutes to read his statement and then looked at his Japanese Seiko watch and realized his time was up.

In brief, persuasive speaking involves more than simply communicating with others in a public setting. It is your responsibility to familiarize yourself with the beliefs, attitudes, and needs of those you hope to persuade. Only by doing so will you be in a position to influence others—and to understand how they may try to influence you.

DELIVERING A PERSUASIVE SPEECH

As a persuasive speaker, you must show a great deal of interest in and enthusiasm for your topic. At the moment of presentation, it must become the most important issue in the world for both you and your listeners. The audience must feel that you have a real sense of conviction about the topic and the solution you suggest.

Be aware that audience members may object to what you say. As a persuader, you need to be able to handle objections in an effective manner. First, be prepared for opposing points of view. Anticipate your audience's concerns and rehearse possible answers. Second, consider the source of objections. For example, audience members may dispute your facts. If you make a statement about the number of millionaires in your state and an audience member has just completed a study on wealth in the United States and has up-to-date statistics, you will need to agree, restate your findings, or suggest that this is a good point which you both should explore. An effective way to handle opposing views is to agree with them as much as possible. "I agree that life insurance may not be the best investment . . ." is a disarming technique often used by sales representatives to counter objections to purchasing insurance.

Answer any argument in a professional manner. Do not become angry that anyone would dare question your reasoning. Remember that your credibility is at stake while you are speaking in front of others. Respond to the question or objection in an authoritative manner and move on to other questions. Maintain control.

✔ SKILL BUILDER

MEETING THE CHALLENGE OF PERSUASIVE SPEAKING

1. Using whatever aids and strategies you believe will increase your ability to influence your listeners, prepare a 5- to 7-minute persuasive speech.

2. Provide an outline and a bibliography—a list of sources consulted.

3. Develop a purpose or goal statement and several valid, well-supported reasons for accepting the argument. Use facts and the well-documented opinions of experts to build as effective a case as you can. Be sure to develop an effective beginning and ending. The ending should reemphasize what you want the audience to do or believe.

4. If time allows, audience members may ask questions. Be prepared to respond to them in an appropriate manner that increases your credibility.

SAMPLE PERSUASIVE PRESENTATIONS

An Outline: "Would You Die for a Drink?"[20]

The purpose statement clearly identifies the persuasive nature of the speech.

Purpose: To persuade the audience to act to keep the drunken driver off the road.

Introduction

Using well-known personalities as examples gets the audience's attention and interest.

Statistics support the argument of the introduction that the problem is serious.

The introduction leads into a preview.

I. How serious is drunken driving?
   A. Johnny Carson and F. Lee Bailey have something in common. On a recent weekend they were both arrested and charged with drunken driving.
      1. Many people chuckled to themselves over this.
      2. Is drunken driving really a laughing matter?
   B. Driving while intoxicated is a very serious problem in this country.
      1. Over 35 percent of all automobile accidents are alcohol-related.
      2. Drunken driving is responsible for more than 25,000 deaths each year.
      3. Drunken driving is responsible for more than 750,000 injuries each year.

II. Today, I will examine how our society treats the drunken driver, and I will suggest what we can do to ensure that drunken drivers stay off the roads.

Body

Announces the first main point of the speech.

Involves the audience by using as examples experiences they're likely to be familiar with.

Explains how and why previous efforts to solve the problem have failed.

I. First, let's look at societal attitudes which permit drunken drivers to remain on the road.
   A. People seem to empathize or identify with the drunken driver.
      1. Since 80 percent of all adult Americans drink, there is an "it could have been me" attitude about drunken driving.
      2. Arrests of Carson, Bailey, and other personalities are a source of gossip, not outrage.
   B. Peer pressure causes many people—including college students—to drink to excess.
   C. Few people act to protect an intoxicated person.
      1. Few offer to call a cab so that the intoxicated person won't drive.
      2. Few encourage the intoxicated person to sleep before getting behind the wheel.
   D. To date, legislative efforts to curb drunken driving have been ineffective.
      1. The National Highway Safety Council estimates that $1 billion is spent annually to reduce drunken driving.
      2. Legislators have tried harsher punishments, only to find that although the number of arrests decreases, the number of drunken drivers does not.

   3. Judges regularly give suspended sentences to drunken drivers.
   4. In New Jersey alone, thousands of drivers simply refuse to take the mandatory informational training seminars on drunken driving.

II. Now, let's look at what you can do to help curb drunken driving.
   A. Avoid drinking and driving yourself.
   B. Since as a host you may be sued in civil court if a guest of yours is involved in an accident, encourage intoxicated guests to stay out of the driver's seat.
   C. Support the efforts of MADD (Mothers Against Drunk Drivers) and RID (Remove Intoxicated Drivers).
   D. Finally, support mandatory use of the PBT (Preliminary Breath Test).
      1. Today, drivers can refuse to take a breath test.
      2. Mandatory breath tests would provide more accurate information for enforcement officials.
      3. In Norway, for example, the PBT is coupled with random road-blocks and a mandatory 21-day sentence in a labor camp.

The second main point is an appeal for the audience to take action.

Subpoints A to D give examples of specific things the audience can do to help.

Conclusion

I. We have seen that societal attitudes contribute to the prevalence of drunk driving and that legislative and personal action need to be taken to correct this problem.
II. The next time you find yourself chuckling over the arrest of some prominent public figure for reportedly driving while intoxicated—think again!

Summarizes the two main points of the speech.

Makes a final appeal to audience members to change their attitudes.

Sources

Bradel, P.: "Preliminary Breath Test in Traffic Enforcement," *Journal of Police Science and Administration*, March 1981, pp. 23–27.
"Drinking and Driving Don't Mix," *Newsday*, December 9, 1981.
Faulkner, S.: "Consultation Report on Drinking and Driving," *Journal of Studies on Alcohol*, vol. 42, March 1980, pp. 151–153.
Mookherjee, H., and H. W. Hogan: "Attitudes and Driving Behavior among Americans," *Journal of Social Psychology*, vol. 112, December 1980, pp. 315–317.
Muscarella, Leni: "Dying for a Drink," *The Record*, March 7, 1982.
"The War against Drunk Drivers," *Newsweek*, September 13, 1982, pp. 34–39.

A Speech: "Censorship of Books—A Problem for Our Time"[21]

Do you believe that you can go to the library and borrow any book you want? According to the Czechoslavakian dissident Milan Simecka, there are countries in the world where you can do this. But what I ask you is, "Is the United States one of those countries?" Though this may surprise you, unfortunately the answer is *not* a resounding yes. Book censorship is a problem that must be alleviated.

The speaker uses a rhetorical question to spark the audience's interest.

Testimony and a question are used to promote curiosity.

The speaker's goal is stated clearly and succinctly. The organization—problem-and-solution order—is also previewed here.

The speaker's position is supported by an abundance of statistical evidence.

The speaker tells us that one of our most basic rights is in danger; fear is used to stimulate agreement.

The speaker clarifies for us the possible motivations of censors and then works to combat these stances.

Books are personified as victims.

The speaker supplies a number of examples of censors' work. The extent and nature of the problem are clarified for us.

The speaker explains the dangers inherent in censorship of books. Both emotional and logical appeals are used.

USA Today reports that in the 1980s complaints about censorship increased in our country from 300 per year to almost 1,000 per year. Even more sadly, in just one 2-year period alone—between 1982 and 1983—there were 22 book burnings in 17 of our states. Book burnings! Where are we living—Nazi Germany? *Freedom of Information*, a publication of the Society of Professional Journalists, reports that our "censors are building a Library of Condemned Books that may soon become the world's fastest-growing but unused collection." As a case in point, efforts to censor books occur in one-fifth of our nation's schools every year—and, surprisingly, half of them succeed. What is happening to one of our most sacred rights—freedom of expression?

What are the censors hoping to accomplish? For what reasons are they banning books? In 1984 the Associated Press reported that the Lindenwald, New Jersey, school board voted to limit access to three books it considered inappropriate for some children—one was about an overweight youngster, and another dealt with divorce and family relations. Are these topics we should not be free to read about? Are children not experiencing these problems themselves, and can't reading about such situations actually increase their ability to cope with and understand them? I would think so. Yet our list of book casualties is increasing, not decreasing, and it is growing at an alarming rate.

Who are the victims? The victims are books we probably grew up with. For example, the journalist Christine Moore notes that in Fairfax County, Virginia, one school administrator is revising *Huckleberry Finn* by deleting "offensive racist" remarks. In a Baton Rouge suburb, the books *Cinderella* and *Snow White* were burned because they contained "satanic" material. Phyllis Schlafly, a notable opponent of ERA, has announced that she will devote her energies to purifying school textbooks of feminist influences. Reports are that she is meeting with success. And in St. David, Arizona, one group succeeded in removing books by Conrad, Hawthorne, Hemingway, Homer, Poe, and Steinbeck from required reading lists. Even more recently, in Panama City, Florida, in 1988, the following books were banned by the school board because, it was said, they contained either the curse "god-damn" or "a lot of vulgarity": Shakespeare's plays *Twelfth Night* and *The Merchant of Venice* and the novels *Mr. Roberts*, *The Great Gatsby*, and *The Red Badge of Courage*.

Why are incidents like these a problem? You forfeit your cultural heritage when you destroy books. You forfeit the stuff that feeds our minds. As President John F. Kennedy noted: "Our young people constitute the greatest resource our country has—and books are essential to their intellectual growth into thoughtful and informed citizens." And as the educator Gilbert Highet observed, it is through books that we "can call into range the voice of a man far distant in time and space, and hear him speaking to us mind-to-mind, heart-to-heart."

We must not take our books for granted. I do not want to read censored thoughts, censored fears, and censored dreams. I do not want to look for a volume to find that its use has been restricted. Our strength as a nation lies in our access to ideas. Censors may have a right to decide what their own children may read, but they should not have a right to decide what I will read.

If you feel the same way as I do, then you will join with me in organizing a school chapter of People for the American Way, a group founded to fight censorship. After all, the book, as our Librarian of Congress Daniel Boorstin likes to put it, is our "TV of the mind." The number of titles we have access to should be increasing, not diminishing. I firmly believe that the world of books is the most wonderful creation of humanity. Nothing should be permitted to destroy them. If we are to live on in freedom our books must live on too.

The speaker proposes a solution that could alleviate the problem.

Sources

Bernstein, Richard: "Opening the Books on Censorship," *The New York Times Magazine*, May 13, 1984.

"If Books Are Gutted Education Will Bleed," *USA Today*, August 9, 1983.

Hentoff, Nat: "Selling the American Heritage for Big Texas Bucks," *The Village Voice*, October 4, 1983, p. 6.

Moore, Christine: "Textbook Censorship Multiplying," *FOI '82*, 1982.

Palmer, Barbara: "Censorship: The Battle Is Heating Up," *USA Today*, June 21, 1984.

SUMMARY

The goal of a persuasive speech is to modify the audience's thoughts, feelings, or actions. To be an effective persuasive speaker you need first to identify your goal and learn as much as you can about the general attitudes and beliefs of the audience members, as well as what their opinion of your specific proposal is likely to be. You should then tailor your presentation accordingly to get their attention, appeal to their needs and goals, and promise them a meaningful reward for accepting your proposal.

Your *credibility*—what the audience thinks of you—will also help determine whether your efforts at persuasion will be successful. A credible speaker is perceived by the audience as someone of good character who is knowledgeable and personable.

SUGGESTIONS FOR FURTHER READING

Cialdini, Robert: *Influence*, Quill, New York; 1984. A fascinating analysis of the persuasion process. Understandable and readable.

Larson, Charles: *Persuasion: Reception and Responsibility*, 5th ed., Wadsworth, Belmont, Calif., 1989. Designed for students who "consume" and "produce" persuasion. Provides an interesting analysis of the communicative and persuasive milieu.

Reardon, Kathleen Kelly: *Persuasion in Practice*, Sage, Newbury Park, Calif., 1991. Defines and explains persuasion at the same time that it debunks a number of myths.

Ross, Raymond: *Understanding Persuasion*, 3d ed., Prentice-Hall, Englewood Cliffs, N.J., 1990. A practical problem-centered introduction to the study of persuasion.

Rybacki, Karyn, and Donald J. Rybacki: *Advocacy and Opposition: An Introduction to Argumentation*, 2d ed., Prentice-Hall, Englewood Cliffs, N.J., 1991. Explores principles of arguing as they apply to daily interaction; also focuses on the role argument plays in society.

Triandes, Harry C.: *Attitude and Attitude Change*, Wiley, New York, 1971. A scholarly examination of attitudes and beliefs.

Zimbardo, Philip G., Ebbe B. Ebbesen, and Christina Maslach: *Influencing Attitudes and Behavior*, 2d ed., Addison-Wesley, Reading, Mass., 1977. A good overview of research and theory.

NOTES

1. For an excellent explanation of why we study persuasion, see Joseph Ilardo, *Speaking Persuasively*, Macmillan, New York, 1981, chap. 1.
2. See Wallace Folderingham, *Perspectives on Persuasion*, Allyn and Bacon, Boston, Mass. 1966, p. 33.
3. For a chapter defining persuasion, Gary Cronkhite, *Persuasion: Speech and Behavioral Change*, Indianapolis, Ind., Bobbs-Merrill, 1969, chap. 1.
4. See M. Herif and C. Hovland, *Social Judgment*, Yale University Press, New Haven, Conn. 1961; and C. Herif, M. Sherif, and R. Nebergall, *Attitude and Attitude Change*, Saunders, Philadelphia, Pa., 1965.
5. Scott Cutlip and Alan Center, *Effective Public Relations*, Prentice-Hall, Englewood Cliffs, N.J., 1985, p. 122.
6. Germaine Greer, *The Female Eunuch*, McGraw-Hill, New York, 1971.
7. A framework for understanding the importance of beliefs is provided by Martin Fishbein and Icek Ajzen, *Belief, Attitude, Intention and Behavior: An Introduction to Theory and Research*, Addison-Wesley, Reading, Mass., 1975. See especially chaps. 1 and 8.
8. Milton Rokeach, *The Open and Closed Mind*, Basic Books, New York, 1960.
9. Prominent theorists such as Leon Festinger, Fritz Hieder, and Theodore Newcomb consider the desire for consistency a central motivator of behavior. For a more contemporary discussion of the topic, see Robert B. Cialdini, *Influence*, Quill, New York, 1984, pp. 66–114.
10. Ibid., p. 117.
11. Ibid.
12. Wayne Minnick, *The Art of Persuasion*, Houghton Mifflin, Boston, Mass., 1968.
13. For a discussion of the role of affect, see, for example, Mary John Smith, *Persuasion and Human Action*, Wadsworth, Belmont, Calif., 1982.
14. From *In Search of Light: The Broadcasts of Edward R. Murrow 1938–1961*, Edward Bliss, Jr. (ed.), Knopf, New York, 1967. Copyright © 1967 by the Estate of Edward R. Murrow. Reprinted by permission of Alfred A. Knopf, Inc.
15. "High Flight" quoted by President Ronald Reagan in his speech to commemorate the *Challenger* crew.
16. Abraham Maslow, *Motivation and Personality*, Harper and Row, New York, 1954, pp. 80–92.
17. Credibility has received much attention from researchers. For sample studies, see R. Applebaum and K. Anatol, "The Factor Structure of Source Credibility as a Function of the Speaking Situation," *Speech Monographs*, vol. 39, 1972, pp. 216–222. A valuable and still worthwhile summary of experimental research on credibility is provided in Kenneth Andersen and Theodore Clevenger, Jr., "A Summary of Experimental Research of Ethos," *Speech Monographs*, vol. 30, 1963, pp. 59–78.
18. Speakers can establish credibility early in a speech. For example, see R. Brooks and T. Scheidel, "Speech as Process: A Case Study," *Speech Monographs*, vol. 35, 1968, pp. 1–7.
19. Nonverbal aspects of credibility are discussed in more detail in Chapter 16.
20. Developed as part of a class exercise by students in the course "Basic Public Speaking" at the College of New Rochelle, New York.
21. Developed as a class exercise by students in the course "Basic Public Speaking" at the College of New Rochelle, New York.

CONTINUING COMMUNICATION: TODAY AND TOMORROW

INTERVIEWING: FROM BOTH SIDES OF THE DESK

After finishing this chapter, you should be able to:

Define *interview*

Explain how an interview differs from a casual conversation

Identify the types of information shared by both participants in an interview

Explain the fears both interviewer and interviewee may bring to the situation

Determine your own level of "interview anxiety"

Describe the stages of an interview

Explain the role of questions in an interview

Formulate closed, open, primary, and secondary questions

Compare and contrast the roles and responsibilities of interviewer and interviewee

Create a favorable impression as an interviewer or interviewee

Enhance your effectiveness in interviews

A t various points during the course of our lives, we will be expected to take part in interviews, assuming the role of interviewer or interviewee. The interview incorporates many of the characteristics and principles of communication that we have discussed. Self-concept, perception, listening and feedback, nonverbal communication, language and meaning, and assertiveness all play a part in determining the effectiveness of communication in an interview setting. Time you spend interviewing or being interviewed can be critical. It can determine whether you give or get a loan, sell or purchase a product, hire the right person, get the job you want, or keep the job you have. By exploring the interview process you can prepare yourself to participate in any interview—from either side of the desk.

WHAT IS AN INTERVIEW?

The Nature of Interviews: Beyond Conversation

Interviews, like other forms of communication, usually involve face-to-face interaction. However, in an interview—unlike ordinary person-to-person communication—at least one of the participants has a purpose that goes beyond interacting informally or simply talking for enjoyment. The conversation that occurs during an interview is planned and is designed to achieve specific objectives. In fact (although sometimes three or more people are involved), you could say that the interview is the most common type of purposeful, planned, decision-making, person-to-person communication. Thus, in the interview, interaction is structured, questions are asked and answered, and behavior is interchanged in an effort to explore predetermined subject matter and realize a definite goal. This description is in keeping with a well-known and often cited definition by Goyer, Redding, and Richey, authors of *Interviewing Principles and Techniques: A Project Text.* They define an interview as a "form of oral communication involving two parties, at least one of whom has a preconceived and serious purpose and both of whom speak and listen from time to time."[1]

No matter how an interview is defined, the participants are involved in a process of personal contact and exchange of information; they meet to give and receive information in order to make educated decisions. Ideally, the interview should be *balanced*: both interviewer and interviewee should give themselves an opportunity to learn from the data given and received during the interchange.

What types of information have you shared during interviews? What information have you received from the other participant in the interview? How do you think the information exchanged affected the decision-making process?

454

In an information-gathering interview, the goal is to obtain information about a topic or person.

Mary Kate Denny/
PhotoEdit

Types of Interviews: Purposes and Goals

Interviews serve a variety of purposes. People engage in interviews to gather information (the *information-gathering* interview), to participate in an evaluation (the *appraisal* interview), to change someone's attitudes or behavior (the *persuasive* interview), to determine why someone is leaving a position (the *exit* interview), to provide guidance (the *counseling* interview), and to gain employment or select the right person for a job (the *hiring* or *selection* interview). Each of these types is characterized by different goals on the part of the participant.

INFORMATION-GATHERING INTERVIEWS

In an information-gathering interview, the interviewer's goal is to collect information, opinions, or data about a specific topic or person. It is the interviewer's job to ask the interviewee questions designed to add to the interviewer's knowledge—questions about the interviewee's views, understanding, insights, predictions, and so on. Examples are interviews conducted with experts to complete an assignment and interviews conducted for the popular media. Whether the interviewer is Barbara Walters, Mike Wallace, or you, the aim is to gather information from someone who has knowledge that you do not yet have.

APPRAISAL INTERVIEWS

In an appraisal interview, the interviewee's performance is assessed by the interviewer, who is usually a superior from management. The goal is to evaluate what the interviewee is doing well and what he or she could do better. Through this means, expectations and behaviors are brought closer together. Interviewees gain perspective on how others view their work, and they also reveal how they see themselves performing.

PERSUASIVE INTERVIEWS

The goal of the interviewer in a persuasive interview is to change the interviewee's attitudes or behavior. It is hoped that as the interview progresses, the interviewee will come to a desired conclusion or give a desired response. Salespeople typically conduct persuasive interviews with customers to close a sale.

EXIT INTERVIEWS

An exit interview is often conducted when an employee leaves an organization; it is an effort to determine why the match between employer and employee did not work or why the employee has decided to leave. Information obtained during an exit interview can be used to refine the hiring process, to help prevent other employees from leaving, or merely to make the departure a more pleasant experience for employer and employee.

COUNSELING INTERVIEWS

A counseling interview is usually conducted by someone trained in psychology and is designed to provide guidance and support for the person being interviewed. Interviewees are helped to solve their problems, to work more productively, to interact with others more effectively, or to improve their relationships with friends and family members—in general, to cope more successfully with daily life.

HIRING INTERVIEWS

A hiring interview is conducted for the purpose of filling an employment position. The interviewer is an agent of the employer—perhaps a member of the personnel or "human resources" department, or perhaps the person who would actually be the interviewee's supervisor. The interviewee, of course, is the person who is applying for the job. Because the hiring interview is experienced so commonly—and because it is so important—we will consider it in detail later in this chapter.

HOW DO YOU FEEL ABOUT INTERVIEWS?
—ASSESSING YOUR "INTERVIEW ANXIETY"

How do you feel about interviewing someone? How do you feel about being interviewed?

Listed on the opposite page are some fears commonly expressed by *interviewers*. Circle the number beneath each statement that most accurately reflects your own level of apprehension: 0 represents "completely unconcerned"; 1, "very mild concern"; 2, "mild concern"; 3, "more apprehensive than not"; 4, "very frightened"; 5, "a nervous wreck."

1. I won't be able to think of good questions to ask.

   0 1 2 3 4 5

2. I will appear very nervous.

   0 1 2 3 4 5

3. I will give the interviewee too little or too much information.

   0 1 2 3 4 5

4. I will not be considered credible.

   0 1 2 3 4 5

5. I will be asked questions about the company that I can't answer.

   0 1 2 3 4 5

6. I will be a poor judge of character.

   0 1 2 3 4 5

7. I will have poor rapport with the interviewee.

   0 1 2 3 4 5

8. I will not appear organized.

   0 1 2 3 4 5

9. I will be ineffective at probing for more information.

   0 1 2 3 4 5

10. I will not hire the right person for the job.

   0 1 2 3 4 5

Total the numbers you circled above to arrive at your "interviewer's anxiety" score.

Below are some fears frequently expressed by *interviewees.* Circle the number that most accurately reflects your own level of apprehension. (0 = "completely unconcerned"; 1 = "very mild concern"; 2 = "mild concern"; 3 = "more apprehensive than not"; 4 = "very frightened"; 5 = "a nervous wreck.")

Interviewee

1. I will be asked questions I cannot answer.

       0   1   2   3   4   5

2. I will not dress properly for the interview.

       0   1   2   3   4   5

3. I will appear very nervous.

       0   1   2   3   4   5

4. I will not appear competent.

       0   1   2   3   4   5

5. The interviewer will cross-examine me.

       0   1   2   3   4   5

6. I will be caught in a lie.

       0   1   2   3   4   5

7. I will talk too much or too little.

       0   1   2   3   4   5

8. I will have poor rapport with the interviewer.

       0   1   2   3   4   5

9. I will undersell or oversell myself.

       0   1   2   3   4   5

10. I won't be hired.

       0   1   2   3   4   5

Total the numbers you circled to arrive at your "interviewee's anxiety" score.

Your scores indicate how frightened you are of assuming the role of interviewer or interviewee. If you accumulated 45 to 50 points, you are a "nervous wreck"; if you scored 35 to 44 points, you are "too frightened"; if you scored 20 to 34 points, you are "somewhat apprehensive"; if you scored 11 to 20 points, you are "too casual"; if you scored 0 to 10 points, you are "not at all concerned"—that is, you simply don't care.

Contrary to what you might assume, not being concerned at all about participating in an interview is just as much of a problem as being a nervous wreck, and being too casual can do as much damage as being too frightened. An interviewer or interviewee should be apprehensive *to a degree*. If you're not concerned about what will happen during the interview, then you won't care about making a good impression and as a result will not perform as effectively as you could.

THE HIRING INTERVIEW

The hiring interview is among the best-known and most widely experienced types of interview and probably is the next major interview you will face. For that reason, this section will focus on hiring interviews.

It is as a result of a hiring interview that we find ourselves accepted or rejected by a prospective employer—an individual, a small business, a large corporation, and so on. The employment interview offers a unique opportunity for the potential employer and the potential employee to share meaningful information that will permit each to determine whether their association would be beneficial and productive. In a sense, the employment interview can be said to give both participants a chance to test each other by asking and answering relevant questions.

The better prepared you are for an employment interview, the better your chances will be of performing effectively and realizing your job objectives. Remember, an interview is certainly not "just talk."[2] Both the interviewer and the interviewee must plan and prepare to participate in an interview. Only with planning and preparation will important questions and answers be shared and "interview anxiety" reduced. Let's begin by familiarizing ourselves with some important aspects of the hiring interview, which are also aspects of interviews in general.

> There is only one person who can tell you whether any candidate is right for the job: the candidate him- or herself.
>
> Kevin J. Murphy, *Effective Listening: Your Key to Career Success*

Most effective interviews have a discernible structure. To put it simply, they have a beginning, a middle, and an end. The *beginning*, or *opening*, is the segment of the process that provides an orientation to what will come. The *middle*, or *body*, is the longest segment and the one during which both parties really get down to business. The *end*, or *close*, is the segment during which the participants prepare to take leave of one another.

Just as the right kind of "hello" at the start of a conversation can help create a feeling of friendliness, so the opening of an interview should be used to establish rapport between interviewer and interviewee.[3] The primary purpose of the opening is to make it possible for both to participate freely and honestly by creating an atmosphere of trust and goodwill and by explaining the purpose and scope of the meeting. Conversational icebreakers and orientation statements perform important functions at this stage. Typical icebreakers include comments about the weather, the surroundings (the "here and now"), and current events—or a compliment. The idea is to use small talk to help make the interview a human encounter rather than a mechanical one. Typical orientation remarks include identification of the interview's purpose, a preview of the topics to be discussed, and statements that motivate the respondent and act as a conduit or transition into the body of the interview.

In the body of the interview, as we noted above, the interactants really get down to business. At this point the interviewer and interviewee might discuss work experiences, including those things the applicant does best, his or her weaknesses, major accomplishments, difficult problems tackled in the past, and career goals. Educational background and activities or interests are relevant areas to probe during this phase of the interview. Breadth of knowledge and the ability to manage time are also common areas of concern.

During the close of the interview, the main points covered are reviewed and summarized. Since an interview can affect any future meetings the interactors may have, care must be taken to make the leave-taking comfortable.[4] Expressing appreciation for the time and effort given is important; neither interviewee nor interviewer should feel "discarded." In other words, the door should be left open for future contacts.

For the next few days, keep track of the verbal and nonverbal messages people use when they say hello or good-bye. Which beginnings and endings were particularly communicative? Which were ineffective? Did you observe any false starts or false endings? How could they have been avoided?

Questions: The "Heartbeat" of the Interview

How many times a day are you asked questions? How many times a day do you ask questions? Questions are obviously a natural part of our daily discourse. Let's see why.

Questions asked in the course of typical everyday interpersonal encounters perform a number of functions. They help us find out needed information, satisfy our curiosity, demonstrate our interest, and test the knowledge of the person we are questioning; at the same time they permit the person we are questioning to reveal himself or herself to us.

The only way to get the accurate answers is to ask the right questions.
Kevin J. Murphy, *Effective Listening: Your Key to Career Success*

For these reasons, questions are the primary means of collecting data in an interview. Not only do questions set the tone for an interview; they also determine whether the interview will yield valuable information or prove to be practically worthless.

The effective interviewer, like the effective newswriter, can benefit from this famous verse by Rudyard Kipling:

I keep six honest serving-men
(They taught me all I know).
Their names are what and why and when
And how and where and who.

The interrogatives *what, where, when, who, how,* and *why* are used throughout an interview because they lay a foundation of knowledge on which to base decisions or conclusions.

During the course of an interview, closed, open, primary, and secondary questions may all be used, and in any combination.[5] *Closed questions* are highly structured and can be answered with a simple yes or no or a few brief words. Following are examples of closed questions:

"How old are you?"

"Where do you live?"

"What schools did you attend?"

"Did you graduate in the top quarter of your class?"

"Would you accept the salary offered?"

"What starting salary do you expect?"

Open questions are broader in nature than closed questions and are less restricting or structured; hence, they offer the interviewee more freedom with regard to the choice and scope of an answer. Following are examples of open questions:

"Tell me about yourself."

"What are your feelings about our industry?"

> Each of you has questions in the interview—both you and the employer. The essence of the interview is to find out the answers to those questions.
> Richard N. Bolles

461

"How do you judge success?"

"Why did you choose to interview for this particular job?"

"What are your career goals?"

Open questions give interviewees a chance to express their feelings, attitudes, and values. Furthermore, they indicate that the interviewer is interested in understanding the interviewee's perspective.

Open and closed questions may be either primary or secondary. *Primary questions* are used to introduce topics or to begin exploring a new area. "What is your favorite hobby?" and "Tell me about your last job" are examples of primary questions; the first is closed, and the second is open. A smart interviewer will prepare a list of primary questions before coming to the interview, and smart interviewees will anticipate the primary questions they may be asked.

Secondary questions—sometimes called *probing questions*—are used to follow up primary questions. They ask for an explanation of the ideas and feelings behind answers to other questions, and they are frequently used when answers to primary questions are vague or incomplete. Following are examples of secondary questions:

"Go on. What do you mean?"

"Would you explain that further?"

"Could you give me an example?"

"What did you have in mind when you said that?"

"Uh huh" and "Hmmm" are typical "comments" to the answers produced by secondary questions. Charles J. Stewart and William B. Cash, Jr., note in their book *Interviewing: Principles and Practices* that effective use of secondary questions distinguishes skilled from unskilled interviewers.[6]

✔ **SKILL BUILDER**

FOLLOW-UP QUESTIONS

What secondary questions would you use to follow up this series of exchanges?

1. INTERVIEWER: How do you feel about a job that requires 50 percent travel?
   INTERVIEWEE: That depends.
   INTERVIEWER: _____

2. INTERVIEWER: Why are you leaving your present position?
   INTERVIEWEE: It's time for a change.
   INTERVIEWER: _____

3. INTERVIEWER: What kind of job are you seeking?
   INTERVIEWEE: An interesting one.
   INTERVIEWER: _____

4. INTERVIEWER: What is your attitude toward overtime?
   INTERVIEWEE: A lot of employees object to overtime.
   INTERVIEWER: _____

5. INTERVIEWER: What do you expect to be earning in 5 years?
   INTERVIEWEE: A decent wage.
   INTERVIEWER: _____

To ask effective follow-up questions, you need to be an effective listener. You must be sensitive to and on the lookout for an interviewee's feelings and attitudes, in addition to the facts and opinions he or she states. You will need to develop techniques that will permit you to see the world through the other person's eyes.

Just as skillful listening is essential if one is to be an effective conversationalist, it is also essential to the give-and-take that characterizes an effective interview. In fact, according to the researcher David Bianculli, the key to the success of professional interviewers like Bryant Gumbel, Ted Koppel, and Phil Donahue is their ability to listen.[7] Of course, it goes without saying that the interviewee must also be an effective listener.

Objectives: Roles and Responsibilities

Let's now examine the roles and responsibilities of each participant in an interview.

Both interviewer and interviewee come to the interview with certain goals in mind. *Interviewers* usually have a threefold objective. They hope to (1) gather information that will enable them to evaluate the interviewees' probable performance accurately; (2) persuade applicants that the business or organization is a good one to work for; and (3) ascertain whether the applicants and the people with whom they will work will be compatible. Interviewers also want to keep their own jobs. Remember that a company invests both time and money in hiring and training a new employee. If the employee doesn't work out, the investment is sacrificed and some of the blame obviously falls on the original interviewer.

To fulfill their objectives, interviewers need to master the art of structuring a successful interview, use effective questioning techniques, and approach each interview with flexibility and sensitivity. Good interviewers work hard during an interview. They wear three "hats": information seeker, information giver, and decision maker (see Figure 19-1 on page 465). They recognize good answers, are aware of word choices, and pick up on silences and hesitations. They are active, not passive, participants.

Interviewees also bear responsibility during an interview. They too need to speak and listen, provide information, and collect information that will help them decide whether or not to accept the job. To accomplish these goals, interviewees need to research the organization to which they are applying and try to anticipate the questions they will be asked. They also need to plan to ask questions themselves. It's unfortunate and unproductive when only the interviewer gains information from an interview. The interviewee can often learn much about work conditions and the prospects for advancement by asking questions and probing for answers. To the extent that interviewees have a right to share the control of the interview, they can affect its direction and content. Like interviewers, interviewees need to be good listeners, adaptable, and sensitive to the image they project.

Effective interviewees work hard at self-assessment. In effect, they take stock of themselves in order to determine who they are, what their career needs and their goals are, and how they can best sell themselves to an employer.

As a prospective interviewee, you will find it useful to prepare by thinking about and answering the following questions:

1. For what types of positions has my training prepared me?
2. What has been my most rewarding experience?
3. What type of job do I want?
4. Would I be happier working alone or with others?
5. What qualifications do I have that make me feel I would be successful in the job of my choice?
6. What type or types of people do I want to work for?
7. What type or types of people do I *not* want to work for?
8. How do I feel about receiving criticism?
9. What salary will enable me to meet my financial needs?
10. What salary will enable me to live comfortably?
11. What will interviewers want to know about me, my interests, my background, and my experiences?

In addition to conducting a self-survey, the interviewee needs to work to withstand the pressure of the interview situation. Are you prepared to maintain your composure while being stared at, interrupted, spoken to abruptly, or asked difficult questions? How do you think you would react? The following questions are favorites among interviewers. How would you answer them?

1. Tell me about yourself.
2. What do you think you're worth?
3. If we hired you, what about this organization would concern you most?
4. What attributes do you think an effective manager should possess?
5. What are your short-term goals? How are they different from your long-term goals?
6. How has your background prepared you for this position?
7. What are your major strengths and weaknesses?
8. How would a former employer or instructor describe you, if asked?
9. What do you consider your greatest accomplishment?
10. How long do you plan to remain with us if you get this job?
11. What would you like to know about us?

Practice in answering questions like these—under both favorable and unfavorable conditions—is essential.[8] It is important that you know what you want to say during the interview and that you use the questions you are asked as an opportunity to say it. Along the way, you can flatter the interviewer by offering comments like "That's a really good question" or "I think you've touched on something really important."

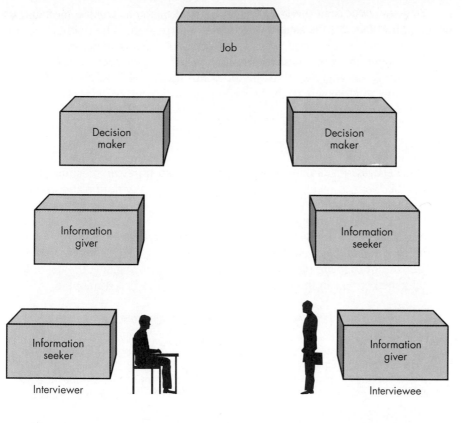

FIGURE 19-1
Responsibilities in an
interview.

The interviewer can of course use a résumé to ascertain information about the applicant—about educational background and previous positions held, for example. However, gathering enough information to evaluate the personal qualities of an applicant is more difficult. Following is a list of personal qualifications, and the questions interviewers typically ask to evaluate them.

1. *Quality:* Skill in managing one's own career.
   Question: What specific things have you deliberately done to get where you are today?

2. *Quality:* Skill in managing others.
   Question: Give me some examples of things you do and do not like to delegate.

3. *Quality:* Sense of responsibility.
   Question: What steps do you take to see that things do not fall through the cracks when you are supervising a project?

4. *Quality:* Skill in working with people.
   Question: If we assembled a group of people you have worked with in one room and asked them to describe what it was like to work with you, what would they be likely to say? What would your greatest supporter say? What would your severest critic say?

What other qualities do you believe interviewers look for in interviewees? If you were an interviewer, what questions would you ask to determine if a person possessed those qualities?

To be effective, an interview requires both participants to work hard. Questioner and respondent constantly exchange information. While either the interviewer or the interviewee speaks, the other is conveying nonverbal information through posture, facial expression, gestures, and so on. You may stop talking during an interview, but this does not mean that you stop communicating. Know what you are trying to accomplish with your verbal and nonverbal messages.

Impression Management: Effective Interviewing

The word *interview* is derived from the French word *entrevoir*, meaning "to see one another" or "to meet." What happens when an interviewer and an interviewee meet for the first time? What variables influence the impressions the interviewer forms of the interviewee? We know, for example, that most interviewers make their decisions about an applicant during the actual course of the interview; in fact, although most decide in the last quarter of the interview whether or not to invite the applicant back, a bias for or against the candidate is established earlier in the interview, often during the first 4 minutes.

In *Your Attitude Is Showing*, Elwood N. Chapman notes:

> First impressions are important because they have a lasting quality. People you meet for the first time appear to have little radar sets tuned into your attitude. If your attitude is positive, they receive a friendly, warm signal, and they are attracted to you; if your attitude is negative, they receive an unfriendly signal, and they try to avoid you.[9]

Apparently, what happens is that once interviewers form an initial impression, they selectively pick up on whatever information supports that impression. In effect, interviewers make self-fulfilling prophecies.

According to the researcher Lois Einhorn, how much of the time allotted for an interview is actually used also sends an important message.[10] She found that interviewees who were not hired had participated in shorter interviews

---

● CULTURE AND COMMUNICATION

VOICES AND IMPRESSION MANAGEMENT

People from different cultures use their voices differently, a fact that could lead to misunderstandings between interviewers and interviewees. People from the middle east, for example, tend to speak louder than westerners, causing westerners to perceive them as overly emotional. In contrast, the Japanese tend to be much more soft-spoken, leading westerners to believe that they are extremely polite and humble.

How could such habitual ways of speaking affect the interview process?

What can interviewers and interviewees do to diminish such perceptual barriers?

YOUR MARKETING PROFILE

1. Identify the assets and talents you would bring to the position of your choice. In other words, attempt to enumerate the qualities and skills that would make you a good investment for an employer.

2. Identify your shortcomings and developmental needs. Enumerate the qualities and skills you wish to develop further and plan how you would do this.

3. Identify those personality strengths you will attempt to communicate during an interview.

4. Identify the communication skills you will use.

5. Now, using the above information, compose a "Position Wanted" advertisement for yourself.

than successful applicants. She also found that successful interviewees spoke a greater percentage of the time than their unsuccessful counterparts. In fact, the successful applicants spoke for some 55 percent of the total interview time, whereas the unsuccessful applicants spoke only 37 percent of the time. Seeming to control the interview also leaves an impression. In Einhorn's research, successful applicants initiated 56 percent of the comments made during their interviews, whereas unsuccessful applicants were viewed as "followers"—they initiated only 37 percent of the comments. It is important for an interviewee to send messages that he or she is active, not passive.

THE JOB APPLICANT

It is important to realize that as a job applicant you will have to work to manage the initial impression you give. You will be evaluated on how you come across during the interview and on how you present yourself. What you say and how you say it are your basic resources—the key tools you have to work with. In effect, you are your own marketing manager; therefore, it's up to you to sell yourself to the interviewer. How you communicate your assets, your values, your attitudes, and your overall credibility will, at least in part, determine whether or not you are hired. Your resources and your ability to share what you are come with you to every interview.

> **Believe in yourself.**
> The wizard of Oz to Dorothy

Of necessity, interviewers need to find out a great deal about you in a short period of time. They want to evaluate your strengths as a communicator, your general personality, your social effectiveness, and your character. The interviewer also wants to determine your needs and wants—including your career and educational goals, interests, and aspirations. Interviewers will assess your appearance, your ability to use body language effectively, and your ability to maintain control during the interview.

To a large extent, the interviewer's assessment of you will determine whether or not you get the job.

The hiring interview is probably the next major interview you will face. Job interviewers judge applicants at least partly on the basis of nonverbal cues—including eye contact; posture that communicates a positive attitude; and indications of a high level of energy, such as hand gestures, facial expression, and appropriate body movements.

Billy E. Barnes/Stock, Boston

At least in part, interviewers will judge you on the basis of the nonverbal cues you send. Interviewers consistently give higher general ratings to applicants who are rated high in nonverbal expression than to applicants who are rated low. A highly rated nonverbal presentation will include (1) maintaining comfortable eye contact with the interviewer rather than looking away; (2) varying the pitch and volume of your voice rather than speaking a monotone, a whisper, or a shout; (3) eliminating hesitations ("uhs" and "ums"); (4) leaning forward from the trunk rather than slumping in your seat; and (5) communicating a high level of energy supported by smiles, hand gestures, and appropriate body movements. In like fashion, avoidance of tightly held hands, twitching feet or fingers, and various other signs of physical tension will influence the interviewer positively.

Obviously, appropriate dress is also important to the impression you make during the interview. The consultant John Molloy (as we discussed in Chapter 5) reports that when interviewing for a job, it is advisable to dress as if you were a candidate for a position one or two steps higher than the one for which you are actually applying.[11] He notes that a man is safe if he wears a dark suit (navy blue, dark gray, or gray pinstripe); a white, blue, or pale-yellow shirt; and a conservative, nondescript tie. Molloy finds that gray suits worn with pale-blue shirts and dark-blue suits worn with pale-yellow shirts increase "likability." He also comments that a solid-gray or a conservative blue or gray pinstripe

What type of clothing would you consider *in*appropriate for a job interview? What type of clothing would you yourself wear to a job interview?

suit—preferably a three-piece suit—is the most powerful and authoritative suit and should therefore be saved for the crucial interview with the most important person you will see. Molloy believes that a woman applying for a professional job should wear a dark-colored, skirted suit and a white or blue blouse; she should avoid tight-fitting clothing or pants.

Why is there so much concern with dress? When all else is comparable—education, aptitude, experience—appearance may well be the deciding factor. The candidate who looks the most professional, competent, and confident will probably be the one who is hired.

▶ POINTS TO PONDER

TO IMPRESS AT AN INTERVIEW, DRESS FOR SUCCESS AND SMILE

"Invest in the right interview outfit, and you'll be investing in your future," advised Jackie Walker, owner of Options Dressing, an image-styling business in Tampa, Fla.

The "right" outfit—for men and women—is a classic suit. Traditional "power" colors such as black, navy, or gray, teamed with a white shirt or blouse, conservative lace-up shoes or pumps, minimal jewelry, and a businesslike briefcase make the best impression, said several personnel managers.

And while it's summer, the hot weather is no excuse for leaving your socks or stockings at home. Coming to interviews without hosiery is the No. 1 mistake young job-seekers make, the personnel managers said.

Leaving a wild and trendy hairstyle untamed is mistake No. 2. And No. 3 is the least forgivable: "They just don't bother to see that everything they wear, down to their shoes, is clean, pressed, and polished," Walker said.

Before leaving home for a job interview, stand in front of a full-length mirror and check your appearance—front and back. Say to yourself, "How will the world see me today? What do I want to accomplish?"

For some jobs, a little more flair or a little less formality may be acceptable—but it's always best to err on the side of conservatism, Walker said. There's plenty of time to "personalize" your outfit once you're safely entrenched in the job.

"Dress appropriately for the job you're seeking," she advised. "In corporate America—banking, law, and so on—you need an image that projects seriousness. If you're going for something in the communications field—real estate, teaching, advertising—you can relax a bit, but not too much. In the creative field—interior design, art, retailing—you can go a little more high-style. The interviewer will be looking at your flair, at how you put things together creatively."

"Do your homework," Walker said. "Go to the place of business ahead of time and check out what people are wearing. Use that as a guide for your interview."

Or call the personnel manager and ask about the dress code at the business, suggested Lisa Maile, owner of Lisa Maile Image, a modeling and acting school in Florida.

"At the end of the day, you want them to remember you," Maile said. "If they've done a lot of interviews that day, they'll probably only remember the best and the worst candidates. You want to make such a good impression that the personnel manager will think, 'I'd better hire this person or they'll be working for the competition.'"

Dress for the job you'd like to have five years from now, rather than an entry-level position, Maile advised.

"And remember, the most important thing to wear is a smile—along with strong eye contact and a power handshake."

Source: From "To Impress at Interview, Dress for Success, Smile" by Jean Patteson. Copyright © 1991 *The Orlando Sentinel*. Reprinted by permission of The Orlando Sentinel.

■ **ETHICS AND COMMUNICATION**

HONESTY IN INTERVIEWS

How essential is it to be absolutely honest during an interview? In your opinion, are lies of omission or commission ever justified? If so, under what circumstances?

"It has come to my attention, Pickarell, that you may have been somewhat less than forthcoming in your résumé."

Drawing by Barsotti; © 1989 The New Yorker Magazine, Inc.

Since every aspect of your nonverbal communication affects the interviewer's judgment of you, you need to work to send out appropriate nonverbal signals. If you consciously or unconsciously send out signals indicating that you're bored, uninterested, or apathetic, you put the interview process in jeopardy. For example, the noted television interviewer Barbara Walters reported the following incident in her book *How to Talk with Practically Anybody about Practically Anything.*

> Some years ago I interviewed Warren Beatty on *Today*. It was before his Bonnie and Clyde fame, and he was fast achieving a reputation among interviewers for being sullen and difficult. However, he was on our program to promote a picture he was currently starring in, and I figured how bad could it be? I smiled warmly and chatted animatedly and asked Mr. Beatty every provocative question I could think of. He answered me monosyllabically with an expression of extreme

boredom bordering on distaste. Finally, I resorted to the hackneyed but spoilproof, "Tell me, Mr. Beatty, what is your new picture about." Well, he slumped in his seat and scratched his chest and rubbed his scalp and yawned and finally after an endless pause he said, "Now that's really a very difficult question."

I'd had it. Right on the air, in front of ten million, I am certain, very sympathetic viewers, I said, "Mr. Beatty, you are the most impossible interview I have ever had. Let's forget the whole thing and I'll do a commercial."[12]

Although this was not a *job* interview, the message still applies. If you do not appear to be a cooperative and willing party to the interview, interviewers will feel that you are wasting their time and effort. Even the most qualified candidate can ruin an interview (and thus forfeit a job opportunity) by communicating a negative rather than a positive image to the interviewer.

You can "cement" a positive image by sending a brief thank-you note to the person or persons who interviewed you. Richard Bolles, author of *What Color Is Your Parachute?* writes: "This is one of the most essential steps in the whole job-seeking process—and the one most overlooked by job-seekers."[13] In fact, one of the authors was actually told that a person who interviewed her for a teaching position had recommended her because she was the only applicant to send him a thank-you note after the interview.

THE INTERVIEWER

It should be remembered that in any interview the interviewer who judges is also judged by the interviewee. To the extent that this judgment is favorable, the interviewer can elicit the interviewee's fullest cooperation in accomplishing the aims and objectives of the interview.

The interviewer's ability to set the tone by reducing the interviewee's initial anxiety is an extremely important factor in the interviewee's first impression. During the body of the interview, the interviewer must work to (1) maintain control of the interchange, (2) deliver information so that it is clearly understood, (3) listen for both facts and feelings, (4) build trust, and (5) distinguish relevant from irrelevant information. Finally, at the conclusion, it is up to the interviewer to explain to the applicant the next course of action to be taken and to terminate the encounter smoothly and graciously.

Like interviewees, interviewers must be adept at using nonverbal cues. They must know when to pause and when to speak. For example, 3- to 6-second silences by interviewers have been found effective in getting interviewees to provide more in-depth information; this is one way the interviewer can increase the amount of time an applicant spends answering a question. Another way to increase the length of an applicant's response is for the interviewer to murmur "Mm-hmm" while nodding affirmatively. In fact, answers to questions posed by interviewers who say "Mm-hmm" have been found to be as much as two times longer than answers given to interviewers who offer no "Mm-hmms." When interviewees rate the interviewer's vocal communication and ability to listen high, they tend to enjoy the interview more and rate the interviewer favorably in general.

WHY DIDN'T I GET THE JOB?

Why does an applicant sometimes receive only a thundering silence from a prospective employer after an interview? A placement director at Northwestern University recently made an interesting survey of 405 well-known firms to find the reasons.

1. *Unrealistic expectations*—Unrealistic about career advancement opportunities and promotion timelines, entry-level job opportunities and responsibilities, and starting salaries. Unrealistic view of workplace, business world, and what they have to offer an employer.

2. *Oral communication skills*—Inability to express themselves effectively. Communication skills inappropriate for business environments.

3. *Writing skills*—Lack of clear, concise, business writing skills, "especially engineers." Poor spelling, grammar. Inarticulate, incoherent.

4. *Knowledge and understanding of the work world*—Poor research and no knowledge of industry, field, company, competitors, job market, or positions. No understanding of business world or actual work environments. "Totally clueless" about life beyond the campus. Not well-rounded—academically, culturally, or socially.

5. *Critical transferable skills*—Deficient in technical skills. Poor math, analytical, problem solving, leadership, creativity, time management, reading, and foreign language abilities. Difficulty in dealing with ambiguity on the job.

6. *Practical work experience*—No relevant or "real life" experience. This includes internships, co-ops, part-time, and meaningful voluntary work experience.

7. *Inappropriate attitudes*—Lack of patience, desire for immediate "paybacks." Exaggerated sense of entitlement. Unwilling to accept responsibility for their actions. Dissatisfied with lateral broadening versus career-ladder progression.

8. *Personal qualities*—Inflexibility. Lack of loyalty, commitment, ethics, maturity, or confidence. Poor professionalism and ignorance of business or social protocol.

9. *Career direction and goals*—Failure to assure personal values, abilities, and interests. Have not set goals and often choose jobs which don't suit them.

10. *Interpersonal and teamwork skills*—Absence of interpersonal skills appropriate for a business setting. Self-centered, with little or no capacity to work and contribute as members of a team.

11. *Initiative and work ethic*—No "go get it" attitude. Many wait for jobs to come to them. Unwilling to work long hard hours and to do "whatever it takes."

12. *Interviewing skills*—Lack strong presentation skills, enthusiasm, energy during the interview process.

Source: From *The Lindquist-Endicott Report 1992* by Victor R. Lindquist, published by The Northwestern University Placement Center, Evanston, Ill.

INCREASING YOUR EFFECTIVENESS IN INTERVIEWS: GUIDELINES

As you can see, an interview, like any other interpersonal relationship, requires the cooperation, skill, and commitment of both participants in order to be effective. Both interviewees and interviewers can benefit from the following guidelines.

1. Be prepared. Understand the purpose of the interview; plan or anticipate the questions you will ask and be asked; understand your goals; and be able to communicate those goals clearly.

2. Practice sending and receiving messages. By its very nature, an interview demands skill at sending and receiving verbal and nonverbal messages. Not only must both interactants clearly encode their messages; each must be skilled at reading the reactions and checking the perceptions of the other.

3. Demonstrate effective listening skills. Problems occur in interviews when either the interviewer or the interviewee fails to listen closely to what the other is saying. As is noted in John Brady's *The Craft of Interviewing*, if participants listen carefully—rather than thinking about what they plan to say next—the interview has a better chance of being productive.[14]

4. Have conviction. Ask and answer questions and express your opinions with enthusiasm. If you aren't excited by your ideas, skills, and abilities, why should anyone else be?

5. Be flexible. Don't overprepare or memorize statements. Think things through thoroughly, but be prepared for questions or answers you didn't anticipate. Be able to adjust to the other person's style and pace.

6. Be observant. Pay attention to the nonverbal signals sent to you and by you. Be sure that the signals you send are positive, not negative. Give the other person your total attention.

7. Consider. Both interviewer and interviewee need to consider the ramifications of a job offer. A typical 40-hour-a-week job done for approximately 50 weeks a year adds up to 6,000 hours in only 3 years. Be sure that your choice is one you and the organization can both live with.

8. Chart your progress. Finally, each time you participate in an interview, fill out a copy of the following evaluation form. Circle the number that best describes your response to each question.

   a. How prepared were you for the interview?

      Not at all prepared   1 2 3 4 5   Fully prepared

   b. What kind of climate did you help create?

      Hostile climate   1 2 3 4 5   Friendly climate

   c. Were the questions you asked clear?

      Not clear   1 2 3 4 5   Clear

   d. Were the responses you offered complete?

      Incomplete   1 2 3 4 5   Complete

e. How carefully did you listen to the other person?

Not at all   1   2   3   4   5   Very carefully

f. How carefully did you pay attention to nonverbal clues?

Not at all   1   2   3   4   5   Very carefully

g. To what extent were you distracted by external stimuli?

Very much   1   2   3   4   5   Not at all

h. How self-confident were you during the interview?

Not at all   1   2   3   4   5   Very confident

i. How flexible were you during the interview?

Not flexible   1   2   3   4   5   Very flexible

j. Would you like to change or improve your behavior for your next interview?

Very much   1   2   3   4   5   Little, or not at all

If your answer to the last question is 1, 2, 3, or 4, consider *how* you would like to change.

SUMMARY

During the course of our lives we all take part in a number of different types of interviews, as either interviewee or interviewer. The interview is the most common type of purposeful, planned, decision-making, person-to-person communication.

Effective interviews are well-structured interactions. They have a beginning, which provides an orientation to what is to come; a middle, when the participants get down to business; and an end, when the main points are reviewed and the participants take leave of one another.

Questions are the heartbeat of the interview and the primary means of collecting data. Four basic types of questions are asked in an interview: closed, open, primary, and secondary. Closed questions are highly structured and can be answered with a simple yes or no or a few words; open questions are broader and offer the interviewee more freedom in responding. Primary questions introduce topics or begin exploring a new area; secondary questions (probing questions) follow up primary questions by asking for further information. (Whatever the type of question, for an interviewee it is essential to maintain honesty in answering.)

Good interviewers and interviewees work hard during an interview, functioning simultaneously as information seekers, information givers, and decision makers. To be a successful interviewee requires specific preparation. Honest self-assessment, practice in answering typical questions, and mastery of the techniques of impression management are of prime importance. To avoid misunderstandings, both interviewer and interviewee need to be aware of cultural differences in voice and vocal tone.

SUGGESTIONS FOR FURTHER READING

Benjamin, Alfred: *The Helping Interview*, Houghton Mifflin, Boston, Mass., 1981. Explores the central issues of the helping interview. Useful for both the nonprofessional and the specialist.

Biegeleisen, J. I.: *Make Your Job Interview a Success*, 3d ed., Prentice-Hall, Englewood Cliffs, N.J., 1991. An advice-packed resource containing easy-to-use techniques.

Bolles, Richard Nelson: *What Color Is Your Parachute?* Ten Speed Press, Berkeley, Calif.; 1991. A manual for job hunters and career changers.

Brady, John: *The Craft of Interviewing*, Vintage, New York, 1977. A helpful guide; covers all aspects of the interview process. Especially strong on the art of questioning.

Caples, John: *The Ultimate Interview*, Doubleday, New York, 1991. A readable, comprehensive guide.

Chapman, Elwood N.: *From Campus to Career Success*, Science Research Associates, Chicago, Ill., 1978. An easy-to-read career-planning manual.

Donaho, Melvin W., and John L. Meyer: *How to Get the Job You Want*, Prentice-Hall, Englewood Cliffs, N.J., 1976. Readable, practical, results-oriented tips on getting a job.

Gifford, Robert, Cheuk Fan'Ng, and Margaret Wilkinson: "Nonverbal Cues in the Employment Interview: Links between Applicant Qualities and Interviewer Judgments," *Journal of Applied Psychology*, vol. 70, no. 4, 1985. Discusses how nonverbal cues can influence the outcome of an interview.

Half, Robert: *How to Get a Better Job in the Crazy World*, Penguin, New York, 1991. An insightful guide to interviewing: what to do and what to avoid. A guidebook for today.

Medley, H. Anthony: *Sweaty Palms Revised: The Neglected Art of Being Interviewed*, Ten Speed Press, Berkeley, Calif., 1991. A widely used source of information for people who are about to endure a job interview. Well written and filled with effective techniques.

Robertson, Jason: *How to Win in an Interview*, Prentice-Hall, Englewood Cliffs, N.J., 1978. How to make who you are and what you know work for you.

Stewart, Charles J., and William B. Cash, Jr.: *Interviewing: Principles and Practices*, 3d ed., Brown, Dubuque, Iowa, 1982. A thorough examination of interviewing principles applicable to all interview settings. Easily translatable into practice.

Walters, Barbara: *How to Talk with Practically Anybody about Practically Anything*, Doubleday, New York, 1970. A description of this famous interviewer's personal rules for successful conversation.

Wolvin, Andrew, and Carolyn Gwynn Coakley: *Listening*, 3d ed., Brown, Dubuque, Iowa, 1988. Contains a valuable section on the listener's role in an interview.

NOTES

1. Robert S. Goyer, W. Charles Redding, and John T. Richey, *Interviewing Principles and Techniques: A Project Text*, Brown, Dubuque, Iowa, 1968, p. 6.
2. For example, Lois J. Einhorn reports in "An Inner View of the Job Interview: An Investigation of Successful Communicative Behavior," *Communication Education*, vol. 30, 1981, pp. 217–228, that successful candidates were able to identify with the employer, support their arguments, organize their thoughts, clarify their ideas, and speak fluently.
3. Leonard Zunin and Natalie Zunin, *Contact: The First Four Minutes*, Nash, Los Angeles, Calif., 1972, pp. 8–12.
4. See Mark L. Knapp, Roderick P. Hart, Gustav W. Friedrich, and Gary M. Schulman, "The Rhetoric of Goodbye: Verbal and Nonverbal Correlates of Human Leave-Taking," *Speech Monographs*, vol. 40, 1973, pp. 182–198.
5. Charles J. Stewart and William B. Cash, Jr., *Interviewing: Principles and Practices*, 3d ed., Brown, Dubuque, Iowa, 1982, pp. 75–85.
6. Ibid.
7. David Bianculli, "Nice Guys Can Interview, but 'Naturals' Get Results," *Baltimore Sun*, May 19, 1984, p. E3.
8. For a study confirming that employers use a candidate's speech characteristics to judge competence and likability, see Robert Hopper, "Language Attitudes in the Employment Interview," *Speech Monographs*, vol. 44, 1974, pp. 346–351.
9. Elwood N. Chapman, *Your Attitude Is Showing*, Science Research Associates, Chicago, Ill., 1987; see also Chapman, *I Got the Job!* Crisp, Los Angeles, Calif., 1988.
10. Einhorn, op. cit.
11. See John T. Molloy, *Dress for Success*, Warner, New York, 1977; and Molloy, *The Woman's Dress for Success Book*, Warner, New York, 1977.
12. Barbara Walters, *How to Talk with Practically Anybody about Practically Anything*, Doubleday, New York, 1978.
13. Richard Bolles, *What Color Is Your Parachute?* Ten Speed Press, Berkeley, Calif., 1992.
14. John Brady, *The Craft of Interviewing*, Vintage, New York, 1977.

LIFELONG DEVELOPMENT OF COMMUNICATION SKILLS

After finishing this chapter, you should be able to:

Explain why developing communication skills is a lifelong task

Use a number of strategies to make your present and future communication more effective

Explain why we need to acknowledge change

Provide examples of important "passages" you have made or expect to make in life

Explain what is meant by changing "communication chairs"

Define *frozen evaluations* and discuss the dangers inherent in them

Identify typical excuses for failing to change

Assess your application of the principles discussed in this text to your own life

Use "checkbacks" to maintain and improve your communication skills

Continue developing communication skills on your own

No one knows the story of tomorrow's dawn.

African proverb

They told me to write about life.
To discover new insights.
To probe my inner soul,
To meditate on my faith,
To reflect on ideals,
And to have it in by Friday.

Anonymous

As we noted in Chapter 1, we wrote this book for you. What we said at the outset is even more relevant now. The topics you have studied should serve you well as you enter into personal and professional relationships. The skills you have mastered should help you fulfill your needs, reach your goals, and improve the quality of your life. But, as we also indicated in Chapter 1, the assignment to develop your abilities in interpersonal, small-group, and public communication has no "due date"; it is a lifelong process. You have completed this term's work, but your lifelong learning program has just begun. As Aldous Huxley remarked, "There's only one corner of the universe you can be certain of improving and that's your own self." Let us now examine a number of strategies you can use to help make your present and future communication experiences as rewarding as you would like them to be. Remember: You *can* surpass yourself.

COMMUNICATION AND CHANGE

As Erich Fromm has observed,

> Actually, the process of birth continues. The child begins to recognize outside objects, to react affectively, to grasp things and to co-ordinate his movements, to walk. But birth continues. The child learns to speak, it learns to know the use and function of things, it learns to relate itself to others, to avoid punishment and gain praise and liking. Slowly, the growing person learns to love, to develop reason, to look at the world objectively. He begins to develop his powers; to acquire a sense of identity, to overcome the seduction of his senses for the sake of an integrated life. . . . The whole life of the individual is nothing but the process of giving birth to himself; indeed, we should be fully born, when we die—although it is the tragic fate of most individuals to die before they are born.[1]

Today is not exactly like yesterday, the day before yesterday, or the day before that. The one thing you can count on is change. We ourselves change with time; the people with whom we interact and relate change with time; and the situations in which we are involved change with time.

Graduation is one experience in which we shed a "shell." Acknowledging the change entailed by such an experience is essential if we are to deal with that change.

David Ryan/Photo 20-20

Acknowledging Change

To deal with change, we must acknowledge it. Only by doing so can we keep ourselves fresh and effective as communicators. In her book *Passages*, Gail Sheehy puts it this way:

> We are not unlike a particularly hardy crustacean. The lobster grows by developing and shedding a series of hard, protective shells. Each time it expands from within, the confining shell must be sloughed off. It is left exposed and vulnerable until, in time, a new covering grows to replace the old.[2]

It could be said that like the lobster, we develop from within; and as we move through the various stages or passages of our lives, we too shed the protections in which we have encased ourselves. What types of "shells" have you shed in your life? Experiences such as graduation, an engagement, moving away from home, marriage, childbirth, death, a broken relationship, divorce, entering the job market, and being fired can make us feel vulnerable because all such transitions require adaptation and change. However, as Sheehy writes,

> We must be willing to change chairs if we want to grow. There is no permanent compatibility between a chair and a person. And there is no one right chair. What is right at one stage may be restricting at another, or too soft.[3]

The message for us is that we must also be prepared to change "communication chairs." The communication strategies we employed successfully at an earlier point in our lives may be inadequate or inappropriate to the situations and people we are interacting with today. Just as the practice of medicine changes as new drugs are discovered and the practice of law changes as laws are revised or overturned, so the practice of communication should change as we leave one life experience and enter another. As this happens, you may notice subtle or dramatic alterations in your sense of self, in your feelings about others, or in your values and attitudes. This is normal, because each change asks you to react and develop in some way. In a sense, everyone is expected to play a "change game"; those who take the time to understand will have an advantage.

Guarding against "Frozen Evaluations"

Has it ever occurred to you that while others can stop you temporarily, you are the only one who can stop yourself permanently?

Consider this. A mature elephant can easily lift a 2-ton load with its trunk. Why is it, then, that a circus elephant will stand quietly for hours tied to a very small, light wooden stake? When the elephant is still young and not very strong, it is restrained by a heavy chain attached to an immovable stake. The small elephant tries to break the chain but realizes that no matter how hard it tries, it cannot break loose. As the elephant matures, even though it gains weight and strength, it no longer tries to break loose—because it *thinks* it can't. Don't we sometimes behave like this? We limit our thought and behavior because of our earlier experiences, and—sadly—sometimes we do not let ourselves move beyond our imaginary boundaries.

Whenever you consciously or unconsciously apply a past evaluation of yourself, someone else, a situation, or an idea to the future—ignoring the changes that have taken place—you are making what William Haney calls a "frozen evaluation." Haney notes that some of our most solidly frozen, and most harmful, evaluations are those we make about ourselves. Evaluations we make about others can be equally harmful, and frozen just as hard.

Think of a situation when someone's frozen evaluation of you—or your frozen evaluation of him or her—caused difficulties. How did the frozen evaluation cause the problem? What could have prevented it?

✔ **SKILL BUILDER**

CHANGES

1. Evaluating yourself:
   a. Compile a list of self-evaluations that have remained relatively unchanged over the years. (For example, "I am shy.")
   b. Identify specific examples—facts, experiences, incidents—that could be used to invalidate each of these self-evaluations.

2. Evaluating others:
   a. Compile a list of evaluations you have made about others that have remained relatively unchanged over a period of time. (For example, "Haynes is a poor teacher.")
   b. As before, identify examples that could be used to invalidate these evaluations.

Frozen evaluations can do us and others a great disservice. People, situations, and ideas are all in constant flux. Try to prevent your judgments from becoming "set" or fixed. Effective communicators have the courage to acknowledge past and future changes in the people, situations, and objects they evaluate. Effective communicators can substitute an awareness of change for the mistaken assumption that things will remain the same.

Since change is inevitable, remember to take it into consideration whenever you make evaluations. People, situations, and things alter with time, and if you refuse to deal with such change, you are in effect refusing to deal with the person, situation, or thing that has changed.

Change and Growth: Avoiding Excuses

The ability to change—
to take a personal
risk—is a skill most of
us need help with.
Ellen Siegelman, *Personal
Risk*

You can do damage to yourself and your relationships with others if you convince yourself that you are unable to change. Such an excuse prevents you from trying out new behaviors, assuming new roles, or interacting successfully in new situations. Change may be difficult, but it can be accomplished.

To be sure, at times our environment constricts and limits our possibilities for change. However, at other times our environment "stretches," and we find ourselves operating within a somewhat different context. The environment we were born into is not the same one we are interacting in now. Although your past certainly influences who you are today, the way you plan and prepare for your future can also influence you. You will permit yourself to grow if you recognize that you are constantly reorganizing and constantly changing. For this reason, the attitudes and values you bring with you from the past into the present day may not apply to the current "you" or the present situation. Remember Alice's answer when the caterpillar asked her who she was:

> I hardly know, sir, just at present—at least I know who I was when I got up this morning, but I think I must have changed several times since then.

Openness, curiosity, and a willingness to take risks and experiment are important assets. You will be wise not to let habits, rigid attitudes, or unyielding opinions hinder your growth by reducing your receptiveness to alternative ways of thinking and behaving.

✔ SKILL BUILDER

"EXCUSES, EXCUSES . . ."

1. Compile a list of excuses that you or others you know use to avoid dealing with change. (For example, "I can't 'unlearn' poverty." "I was spoiled as a child, so I always have to get my way." "I was taught that men don't do dishes and that women belong in the home.")

2. Explain why the concept of change makes the validity of each of these excuses doubtful.

AN ALL TOO COMMON STORY
Kati Marton

In your opinion, did excuses for failing to change contribute to the situation described here? How would you respond today to such a situation? Why?

Is there a woman in the American workplace for whom Prof. Anita Hill's painful revelations regarding sexual harassment do not resonate? For me, her recollections revived an incident I had suppressed for more than a decade and a half. Unlike Professor Hill's experience, my memory of sexual harassment will not leave a deep imprint on the nation's psyche. Mine is but one woman's story. The professor and I are products of vastly different cultures and professions: she an Oklahoma farm girl; I, Budapest-born and -raised, a relative newcomer to this land. In common we had this: both of us were determined to succeed in highly competitive and conspicuously male-dominated professions: hers the law, mine the media. Yet, listening to her testimony, I was struck by how similarly she and I, different in almost every way, responded to sexual pressures in our professional lives. In the wake of Anita Hill's searing memories, I now see my own experience as part of a sad, pervasive pattern of sexual blackmail in offices across the land.

I was 25 years old at the time, the same age as Professor Hill when she worked for Judge Clarence Thomas at the Equal Employment Opportunity Commission. I was only six months into my job as an on-air reporter for a network affiliate in Philadelphia. Like Professor Hill, I, too, lacked a résumé. I, too, loved my job. On the day in question, a station news executive and I traveled by train to New York so that I could receive a George Foster Peabody Award for my work on a documentary on the Philadelphia Orchestra's visit to China. I delivered an earnest and self-conscious acceptance speech to the media heavyweights gathered in the gold-trimmed room. At one point, I momentarily lost my composure and my newly acquired American accent when I mentioned that only a few years before, I did not even speak English. But through it all I basked in the warm glow of my peers' approval. It should have been a proud day for a neophyte reporter. It did not turn out that way.

My executive escort, seemingly bristling with pride (it was the first time a local Philadelphia television reporter had won the coveted Peabody), invited me and a childhood friend from Budapest to the Russian Tea Room to toast the event. The hours passed in a happy haze. "Isn't it time we headed for the Metroliner back to Philadelphia?" I asked the executive around nightfall. Having said goodnight to my friend, we walked to the limousine my colleague had hired for the occasion. But the car did not follow the familiar route to Penn Station. Without a word of prompting, the limo pulled up in front of the Hilton hotel. Too astonished and too intimidated to muster anything like a firm protest, I found myself following the executive into the hotel elevator. "I only want to get to know you better," he explained. "To talk to you."

And talk I did, with the feverish urgency of a drowning person clinging to a life raft. I saw talk as my only escape from certain disaster, a compromise between humiliating the man to whom I owed my career and my own revulsion at the situation he had placed me in. So I talked about my childhood, embellishing and dramatizing, in the manner of a stand-up comic auditioning for the big time. By midnight I had run out of steam and stories so I prodded him to talk about his life, his troubles. It was the most exhausting tap dance of my life, but it was the only way I could think of to deflect this man from pursuing what I assumed to be his own objectives. There was no time to even wonder how in God's name he presumed this was where I wanted to spend the proudest night of my short career. What gave a man with whom I had exchanged one handshake—and that on the day I was hired—this right? He assumed that right. I, loving my job, thinking I got it only by a stroke of luck, became his accomplice by not walking out, by not even voicing outrage. I did not have the nerve.

(Continued)

Belittling comments: At dawn, he finally drifted off to sleep and I made my bleary-eyed way to the train and to Philadelphia. Toward evening, as I faced the bright lights of the studio cameras, I saw him just arriving to work. He looked much more rested than I. By then all memories of the previous day's brief moment of glory had been supplanted by other memories. Irrational feelings of guilt regarding my conduct began to nag at me. Had I given the wrong signals? He seemed such a nice, square sort of family man. And why had I not walked out on him? The minute a woman decides to stay and stay silent, in her own mind at least, she loses the moral edge. Like thousands of women in newsrooms, offices and factories, I had swapped the moral edge for job security. I did not think I had the luxury of choice in the matter.

I suppose the executive felt sure I would never talk about his abortive attempt at seduction. He was right. I never have, until now. Nor have I let myself take much pride in that hard-won Peabody Award, fearing that the other memories would rush in beside them. But hearing Professor Hill's taut recitation, accompanied by the belittling comments of certain members of the gentleman's club on Capitol Hill, forced me to mentally revisit that room in the Hilton. Professor Hill's dignity did not mask the lasting humiliation that is the inevitable residue of such moments.

There is more than personal catharsis at stake in owning up to this long-suppressed incident. I am writing this not only because the memory would not let go. I am writing because Professor Hill's voice moved me to do so. I wanted to say to the Senate panel, "Look, I know why she stayed on with the man who insulted her. So many of us have been there, not liked ourselves for it, but have stayed." And there is another impulse to my speaking out now. If men and women alike pronounce such degrading episodes unacceptable, perhaps our daughters might be spared similar choices in their professional lives. No one should have to purchase job security at so high a price.

Source: From "An All Too Common Story" by Kati Marton, Newsweek, October 21, 1991. Reprinted by permission of Kati Marton, Media Studies Center, School of Journalism, Columbia University.

COMMUNICATION AND YOUR "PEOPLE ENVIRONMENT": FAMILY, FRIENDS, EDUCATION, AND WORK

The extent to which you develop skills for communicating with others will influence your success in making your way through your "people environment." Your *people environment* has at least four different areas: family, friends, education, and work. One reason we wrote this book is to give you skills in interpersonal, small-group, and public communication that will enable you to relate effectively in any of these contexts—that is, wherever you happen to find yourself.

It is now time for you to assess your ability to function in each of these environments. Doing so will let you identify your needs and the demands placed on you when you communicate with others in the vital areas of your life. Your assessments should indicate how communication influences your relationships with others in each of these sectors. As Virginia Satir notes in *Peoplemaking*, "communication is a huge umbrella that covers and affects all that goes on between human beings."[4] Let us be certain to examine the umbrella's "spokes." Use the following exercises to recognize, reaffirm, and set priorities in communication skills. Once you understand your own priorities in each of the major arenas, you will be able to act more consistently to achieve your goals.

● CULTURE AND COMMUNICATION

TOLERANCE

Whether or not we are able to function effectively with people from other cultures will become increasingly significant for success—personally and on the job—in the years ahead.

What steps, if any, are you willing to take to help you increase your own tolerance for ambiguity, your willingness to be nonjudgmental, and your ability to empathize with people from cultures different from your own?

Whether we are interacting interpersonally, participating in a small group, or delivering a speech, we sometimes communicate in ways that are harmful to ourselves or others. Identifying behaviors that impede our functioning and recognizing behaviors that can be substituted for them are important steps in improving our communication abilities. What happens to us in one area may be quite different from what happens to us in another, and our perception of ourselves can also change from one area to another. Accounting for such differences is part of the process of growth. By now it should be apparent that one key to effective communication is *behavioral flexibility*.

✔ SKILL BUILDER

WHERE AM I NOW?—TARGET BEHAVIORS

1. On a separate sheet, for each area of your "people environment," identify specific behaviors that you would like to *avoid* in communication with specific people.

2. On a separate sheet, for each area, identify specific behaviors you want to *use* in communication with specific people.

Family

Person 1
Person 2

Friends

Person 1
Person 2

Education

Person 1
Person 2

Work

Person 1
Person 2

Family

Person 1
Person 2

Friends

Person 1
Person 2

Education

Person 1
Person 2

Work

Person 1
Person 2

✔ SKILL BUILDER

WHERE AM I NOW?—ASSESSING YOUR CONFIDENCE

1. Use the following scales to measure your ability to apply the skills discussed in this book to each area of your "people environment." The number 1 represents "little or no confidence" and the number 5 indicates "total confidence." Circle the number that best reflects your assessment.

	Family	Friends	Education	Work
Self-concept	1 2 3 4 5	1 2 3 4 5	1 2 3 4 5	1 2 3 4 5
Perceptual skills	1 2 3 4 5	1 2 3 4 5	1 2 3 4 5	1 2 3 4 5
Listening skills	1 2 3 4 5	1 2 3 4 5	1 2 3 4 5	1 2 3 4 5
Ability to send and receive nonverbal cues	1 2 3 4 5	1 2 3 4 5	1 2 3 4 5	1 2 3 4 5
Ability to communicate verbally	1 2 3 4 5	1 2 3 4 5	1 2 3 4 5	1 2 3 4 5
Assertiveness	1 2 3 4 5	1 2 3 4 5	1 2 3 4 5	1 2 3 4 5
Ability to interact with others to solve problems	1 2 3 4 5	1 2 3 4 5	1 2 3 4 5	1 2 3 4 5
Leadership	1 2 3 4 5	1 2 3 4 5	1 2 3 4 5	1 2 3 4 5
Conflict-management skills	1 2 3 4 5	1 2 3 4 5	1 2 3 4 5	1 2 3 4 5
Public speaking	1 2 3 4 5	1 2 3 4 5	1 2 3 4 5	1 2 3 4 5
Ability to adapt to a specific audience	1 2 3 4 5	1 2 3 4 5	1 2 3 4 5	1 2 3 4 5

2. What do your ratings tell you about your mastery of communication skills? Which skills pose problems for you in every area? Which pose problems for you in only one area? In which area do you experience the most problems? The fewest problems? Why?

The goal of the "Skill Builders" above and on the preceding page is to identify ways in which your evaluation of your communication assets and liabilities affects your ability to function in each area of your "people environment." You can choose to ignore your weaker behaviors and drift through an encounter, or you can choose to deal with problem behaviors and face communicative challenges.

To develop a skill fully, you must want to improve. You must be willing to work, and you must be personally committed. You must believe that the goal you seek is desirable—a target worth striving for. You will probably want to improve your communication in all four areas. Your chances of succeeding will be increased if you practice all the communication skills—interpersonal, small-group, and public—that we have considered. These skills are vital to success in each area of your life.

Lloyd Jones tells us, "The men (or women) who try to do something and fail are infinitely better than those who try to do nothing and succeed." Why?

MOTHER TO SON
Langston Hughes

Well, Son, I'll tell you
Life for me ain't been no crystal stair.
It's had tacks in it.
And splinters.
And boards torn up.
And places with no carpets on the floor.
Bare.
But all the time
I'se been climbin' on
And reachin' landin's
And turning corners
And sometimes goin' on in the dark
Where there ain't been no light.
So, Boy, don't you turn back.
Don't you set down on the steps
'Cause you find it's kinder hard.
Don't you fall now—
For I'se still goin', Honey,
I'se still climbin'
And life for me ain't been no crystal stair.[5]

We wrote this text hoping that you would find it a practical manual for developing communication skills—one you could use again and again. Thus, each of the Skill Builders can be repeated at various points throughout your life. Your responses will trace your growth and development as a communicator. We have also included a number of key "Checkback" exercises that you can repeat through the years to help ensure that you are continually working to maintain, nourish, and improve your communication skills.

✔ CHECKBACK 1

AN ANNUAL REVIEW

1. Describe your self-concept. In your description, include an analysis of the roles you believe you have performed effectively this year, the roles you feel you need to work on, and new discoveries you have made about yourself.

2. Discuss the relationships you've shared with "significant others" during the year. Include a description of relationships that have ended, relationships that have been maintained, and relationships that have just begun.

3. Discuss your ability to communicate on the job. What are your strengths? What are your problem areas?

4. Identify your communication goals for the coming year.

5. Repeat this exercise annually.

✔ CHECKBACK 2

UP TO DATE

Describe yourself 10 years ago, 5 years ago, and today in terms of physical appearance, personality characteristics, intellectual ability, and communication skills. Use the following chart to guide your observations. Repeat this exercise every 5 years.

1. **Ten years ago:**
   Physical appearance _____
   Personality characteristics _____
   Intellectual ability _____

   Communication skills:
   Interpersonal _____
   Small-group _____
   Public _____

2. **Five years ago:**
   Physical appearance _____
   Personality characteristics _____
   Intellectual ability _____

   Communication skills:
   Interpersonal _____
   Small-group _____
   Public _____

3. **Today:**
   Physical appearance _____
   Personality characteristics _____
   Intellectual ability _____

   Communication skills:
   Interpersonal _____
   Small-group _____
   Public _____

Which aspects of yourself have undergone the most change? Why?

LIFE LINES

1. Do this exercise every year, on the same day. It will give you an opportunity to plot the development of your communication skills in the main areas of your life.

2. On the chart that follows, use a pen or pencil of one color to plot your personal communication abilities and another color to plot your professional communication abilities. Label each line with this year's date. Redraw the lines each year as necessary, or reproduce the graph for every yearly self-examination.

3. What do your "life lines" reveal about your ability to communicate effectively in each area?

4. Identify factors that might account for stability or change in your life lines.

Year: _____ Color code: _____ Professional life: _____ Personal life: _____

Skills

Mastery	Self-concept	Perception	Listening	Nonverbal	Verbal	Assertion	Group problem solving	Public speaking	Interviewing
High 5									
4									
3									
2									
1 Low									

487

THE SEARCH

Shel Silverstein

I went to find the pot of gold
That's waiting where the rainbow ends,
I searched and searched and searched and searched
And searched and searched, and then—
There it was, deep in the grass,
Under an old and twisty bough.
It's mine, it's mine, it's mine at last. . . .
What do I search for now?[6]

We hope that we have provided you with an impetus to continue to develop your communication skills. You now have a body of knowledge and a series of exercises you can use to gain a better understanding of yourself, of others, and of the relationships you share. Certainly, we have not covered everything there is to say about communication. However, we believe that the materials in this text will help make you a more effective communicator.

Since communication occupies most of your time, it makes sense to try to do it well. Good luck!

SUMMARY

Developing the ability to communicate is a lifelong task. For that reason, it is important that you make a commitment to continue improving your skills, even though this communications course is ending.

A number of strategies can help you: (1) Be prepared to adapt your communication strategies to changes in your life. (2) Guard against "frozen evaluations." (3) Avoid making excuses for not changing. (4) Analyze how your "people environment" affects the nature of your interactions. (5) Use the "Checkbacks" to monitor your progress.

SUGGESTIONS FOR FURTHER READING

Bolles, Richard Nelson: *The Three Boxes of Life*, Ten Speed Press, Berkeley, Calif., 1979. A valuable resource for job-seekers and job-changers.

Bolles, Richard Nelson: *What Color Is Your Parachute?* Ten Speed Press, Berkeley, Calif., 1991. A best-selling career and self-development guide.

Fulghum, Robert: *It Was on Fire When I Lay Down on It*, Villards/Random House, New York, 1989. Collection of essays that relate directly to the effect of communication on your life. Enjoyable reading.

John-Roger and Peter McWilliams: *Do It! Let's Get Off Our Buts*, Prelude, Los Angeles, Calif., 1991. A popular book of interesting readings. Takes the position that most people avoid doing what they know they should do.

Heller, Robert: *Super Self: The Art and Science of Self Management*, Atheneum, New York, 1979. A practical guide to self-control and self-development.

Roane, Susan: *How to Work A Room*, Warner, New York, 1988. Presents strategies for socializing in business and personal settings. Offers specific techniques to help you become more proficient at communicating in informal settings.

Satir, Virginia: *Peoplemaking*, Science and Behavior Books, Palo Alto, Calif., 1972. How to develop a healthy, supportive family communication.

Sheehy, Gail: *Passages: Predictable Crises of Adult Life*, Dutton, New York, 1976. Identifies changes and strains in person-to-person relationships that occur during various stages of life.

NOTES

1. Erich Fromm, *The Art of Loving*, Harper and Row, New York, 1974.
2. Gail Sheehy, *Passages: Predictable Crises of Adult Life*, Dutton, New York, 1976.
3. Ibid.
4. Virginia Satir, *Peoplemaking*, Science and Behavior Books, Palo Alto, Calif., 1972.
5. Langston Hughes, "Mother to Son," from *Selected Poems of Langston Hughes*, Knopf, New York, 1926. Copyright 1926 by Alfred A. Knopf, Inc., and renewed 1954 by Langston Hughes. Reprinted by permission of the publisher.
6. "The Search," from *Where the Sidewalk Ends*, by Shel Silverstein. Copyright © 1974 Evil Eye Music, Inc. Used by permission of HarperCollins Publishers.

ANSWER KEY

Blindering Problem (Chapter 3, page 70)

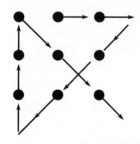

The Detective (Chapter 3, page 73)

1. ?
2. ?
3. F
4. ?
5. ?
6. T
7. ?
8. ?
9. ?
10. ?
11. ?

Business Babble Quiz (Chapter 4, page 97)

1. h
2. f
3. i
4. j
5. g
6. b
7. d
8. a
9. e
10. c

The States (Chapter 9, page 239)

1. Maine	11. Arkansas
2. New York	12. Minnesota
3. New Jersey	13. Oklahoma
4. Delaware	14. North Dakota
5. Ohio	15. Colorado
6. Georgia	16. New Mexico
7. Alabama	17. Wyoming
8. Illinois	18. Utah
9. Mississippi	19. Idaho
10. Wisconsin	20. Washington

Lost on the Moon (Chapter 9, page 243)

1. Two 100-pound tanks of oxygen (necessary for breathing)
2. Five gallons of water (necessary to replace fluid lost through perspiration, etc.)
3. Map constellations (necessary to find directions)
4. Food concentrate (supplies daily food requirements)
5. Solar-powered FM receiver-transmitter (can transmit a distress signal)
6. Nylon rope (50 feet) (good for tying the injured; also helps in climbing)
7. First-aid kit with injection needles (medicine and bandages may be needed)
8. Parachute silk (can be used for shelter from the sun's rays)
9. Life raft (could function as a self-propulsion device)
10. Signal flares (could be used as a distress signal)
11. Two .45-caliber pistols (could be used to make self-propulsion devices)
12. One case of dehydrated milk (provides food; can be mixed with water for drinking)
13. Portable heating unit (useful only if the landing had been on the *dark* side of the moon)
14. Magnetic compass (almost useless, since the moon probably has no magnetic poles)
15. One box of matches (useless on the moon)

INDEX

386 D/1